OXFORD WORLD'S CLASSICS

LEAVES FROM THE JOURNAL OF OUR LIFE IN THE HIGHLANDS, FROM 1848 TO 1861 AND MORE LEAVES FROM THE JOURNAL OF A LIFE IN THE HIGHLANDS, FROM 1862 TO 1882

This volume makes accessible for contemporary readers two books authored by Queen Victoria: *Leaves from the Journal of Our Life in the Highlands, from 1848 to 1861*, a best-seller when it was published in 1868, and its sequel, *More Leaves from the Journal of a Life in the Highlands*, published in 1884. The books are selections from the diary the Queen wrote nearly every day of her life. Originally intended for private circulation, later expanded to appeal to a wider public, these published diary entries cover not only the family holidays at Balmoral Castle in the Scottish Highlands, which the Queen and Prince Albert enjoyed up to his death in 1861, but also the Queen's journeys—as sovereign and as 'Royal Tourist'—around Scotland, Ireland, and other regions within the British Isles.

QUEEN VICTORIA (1819–1901) succeeded her uncle King William IV to the throne of Great Britain and Ireland in 1837. In 1840 she married Prince Albert of Saxe-Coburg and Gotha. The couple had nine children. Before Queen Elizabeth II, she was the longest-reigning monarch in British history, and, in the same way as Elizabeth I in 'Elizabethan' times, she played a central role in shaping the era known as 'Victorian'.

MARGARET HOMANS is Professor of English and of Women's, Gender, and Sexuality Studies at Yale University, and the author of *Royal Representations: Queen Victoria and British Culture, 1837–1876* (1998) and *Bearing the Word: Language and Female Experience in Nineteenth-Century Women's Writing* (1986).

JOANNA MARSCHNER is Senior Curator of Historic Royal Palaces, and co-editor of *Queen Victoria's Self-Fashioning: Curating the Royal Image for Dynasty, Nation and Empire* (2022) and *Enlightened Princesses: Caroline, Augusta, Charlotte and the Shaping of the Modern World* (2017), and author of *Queen Caroline: Cultural Politics at the Early Eighteenth-Century Court* (2014).

ADRIENNE MUNICH is co-editor emerita of the journal *Victorian Literature and Culture*, Professor emerita of English, Cultural Studies, and Art at Stony Brook University, NY, author of *Queen Victoria's Secrets* (1996) and *Empire of Diamonds: Victorian Gems in Imperial Settings* (2020), and co-editor with Margaret Homans of *Remaking Queen Victoria* (1997).

OXFORD WORLD'S CLASSICS

*For over 100 years Oxford World's Classics have brought
readers closer to the world's great literature. Now with over 700
titles—from the 4,000-year-old myths of Mesopotamia to the
twentieth century's greatest novels—the series makes available
lesser-known as well as celebrated writing.*

*The pocket-sized hardbacks of the early years contained
introductions by Virginia Woolf, T. S. Eliot, Graham Greene,
and other literary figures which enriched the experience of reading.
Today the series is recognized for its fine scholarship and
reliability in texts that span world literature, drama and poetry,
religion, philosophy, and politics. Each edition includes perceptive
commentary and essential background information to meet the
changing needs of readers.*

OXFORD WORLD'S CLASSICS

QUEEN VICTORIA

Leaves from the Journal of Our Life in the Highlands, from 1848 to 1861

and

More Leaves from the Journal of a Life in the Highlands, from 1862 to 1882

Edited with an Introduction and Notes by
MARGARET HOMANS
JOANNA MARSCHNER
and
ADRIENNE MUNICH

OXFORD
UNIVERSITY PRESS

OXFORD
UNIVERSITY PRESS

Great Clarendon Street, Oxford, OX2 6DP,
United Kingdom

Oxford University Press is a department of the University of Oxford.
It furthers the University's objective of excellence in research, scholarship,
and education by publishing worldwide. Oxford is a registered trade mark of
Oxford University Press in the UK and in certain other countries

© Editorial material Margaret Homans, Joanna Marschner, and Adrienne Munich 2024

The moral rights of the authors have been asserted

All rights reserved. No part of this publication may be reproduced, stored in
a retrieval system, or transmitted, in any form or by any means, without the
prior permission in writing of Oxford University Press, or as expressly permitted
by law, by licence or under terms agreed with the appropriate reprographics
rights organization. Enquiries concerning reproduction outside the scope of the
above should be sent to the Rights Department, Oxford University Press, at the
address above

You must not circulate this work in any other form
and you must impose this same condition on any acquirer

Published in the United States of America by Oxford University Press
198 Madison Avenue, New York, NY 10016, United States of America

British Library Cataloguing in Publication Data

Data available

Library of Congress Control Number: 2023913085

ISBN 978–0–19–289385–7

Printed and bound in the UK by
Clays Ltd, Elcograf S.p.A.

Links to third party websites are provided by Oxford in good faith and
for information only. Oxford disclaims any responsibility for the materials
contained in any third party website referenced in this work.

ACKNOWLEDGEMENTS

THE editors of this volume must express their deep gratitude to HM The King, who graciously allowed access to the Royal Archives and the Royal Library, and has generously given permission for material retrieved there to be published. We thank Tim Knox and the staff of the Royal Collection Trust. We are especially grateful to Bill Stockting, Julie Crocker, and Allison Derrett in the Royal Archives, and Emma Stuart and Elizabeth Ashby in the Royal Library for their kind help in facilitating our research visits, and for their encouragement and support of the project, which are much appreciated. We would also like to thank Dr Jana Riedel for her help with research for the Cast of Characters and Martin Brown for his creation of the maps for this edition.

CONTENTS

Introduction	ix
Note on the Texts	li
Select Bibliography	lvii
A Chronology of Queen Victoria	lxi
Cast of Characters	lxv
Maps	xcvii

LEAVES FROM THE JOURNAL OF OUR LIFE IN THE HIGHLANDS, FROM 1848 TO 1861	1
MORE LEAVES FROM THE JOURNAL OF A LIFE IN THE HIGHLANDS, FROM 1862 TO 1882	171
Explanatory Notes	379
Glossary	449

INTRODUCTION
'LAND OF BROWN HEATH AND SHAGGY WOOD': QUEEN VICTORIA'S MONARCHY IN THE SCOTTISH HIGHLANDS

THE influence and importance of *Leaves from the Journal of Our Life in the Highlands* (1868) and its sequel, *More Leaves from the Journal of a Life in the Highlands* (1884), cannot be overstated. No English monarch had published such personal volumes as appeared under Queen Victoria's signature, a fact that early reviews of the first volume noted: 'the book, though written by a Queen, is in essence democratic. In this respect, it is unique in the annals of all literature.'[1] Victoria's publications were 'a unique form of writing on the Highlands' that 'fashion[ed] a unique form of British imperial subjectivity.'[2] The Queen and Prince Albert had become entranced with the Highlands when visiting Scotland early in their marriage; they soon acquired Balmoral Castle as a holiday home, and Victoria—a lifelong diarist—wrote daily about the happy novelty of 'our life in the Highlands'. The Queen's original intention in 1864 was to print selected diary entries about the Highlands for her family and friends, starting with the short countryside adventures in the Cairngorms that she calls 'great expeditions', and sixty-three copies were distributed in 1865. But as the private edition was sure to be leaked to the media, this initial plan was overtaken by the political imperative to reach a wider readership by publishing these selections, and adding to them accounts of her visits to other regions within Great Britain—Ireland, Wales, Cornwall, the Channel Islands. The Queen worked closely with Sir Arthur Helps, Clerk of the Privy Council and her trusted advisor, in fashioning the first volume.

The books invite the reader to know the Queen as a real person. Some of her advisors and most of her family believed that monarchy should preserve its mystique—General Charles Grey, for example, feared the public would get 'too much of the private thoughts of the Sovereign'—but she defended her wish to reveal herself, insisting 'Age will make itself felt & this stupid & selfish "world" will learn to see that the Queen is

---

[1] *Contemporary Review* 7 (February 1868), 289.
[2] Kenneth McNeil, *Scotland, Britain, Empire: Writing the Highlands, 1760–1860* (Oxford: Oxford University Press, 2007), 147.

made of flesh & blood like other people.'³ Illustrated with her sketches, *Leaves* became a best-seller in 1868. It was soon reissued in a cheaper 'people's edition' and in a large-format illustrated edition, and it was translated into many languages, both within and beyond the empire.

Although *Leaves* and *More Leaves* appear to be 'simple records', their 'perfect faithfulness of narration' flowing naturally from the Queen's pen, great care and extensive labour went into the selecting and editing of the diary entries (*Leaves*, Dedication and 8). Smith, Elder, & Co., the prestigious publisher of Charlotte Brontë, Robert Browning, and other major literary figures, had printed the private edition and now became the book's commercial publisher. Although the Queen had judiciously chosen content for the private edition, a still more lengthy process of expanding and editing ensued. While the Queen continued selecting entries, Smith, Elder assigned a junior assistant, Frederick Enoch, to aid with editorial tasks, ranging from checking her spelling of place names to marking places where her phrasing could be improved. Proofs of subsections of the book were sent back and forth between Helps, Enoch, and the Queen. She told her daughter Vicky (Victoria, Crown Princess of Prussia) that she had been 'cutting out some of the more familiar descriptions and being subjected by Mr. Helps and others to a very severe scrutiny of style and grammar'. She reported adding the entries about further journeys, while cutting and amending other sections; 'It has given a great deal of trouble for one had so carefully to exclude even the slightest observation which might hurt anyone's feeling . . . no-one can conceive the trouble of printing a book, and the mistakes, which are endless.'⁴ She accepted some proposed edits but rejected others. Negotiations about sensitive points continued to the last minute: in December 1867 she wrote to Helps's daughter Alice: 'I was not <u>offended</u> but <u>distressed</u> & <u>alarmed</u> at seeing <u>so much</u> changed when I had thought <u>all</u> was <u>settled</u> completely. . . . I felt too that my <u>own</u> feelings and the reasons for <u>things</u> were being overlooked & not understood & this alarmed me.'⁵

Above all, the Queen insisted that the book convey her true feelings. Helps's canny and diplomatic Preface introduces a humanized Queen Victoria, the Queen whom he was certain *Leaves* itself would put on lively display. He points to the intimate, authentic, and unpretentious style that

---

[3] Grey is quoted in John R. DeBruyn, 'Sir Arthur Helps and the Royal Connection', pts 1, 2, *Bulletin of the John Rylands Library* 66 (1983–4), 54–87, 141–76, at pp. 73–4; letter to Arthur Helps, 26 January 1870, Royal Archives (hereafter abbreviated RA), Vic Add MSS A32/17.

[4] 21 December 1867, in *Your Dear Letter: Private Correspondence of Queen Victoria and the Crown Princess of Prussia, 1865–1871*, ed. Roger Fulford (New York: Scribner's, 1971), 166.

[5] RA Vic Add MSS A32/8.

brings the Queen to the level of ordinary folks, 'for in every page the writer describes what she thinks and feels, rather than what she might be expected to think and feel' (*Leaves*, 8). Because neither volume was purposely written for publication, this claim of authenticity is patently true, yet it is also complex in its effects and influence. Whether or not by design, both volumes serve wide-ranging strategic ends.

'*I am known and understood*': Leaves *and* More Leaves *as the Queen's Books*

The first of those strategic ends was to create a new mode of appearance for a queen who had removed herself from public view. With the death of her beloved consort, Prince Albert, in December 1861, Victoria abruptly went into seclusion, avoiding all public events, although she continued to fulfil her obligations as sovereign behind the scenes. As the central performer of the nation, her visibility in pomp and circumstance justified the existence of a queen in a constitutional monarchy, yet she remained out of view through the 1860s. The Representation of the People Act of 1867 doubled the size of the British electorate and enfranchised working-class men for the first time, putting fresh pressure on the monarchy to justify itself. Her disappearance left a void, and publishing *Leaves* served as a substitute for her bodily presence. When her diaries entered private homes in the hands of readers, Victoria's voice echoed, not only in the British Isles but in countries that spoke the many languages into which the volumes were translated. Her journals made her intimately present in domestic spaces as a 'broken-hearted' member of the human family.

Albert's death at the age of 42 left his wife inconsolable for the rest of her life, though she eventually was to turn her widowed state into an identity.[6] Loss infuses both volumes. *Leaves* retrospectively invites readers into the happy, indeed blissful, private spaces of the royal family that Victoria has lost, but that her writing brings to life; *More Leaves*, opening with the building of Prince Albert's memorial cairn at Balmoral Castle, overtly grieves for Albert, as Victoria recalls in many entries the Highland locales that she had visited in happier times with her spouse. Victoria particularly identified *More Leaves* as 'records of my widowed life', and, intensifying its mournful remembrance, this volume was

---

[6] Adrienne Munich, *Queen Victoria's Secrets* (New York: Columbia University Press, 1996), 79–103; Margaret Homans, *Royal Representations: Queen Victoria and British Culture, 1837–1876* (Chicago: Chicago University Press, 1998), 58–66, 100–56.

dedicated 'to the memory of my devoted personal attendant and faithful friend John Brown' (*More Leaves*, Dedication). The family constructed eleven commemorative cairns in the Balmoral grounds, creating a graveyard of sorts, a landscape of memory, which is doubly memorialized by Victoria's later writing about it. As her losses mounted up, she added more monuments: statues of Albert, of John Brown, even of a favourite dog, Noble. She describes walking to see the cross she had erected to mark her daughter Alice's untimely death, with a series of footnotes on the deaths of Alice's children trailing after her account. In her descriptions of places beyond Balmoral, too, memorials abound. Returning to a moorland spring, which she visited with Albert in 1861, the lonely Queen finds built above it a stone monument that commemorates the earlier visit and marks her loss with its inscription, '. . . drink and pray for Scotland's Queen' (*More Leaves*, 197). Year after year, she records her sorrowful ceremonial unveiling of statues of Prince Albert both at Balmoral and in Scotland's cities. Ghosts inhabit the volumes, as they also inhabit the landscapes she describes travelling through.

In *Leaves*, through her rigorous selection and editing of diary entries from which matters of state, other travels, and events at her other homes are stripped away, she constructs her essential story: that of a wife looking with new eyes on new places and people at the side of her beloved husband, and that of a woman fostering community through charitable deeds, and building character by seeking out the challenges of rough country adventure. Her ambition to scale mountain peaks, even with copious assistance, was highly unusual for a Briton in the 1840s and 1850s, perhaps inspired by her husband's delight in exploring the mountains of Germany and Switzerland. *More Leaves* continues the story of the wife after she became a widow, opening with her transformation from the intrepid hill-walker and pony-rider of 'The Last Expedition', when Victoria and Albert climbed rugged Cairn Turc and remote Cairn Glaishie and looked over 'the wonderful panorama which lay stretched out before us' (*Leaves*, 135), into the widow, who, placing stones for Albert's memorial cairn on Craig Lowrigan the summer after his death, 'felt very shaky and nervous,' and was tired out by even a short walk (*More Leaves*, 183). But as *More Leaves* proceeds, the anxious widow averse to appearing in public re-emerges as the curious tourist eager to learn about local histories and the grateful Queen who does not shy away from crowds of adoring subjects. She attributes her recovery to her life in the Highlands, where she spent far more time after Albert's death than before it. In the many entries about the deaths of common people as well as members of the royal family, *More Leaves* finds Victoria humbly praising the healing qualities of the Highlands and their people. It is a place where people understand pain; Victoria claims that she has 'learnt many a lesson of resignation and faith' (*More Leaves*, 175). Such character building subtends the entries, and as readers observe her overcoming her own great loss, they too are to be improved and edified by indirectly participating in the Queen's Highlands experience.

Together, the two volumes presented an intimate view of the royal family that all subjects could identify with. The abundance of the Queen's mourning presented her as an emotional woman to her subjects, 'who had always shown a sincere and ready sympathy with the personal joys and sorrows of their Sovereign' (*Leaves*, 7). Victoria wanted the book to be widely accessible, wishing that it be '<u>as good</u> as possible, & that it <u>shld.</u> be much read, especially by the people—her <u>real</u> friends. It <u>shld</u> not be a <u>dear</u> book, so that <u>everyone</u> can buy it.'[7] When *Leaves* appeared on 10 January 1868, priced at 10s. 6d., it sold 18,000 copies within the first week and sold out the entire first edition of 20,000 within two weeks so that a second edition was needed immediately. (The people's edition of March 1868, which cost 2s. 6d. and sold 103,000 copies in 1868, was still not priced for the working classes, who typically could afford books only when the price was 6d. or lower; an edition at 6d. was eventually published in 1882.[8]) The Queen believed that the impressively high sales contributed to a change in the public's perception of her, and, indeed, during her sequestered mourning, publication of the volumes steadied eroding support for the monarchy, defending her to some extent from populist attacks as it forged a new rapport between the monarch and the nation at a challenging time. She wrote to Vicky that the public response shows 'extreme loyalty':

From all and every side, high and low, the feeling is the same the letters flow in, saying how much more than ever I shall be loved, now that I am known and understood . . . It is very gratifying to see how people appreciate what is simple and right and how especially my truest friends—the people—feel it. They have (as a body) the truest feeling for family life.[9]

As the weeks go by, she adds that the success of the book is bringing renewed support for her monarchy: 'everyone is so full of gratitude and loyal affection, saying it is not to be told the good it will do the Throne'.[10]

---

[7] RA Vic Add MSS A32/4.

[8] See Simon Eliot, 'What price books?', *OUPblog*, at https://blog.oup.com/2014/02/19th-century-book-pricing-oxford-university-press/; Leonard Huxley, *The House of Smith, Elder* (London: William Clowes & Sons, 1923), 149.

[9] 18 January 1868, in *Your Dear Letter*, ed. Fulford, 171.

[10] 29 January 1868, in ibid., 173.

Leaves was published at the same time in the USA and Canada, and the London *Times* predicted the book's popularity not only in Britain but 'in myriads of homes throughout an empire which circles the globe'.[11] The *New York Times* found that the Queen 'will be more beloved than ever from the frankness with which she has taken them into her confidence', and praised the book's 'very simple and womanly style', its 'naturalness', and its lack of 'the etiquette or dignity which usually surround a monarch's life'.[12] Initial reviews in Britain vindicated the Queen's view that the book would aid her politically. The *Daily Telegraph* asserted that the book 'consoled' readers who missed her, sympathizing with her withdrawal: 'Those who have been impatient with the wish to see Her Majesty more in public will at least comprehend how real was the home in the ruins of which she has had to mourn the stroke of Death.'[13] The review in the London *Times* mentioned above emphasized the feeling of intimacy the book creates, echoing the identification between book and person that Victoria intended: 'In the green cloth dress of her book she enters familiarly into our houses. She takes us by the hand, she sits by our firesides, and she opens to us her heart. . . . She lays aside her robes of State and enters into friendly conversation with her subjects.' Because the Queen shares such ordinary experiences, the book 'will touch the popular heart as it cannot be touched by the extraordinary and the unknown', and will 'deepen . . . the national sentiment of loyalty which the Queen has inspired'. Other reviews focus on the book's memorialization of Prince Albert and on the Queen's frankness about her grief: even *Punch*, famed for its cynical wit, published an uncynical poem that ends:

> The Royal Widow has done well
> Thus on her people's love to call,
> Her simple wifely tale to tell,
> And trust her joys and griefs to all.[14]

The reviews promised that the book would increase the Queen's appeal for her subjects by showing that 'the most unalloyed happiness she has tasted is that which she found in a sphere within the reach of her humblest subjects—the circle of domestic life'.[15] Helps urged her to capitalize on the book's success by appearing once again in public to receive in person 'the loyal feeling which is only longing for an occasion to express

---

[11] 'The Queen's Journal', *The Times*, 10 January 1868, 8.
[12] *New York Times*, 2 February 1868, 2.   [13] *Daily Telegraph*, 10 January 1868.
[14] *Punch* 54 (25 January 1868), 38.
[15] *Edinburgh Review* (January 1868), 281–300, at p. 300.

itself.... It would be an immense advantage politically speaking.'[16] And when she laid the foundation stone for the new buildings at St Thomas's Hospital in London in May 1868, Helps was happy to inform her that *The Times* reported positively on her appearing in public for the ceremony.[17]

Once *Leaves* was out, she corrected errors for a second edition and communicated her views on the cheaper edition that was to appear in March: she wanted it to be 'a <u>well</u> & not too <u>closely</u> printed edition so that the <u>poor</u> people may read it clearly'.[18] She continued her enthusiastic work of authorship, taking an active role in selecting pictures for the illustrated edition of December 1868 and, as early as autumn 1869, writing to Helps about adding recent trips to a new edition of *Leaves*, an idea that led eventually to the sequel, *More Leaves*. When John Brown died suddenly in 1883, his loss may have precipitated her decision to complete the sequel. Brown, who had become notorious as the object of the Queen's affection after Albert's death, remained a source of contention with her advisors, as his role in *More Leaves* is far more prominent than in *Leaves*. (Soon after the publication of *More Leaves*, the Queen wanted to publish Brown's diary and a memoir she had written about him. Both were destroyed.[19]) As the Queen chose new material she demanded: 'nothing to be altered <u>except</u> in pencil & then herself to be asked and suggestions made so she can explain <u>what</u> she means'.[20] She defended her choices to her adult children when they raised objections (for their specific quarrels, see Explanatory Notes to *More Leaves*, 261 and 322). Days before the date of publication, Bertie (Albert Edward, the Prince of Wales) wrote to request that the book remain in private circulation only. She replied: 'with respect to your dislike of the publication of what you call my '<u>private life</u>' . . . I certainly <u>cannot</u> agree with you', listing five reasons, including: '4thly I <u>know</u> that the publication of my first book did me more good than anything else.'[21] She defended herself similarly to Vicky: 'I have <u>always</u> been <u>fully aware</u> of what I was doing, and know <u>perfectly well what my</u> people like and appreciate and that is, "Home Life," and simplicity.'[22] Victoria remained

---

[16] RA L25/105, quoted in DeBruyn, 'Sir Arthur Helps', 142–3.
[17] DeBruyn, 'Sir Arthur Helps', 143, citing RA L25/106.
[18] Letter to Sir Arthur Helps, 13 January 1868, RA Vic Add MSS A32/15, quoted in DeBruyn, 'Sir Arthur Helps', 142.
[19] A. N. Wilson, *Victoria: A Life* (London: Atlantic Books, 2014), 426–9.
[20] 2 March 1879, RA Vic Add MSS A32/19, quoted in DeBruyn, 'Sir Arthur Helps', 148.
[21] Letter 5 in 'Letters Referring to the Queen's Book, 1883–1884', RA VIC/MAIN/Z/173.
[22] Letter 16 in ibid.

determined to present herself, her observations and her feelings, on her own terms and in her own voice.

As in the case of *Leaves*, she received appreciative letters, most of them ignoring the travelogue and focusing on the book's emotional presentation of her widowhood. A reader whose name was not recorded wrote:

> I dare hardly address your Gracious Majesty but reading the new Leaves from the Highland Journal has left me with such an intense yearning to tell the deep sympathy it has evoked that I cannot express it. I am sure to all your people who, too, have 'loved and lost' it must call forth deep earnest loving sympathy and it seems to speak so personally to one that it feels to me as impossible to keep back the word of loving sympathy and esteem as it would be if a personal friend told me her heart sorrow.[23]

The British and American reviews, unsurprisingly, are shorter and less glowing than those that greeted *Leaves*, as the impact of a sequel was bound to be less; the book is 'precisely similar' to *Leaves*, which 'every one has read', but with this difference, that as she travels through 'the most romantic scenery . . . an eternal sense of pain underlies superficial distractions'.[24] The reviews note, with barely concealed disapproval, the prominence given to Brown, and about the reviews the Prince of Wales remarks: 'some of them I should have preferred to have left unread'.[25] But the Queen in reply finds the same reviews 'loyal' and 'beautiful',[26] and the book sold well: a month after publication it had sold out the first two editions of 10,000 and 25,000, and further editions were in preparation; and plans were made, as they had been for *Leaves*, for a cheap edition and for translations into other languages.[27]

What can account for the great success of *Leaves* and *More Leaves*; what made readers feel the books brought the Queen into their homes? To begin with, her evident affection for ordinary people: her servants, the villagers in Crathie and other places near Balmoral Castle, and people she met on excursions. Victoria frequently added footnotes to her journal entries, to identify her servants, drafting them in pen or pencil at the bottom of a page proof and often providing family histories extending far beyond what was needed in the immediate context. She also narrates lively interactions with those who work for her and points out

---

[23] Letter 11, in ibid.
[24] *Saturday Review*, 16 February 1884, 217–18.
[25] Letter 18, in 'Letters Referring to the Queen's Book, 1883–1884', RA VIC/MAIN/Z/173.
[26] Letter 19, in ibid.
[27] Letter to the Marquess of Lorne, 4 March 1884, RA Add MSS A/17.

that she and Albert 'were always in the habit of conversing' with their Highland servants, conversations they found 'pleasant' and 'instructive' (*Leaves*, 111). Helps's Preface highlights her feeling 'keenly what are the reciprocal duties of masters and servants'; her 'abiding interest' in her servants, Helps believes, signifies Victoria's wish to see 'a gradual blending together of all classes . . . in the great brotherhood that forms a nation' (*Leaves*, 9). Whether performed or authentic, *Leaves* portrays the Queen acting on that hope, never 'tak[ing] for granted the services and attentions which are rendered to her' but seeing them 'as especial kindnesses shown to herself' (*Leaves*, 9–10), as if she were neither her servants' employer nor their sovereign. When *Leaves* was translated into Gujarati, the preface added for the translation recommended 'the deep and abiding interest felt by the Sovereign for the welfare of her subjects' as 'deserving of very careful study both by [India's] Princes and people', echoing the Queen's own assessment that the kindly feelings towards her servants and the poor expressed in her book would serve as a model for the upper classes.[28] In *More Leaves*, she lists the servants she invited to attend, among honoured guests, an unveiling of Albert's statue (*More Leaves*, 192), an unusual proceeding that irritated her family. She published the books, she claimed, 'to show my affection for, and gratitude towards those whom History should perhaps not think of mentioning'.[29]

In keeping with her expressions of affection for her servants, the Queen depicts her participation in local events such as christenings and funerals when she acts and is treated as part of the community. She is a good neighbour: old Mrs Grant on her deathbed wears a pair of socks the Queen gave her a few days earlier. In remote Highland towns, she meets townspeople who do not know who she is and enjoys being addressed as one of them. She and Albert enjoyed travelling incognito when they made their 'great expeditions' in and around the mountains and glens of the Cairngorms, concealing visual signs of their identity (although an editor pencilled an objection to these 'falsehoods' at the back of a proof volume[30]) and interacting with townspeople and hotel staff. Through such incidents, the books envision social classes allying to form a harmonious nation, positioning the Queen not as a cynosure atop

---

[28] The translation, by M. M. Bhownaggree, was published in 1877. Preface quoted from the review in the *Times of India*, 27 January 1877, 3.

[29] Letter 16, 24 February 1884, in 'Letters Referring to the Queen's Book, 1883–1884', RA VIC/MAIN/Z/173.

[30] Royal Collection Inventory Number (hereafter abbreviated RCIN) 1053115.

a lofty hierarchy but as a friendly, familiar presence. She relates to readers as she describes herself relating to people in the Highlands, and indeed to communities in other parts of the nations and regions that she visits, drawing them into a fellowship of shared interests and concerns. Tellingly, however, she also wrote about her great pleasure in adoring crowds and the visible signs of her sovereignty: she saw no contradiction between her wish to see social classes draw closer together and her belief in her own divinely bestowed monarchy.

Identifying herself as a member of her community, the Queen also portrays herself in *Leaves* primarily as a wife, deferring to Albert's superior opinions, crediting him with the new castle's excellent design, and positioning herself within domestic spaces or, when out of doors, arranging her enjoyments around his. Deer-stalking and shooting other game were among Prince Albert's chief occupations when in Scotland, and his arduous hunting of native fauna, while Queen Victoria sketches or awaits his return, narratively conjures a conventional gender hierarchy that mitigates her sovereignty. Her community activities also emphasize her proper Victorian woman's domestic role: distributing shawls and petticoats to warm ageing women in winter, comforting struggling families during illness, and celebrating births and deaths—these too served to reinforce traditional gender hierarchy. Through her writing, she enters the homes of a world-wide audience, not only as an intimate human voice but specifically as a woman and wife. Throughout her reign, Queen Victoria was engaged in an evolving project to redefine the monarchy to suit her gender, changing the sovereign's image from that of soldier or statesman to that of the matriarch, the wife, mother, and widow.[31]

Although publishing books was still somewhat outside a woman's proper sphere of activity in the 1860s, the diary or journal was considered quintessentially female, and choosing to publish in this socially acceptable genre enabled Victoria to write her own story while remaining within proper gender boundaries.[32] While at work on *Leaves*, she was also overseeing the publication of substantial works about her late husband in conventional masculine forms: a collection of his speeches and

---

[31] Dorothy Thompson, *Queen Victoria: Gender and Power* (London: Virago, 1990); Homans, *Royal Representations*; Munich, *Queen Victoria's Secrets*; Susan Kingsley Kent, *Queen Victoria: Gender and Empire* (Oxford: Oxford University Press, 2016).

[32] Rebecca Steinitz, 'Travel, Domesticity and Genre in Victoria's *Journal of Our Life in the Highlands*', *Victorians Institute Journal* 29 (2001), 149–68; Cynthia Huff, 'Private Domains: Queen Victoria and Women's Diaries', *a/b: Auto/Biography Studies* 4 (1988), 46–52.

addresses, followed by two versions of his biography.[33] These works solidify Albert's identity as an important statesman. In contrast, by publishing 'leaves from [a] journal' and selecting entries primarily about domestic and holiday life, the Queen continued to shape her royal image as a traditionally female one. Girls and women were expected to share their journals and letters with family and close friends (if not to publish them). For upper-class British girls, writing a diary was intended to develop moral character, and Victoria, who began writing a diary at the age of 13, maintained the habit of experiencing her life through writing about it long after her mother insisted on such activity. Her diary became the place where her life story unfolded, the place where she created her own character as queen, wife, mother, and widow. *Leaves* and *More Leaves*, although they do not follow the conventional narrative arc of autobiography, constitute her presentation of that life: the form in which she chose to enter readers' homes in 'the green cloth dress of her book'.

Scotland's Highlands: The Place, the People

But why Scotland, why the Highlands? Queen Victoria wrote in her diary nearly every day of her life; the strategic aim of becoming 'known and understood' by her subjects could have been achieved by publishing a different selection. The first two parts of *Leaves* trace in chronological sequence two decades of life in Scotland, from Victoria and Albert's enjoyment of stately official travel in 1842, through their establishment of new patterns of domestic life starting in 1848, and the delights of casual rustic excursions up until two months before Albert's death. The third part supplements that chronology with trips to other regions of the British Isles outside Scotland during the same period. Choosing to select the majority of the entries to reflect life and travel in Scotland not only placed an avatar of the Queen before her subjects; it achieved state and imperial goals as well. Although Helps's Preface to *Leaves* claims that 'all references to political questions, or to the affairs of Government, have . . . been studiously omitted' (*Leaves*, 8), both *Leaves* and *More Leaves* tacitly articulate and promote the Queen's attitude to Britain's internal colonization of Scotland and other parts of the United Kingdom, and

---

[33] *Principal Speeches and Addresses of His Royal Highness the Prince Consort*, ed. Arthur Helps (London: John Murray, 1862); Charles Grey, *The Early Years of His Royal Highness the Prince Consort, Compiled under the Direction of Her Majesty the Queen* (London: Smith, Elder, & Co., 1867); Theodore Martin, *The Life of His Royal Highness the Prince Consort*, 5 vols. (London: Smith, Elder, & Co., 1874–80).

even her perspective on Britain's global engagements and its growing empire.[34]

The relationship between England and Scotland had long been vexed. Two distinct nations, one larger and more powerful than the other, had been uneasily combined in 1603. Although England did not conquer Scotland, some aspects of the Union were experienced as imperial control. Differences of language, religion, and culture as well as of perceived race or ethnicity had long reinforced the border between the two nations; differences of military and economic power created imbalance between them. In the late medieval period, Scotland and England fought a series of wars over Scottish independence, in which Scotland fended off English attempts at conquest. Yet so intertwined were the two royal families that in 1603, on the death of Queen Elizabeth with no direct heir, King James VI of Scotland became King James I of England. Following this merging of the two monarchies, Scotland's Parliament was dissolved through the Acts of Union in 1707.

While the English-speaking southern part of Scotland, later known as the Lowlands, adapted to integration into Great Britain under the Union of the Crowns, other Scottish regions, especially the mountainous, sometimes Catholic, Gaelic-speaking north and west, which came to be known as the Highlands (together with the northern and western islands), continued to resist rule from London. The United Kingdom was by law a Protestant country, requiring a Protestant monarch since 1603. Armed revolts were quelled by the British Army in 1688–9, 1715, 1719, and 1745–6. In the last rising, known as 'the '45' (Scottish Gaelic Bliadhna Theàrlaich: 'The Year of Charles'), Prince Charles Edward Stuart, the Young Pretender, attempted to reclaim the thrones of Scotland and England for his father, who would have been King James VIII of Scotland and III of England had the Catholic King James VII and II not been deposed in 1688 in favour of his Protestant daughter Mary II and her husband, William III. Charles launched the rebellion at Glenfinnan in the western Highlands, capturing Edinburgh and winning other battles nearby, but defeat in the Battle of Culloden in April 1746 ended the rising and brought organized military resistance to an end. The carrying of weapons was banned, and a permanent military occupation was imposed to ensure that it did not recur.

---

[34] Michael Hechter, *Internal Colonialism: The Celtic Fringe in British National Development, 1536–1966* (Berkeley: University of California Press, 1975; reissued with new introduction, London: Transaction, 1999); Silke Stroh, *Gaelic Scotland in the Colonial Imagination: Anglophone Writing from 1600 to 1900* (Evanston, IL: Northwestern University Press, 2016).

However, the legendary glamour and heroism of 'Bonnie Prince Charlie' and his Highland allies lived on in story and song. Symbols of Highlands resistance, such as wearing tartan, playing bagpipe music, and performing Highland games, banned by the Disarming Act (described by a government minister as 'disarming and undressing those savages') between 1746 and its repeal in 1782, were converted into harmless emblems of cultural pride and, increasingly, alluring sources of tourist appeal.[35] Scottish Gaelic, once considered a threat to British hegemony and proscribed after 1746, was, by the time of Victoria and Albert, a harmless and attractive relic.[36] Victoria notes that a few people she meets in remote locations speak only Gaelic, in the mountains between Balmoral and Dunkeld in 1866 and at Loch Maree in the far north-west in 1877; Prince Albert took Gaelic lessons when in Scotland.

Victoria saw the Highlanders as a distinct people, different even from other Scots. Often though she writes about individuals, she also writes about them ethnographically, drawing on stereotypes and the notion of race. Not only visitors from the south but Scots themselves touted the Highlands' 'racial' difference from other parts of Scotland and, by implication, the rest of the British Isles.[37] Highlanders were complexly Celt, not Anglo-Saxon or Briton, in the messy racializing of the period that tended to attribute differences of culture to heritable race. The Highland 'race' was deemed inferior of mind and not industrious, though at the same time the men were considered to be of superior military ability. Calling them Celts implied that they were primitive, tribal peoples, heroic yet warring with each other as well as outsiders; the eighteenth century saw the Highlander as 'a rude savage in an uncultivated landscape'.[38] Such attitudes persisted into the nineteenth century: the review of *Leaves* in *The Times* observes that 'in Scotland there are two distinct races' and that 'the Highlanders, chiefly Celtic and Norse',

---

[35] Quoted in T. M. Devine, *The Scottish Nation: A History, 1700–2000* (London: Viking, 1999), 233.

[36] Stroh, *Gaelic Scotland in the Colonial Imagination*.

[37] For example, William F. Skene, *The Highlanders of Scotland, their Origin, History, and Antiquities: With a sketch of their Manners and Customs, and an Account of the Clans into which they were Divided, and of the State of Society which Existed among them*, 2 vols. (London: John Murray, 1837).

[38] Charles Withers, 'The Historical Creation of the Scottish Highlands', in *The Manufacture of Scottish History*, ed. Ian Donnachie and Christopher Whatley (Edinburgh: Polygon, 1992), 143–56, at p. 147. See also Murray G. H. Pittock, *The Invention of Scotland: The Stuart Myth and the Scottish Identity, 1638 to the Present* (London: Routledge, 1991); Morna O'Neill, 'Queen Victoria's *Leaves from the Journal of Our Life in the Highlands*: Illustrated Print Culture and the Politics of Representation', *19: Interdisciplinary Studies in the Long Nineteenth Century* 33 (2022), at https://doi.org/10.16995/ntn.4711.

are 'manly, courageous, and courteous', 'strong' and 'handsome', if also characterized by 'laziness and hot temper'.[39]

Consistent with these racializing attitudes, Victoria's first impression of Scotland is that 'The country and people have quite a different character from *England* and the English', as she notices the children's bare feet and the 'loose flowing' red hair of the 'handsome girls' (*Leaves*, 20). Travelling into the Highlands, she observes, 'the people [are] so different'; she links differences of heritable physique with those of culture and also of economic privation ('sandy hair, high cheek-bones; children with long shaggy hair and bare legs and feet', *Leaves*, 37). Eventually the strangeness fades, for Victoria will later consider these her people, yet she never ceases to refer to the Highlanders as a people with their own look and 'character', sometimes resorting to Victorian stereotypes about race, if positive ones. Since Lowlanders had commonly characterized the Highlanders as violent or lazy, 'savage' or 'barbarous', her simplistic, positive racial generalizations are made as if over-correcting these common stereotypes.[40] As she writes of John Brown: 'He has all the independence and elevated feelings peculiar to the Highland race' (*Leaves*, 77).

By the nineteenth century, the Highlands were much altered from earlier times. The military roads built following the rebellions of 1715, 1719, and 1745–6 and the expanding railway system made its mountainous terrain newly accessible to visitors and influences from the south. The impact of industrialization in the Lowlands was reaching deep into the Highlands. Nonetheless, the Highlands as Victoria and Albert enjoyed them were alluringly different from England, not only in the character of the people but in the look of the landscapes. The region has a unique biota, the only part of the British Isles to have the *taiga* (boreal forest) biome, as it features a concentrated population of Scottish pine forest. It is mountainous and covered with boggy moors and, in autumn, the royal couple's favourite season there, with purple heather, and it was comparatively empty. The Highland Clearances of the eighteenth and nineteenth centuries had reduced the population, as long-standing subsistence farming communities were 'cleared' by their landlords in favour of tenants paying higher rents to graze sheep on large open tracts, or of deer forests for lease to wealthy hunters. What looked timeless and ancient was the comparatively recent result of sheep and deer displacing

---

[39] 'The Queen's Journal', *The Times*, 10 January 1868, 8.
[40] Peter Womack, *Improvement and Romance: Constructing the Myth of the Highlands* (London: Palgrave Macmillan, 1989), 4, quoting a source of 1754.

people and the crops and cattle they had depended on. The Hunger of the 1840s to 1850s, which afflicted Scotland as well as Ireland, further emptied the landscape.

The Highlands' emptiness and ruined stone buildings may have been part of their romantic appeal, but they were also signs of poverty. The legacies of the Clearances and of other rapid changes in the Scottish economy were long and deep. As the Queen travels in Scotland, she observes the marks of extreme poverty: people living in inadequate shelter, ragged children with no shoes. In a remote spot on Loch Torridon, where she has been picnicking and sketching, she describes seeing 'a row of five or six wretched hovels, before which stood barelegged and very ill-clad children, and poor women literally squatting on the ground'; but next she observes only that 'The people cheered us and seemed very much pleased' (*More Leaves*, 351). Seeing poverty in no way compromises her enjoyment of a picturesque landscape or of her subjects' expressions of love. The poverty she observes seems to be in the nature of things, without connection either to estate management practices—her own, or those of her aristocratic friends—or to her own government's policies. Her interactions with the poor are individual and sentimental, as with her charitable gifts to neighbours around Balmoral. She also observes the traces of traditional economic practices that had supported the population but had been erased or were dying out, such as the communal farming practices she learned about on a visit to Scotland's west (which she seemed not to know had also characterized her own estate), or the cattle drovers bringing their herds to 'trysts' along the 'drove roads' that now smooth the way for her mountainside picnics. She reads the landscape in terms of the pleasures it affords her, not in terms of the marginal lives of her subjects.

When first describing her northern territory, Queen Victoria regards it as strange, often depicting its landscapes as 'wild'. Sighting the coast of Scotland for the first time in 1842, she experiences it as formidable, in contrast to the English coast, which she knows as 'our coast': 'We then came in sight of the Scotch coast, which is very beautiful, so dark, rocky, bold, and wild, totally unlike our coast' (*Leaves*, 18), the possessive indicating not only Scotland's unfamiliarity but also its foreignness. Yet on returning from her second visit in October 1844, England looks 'flat' to her, a fine metaphor for the Queen's altering perceptions of her realm, for she has begun to experience the Highlands as 'ours' too. She writes that she felt 'so attached to the dear, dear *Highlands*, and missed the fine hills so much', praising the Highlanders as 'such a chivalrous, fine, active people' and the Highlands for having 'a quiet, a retirement, a wildness, a liberty, and a solitude that had such a charm for us' (*Leaves*, 44). 'Dear, dear' implies intimacy and familiarity, but in its 'wildness' the Scottish Highlands seemed thrillingly different from her everyday England. Since the eighteenth century, the Highlands had ceased to pose any actual political threat, yet their history of rebellion lingered in the air and, when in Scotland, the Queen was at once on holiday and on a soft-power diplomatic mission to ensure the political unity of the two unequal nations.

Progresses, Tourism, and Scott's Romantic Myth

As a private edition, *Leaves* was restricted to journal entries about the royal family's happy life at Balmoral Castle, but even this limited selection portrays Scotland as more than a holiday home, with the castle becoming both a private family retreat and a royal outpost in Aberdeenshire, close to the Lowlands but firmly positioned as a Highlands royal settlement. When the published edition added the journeys beyond Scotland, Arthur Helps describes them as 'her Majesty's progresses in England, Ireland, and the Channel Islands' (*Leaves*, 7). By calling these excursions 'progresses', Helps suggests their openly political aim, invoking comparisons with Queen Elizabeth I visiting her nobles' houses to remind them of her sovereignty, and recalling earlier journeys of the young Princess Victoria, arranged by her mother to affirm her proximity to the throne.[41] Moreover, by including the earlier Scottish visits, the Queen provided a political context for the royal acquisition of an estate there; the accounts of those earlier visits convey her love for Scotland, even as she attended to her official duties as sovereign, the first trip including a naval squadron and ceremonial appearances accompanied by local regiments in and around Edinburgh. Later, especially in the period covered in *More Leaves*, the Queen would visit the haunted landmarks of Scottish resistance: Bannockburn, Stirling Castle, the Pass of Killiekrankie, Glencoe, Culloden, the monument to Prince Charles Edward Stuart at Glenfinnan. Balmoral Castle, though privately owned to this day, became analogous with other royal residences such as Windsor Castle, requiring the Queen's ministers to travel north on official business during her stays. It also counted as one of the historic Highlands castles, abandoned and ruined or rebuilt and domesticated, that once served as Highland defences against differing enemies over the centuries, some of which

---

[41] Munich, *Queen Victoria's Secrets*, 35–48.

were taken over as garrisons for British troops after the final suppression of the Jacobite cause, and which the Queen found fascinating as well as romantic. Living at Balmoral, both a refuge from and an outpost of the British Empire, achieved a gentle and symbolic 'conquest' of the Highlands, confirming Victoria's role not only as Queen of the United Kingdom but specifically as Scotland's Queen.

At times, the Queen's accounts of her travels do indeed read like royal progresses—Helps's archaic yet apt term. On the earlier visits to Scotland, by sea and road, the royal couple stayed at the palaces or castles of members of the nobility, some of whom, such as Lord and Lady Glenlyon at Blair Castle in 1844, moved out to allow the Queen's large household the space it required. Later travels made by train were progresses too, as when, stopping at the town of Elgin in 1872 on her way to visit the Duke and Duchess of Sutherland, she proudly announces that 'No British sovereign has ever been so far north' (*More Leaves*, 274), and town after town on this remote trainline is decorated to celebrate her brief visits. Triumphal arches 'adorned with flowers and heather' (*More Leaves*, 274), crowds of people, and military 'volunteers' greet her; at Golspie, signs in Gaelic and in English welcome her with gratitude and love, loyalty and enthusiasm (although ironically one of these signs repurposed a Jacobite song summoning Bonnie Prince Charlie's return). This kind of welcome greets her again and again as she moves around Scotland.

But Helps also calls Victoria and Albert 'Royal Tourists' (*Leaves*, 8), and some travels read less as royal progresses and more like private tourism. They climb the mountains around Balmoral for the adventure of it and to enjoy the relative solitude. On their 'great expeditions' in 1860 and 1861, Victoria and Albert stayed overnight in country hotels, putting up with meagre food and uncomfortable lodging, travelling incognito so as to experience—to the extent they could—what travel was like for ordinary people. On her 'Expedition to Loch Maree' in 1877, the Queen again stayed in a hotel and shopped for souvenirs at a local store. Sometimes her accounts merge the language of the royal progress with that of tourism. Writing about her visit to Inveraray Castle in 1875, she both affirms the dynastic connection created by the marriage of her daughter Princess Louise to the Marquess of Lorne (heir to the Duke of Argyll, whose castle this is) and follows closely the route described by a guidebook which directs travellers to the famously pretty drive along Loch Fyne and the celebrated 'avenue of fine old beeches' (*More Leaves*, 328). The Queen's travels both affirmed her sovereignty and encouraged the 'opening up of Scotland' to a new industry: tourism. In

1846 Cook's Tours began bringing travellers from the south into the Highlands by railway and steamboat; following the royal couple's well-publicized 1847 tour up the west coast, MacBrayne's steamship line was able to advertise a 'Royal Route' tour from Glasgow to Oban. The royal couple's residence in Scotland encouraged still more tourism from the south, helping to 'fashion a taste among the wealthy and the nobility for the ownership of highland estates and the enjoyment of field sports'.[42] In the later 1860s and 1870s, the Queen travelled to what had by then become popular Scottish tourist destinations; in 1873 the fame of Glencoe (scene of the massacre of 1692), combined with her own celebrity, brought the news media to the remote site, where John Brown had to scare away an aggressive reporter who spied on the Queen's hillside picnic (*More Leaves*, 312).[43]

The Scotland that Victoria came to love, to identify with, and to take possession of was not only a geographic location and a political entity; it was also a myth, an imagined place. As a young reader, Victoria was known to have loved Jane Porter's best-selling historical romance *The Scottish Chiefs* (1809), with its highly coloured portrayal of William Wallace and the stirring events of Scotland's long-ago fight for independence.[44] As an adult, she became absorbed by the mythical Scotland created by Sir Walter Scott, whose poem *The Lay of the Last Minstrel* (1805) is quoted as the epigraph to the 'Life in the Highlands' section of *Leaves*. Victoria describes reading most of this long narrative poem aloud with Albert during and on their way home from their first visit to Scotland in 1842, and, with other Scott works they read together (although Scott's myriad works do not convey a single, unified picture of Scotland[45]), it helped to create their sense of Scotland's reality, in the way that readers often unconsciously construct their experiences from absorbing influential texts. The Scottish history they entered was draped

---

[42] John R. Gold and Margaret M. Gold, *Imagining Scotland: Tradition, Representation, and Promotion in Scottish Tourism since 1750* (Aldershot: Scolar Press, 1995), 83. See also Richard W. Butler, 'The History and Development of Royal Tourism in Scotland: Balmoral, the Ultimate Holiday Home?' in *Royal Tourism: Excursions around Monarchy*, ed. Philip Long and Nicola J. Palmer (Clevedon, Somerset: Channel View, 2008), 51–61; Richard W. Butler, 'Evolution of Tourism in the Scottish Highlands', *Annals of Tourism Research* 12 (1985), 371–91.
[43] On Victoria and the rapid growth of the nineteenth-century media, see John Plunkett, *Queen Victoria: First Media Monarch* (Oxford: Oxford University Press, 2003).
[44] Graeme Morton, *William Wallace: A National Tale* (Edinburgh: Edinburgh University Press, 2014), 133–4; Devoney Looser, *Sister Novelists: The Trailblazing Porter Sisters, who Paved the Way for Austen and the Brontës* (New York: Bloomsbury, 2022), xiii.
[45] Pittock, *The Invention of Scotland*; McNeil, *Scotland, Britain, Empire*.

in the rosy mantle of Scott's imagining. *The Lay of the Last Minstrel* is set in the Scottish Borders in the mid-sixteenth century; Scott wrote that his intent was 'to illustrate the customs and manners which anciently prevailed . . . combining habits of constant depredation with the influence of a rude spirit of chivalry',[46] and the poem does so by means of a story about a deadly feud between two clans and the forbidden romance that eventually resolves it. The 'last minstrel' recalls Ossian, the mythic third-century bard of Scotland (largely, if not wholly, fabricated by eighteenth-century poet James Macpherson), whose songs, presented as translations from ancient Gaelic, served as an earlier generation's guide to Scotland's wild essence. Scott continued to write romances and historical novels that dramatize the powerful appeal of Scottish and especially the Highlands' fierce independence, even while advocating for the Union and the consequent taming of the Highlands.

How very vivid and medieval were Victoria's and Albert's experiences of the Highlands, with the writings of Scott guiding them: for Victoria, Scott serves both as a travel guide through the rough land and as a model for her own travel writing. Her entries enchant the reader with colourful descriptions reminiscent of Scott's magical kingdom. Both Scott and the guidebooks that rely on him represent the Highlands as an untamed place, where clans dominate, where the ethic differs from the rest of the British Isles, where a romantic wildness predominates. In 1869 the Queen visited the scenes around Loch Lomond and Loch Katrine that Scott brought to life in his narrative poem *The Lady of the Lake* (1810) and his novel *Rob Roy* (1818), these works of fiction with their sympathetic outlaws shaping her itineraries around the Trossachs, as they did for many nineteenth-century tourists. Nineteenth-century guidebooks often rely on and quote these works. As George and Peter Anderson write in their guide to the Trossachs: 'the scenery of the chain of lakes . . . has acquired a degree of celebrity almost unparalleled, the genius of Scott having invested it with all the charms of perhaps the most generally engaging and popular . . . of his creations'; so their explicit purpose is 'to direct the traveller to the position of the more prominent localities of "The Lady of the Lake"'.[47] *The Lady of the Lake* is set in the time of King James V of Scotland (1512–1542); the plot pits a dashing outlaw

---

[46] Walter Scott, *The Lay of the Last Minstrel: A Poem* (London: Longman et al.; Edinburgh: A. Constable, 1805), Preface (unpaginated).

[47] George Anderson and Peter Anderson, *Guide to the Highlands and Islands of Scotland, Including Orkney and Zetland*, 3rd edn (Edinburgh, 1851), 166–7. Other guides in the Royal Library that quote *The Lady of the Lake* and *Rob Roy* include *Black's Guide to the Trossachs* and *Maclure and Macdonald's Illustrated Guide to the Western Highlands of Scotland*.

clan leader against the heroic king, and has a romantic resolution. To visit the poem's 'localities' is to see a mythic Scotland. Such tales and the landscapes they made visible allowed Victoria and Albert to enjoy the romantic legacy of the clan-dominated past while occupying a contemporary Scotland that embraces the Union. 'Highlandism', one name for this myth, 'answered the emotional need for the maintenance of a distinctive Scottish identity without in any way compromising the union'.[48]

Victoria's choice to publish extracts chiefly about the Highlands thus was a brilliant political and cultural decision, as, via Sir Walter Scott, Victoria and Albert entered and then enhanced the creation of the myth of the Highlands. Victoria was one of 'the authors of nineteenth-century Highland sentimentality'.[49] She helped to transform legendary Jacobite resistance into endorsement of the Union, when 'she inherited and reinforced the colourful, picturesque, and partial accounts of Scottish history fabricated by the previous generation's biased borrowing from Jacobite propaganda'.[50] Readers could follow her visits to famous locations from Scottish history and fiction, as she had followed Scott, *Black's Guide to the Trossachs*, and other guides. She even chose to evoke guidebook format typographically, emphasizing place names by having them italicized. *Leaves* and *More Leaves* provide information for those seeking short excursions by land or water, and they sometimes—whether in Edinburgh, Fingal's Cave, or the Trossachs—lapse into prose that sounds as if it has been lifted directly from a travel guide, although unlike other travel guides, the Queen's books allow travellers to feel that they are emulating royalty by following in her footsteps. Guiding her readers through Scotland, the Queen confers royal authority on a timeless mythic reality that travellers under her influence can see through their own eyes.

Queen Victoria was not the first British monarch to be guided through Scotland by Sir Walter Scott. George IV had made a state visit in August 1822, staying for two weeks in and around Edinburgh. He was the first reigning British monarch to set foot in Scotland since before the Union of the two Crowns: the British monarch was constitutionally obliged to make an appearance as monarch of Scotland, but Scotland had been deemed too dangerous for such visits in the eighteenth century. Although Victoria mentions his visit only obliquely, it was a meaningful precursor to her far more extensive tours and residency in Scotland. Scott himself

---

[48] Devine, *The Scottish Nation*, 244.
[49] Womack, *Improvement and Romance*, 177. See also Withers, 'The Historical Creation of the Scottish Highlands'.
[50] Pittock, *The Invention of Scotland*, 103.

served as master of ceremonies, planning displays of royal pageantry featuring the clans, and even publishing a pamphlet to instruct the populace on what to do once the king arrived.[51] As if George IV's arrival were to be imagined as a stylized, theatrical return of Bonnie Prince Charlie, he made good use of historic sites, such as the Palace of Holyroodhouse, and costumed the male participants in tartans. It was for this occasion that Scott promoted the notion that each clan had its own design of tartan.[52] Because Scottish dress and weapons had been proscribed by the Disarming Act, two generations of Highlanders had not been able to wear their traditional dress. After 1782 many continued wearing breeches rather than kilts, hence the unfamiliarity of the kilt in Edinburgh at the time of George IV's visit. Scott dressed the king in a bright red Royal Stewart kilt (in line with a portrait of 1742 showing George III as a little boy in a Royal Stewart suit), which visually asserted that the king was an ancestral clan chief. These performances were intended to solidify the Union of Scotland and England by representing King George as both a Hanoverian and the heir to the Stuart line, King of Scotland as well as of England. The re-enactment was backed up by claims about his bloodline: as Scott wrote in his pamphlet, the king is 'our kinsman', who 'comes hither as the descendent of a long line of Scottish Kings. . . . In short, we are the CLAN, and our King is the CHIEF.'[53]

Queen Victoria's first visit to Scotland in 1842 involved pageantry and ceremony reminiscent of George IV's visit twenty years earlier. In Edinburgh Castle she was shown the Crown Jewels of Scotland; visiting Scone to see where the kings of Scotland were traditionally crowned, Victoria and Albert were asked to sign 'a curious old book' in which the last signatures were those of James VI of Scotland and Charles I (*Leaves*, 25), an event that inscribed the couple in the ancient royal lineage.[54] Later Victoria explicitly took up the same notion that Scott emphasized in his *Hints Addressed to the Inhabitants of Edinburgh* (1822), believing that she combined in her person the bloodlines of the Stuarts and the Hanoverians:

---

[51] Anonymous [Walter Scott], *Hints Addressed to the Inhabitants of Edinburgh and Others in Prospect of His Majesty's Visit by an Old Citizen* (1822); see Ian Duncan, *Scott's Shadow: The Novel in Romantic Edinburgh* (Princeton, NJ: Princeton University Press, 2007), 4–8; Devine, *The Scottish Nation*, 235–6.

[52] Hugh Trevor-Roper, 'The Invention of Tradition: The Highland Tradition of Scotland', in *The Invention of Tradition*, ed. Eric Hobsbawm and Terence Ranger (Cambridge: Cambridge University Press, 1983), 15–41; Womack, *Improvement and Romance*, 144.

[53] [Scott], *Hints Addressed to the Inhabitants of Edinburgh*, quoted in McNeil, *Scotland, Britain, Empire*, 73.

[54] Munich, *Queen Victoria's Secrets*, 36.

I feel a sort of reverence in going over these scenes in this most beautiful country, which I am proud to call my own, where there was such devoted loyalty to the family of my ancestors—for Stuart blood is in my veins, and I am *now* their representative, and the people are as devoted and loyal to me as they were to that unhappy race. (*More Leaves*, 309)

Victoria makes this awestruck observation in 1873, while touring Prince Charles Edward Stuart's landing-place of 1745 in the west of Scotland, claiming that a long historic conflict is now resolved through her presence. This moment displays the advantage gained by perpetuating 'Highlandism', the myth of the Highlands' picturesque wildness and liberty: Jacobite passion can safely flow unchecked, for the object of its loyal enthusiasm is now the Queen herself, the embodiment of Scottish as well as British sovereignty.[55]

Balmoral Castle and 'Tartanitis'

Scott's romantic vision of Scotland is reflected as well in Victoria and Albert's acquisition of Balmoral Castle and the choices they made in rebuilding, decorating, and staffing it. The couple had spent a month in 1847 at Ardverikie on Loch Laggan in the west of Scotland, before taking on Balmoral, which had been recommended to them by Lord Aberdeen, who had inherited the lease on the death of his brother Sir Robert Gordon: 'the place is so situated as to permit of great privacy. . . . it wd. be very difficult to find a place combining soil, climate, scenery, house, and comparative civilisation of roads etc., with excellent Deer and other shooting all readymade'.[56] Located in the fertile valley of the River Dee, it is adjacent to the Cairngorm mountains and close to the 'Highland Line', the imaginary boundary (roughly following the country's geological and linguistic contours) between the Gaelic-speaking Highlands and the English-speaking Lowlands. Prince Albert first leased the estate in 1848, mainly for the autumn shooting; but the Highlands grew on the royal couple, and they purchased it outright in 1852 for £32,000 (equivalent to about £4 million today) on Victoria's receiving a timely legacy of £500,000 (roughly £60 million today) from John Camden Neild (1780–1852), who was known to be generous to others and miserly towards himself. In acquiring the estate, they replaced, if

---

[55] Womack, *Improvement and Romance*; Pittock, *The Invention of Scotland*; James J. Coleman, *Remembering the Past in Nineteenth-Century Scotland: Commemoration, Nationality and Memory* (Edinburgh: Edinburgh University Press, 2014), 155–64.

[56] Lord Aberdeen, letter to Prince Albert's secretary George Anson, 18 January [no year]; RA PP. Balmoral 22/4/.

they did not directly displace, a branch of an authentic Highland family, the Farquharsons, staunch Jacobites in the eighteenth century, who retained relics of Bonnie Prince Charlie and who had owned and lived in the castle until 1799. The last family owner had had to sell to the Earl of Fife, to whom he was in debt. The Earl of Fife leased out Balmoral, the last tenant before Victoria and Albert having been Sir Robert Gordon, whose death in 1847 left the remainder of his lease available.[57]

The new tenants, soon to be owners, took the decision to retain Sir Robert's local household servants, gamekeepers, and foresters, rather than bring staff from the south, and to hire locals even for professional positions, such as Commissioner and Clerk of Works who would carry out their building plans. This choice meant that the royal family were intimately immersed in Highlands culture from the start, hearing Scots English daily and overhearing the Gaelic that many of their employees spoke among themselves. The Queen took to visiting her servants' families in their homes, taking tea, complimenting them on their scones, and concerning herself with their family matters.

The original Balmoral Castle, 'a pretty little castle in the old Scottish style' (*Leaves*, 63), deemed inadequate for royal uses, was replaced by a grander castle designed by the Aberdeen architects John and William Smith. The new castle was located next to the old, on a site with better views and closer to the Dee, and entries in *Leaves* from 1852 to 1856 describe the stages of construction and demolition. In 1842 Victoria and Albert had enjoyed their three-day stay at Taymouth Castle, a vast, freshly completed neo-medieval castle, adorned with crenellations and turrets, and their new castle's design (for which Victoria credited Albert) included medieval-style turrets and windows. Its architectural style resembles other Scottish baronial structures, a style that had become popular from the 1820s and that made the modern castle, with its central keep-like tower, appear more authentically ancient and Scottish than the castle it replaced, although the old castle had in fact retained at its heart a late-medieval tower house. The new castle's design blended historically Scottish and British/English architectural styles in the interests of 'expressing British glory through purportedly local forms', even as it also incorporated allusions to German palaces from Albert's youth.[58] Newly minted antiquity is a quality that fits the image

---

[57] The Revd John Stirton, *Balmoral in Former Times: An Historical Sketch* (Forfar: W. Shepherd, 1921); Appendix to the illustrated edition of *Leaves*; Aonghus MacKechnie and Florian Urban, 'Balmoral Castle: National Architecture in a European Context', *Architectural History* 58 (2015), 159–96.

[58] MacKechnie and Urban, 'Balmoral Castle', 170.

created also by the couple's readings of Walter Scott, who had completed his own neo-medieval castle, Abbotsford, near the town of Galashiels in the Scottish Borders, in the 1820s (the Queen visited it in 1867).

For the new castle, Victoria and Albert acquired furnishings from Holland & Sons of Mount Street, London. Many items were embellished with silver or pewter plaques cast with Victoria and Albert's cypher or with Scottish devices such as thistles, 'in such abundance that they would rejoice the heart of a donkey'.[59] Frieda Arnold, the Queen's Dresser, noted the dense hunting imagery: 'the wall lights are silver antlers, guns or game bags, and if one's pen needs dipping, one must look for ink in the back of a hound or boar'.[60] The couple adopted tartan as a shorthand signifier of Scottishness, believing in its connection to venerable clan traditions. An 1842 forgery purporting to be a sixteenth-century manuscript, *Vestiarium Scoticum*, produced by John Allen under the pseudonym John Sobieski Stuart (who claimed to be the heir of the Stuarts), further popularized the notion of clan tartans; the Queen bought a copy for the Royal Library. The royal couple deployed tartan to decorate not only their persons but also their castle, where even the rugs, curtains, and upholstery were tartan, as can be seen in James Roberts's watercolours of Balmoral interiors of 1857. No longer suspected of inflaming rebellious spirits, tartan had now returned as a Scott-inspired souvenir of a romantic history. One historian of Balmoral affectionately terms its pervasive use 'tartanitis': red Royal Stewart, green Hunting Stewart, and red and white Dress Stewart mingled with a new 'Balmoral' tartan in two shades of grey, red, and black, and with the 'Victoria' tartan, a lighter variant of the Royal Stewart.[61] A memorandum from the Queen in 1870 required the gillies and other staff to wear a kilt and jacket of the Balmoral tartan.[62]

The royal family, too, wore tartan 'Highland dress', Albert and the boys wearing the kilt and the Queen adorning herself and the princesses in tartan, in the form of a 'plaid scarf over my shoulder' (*Leaves*, 78) for a Highland ball, or as the fabric of skirts worn with velvet bodices. In the Royal Ceremonial Dress Collection of Historic Royal Palaces, several tartan

---

[59] Sir Herbert Maxwell, *Life and Letters of Lord Clarendon, K.G., G.C.B*, 2 vols. (London: Longmans, 1913), i, 128.
[60] Frieda Arnold, *My Mistress the Queen: The Letters of Frieda Arnold, Dresser to Queen Victoria, 1854–9*, ed. Benita Stoney and Heinrich C. Weltzien, trans. Sheila de Bellaigue (London: Weidenfeld and Nicolson, 1994), 127.
[61] Ivor Brown, *Balmoral: The History of a Home* (London: Collins, 1955), 18. See also Gold and Gold, *Imagining Scotland*, 81; Munich, *Queen Victoria's Secrets*, 45–6.
[62] Cited in MacKechnie and Urban, 'Balmoral Castle', 176.

clothing items are preserved from this era, including a Dress Stewart silk sash probably worn by the Queen when dancing. A girl's dress of silk satin woven in a pattern similar to Royal Stewart, dating from 1850–52 and worn probably by Vicky, is in the Royal Collection. These furnishings and costumes, added to the purchase of an ancient Highland estate and the building of a neo-medieval castle, identified the monarch as Scotland's Queen.

Victoria and Albert eventually expanded the estate's holdings to 50,000 acres. At the same time that they purchased Balmoral, they acquired Abergeldie Castle on the River Dee, about two miles (3 km) to the east, which became a summer home for Victoria's mother, the Duchess of Kent, and later for Bertie, the Prince of Wales. In addition to building the new castle and laying out new gardens, grounds, and stables, the royal couple added to the estate by building roads and bridges, draining bogs, planting forests, building cairns and other monuments, building a Garden Cottage for the children and cottages for workers, and rebuilding Alt-na-Giuthasach and later Glassalt Shiel as rustic outposts. In 1861 Albert planned a dairy similar to one constructed in the grounds of Windsor Castle; Victoria fulfilled his plans, completing the dairy in 1863. Later, she built the houses Baile-na-Coille for John Brown and Karim Cottage for her Indian Secretary, the Munshi Abdul Karim.[63]

The Clans and the Clearances

Queen Victoria's sentimental enjoyment of the Highlands included picturing herself as a pre-modern monarch presiding over clan chiefs or feudal lords in a land imagined to be insulated from the economic changes that were transforming and disrupting contemporary Highland life. Calling the Highlanders 'chivalrous' (*Leaves*, 44) identified them with the clans, a form of militarized local governance that, in the Highlands, long pre-dated the dominance of the British monarchy. At Taymouth Castle in 1842, Victoria and Albert had been treated to a spectacular Highland welcome, including kilted soldiers firing salutes and pipers playing: 'It seemed as if a great chieftain in olden feudal times was receiving his sovereign' (*Leaves*, 27). The clan in theory (if not literally) consisted of blood relations bound by ties of kinship and loyalty to ancestral homelands, with the clan chief in the role of patriarch. In return for enjoying their chief's protection, sharing common agricultural

---

[63] His Royal Highness the Prince of Wales, *The Buildings and Other Works Executed on the Balmoral Estate from 1848 to 1875* (privately printed 1876), RCIN 1077598.

and grazing lands, and receiving economic support in times of hardship, clan families were expected to provide young men for the clan chief's private armed force. In return for such sacrifices, families expected to continue making a subsistence livelihood on lands where their ancestors had farmed for generations.

Implicitly, Queen Victoria was the chief of clan chiefs. Sir Walter Scott, contemplating the role of clan chief for George IV in 1822, studied *Burt's Letters from the North of Scotland* (1754), which defines 'the Power of the Chiefs' not as the economic power of 'Landlords, but as lineally descended from the old Patriarchs, or Fathers of the Families; for they hold the same Authority when they have lost their Estates'.[64] Clan chiefs were fathers, not landlords; obligations were inherited and reciprocal, not transactional. Sir Arthur Helps confirms the Queen's identification with this archaic political system in his Preface to *Leaves*. When he praises Victoria's care for those who serve her, his words evoke the clan as a kin-based social structure: the Queen's journals 'illustrate . . . the Patriarchal feeling (if one may apply such a word as "patriarchal" to a lady) which is so strong in the present occupant of the Throne' (*Leaves*, 8). Helps's awkward 'Patriarchal' echoes Burt's definition, and when he exalts her feeling 'keenly what are the reciprocal duties of masters and servants', he is describing her as a feudal clan chief, not an employer or landlord. Just as Scott encouraged George IV to imagine himself a grand clan chief, Victoria's Highland servants helped her play the role of sovereign in a land of 'great chieftains', as she wrote of her visit to Taymouth in 1842. And, indeed, their neighbours in the Dee valley included two nominal clan chiefs who still presided over substantial estates: the Earl of Fife, head of the Duff clan on the Mar estate, and the Laird of Invercauld, owner of Braemar Castle and chief of the Farquharsons.

Ironically, however, Victoria and Albert's enjoyment of Balmoral depended on the cessation of the clan as a viable economic, social, and political structure. The persistence of the clans was incompatible with the extension of British sovereignty over the whole of Scotland, beginning with the Union of the Crowns in 1603. Some of the clans (including those of her neighbours) joined the Jacobite fight for the restoration of James VII and II and his heirs, but after the Battle of Culloden in 1746 the banning of armed clan militias undermined their governance and completed the transformation of the clan chief

---

[64] Quoted in McNeil, *Scotland, Britain, Empire*, 75.

into a landlord.[65] If young men were no longer required to serve in the chief's militia, the chief was no longer obliged to support his followers, and Highlands subsistence agriculture as a form of social welfare—the chief sometimes receiving little or no rent from his tenants—gave way to the modern, transactional relationship of landlord and tenant. Some clan chiefs sought to maximize profits, while others sold clan lands to wealthy capitalists from the south, 'a new dissociated élite in a region of traditional family allegiance'.[66] Oftentimes landlords saw the resulting changes as 'improvements' not only for themselves but for their tenants, who, however, sometimes put up strong resistance. In what are now known as the Highland Clearances, landlords cleared their land of people in favour of open grazing for sheep; they evicted families that had farmed the same land for generations and sometimes burned their houses and villages to prevent them from returning. One agent of this transformation justified the evictions on the grounds that traditional farmers 'added little to the wealth of the empire' because they 'deemed . . . no improvement worthy of adoption if it was to be obtained at the expense of sacrificing the customs or leaving the hovels of their ancestors'.[67] Other agents who encountered resistance disparaged the farmers as savages, idlers, '"banditti" threatening the entire course of progress'.[68]

Many of the evicted families either emigrated to Canada or Australia or received small allotments on the unfertile coasts of the estates they lived on, where they could attempt to make a living from the sea or find work in other industries. But those relocated to the coasts often emigrated later, as knowledge of fishing on such rugged coasts did not come easily to farmers, and the mining, factories, and other alternative occupations that landlords sometimes tried to establish often failed.[69] The economic transformation of the Highlands would no doubt have happened eventually as Britain's general economy shifted from agriculture to industry,

---

[65] T. M. Devine, *Clanship to Crofters' War: The Social Transformation of the Scottish Highlands* (Manchester: Manchester University Press, 1994); Devine, *The Scottish Nation*, 170–95; Robert A. Dodgshon, *From Chiefs to Landlords: Social and Economic Change in the Western Highlands and Islands, c.1493–1820* (Edinburgh: Edinburgh University Press, 1998).
[66] Eric Richards, *The Highland Clearances: People, Landlords and Rural Turmoil* (Edinburgh: Berlinn, 2013), 360.
[67] James Loch, quoted in John Prebble, *The Highland Clearances* (London: Secker and Warburg, 1963), 64.
[68] Richards, *The Highland Clearances*, 170.
[69] Richards, *The Highland Clearances*; Prebble, *The Highland Clearances*; Devine, *Clanship to Crofters' War*; Dodgshon, *From Chiefs to Landlords*; James Hunter, *Set Adrift upon the World: The Sutherland Clearances* (Edinburgh: Berlinn, 2015).

but it happened suddenly and violently in the Highlands, this economic change bringing about a 'social revolution'.

Sheep had become newly profitable, beginning in the eighteenth century, owing to the rapidly growing textile industry in the north of England; soon, clearing the land again to replace sheep with deer and planting forests for them became still more profitable, as southerners, grown wealthy from the new industries, sought to rent or buy Scottish estates for recreational shooting. An observer in 1846 said of 'the sporting tenants' that 'they increase rents, they spend money', while their 'general tendency is to accelerate the obliteration of everything peculiarly Highland'; by the 1880s 'two thirds of the Highlands' were in 'Lowland, English or even American hands'.[70] The area around the River Dee followed this pattern. Glen Dee began to be cleared for deer in 1829; Balmoral itself, having already become available to wealthy southerners, was cleared for sheep in 1833 and cleared again to be 'switched to deer' just before the arrival of Victoria and Albert.[71] On their delightful pony rides into nearby glens and up mountainsides, they would have passed the fresh ruins of farming families' dwellings in such places as Ruighacail and Rachaish (in Glen Gelder) and Bualtaich (near the Genechal forest), abandoned yet still marked on maps to this day. The fashion for clearing for deer accelerated once Victoria and Albert acquired Balmoral, purchased adjoining forests, and planted more. In *Leaves*, when Victoria and Albert journey south into Glen Tanar, cleared for deer in 1855, she records that Albert discussed with estate manager John Grant their plans for planting two new forests, one of which 'he intended as a deer-forest for the Prince of Wales' (*Leaves*, 123). For the Queen, this conversation of 1861 is significant for Albert's uncanny prediction of his own death as likely to happen before the forests were mature; but it also testifies to the royal family's participation in Scotland's often brutal post-clan economy. The many-pointed antlers from a stag became the emblem of Balmoral Castle: Edwin Landseer's drawing of deer decorates their Balmoral Castle stationery, and the heads of especially impressive stags, mostly Albert's trophies, adorned the castle's interior walls. What seemed 'wild' and aboriginal was constructed with purchasers such as them in mind.

In her writing about Balmoral, the Queen seems unaware of the toll that the Highlands' rapid economic transformation took on the local population. Victoria and Albert were not directly responsible for any evictions,

---

[70] Henry Cockburn, quoted in Richards, *The Highland Clearances*, 369; Richards, *The Highland Clearances*, 360.
[71] Richards, *The Highland Clearances*, 241.

yet in a long footnote about John Brown, the son of a farmer, she notices that two of his brothers emigrated to New Zealand and Australia (*Leaves*, 77). Albert became a patron of the Society for Assisting Emigration from the Highlands and Islands, beginning in 1851.[72] On her visit to the third Duke and Duchess of Sutherland in 1872, Victoria quotes in full the celebratory words carved on a memorial to James Loch, who as Commissioner for the first Duke and Duchess put the Sutherland Clearance policies into effect, starting in the mid-1810s. Historians of the Clearances tend to cite Sutherland as the most egregious example of the suffering they caused, both for the force and speed with which tenants were removed and for the scale of the evictions. Under James Loch, Sutherland's farmed 'straths' or valleys were depopulated; 1,300 people were removed from Strathnaver alone in May 1819, and by 1821 between 6,000 and 10,000 people had been evicted.[73] 'What was destroyed', writes James Hunter about the Sutherland Clearances, 'was not simply a set of farming townships. Also eradicated was a way of life that had sustained a complex body of belief, ideas and tradition through as many as 2,000 years.'[74] Removals continued, though at a slower pace, under the second Duke and Duchess, and went on during the Hunger of the 1840s. Visiting Sutherland, Queen Victoria marvels at the expansion of the estate, which became Scotland's largest and most valuable, thanks to the profits from sheep farming, eventually covering 1.5 million acres. She accepts the owners' view that the removals led to improvements for tenants as well as landlords. In 1875 on her visit to Inveraray in the western Highlands, she was shown the nearby townships of Achnagoul and Achindrain, which maintained until 1847 the clan-based, communal farming practice known as 'runrig', which was destroyed elsewhere by 'improving' landlords; she quotes approvingly a description of it as '*primitive*', 'rude', 'semi-barbarous', and inimical to improvement (*More Leaves*, 331).

The demise of the clans benefitted the Queen because it ended their challenge to British state power, and because the ensuing Clearances made possible Balmoral's deer forests. Equally important was the Queen's enjoyment of aesthetic experiences dependent on the clans' sentimentalized revival. Victoria's charmed picture of Highlands life often includes local militias at special events at home or away, as in the neo-medieval scene of her welcome to Taymouth Castle. Once disarmed for their potential hostility to the British Crown, some clan militias became British

---

[72] Prebble, *The Highland Clearances*, 215.
[73] Hunter, *Set Adrift upon the World*, 285; Devine, *The Scottish Nation*, 177.
[74] Hunter, *Set Adrift upon the World*, 115.

regiments that, uniformed in the kilt from the early nineteenth century onwards, fought in Britain's imperial wars and maintained its military occupations, from the American Revolution to post-Mutiny India, even if, owing to the Clearances, some clans had become less willing as well as less able to supply fighting troops.[75] These revived clan militias or 'volunteers' now served to enhance Victoria's sense of herself as chief of clan chiefs, for just as clan families owed soldiers to their chiefs, so the landowners owed fighting forces to their monarch. Now tamed to ornament formal occasions, clan militias—or men dressed as such—appear throughout *Leaves* and *More Leaves*; these performances were inspired by the neo-medieval Eglington Tournament of 1839, which Lord Glenlyon attended with a 'tail' of local men in military costumes. In 1842, when the Queen reached Dunkeld, 'Lord Glenlyon's Highlanders, with halberds, met us, and formed our guard—a piper playing before us' (*Leaves*, 25); arriving at Golspie in 1872, she is greeted by a detachment of the Duchess of Sutherland's Volunteers, looking 'very handsome in red jackets and Sutherland tartan kilts' (*More Leaves*, 276). With her male retainers customarily dressed in Balmoral or Stewart tartan kilts, the Queen eventually mustered her own 'clan' militia, the Balmoral Highlanders; she describes them as 'all our people in full dress' alongside other local 'volunteers' formally welcoming her son Alfred back to Balmoral following his wedding in 1874 (*More Leaves*, 321).

Such portrayals of a domesticated Scots military enhance the mythic, sentimental view of Scotland, as do the Queen's two accounts of the traditional Highland Games known as the Braemar Gathering. Braemar, just up the valley of the River Dee west of Balmoral, was where the Stuart standard was first raised in 1715, a centre of Jacobite clan resistance, which the Hanoverian army suppressed in 1715 and again in 1745–6. After 1746, British Army troops were stationed in Braemar Castle, remaining until 1831, and an extension of the military roads, built by General Wade from 1715 to facilitate control of the Highlands, was constructed linking Braemar to the south. No mere entertainment, the yearly Braemar Gathering of the 1850s originated in the clan gathering, which, although it had lapsed until its revival in the 1820s, had once had the serious purpose of organizing and training military forces.[76] In the

---

[75] Andrew Mackillop, *'More fruitful than the soil': Army, Empire and the Scottish Highlands, 1715–1815* (East Linton, Scotland: Tuckwell, 2000); Richards, *The Highland Clearances*, 345–6.
[76] Donald Fox, 'Queen Victoria and the Braemar Gathering', 13 April 2020, at http://donaldpfox.blogspot.com/2020/04/queen-victoria-and-braemar-gathering.html.

1850 journal entry 'The Gathering', the Queen describes the athletic contests—'There were the usual games of "putting the stone," "throwing the hammer" and "caber," and racing up the hill of *Craig Cheunnich'*— and adds in a footnote that the Balmoral gillie who won the race 'spit blood' and became permanently disabled (*Leaves*, 74). These modified battle games mimic the handling of weapons and other strategic skills and derive from long-ago displays of actual military prowess. The final competition is the Ghillie Callum, a solo sword dance over two crossed swords, evoking armed combat. By 1850 the occupying troops were gone, yet echoes of war persist in the festive scene, if transformed into entertainment.

Victoria's journal entry about the 1859 games describes a restaging at Balmoral Castle of that year's Braemar Gathering: Prince Albert, president of the British Association for the Advancement of Science in 1859, had invited the members to observe the Highlanders perform. The pseudo-scientific perspective of the BAAS (which had never before met in the Highlands) racialized the Highlanders, as did Egron Lundgren's primitivising caricatures for the illustrated edition of *Leaves*; the Prince's speech to the group earlier in the week, too, alluded to the Highlands' distinctive racial composition.[77] The Queen's account includes not only contests that recall military skills but also the 'beautiful sight' of local militias on the march in their kilts and plaids and standing in their ranks: 'There were gleams of sunshine, which, with the Highlanders in their brilliant and picturesque dresses, the wild notes of the pipes, the band, and the beautiful background of mountains, rendered the scene wild and striking in the extreme' (*Leaves*, 106). Kilts and plaids, once feared as signs of resistant Scots militarism, are now 'picturesque'; the militias, which she lists by name, are her neighbours and include members of the ancient Farquharson family which once owned Balmoral. At the end of the sword dance, the tartan-clad royal party watches 'the Highlanders marching away' (*Leaves*, 107), and after dinner in the castle, 'We could see the fire of Forbes's encampment on the opposite side' (that is, of the River Dee; *Leaves*, 107). In later years when the Braemar Gathering was held at Balmoral, the Queen's Balmoral Highlanders would march alongside these local clan militias.

The Highland militias under the command of local landowners are decorative additions to the scene, yet their presence summons an old and complex history of real conflicts, and their performances put on display

---

[77] O'Neill, 'Queen Victoria's *Leaves* . . . and the Politics of Representation'.

the historical process of the Highlands' military subordination. About the change in 'national manners' since the 'conquest' in 1746, Samuel Johnson had written: 'the clans retain little now of their original character, their ferocity of temper is softened, their military ardour is extinguished, their dignity of independence is depressed, their contempt of government subdued, and their reverence for their chiefs abated'.[78] The docility of the militias that perform for the Queen accentuates the state power she represents as well as making visible the disappearance of a once flourishing political and economic system. At the 1859 games at Balmoral, as at Dunkeld and Taymouth in 1842, the Queen and Prince live a Highland fantasy of clan life, made gracious by colourful militias, loyal retainers, and 'reciprocal duties', without the dangerous clan resistance for which Braemar was historically known and with no concern for the fates of the evicted former inhabitants. The internal colonization of the Highlands is safely confirmed, even as royal identity becomes—at least temporarily—more vivid.

Seeing the Highlands through Art

Just as the Queen experienced Scotland from the romantic perspective of Sir Walter Scott, she also saw Scotland through the lens of visual artists such as Sir Edwin Landseer, whose sketches and paintings amplified the romance by portraying Highland landscapes as wild and free. And just as Victoria's training as a diarist meant she experienced her life through the act of writing about it, her lifelong practice of sketching and painting led her to see the Highlands and other parts of her nation through her own experience as an artist, as well through the study of works by others. Victoria's art education, a standard part of an elite girl's schooling in the early 1800s, began when she was eight years old. She became a skilled and devoted artist and, with Albert, an avid collector of fine art. She continued as an adult to employ drawing masters, working with William Leighton Leitch from 1846 until his death; Edward Lear taught her watercolour painting for a few weeks in 1846, and Carl Haag and others also served as art teachers for Victoria and her family for shorter periods. During the 1840s Victoria and Albert experimented with etching and lithography; as the Queen and her dresser Marianne Skerrett became increasingly proficient in these techniques, a printing

---

[78] Samuel Johnson and James Boswell, *A Journey to the Western Islands of Scotland* (1775), and *The Journal of a Tour to the Hebrides* (1785), ed. Celia Barnes and Jack Lynch (Oxford: Oxford University Press, 2020), 46.

press set up at Buckingham Palace allowed the royal artwork to be easily circulated to family and friends. The royal family were also enthusiastic commissioners of, and indeed practitioners in, the new art of photography, to which they were introduced in the early 1840s. By the 1850s Ernst Becker, a skilled photographer who served as the Prince's Private Secretary, was acting as tutor to the young princes and helping the royal family acquire cameras and all the necessary equipment.

The Queen and the Prince kept albums of their own artwork, and thousands of drawings, watercolours, and photographs are preserved in the Royal Collection, many gathered in volumes that might be considered visual diaries. They also compiled albums of watercolours and drawings by professional artists recording their life together, known as the Souvenir or View Albums. Many artists were approached to produce content, and during the autumn visits to Balmoral an artist was often invited to join the royal party.[79] Landseer was one such artist.

Edwin Landseer had from the 1820s been commissioned to paint subjects for aristocratic clients who were in Scotland for the hunting, including animal portraits and romantic landscapes featuring its wildlife. Landseer's vision of the Highlands included the heroic *Monarch of the Glen* (1851), portraying a stag with enormous antlers, which is both an emblem of Highland liberty and a lure for wealthy hunters. With his brother Thomas, he turned his Highlands scenes into engravings for a popular market, and the success of this venture led to a commission from Sir Walter Scott for illustrations for a new and complete edition of the Waverley novels (1830–33). *Leaves* notes the presence of Landseer's work in aristocratic homes: at 'the scene of all Landseer's glory', the Bedford estate at Invereshie, where he had worked in the 1820s, there was 'a fresco of stags ... over a chimney-piece' in an abandoned hunting camp (*Leaves*, 113 and 128), and the artist's 'beautiful drawings of stags' (probably engravings) decorated the walls of the shooting lodge Ardverikie where the royal couple spent a month in 1847 (*Leaves*, 55). Even before their residence in Scotland, Victoria and Albert had a special affinity with Landseer's work: they commissioned him to paint portraits of their family and their pets, and in 1842 Victoria purchased his stag portrait *The Sanctuary* as a gift for Albert. In 1848 he was commissioned to start work on his painting *Royal Sports on Hill and Loch*, which depicts Victoria and Albert in a wild mountain scene by the side of Loch Muick, surrounded by kilt-clad gillies and gazing at a stag

---

[79] Delia Millar, *Queen Victoria's Life in the Scottish Highlands Depicted by her Watercolour Artists* (London: Philip Wilson, 1985).

Albert has just shot; and he later painted Albert as a successful hunter in *Sunshine: Balmoral in 1860, or Death of the Royal Stag with the Queen Riding up to Congratulate His Royal Highness*. A Landseer drawing of a stag watching over his reclining mate served as the Balmoral Castle letterhead.

William Wyld succeeded Landseer as resident painter in 1853, and in the years leading up to Prince Albert's death, Haag, Lundgren, and George Fripp took their place too; after Albert's death, the Queen settled on employing Leitch or Haag exclusively. Like Landseer, Haag excelled at placing the royal family in their Highland setting: his watercolour *Balmoral, Bringing Home the Stag* (1854) portrays Albert as successful hunter at the castle's warmly lit entry, displaying a dead stag for the admiration of Victoria and Bertie.[80] His *The Queen and Prince Consort Fording Poll Tarf* (1865)—the royal couple and their gillies on horseback crossing a notoriously deep and fast-running stream near Blair Castle, an episode recounted in the 'Third Great Expedition' in *Leaves*—locates a grand royal procession in Victoria's favourite kind of wild scene. To support a publishing venture, *The Highlanders of Scotland* (announced by the Queen in a footnote in *Leaves*, 74, and published in 1870), she commissioned the Edinburgh portrait painter Kenneth Macleay to create detailed watercolours of her Highland servants and representatives of the clans. She also continued to employ leading contemporary photographers, such as Roger Fenton and William Bambridge, to record places or occasions important to the royal family.

Whether in residence at Balmoral or while travelling, the Queen would walk or ride out almost every day with a drawing book to record the changing light.[81] In *Leaves* and *More Leaves*, she often depicts herself pausing to sketch a scene, whether from the deck of a ship or the window of a stately home, or on a mountain pass. Leitch conjures a compelling image of the Queen painting, 'sitting in the middle of a country road, with a great rough stone out of the river to put her paintbox on . . . Lady Churchill holding an umbrella over the Queen's head'.[82] (Jane, Baroness Churchill, was one of Queen Victoria's ladies of the bedchamber and her frequent companion on the journeys depicted in *Leaves* and *More Leaves*.) Frustration at her lack of time led her on occasion to task one of her artistically skilled ladies-in-waiting either to set up a composition— referred to as 'taking a view'—or to finish a sketch for her. Lady Canning,

---

[80] Munich, *Queen Victoria's Secrets*, 41–4.

[81] Marina Warner, *Queen Victoria's Sketchbook* (London: Macmillan, 1979), 167–93.

[82] Andrew MacGeorge, *William Leighton Leitch: Landscape Painter* (London: Blackie, 1884), 65.

a lady-in-waiting from 1842 to 1855, recounts: 'The Queen sent for me before breakfast to know whether I had drawn anything & to bespeak a sketch of the house from the road, the spot from which we first saw it when we arrived.'[83]

While Victoria often quotes Albert comparing a scene to a place he has visited in Europe, her own view remains closely observant of the actual sites she visits. Her landscape descriptions, full of colours and textures, sometimes read like notes for a painting to be made later. On the morning of what turned out to be the 'last expedition', in October 1861, she observes the effect of a sharp frost seen at a distance: 'the mountains were beautifully lit up, with those very blue shades upon them, like the bloom on a plum' (*Leaves*, 134). She describes scenes using visual artists' terms, as if she were contemplating how to frame a sketch had she time to make one: on taking a walk around Blair Castle in September 1844, she describes the clear streams, 'the peeps between the trees', the shadows and mossy stones, and she comments: 'at every turn you have a picture' (*Leaves*, 38). She describes other sights as 'a panorama' (e.g. *Leaves*, 21) or 'picturesque' (e.g. *Leaves*, 22). As a young art student, she copied her masters' drawings; time and again she wishes to frame and capture the scene as Landseer would have done. His work evidently fired her ambition: as she remarked on one occasion, 'I wish we could have had Landseer with us to sketch our party, with the background, it was so pretty, as were the various "halts," &c. If I only had had time to sketch them!' (*Leaves*, 42). On this 1844 visit to Scotland the royal couple were travelling with a collection of Landseer's work, which they looked over with appreciation on their homeward journey. She 'wished for Landseer's pencil' again later on, when observing a 'picturesque' scene of people spearing salmon in the river near the castle (*Leaves*, 75), a scene she herself sketched, her idea of what is picturesque shaped by his.

With the exception of the people's edition, all published versions of *Leaves* and *More Leaves* are illustrated. The private edition of 1865 included pasted-in reproductions of photographs and engravings, which were not carried over into the public edition. The regular 1868 edition of *Leaves* was illustrated with some of the many sketches the Queen made in Scotland and on her other journeys, engraved by William and Francis Holl, and appearing as simple line drawings inserted directly into the appropriate place in the text. These casual-looking drawings of subjects, ranging from landscapes and seascapes to working people in Wales and

---

[83] Virginia Surtees, *Charlotte Canning: Lady-in-Waiting to Queen Victoria and Wife of the First Viceroy of India, 1817–1861* (London: John Murray, 1975), 101.

Cornwall, enhance the sense of intimacy with her readers that the Queen projects through her writing, as well as highlighting her curiosity about her realm. Occasional small rectilinear spaces were left blank in the formatting of the earliest proofs, suggesting that she planned to include still more of her drawings. Stipple engravings of two views of Balmoral were also included as tipped-in plates.

The care she took in editing the text also extended to the illustrations, where she would draw alterations in a fine pencil or write comments in the margins. 'The engravers' proofs, always scrutinised by the Queen, were never returned to me without some pertinent comment, sometimes illustrated by a drawing by the Queen in the margin,' wrote her advisor Theodore Martin in his memoir.[84] In one of the earliest proofs, she noted that the man holding the oar in her sketch of a small ferry boat—John Grant, who was exempt from the dress code at Balmoral—should be wearing 'trowsers & no kilt', and the Queen and Lady Churchill were to be depicted without veils (*Leaves*, 113). After the publication of *Leaves*, photographer George Washington Wilson produced a portfolio of forty-two albumen prints of picturesque Highland landscapes, which were marketed to be bound as extra illustrations into copies of the book.

For the lavish, large-format illustrated edition of December 1868, the Queen introduced additional illustrations, including seven more drawings by herself and two by Albert. (The Explanatory Notes to this edition of *Leaves* indicate where one of her drawings or Albert's appears in the illustrated edition.) The remaining seventy images were drawn from the Souvenir Albums and from the photograph albums she had earlier compiled to record royal excursions and scenes from royal family life. Two chromolithographs of Balmoral Castle interiors that replicate watercolours by James Roberts were included, with a generous selection of full-page steel engravings, including reproductions of paintings and drawings by Landseer, Haag, and Wyld, and numerous smaller in-text woodcuts made by Edmund Wimperis and James Cooper after photographs by Washington Wilson and Roger Fenton. Wimperis and Cooper also reproduced watercolours and drawings made by professional artists such as Leitch and Lundgren, as well as by Lady Canning, the Hon. Eleanor Stanley, and the Hon. Mrs Gordon, members of the Queen's Household.

The illustrated edition conveys the impression of a scrapbook or keepsake album, with its variety of media, styles, and subjects—landscapes and seascapes, portraits of Highland retainers, depictions of

---

[84] Theodore Martin, *Queen Victoria as I Knew Her* (Edinburgh: Blackwood, 1908), 49.

rural pursuits, and graphic records of Prince Albert's hunting trophies—sometimes more than one image on a two-page opening. Preparing the illustrated edition, the Queen exerted the same care as before, making selections and supervising the transformation of images into engravings, consulting her artist daughter Princess Louise, and sending detailed critiques of early states of some prints. For the image of John Brown seated in a chair that appears at the end of the 'Loch Muich' entry, an engraving taken from a photograph, she asked for alterations to his face ('the nose is too thick and the eyes stare a little') and commented: 'The heather is altogether wrong. The woodcut is "Bell" or "Cat" heather, and white heather is totally different! The Queen sends a small sprig of it, though the blossom has closed.'[85]

More Leaves was only modestly and sparingly illustrated. The Queen included no images of her own, but she made extensive notes on the proof of her engraved portrait that would serve as the frontispiece.[86] There are three engravings made after watercolours by Nathaniel Everett Green, who was the Queen's and Princess Beatrice's drawing tutor in the 1880s: the images of the monument to Princess Alice, Duchess of Hesse, and views of the Glassalt Shiel and Glen Gelder Shiel. The majority of the images, producing the effect of an album of personal reminiscences, were drawn up following a simple formula: small engraved portraits after photographs of royal family members or of Highland servants were set up on a page above an engraved rendering of their signature, which served as caption. The Queen's decisive hand can be detected in the unconventional selection of portraits, mingling servants with royal family members, and especially in the inclusion of two dog portraits: photographs by Hill and Saunders made at Balmoral in 1872 were used as the basis for the engravings of Sharp, Queen Victoria's favourite collie, then eight years old, and Noble III, a border collie fourteen months old. Taken together, the illustrations of *Leaves* and *More Leaves* support Queen Victoria's inclusive values, providing insight into both her political agenda and her personal interests and interactions.

Travels in the Wider British Isles

The three visits to Scotland that open *Leaves*, as well as many episodes of *More Leaves*, see the Queen travelling far afield around Scotland: to Edinburgh; to the Trossachs, Inveraray, Inverlochy, and Glencoe in the rugged west; to Dunrobin and to Loch Maree in the north-east and north-west; and south to Broxmouth and to Scott's Borders region. She

---

[85] Frederick Enoch's scrapbook of proofs, RCIN 1053051.
[86] Stipple with engraving of Queen Victoria, with touches of pencil on the portrait and pencil inscription by Queen Victoria. RCIN 605709.

never travelled to the Outer Hebrides or the northern islands of Orkney and Shetland, but her route to Scotland's west in 1847 took her to Wales, Iona, and Fingal's Cave, and within sight of other islands of the Inner Hebrides; yachting trips in 1846 took her to Cornwall, the Scilly Isles, and the Channel Islands. The books extend well beyond Scotland by including 'progresses' in Ireland and elsewhere in the British Isles; by alluding to her sons' military and diplomatic adventures across the empire in Canada, India, and South Africa; and through the ever present, if implicit, analogy between the internal colonization of Scotland and the imperial domination of lands beyond Britain.

At Britain's periphery, the Queen's attitude towards unfamiliar locales recalls her way of writing about the Highlands: differences of clothing, style, and language strike her forcefully and tend to blur together with differences of physiognomy; these differences are ethnographically stereotyped and sometimes racialized. Her first impression of Ireland is that the place and the people are 'foreign'. In Cork, 'not at all like an English town. . . . The crowd is a noisy, excitable, but very good-humoured one, running and pushing about, and laughing, talking, and shrieking. The beauty of the women is very remarkable, and struck us much.' Irish clothing is peculiar too: the women 'wear no bonnets, and generally long blue cloaks; the men are very poorly, often raggedly dressed' (*Leaves*, 142-3). Her observations, especially of her impoverished subjects, tend to use stereotypes. In the 'First Great Expedition' in 1860, the Queen describes Tomintoul as 'the dirtiest, poorest village in the whole of the *Highlands*' (*Leaves*, 116); cut from this passage at an early proof stage is Lady Churchill's comparison of the town's 'look of wretched disreputability' to 'an Irish village: Grant said they were chiefly Catholics'. Being poor, being Irish, and being Catholic are here signs of moral failure, though the Queen knew this offensive line had to be cut for publication. Observing poverty in Ireland itself, she uses similar stereotypes: when she watches 'country people dance jigs, which was very amusing. . . . The people were very poorly dressed. . . . There was one man who was a regular specimen of an Irishman, with his hat on one ear' (*Leaves*, 147). Unaware of her patronizing views, the Irish crowds apparently adore her. These places and their people are foreign, but they are hers, and these visits confirm the connection.

The 'First Visit to Ireland', a week-long state visit to Cork, Dublin, and Belfast in August 1849, was the first of the additional sections to be added to the Balmoral entries, and in the published *Leaves* it appears out of chronological sequence as the first of the four 'Tours in England and

Ireland and Yachting Excursions'. Despite Helps's claim, in the Preface, to have omitted political matters, the prominent position given to her visit to Ireland registers its political significance, ranking next after the more extensive accounts of Scotland, despite the Queen's visiting Ireland only four times during her reign. Ireland's situation with regard to Britain differed from that of Scotland, even though the two nations initially posed similar challenges to British rule. Ireland had been invaded, conquered, colonized (in part by Scottish immigrants 'cleared' from the Highlands), and ruled by Britain since the 1500s. In 1689-90 William III quelled Irish resistance with a hand even heavier than that with which he suppressed the clans in Scotland, and another Irish rebellion was violently suppressed in 1798. Like Scotland in 1707, by 1800 Ireland had become part of Great Britain through the Acts of Union, its parliament dissolved and replaced by representatives—but only Protestant ones—in parliament in London. Replacing Catholicism with Protestantism and Gaelic with English were imperial goals. The government suspended habeas corpus and instituted other repressive measures in response to the Young Ireland Rebellion in 1848; popular assertions of nationalism and agitation to repeal the 1800 Acts of Union began by 1849. (Unlike Scotland, Ireland would continue to resist until and after 1921, when the Irish Free State separated from Great Britain to become an independent nation.)

Most salient for the timing of the Queen's visit was the famine that began with the potato blight in 1845 and continued to bring mass illness and death to Ireland with the failure of another crop in 1849 after the British prematurely ended their relief efforts. Political unrest in Ireland made the Queen's visit both timely and risky. Victoria sympathized with the starving but condemned the murders of aristocratic landlords, rejected the notion of independence entirely, and did not question Ireland's integration into the Union. That she was warmly welcomed by both unionists and nationalists surprised some observers. On first arriving in the outer harbour of Cork, she evidently saw only celebration: 'to give the people the satisfaction of calling the place *Queenstown*, in honour of its being the first spot on which I set foot upon Irish ground, I stepped on shore amidst the roar of cannon . . . and the enthusiastic shouts of the people' (*Leaves*, 142). Proceeding up the river towards Cork, they stopped to receive the gift of a salmon and listen to 'a very pretty address from the poor fishermen of *Blackrock*' (*Leaves*, 142). It hardly seems right for the Queen to have accepted food from the hands of poor fishermen in the midst of the Great Hunger, and yet everywhere they went, as in Dublin, 'the crowd in the streets [was] immense, and so loyal' (*Leaves*, 145). On departing Dublin, the Queen stood at the stern of her ship 'amidst the cheers of thousands and thousands, and salutes from all the ships; and I waved my handkerchief as a parting acknowledgment of their loyalty' (*Leaves*, 148). In the original diary, the Queen had also recorded: 'We feel so deeply [tou]ched at the affect[ion]ate loyalty of the poor Irish, who called out "come every year",—"when will you come back" & one man gave "3 cheers for next summer".'[87] But the Queen heard no dissenting voices and did not take this opportunity to exert her soft power in Ireland as she had in Scotland.

More distant realms appear in Victoria's writing, too, though usually only as they relate to home, family, and community. In 'News of the Fall of Sevastopol', this decisive battle of the Crimean War comes into *Leaves* by way of the celebratory bonfire lit on Craig Gowan. The entry's focus is on local festivity, as the entire Balmoral and Crathie community— 'Albert and all the gentlemen . . . followed by all the servants, and gradually by all the population of the village' (*Leaves*, 89)—gather around the bonfire that 'blazed forth brilliantly' to dance and shout, play the bagpipes, shoot off guns, and drink whisky. The Queen, her family, and her Household celebrate her armies' successes through a local lens, marking local pride in the Highland regiments that served in the war.

At the end of *More Leaves*, another bonfire is lit, to celebrate the 1882 victory of Tel El Kebir in Britain's imperial war with Egypt. Explicitly pairing these celebrations, Victoria writes: 'A bonfire was to be lit by my desire on the top of *Craig Gowan* at nine, just where there had been one . . . after the fall of *Sevastopol*, when dearest Albert went up to it at night with Bertie and Affie.' Once again, the community gathers around a 'blazing' fire with 'cheering and pipes' (*More Leaves*, 377). The Queen's worry in the days preceding the battle, like her relief now—she is 'upset' and 'overcome' by the good news—is all the greater because 'Affie' (Prince Alfred), aged 5 at the celebration in 1855, is now a British officer serving in Egypt. A telegram tells her that the 'Duke of Connaught is well, and behaved admirably, leading his brigade to the attack' (*More Leaves*, 376), so the victory in Egypt is at once personal and imperial.

The Queen was more actively involved in foreign policy than was once recognized.[88] When she urges the extension of Britain's power in ever more distant places, she both elevates her family's and her beloved

---

[87] 10 August 1849, RA VIC/MAIN/QVJ/1849; http://www.queenvictoriasjournals.org/home.do.

[88] Miles Taylor, *Empress: Queen Victoria and India* (New Haven, CT: Yale University Press, 2018).

Highlanders' service to her, and risks their lives, mourning the murderous cost of empire to herself without weighing the violence inflicted in her name on those she would conquer. Although the book finishes on a triumphant note, in the pages preceding the end she has recorded another imperial adventure, which, while succeeding in its strategic aim for the British, has ended badly for her personally: in Natal (South Africa), in Britain's 1879 war of choice to subjugate 'those horrid Zulus' (*More Leaves*, 368), the Prince Imperial—the only child of her friend, the former Empress Eugenie, widow of Emperor Napoleon III of France—has been killed. Again, a matter of state is included in the book for its personal impact, and she repeats the words 'dreadful' and 'frightful' in evoking the emotions that afflict her on receiving the news. Princess Beatrice's transcription of the original diary reveals that her thoughts have been full of the Zulu war and another war in Afghanistan for many days. Haunted at its beginning by the loss of Prince Albert and by the ghosts of Scotland's past, the Queen's book is haunted at the end by the 'dreadful' consequences of exercising global imperial power in the present. Despite the careful editing to exclude politics, even—or especially—in this mythologized and domesticated Highlands location, the empire's violence is never far away.

NOTE ON THE TEXTS

On 10 January 1868 the London publishing house Smith, Elder, & Co. brought out—to give the book its full title—*Leaves from the Journal of Our Life in the Highlands, from 1848 to 1861. To which are Prefixed and Added Extracts from the Same Journal giving an Account of Earlier Visits to Scotland, and Tours in England and Ireland, and Yachting Excursions*. No author's name appears on the title page: the reader would understand to whom 'Our' referred. Arthur Helps appears on the title page as editor. Smith, Elder also published *More Leaves from the Journal of a Life in the Highlands, from 1862 to 1882*, on 12 February 1884. Again, no author's name appears, but the title page is preceded by an engraved portrait of the Queen from 1866 with her signature, Victoria R, beneath it.

The texts that follow reproduce the second edition of *Leaves* and the fourth edition of *More Leaves*. The second edition of *Leaves* was more widely distributed than the first, which it rapidly followed owing to brisk sales, and it corrects minor errors in the first. The choice to reprint the fourth edition of *More Leaves* requires more explanation. All editions after the second are three pages longer than the first two, because the Queen inserted a new entry, 'Departure of the Prince of Wales from Abergeldie before leaving for India' (*More Leaves*, 322–3) in response to her son's complaint that he was rarely mentioned. Because the third edition was very small and is nearly impossible to find, the much larger and more widely circulated fourth edition is used as the default edition for reference by most readers and scholars, and is the one chosen for reprinting here.

To target a still wider readership after its initial popular success, *Leaves* went on to be published both in a more modestly priced edition (in a smaller format and without the illustrations and decorative borders) in March 1868, and in a larger format with additional illustrations and a fine binding for the lucrative Christmas market that year. *Leaves* also had global reach. Translations included Welsh, Irish, Scottish Gaelic, French, Spanish, German, Swedish, Italian, Gujarati, and Marathi. The Queen envisioned a bilingual, double-column English–Scottish Gaelic edition, of chiefly symbolic value, since few of her Scottish subjects by this time lacked English. An elaborately decorated Hindi translation with a jewel-encrusted cover was brought back from India by the Prince of Wales as a tribute to the Queen in 1875.

Both published texts derived originally from the Queen's handwritten diaries, transformed through lengthy processes of selection and editing by several hands, as described in the Introduction (ix–x and xv). Initially printed for circulation only among family and friends, the limited private edition of *Leaves* (also produced by Smith, Elder, & Co.) contained only those entries that appear under the section heading 'Life in the Highlands'; the selection was later expanded for publication with two inserted entries (about the Crown Princess's engagement and the death of the Duke of Wellington), with journeys to Scotland preceding the acquisition of Balmoral Castle, and with descriptions of royal journeys to other parts of the British Isles.

Despite the sometimes heavy editing, *Leaves* and *More Leaves* undoubtedly preserve the Queen's authentic voice more effectively than other sources. It was she herself who made the selections from her diary for the two volumes, and her involvement at every stage is documented in her letters. Long after the publication of the two books, after the Queen's death, and at her request, her youngest daughter, Princess Beatrice, destroyed all but two short fragments of the handwritten diary after transcribing and editing it. It is Princess Beatrice's edited transcription that is held by the Royal Archives and is available to contemporary readers. The texts of *Leaves* and *More Leaves*, derived from the original handwritten diary, may thus offer a particularly valuable example of what Victoria actually wrote. In this Oxford World's Classics edition, the Explanatory Notes indicate where the princess's transcription omits something from the original; they also indicate additions and changes the Queen made to her original diary, and changes where it is not possible to know the author. Princess Beatrice cuts expressions of feeling, but not all of them; eliminates household details; and, most tellingly, removes many references to John Brown, the Queen's treasured gillie and companion, who appears far more often, doing more important things, in the books than in the diary as the princess transcribed it. Thus, both *Leaves* volumes provide close to an original account of Queen Victoria's daily feelings, interests, concerns, and worries, as well as a more authentic representation of her voice.

The editors of this Oxford World's Classics uncovered these and other alterations not only by comparing the texts of the two books with Princess Beatrice's transcription, but also by consulting a set of proofs for *Leaves* in the Royal Library at Windsor Castle (no proofs remain from the publishing process of *More Leaves*). The private edition went through four printed proofs, with corrections by the Queen and others, before it was ready for its limited distribution in 1865. These proofs are bound in green morocco leather with gold stamping on the covers (they were kept by Frederick Enoch, the editorial assistant at Smith, Elder, & Co., and later bound by him and eventually returned). The later, longer proofs, which include the additional journeys, are bound in workaday cloth covers in shades of green, red, and dark blue. Additional proofs of short sections, unbound, are gathered in boxes and folders tied with cotton tape.

All of the proofs are marked by many hands, in pencil and pen, revealing in detail the collaborative process of editing. Enoch asserts that evidence of the Queen's revisions—she wrote on some of the proofs, proposed changes that others pencilled in, and indicated her approval of others' suggestions—appears throughout the proof volumes, and that title-page and chapter headings are in the Queen's handwriting. A later proof volume, one of those that contains the additional journeys, bears a pencilled message opposite the title page: 'Has corrections in the handwriting of Queen Victoria.' Frederick Enoch's most detailed compendium volume in the Royal Library comprises two-page spreads of proof pages with his annotations pasted into a copy of the illustrated edition of *Leaves*, bound together with such additional materials as discarded illustrations and his Supplementary Preface and Supplementary Appendix explaining the editing history.

When the decision was made to treat the private edition of *Leaves* as a first proof for the published version, diary entries were revised for reasons of privacy and discretion as well as style and grammar. Entries are edited to create a rounded travel narrative, omitting domestic details at the beginning or ending of an entry. Pet names for family members are replaced or explained; some comments on the Queen's health, on her hearty appetite, and the meals she consumed are omitted, as are the alarmingly long lists of 'game' killed by Albert. Most notable among the Queen's additions are footnotes about those who worked for her, some of which can be seen drafted in her hand in early proofs, and to which, once they were typeset, she added more detail in subsequent proofs. (She lamented that the type for the footnotes was so small.) The note about John Brown was a source of contention and went through countless edits as Victoria pushed for fuller expression of her feelings and her editors pushed for less. The Queen also edited to preserve the dignity of her subjects, about whom in private she sometimes wrote patronizingly; for example, when she characterized a group of visitors as 'amusing', Helps pencilled 'will offend', and she cut accordingly. Descriptions of rowdy urban crowds were made less threatening; an 'oldish' man became 'elderly' (*Leaves*, 110). Sometimes the Queen rejected proposed edits that may have sounded too decorous to her ear: she was encouraged to revise 'went away, to begin undressing' to read, 'retired', but she rejected the suggestion; she did, however, agree to cut a discussion of her bedsheets in the same episode (*Leaves*, 115).

Small style and grammar edits abound as well. Victoria searched for the right level of intimacy with the reader: 'we' or 'we two' was typically changed to the less intimate 'Albert and I', but the formality of the third person was avoided, as in the footnote where 'the Queen's half-brother' in proof became 'my half-brother' (*Leaves*, 31). Sound was attended to, as small edits were made to avoid graceless echoes. 'Vicky was safely put into the boat, and equally safely carried on deck' was edited to: 'Vicky was safely put into the boat, and carefully carried on deck' (*Leaves*, 36); 'at length we began' was changed to 'we then began', because the next paragraph opens 'At length Albert met us' (*Leaves*, 43). Pencilled above a chapter title in an editor's hand are the words 'too many gots', and the Queen obliged by revising several sentences accordingly, starting with changing 'I got on my pony' to 'I mounted my pony' (*Leaves*, 69). The description of Kitty Kear in 'Visits to Old Women', 'with a great air of dignity in welcoming us', became 'who welcomed us with a great air of dignity' (*Leaves*, 98), a barely noticeable revision that testifies to the care with which every expression was examined.

Less can be learned about the selecting and editing of *More Leaves* than is known about *Leaves*. The Queen had begun choosing diary entries about trips taken after 1861 almost as soon as *Leaves* appeared, first with the thought of an expanded edition of *Leaves*, then with the intent to create a sequel. *More Leaves* follows the same principles of selection used for *Leaves* but was produced with the assistance of other editors. Until his death in 1875, she worked with Sir Arthur Helps on this new volume; afterwards, she enlisted his daughter, Alice Helps, who had worked on *Leaves*, and her own private secretary, Henry Ponsonby; but no single figure is named as editor, in the way that Helps was for *Leaves*.

Because Queen Victoria took such trouble over composing the original footnotes and because she supervised the editing and production of her books, the present edition prints her footnotes at the foot of the page, as close as possible to their original locations (given that pages in the original publications had fewer words per page). The Queen's footnotes are signalled in the text by plus signs (+), which she used when adding footnotes to proofs by hand, followed by daggers, double daggers, and other symbols in the traditional sequence. The editors' Explanatory Notes are signalled in the texts by asterisks and printed following the texts of the two books (379–448).

Information about the many individuals Queen Victoria knew, met, or refers to can be found in the Cast of Characters (lxv–xcv). Maps are included to help the reader to follow the Queen's many journeys within and beyond Scotland (xcvii–c). This edition also includes a Glossary (449–55) for terms that may be unfamiliar to modern readers and to those unfamiliar with the Scots English that the Queen took pleasure in knowing.

Some features of this edition may strike readers as unconventional or awkward, such as the punctuation, the italicization of place names, and the format and placement of the illustrations, which differ markedly between the two volumes. These features result from the editors' choice to replicate as closely as possible the style and appearance of the Queen's original publications.

SELECT BIBLIOGRAPHY

Brown, Ivor, *Balmoral: The History of a Home* (London: Collins, 1955)

Butler, Richard W., 'Evolution of Tourism in the Scottish Highlands', *Annals of Tourism Research* 12 (1985), 371–91

Butler, Richard W., 'The History and Development of Royal Tourism in Scotland: Balmoral, the Ultimate Holiday Home?', in *Royal Tourism: Excursions around Monarchy*, Philip Long and Nicola J. Palmer, eds (Clevedon, Somerset: Channel View, 2008), 51–61

Coleman, James J., *Remembering the Past in Nineteenth-Century Scotland: Commemoration, Nationality and Memory* (Edinburgh: Edinburgh University Press, 2014)

Collier, Carly, *Victoria & Albert: Our Lives in Watercolour* (London: Royal Collection Trust, 2019)

DeBruyn, John R., 'Sir Arthur Helps and the Royal Connection', pts 1, 2, *Bulletin of the John Rylands Library* 66 (1983–4), 54–87, 141–76

Devine, T. M., *Clanship to Crofters' War: The Social Transformation of the Scottish Highlands* (Manchester: Manchester University Press, 1994)

Devine, T. M., *The Scottish Nation: A History, 1700–2000* (London: Viking, 1999)

Dimond, Frances, and Roger Taylor, *Crown and Camera: The Royal Family and Photography, 1842–1910* (London: Viking, 1987)

Duncan, Ian, *Scott's Shadow: The Novel in Romantic Edinburgh* (Princeton, NJ: Princeton University Press, 2007)

Gold, John R., and Margaret M. Gold, *Imagining Scotland: Tradition, Representation and Promotion in Scottish Tourism since 1750* (Aldershot: Scolar Press, 1995)

Hatt, Michael, and Joanna Marschner, eds, *Victoria's Self-Fashioning: Curating the Royal Image for Dynasty, Nation, and Empire* (2022) [special issue, *19: Interdisciplinary Studies in the Long Nineteenth Century* 33], at https://19.bbk.ac.uk/issue/822/info/

Hatt, Michael, and Joanna Marschner, 'Introduction: Victoria's Self-Fashioning: Curating the Royal Image for Dynasty, Nation, and Empire', *19: Interdisciplinary Studies in the Long Nineteenth Century* 33 (2022), at https://doi.org/10.16995/ntn.8185

Hibbert, Christopher, *Queen Victoria: A Personal History* (London: HarperCollins, 2000)

Homans, Margaret, *Royal Representations: Queen Victoria and British Culture, 1837–1876* (Chicago: Chicago University Press, 1998)

Homans, Margaret, and Adrienne Munich, eds, *Remaking Queen Victoria* (Cambridge: Cambridge University Press, 1997)

Huff, Cynthia, 'Scripting the Materimperium: The Queen's Highland Journals, Colonial Women's Diaries, and the Victorian Imagined Community', *Prose Studies* 24 no. 1 (2001), 41–62

Johnson, Samuel, and James Boswell, *A Journey to the Western Islands of Scotland* (1775), and *The Journal of a Tour to the Hebrides* (1785), Celia Barnes and Jack Lynch, eds (Oxford: Oxford University Press, 2020)

Kent, Susan Kingsley, *Queen Victoria: Gender and Empire* (Oxford: Oxford University Press, 2016)

Lauder, Thomas Dick, *Memorial of the Royal Progress in Scotland* (Edinburgh: Adam and Charles Black, 1843)

Leask, Nigel, *Stepping Westward: Writing the Highland Tour, c. 1720–1830* (Oxford: Oxford University Press, 2020)

Longford, Elizabeth, *Victoria R.I.* (London: Weidenfeld and Nicolson, 1964) [first pubd in the USA as *Queen Victoria: Born to Succeed* (New York: Harper & Row, 1964)]

Lyden, Anne M., *A Royal Passion: Queen Victoria and Photography*, exh. cat., J. Paul Getty Museum, Los Angeles (2014)

MacKechnie, Aonghus, and Florian Urban, 'Balmoral Castle: National Architecture in a European Context', *Architectural History* 58 (2015), 159–96

Macleay, Kenneth [and Amelia Murray Macgregor], *Highlanders of Scotland: Being a Series of Portraits Illustrative of the Principal Clans and Followings, and the Retainers of the Royal Household at Balmoral, in the Reign of Her Majesty Queen Victoria. With copious notices from authentic sources. In coloured lithographs by V. Brooks*, 2 vols. (London: Mitchell, 1870)

McNeil, Kenneth, *Scotland, Britain, Empire: Writing the Highlands, 1760–1860* (Oxford: Oxford University Press, 2007)

Marschner, Joanna, 'Shaping Royal Image through Repurposed Royal Residences in the Late Nineteenth Century: Queen Victoria's Museum at Kensington Palace', *19: Interdisciplinary Studies in the Long Nineteenth Century*, 33 (2022), at https://doi.org/10.16995/ntn.4712

Marsden, Jonathan, ed., *Victoria and Albert: Art and Love* (London: Royal Collection Publications, 2010)

Martin, Theodore, *Queen Victoria as I Knew her* (Edinburgh: Blackwood, 1908)

Millar, Delia, *Queen Victoria's Life in the Highlands Depicted by her Watercolour Artists* (London: Philip Wilson, 1985)

Munich, Adrienne, *Queen Victoria's Secrets* (New York: Columbia University Press, 1996)

O'Neill, Morna, 'Queen Victoria's *Leaves from the Journal of Our Life in the Highlands*: Illustrated Print Culture and the Politics of Representation', *19: Interdisciplinary Studies in the Long Nineteenth Century* 33 (2022), at https://doi.org/10.16995/ntn.4711

Pittock, Murray G. H., *Celtic Identity and the British Image* (Manchester: Manchester University Press, 1999)

Pittock, Murray G. H., *The Invention of Scotland: The Stuart Myth and the Scottish Identity, 1638 to the Present* (London: Routledge, 1991)

Plunkett, John, *Queen Victoria: First Media Monarch* (Oxford: Oxford University Press, 2003)

Ponsonby, Arthur, *Henry Ponsonby, Queen Victoria's Private Secretary: His Life from his Letters* (London: Macmillan and Co., 1942)

Reed, Charles V., *Royal Tourists, Colonial Subjects, and the Making of a British World, 1860–1911* (Manchester: Manchester University Press, 2016)

Richards, Eric, *The Highland Clearances: People, Landlords, and Rural Turmoil* (Edinburgh: Berlinn, 2013)

Rigney, Ann, *The Afterlives of Walter Scott: Memory on the Move* (Oxford: Oxford University Press, 2012)

Roberts, Jane, *Royal Artists from Mary Queen of Scots to the Present Day* (London: Grafton Books, 1987)

Steinitz, Rebecca, 'Travel, Domesticity and Genre in Victoria's *Journal of Our Life in the Highlands*', *Victorians Institute Journal* 29 (2001), 149–68

Stroh, Silke, *Gaelic Scotland in the Colonial Imagination: Anglophone Writing from 1600 to 1900* (Evanston, IL: Northwestern University Press, 2016)

Surtees, Virginia, *Charlotte Canning: Lady-in-Waiting to Queen Victoria and Wife of the First Viceroy of India, 1817–1861* (London: John Murray, 1975)

Thompson, Dorothy, *Queen Victoria: Gender and Power* (London: Virago, 1990)

Trevor-Roper, Hugh, 'The Invention of Tradition: The Highland Tradition of Scotland', in *The Invention of Tradition*, Eric Hobsbawm and Terence Ranger, eds (Cambridge: Cambridge University Press, 1983), 15–41

Tyrrell, Alex, 'The Queen's "Little Trip": The Royal Visit to Scotland in 1842', *Scottish Historical Review* 82 (2003), 47–73

Victoria, Queen of the United Kingdom of Great Britain and Ireland, *The Girlhood of Queen Victoria: A Selection from Her Majesty's Diaries between the Years 1832 and 1840*, ed. Viscount Esher (London: John Murray, 1912)

Victoria, Queen of the United Kingdom, *The Letters of Queen Victoria: A Selection of Her Majesty's Correspondence between the Years 1837 and 1861*, A. C. Benson and Reginald Brett, Viscount Esher, eds, 3 vols. (London: John Murray, 1908)

Victoria, Queen of the United Kingdom, *The Letters of Queen Victoria, 2nd ser.: A Selection from Her Majesty's Correspondence and Journal between the Years 1862 and 1878*, ed. George Earle Buckle, 3 vols. (London: John Murray, 1926–8)

Victoria, Queen of the United Kingdom, *Queen Victoria in her Letters and Journals*, ed. Christopher Hibbert (New York: Viking, 1985)

Victoria, Queen of the United Kingdom, 'Queen Victoria's Journal', RA VIC/MAIN/QVJ/[year and date]; available online at http://www.queenvictoriasjournals.org/home.do

Victoria, Queen of the United Kingdom, and Victoria, Crown Princess of Prussia, *Your Dear Letter: Private Correspondence of Queen Victoria and the Crown Princess of Prussia*, ed. Roger Fulford (New York: Scribner's, 1971)

Ward, Yvonne, *Censoring Queen Victoria: How Two Gentlemen Edited a Queen and Created an Icon* (London: Oneworld, 2014)

Warner, Marina, *Queen Victoria's Sketchbook* (London: Macmillan, 1979)

Wilson, A. N., *Victoria: A Life* (London: Atlantic Books, 2014)

Wilson, G. W., *Photographs to Illustrate the Queen's Book, 'Leaves from the Journal of Our Life in the Highlands'*: 42 Views (Aberdeen: G. W. Wilson, 1868)

Womack, Peter, *Improvement and Romance: Constructing the Myth of the Highlands* (London: Palgrave Macmillan, 1989)

Woodham-Smith, Cecil, *Queen Victoria: Her Life and Times, 1819–1861* (London: Hamish Hamilton, 1972)

Further Reading in Oxford World's Classics

Carlyle, Thomas, *Past and Present*, David R. Sorensen and Brent E. Kinser, eds

Catherine the Great, *Selected Letters*, Andrew Kahn and Kelsey Rubin-Detlev, eds

Disraeli, Benjamin, *Sybil, or The Two Nations*, ed. Nicholas Shrimpton

Eliot, George, *Adam Bede*, Carol A. Martin

Eliot, George, *Middlemarch*, ed. David Carroll and David Russell, eds

Gaskell, Elizabeth, *North and South*, ed. Angus Easson, introduction by Sally Shuttleworth

Johnson, Samuel, and James Boswell, *A Journey to the Western Islands of Scotland* and *The Journal of a Tour to the Hebrides*, Celia Barnes and Jack Lynch, eds

Scott, Walter, *Rob Roy*, ed. Ian Duncan

Scott, Walter, *Waverley*, ed. Kathryn Sutherland

lxi

A CHRONOLOGY OF QUEEN VICTORIA

1819	24 May	Birth of Queen Victoria.
	26 August	Birth of Prince Albert.
1821		Highland Clearances in Sutherland, begun 1807, are largely completed.
1822	15–29 August	Visit of King George IV to Scotland, the first reigning British monarch to visit since 1650.
	22 October	Opening of the Caledonian Canal.
1830	26 June	Death of King George IV, and accession of William IV.
1832	1 August	Princess Victoria begins her diary.
	21 September	Death of Sir Walter Scott (b. 1771). First Reform Act.
1833		Balmoral Castle estate cleared of farms to make way for sheep.
1836	22 May – 7 June	First visit to England of Prince Albert.
1837	20 June	Death of William IV, and accession of Queen Victoria.
1838	28 June	Coronation of Queen Victoria.
	17 September	London to Birmingham railway opens.
1838–42		First Anglo-Afghan War.
1839	10–15 October	Prince Albert's second visit to England; Victoria proposes marriage.
1840	10 February	Marriage of Queen Victoria and Prince Albert.
	21 November	Birth of Princess Victoria (Vicky), Princess Royal.
1841	8 November	Birth of Prince Albert Edward (Bertie), Prince of Wales.
1842	29 August	First visit to Scotland. Edwin Landseer, *The Sanctuary*, purchased by Victoria for Albert.
1843	25 April	Birth of Princess Alice. Lease taken of Osborne House on the Isle of Wight.
1844	6 August	Birth of Prince Alfred.
	9 September	Visit to Blair Athole.
1845	September	Failure of the potato crop in Ireland leading to the Irish Potato Famine. Purchase of Osborne House on the Isle of Wight.
1846	25 May	Birth of Princess Helena.
	20 August	Tour of the south coast of England and the Channel Islands.
	2 September	Tour of Cornwall. Thomas Cook first organizes tourist trips to Scotland. Repeal of the Corn Laws, and the beginning of the free-trade era.

1847	11 August	Tour round the west coast of Scotland and visit to Ardverikie.
1848	18 March	Birth of Princess Louise.
	April	Last Chartist petition to Parliament, following a decade of meetings, petitions, and strikes. Lease taken by the royal family of the estate of Balmoral.
1849	29 March	British annexation of the Punjab; Maharajah Duleep Singh deposed.
	2–11 August	First visit to Ireland.
1850	1 May	Birth of Prince Arthur.
1851	1 May	The Great Exhibition opened by Queen Victoria. John Brown enters royal service. Edwin Landseer, *The Monarch of the Glen*. First telegraph cable laid across the English Channel.
1852	June	Purchase of the Balmoral estate by the royal family.
	14 September	Death of the Duke of Wellington (b. 1769).
1853	7 April	Birth of Prince Leopold.
1854	28 March	Britain and France declare war on Russia, joining the Crimean War on the side of the Ottoman Empire.
1855	August	Reciprocal visits between Victoria and Albert and Emperor Napoleon III and Empress Eugenie of France, the first visit to Paris by an English sovereign since 1431.
	29 September	Engagement of Vicky to Prince Frederick of Prussia (Fritz).
1856	30 March	Crimean War ends.
	August	New Balmoral Castle completed, and the old castle demolished.
1857	14 April	Birth of Princess Beatrice.
	10 May	Start of the 'Indian Mutiny', also called the Sepoy Rebellion
	16 August	First telegraph cable laid across the Atlantic. Prince Albert granted the title of Prince Consort.
1858	25 January	Marriage of Princess Victoria to Prince Frederick of Prussia, later Emperor Frederick III of Germany.
	2 August	The British Parliament passes the Government of India Act, ending the rule of the East India Company and bringing India under British rule.
1859	22 September	Braemar Games restaged at Balmoral Castle.
1861	16 March	Death of the Queen's mother, the Duchess of Kent (b. 1786).
	27 August	Visit to the Lakes of Killarney.
	16 October	Last 'great expedition' in the Cairngorms recorded in *Leaves*.
	30 November	Prince Albert keeps Britain out of the American Civil War by drafting a diplomatic memo on the 'Trent Affair'.
	14 December	Death of Prince Albert.

1863	10 March	Marriage of Prince Albert Edward, Prince of Wales, and Princess Alexandra of Denmark.
	13 October	Queen Victoria unveils the memorial statue of Prince Albert in Aberdeen
1864		John Brown becomes Queen Victoria's servant at Windsor as well as in Scotland.
1865	3 June	Private edition of *Leaves of the Journal of Our Life in the Highlands* circulated.
		Birth of Prince George (George V) to the Prince of Wales and Princess Alexandra.
1866	6 February	Queen Victoria opens Parliament for the first time since the death of Prince Albert.
1867	15 August	Second Reform Act extends the vote to tax-paying males of the urban working class.
	20 August	Queen Victoria visits the Borders region and Sir Walter Scott's Abbotsford.
		Publication of *The Early Years of the Prince Consort*, compiled by Lord Grey under the direction of Queen Victoria.
1868	10 January	*Leaves from the Journal of Our Life in the Highlands* published.
	March	People's edition of *Leaves* published.
	December	Special extra illustrated edition of *Leaves* published.
1870–71		Franco-Prussian War, ending with the proclamation of the German Empire.
1869		Suez Canal built, which dramatically reduces the journey time to and from Australia and the Far East.
1873	12–13 September	The Queen visits Glenfinnan and Glencoe.
1875–6		The Prince of Wales tours India.
1876	1 May	Queen Victoria proclaimed Empress of India.
	17 August	Queen Victoria unveils the memorial to Prince Albert in Edinburgh.
1878	14 December	Death of Princess Alice.
1878–80		Second Anglo-Afghan War.
1879	1 June	Death in Natal of Louis-Napoleon, Prince Imperial, only child of Emperor Napoleon III and Empress Eugenie.
		The Anglo-Zulu War between the British Empire and the Zulu Kingdom.
1880–81		First Boer War.
1882	13 September	In the war to occupy Egypt, the British win the battle of Tel El Kebir.
1883	January	Britain takes control of Egypt.
	27 March	Death of John Brown.
1884	12 February	Publication of *More Leaves from the Journal of a Life in the Highlands*.
		Third Reform Act extends voting rights to agricultural workers.

Chronology

1886	Defeat in Parliament of the first Home Rule Bill for Ireland.
1887 June	Golden Jubilee celebration for the 50th anniversary of Victoria's reign.
1888	Accession of Emperor and Empress Frederick III (Vicky and Fritz); death of Fritz and accession of Kaiser Wilhelm II.
1894 23 June	Birth of Prince Edward (Edward VIII) to Prince George and Princess Mary.
1895 14 December	Birth of Prince George (George VI) to Prince George and Princess Mary.
1897 June	Diamond Jubilee celebration for the 60th anniversary of Victoria's reign.
1899–1902	Second Boer War.
1901 22 January	Death of Queen Victoria.

CAST OF CHARACTERS

THE headwords of the entries in this biographical glossary reflect Queen Victoria's references to the people concerned in *Leaves* and *More Leaves*. Cross-references are included where an alternative name differs significantly from the name under which the entry appears.

Abby. *See* Albert.

Abercorn, Lord. James Hamilton, 2nd Marquess and from 1868 1st Duke of Abercorn (1811–1885), served as Groom of the Stole to Prince Albert, 1846–59, and Lord Lieutenant of Ireland, 1866–8 and 1874–6. He lent Ardverikie, his house in the Scottish Highlands, to Queen Victoria in 1847.

Aberdeen, Lord. George Hamilton-Gordon, 4th Earl of Aberdeen (1784–1860), was the brother of Sir Robert Gordon, the last tenant of Balmoral. He was a Tory member of the House of Lords from 1806, and became Foreign Secretary during the administration of the Duke of Wellington in 1828 and under Sir Robert Peel in 1841. He served as Prime Minister, 1852–5.

Aberdeen, Lord Provost of. Sir Alexander Anderson of Blelack (1802–1887) was a Scottish lawyer and politician, who served as Lord Provost of Aberdeen, 1859–66.

Abinger, Lord and Lady. Lieutenant General William Frederick Scarlett, 3rd Baron Abinger (1826–1892), a captain of the Scots Fusilier Guards in the British Army, served in the Crimean War in 1854–5. In 1863 he married Helen Magruder, daughter of Commodore George Allan Magruder of the United States Navy.

Affie / Prince Alfred / Duke of Edinburgh. Prince Alfred Ernest Albert (1844–1900), fourth child of Queen Victoria and Prince Albert, was created Duke of Edinburgh in 1866. A naval officer, in 1893 he succeeded his uncle, Ernest II, as Duke of Saxe-Coburg and Gotha (his eldest brother, Albert Edward, Prince of Wales, having renounced the title in 1863). Alfred married the Grand Duchess Marie Alexandrovna (1853–1920; q.v.), daughter of Alexander II, Tsar of Russia, in 1874.

Airlie, Lord and Lady. David Graham Drummond Ogilvy, known as Lord Ogilvy to 1849, then 10th and 5th Earl of Airlie (1826–1881), was a Deputy Lieutenant for Forfarshire in 1847, and served as Captain of the Forfarshire Yeomanry Cavalry and the 12th Forfarshire Rifle Volunteers from 1856. After he succeeded to the earldom in 1849, he was elected a representative peer to the House of Lords in 1850. He married Henrietta Blanche (1830–1921), second daughter of Edward Stanley, 2nd Baron Stanley of Alderley, in 1851.

Albany, Duke and Duchess of. *See* Leopold / Duke of Albany; Helen / Duchess of Albany.

Albert / Abby. Prince Albert of Schleswig-Holstein (1869–1931) was the son of Princess Helena and Prince Christian of Schleswig-Holstein. The Queen refers to Prince Albert and his elder brother, Prince Christian Victor (q.v.), as 'Helena's boys'. He later served in the Prussian Army. After the deaths of his brother and father, Prince Albert became heir to the Duchy of Schleswig-Holstein, to which he succeeded in 1921 as head of the House of Schleswig-Holstein-Sonderburg-Augustenburg.

Albert / Prince Albert. Prince Albert, the Prince Consort (1819–1861), was the second son of Ernest III, Duke of Saxe-Coburg-Saalfeld (1784–1844), and his first wife, Louise of Saxe-Gotha-Altenburg (1800–1831), who was the sister of Queen Victoria's mother. A studious but playful person, interested in the newest technologies, such as the railway, Prince Albert of Saxe-Coburg and Gotha married his cousin in 1840 after she had been monarch for nearly three years. He died unexpectedly at the age of 42.

Alexander II, King of Scotland. Alexander II, King of Scots (1198–1249), was the only son of William (William the Lion), King of Scots, and his wife, Ermengarde. He succeeded his father in 1214 and reigned until his death. Alexander married Joan (1210–1238), the eldest daughter of King John of England, in 1221, and, after her death, Marie de Coucy (d. 1284). He concluded the Treaty of York in 1237, which defined the boundary between England and Scotland (virtually unchanged today). In 1867 Queen Victoria saw his burial place at Melrose Abbey (not at Dunstaffnage Castle, as she suggested earlier in *Leaves*).

Alexandra. *See* Alix / Alexandra / Princess of Wales.

Alfred. *See* Affie / Prince Alfred / Duke of Edinburgh.

Alice / Princess Alice. Princess Alice Maud Mary, later Princess Louis of Hesse (1843–1878), third child of Queen Victoria and Prince Albert, married Prince Louis of Hesse and by Rhine (1837–1892; q.v.) in 1861, becoming Grand Duchess of Hesse and by Rhine in 1877. A sensible person, whom Victoria often consulted, Alice died from diphtheria at the age of 35. She was the great-grandmother of Prince Philip of Greece and Denmark (1921–2021), husband of Queen Elizabeth II.

Alice's son. *See* Ernie / Alice's son.

Alison, Mr. Sir Archibald Alison (1792–1867) was an English-born Scottish lawyer and historian, author of the ten-volume *History of Europe from the Commencement of the French Revolution to the Restoration of the Bourbons* (1835–42), the first scholarly English-language study of the French Revolution.

Alix / Alexandra / Princess of Wales. Princess Alexandra of Denmark, later Queen of the United Kingdom of Great Britain and Ireland (1844–1925), was daughter of Prince Christian of Schleswig-Holstein-Sonderburg-Glücksburg, King of Denmark (1818–1906), and Princess Louise of Hesse-Kassel (1817–1898). Glamorous and fashionable, she married Albert Edward, Prince of Wales (*see* Bertie / Prince of Wales), eldest son of Queen Victoria and Prince Albert, in 1863. She became queen consort in 1901, when her husband succeeded Queen Victoria as Edward VII.

Anderson, the Rev. Mr. The Revd Archibald Anderson (1794–1866) was the minister of the parish of Crathie, 1840–66. He married Grace Cumming (1799–1887) in 1826.

Andrews, Mary. Mary Ann Andrews was the daughter of Charles Andrews, who was in the service of King Leopold I of Belgium. Appointed wardrobe maid to Queen Victoria in 1854, she served until 1866, when she became dresser to Princess Helena on her marriage to Prince Christian of Schleswig-Holstein.

Angus, Earl of. Archibald Douglas, 6th Earl of Angus (1489–1557), was the second husband of Princess Margaret Tudor (1489–1541), the elder sister of King Henry VIII of England. Margaret was Queen of Scots, 1503–13, as consort of King James IV. Her marriage to Angus was annulled in 1527.

Ansdell, Mr. Richard Ansdell (1815–1885) was a painter of animals and genre scenes; he exhibited at the Royal Academy from 1840. After he refused to paint Queen Victoria's dogs unless they were brought to his studio, he received no royal commissions.

Anson, Mr. George Edward Anson (1812–1849), courtier and politician, son of the Very Revd Frederick Anson, Dean of Chester, was Prince Albert's Private Secretary and served as Keeper of Her Majesty's Privy Purse and Treasurer of the Household to Prince Albert. He was married to the Hon. Georgiana Mary Harbord, who was a woman of the bedchamber to Queen Victoria.

Argyll, Duke and Duchess of. Elizabeth Georgiana Campbell (née Leveson-Gower), Duchess of Argyll (1824–1878), was the eldest daughter of the 2nd Duke of Sutherland and Lady Harriet Howard. In 1844 she married George John Douglas Campbell, Marquess of Lorne (1823–1900), heir of the 7th Duke of Argyll, and she became Duchess of Argyll in 1847, when her husband succeeded his father to become the 8th Duke. She and her mother were instrumental in circulating a celebrated anti-slavery petition from the women of Great Britain to the women of the USA in 1853. She was Queen Victoria's Mistress of the Robes, 1868–70. Her husband was a Liberal statesman and polymath, who made a significant geological discovery in the 1850s, when his tenant found fossilized leaves on the Isle of Mull. He also helped to popularize ornithology. Victoria and Albert's daughter Louise married the Argylls' eldest son, John (to whom the Queen always refers as Lorne), who became the 9th Duke.

Arthur / Prince Arthur / Duke of Connaught. Prince Arthur William Patrick Albert, 1st Duke of Connaught and Strathearn, Earl of Sussex (1850–1942), was the seventh child of Queen Victoria and Prince Albert. He was Colonel-in-Chief of nineteen army regiments and Colonel of three, serving in Egypt and India. Later, he was Commander-in-Chief of Ireland,

1900–04, and Governor General of Canada, 1911–16. In 1879 he married Princess Louise Margaret of Prussia (1860–1917; q.v.).

Atholl, Duke and Duchess of. Anne Murray (née Home-Drummond), Duchess of Atholl (1814–1897), was known as Lady Glenlyon, 1839–46; as Duchess of Atholl, 1846–64; and as Dowager Duchess of Atholl, 1864–97. She served as Mistress of the Robes to Queen Victoria in Lord Derby's government of 1852; she later served as a lady of the bedchamber for almost forty years and was one of Victoria's closest friends. In 1839 she married George Murray, 2nd Baron Glenlyon (1814–1864); in the same year he formed the Atholl Highlanders militia as his personal bodyguard, which was much admired by Queen Victoria on her visits to Blair Castle in 1842, 1844, and 1861. In 1846 he succeeded his uncle as 6th Duke of Atholl, and Anne, Lady Glenlyon, became Duchess of Atholl. Their son John succeeded as the 7th Duke in 1864, when Anne became the Dowager Duchess of Atholl.

Baby / Princess Beatrice. Princess Beatrice Mary Victoria Feodore, later Princess Henry of Battenberg (1857–1944), the fifth daughter and youngest child of Queen Victoria and Prince Albert, was four years old when Prince Albert died. She later became the Queen's companion, confidante, and secretary. In 1885 Beatrice married Prince Henry of Battenburg (1858–1896). After the Queen's death, she transcribed and edited Victoria's diaries, eliminating much valuable information.

Bauer, Fräulein. Ottilie Bauer (*c*. 1834–1920) was German Governess to Queen Victoria's daughters from 1858. She was a distant relative of Baron Stockmar (q.v.). She later served as reader to Queen Victoria, Lady-in-Waiting to Princess Alice, and sometime governess to Princess Beatrice's children.

Beatrice. *See* Baby / Princess Beatrice.

Becker, A. August Becker (1821–1887) was a German landscape painter associated with the Düsseldorfer Malerschule (the Düsseldorf school of painters). He was the brother of Dr Ernst Becker, Prince Albert's German Private Secretary and Librarian.

Becker, Dr. Ernst. A trained scientist from Darmstadt, Ernst Becker (1826–1888) was Prince Albert's German Private Secretary from 1851. He also served as tutor to the royal children, reorganized the royal library, and introduced the family to the practice of photography.

Belgians, King of the. *See* Leopold / Uncle Leopold / King of the Belgians.

Benda. Carl Siegmund Friedrich Benda (1817–1876) was a forester from Coburg; he served as personal hunter (Jäger) to Prince Albert, 1840–48.

Bertie / Prince of Wales. Prince Albert Edward, Prince of Wales (1841–1910), second child and eldest son of Queen Victoria and Prince Albert, was also Duke of Cornwall and Duke of Rothesay, and was named Duke of Dublin in 1850. Victoria blamed Bertie for causing the illness that killed Prince Albert, who, already ailing, went to his son's rescue after an amorous scrape at university. Bertie married Princess Alexandra of

Denmark in 1863. When he was sixty years old, he succeeded his mother as Edward VII.

Biddulph, Sir Thomas. Sir Thomas Myddleton Biddulph (1809–1878) was Master of the Household to Queen Victoria from 1851, and an officer in the British Army. From 1866 he shared the office of Keeper of the Privy Purse with Lieutenant General Charles Grey. In 1857 he married Mary Frederica Seymour (q.v.), one of the Queen's maids of honour.

Blakeney, Sir Edward. Field Marshal Sir Edward Blakeney (1778–1868) was a Lord Justice of Ireland and was Commander-in-Chief in Ireland, 1836–55.

Bouch, Mr. Sir Thomas Bouch (1822–1880), a railway engineer, as manager of the Edinburgh and Northern Railway introduced the first roll-on/roll-off train ferry service in the world. He was knighted after the 1878 completion of the first Tay Railway Bridge, but his reputation was destroyed when the bridge collapsed in 1879.

Bourner. George Bourner (1821–1895) entered the service of Queen Victoria as 'Helper' in 1845, and was appointed, successively, postillion in 1862, Queen's Postillion in 1865, and finally Head Coachman.

Bouverie, Colonel. Jacob Pleydell-Bouverie, Viscount Folkestone from 1828, and from 1869 4th Earl of Radnor (1815–1889), was the son of William Pleydell-Bouverie, 3rd Earl of Radnor, and Anne Judith (née St John-Mildmay). He was Equerry to Prince Albert on the first visit to Scotland and a lieutenant in the Royal Wiltshire Regiment of Yeomanry, 1840–47. He married Lady Mary Augusta Frederica Grimston, daughter of James Walter Grimston, 1st Earl of Verulam, in 1840. Lady Mary was one of the train-bearers to Queen Victoria at the coronation in 1838.

Breadalbane, Lord and Lady. John Campbell, from 1834 2nd Marquess of Breadalbane (1796–1862), was appointed Lord Lieutenant of Argyllshire in 1839, a post he held until his death. His other public roles in Scotland included those of Rector at the University of Glasgow and President of the Society of Antiquaries. Appointed Lord Chamberlain of the Household, he served in that capacity, 1848–52 and 1853–8. In 1821 he married Lady Elizabeth Baillie (1803–1861), daughter of George Baillie and sister of George Baillie-Hamilton, 10th Earl of Haddington. In 1842 Lord and Lady Breadalbane entertained Queen Victoria and the Prince Consort at Taymouth Castle.

Brewster, Mr. Abraham Brewster (1796–1874) was an Irish judge and Lord Chancellor of Ireland, 1867–8.

Brown, Donald. The first of three younger brothers of John Brown, Donald Brown (1832–1918) was appointed porter and livery porter to Queen Victoria and Keeper of the Queen's Lodge at Osborne.

Brown, Hugh. The youngest brother of John Brown, Hugh Brown (1838–1896) was first a ploughman, but entered royal service after the death of

Prince Albert, serving as Extra Highland Attendant to Queen Victoria and Keeper of the Royal Kennels at Windsor.

Brown, James. The elder brother of John Brown, James (or Jemmie) Brown (1825–1922) entered royal service in about 1864, serving Queen Victoria as a shepherd.

Brown, John. The second of five brothers, John Brown (1826–1883) was born in Crathie, the son of John Brown (1790–1875), a farmer, and Margaret Leys (1799–1876). Engaged as a stable boy on the Balmoral estate in 1842 at the age of 15, he was kept on as a gillie when Victoria and Albert acquired the property in 1848, and in 1858 was appointed to Prince Albert's Household in Scotland. He was sent to Osborne House in December 1864 to assist in the stables, from then on serving as groom and personal attendant to Queen Victoria. She gave him the official title of The Queen's Highland Servant. Their close relationship was the subject of gossip; in the late 1860s the Queen was familiarly referred to as 'Mrs. Brown'.

Brown, William. The second youngest brother of John Brown, William (or Willie) Brown (1835–1906) did not enter royal service like his four brothers, but ran the family farm in Crathie. When he retired in 1884, his family went to live at Baile-na-Coile, the house that the Queen had built for his brother John on the Balmoral estate.

Bruce, General. Major General Robert Bruce (1813–1862), son of Thomas Bruce, 7th Earl of Elgin, and brother of Lady Augusta Bruce, was a British Army officer, who served from 1858 as Governor to the Prince of Wales. He married in 1848 Katherine Mary, second daughter of Sir Michael Shaw Stewart; she was appointed a woman of the bedchamber to Queen Victoria in 1866.

Bruce, Lady Augusta. Lady Augusta Elizabeth Frederica Bruce (1822–1876) was the daughter of Thomas Bruce, 7th Earl of Elgin, a British diplomat. Having served in the household of Queen Victoria's mother, the Duchess of Kent, Augusta Bruce was appointed Woman of the Bedchamber to Queen Victoria in 1861 and Extra Woman of the Bedchamber in 1863. In 1863 she married Arthur Penrhyn Stanley (1815–1881), who became Dean of Westminster in 1864.

Buccleuch, Duke and Duchess of. Walter Francis Montagu Douglas Scott, 5th Duke of Buccleuch, 7th Duke of Queensberry (1806–1884), succeeded to his titles at the age of 19. A large landholder and Conservative politician, he was Lord Keeper of the Privy Seal, 1842–6. In 1829 he married Charlotte Anne (1811–1895), daughter of Thomas Thynne, 2nd Marquess of Bath, and Isabella, daughter of George Byng, 4th Viscount Torrington. The Duchess of Buccleuch served as Mistress of the Robes to Queen Victoria, 1841–6. Victoria and Albert stayed with the Duke and Duchess of Buccleuch at Dalkeith Palace on their first visit to Scotland.

Burns. Robert Burns (1759–1796), a tenant farmer, became known as the ploughman poet, the Bard of Ayrshire. His poems, such as 'My love is like a red, red rose', and 'Auld Lang Syne', appealed to a wide audience. He wrote in both the Scots language and English. Perhaps because of his rebellious views and his fathering children outside conventional marriage, Queen Victoria does not quote from him, even though he was known as the 'Bard of Scotland'.

Caird, the Rev. J. The Revd John Caird (1820–1898) was a Church of Scotland minister, theologian, and university principal. Queen Victoria appointed him one of her Chaplains-in-Ordinary in Scotland in 1857, and he served her in this role until 1886. He championed religious tolerance, refusing to censor unbelief as a moral or intellectual fault.

Cambridge, Duke of. Prince Adolphus Frederick, 1st Duke of Cambridge (1774–1850), the tenth child of King George III and Queen Charlotte, was Queen Victoria's uncle. In 1818 he married Princess Augusta Wilhelmina Louisa of Hesse-Kassel (1797–1889). He served until 1837 as Viceroy of Hanover on behalf of his brothers George IV and William IV.

Campbell, Mr. The Revd Archibald Alexander Campbell was minister of Crathie Church from 1874 to 1896.

Campbell of Monzie. Alexander Cameron Campbell of Monzie (1812–1869), a large landowner in the west of Scotland, was elected Conservative MP for Argyllshire in 1841 but resigned two years later; he ran again, unsuccessfully, in the 1850s. In 1844 Campbell married Christina, only child of Sir Duncan Cameron of Fassifern, who owned 'a good deal of Ben Nevis' (*More Leaves*, 314).

Canning, Lady. Charlotte Elizabeth Canning (née Stuart), Countess Canning (1817–1861), was the daughter of Sir Charles Stuart (later 1st Baron Stuart de Rothesay). An accomplished artist, in 1835 she married Charles Canning (1812–1862), who was Viscount and later Earl Canning. She was Lady of the Bedchamber to Queen Victoria, 1842–55. She died in India, where her husband served as Governor General and then Viceroy.

Carl / Charles / Prince Leiningen Carl Friedrich Wilhelm Emich, 3rd Prince of Leiningen (1804–1856), was the son of Emich Carl, 2nd Prince of Leiningen, and Princess Victoria of Saxe-Coburg-Saalfeld; he was Queen Victoria's half-brother. Prince Carl married Countess Marie of Klebelsberg (1806–1880) in 1829.

Carnarvon, Lord. Henry Howard Molyneux Herbert, 4th Earl of Carnarvon (1831–1890), was a leading member of the Tory party. He was twice Secretary of State for the Colonies, and also served as Lord Lieutenant of Ireland. In 1867 he introduced the British North America Act, which conferred self-government on Canada and created a federation.

Castlerosse, Lord and Lady. Valentine Augustus Browne, 4th Earl of Kenmare (1825–1905), Viscount Castlerosse from 1853 to 1871, held office in every Liberal (or Whig) administration between 1856 and 1886, notably as Lord Chamberlain of the Household under William Gladstone, 1880–86. The Kenmare estate amounted, in the 1870s, to over 117,000 acres, predominantly in County Kerry, Ireland. In 1858 Lord Kenmare married Gertrude Thynne (d. 1913), daughter of the Revd Lord Charles Thynne, Canon of Canterbury, and granddaughter of Thomas Thynne, 2nd Marquess of Bath.

Cathcart, Emily. The Hon. Emily Sarah Cathcart (1834–84), daughter of Lieutenant General Sir George Cathcart, was successively Maid of Honour, 1855–80, Extra Woman of the Bedchamber, 1880–81, and Woman of the Bedchamber, 1891–1901, to the Queen.

Charles. *See* Carl / Charles / Prince Leiningen.

Charles I. Charles I, King of England, Scotland, and Ireland (1600–1649), was the second son of King James VI of Scotland (later King James I of England) and Anne of Denmark. He married Princess Henrietta Maria, sister of King Louis XIII of France. He succeeded his father to the throne as Charles I of England and Scotland. His authoritarian rule and quarrels with parliament eventually provoked a civil war and led to his execution on 30 January 1649.

Charles Edward, Prince / Prince Charlie. Prince Charles Edward Stuart (1720–1788), was the elder son of James Francis Edward Stuart ('the Old Pretender'), grandson of King James VII of Scotland and II of England, and the Stuart claimant to the thrones of England, Scotland, and Ireland after 1766 as Charles III. During his lifetime, he was also known as 'the Young Pretender' and 'the Young Chevalier'; in popular memory, he is known as 'Bonnie Prince Charlie', best remembered for his role in the Jacobite rising of 1745. His defeat at Culloden in April 1746 effectively ended the Stuart campaign for royal power. His escape from Scotland after the uprising led to his portrayal as a romantic figure of heroic failure.

Christian Victor / Christle. Prince Christian Victor of Schleswig-Holstein (1867–1900) was the elder son of Princess Helena and Prince Christian of Schleswig-Holstein. The Queen referred to Prince Christian and his brother, Prince Albert (*see* Abby / Albert), as 'Helena's boys'. A soldier, he died of typhoid while fighting in South Africa.

Churchill, Jane / Lady Churchill. Jane Spencer (née Conyngham), Lady Churchill (1826–1900), daughter of Francis Conyngham, Earl of Mount Charles, then 2nd Marquess Conyngham, married Francis George Spencer, 2nd Baron Churchill from 1845 (d. 1886), in 1849. From 1854 Lady Churchill was Lady of the Bedchamber to Queen Victoria, a position she kept until her death.

Clarendon, Lord. George William Frederick Villiers, 4th Earl of Clarendon (1800–1870), was a diplomat and statesman who served as Foreign Secretary three times. He was the leading British representative at the Congress of Paris in 1856, which ended the Crimean War.

Clark, Francie. Born in Crathie, Francis Clark (1841–1895) was a cousin of John Brown and a ploughman. He entered royal service in 1870 as a Highland servant to Queen Victoria. He drove the Queen's carriage and from 1879 looked after her dogs. He took over the role played by John Brown in the Queen's Household after Brown's death.

Clark, Sir James. Sir James Clark, 1st Baronet (1788–1870), was Physician-in-Ordinary to Queen Victoria between 1837 and 1860, and was appointed Physician also to Prince Albert. Clark is famous for having contributed to John Keats's agonizing death, and also to the scandal surrounding Lady Flora Hastings, whose cancerous liver tumour he diagnosed as pregnancy. When Albert himself was on his deathbed, Clark assured the Queen that he would be better in two to three days. Victoria never doubted his competency.

Connaught, Duke of. *See* Arthur / Prince Arthur / Duke of Connaught.

Coutts, Charlie. Charles Coutts was a gillie on the Balmoral estate.

Coutts, Jemmie. James Coutts, sometimes called Jemmie Coutts, was a gillie on the Balmoral estate.

Cross, Mr. Richard Assheton Cross, 1st Viscount Cross (1823–1914), was a statesman and Conservative politician, who served as Home Secretary in 1874–80 and 1885–6.

Crum Ewing, Mr. H. E. Humphrey Ewing Crum-Ewing (1802–1887) was a Scottish Liberal politician, who sat in the House of Commons from 1857 to 1874. He was Lord Lieutenant of Dumbartonshire, 1874–87.

Dalhousie, Lord. James Andrew Broun-Ramsay, 1st Marquess of Dalhousie (1812–1860), known as Earl of Dalhousie between 1838 and 1849, was the third and youngest son of George Ramsay, 9th Earl of Dalhousie. In 1836 he married Lady Susan Hay, daughter of the Marquess of Tweeddale. As Governor General of India from 1848 to 1856, he consolidated East India Company rule and laid the groundwork for India's absorption into the British Empire after 1857. After Britain won the Second Anglo-Sikh War, he presided over the transfer of the Punjab to British rule, and of the Koh-i-noor diamond into British possession, organizing Maharajah Duleep Singh's guardianship and ultimate exile to England. Victoria and Albert briefly visited the Marquess and his wife at Dalhousie, their castle in Midlothian, on an excursion from Dalkeith on their first visit to Scotland.

Dalhousie, Lord / Lord Panmure. Fox Maule-Ramsay, 2nd Baron Panmure, 11th Earl of Dalhousie (1801–1874), was the eldest son of William Maule, 1st Baron Panmure, and a grandson of George Ramsay, 8th Earl of Dalhousie. Before 1852 he was known as Fox Maule; after becoming the 2nd Baron Panmure in 1852, he was known as Lord Panmure; and, from 1860, when he became 11th Earl of Dalhousie, he was known as Lord Dalhousie. In 1835 he entered the House of Commons as MP for Perthshire. He was Secretary at War, 1846–52, and later Palmerston's Secretary of State for War, 1855–8, during the conclusion of the Crimean War. He was Keeper of the Privy Seal of Scotland from 1853 until his death. As landowner of a large property just south of Balmoral, he was Victoria and Albert's neighbour and occasional host on their expeditions. The Queen refers to him as Lord Panmure in 1852

(*Leaves*, 79) and as Lord Dalhousie in 1861 (*Leaves*, 119) and 1865 (*More Leaves*, 197).

Darnley, Lord. Henry Stewart, Duke of Albany, Earl of Ross, Lord Darnley (1545/6–1567), was the son of Matthew Stewart, 4th Earl of Lennox, and Lady Margaret Douglas, who was the daughter of Margaret Tudor, Queen Consort of James IV, King of Scots, by her second husband Archibald Douglas, 6th Earl of Angus. Darnley married Mary Queen of Scots in 1565, and was assassinated at the Palace of Holyroodhouse in 1567.

Dawson, Caroline. Caroline Margaret Dawson (1822–1896), daughter of the Hon. Lionel Charles Dawson, was Maid of Honour to Queen Victoria, 1845–51. In 1851 she married her cousin the Hon. Henry William Parnell.

Denvir, Bishop. Cornelius Denvir (1791–1866), was an Irish Roman Catholic prelate, mathematician, natural philosopher, and sometime Bishop of Down and Connor. He is noted for ministering in Belfast amid growing sectarian tension, taking a moderate and non-confrontational stance.

Dittweiler, Emilie. A native of Baden-Württemburg, Emilie Dittweiler (*c.* 1831–*c.* 1899) served as a dresser to Queen Victoria, 1857–92.

Donegal, Lord. George Hamilton Chichester, 3rd Marquess of Donegall (1797–1883), Earl of Belfast between 1799 and 1844, was an Anglo-Irish landowner, courtier, and politician. He served as Vice-Chamberlain of the Household in 1830–34 and 1838–41, and as Captain of the Yeomen of the Guard in 1848–52. He was also Lord Lieutenant of Antrim, Ireland, 1841–83, and was made a Knight of St Patrick in 1857. He married Lady Harriet Anne Butler (d. 1860), daughter of the 1st Earl of Glengall, in 1822.

Douro, Lady. Elizabeth Hay, later Duchess of Wellington (1820–1904), married in 1839 Lieutenant General Arthur Richard Wellesley (1807–1884), Marquess of Douro from 1814 to 1852, a British soldier and politician, who served as Master of the Horse in the 1850s and became the 2nd Duke of Wellington in 1852 on the death of his father. She served as Queen Victoria's Mistress of the Robes in 1861–8 and 1874–80.

Down, Bishop of. Robert Bent Knox (1808–1893) was the Church of Ireland Bishop of Down, Connor, and Dromore from 1849 to 1886, and then Archbishop of Armagh and Primate of All Ireland from 1886 until his death.

Duff, Mr. and Lady Agnes. *See* Fife, Earl and Countess of.

Dufferin, Lord and Lady. Frederick Temple Hamilton-Temple-Blackwood, 1st Marquess of Dufferin and Ava (1826–1902), was appointed a Lord-in-Waiting to Queen Victoria in 1849. He became Governor General of Canada in 1872 and Viceroy of India in 1884. He married Hariot Georgina Rowan-Hamilton (1843–1936) in 1862, who is known for leading an initiative to improve medical care for women in British India.

Duncan, Charles. Engaged as a gillie at Balmoral from 1849, Charles Duncan (1826–1904) was promoted to keeper in 1851. From 1868, he served as forester to the Prince of Wales at Birkhall, near Balmoral.

Edinburgh, Duchess of. *See* Marie / Duchess of Edinburgh.
Edinburgh, Duke of. *See* Affie / Prince Alfred / Duke of Edinburgh.
Edward I. Edward I, King of England, Lord of Ireland, and Duke of Aquitaine (1239–1307), known as 'Edward Longshanks' and 'the Hammer of the Scots', was the eldest son of King Henry III and Eleanor of Provence. He was married to Eleanor of Castille (1241–1290) in 1254. Her death was commemorated by the erection of 'Eleanor Crosses' (some still extant). Edward I then married Margaret of France (*c.* 1279–1318), daughter of Philip III of France and Maria of Brabant, in 1299.
Elcho, Lord / Earl of Wemyss. Francis Wemyss-Charteris-Douglas, 9th Earl of Wemyss and 5th Earl of March (1795–1883), succeeded to the earldom in 1853. Until that time, he was known as Lord Elcho, a junior courtesy title for Wemyss-Charteris family members, and appears under that title in the Queen's account of her visit in 1842; he had become Earl by the time of the book's publication, as her footnote indicates. He was a member of the Royal Company of Archers, gaining the rank of Lieutenant General in 1842. He served as Lord Lieutenant of Peeblesshire, 1853–80. In 1817 he married Lady Louisa Bingham (1798–1882).
Elphinstone, Colonel. Major General Sir Howard Craufurd Elphinstone (1829–1890) was a British Army officer. He joined the Corps of Royal Engineers and was commissioned as a second lieutenant in 1847. He won the Victoria Cross for his service in the Crimean War. In 1859 he joined the Royal Household as Governor to Prince Arthur, later serving as Prince Arthur's Comptroller of the Household and also as Governor to Prince Leopold.
Elphinstone, Lord and Lady. William Buller Fullerton Elphinstone, 15th Lord Elphinstone, later 1st Baron Elphinstone (1828–1893), known as William Elphinstone until 1861, was a Scottish Conservative politician. He succeeded his second cousin as Lord Elphinstone in 1861 and was elected a Scottish representative peer in 1867, serving as a lord-in-waiting (government whip in the House of Lords) under various prime ministers for periods between 1874 and 1889. In 1885 he was created Baron Elphinstone, of Elphinstone in the County of Haddington. He married Lady Constance Euphemia Murray (1838–1922), daughter of Alexander Murray, 6th Earl of Dunmore, in 1864.
Elphinstone, Sir J. D. H. Sir James Dalrymple-Horn-Elphinstone, 2nd Baronet (1805–1886), was a Conservative politician, who sat in the House of Commons for two periods between 1857 and 1880.
Ely, Lady. Jane Loftus, Marchioness of Ely (1821–1890), daughter of James Hope-Vere and Lady Elizabeth Hay, married John Loftus, 3rd Marquess of Ely, in 1844. She was appointed a lady of the bedchamber to Queen Victoria in 1851, and became one of the Queen's most trusted attendants. After the marriage of Princess Louise in 1871, Lady Ely was asked to live with the Queen, which she did until April 1889, when she resigned

following the death of her son. In recognition of her service, she was granted the honorary title of Extra Lady of the Bedchamber.

Ernie / 'Alice's son'. Prince Ernest Louis of Hesse and by Rhine (1868–1937) was the eldest son of Princess Alice and Prince Louis of Hesse and by Rhine. Prince Ernest married Princess Victoria Melita of Saxe-Coburg and Gotha (1876–1936), the daughter of his uncle Prince Alfred. On his father's death in 1892, Prince Ernest became Grand Duke of Hesse and by Rhine.

Erroll, Leila. Lady Cecilia Leila Hay of Erroll (1860–1935), daughter of William Harry Hay, 19th Earl of Erroll, and Eliza Amelia, Countess of Erroll, was a lady-in-waiting to Queen Victoria.

Erroll, Lord and Lady. William Harry Hay, 19th Earl of Erroll (1823–1891), was known as Lord Hay, 1823–31, and Lord Kilmarnock, from 1831, until he succeeded to the earldom in 1846. He served as Page of Honour to his grandfather, King William IV, 1831–7, and to Queen Victoria, 1837–9. In 1848 he married Eliza Amelia Gore (1829–1916). The Countess of Erroll served as Lady of the Bedchamber to Alexandra, Princess of Wales, from 1872.

Ettrick Shepherd, the. James Hogg, known as the Ettrick Shepherd (1770–1835), was a self-taught poet and novelist from a remote part of the Scottish Borders, where he worked as a shepherd as a young man. Recruited to discover ballads for Walter Scott's *Minstrelsy of the Scottish Border* (1802–3), he became a friend of Scott and an international celebrity for poems that drew on local oral poetry and ballad traditions. His best-known work is the novel *The Private Memoirs and Confessions of a Justified Sinner* (1824). In 1831 he published a collection of his own poetry, *The Ettrick Shepherd*.

Farquharson, Mr. / Farquharson of Invercauld. James Farquharson (1808–1862) became the 12th Laird of Invercauld in 1845; the Farquharsons were patrons of the Braemar Gathering and owners of Invercauld House, Braemar Castle, and the Invercauld estate, adjacent to Balmoral. His son, Colonel James Ross Farquharson (1834–1888), became Laird in 1862.

Farquharson, Mrs. P., and P. Farquharson. Margaret (McHardy) Farquharson was the wife of Peter Farquharson (1804–1874), a distant relative of the Farquharsons of Invercauld. He had worked as gamekeeper for Sir Robert Gordon, the last tenant of Balmoral, and continued as gamekeeper for the royal family at Abergeldie and in Glen Girnock. The Farquharsons lived on a small farm, Balnacroft, near Abergeldie.

Fayrer, Dr. Sir Joseph Fayrer (1824–1907) was an English physician and surgeon, known for his writings on medicine, public health, and the treatment of snake bites in India. His book on snakes that Victoria refers to in *More Leaves* is *The Thanatophidia of India* (1872). In 1875 he accompanied Bertie, the Prince of Wales, on his tour of India.

Fife, Earl and Countess of. Agnes Duff (née Lady Agnes Georgiana Elizabeth Hay), Countess Fife (1829–1869), was the daughter of William Hay, 18th Earl of Erroll. In 1846 she married James Duff (1814–1879), son of General the Hon. Sir Alexander Duff and Anne Stein. Duff later inherited the earldom of Fife upon the death of his uncle in 1857, becoming the 5th Earl Fife as well as the head of Clan Duff. They owned the Mar estate near Balmoral.

FitzClarence, Lord Adolphus. Lord Adolphus FitzClarence (1802–1856), an illegitimate child of Prince William, Duke of Clarence (later William IV), and his mistress, Dorothy Jordan, was a British naval officer. On the accession of his father as king in 1830, FitzClarence took command of the royal yacht *Royal George*, retaining this duty on the accession of his cousin Victoria in 1837, until he was promoted to Rear-Admiral in 1853. In 1848 he also became a naval aide-de-camp to the Queen and remained in office until he died.

Fortescue, Lord. Thomas Fortescue, 1st Baron Clermont of Ravensdale Park in County Louth, Ireland (1815–1887), was an Irish Whig politician.

Fritz / Crown-Prince of Prussia. Prince Frederick William of Prussia (1831–1888) was the eldest son of Wilhelm I (1797–1888), King of Prussia and, from 1871, first German emperor, and Augusta of Saxe-Weimar-Eisenach (1811–1890). He married Vicky (q.v.), the eldest child of Queen Victoria and Prince Albert, in 1858. He succeeded his father, as Emperor Frederick III, King of Prussia, in 1888, but he died just months later of cancer.

Gordon, Colonel. George Grant Gordon (1836–1912), the son of Lord Francis Arthur Gordon, was a colonel in the British Army, who served in Crimea. He became Equerry and Controller of the Household to Prince and Princess Christian of Schleswig-Holstein (Princess Helena), whom he served from 1866 to 1896.

Gordon, Duchess of. Elizabeth Gordon (née Brodie), Duchess of Gordon (1794–1864), was the daughter of Alexander Brodie, a wealthy India merchant and politician. In 1813 she married George Gordon, Marquess of Huntly, later 5th Duke of Gordon (1770–1836). From 1830 she served as Mistress of the Robes to Queen Adelaide. Often referred to as 'the Good Duchess', she is remembered as an important supporter of the Free Church of Scotland.

Grant, John. First employed as a gillie then keeper by Sir Robert Gordon, tenant of Balmoral until 1847, John Grant (1810–1879) served the Queen as gamekeeper from 1848 until his death. When Victoria and Albert purchased Balmoral, Albert employed him as Head Forester and attendant when the Prince went deer-stalking. Victoria promoted Grant to Head Gamekeeper after Albert's death.

Grant, Mrs. Elizabeth Grant (née Robbie) (1817–1887) was the wife of John Grant, the Head Gamekeeper at Balmoral. 'Old Mrs. Grant', whom the Queen also calls 'Widow Grant' (1780–1869), was John Grant's mother.

Grant-Sutties, the. Lady Susan Harriet Grant-Suttie (née Innes-Ker) (1837–1909) was the daughter of James Innes-Ker, 6th Duke of Roxburghe, and Susanna Innes-Ker (née Dalbiac). Lady Susan married James Grant-Suttie, son and heir of Sir George Grant-Suttie, 5th Baronet of Balgone and Prestongrange, in 1857.

Granville, Lord and Lady. Granville George Leveson-Gower, 2nd Earl Granville (1815–1891), was first elected to parliament in 1836 as Whig MP for Morpeth; he is best remembered for his service as Secretary of State for Foreign Affairs (1870–74, 1880–85). After the death of his first wife, Marie Louise Pelline de Dalberg, he married, in 1865, Castila (or Castalia) Rosalind Campbell, daughter of Walter Frederick Campbell. It is to the second Lady Granville that the Queen refers in her account of her visit to Dunrobin in 1872.

Grey, General. General Charles Grey (1804–1870), second son of the 2nd Earl Grey, was a British army officer and member of the House of Commons. He served as Private Secretary to Prince Albert from 1849 to 1861, and as Private Secretary to the Queen from 1861 until his death.

Grey, Lord. Sir George Grey, 2nd Baronet (1799–1882), was the son of George Grey, 1st Baronet (1767–1828), and nephew of Charles Grey, 2nd Earl Grey (1764–1845), Prime Minister, 1830–34. Grey worked in the administration of four prime ministers, Lord Melbourne, Lord John Russell, Lord Aberdeen, and Lord Palmerston, and was Home Secretary (formally called the Secretary of State for the Home Department) three times. He was a cousin of Charles Grey, Queen Victoria's Private Secretary.

Gruner, Mlle. Charlotte Gruner was German Governess to Victoria and Albert's children from 1844 to 1850, when she married and left royal service.

Haddington, Lord. Thomas Hamilton, 9th Earl of Haddington (1780–1858), was a Scottish Conservative statesman. In 1802 Lord Haddington married Lady Maria Parker (d. 1861), heir of George Parker, 4th Earl of Macclesfield.

Hatherley, Lord. William Page Wood, 1st Baron Hatherley (1801–1881), was a Liberal lawyer and statesman, who served as Lord High Chancellor, 1868–72, in William Gladstone's first ministry.

Helen / Duchess of Albany. Princess Helen of Waldeck and Pyrmont, later Duchess of Albany (1861–1922), was daughter of George Victor, Prince of Waldeck and Pyrmont, and his first wife, Princess Helena of Nassau. In 1882 Princess Helen married Prince Leopold (q.v.), Duke of Albany, son of Queen Victoria and Prince Albert.

Helena / Princess Helena / Lenchen. Helena Augusta Victoria, later Princess Christian of Schleswig-Holstein (1846–1923), fifth child of Queen Victoria and Prince Albert, married Prince (Frederick) Christian of Schleswig-Holstein-Sonderburg-Augustenburg (1831–1917) in 1866. Devoted to charitable causes, she was a founder of the Red Cross and what became the Royal School of Needlework, established to provide employment for women.

Helena's boys. *See* Albert / Abby; Christian Victor / Christle.

Helps, Arthur. Sir Arthur Helps (1813–1875) was an essayist and historian who served as Clerk of the Privy Council from 1860. As an undergraduate, he was a member of the Cambridge Apostles, a literary society among whose members was Alfred Tennyson. After the death of Prince Albert, Helps assisted Queen Victoria to edit *The Principal Speeches and Addresses of His Royal Highness the Prince Consort* (1862), for which he also wrote the biographical introduction. As the Queen's chief literary advisor, he assisted in editing and wrote a preface to *Leaves from the Journal of Our Life in the Highlands*, a work he had urged her to publish; he is named on the title page as editor.

Hildyard, Miss. Sarah Ann Hildyard became Sub-Governess to Victoria and Albert's elder children in the royal nursery in 1847. She left royal service in 1865 owing to ill health, and died in 1889.

Hogg, James. *See* Ettrick Shepherd, the.

Hope, Sir J. Sir John Hope, 11th Baronet (1781–1853), was the Conservative MP for Midlothian in 1845, re-elected in 1847 and 1852. He was Vice-Lieutenant of the county and also a member of the Royal Company of Archers.

James I. For King James I of England, *see* James VI.

James II. James II, King of Scots (1430–1460), was the younger of twin sons of James I, King of Scots (1394–1437), and Joan Beaufort (d. 1445), the daughter of John Beaufort, Marquess of Dorset and of Somerset (d. 1410). When his father was murdered, James succeeded to the throne at the age of 6. In 1449 he married Mary of Guelders (d. 1463). In 1460, James died, aged 29, from wounds caused by the accidental discharge of a gun, and was succeeded by his son, James III (1452–1488).

James II. Prince James Stuart, Duke of York, Duke of Albany (1633–1701), later James II and VII, King of England, Scotland, and Ireland, was the second son of King Charles I and Henrietta Maria of France. In 1660 he married Anne Hyde, the daughter of Edward Hyde, chief minister to James's brother, King Charles II. Following Anne's death, James married Princess Mary Beatrice of Modena (their son was James, later known as the 'Old Pretender'). James succeeded to the throne when Charles II died without issue in 1685. A convert to Catholicism, his religious policy created unrest, and he was deposed in 1688 in favour of his Protestant daughter Mary and her husband William of Orange (who ruled as William III and Mary II). He died in exile in France.

James IV. James IV, King of Scots (1473–1513), was the eldest son of James III (1452–1488) and his wife, Margaret of Denmark (1456/7–1486). In 1503 he married Princess Margaret Tudor (1489–1541), the eldest daughter of King Henry VII of England and Elizabeth of York. James IV was killed at the Battle of Flodden Field. Their son James V (1512–1542) was the father of Mary Queen of Scots.

James VI. of Scotland. James VI and I, King of Scotland, England, and Ireland (1566–1625), was the son of Mary Queen of Scots and her second husband, Henry Stewart, Lord Darnley. In 1567 the throne of Scotland passed to Prince James Charles Stuart when he was thirteen months old, after his mother was forced to abdicate. In 1589 James married Princess Anne (1574–1619), daughter of Frederick II, King of Denmark, and Sophie of Mecklenburg-Güstrow. When Queen Elizabeth I died in 1603 without issue, given his lineage from King Henry VII's elder daughter, Margaret (*see* James IV.), James succeeded to the throne of England, as James I.

Jenner, Sir William / Dr. Jenner. Sir William Jenner, 1st Baronet (1804–1870), was Court Physician and, from 1862 to 1890, Physician-in-Ordinary to Queen Victoria. He was President of the Royal College of Physicians, 1881–8.

Jungbluth. Friedrich (or Frederick) Jungbluth (1820–1895) entered Queen Victoria's service in 1847, and was appointed German Cook in 1848, Third Master Cook in 1854, Second Master Cook in 1866, and First Master Cook in 1869. He was awarded the Victoria Faithful Service Medal at Balmoral in 1873, and a bar for a further ten years' service in 1883. He retired with a pension in 1887.

Kanné. Joseph Julius Kanné (*c.* 1818–1888), who was Austrian, entered royal service in 1857. He served as Director of the Queen's Continental Journeys for thirty years.

Kent, Duchess of / Mama. Princess Victoria Mary Louise of Saxe-Coburg-Saalfeld (1786–1861) was Queen Victoria's mother. The fourth daughter of Franz Friedrich Anton, Duke of Saxe-Coburg-Saalfeld (1750–1806), and his second wife, Augusta Caroline, Countess of Reuss-Ebersdorf (1757–1831), she married, in 1803, Emich Carl, Prince of Leiningen (1763–1814), with whom she had a son, Prince Carl, and a daughter, Princess Feodore. After the death of Prince Emich, she married, in 1818, Prince Edward, Duke of Kent and Strathearn (1767–1820), the fourth son of George III and Queen Charlotte. Victoria was their only child.

Kinnoull, Lord. Thomas Robert Hay-Drummond, 11th Earl of Kinnoull (1785–1866), married Louisa Burton Rowley, daughter of Sir Charles Rowley, 1st Baronet, in 1824. The Queen and Prince briefly visited Lord Kinnoull at Dupplin Castle on their first visit to Scotland.

Knollys, Charlotte. Elizabeth Charlotte Knollys (1835–1930), known as Charlotte Knollys, was the daughter of Sir William Thomas Knollys, Comptroller of the Household of the Prince of Wales, and his wife, Elizabeth St Aubyn. From 1863 she was Lady of the Bedchamber and Private Secretary (the first woman to fill that role in royal service) to Princess Alexandra of Denmark, later Queen Alexandra.

Knox. John Knox (1514–1572), Scottish theologian, led Scotland's Reformation and founded the Presbyterian Church of Scotland, known as the Kirk; he wrote *The History of the Reformation in Scotland* in five volumes (1559–66). Serving as the Kirk's religious leader during the reign of Mary Queen of Scots, he called for her execution.

Landseer. Sir Edwin Henry Landseer (1802–1873), English painter and sculptor, specialized in animal subjects. In 1824 he travelled to Scotland, where he received painting commissions from Sir Walter Scott and John Murray, 4th Duke of Atholl. Elected to the Royal Academy in 1831, he became one of Queen Victoria's and Prince Albert's favourite British painters; he was knighted in 1850. He is buried in St Paul's Cathedral, London.

Leiningen, Ernest / 'our nephew'. Ernest Leopold, 4th Prince of Leiningen (1830–1904), was the son of Carl, Prince of Leiningen, Victoria's maternal half-brother, and the Countess Marie of Klebelsberg. In 1858 he married Princess Marie Amalie of Baden (1834–1899). He became a Vice-Admiral in the Royal Navy.

Leiningen, Prince. *See* Carl / Charles / Prince Leiningen.

Leinster, Duke and Duchess of. Charles William FitzGerald, Marquess of Kildare, then from 1874 4th Duke of Leinster (1819–1887), was an Irish peer and politician. He was High Sheriff of Kildare for 1843 and MP for Kildare from 1847 to 1852. In 1870 he entered the House of Lords as Baron Kildare; he succeeded his father as Duke in 1874. He married Lady Caroline Sutherland-Leveson-Gower (1827–1887), daughter of the 2nd Duke and Duchess of Sutherland.

Lenchen. *See* Helena / Princess Helena / Lenchen.

Leopold / Prince Leopold / Duke of Albany. Prince Leopold George Duncan Albert (1853–1884) was the eighth child of Queen Victoria and Prince Albert. Scholarly like his father, he was elected President of the Royal Society of Literature in 1878 and Vice-President of the Society of Arts in 1879. In 1882 he married Princess Helen of Waldeck and Pyrmont. A haemophilia sufferer, he died following a fall.

Leopold / Uncle Leopold / King of the Belgians. Leopold I, King of the Belgians (1790–1865), was the youngest son of Franz Friedrich Anton, Duke of Saxe-Coburg-Saalfeld, and his second wife, Augusta Caroline, Countess of Reuss-Ebersdorf. In 1816 Leopold married Princess Charlotte of Wales, the only child of King George IV; she died in childbirth in 1817. In 1832 he married his second wife, Louise-Marie Thérèse Charlotte Isabelle of Orléans, eldest daughter of the French king Louis Philippe I and his wife, Maria Amalia of the Two Sicilies. He was Queen Victoria's uncle and an important advisor in her youth and early reign.

Leslie, Provost. William Leslie (1814–1880) was Lord Provost of Aberdeen, 1869–73.

Leys, Francis. The brother of John Brown's mother, Margaret Leys, Francis Leys (1810–1886) was the uncle of John Brown. He married Mary Coutts in 1842 and served as an elder of the church at Crathie.

Liverpool, Lord. Charles Cecil Cope Jenkinson, 3rd Earl of Liverpool (1784–1851), was MP for East Grinstead. His eldest daughter, Lady Catherine Julia Jenkinson (1811–1877), was Lady-in-Waiting to the Duchess of Kent, Queen Victoria's mother.

Löhlein. Rudolph Löhlein (1827–1896), a native of Coburg, was appointed Second Valet to Prince Albert in 1847, then served as First Valet, 1858–61. Löhlein remained in Queen Victoria's service after Prince Albert's death.

Londonderry, Lord and Lady. George Henry Robert Charles William Vane-Tempest, 5th Marquess of Londonderry (1821–1884), known as Viscount Seaham, 1823–54, and as Earl Vane, 1854–72, was a British aristocrat, businessman, diplomat, and Conservative politician. In 1846 he married Mary Cornelia Edwards (d. 1906), daughter of Sir John Edwards, 1st Baronet. In 1872 he inherited the title as 5th Marquess, and in 1880 he became Lord Lieutenant of County Durham, a post he held until his death.

Lorne / Lord Lorne / Marquis of Lorne. John George Edward Henry Douglas Sutherland Campbell, Marquess of Lorne, later 9th Duke of Argyll (1845–1914), was the eldest son of George, Marquess of Lorne, and Lady Elizabeth Sutherland-Leveson-Gower, daughter of the 2nd Duke of Sutherland. Earl of Campbell from birth, he became Marquess of Lorne in 1847 and 9th Duke of Argyll on the death of his father in 1900. He served as Governor General of Canada, 1878–83. In 1871 he married Princess Louise (q.v.), daughter of Queen Victoria and Prince Albert.

Lothian, Lord. Schomberg Henry Kerr, 9th Marquess of Lothian (1833–1900), second son of John Kerr, 7th Marquess of Lothian, and Lady Cecil Kerr, was known as Lord Schomberg Kerr until 1870; after he succeeded to the title he was usually known simply as Lothian. He was a diplomat and Conservative politician, and served as Secretary for Scotland under Lord Salisbury between 1887 and 1892. He married, in 1865, Lady Victoria Alexandrina (1844–1938), daughter of Walter Francis Montagu Douglas Scott, 5th Duke of Buccleuch.

Louis / Louis of Hesse. Prince Louis of Hesse and by Rhine (1837–1892) was the eldest son of Prince Charles of Hesse and by Rhine and Princess Elisabeth of Prussia. In 1862 he married Princess Alice (q.v.), daughter of Queen Victoria and Prince Albert. In 1877 Louis became Grand Duke of Hesse and by Rhine.

Louise / Princess Louise / Louischen. Princess Louise Caroline Alberta (1848–1939), sixth child of Queen Victoria and Prince Albert, was a talented artist, whose marble sculpture of her mother stands in the grounds of Kensington Palace. In 1871 she married the Marquess of Lorne (*see* Lorne), heir of the Duke of Argyll. After Lorne became Canada's Governor General in 1878, Louise, as viceregal consort, used her position to support the arts, higher education, and female equality. Louise became Duchess of Argyll when Lorne succeeded his father as 9th Duke of Argyll in 1900.

Louise Margaret / Princess Louise Margaret. Princess Louise Margaret Alexandra Victoria Agnes of Prussia (1860–1917) was daughter of Prince Friedrich Karl of Prussia and Princess Maria Anna of Anhalt. In 1879 she married Prince Arthur (q.v.), Duke of Connaught and Strathearn, son of Queen Victoria and Prince Albert.

Lovat, Lord. Simon Fraser, 13th Lord Lovat and 2nd Baron Lovat (1828–1887), succeeded his father in 1875. He resided at Beaufort Castle, and was the 22nd Chief of Clan Fraser of Lovat, or MacShimidh. He served as a lieutenant colonel in the 2nd Battalion of the Queen's Own Cameron Highlanders Militia, and as Lord Lieutenant of Inverness, 1873–87. From 1883 to 1887, he served as Aide-de-camp to Queen Victoria.

Macdonald, Annie / Mrs. Macdonald. Annie Mitchell (1832–1897), daughter of a blacksmith at Balmoral, entered royal service as a Balmoral housemaid, rising to wardrobe maid and, later, First Wardrobe Woman to Queen Victoria on the retirement of Marianne Skerrett in 1862. In 1863 Mitchell married John Alexander Macdonald (q.v.), a footman at Balmoral.

Macdonald, Flora. The Hon. Flora Clementine Isabella Macdonald (1822–1899), was the daughter of Reginald George Macdonald, 25th Chief of Clanranald. She was Maid of Honour to Queen Victoria, 1847–74, Woman of the Bedchamber, 1874–97, and Extra Woman of the Bedchamber from 1897.

Macdonald, John. Personal hunter (Jäger) to Prince Albert from 1847, John Macdonald (d. 1860) was also Keeper of the Royal Kennels at Windsor from 1848. His brother later served as Head Keeper for the Duke of Sutherland at Dunrobin.

Macdonald, John Alexander. Footman to Queen Victoria from 1850, John Alexander Macdonald (1828–1865) married Annie Mitchell, who served Queen Victoria as a wardrobe maid, in 1863 (*see* Macdonald, Annie / Mrs. Macdonald).

MacGregor, Miss. Amelia Georgiana Murray MacGregor (1829–1917), daughter of Evan John MacGregor, Baronet, and Elizabeth Murray, was the author of a book on Clan MacGregor, and provided the text and assisted in the production of Kenneth Macleay's *Highlanders of Scotland* (1870). She was a trusted friend of the Dowager Duchess of Atholl.

MacGregor, Sir Malcolm. Rear-Admiral Sir Malcolm Murray-Macgregor of Macgregor, 4th Baronet (1834–1879), was a senior officer in the Royal Navy.

Mackay. Angus Mackay (1813–1859), a distinguished composer and performer on the bagpipe, and compiler and publisher of Scottish traditional music, was Piper to Queen Victoria from 1843 to 1854.

Macleod, Dr. Norman. Queen Victoria's trusted spiritual advisor after the death of Prince Albert, the Revd Norman Macleod (1812–1872) was a Scottish clergyman and author, who sometimes performed religious services at Balmoral. He served as Moderator of the General Assembly of the Church of Scotland, 1869–70.

McNeill, Sir John and Lady Emma. Sir John McNeill (1795–1883) was born on the Hebridean Island of Colonsay. He worked for the East

India Company from 1816, in Bombay and Persia, as a medical doctor and as a diplomat. In 1845 he was appointed Chairman of the Board of Supervision, entrusted with the working of the new Poor Law (Scotland) Act 1845. After the Crimean War, he co-authored a report on the disastrous conditions of army service, which led to reforms. The Queen recalls that he 'was formerly my minister in Persia' (*More Leaves*, 326). In 1871 he married his third wife, Lady Emma Augusta Campbell, sister of the 8th Duke of Argyll, who hosted Sir John and Lady Emma, together with Queen Victoria, at Inveraray Castle in September 1875.

Macpherson, James. *See* Ossian.

Malcolm IV, King. Malcolm IV, King of Scots (1141–1165), was the eldest son of Henry, Earl of Huntingdon and of Northumberland, and Ada de Warenne. He succeeded his grandfather David I, King of Scots, in 1153 at the age of 12, his father having died in 1152. While he was forced to surrender the modern counties of Northumberland and Cumbria, he succeeded in maintaining peace and royal authority in Scotland. Malcolm IV died at the age of 24, with no issue. He is buried at Dunfermline Abbey.

Mama. *See* Kent. Duchess of / Mama.

Mansfield, Lord. William David Murray (1806–1898) was both 4th and 3rd Earl of Mansfield, having inherited two distinct titles (one in 1840 from his father, David William Murray, 3rd Earl of Mansfield; the other from his grandmother, Louisa Murray, 2nd Countess of Mansfield, in 1843). In 1829 he married Louisa, daughter of Cuthbert Ellison. He was a Tory MP, 1830–40, and served as Lord of the Treasury, 1834–5. Scone Palace is the family seat of the Earls of Mansfield, where Lord Mansfield hosted Victoria and Albert during their first visit to Scotland.

Marie / Duchess of Edinburgh. Grand Duchess Maria Alexandrovna of Russia (1853–1920) was daughter of Alexander II, Tsar of Russia, and his first wife, Princess Marie of Hesse and by Rhine. In 1874 she married Prince Alfred (q.v.), Duke of Edinburgh, son of Queen Victoria and Prince Albert.

Marochetti. Baron Carlo Giovanni Battista Marochetti (1805–1867), was an Italian-born sculptor, who worked in Britain from 1848. Having made a portrait bust of Prince Albert in 1849, Marochetti was commissioned to sculpt the private monument of Prince Albert (and later of Queen Victoria) at the Royal Mausoleum at Frogmore in Windsor Great Park. He also created the statue of Prince Albert for Aberdeen, which the Queen unveiled in 1863.

Mary, Queen of Scots. Mary Stuart, Mary I of Scotland (1542–1587), known as Mary Queen of Scots, was daughter of James V and Mary of Guise. She acceded to the throne when she was six days old, on the death of her father. During her childhood, Scotland was ruled by regents. In 1558 she married Francis, Dauphin of France, becoming Queen Consort of France from his accession as Francis II of France in 1559. After his death in December 1560, Mary returned to Scotland, and, in 1565, married her half-cousin Henry Stewart, Lord Darnley (1545/6–1567; *see* Darnley, Lord), who was assassinated in 1567. This marriage produced one male heir, the future James VI of Scotland and I of England. The Queen was forced to abdicate in 1567. In 1586 she was convicted of plotting to overthrow her cousin Queen Elizabeth I of England, and she was executed in 1587 at Fotheringhay Castle in Northamptonshire.

Matheson, Sir Alexander. A China merchant and railway entrepreneur, Sir Alexander Matheson, 1st Baronet (1805–1886), became a Liberal MP. He also served as a magistrate and was appointed Deputy Lieutenant of the Counties of Ross and Cromarty and Invernessshire.

May. Princess Marie of Hesse and by Rhine (1874–1878), was the youngest child of Princess Alice and Prince Louis of Hesse and by Rhine, and Queen Victoria's granddaughter. She died of diphtheria at the age of 4.

Morgan. James Morgan (1838–1890) was appointed a gillie at Balmoral in 1857. After Prince Albert's death, he worked, 1866–71, for Prince and Princess Christian of Schleswig-Holstein (Princess Helena). He later returned to Queen Victoria's service as a gillie, footman, and livery porter, before retiring to Scotland. He was sometimes called Jemmie.

Mount Edgcumbe, Lord and Lady. Ernest Augustus Edgcumbe, 3rd Earl of Mount Edgcumbe (1797–1861), was a peer and politician. He was returned to parliament for Fowey, Cornwall, in 1819, serving until 1826, and then represented Lostwithiel until 1830. In 1839 he succeeded his father in the earldom and entered the House of Lords. He married Caroline Augusta, daughter of Rear-Admiral Charles Feilding, in 1831. She was a half-sister of Henry Fox Talbot, the photographer.

Nestor. Jean Nestor Marie Tirard was the son-in-law of Isidore Marchand, hairdresser to the Duchess of Kent and to Queen Victoria as a child. He served as Hairdresser in Ordinary to Queen Victoria from 1846. After he retired from royal service in 1867, his son Albert Victor continued the dressing of the Queen's hair. Haberdashery and trimmings were supplied by his business, run under the name Nestor Tirard and managed by his two sons.

Noble. A border collie (1870?–1887) given to Queen Victoria in 1872 by Lady Charles Ker when he was fourteen months old. (He is sometimes referred to as Noble III.) He had a sweet disposition, and his special role was guarding the Queen's gloves. He is buried in the grounds of Balmoral, memorialized by a bronze statue on a marble plinth.

Norfolk, Duke and Duchess of. Henry Charles Howard, 13th Duke of Norfolk (1791–1856), bore the title Earl of Surrey between 1815 and 1842. He married Lady Charlotte Sophia Leveson-Gower (1788–1870), daughter of the 1st Duke and Duchess of Sutherland, in 1814. In 1829 he was elected to the House of Commons for Horsham, the first Roman Catholic to sit in the House after Catholic emancipation. He served as Master of the Horse,

1846–52, and as Lord Steward of the Household in 1853–4. He was made a Knight of the Garter and a Privy Councillor. 'The young Duke of Norfolk', whom the Queen encounters at Abbotsford in 1867 (*More Leaves*, 226), is his heir, the 14th Duke.

Northcote, Sir Stafford. Stafford Henry Northcote, 8th Baronet from 1851, 1st Earl of Iddesleigh from 1885 (1818–1887), was a Conservative politician, first elected to parliament in 1855. He was Chancellor of the Exchequer, 1874–80, and later served as Foreign Secretary.

Ossian. James Macpherson (1736–1796), Scottish poet, presented his poems as the work of 'Ossian', an epic poet of third-century Scotland, whose existence he invented. Macpherson's 'discovery' of Ossian was based partly on Gaelic ballads. In 1760 he published translations from Scottish Gaelic as *Fragments of Ancient Poetry Collected in the Highlands of Scotland*. In 1761, claiming to have obtained ancient manuscripts in the Hebrides islands, he announced that he had discovered and translated Ossian's epic, which he published as *Fingal: An Ancient Epic Poem in Six Books*. Further works by Ossian followed. Although the authenticity of the poems was immediately challenged by those with knowledge of Gaelic traditions and poetry, the term 'Ossianic ballads' refers to genuine Gaelic poems in the Scottish / Irish tradition, and Macpherson's 'Ossian' works, regarded as a tribute to Scotland's heroic past, remained popular through the nineteenth century. Macpherson later served in parliament.

Paget, Lord Alfred. Alfred Henry Paget, Lord Alfred Paget (1816–1888), was the son of Henry William Paget, 1st Marquess of Anglesey. Equerry to Queen Victoria, 1837–41, and Chief Equerry and Clerk-Marshall, 1846–74, he resigned as Chief Equerry in 1874, but remained Clerk-Marshall until his death. He served as Liberal MP for Lichfield from 1837 to 1865. In 1847 he married Cecilia Wyndham, daughter of George Thomas Wyndham of Cromer Hall, Norfolk.

Paget, Miss Matilda. The daughter of the Hon. Berkeley Paget, Matilda Paget (1811–1871) was Maid of Honour to Queen Victoria, 1837–55.

Palmerston, Lord. Henry John Temple, 3rd Viscount Palmerston (1784–1865), was Prime Minister, 1855–8 and 1859–65. He dominated Britain's expansionist foreign policy during the period 1830 to 1865, when Britain stood at the height of its imperial power. Victoria's and Albert's disagreements with him were notorious for testing the limits of the monarchy's prerogatives. Holding office almost continuously from 1807 until his death in 1865, he began his parliamentary career as a Tory, defected to the Whigs in 1830, and became the first Prime Minister from the newly formed Liberal Party in 1859.

Panmure, Lord. *See* Dalhousie, Lord / Lord Panmure.

Peel, Sir Robert. Sir Robert Peel, 2nd Baronet (1788–1850), son of a textile manufacturer, was Prime Minister at the time of Victoria and Albert's first two visits to Scotland. A Tory who helped to found the modern Conservative party, he served as Prime Minister in 1834–5 and 1841–6. Victoria had initially been reluctant to accept the transfer of power from her first Prime Minister, Lord Melbourne, a Whig, to Peel, as she was required to do as a constitutional monarch, but she eventually came to respect him.

Philip / 'our cousin Philip' / Philip (Count of Flanders). Prince Philippe of Belgium, Count of Flanders (1837–1905), was the son of King Leopold I of Belgium and his second wife, Princess Louise-Marie of Orléans. He was the first cousin of both Queen Victoria and Prince Albert.

Phipps, Captain Charles. Charles Edmund Phipps (1844–1906), son of Sir Charles Beaumont Phipps, was Page of Honour to Queen Victoria from 1853. He was later Assistant Adjutant Quartermaster-General and Groom-in-Waiting to Queen Victoria, and, from 1874, Gentleman Usher Daily Waiter in Ordinary. In 1868 he married the Canadian Susan Stewart Geddes, daughter of the Very Reverend John Geddes, Dean of Niagara.

Phipps, Colonel / Sir Charles Phipps. Sir Charles Beaumont Phipps (1801–1866), son of Henry Phipps, 1st Earl of Mulgrave, was appointed Equerry in Ordinary to Queen Victoria in 1846 and Private Secretary to Prince Albert in 1847. In 1849 he succeeded George Edward Anson as Keeper of the Privy Purse. In 1851 he was promoted to Colonel in the Scots Fusilier Guards and also became Treasurer to Prince Albert. From 1851 he served the Prince of Wales as Treasurer and Secretary, and in various other offices.

Phipps, Harriet. Harriet Lepel Phipps (1841–1922), daughter of Sir Charles Beaumont Phipps, was appointed Maid of Honour to Queen Victoria in 1862, and Woman of the Bedchamber in 1889.

Pickard, Lieutenant-Colonel. Arthur Frederick Pickard (1844–1880) was a British Army officer and courtier. For his actions in New Zealand in 1863, he was awarded the Victoria Cross. He was appointed an equerry to Prince Arthur in 1871, and in 1878 he was made Assistant Keeper of the Privy Purse and Assistant Private Secretary to the Queen, at which time he was promoted to Lieutenant Colonel.

Ponsonby, General / Colonel Ponsonby. Major-General Sir Henry Frederick Ponsonby (1825–1895) was the son of Major-General Sir Frederick Cavendish Ponsonby, an Anglo-Irish nobleman. He joined the army in 1842, later serving in the Crimean War. After the war he was appointed Equerry to Prince Albert. In 1862 was sent to Canada in command of a battalion of the Grenadier Guards. From 1870 he served as Keeper of the Privy Purse and Private Secretary to Queen Victoria, succeeding General Sir Charles Grey. In 1861 Ponsonby married the Hon. Mary Elizabeth Bulteel, Maid of Honour to Queen Victoria.

Profeit, Dr. Dr Alexander Profeit (1834–1897), son of a farmer, studied at Aberdeen University and became a licentiate of the Royal College of Surgeons of Edinburgh, before moving to Crathie. From 1854 he provided medical services to the employees at Balmoral and in 1875 became the

Royal Commissioner, succeeding Dr Andrew Robertson and serving until his death. Mrs. Profeit was Isabella Anderson (1842–1888).

Provost Leslie. *See* Leslie, Provost.

Renwick. Robert Renwick was Sergeant Footman to Queen Victoria between 1844 and 1859, and Gentleman Porter from 1855 to 1862. He was attendant on Queen Victoria when she was assaulted by Robert Pate in 1850.

Reynolds, Sir Joshua. The English portrait and history painter Sir Joshua Reynolds (1723–1792) was one of the earliest members of the Royal Society of Arts, helped to found the Society of Artists of Great Britain, and in 1768 became the first President of the Royal Academy of Arts, a position he held until his death. In 1769 he was knighted by George III, only the second artist to be so honoured.

Richmond, Duke of. Charles Henry Gordon-Lennox, 6th Duke of Richmond, 6th Duke of Lennox, and 1st Duke of Gordon (1818–1903), was known as Earl of March until 1860, when he inherited his titles from his father. He was a Conservative politician. The main seat of the Dukes of Gordon was Gordon Castle in Fochabers, Morayshire, but between the sixteenth and early twentieth century they also held the Glenlivet estate, with its shooting-lodge, Glenlivet House, at Ballindolloch, which the Queen visited in September 1867. Glenlivet is now part of the Cairngorms National Park.

Riddell, General. General Henry James Riddell (d. 1861) was a British Army officer, who took part in the Napoleonic wars and served as Commander-in-Chief in Scotland and as Governor of Edinburgh Castle, 1847–52.

Robert, Duke of Normandy. Sometimes called Robert Curthose, Robert, Duke of Normandy (1050s–1134), was the son of William II, Duke of Normandy, later William I of England (William the Conqueror), and his wife, Matilda, daughter of the Count of Flanders.

Robert Bruce / Robert I. Robert I, King of Scots (1274–1329), was the son of Robert (VI) de Brus (1243–1304) and Marjory, Countess of Carrick. Taking the throne in 1306, he played an important role in ensuring the independence and survival of the kingdom of Scotland. He had two spouses, Isabella of Mar (*c.* 1277–1296) and Elizabeth de Burgh (*c.* 1284–1327). The body of Robert I was buried at Dunfermline Abbey, but his heart was buried at Melrose Abbey.

Robertson, Dr. Andrew Robertson (1799–1881), born at Perth, became a licentiate of the Royal College of Surgeons of Edinburgh in 1818, and set up a medical practice at Crathie. He gave up medicine soon after being appointed Royal Commissioner in 1848 and served in this position until 1875, managing improvements to the Balmoral estate, including the construction of the new Balmoral Castle, the new bridge at Crathie, the construction and improvement of various cottages on the estate, and the erection of the Glassalt Shiel on Loch Muick. He left royal service in 1875.

Rob Roy. Robert Roy MacGregor (Scottish Gaelic Raibeart Ruadh MacGriogair) (baptised 1671, d. 1734) was a Scottish outlaw, who later became a folk hero. Born at Glengyle at the head of Loch Katrine, he joined the Jacobite rising of 1689, at the age of 18, to support King James VII and II, who had fled Britain after being deposed by parliament in 1688. Later Rob Roy became a respected cattleman, but after borrowing a large sum to increase his herd, he defaulted on his loan. His principal creditor, James Graham, 1st Duke of Montrose, seized his lands and he was branded an outlaw. Rob Roy continued waging a private blood feud against the Duke, raiding his cattle and robbing his rents until 1722, when he was forced to surrender. After being imprisoned he was finally pardoned in 1727. He died at Balquhidder, where his wife, Helen (Mary) McGregor (1671–1745), and their two sons are also buried. Walter Scott wrote a novel about him, and guidebooks to the Scottish regions where he lived often conflate the historical and the fictional Rob Roy.

Rosebery, Lord. Archibald John Primrose, 4th Earl of Rosebery (1783–1868), succeeded to the earldom in 1814, and was created Baron Rosebery, of Rosebery in the County of Edinburgh, in 1828. In 1819 he married his second wife, Anne Margaret Anson, daughter of Thomas Anson, 1st Viscount Anson. Victoria and Albert visited the Roseberys at Dalmeny House outside Edinburgh on their first visit to Scotland. (The Queen misspells their name 'Roseberry' in *Leaves*.) Lord Rosebery's eldest son, Archibald Primrose, Lord Dalmeny (1809–1851), married, in 1834, Lady Catherine Lucy Wilhelmina Stanhope (1819–1901), a historian and the daughter of Philip Stanhope, 4th Earl Stanhope; she had served as bridesmaid to Queen Victoria. Lord Rosebery was the grandfather of the Prime Minister of the same title in the 1890s.

Ross, William. Having served in the 42nd Highlanders, William Ross (1832–1891) was appointed Piper to Queen Victoria in 1854 and served her until 1891.

Roxburghe, Duke and Duchess of. James Henry Robert Innes-Ker, 6th Duke of Roxburghe (1816–1879), a Scottish peer, married, in 1836, Susanna Dalbiac (1814–1895), who became a lady of the bedchamber to Queen Victoria, and her friend. Susanna Innes-Ker was one of Victoria's longest serving ladies-in-waiting, holding the appointment from 1865 until her death.

Russell, Lord John. Known by his courtesy title Lord John Russell until 1861, John Russell, 1st Earl Russell (1792–1878), was the third son of John Russell, 6th Duke of Bedford. He was a Whig and Liberal statesman, who served as Prime Minister, 1846–52 and 1865–6.

Ruthven, Dowager Lady. Lady Mary Hamilton Ruthven (née Campbell), Lady Ruthven (1789–1885). In 1813 she married James Ruthven, 6th Baron Ruthven (1777–1853), a Scottish peer and professional soldier. He succeeded his father as 7th Lord Ruthven of Freeland in 1789; after his death, his widow was known as the Dowager Lady Ruthven.

St. Aubyn, Sir J. John St Aubyn, 1st Baron St Levan (1829–1908), was the son of Sir Edward St Aubyn, 1st Baronet, of St Michael's Mount, Cornwall, and his wife, Emma, daughter of General William Knollys. He succeeded to the baronetcy in 1872 and was known as Sir John St Aubyn from that time until 1887, when he was created Baron St Levan. He was a Liberal politician and sat in the House of Commons from 1858 until he was raised to the peerage. He married Lady Elizabeth Clementina, daughter of John Townshend, 4th Marquess Townshend, in 1856.

Scott, Sir Walter. The celebrated and prolific Scottish writer Sir Walter Scott, 1st baronet (1771–1832), was born in Edinburgh and raised there and in the Borders region; he trained as a barrister and worked all his life as a judge and legal administrator. He published a collection of ballads, *Minstrelsy of the Scottish Border*, in 1802–3; thereafter he became famous as a poet with *Lay of the Last Minstrel*, *Marmion*, and *The Lady of the Lake*, all of which Queen Victoria cites in *Leaves* and *More Leaves*. The popularity of his first novel, *Waverley* (1815), about the Jacobite rising of 1745, led to his writing further historical novels, several of which (especially *Rob Roy*) the Queen also references. He built an elaborate mansion, Abbotsford, near Melrose Abbey in the Borders region and was made a baronet in 1818; he managed King George IV's visit to Scotland in 1822, and his writing helped to launch Scotland as a popular tourist destination.

Seymour, Miss. Mary Frederica Seymour (1824–1902), daughter of Charles William Seymour of the 7th Regiment of Light Dragoons (Hussars), was Queen Victoria's Maid of Honour, 1850–57, and later Honorary Woman of the Bedchamber to the Queen, and Lady-in-Waiting to Princess Beatrice, Princess Henry of Battenberg. In 1857 she married Sir Thomas Biddulph (q.v.), the Queen's Master of the Household.

Shackle, Jane. The daughter of William Shackle, a member of the Queen's Household, Jane Shackle (c. 1841–1914) was appointed a wardrobe maid to Queen Victoria in the late 1850s. Jane had left royal service by the time her father retired in about 1870.

Shackle. William Shackle (1813–1892) had served in the household of the Duke of Wellington before he was appointed footman in the Royal Household in the 1840s. In about 1847 he was promoted and served as page to Queen Victoria. He retired from royal service about 1870.

Sharp. The first collie to be kept by Queen Victoria as a pet, Sharp, a border collie (1864–1879), was named after a government minister. He had a fierce temperament and guarded John Brown's door. He died in 1879 at the age of 15, and was buried at Windsor Castle with a bronze likeness on his tomb.

Singh, Maharajah Duleep. The last maharajah of the Sikh Empire, Duleep Singh, Maharajah of Lahore (1838–1893), was the youngest son of Maharajah Ranjit Singh. He succeeded his father at the age of 5, his mother Maharani Jind Kaur ruling as regent. When he was 10, after the Sikh Empire was defeated in the Second Anglo-Sikh War, Duleep Singh was deposed by the British Crown and signed a treaty ceding the vast Punjab to Britain. As part of the agreement, he 'gave' Queen Victoria the Koh-i-noor, the most famous diamond in the world. Converted to Christianity and exiled to Britain aged 15, he became a favourite of the Queen. He leased homes in Scotland from the late 1850s to the early 1860s, and from 1863 he lived at Elveden in Norfolk. He married twice: first Bamba Müller in 1864, then Ada Douglas Wetherill in 1889; his eight children had no offspring. In later life he reconverted to his Sikh faith and tried unsuccessfully to join anti-British forces in what was called the Great Game, the imperial struggle for supremacy in Eurasia. However, when he died, disgraced, in Paris, he received a Christian burial in England, at Elveden church, which he had endowed.

Smithett, Captain. Captain Sir Luke Smithett (1800–1871) was Commodore of the Dover Packet Service and Captain of the royal yacht *Victoria and Albert*. He was knighted for his services as Commodore of the Royal Packets on the Dover passage.

Smith of Aberdeen, Mr. William Smith (1817–1891) was the city architect of Aberdeen, and a partner in a family architectural practice, J. & W. Smith. Smith's first major architectural commission was Trinity Hall, built in 1846 in the Gothic style, on Union Street in Aberdeen, which attracted Prince Albert's attention. The Prince commissioned J. & W. Smith in 1848 to remodel old Balmoral Castle, starting in 1852. The commission was extended to the construction of a completely new house between 1853 and 1855, followed by other buildings on the royal estate.

Sodor and Man, Bishop of. Robert John Eden, 3rd Baron Auckland (1799–1870), Church of England clergyman and chaplain to Queen Victoria, 1837–47; he had been chaplain to King William IV. He was Bishop of the diocese of Sodor and Man (the Isle of Man) from 1847 to 1854 and Bishop of Bath and Wells from 1854 to 1869.

Steell, Mr. Sir John Robert Steell (1804–1891) was a sculptor, who modelled many of the leading figures of Scottish history and culture, and is best known for a number of sculptures displayed in Edinburgh, including the statue of Sir Walter Scott at the base of the Scott Monument. He was knighted in 1876 following the unveiling, by Queen Victoria, of his statue of the Prince Consort, which stands in the centre of Charlotte Square in Edinburgh.

Stanley, Lady Augusta. *See* Bruce, Lady Augusta.

Stewart, Lizzie. Elizabeth Stewart, a native of Crathie, was Queen Victoria's Second Wardrobe Maid from 1879.

Stockmar, Baron. Christian Friedrich Stockmar, Baron Stockmar (1787–1863), a native of Coburg, was a physician and statesman, a friend and unofficial advisor to Albert and Victoria. From 1816 he had been Physician and later Private Secretary, Comptroller of the Household, and political advisor to Prince Leopold, later King of the Belgians. At King Leopold's suggestion, Stockmar advised Queen Victoria from 1837 on her plans for marriage. In 1848 he was made Ambassador of the Duchy of Saxe-Coburg and Gotha.

Sutherland, 2nd Duke and Duchess of. Harriet Elizabeth Georgiana Howard (1806–1868), married, in 1823, her cousin George Sutherland-Leveson-Gower (1786–1861), who succeeded his father as 2nd Duke of Sutherland in 1833. The Duchess of Sutherland was Mistress of the Robes under several Whig administrations between 1837 and 1861, and a great friend of Queen Victoria. She was an important figure in London society, using her social position to undertake various philanthropic activities, including supporting the protest of English ladies against American slavery. The couple inherited the enormous industrial wealth of the 1st Duke and the vast Sutherland landholdings of the 1st Duchess, the former Lady Stafford, who, in the early 1800s, in what were later termed the Highland Clearances, evicted their long-standing farming tenants to give the land over to sheep farming. The 2nd Duchess of Sutherland and her then unmarried daughter Elizabeth, later the Duchess of Argyll, joined the royal party at Taymouth Castle in 1842. In 1872, in *More Leaves*, the Queen refers to the 1st Duke (1758–1833) as 'the old Duke;' to the 2nd Duke as 'the late Duke;' and to the (current) 3rd Duke, as 'the Duke.'

Sutherland, 3rd Duke and Duchess of. George Granville William Sutherland-Leveson-Gower (1828–1892), was Marquess of Stafford from 1833 until 1861, when he inherited his father's title. He married Anne Hay-Mackenzie (1829–1888) in 1849. A Liberal MP, he was instrumental in expanding the Highlands railway, building the Duke of Sutherland's Railway and supporting other Highland lines. Queen Victoria visited, and was driven in a train by, the 3rd Duke when she travelled to Dunrobin in 1872 to commemorate his mother, her friend Harriet, the 2nd Duchess of Sutherland. The Queen refers to the 3rd Duchess as Annie Sutherland.

Suttie. *See* Grant-Sutties, the.

Taylor, Dr. Malcolm Campbell Taylor (1832–1922), minister of Crathie church, 1867–73, was then appointed Extraordinary Chaplain to the Queen in Scotland by Victoria, who also recommended him for the post of professor of ecclesiastical history at Edinburgh University, to which he was appointed in 1876.

Taylor, Mr. Richard Taylor (1810–1883) worked for mining engineers John Taylor and Sons. After returning from a study visit to Germany, he took on the management of the Consolidated Mines and the United Mines at Gwennap, Cornwall, and of other mines in that county. He was also appointed Mineral Agent to the Duchy of Cornwall, a post he held for many years.

Teck, Prince and Princess of / Duke and Duchess of Teck. Princess Mary Adelaide of Cambridge (1833–1897) was the youngest child of Prince Adolphus, 1st Duke of Cambridge, and Princess Augusta Wilhelmina Louisa of Hesse-Cassel. She became Duchess of Teck following her marriage to Francis, Duke of Teck (1837–1900), in 1866. One of their children, Princess Victoria Mary (1867–1953), married Prince George, Duke of York (1865–1936), who would succeed his father, King Edward VII, to the throne in 1910.

Todd, Dr. James Henthorn Todd (1805–1869) was a biblical scholar, educator, and Irish historian. He co-founded the Irish Archaeological Society in 1840 and acted as its honorary secretary. From 1847 to 1855 he served as Secretary of the Royal Irish Academy, and in 1849 he was made Regius Professor of Hebrew at Trinity College, Dublin.

Van de Weyer, Mr. Jean-Sylvain Van de Weyer (1802–1874) served as the Belgian Minister at the Court of St James—effectively the ambassador—and, briefly, as the Prime Minister of Belgium, under King Leopold I. In 1839 he married Elizabeth Anne Sturgis Bates (1817–1878), daughter of Joshua Bates of Barings Bank, formerly of Boston. Mrs Van de Weyer became a close friend of Queen Victoria following Prince Albert's death. Louise Van de Weyer, one of their daughters, was a friend of Princess Louise.

Vicky / Crown-Princess of Prussia. Princess Victoria Adelaide Mary Louisa, Princess Royal (1840–1901), was the first child of Queen Victoria and Prince Albert. She was married in 1858 to Crown Prince Frederick William of Prussia (*see* Fritz / Crown-Prince of Prussia) when she was only seventeen years old. She was Empress of Germany from her husband's accession as emperor on 9 March 1888 to his death on 15 June of the same year. She and the Queen conducted an extensive correspondence.

Victoria, Queen. Princess Alexandrina Victoria, later Queen Victoria (1819–1901), was the only child of Prince Edward, Duke of Kent and Strathearn (1738–1820), fourth son of King George III and Charlotte of Mecklenburg-Strelitz, and Princess Victoria of Saxe-Coburg-Saalfeld. Victoria succeeded her uncle King William IV to the throne in 1837. In 1840 she married Prince Albert (q.v.) of Saxe-Coburg and Gotha. The couple had nine children. Before Elizabeth II, Victoria was the longest-reigning monarch in British history, and, like Elizabeth I in 'Elizabethan' times, was central in shaping the era in which she reigned, known as 'Victorian'.

Wagland. John George Wagland (1814–1892) was born into royal service: his father, John Wagland, was gate porter at Windsor Castle, and his grandfather, George Wagland, began the family's service to the royal family in 1788. John George was serving as a groom in 1840 and was later promoted to coachman.

Waldemar, Prince. Prince Joachim Friedrich Ernst Waldemar of Prussia (1868–1879) was the youngest son of Vicky, daughter of Queen Victoria and Prince Albert, and Crown Prince Frederick William of Prussia. The Queen refers to him as Waldemar in recording his death from diphtheria at the age of 11.

Wallace. Sir William Wallace (1270–1305), legendary fighter for Scottish freedom, and leader in the First War of Scottish Independence (1296–1328), defeated the army of King Edward I at the Battle of Stirling Bridge in 1297.

Wellesley, Lord Charles. Major-General Lord Charles Wellesley (1808–1858) was a politician, soldier, and courtier. He was the second son of Arthur Wellesley, 1st Duke of Wellington, and Catherine Pakenham.

Wellington, 1st Duke of. Arthur Wellesley, 1st Duke of Wellington (1769–1852), born in Ireland, was both a military hero, who, commanding Britain's armed forces, defeated the Emperor Napoleon at the battle of Waterloo in 1815, and a politician who served as Prime Minister, 1828–30 and 1834. As a politician he favoured conservative, even repressive positions on issues such as expansion of the vote, but in old age he was idolized as a great public servant. He was made Duke of Wellington in 1814. With Prince Albert, he presided over the re-cutting of the Koh-i-noor diamond.

Wemyss, Earl of. *See* Elcho, Lord / Earl of Wemyss.

Wemyss, General. William Wemyss (1790–1852), Colonel and later Lieutenant General of the 93rd Foot, was Equerry to Queen Victoria during her visit to Scotland in 1842. He married Lady Isabella Hay, daughter of William Hay, 17th Earl of Erroll. His brother (mentioned in *Leaves*, 24) was James Eskine Wemyss (1789–1854), Rear-Admiral in the Royal Navy, who married Lady Emma Hay, another daughter of the 17th Earl of Erroll. They were distant cousins of Lord Elcho, 9th Earl of Wemyss, being descendants of the third son of the 5th Earl.

Willem. In 1863 Princess Alice took into her household in Darmstadt a 13-year-old Malay boy. Two years before that, his family had given him to a German settler in maritime South-East Asia in return for an unidentified service rendered, and he was brought to Germany by this employer. Alice ensured that he was taught to read and write and had him christened in the Christian faith, when he was given the name Willem. Alice describes him as 'very intelligent'.

William III. William of Orange (1650–1702) was the sovereign Prince of Orange from birth, Stadtholder of Holland, Zeeland, Utrecht, Guelders, and Overijssel in the Dutch Republic from the 1670s, and King of England, Scotland, and Ireland from 1689 until his death. He was only the child of Stadtholder William II, Prince of Orange, and Mary, Princess Royal, the eldest daughter of King Charles I of England, Scotland, and Ireland, and sister of King Charles II and King James II and VII. In 1677 he married his first cousin the Protestant Princess Mary (1662–1694), eldest daughter of King James II and VII by his first wife, Anne Hyde. After the deposition of King James II, William and Mary were invited, under the terms of the Bill of Rights of 1689, to reign over England, Scotland, and Ireland, taking the royal titles William III and Mary II.

William of Hesse. Prince William of Hesse and by Rhine (1845–1900) was the younger brother of Louis of Hesse, husband of Princess Alice.

Willoughby, Lord and Lady. Peter Robert Drummond-Burrell, 2nd Baron Gwydyr, 22nd Baron Willoughby de Eresby (1782–1865), was the eldest son of Peter Burrell, 1st Baron Gwydyr, and Priscilla Bertie, 21st Baroness Willoughby de Eresby. Through his mother's death in 1828, he inherited the office of Lord Great Chamberlain, and in this capacity played a leading role at the coronation of Queen Victoria in 1838, holding the crown. In 1807 he married Sarah Clementina Drummond (1786–1865), daughter of James Drummond, 11th Earl of Perth, and of Clementina Elphinstone (a daughter of Charles Elphinstone, 10th Lord Elphinstone). The Queen and Prince Albert stayed at Drummond Castle with Lord and Lady Willoughby in September 1842.

Wilmore, C. Charlotte Wilmore (b. *c.* 1834) was appointed Second Dresser to Queen Victoria in 1866, She left royal service on her marriage in 1881.

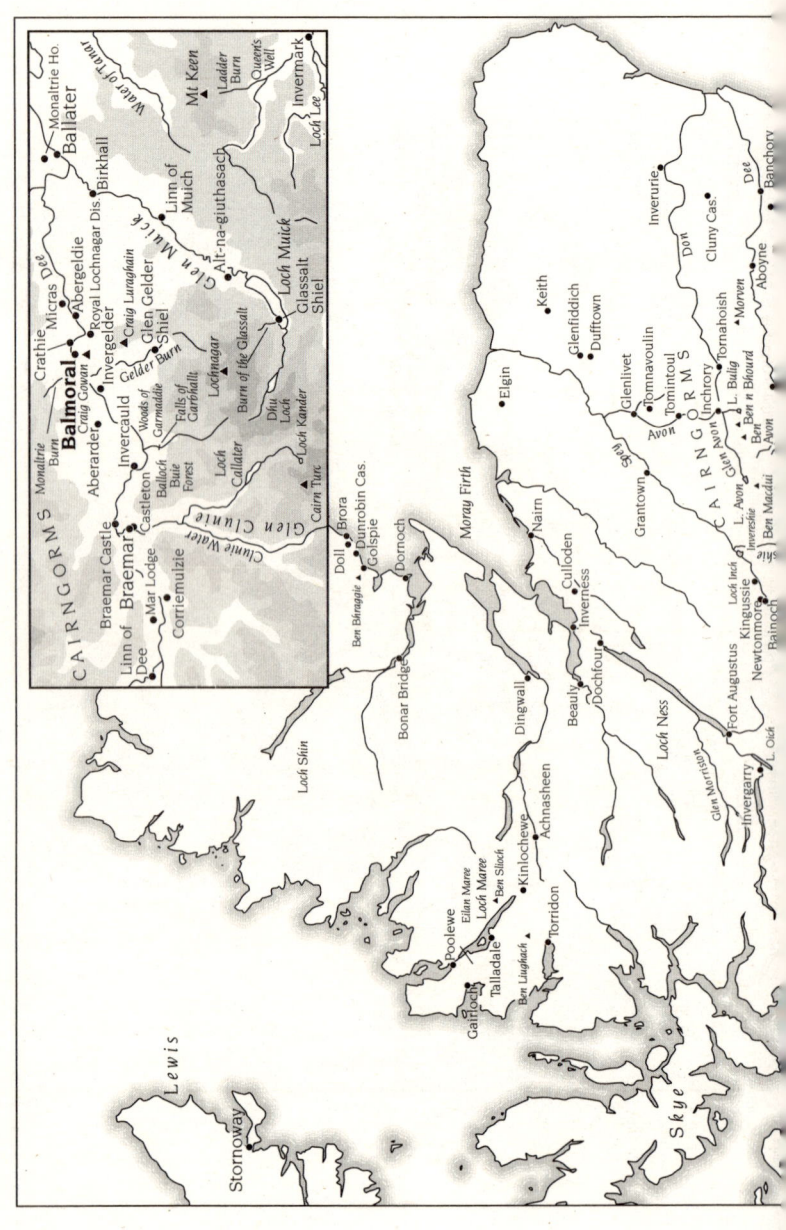

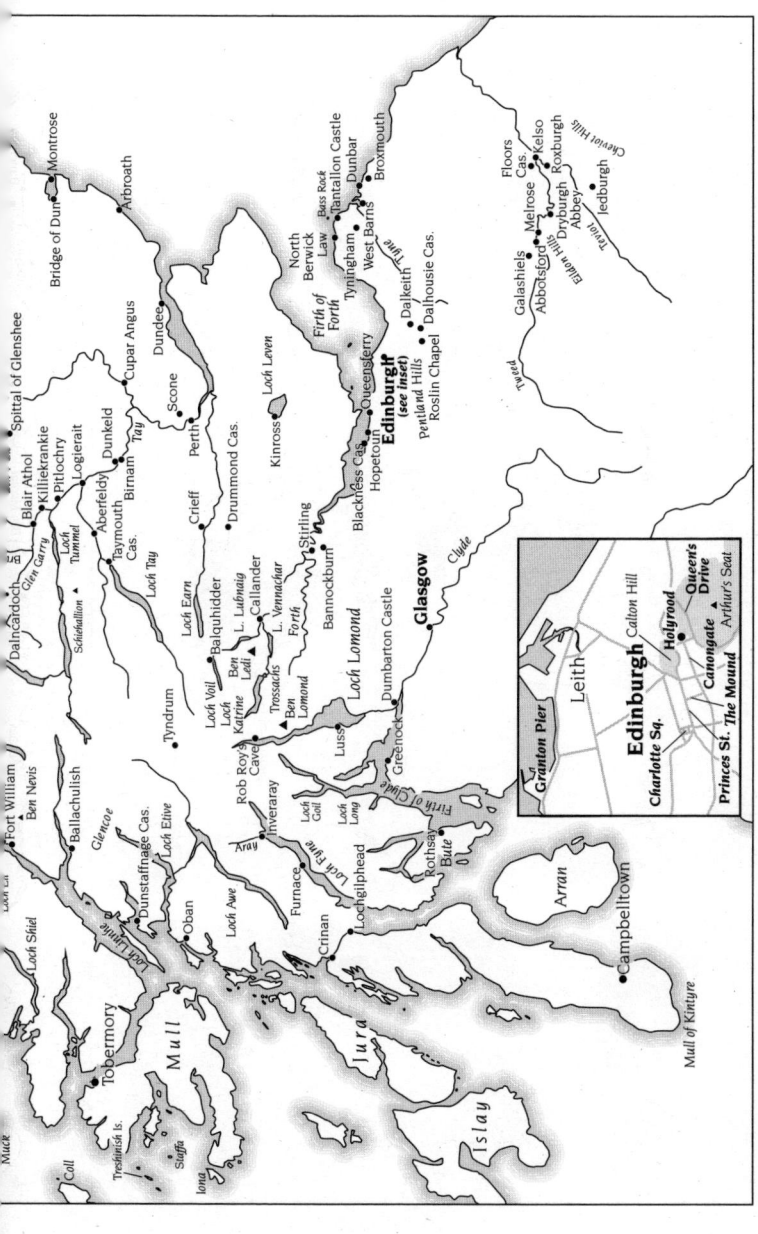

c

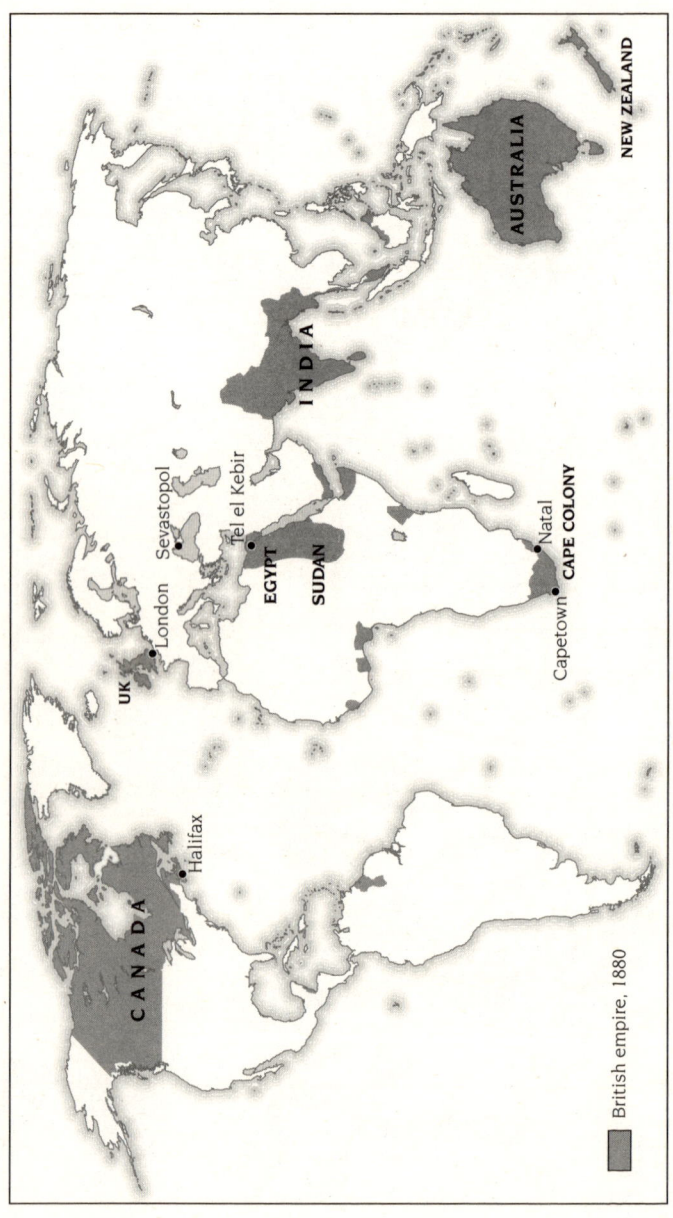

LEAVES
FROM THE JOURNAL
OF
OUR LIFE IN THE HIGHLANDS,
FROM 1848 TO 1861

[Balmoral Castle from the South-East.]

LEAVES

FROM THE JOURNAL

OF

OUR LIFE IN THE HIGHLANDS,

FROM 1848 TO 1861.

TO WHICH ARE PREFIXED AND ADDED EXTRACTS FROM THE SAME
JOURNAL GIVING AN ACCOUNT OF

EARLIER VISITS TO SCOTLAND,

AND TOURS IN ENGLAND AND IRELAND,

AND

YACHTING EXCURSIONS.

EDITED BY ARTHUR HELPS.

SECOND EDITION.

LONDON:

SMITH, ELDER AND CO.

1868.

[THE RIGHT OF TRANSLATION IS RESERVED]

TO

THE DEAR MEMORY OF HIM

WHO MADE THE LIFE OF THE WRITER BRIGHT AND HAPPY,

THESE SIMPLE RECORDS

ARE LOVINGLY AND GRATEFULLY INSCRIBED.

EDITOR'S PREFACE.

The circumstances which have led to the publication of this Volume are, briefly, these.

During one of the Editor's official visits to Balmoral, her Majesty very kindly allowed him to see several extracts from her journal, relating to excursions in the Highlands of Scotland. He was much interested by them; and expressed the interest which he felt. It then occurred to her Majesty that these extracts, referring, as they did, to some of the happiest hours of her life, might be made into a book, to be printed privately, for presentation to members of the Royal Family and her Majesty's intimate friends; especially to those who had accompanied and attended her in these tours.

It was then suggested to her Majesty by some persons, among them a near and dear relative of the Queen, and afterwards by the Editor, that this work, if made known to others, would be very interesting to them as well as to the Royal Family and to her Majesty's intimate friends. The Queen, however, said, that she had no skill whatever in authorship; that these were, for the most part, mere homely accounts of excursions near home; and that she felt extremely reluctant to publish anything written by herself.*

To this the Editor respectfully replied, that, if printed at all, however limited the impression, and however careful the selection of persons to whom copies might be given, some portions of the volume, or quite as probably incorrect representations of its contents, might find their way into the public journals. It would therefore, he thought, be better at once to place the volume within the reach of her Majesty's subjects, who would, no doubt, derive from it pleasure similar to that which it had afforded to the Editor himself. Moreover, it would be very gratifying to her subjects, who had always shown a sincere and ready sympathy with the personal joys and sorrows of their Sovereign,—to be allowed to know how her rare moments of leisure were passed in her Highland home, when every joy was heightened, and every care and sorrow diminished, by the loving companionship of the Prince Consort. With his memory the scenes to which this volume refers would always be associated.

Upon these considerations her Majesty eventually consented to its publication.

While the book was being printed, the Editor suggested that it would gain in interest if other extracts were added to it, describing her Majesty's progresses in England, Ireland, and the Channel Islands.

The Queen was pleased to assent; and the additions were accordingly made.*

It will easily be seen that this little work does not make any pretension to be more than such a record of the impressions received by the Royal Author in the course of these journeys, as might hereafter serve to recall to her own mind the scenes and circumstances which had been the source of so much pleasure. All references to political questions, or to the affairs of Government, have, for obvious reasons, been studiously omitted. The book is mainly confined to the natural expressions of a mind rejoicing in the beauties of nature, and throwing itself, with a delight rendered keener by the rarity of its opportunities, into the enjoyment of a life removed, for the moment, from the pressure of public cares.*

It would not be becoming in the Editor to dwell largely upon the merits of this work. He may, however, allude to the picturesque descriptions of scenery in which the work abounds; to the simplicity of diction throughout it; and to the perfect faithfulness of narration which is one of its chief characteristics; for in every page the writer describes what she thinks and feels, rather than what she might be expected to think and feel.

Moreover, he may point out the willingness to be pleased, upon which so much of the enjoyment of any tour depends: and also the exceeding kindliness of feeling—the gratitude even—with which the Royal Tourists recognize any attention paid to them, or any manifestation of the cordial attachment felt towards them, by any of her Majesty's subjects, from the highest to the humblest, whom they happen to meet with in the course of their journeys.

The Editor thinks that he should not be doing justice to the Royal Author's book—not doing what, if it were any other person's work which was entrusted to his editing, he should do—if he were to forbear giving utterance to the thoughts which occurred to him in reference to the notes to the Volume.*

These notes, besides indicating that peculiar memory for persons, and that recognition of personal attachment, which have been very noticeable in our Sovereigns, illustrate, in a striking manner, the Patriarchal feeling* (if one may apply such a word as "patriarchal" to a lady) which is so strong in the present occupant of the Throne. Perhaps there is no person in these realms who takes a more deep and abiding interest in the welfare of the household committed to his charge than our gracious

Queen does in hers, or who feels more keenly what are the reciprocal duties of masters and servants.

Nor does any one wish more ardently than her Majesty, that there should be no abrupt severance of class from class, but rather a gradual blending together of all classes,—caused by a full community of interests, a constant interchange of good offices, and a kindly respect felt and expressed by each class to all its brethren in the great brotherhood that forms a nation.

Those whose duty it has been to attend upon the Queen in matters of business, must have noticed that her Majesty, as a person well versed in the conduct of affairs, is wont to keep closely to the point at issue, and to speak of nothing but what is directly connected with the matter before her. But whenever there is an exception to this rule, it arises from her Majesty's anxious desire to make some inquiry about the welfare of her subjects—to express her sympathy with this man's sorrow, or on that man's bereavement—to ask what is the latest intelligence about this disaster, or that suffering, and what can be done to remedy or assuage it—thus showing, unconsciously, that she is, indeed, the Mother of her People, taking the deepest interest in all that concerns them, without respect of persons, from the highest to the lowest.

The Editor thinks that one point of interest which will incidentally be disclosed by this publication, is the aspect of the Court in these our times. What would not the historian give to have similar materials within his reach, when writing about the reigns of the great Queen Elizabeth or the good Queen Anne? There is always something in the present which has the appearance of being trivial and prosaic; but the future historian will delight in having details before him furnished by this book and by the Life of the Prince Consort,[+] which will enable him fully to describe the reign of Victoria, and justly to appreciate the private life of a Sovereign whose public life will enter so largely into the annals of the nineteenth century.

One more remark the Editor cannot refrain from making; namely, that it is evident that her Majesty never takes for granted the services and attentions which are rendered to her, and which we all know would be rendered to her from dutiful respect and regard, but views them as

---

[+] A work which has met with a very cordial reception from the public, and which, from what the Editor has seen, will not by any means diminish in interest as it proceeds to describe the full and busy life of the Prince as a man.

especial kindnesses shown to herself, and to which she makes no claim whatever from her exalted position as a Sovereign.

This latter trait, very characteristic of the Royal Author, gives, throughout, an additional charm to the book, which, on that account alone, and apart even from its many other merits, will, the Editor doubts not, be gratefully and affectionately welcomed by the public.

LONDON,
    January, 1868.

CONTENTS.

Earlier Visits to Scotland.

	DATE	PAGE
First Visit to Scotland	29 Aug. 1842	17
Visit to Blair Athole	9 Sept. 1844	36
Tour round the West Coast of Scotland and Visit to Ardverikie	11 Aug. 1847	45

Life in the Highlands, 1848–1861.

First Impressions of Balmoral	8 Sept. 1848	63
First Ascent of Loch-na-Gar	16 Sept. 1848	64
A "Drive" in the Balloch Buie	18 Sept. 1848	66
The First Stay at Alt-na-Giuthasach	30 Aug. 1849	67
A Beat in the Abergeldie Woods	3 Sept. 1849	69
Visit to the Dhu Loch, &c	11 Sept. 1849	70
Ascent of Ben-na-Bhourd	6 Sept. 1850	72
The Gathering	12 Sept 1850	74
Salmon Leistering	13 Sept. 1850	75
Loch Muich	16 Sept. 1850	77
Torch-light Ball at Corriemulzie	10 Sept. 1852	78
Account of the News of the Duke of Wellington's Death	16 Sept. 1852	79
Building the Cairn on Craig Gowan, &c	11 Oct. 1852	81
Laying the Foundation Stone of our New House	28 Sept. 1853	84
The Kirk	29 Oct. 1854	86

Arrival at the New Castle at Balmoral	7 Sept. 1855	87
Impressions of the New Castle	8 Sept. 1855	88
News of the Fall of Sevastopol	10 Sept. 1855	89
The Betrothal of the Princess Royal	29 Sept. 1855	91
The Kirk	14 Oct. 1855	92
Finding the Old Castle Gone	30 Aug. 1856	93
Gardens, &c. round the New Castle	31 Aug. 1856	94
Love for Balmoral	13 Oct. 1856	95
Opening of the New Bridge over the Linn of Dee	8 Sept. 1857	97
Visits to the Old Women	26 Sept. 1857	98
Visit to the Prince's Encampment at Feithort	6 Oct. 1857	100
A Fall of Snow	18 Sept. 1858	102
Ascent of Morven	14 Sept. 1859	104
The Prince's Return from Aberdeen	15 Sept. 1859	105
Fête to the Members of the British Association	22 Sept. 1859	106
Expedition to Inchrory	30 Sept. 1859	108
Ascent of Ben Muich Dhui	7 Oct. 1859	110
First Great Expedition:—To Glen Fishie and Grantown	4 Sept. 1860	112
Second Great Expedition:—To Invermark and Fettercairn	20 Sept. 1861	119
Expedition to Loch Avon	28 Sept. 1861	125
Third Great Expedition:—To Glen Fishie, Dalwhinnie, and Blair Athole	8 Oct. 1861	127
Last Expedition	16 Oct. 1861	134

Tours in England and Ireland, and Yachting Excursions.

First Visit to Ireland	2 Aug. 1849	141
Yachting Excursion	20 Aug. 1846	155
Second Yachting Excursion	2 Sept. 1846	160
Visit to the Lakes of Killarney	27 Aug. 1861	168

Illustrations.

Balmoral Castle from the South-East	FRONTISPIECE
Balmoral Castle from the North-West	96

EARLIER VISITS TO SCOTLAND.

First Visit to Scotland.

On Board the Royal George Yacht,*
Monday, August 29, 1842.

AT five o'clock in the morning we left *Windsor* for the railroad,* the Duchess of Norfolk, Miss Matilda Paget, General Wemyss, Colonel Bouverie, and Mr. Anson following us. Lord Liverpool, Lord Morton, and Sir James Clark, who also accompany us, had already gone on to *Woolwich.**

We reached *London* at a quarter to six, got into our carriages, and arrived at *Woolwich* before seven. Albert and I immediately stepped into our barge.* There was a large crowd to see us embark. The Duke of Cambridge, Lord Jersey, Lord Haddington, Lord Bloomfield, and Sir George Cockburn were present in full uniform. Sir George handed me into the barge. It was raining very hard when we got on board, and therefore we remained in our sitting-room.

I annex a list of our squadron:—

1. The ship "Pique," 36 guns.
2. The sloop "Daphne," 18 guns—(both of which join us at the *Nore*).
3. The steam-vessel "Salamander" (with the carriages on board).
4. The steam-vessel "Rhadamanthus" (Lord Liverpool and Lord Morton on board).
5. The steam-vessel "Monkey" Tender, which has towed us till nine o'clock (Mr. Anson and the equerries on board).
6. The steam-vessel "Shearwater," which is now towing us (Sir James Clark on board).
7. The steam-vessel "Black Eagle" (which has the ladies on board, and which tows us in front of the "Shearwater").
8. The steam-vessel "Lightning" (with the Jäger Benda, and our two dogs, "Eôs" and "Cairnach," on board) in front, which has gone to take our barge on board from the "Pique."
9. The steam-vessel "Fearless" (for survey).

This composes our squadron, besides which the Trinity-House steamer goes with us,* and, also, a packet. Innumerable little pleasure steamboats have been following us covered with people.

Tuesday, August 30.

We heard, to our great distress, that we had only gone 58 miles since eight o'clock last night. How annoying and provoking this is! We remained on deck all day lying on sofas; the sea was very rough towards evening, and I was very ill. We reached *Flamborough Head** on the Yorkshire coast by half-past five.

Wednesday, August 31.

At five o'clock in the morning we heard, to our great vexation, that we had only been going three knots an hour in the night, and were 50 miles from *St. Abb's Head.**

We passed *Coquet Island* and *Bamborough Castle** on the Northumberland coast, which I was unfortunately unable to see; but from my cabin I saw *Ferne Island*, with Grace Darling's lighthouse on it; also *Rocky Islands* and *Holy Island*.* At half-past five I went on deck, and immediately lay down. We then came in sight of the Scotch coast, which is very beautiful, so dark, rocky, bold, and wild, totally unlike our coast. We passed *St. Abb's Head* at half-past six. Numbers of fishing-boats (in one of which was a piper playing) and steamers full of people came out to meet us, and on board of one large steamer they danced a reel to a band. It was a beautiful evening, calm, with a fine sunset, and the air so pure.

One cannot help noticing how much longer the days are here than they were in *England*. It was not really dark till past eight o'clock, and on Monday and Tuesday evening at *Windsor* it was nearly dark by half-past seven, quite so before eight. The men begged leave to dance, which they did to the sound of a violin played by a little sailor-boy;* they also sang.

We remained on deck till twenty-five minutes to nine, and saw many bonfires* on the Scotch coast—at *Dunbar*—Lord Haddington's place, *Tyninghame*, and at other points on the coast. We let off four rockets, and burned two blue lights. It is surprising to see the sailors climb on the bowsprit and up to the top of the masthead—this too at all times of the day and night. The man who carried the lantern to the main-top ran up with it in his mouth to the top. They are so handy and so well conducted.*

We felt most thankful and happy that we were near our journey's end.

Thursday, September 1.

At a quarter to one o'clock, we heard the anchor let down—a welcome sound. At seven we went on deck, where we breakfasted. Close on one side were *Leith* and the high hills towering over *Edinburgh*, which was in fog; and on the other side was to be seen the *Isle of May* (where it is said Macduff held out against Macbeth*), the *Bass Rock* being behind us. At ten minutes past eight we arrived at *Granton Pier*, where we were met by the Duke of Buccleuch, Sir Robert Peel and others. They came on board to see us, and Sir Robert told us that the people were all in the highest good humour, though naturally a little disappointed at having waited for us yesterday.* We then stepped over a gangway on to the pier, the people cheering and the Duke saying that he begged to be allowed to welcome us. Our ladies and gentlemen had landed before us, safe and well, and we two got into a barouche, the ladies and gentlemen following. The Duke, the equerries, and Mr. Anson rode.

There were, however, not nearly so many people in *Edinburgh*, though the crowd and crush were such that one was really continually in fear of accidents. More regularity and order would have been preserved had there not been some mistake on the part of the Provost* about giving due notice of our approach. The impression *Edinburgh* has made upon us is very great; it is quite beautiful, totally unlike anything else I have seen; and what is even more, Albert, who has seen so much, says it is unlike anything *he* ever saw; it is so regular, everything built of massive stone, there is not a brick to be seen anywhere. The *High Street*, which is pretty steep, is very fine. Then the Castle, situated on that grand rock in the middle of the town, is most striking. On the other side the *Calton Hill*, with the *National Monument*, a building in the Grecian style; *Nelson's Monument*; *Burns' Monument*;* the *Gaol*; the *National School*, &c.; all magnificent buildings, and with *Arthur's Seat** in the background, over-topping the whole, form altogether a splendid spectacle. The enthusiasm was very great, and the people very friendly and kind. The Royal Archers Body Guard[†] met us and walked with us the whole way through the town. It is composed entirely of noblemen and gentlemen, and they all walked close by the carriage; but were dreadfully pushed about. Amongst them were the Duke of Roxburgh and Lord Elcho on my side; and Sir J. Hope on Albert's side. Lord Elcho[†] (whom I did not know at the time) pointed out the various monuments and places to me as we came along. When we were out of the town, we went faster. Every cottage is built of stone, and so are all the walls that are used as fences.

[†] The Duke of Buccleuch told me the other day, that the Archers Guard was established by James 1., and was composed of men who were mounted and armed from head to foot, and who were bound always to be near the Sovereign's person. At Flodden Field, King James IV.'s body, it is said, was found covered and surrounded by the bodies of the Archers Guard.*
[†] Now Earl of Wemyss.

The country and people have quite a different character from *England* and the English. The old women wear close caps, and all the children and girls are barefooted. I saw several handsome girls and children with long hair; indeed all the poor girls from sixteen and seventeen down to two or three years old, have loose flowing hair; a great deal of it red.

As we came along, we saw *Craigmillar Castle*,* a ruin, where Mary, Queen of Scots, used to live. We reached *Dalkeith** at eleven; a large house, constructed of reddish stone, the greater part built by the Duchess of Monmouth, and the park is very fine and large. The house has three fronts, with the entrance on the left as you drive up. The Duchess of Buccleuch arrived directly after us, and we were shown up a very handsome staircase to our rooms, which are very comfortable. We both felt dreadfully tired and giddy.

We drove out together. The park is very extensive, with a beautiful view of *Arthur's Seat* and the *Pentland Hills*; and there is a pretty drive overhanging a deep valley. At eight we dined—a large party. Everybody was very kind and civil, and full of inquiries as to our voyage.

Dalkeith House,
Friday, September 2.

At breakfast I tasted the oatmeal porridge, which I think very good, and also some of the "Finnan haddies." We then walked out. The pleasure-grounds seem very extensive and beautiful, wild and hilly. We walked down along the stream (the river *Esk*), up a steep bank to a little cottage, and came home by the upper part of the walk. At four o'clock we drove out with the Duchess of Buccleuch and the Duchess of Norfolk—the Duke and equerries riding—the others in another carriage. We drove through *Dalkeith*, which was full of people, all running and cheering.

Albert says that many of the people look like Germans. The old women with that kind of cap which they call a "mutch," and the young girls and children with flowing hair, and many of them pretty, are very picturesque; you hardly see any women with bonnets.

Such a thick "Scotch mist" came on that we were obliged to drive home through the village of *Lasswade*, and through Lord Melville's Park, which is very fine.

Saturday, September 3.

At ten o'clock we set off—we two in the barouche—all the others following, for *Edinburgh*. We drove in under *Arthur's Seat*, where the crowd began to be very great, and here the Guard of Royal Archers met us; Lord Elcho walking near me, and the Duke of Roxburgh and Sir J. Hope on Albert's side. We passed by *Holyrood Chapel*, which is very old and full of interest, and *Holyrood Palace*,* a royal-looking old place. The procession moved through the *Old Town* up the *High Street*, which is a most extraordinary street from the immense height of the houses, most of them being eleven stories high, and different families living in each story. Every window was crammed full of people.

They showed us *Knox's House*,* a curious old building, as is also the *Regent Murray's House*,* which is in perfect preservation. In the *Old Town* the *High Church*, and *St. Paul's* in the *New Town*, are very fine buildings. At the barrier, the Provost presented us with the keys.

The girls of the *Orphan Asylum*, and the Trades in old costumes, were on a platform. Further on was the *New Church*, to which—strange to say, as the church is nearly finished—they were going to lay the foundation stone. We at length reached the Castle, to the top of which we walked.

The view from both batteries is splendid, like a panorama in extent. We saw from them *Heriot's Hospital*, a beautiful old building, founded, in the time of James, by a goldsmith and jeweller, whom Sir Walter Scott has made famous in his *Fortunes of Nigel*.* After this, we got again into the carriages and proceeded in the same way as before, the pressure of the crowd being really quite alarming; and both I and Albert were quite terrified for the Archers Guard, who had very hard work of it; but were of the greatest use. They all carry a bow in one hand, and have their arrows stuck through their belts.

Unfortunately, as soon as we were out of *Edinburgh*, it began to rain, and continued raining the whole afternoon without interruption. We reached *Dalmeny*, Lord Roseberry's,* at two o'clock. The park is beautiful, with the trees growing down to the sea. It commands a very fine view of the *Forth*, the *Isle of May*, the *Bass Rock*,* and of *Edinburgh*; but the mist rendered it almost impossible to see anything. The grounds are very extensive, being hill and dale and wood. The house is quite modern: Lord Roseberry built it, and it is very pretty and comfortable. We lunched there. The Roseberrys were all civility and attention. We left them about half-past three, and proceeded home through *Leith*.

The view of *Edinburgh* from the road before you enter *Leith* is quite enchanting; it is, as Albert said, "fairy-like," and what you would only imagine as a thing to dream of, or to see in a picture. There was that beautiful large town, all of stone (no mingled colours of brick to mar it), with the bold Castle on one side, and the *Calton Hill* on the other, with those high sharp hills of *Arthur's Seat* and *Salisbury Crags* towering above all, and making the finest, boldest background imaginable. Albert said he felt sure the *Acropolis* could not be finer; and I hear they sometimes call *Edinburgh* "the modern *Athens*." The Archers Guard met us again at *Leith*, which is not a pretty town.

The people were most enthusiastic, and the crowd very great. The Porters all mounted, with curious Scotch caps, and their horses decorated with flowers, had a very singular effect; but the fishwomen are the most striking-looking people, and are generally young and pretty women—very clean and very Dutch-looking, with their white caps and bright-coloured petticoats.* They never marry out of their class.

At six we returned well tired.

Sunday, September 4.

We walked to see the new garden which is being made, and saw Mackintosh there, who was formerly gardener at *Claremont*. The view of *Dalkeith* (the village, or rather town) from thence is extremely picturesque, and Albert says very German-looking. We returned over a rough sort of bridge, made only of planks, which crosses the Esk, and which, with the wooded banks on each side, is excessively pretty. Received from Lady Lyttelton good accounts of our little children.* At twelve o'clock there were prayers in the house, read by Mr. Ramsay, who also preached.

At half-past four the Duchess drove me out in her own phaeton, with a very pretty pair of chestnut ponies, Albert riding with the Duke and Colonel Bouverie. We drove through parts of the park, through an old wood, and along the banks of the *South Esk* and the *North Esk*, which meet at a point from which there is such a beautiful view of the *Pentland Hills*. Then we drove, by a private road, to *Newbattle*, Lord Lothian's place.* The park is very fine, and the house seems large; we got out to look at a most magnificent beech-tree. The *South Esk* runs close before the house, by a richly wooded bank.

From thence we went to *Dalhousie*, Lord Dalhousie's.* The house is a real old Scotch castle, of reddish stone. We got out for a moment, and the Dalhousies showed us the drawing-room. From the window you see a beautiful wooded valley, and a peep of the distant hills.

Lord Dalhousie said there had been no British sovereign there since Henry IV. We drove home by the same way that we came. The evening was—as the whole day had been—clear, bright, and frosty, and the *Moorfoot Hills* (another range) looked beautiful as we were returning. It was past seven when we got home.

Monday, September 5.

I held a Drawing-room* at *Dalkeith* to-day, in the gallery. The Ministers and Scotch Officers of State were in the room, and the Royal Archers were in attendance in the room and outside of it, like the Gentlemen at Arms in *London*. Before the Drawing-room I received three addresses—from the Lord Provost and Magistrates, from the Scotch Church, and from the Universities of *St. Andrews, Glasgow,* and *Edinburgh*—to which I read answers. Albert received his just after I did mine, and read his answers beautifully.

Tuesday, September 6.

At nine o'clock we left *Dalkeith* as we came. It was a bright, clear, cold, frosty morning. As we drove along we saw the *Pentlands*, which looked beautiful, as did also *Arthur's Seat*, which we passed quite close by. The *Salisbury Crags*, too, are very high, bold, and sharp. Before this we saw *Craigmillar*. We passed through a back part of the town (which is most solidly built), close by *Heriot's Hospital*, and had a very fine view of the Castle.

I forgot to say that, when we visited the Castle, we saw the Regalia,* which are very old and curious (they were lost for one hundred years); also the room in which James VI. of Scotland and the First of England was born—such a very, very small room, with an old prayer written on the wall. We had a beautiful view of *Edinburgh* and the *Forth*. At *Craigleith* (only a half-way house, nine miles) we changed horses. The Duke rode with us all the way as Lord Lieutenant of the county, until we arrived at *Dalmeny*, where Lord Hopetoun met us and rode with us. At eleven we reached the *South Queensferry*, where we got out of our carriage and embarked in a little steamer; the ladies and gentlemen and our carriages going in another. We went a little way up the *Forth*, to see *Hopetoun House*, Lord Hopetoun's, which is beautifully situated between *Hopetoun* and *Dalmeny*. We also saw *Dundas Castle*, belonging to Dundas of Dundas, and further on, beyond *Hopetoun*, *Blackness Castle*,* famous in history. On the opposite side you see a square tower, close to the water, called *Rosyth*, where Oliver Cromwell's mother was said to have been born, and in the distance *Dunfermline*, where Robert Bruce is buried. We passed close by a very pretty island in the *Forth*, with an old castle on it, called *Inchgarvie*; and we could see the *Forth* winding beautifully, and had a distant glimpse of *Edinburgh* and its fine Castle. We landed safely on the other side at *North Queensferry*, and got into our carriages. Captain Wemyss, elder brother to General Wemyss, rode with us all the way beyond *Cowdenbeath* (eight miles). The first village we passed through on leaving the *Queensferry*, was *Inverkeithing*. We passed by Sir P. Durham's property.

We changed horses at *Cowdenbeath*. At a quarter-past one we entered *Kinross-shire*. Soon after, the country grew prettier, and the hills appeared again, partly wooded. We passed *Loch Leven*, and saw the castle on the lake* from which poor Queen Mary escaped. There the country is rather flat, and the hills are only on one side. We changed horses next at *Kinross*. Soon after this, the mountains, which are rather barren, began to appear. Then we passed the valley of *Glen Farg*; the hills are very high on each side, and completely wooded down to the bottom of the valley, where a small stream runs on one side of the road—it is really lovely.

On leaving this valley you come upon a beautiful view of *Strathearn* and *Moncrieffe Hill*. We were then in *Perthshire*. We changed horses next at the *Bridge of Earn* (12 miles). At half-past three we reached *Dupplin*, Lord Kinnoull's. All the time the views of the hills, and dales, and streams were lovely. The last part of the road very bad travelling, up and down hill. *Dupplin* is a very fine modern house, with a very pretty view of the hills on one side, and a small waterfall close in front of the house. A battalion of the 42nd Highlanders* was drawn up before the house, and the men looked very handsome in their kilts. We each received an address from the nobility and gentry of the county, read by Lord Kinnoull; and from the Provost and Magistrates of *Perth*. We then lunched. The Willoughbys, Kinnairds, Ruthvens, and Lord Mansfield, and one of his sisters, with others, were there. After luncheon, we walked a little way in the grounds, and then at five o'clock we set off again. We very soon came upon *Perth*, the situation of which is quite lovely; it is on the *Tay*, with wooded hills skirting it entirely on one side, and hills are seen again in the distance, the river winding beautifully.

Albert was charmed, and said it put him in mind of the situation of *Basle*. The town itself (which is very pretty) was immensely crowded, and the people very enthusiastic; triumphal arches* had been erected in various places. The Provost presented me with the keys, and Albert with the freedom of the city. Two miles beyond is *Scone* (Lord Mansfield's), a fine-looking house of reddish stone.

Lord Mansfield and the Dowager Lady Mansfield received us at the door, and took us to our rooms, which were very nice.

Wednesday, September 7.

We walked out, and saw the mound on which the ancient Scotch kings were always crowned;* also the old arch with James VI.'s arms, and the old cross, which is very interesting.

Before our windows stands a sycamore-tree planted by James VI.* A curious old book was brought to us from *Perth*, in which the last signatures are those of James I. (of England) and of Charles I., and we were asked to write our names in it, and we did so. Lord Mansfield told me yesterday that there were some people in the town who wore the identical dresses that had been worn in Charles I.'s time. At eleven o'clock we set off as before. We drove through part of *Perth*, and had a very fine view of *Scone*. A few miles on, we passed the field of battle of *Luncarty*,* where tradition says the Danes were beaten by Lord Erroll's ancestor. We also passed Lord Lynedoch's property. We then changed horses at the "New Inn" at *Auchtergaven*. The *Grampians* came now distinctly into view; they are indeed a grand range of mountains.

To the left we saw *Tullybugles*, where it is said the Druids used to sacrifice to Bel;* there are a few trees on the top of the mountain.

To the left; but more immediately before us, we saw *Birnam*, where once stood *Birnam Wood*, so renowned in *Macbeth*.* We passed a pretty shooting place of Sir W. Stewart's, called *Rohallion*, nearly at the foot of *Birnam*. To the right we saw the *Stormont* and *Strathtay*. Albert said, as we came along between the mountains, that to the right, where they were wooded, it was very like *Thüringen*,* and on the left more like *Switzerland*. *Murthly*, to the right, which belongs to Sir W. Stewart, is in a very fine situation, with the *Tay* winding under the hill. This lovely scenery continues all along to *Dunkeld*. Lord Mansfield rode with us the whole way.

Just outside *Dunkeld*,* before a triumphal arch, Lord Glenlyon's Highlanders, with halberds,* met us, and formed our guard—a piper playing before us. *Dunkeld* is beautifully situated, in a narrow valley, on the banks of the *Tay*. We drove in to where the Highlanders were all drawn up, in the midst of their encampments, and where a tent was prepared for us to lunch in. Poor Lord Glenlyon[+] received us; but he had suddenly become totally blind, which is dreadful for him. He was led about by his wife; it was very melancholy. His blindness was caused by over-fatigue. The Dowager Lady Glenlyon, the Mansfields, Kinnoulls,

---

[+] The late Duke of Athole.

Buccleuchs, and many others were there. We walked down the ranks of the Highlanders, and then partook of luncheon, the piper played, and one of the Highlanders[+] danced the "sword dance."* (Two swords crossed are laid upon the ground, and the dancer has to dance across them without touching them.) Some of the others danced a reel.

At a quarter to four we left *Dunkeld* as we came, the Highland Guard marching with us till we reached the outside of the town. The drive was quite beautiful all the way to *Taymouth*.[†]* The two highest hills of the range on each side are (to the right, as you go on after leaving *Dunkeld*) *Craig-y-Barns* and (to the left, immediately above *Dunkeld*) *Craigvinean*. The *Tay* winds along beautifully, and the hills are richly wooded. We changed horses first at *Balanagard* (nine miles), to which place Captain Murray, Lord Glenlyon's brother, rode with us. The hills grew higher and higher, and Albert said it was very Swiss-looking in some parts. High ribbed mountains appeared in the distance, higher than any we have yet seen. This was near *Aberfeldy* (nine miles), which is charmingly situated and the mountains very lofty. At a quarter to six we reached *Taymouth*. At the gate a guard of Highlanders, Lord Breadalbane's men, met us. *Taymouth* lies in a valley surrounded by very high, wooded hills; it is most beautiful. The house is a kind of castle, built of granite. The *coup-d'œil* was indescribable. There were a number of Lord Breadalbane's Highlanders, all in the Campbell tartan, drawn up in front of the house, with Lord Breadalbane himself in a Highland dress at their head, a few of Sir Neil Menzies' men (in the Menzies red and white tartan), a number of pipers playing, and a company of the 92nd Highlanders,* also in kilts. The firing of the guns, the cheering of the great crowd, the picturesqueness of the dresses, the beauty of the surrounding country, with its rich background of wooded hills, altogether formed one of the finest scenes

---

[+] Charles Christie, now steward to the present Dowager Duchess of Athole.

[†] I revisited Taymouth last autumn, on the 3rd of October, from Dunkeld (incognita), with Louise, the Dowager Duchess of Athole, and Miss MacGregor. As we could not have driven through the grounds without asking permission, and we did not wish to be known, we decided upon not attempting to do so, and contented ourselves with getting out at a gate close to a small fort, into which we were led by a woman from the gardener's house, near to which we had stopped, and who had no idea who we were.

We got out, and looked from this height down upon the house below, the mist having cleared away sufficiently to show us everything; and then, unknown, quite in private, I gazed—not without deep emotion—on the scene of our reception twenty-four years ago,* by dear Lord Breadalbane, in a princely style, not to be equalled in grandeur and poetic effect.

Albert and I were then only twenty-three, young and happy. How many are gone that were with us then!

I was very thankful to have seen it again.

It seemed unaltered.—1866.

imaginable. It seemed as if a great chieftain in olden feudal times was receiving his sovereign. It was princely and romantic. Lord and Lady Breadalbane took us upstairs, the hall and stairs being lined with Highlanders.

The Gothic staircase is of stone and very fine; the whole of the house is newly and exquisitely furnished. The drawing-room, especially, is splendid. Thence you go into a passage and a library, which adjoins our private apartments. They showed us two sets of apartments, and we chose those which are on the right hand of the corridor or ante-room to the library. At eight we dined. Staying in the house, besides ourselves, are the Buccleuchs and the two Ministers, the Duchess of Sutherland and Lady Elizabeth Leveson Gower,[+] the Abercorns, Roxburghs, Kinnoulls, Lord Lauderdale, Sir Anthony Maitland, Lord Lorne,[†] the Fox Maules, Belhavens, Mr. and Mrs. William Russell, Sir J. and Lady Elizabeth, and the Misses Pringle, and two Messrs. Baillie, brothers of Lady Breadalbane. The dining-room is a fine room in Gothic style, and has never been dined in till this day. Our apartments also are inhabited for the first time. After dinner the grounds were most splendidly illuminated,—a whole chain of lamps along the railings, and on the ground was written in lamps, "Welcome Victoria—Albert."

A small fort, which is up in the woods, was illuminated, and bonfires were burning on the tops of the hills. I never saw anything so fairy-like. There were some pretty fireworks, and the whole ended by the Highlanders dancing reels, which they do to perfection, to the sound of the pipes, by torchlight, in front of the house. It had a wild and very gay effect.

Taymouth,
Thursday, September 8.

Albert went off at half-past nine o'clock to shoot with Lord Breadalbane. I walked out with the Duchess of Norfolk along a path overlooking the *Tay*, which is very clear, and ripples and foams along over the stones, the high mountains forming such a rich background. We got up to the dairy, which is a kind of Swiss cottage,* built of quartz, very clean and nice. From the top of it there is a very pretty view of *Loch Tay*.

[+] Now Duchess of Argyll.   [†] The present Duke of Argyll.

We returned home by the way we came. It rained the whole time, and very hard for a little while. Albert returned at half-past three. He had had excellent sport, and the trophies of it were spread out before the house—nineteen roe-deer, several hares and pheasants, and three brace of grouse; there was also a capercailzie that had been wounded, and which I saw afterwards, a magnificent large bird.

Albert had been near *Aberfeldy*, and had to shoot and walk the whole way back, Lord Breadalbane himself beating, and 300 Highlanders out. We went out at five, with Lady Breadalbane and the Duchess of Sutherland; we saw part of *Loch Tay*, and drove along the banks of the *Tay* under fine trees, and saw Lord Breadalbane's American buffaloes.

Friday, September 9.

Albert off again after nine o'clock, to shoot. Soon after he left I walked out with the Duchess of Norfolk across the iron bridge, and along a grass walk overhanging the *Tay*.

Two of the Highland Guard (they were stationed at almost every gate in the park) followed us, and it looked like olden times to see them with their swords drawn.

We then walked to a lodge on the same road. A fat, good-humoured little woman, about forty years old, cut some flowers for each of us, and the Duchess gave her some money, saying, "From Her Majesty." I never saw any one more surprised than she was; she, however, came up to me and said very warmly, that my people were delighted to see me in *Scotland*. It came on to rain very heavily soon afterwards, but we walked on. We saw a woman in the river, with her dress tucked up almost to her knees, washing potatoes.

The rain ceased just as we came home, but it went on pouring frequently. Albert returned at twenty minutes to three, having had very hard work on the moors, wading up to his knees in bogs every now and then, and had killed nine brace of grouse. We lunched; then we went to the drawing-room, and saw from the window the Highlanders dancing reels; but unfortunately it rained the whole time. There were nine pipers at the castle; sometimes one, and sometimes three played. They always played about breakfast-time, again during the morning, at luncheon, and also whenever we went in and out; again before dinner, and during most of dinner-time. We both have become quite fond of the bagpipes.

At a quarter-past five we drove out with the Duchess of Buccleuch and the Duchess of Sutherland (poor Lady Breadalbane not being very well), Lord Breadalbane riding the whole time before us. We took a most beautiful drive, first of all along part of the lake and between the hills—such thorough mountain scenery,—and with little huts, so low, so full of peat smoke, that one could hardly see anything for smoke. We saw *Ben Lawers*, which is said to be 4,000 feet high, very well, and further on, quite in the distance, *Ben More*—also the *Glenlyon*, and the river *Lyon*, and many fine glens. It was quite dark when we came home at half-past seven. At eight we dined; Lord and Lady Ruthven and Lord and Lady Duncan dined here. After dinner came a number of people, about ninety, and there was a ball. It opened with a quadrille, which I danced with Lord Breadalbane, and Albert with the Duchess of Buccleuch. A number of reels were danced, which it was very amusing and pretty to see.*

Saturday, September 10.

We walked to the dairy and back—a fine bright morning; the weather the two preceding days had been very unfortunate. I drove a little way with Lady Breadalbane, the others walking, and then got out, and each of us planted two trees, a fir and an oak.* We got in again, and drove with the whole party down to the lake, where we embarked. Lady Breadalbane, the Duchess of Sutherland and Lady Elizabeth went by land, but all the others went in boats. With us were Lord Breadalbane and the Duchess of Norfolk and Duchess of Buccleuch; and two pipers sat on the bow and played very often. I have since been reading in *The Lady of the Lake*, and this passage reminds me of our voyage:—

> "See the proud pipers on the bow,
> And mark the gaudy streamers flow
> From their loud chanters down, and sweep
> The furrow'd bosom of the deep,
> As, rushing through the lake amain,
> They plied the ancient Highland strain."*

Our row of 16 miles up *Loch Tay* to *Auchmore*, a cottage of Lord Breadalbane's, near the end of the lake, was the prettiest thing imaginable. We saw the splendid scenery to such great advantage on both sides: *Ben Lawers*, with small waterfalls descending its sides, amid other high mountains wooded here and there; with *Kenmore* in the distance; the view, looking back, as the loch winds, was most beautiful. The boatmen sang two Gaelic boat-songs,* very wild and singular; the language so guttural and yet so soft. Captain McDougall, who steered, and who is the head of the McDougalls, showed us the real "brooch of Lorn," which was taken by his ancestor from Robert Bruce in a battle.* The situation of *Auchmore* is exquisite; the trees growing so beautifully down from the top of the mountains, quite into the water, and the mountains all round, make it an enchanting spot. We landed and lunched in the cottage, which is a very nice little place. The day was very fine; the Highlanders were there again. We left *Auchmore* at twenty minutes past three, having arrived there at a quarter before three. The kindness and attention to us of Lord and of Lady Breadalbane (who is very delicate) were unbounded. We passed *Killin*, where there is a mountain stream running over large stones, and forming waterfalls.

The country we came to now was very wild, beginning at *Glen Dochart*, through which the *Dochart* flows; nothing but moors and very high rocky mountains. We came to a small lake called, I think, *Laragilly*, amidst the wildest and finest scenery we had yet seen. *Glen Ogle*, which is a sort of long pass, putting one in mind of the prints of the *Kyber Pass*,* the road going for some way down hill and up hill, through these very high mountains, and the escort in front looking like mere specks from the great height. We also saw *Ben Voirlich*. At *Loch Earn Head* we changed horses. Lord Breadalbane rode with us the whole way up to this point, and then he put his Factor (in Highland dress) up behind our carriage. It came on to rain, and rained almost the whole of the rest of the time. We passed along *Loch Earn*, which is a very beautiful long lake skirted by high mountains; but is not so long or so large as *Loch Tay*. Just as we turned and went by *St. Fillans*, the view of the lake was very fine. There is a large detached rock with rich verdure on it, which is very striking.

We also saw *Glenartney*, the mountain on which Lord Willoughby has his deer forest. We passed by Sir D. Dundas's place, *Dunira*, before we changed horses at *Comrie*, for the last time, and then by Mr. Williamson's, and by *Ochtertyre*, Sir W. Keith Murray's.

Triumphal arches were erected in many places. We passed through *Crieff*, and a little past seven reached *Drummond Castle*,* by a very steep ascent. Lord Willoughby received us at the door, and showed us to our rooms, which are small but nice. Besides Lord and Lady Willoughby and the two Misses Willoughby, and our own people, the dinner-party was composed of the Duchess of Sutherland and Lady Elizabeth L. Gower, Lord and Lady Carington, Mr. and Mrs. Heathcote, the Duke de Richelieu, Lord Ossulston, Mr. Drummond, and the officers of the Guard.

Drummond Castle,
Sunday, September 11.

We walked in the garden, which is really very fine, with terraces, like an old French garden. Part of the old castle and the archway remains.

At twelve o'clock we had prayers in the drawing-room, which were read by a young clergyman, who preached a good sermon.

It poured the whole afternoon, and, after writing, I read to Albert the three first cantos of *The Lay of the Last Minstrel*,* which delighted us both; and then we looked over some curious, fine old prints by Ridinger.* At eight we dined. The Duchess of Sutherland and Lady Elizabeth had gone; but Lord and Lady Abercorn and Lord and Lady Kinnoull and their daughter added to the party.

Monday, September 12.

Albert got up at five o'clock to go out deer-stalking. I walked out with the Duchess of Norfolk.

All the Highlanders (Lord Willoughby's people, 110 in number), were drawn up in the court, young Mr. Willoughby and Major Drummond being at their head, and I walked round with Lady Willoughby. All the arms they wore belonged to Lord Willoughby; and there was one double-hilted sword, which had been at the battle of *Bannockburn*.* I hear that at *Dunkeld* there were nearly 900 Highlanders, 500 being *Athole* men;* and, altogether, with the various Highlanders who were on guard, there were 1,000 men.

At length—a little before three—to my joy, Albert returned, dreadfully sunburnt, and a good deal tired; he had shot a stag. He said the exertion and difficulty were very great. He had changed his dress at a small farm-house. *Glenartney* is ten miles from *Drummond Castle*; he drove there. Campbell of Monzie (pronounced "Monie"), a young gentleman who has a place near here, went with him and was, Albert said, extremely active. To give some description of this curious sport, I will copy an extract from a letter Albert has written to Charles,[+] giving a short account of it:—

"Without doubt deer-stalking is one of the most fatiguing, but it is also one of the most interesting of pursuits. There is not a tree, or a bush behind which you can hide yourself . . . One has, therefore, to be constantly on the alert in order to circumvent them; and to keep under the hill out of their wind, crawling on hands and knees, and dressed entirely in grey."

At half-past four we drove out with Lady Willoughby and the Duchess of Buccleuch. We drove through *Fern Tower* (belonging to the widow of the first Sir D. Baird), where we stopped the carriage; then to

---

[+] My half-brother, Prince Leiningen, who died in 1856.*

Abercairny, Major Moray's. We got out there a moment to look at the very fine house he is building, then drove home by *Monzie* (Campbell of Monzie's), and Sir W. Murray's, and had a very good view of the Highland hills—a very fine day. At eight we dined. The Belhavens, Seftons, Cravens, Campbell of Monzie, and various others composed the party. After dinner more people came—several in kilts; and many reels were danced; Campbell of Monzie is an exceedingly good dancer. We danced one country dance—I with Lord Willoughby—and Albert with Lady Carington.

Tuesday, September 13.

We had to start early, and therefore got up soon after seven o'clock; breakfast before eight. At nine we set off. The morning was very foggy and hazy. We passed near Lord Strathallan's place and stopped for a moment where old Lady Strathallan was seated. Lord Willoughby rode with us the whole way till we arrived here. Soon after this we came to a very extraordinary Roman encampment at *Ardoch*, called the "Lindrum."* Albert got out; but I remained in the carriage, and Major Moray showed it to him. They say it is one of the most perfect in existence.

We changed horses at *Greenloaning*, and passed through *Dunblane*. At twelve o'clock we reached *Stirling*, where the crowd was quite fearful, and the streets so narrow, that it was most alarming; and order was not very well kept. Up to the Castle,* the road or street is dreadfully steep; we had a foot procession before us the whole way, and the heat was intense. The situation of the Castle is extremely grand; but I prefer that of *Edinburgh Castle*. Old Sir Archibald Christie explained everything to us very well. We were shown the room where James II. killed Douglas, and the window out of which he was thrown.* The ceiling is most curious. A skeleton was found in the garden only twenty-five years ago, and there appears to be little doubt it was Douglas's. From the terrace the view is very extensive; but it was so thick and hazy, that we could not see the Highland hills well. Sir A. Christie showed us the field of the battle of *Bannockburn*; and the "Knoll," close under the walls of the Castle, from which the ladies used to watch the tournaments; all the embankments yet remain.* We also saw Knox's pulpit.

We next passed through *Falkirk*, and changed horses at *Callander Park*, Mr. Forbes's; both he and Sir Michael Bruce having ridden with us from beyond *Stirling*. We passed Lord Zetland on the road, and shortly before reaching *Linlithgow*, where we changed horses, Lord Hopetoun met us. Unfortunately, we did not see the Palace, which, I am told, is well worth seeing.* The Duke of Buccleuch met us soon after this, and, accompanied by a large number of his tenants, rode with us on horseback to *Dalkeith*. We changed horses at *Kirkliston*, and lastly at the outskirts of *Edinburgh*. There were a good many people assembled at *Edinburgh*; but we were unable to stop. We reached *Dalkeith* at half-past five. The journey was 65 miles, and I was very tired, and felt most happy that we had safely arrived here.

Dalkeith,
Wednesday, September 14.

This is our last day in *Scotland*; it is really a delightful country, and I am very sorry to leave it. We walked out and saw the fine greenhouse the Duke has built, all in stone, in the Renaissance style. At half-past three o'clock we went out with the Duchess of Buccleuch, only Colonel Bouverie riding with us. We drove through *Melville Park*, and through one of the little collier villages (of which there are a great many about *Dalkeith*), called *Loanhead*,* to *Rosslyn*.

We got out at the chapel,* which is in excellent preservation; it was built in the fifteenth century, and the architecture is exceedingly rich. It is the burying place of the family of Lord Rosslyn, who keeps it in repair. Twenty Barons of Rosslyn are buried there in armour. A great crowd had collected about the chapel when we came out of it.

From *Rosslyn* we then drove to *Hawthornden*, which is also beautifully situated at a great height above the river. To our great surprise we found an immense crowd of people there, who must have run over from *Rosslyn* to meet us.

We got out, and went down into some of the very curious caves in the solid rock, where Sir Alexander Ramsay and his brave followers concealed themselves, and held out for so long a time.* The Duchess told us there were many of these caves all along the river to *Rosslyn*.

We came home through *Bonnyrigg*, another collier village, and through *Dalkeith*.

Thursday, September 15.

We breakfasted at half-past seven o'clock, and at eight we set off, with the Duchess of Buccleuch, Lord Liverpool and Lord Hardwicke following. The ladies and equerries had embarked earlier. The day was very bright and fine. The arrangements in *Edinburgh*, through which we had to pass, were extremely well managed, and excellent order was kept. We got out of the carriage on the pier, and went at once on board the "Trident," a large steamboat belonging to the General Steam Navigation Company.* The Duke and Duchess of Buccleuch, Lady J. Scott, the Emlyns, Lord Cawdor, and Lady M. Campbell, came on board with us, and we then took leave of them. We both thanked the Duke and Duchess for their extreme kindness, attention, and hospitality to us, which really were very great—indeed we had felt ourselves quite at home at *Dalkeith*.

As the fair shores of *Scotland* receded more and more from our view, we felt quite sad that this very pleasant and interesting tour was over; but we shall never forget it.

On board the "Trident" (where the accommodation for us was much larger and better than on board the "Royal George," and which was beautifully fitted up,) were Admiral Sir E. Bruce, a pleasant old man, Commander Bullock, and three other officers. The "Rhadamanthus," with some servants and carriages, set off last night, as well as the "Shearwater," with Lord Liverpool and Lord Hardwicke on board.

The "Salamander" (with Mr. and Mrs. Anson on board), the "Fearless," and the "Royal George" yacht set off at the same time with us, but the wind being against us, we soon lost sight of the yacht, and, not very long after, of all our steamers, except the "Monarch," which belongs to the General Steam Navigation Company, and had some of our horses on board. It started nearly at the same time, and was the only one which could keep up with us. We passed *Tantallon Castle*,* a grand old ruin on the coast, and quite close to the *Bass Rock*, which is very fine, and nearly opposite *Tantallon*. It was entirely covered with sea-gulls and island geese, which swarm in thousands and thousands, quite whitening its sides, and hovering above and around it.

At two o'clock we passed the famed *St. Abb's Head*, which we had so longed to see on our first voyage to *Scotland*. I read a few stanzas out of *Marmion*,* giving an account of the voyage of the nuns to *Holy Island*, and saw the ruins of the convent on it; then *Bamborough Castle*, and a little further on the *Ferne Islands*. We were very sorry to hear that poor Grace Darling had died* the night before we passed the first time.

Friday, September 16.

We heard that we had passed *Flamborough Head* at half-past five in the morning. The "Black Eagle" we passed at half-past eight last night, and we could only just see her smoke by the time we came on deck. At half-past nine I followed Albert on deck; it was a fine, bright morning. We had some coffee, and walked about; we were then quite in the open sea; it was very fine all day. At five we were close to the "Rhadamanthus," which had been in sight all day. We had a very pleasant little dinner on deck, in a small tent made of flags, at half-past five.* We passed *Yarmouth* at about a quarter to six—very flat—and looking, Albert said, like a Flemish town. We walked up and down on deck, admiring the splendid moonlight, which was reflected so beautifully on the sea.

We went below at half-past seven, and I read the fourth and fifth cantos of *The Lay of the Last Minstrel* to Albert, and then we played on the piano.

Saturday, September 17.

At three o'clock in the morning we were awakened by loud guns, which, however, were welcome sounds to us, as we knew that we were at the *Nore*, the entrance of the river. About six we heard the "Rhadamanthus" had just passed us, and they said we were lying off *Southend*, in order to let the "Black Eagle" come up. It was a very bright day, though a little hazy.

The shipping in the river looked very pretty as we passed along. At ten minutes past ten we got into the barge and landed. The Duchess of Norfolk and Miss Matilda Paget and the equerries were all there, but the others we knew nothing of. Sir James Clark had been on board the "Trident" with us. We drove off at once to the railway terminus, and reached *Windsor Castle* at half-past twelve o'clock.*

Visit to Blair Athole.*

Monday, September 9, 1844.

We got up at a quarter to six o'clock. We breakfasted. Mama came to take leave of us; Alice and the baby[+] were brought in, poor little things, to wish us "good-by." Then good Bertie[†] came down to see us, and Vicky[‡] appeared as "voyageuse," and was all impatience to go. At seven we set off with her for the railroad, Viscountess Canning and Lady Caroline Cocks[§] in our carriage. A very wet morning. We got into the carriage again at *Paddington*, and proceeded to *Woolwich*, which we reached at nine. Vicky was safely put into the boat, and then carefully carried on deck of the yacht by Renwick,[¶] the sergeant-footman, whom we took with us in the boat on purpose. Lord Liverpool, Lord Aberdeen, and Sir James Clark met us on board. Sir Robert Peel was to have gone with us, but could not, in consequence of his little girl being very ill.*

Blair Athole,
Wednesday, September 11.

At six o'clock we inquired and heard that we were in the port of *Dundee*. Albert saw our other gentlemen, who had had a very bad passage. Tuesday night they had a dreadful storm. *Dundee* is a very large place, and the port is large and open; the situation of the town is very fine, but the town itself is not so. The Provost and people had come on board, and wanted us to land later, but we got this satisfactorily arranged. At half-past eight we got into our barge with Vicky,* and our ladies and gentlemen. The sea was bright and blue; the boat danced along beautifully. We had about a quarter of a mile to row.

A staircase, covered with red cloth, was arranged for us to land upon, and there were a great many people; but everything was so well managed that all crowding was avoided, and only the Magistrates were below the platform where the people were. Albert walked up the steps with me, I holding his arm and Vicky his hand, amidst the loud cheers of the

---

[+] Prince Alfred, then only five weeks old.
[†] Name by which the Prince of Wales is always called in his family.
[‡] Victoria, Princess Royal.
[§] Now Lady C. Courtenay.
[¶] Now pensioned: promoted to Gentleman Porter in 1854. A very good servant; and a native of Galashiels.

people, all the way to the carriage, our dear Vicky behaving like a grown-up person—not put out, nor frightened, nor nervous. We got into our postchaise, and at the same time Renwick took Vicky up in his arms and put her in the next carriage with her governess and nurse.

There was a great crowd in *Dundee*, but everything was very well managed, and there would have been no crowding at all, had not, as usual, about twenty people begun to run along with the carriage, and thus forced a number of others to follow. About three miles beyond *Dundee* we stopped at the gate of Lord Camperdown's place: here a triumphal arch had been erected, and Lady Camperdown and Lady Duncan and her little boy, with others, were all waiting to welcome us, and were very civil and kind. The little boy, beautifully dressed in the Highland dress, was carried to Vicky, and gave her a basket with fruit and flowers. I said to Albert I could hardly believe that our child was travelling with us—it put me so in mind of myself when I was the "little Princess." Albert observed that it was always said that parents lived their lives over again in their children, which is a very pleasant feeling.*

The country from here to *Cupar Angus* is very well cultivated, and you see hills in the distance. The harvest is only now being got in, but is very good; and everything much greener than in *England*. Nothing could be quieter than our journey, and the scenery is so beautiful! It is very different from *England*: all the houses built of stone; the people so different,—sandy hair, high cheek-bones; children with long shaggy hair and bare legs and feet; little boys in kilts. Near *Dunkeld*, and also as you get more into the *Highlands*, there are prettier faces. Those jackets which the girls wear are so pretty; all the men and women, as well as the children, look very healthy.

Cupar Angus is a small place—a village—14 miles from *Dundee*. There you enter *Perthshire*. We crossed the river *Isla*, which made me think of my poor little dog "Isla." For about five or six miles we went along a very pretty but rough cross-road, with the *Grampians* in the distance. We saw *Birnam Wood* and Sir W. Stewart's place in that fine valley on the opposite side of the river. All along such splendid scenery, and Albert enjoyed it so much—rejoicing in the beauties of nature, the sight of mountains, and the pure air.

The peeps of *Dunkeld*, with the river *Tay* deep in the bottom, and the view of the bridge and cathedral, surrounded by the high wooded hills, as you approached it, were lovely in the extreme. We got out at an inn (which was small, but very clean) at *Dunkeld*, and stopped to let Vicky have some broth. Such a charming view from the window! Vicky stood and bowed to the people out of the window. There never was such a good traveller as she is, sleeping in the carriage at her usual times, not put out, not frightened at noise or crowds; but pleased and amused. She never heard the anchor go at night on board ship; but slept as sound as a top.

Shortly after leaving *Dunkeld*, which is 20 miles from *Blair* and 15 from *Cupar Angus*, we met Lord Glenlyon in a carriage; he jumped out and rode with us the whole way to *Blair*,—and a most beautiful road it is. Six miles on, in the woods to the left, we could see *Kinnaird House*, where the late Lady Glenlyon (Lord Glenlyon's mother, who died about two or three months ago) used to live. Then we passed the point of *Logierait*, where there are the remains of an ancient castle,—the old Regality Court of the Dukes of Athole.* At *Moulinearn* we tasted some of the "*Athole brose*," which was brought to the carriage.

We passed *Pitlochrie*, a small village, *Faskally*, a very pretty place of Mr. Butter's, to the left, and then came to the *Pass of Killiecrankie*,* which is quite magnificent; the road winds along it, and you look down a great height, all wooded on both sides; the *Garry* rolling below it. I cannot describe how beautiful it is. Albert was in perfect ecstasies. *Lude*, Mr. McInroy's, to the right, is very pretty. *Blair Athole* is only four or five miles from the *Killiecrankie Pass*. Lord Glenlyon has had a new approach made. The house is a large plain white building, surrounded by high hills, which one can see from the windows. Lord and Lady Glenlyon, with their little boy, received us at the door, and showed us to our rooms, and then left us.*

Blair Castle, Blair Athole,
Thursday, September 12.

We took a delightful walk of two hours. Immediately near the house the scenery is very wild, which is most enjoyable. The moment you step out of the house you see those splendid hills all round. We went to the left through some neglected pleasure-grounds, and then through the wood, along a steep winding path overhanging the rapid stream. These Scotch streams, full of stones, and clear as glass, are most beautiful; the peeps between the trees, the depth of the shadows, the mossy stones, mixed with slate, &c., which cover the banks, are lovely; at every turn you have a picture. We were up high, but could not get to the top; Albert in such delight; it is a happiness to see him, he is in such spirits. We came back by a higher drive, and then went to the Factor's house, still higher up, where Lord and Lady Glenlyon are living, having given *Blair* up to us. We walked on, to a corn-field where a number of women were cutting and reaping the oats ("shearing" as they call it in *Scotland*), with a splendid view of the hills before us, so rural and romantic, so unlike our daily *Windsor* walk (delightful as that is); and this change does such good: as Albert observes, it refreshes one for a long time. We then went into the kitchen-garden, and to a walk from which there is a magnificent view. This mixture of great wildness and art is perfection.

At a little before four o'clock Albert drove me out in the pony phaeton till nearly six—such a drive! Really to be able to sit in one's pony carriage, and to see such wild, beautiful scenery as we did, the farthest point being only five miles from the house, is an immense delight. We drove along *Glen Tilt*, through a wood overhanging the river *Tilt*, which joins the *Garry*, and as we left the wood we came upon such a lovely view,— *Ben-y-Ghlo* straight before us—and under these high hills the river *Tilt* gushing and winding over stones and slates, and the hills and mountains skirted at the bottom with beautiful trees; the whole lit up by the sun; and the air so pure and fine; but no description can at all do it justice, or give an idea of what this drive was.

Oh! what can equal the beauties of nature! What enjoyment there is in them! Albert enjoys it so much; he is in ecstasies here. He has inherited this love for nature from his dear father.*

We went as far as the *Marble Lodge*, a keeper's cottage, and came back the same way.

Monday, September 16.

After our luncheon at half-past three, Albert drove me (Lord Glenlyon riding with us) to the *Falls of the Bruar*. We got out at the road, and walked to the upper falls, and down again by the path on the opposite side.* It is a walk of three miles round, and a very steep ascent; at every turn the view of the rushing falls is extremely fine, and looking back on the hills, which were so clear and so beautifully lit up, with the rapid stream below, was most exquisite. We threw stones down to see the effect in the water. The trees which surround the falls were planted by the late Duke of Athole in compliance with Burns's "*Petition*."*⁺

The evening was beautiful, and we feasted our eyes on the ever-changing, splendid views of the hills and vales as we drove back. Albert said that the chief beauty of mountain scenery consisted in its frequent changes. We came home at six o'clock.*

Tuesday, September 17.

At a quarter to four o'clock we drove out, Albert driving me, and the ladies and Lord Glenlyon following in another carriage. We drove

---

⁺ *The Humble Petition of Bruar Water to the Noble Duke of Athole** to the *Pass of Killiecrankie*, which looked in its greatest beauty and splendour, and appeared quite closed, so that one could not imagine how one was to get out of it. We drove over a bridge to the right, where the view of the pass both ways, with the *Garry* below, is beautiful. We got out a little way beyond this and walked on a mile to the *Falls of the Tummel*, the stream of which is famous for salmon; these falls, however, are not so fine, or nearly so high, as those of the *Bruar*. We got home at half-past six; the day was fast fading, and the lights were lovely.

We watched two stags fighting just under our window; they are in an enclosure, and roar incessantly.

Wednesday, September 18.

At nine o'clock we set off on ponies, to go up one of the hills, Albert riding the dun pony and I the grey, attended only by Lord Glenlyon's excellent servant, Sandy McAra, in his Highland dress. We went out by the back way across the road, and to the left through the ford, Sandy leading my pony and Albert following closely, the water reaching up above Sandy's knees. We then went up the hill of *Tulloch*, first straight up a very steep cabbage-field, and then in a zigzag manner round, till we got up to the top; the ponies scrambling up over stones and everything, and never making a false step; and the view all round being splendid and most beautifully lit up. We went up to the very highest top, which cannot be seen from the house or from below; and from here the view is like a panorama: you see the *Falls of the Bruar*, *Ben-y-Chat*, *Ben Vrackie*, *Ben-y-Ghlo*, the *Killiecrankie Pass*, and a whole range of distant hills on the other side, which one cannot at all see from below. In the direction of *Taymouth* you also see *Dalnacardoch*, the first stage from *Blair*. *Blair* itself and the houses in the village looked like little toys from the great height we were on. It was quite romantic. Here we were with only this Highlander behind us holding the ponies (for we got off twice and walked about)—not a house, not a creature near us, but the pretty Highland sheep, with their horns and black faces,—up at the top of *Tulloch*, surrounded by beautiful mountains.

We came back the same way that we went, and stopped at the ford to let the ponies drink before we rode through. We walked from inside the gate, and came home at half-past eleven,—the most delightful, most romantic ride and walk I ever had. I had never been up such a mountain, and then the day was so fine. The hill of *Tulloch* is covered with grass, and is so delightfully soft to walk upon.

Thursday, September 19.

Albert set off, immediately after luncheon, deer-stalking, and I was to follow and wait below in order to see the deer driven down. At four o'clock I set off with Lady Glenlyon and Lady Canning. Mr. Oswald and Lord Charles Wellesley riding, by the lower *Glen Tilt* drive. We stopped at the end; but were still in the wood; Sandy was looking out and watching. After waiting we were allowed to come out of the carriage, and came upon the road, where we saw some deer on the brow of the hill. We sat down on the ground, Lady Canning and I sketching, and Sandy and Mr. Oswald, both in Highland costume, (the same that they all wear here, viz. a grey cloth jacket and waistcoat, with a kilt and a Highland bonnet,*) lying on the grass and looking through glasses. After waiting again some time, we were told in a mysterious whisper that "they were coming," and indeed a great herd *did* appear on the brow of the hill, and came running down a good way, when most provokingly two men who were walking on the road—which they had no business to have done—suddenly came in sight, and then the herd all ran back again and the sport was spoilt. After waiting some little while we observed Albert, Lord Glenlyon, and the keepers on the brow of the hill, and we got into the carriage, drove a little way, went over the bridge, where there is a shepherd's "shiel," and got out and waited for them to join us, which they did almost immediately,—looking very picturesque with their rifles. My poor Albert had not even fired one shot for fear of spoiling the whole thing, but had been running about a good deal. The group of keepers and dogs was very pretty. After talking and waiting a little while, we walked some way on, and then Albert drove home with us.

Saturday, September 21.

After breakfast Albert saw Lord Glenlyon, who proposed that he should go deer-stalking and that I should follow him. At twenty minutes to eleven we drove off with Lady Canning for *Glen Tilt*. The day was glorious and it would have been a pity to lose it, but it was a long hard day's work, though extremely delightful and enjoyable, and unlike anything I had ever done before. I should have enjoyed it still more had I been able to be with Albert the whole time.

We drove nearly to Peter Fraser's house, which is between the *Marble Lodge* and *Forest Lodge*.* Here Albert and I walked about a little, and then Lady Canning and we mounted our ponies and set off on our journey, Lord Glenlyon leading my pony the whole way, Peter Fraser, the head-keeper (a wonderfully active man) leading the way; Sandy and six other Highlanders carrying rifles and leading dogs, and the rear brought up by two ponies with our luncheon-box. Lawley,[+] Albert's Jäger, was also there, carrying one of Albert's rifles; the other Albert slung over his right shoulder, to relieve Lawley. So we set off and wound round and round the hill, which had the most picturesque effect imaginable. Such a splendid view all round, finer and more extensive the higher we went! The day was delightful; but the sun very hot. We saw the highest point of *Ben-y-Ghlo*, which one cannot see from below, and the distant range of hills we had seen from *Tulloch* was beautifully softened by the slightest haze. We saw *Loch Vach*. The road was very good, and as we ascended we had to speak in a whisper, as indeed we did almost all day, for fear of coming upon deer unawares. The wind was, however, right, which is everything here for the deer. I wish we could have had Landseer with us to sketch our party,* with the background, it was so pretty, as were also the various "halts," &c. If I only had had time to sketch them!

We stopped at the top of the *Chrianan*, whence you look down an immense height. It is here that the eagles sometimes sit. Albert got off and looked about in great admiration, and walked on a little, and then remounted his pony. We then went nearly to the top of *Cairn Chlamain*, and here we separated, Albert going off with Peter, Lawley, and two other keepers, to get a "quiet shot" as they call it; and Lady Canning, Lord Glenlyon, and I went up quite to the top,* which is deep in moss. Here we sat down and stayed some time sketching the ponies below; Lord Glenlyon and Sandy remaining near us. The view was quite beautiful, nothing but mountains all around us, and the solitude, the complete solitude, very impressive. We saw the range of *Mar Forest*, and the inner range to the left, receding from us, as we sat facing the hill, called *Scarsach*, where the counties of *Perth*, *Aberdeen*, and *Inverness* join. My pony was brought up for me, and we then descended this highest pinnacle, and proceeded on a level to meet Albert, whom I descried coming towards us. We met him shortly after; he had had bad luck, I am sorry to say. We then sat down on the grass and had some luncheon; then I walked a little with Albert and we got on our ponies. As we went on towards home some deer were seen in *Glen Chroime*, which is called the "Sanctum;" where it is supposed that there are a great many. Albert went off soon after this, and we remained on *Sron a Chro*, for an hour, I am sure, as Lord Glenlyon said by so doing we should turn the deer to Albert, whereas if we went on we should disturb and spoil the whole

---

[+] A very good man. His health obliged him to give up being a Jäger in 1848; he was then appointed a Page, in which position he continued till he died, in November, 1865.

thing. So we submitted. Albert looked like a little speck creeping about on an opposite hill. We saw four herds of deer, two of them close to us. It was a beautiful sight.

Meanwhile I saw the sun sinking gradually, and I got quite alarmed lest we should be benighted, and we called anxiously for Sandy, who had gone away for a moment, to give a signal to come back. We then began our descent, "squinting" the hill, the ponies going as safely and securely as possible. As the sun went down the scenery became more and more beautiful, the sky crimson, golden-red and blue, and the hills looking purple and lilac, most exquisite, till at length it set, and the hues grew softer in the sky and the outlines of the hills sharper. I never saw anything so fine. It soon, however, grew very dark.

At length Albert met us, and he told me he had waited all the time for us, as he knew how anxious I should be. He had been very unlucky, and had lost his sport, for the rifle would not go off just when he could have shot some fine harts; yet he was as merry and cheerful as if nothing had happened to disappoint him.* We got down quite safely to the bridge; our ponies going most surely, though it was quite dusk when we were at the bottom of the hill. We walked to the *Marble Lodge*, and then got into the pony carriage and drove home by very bright moonlight, which made everything look very lovely; but the road made one a little nervous.

We saw a flight of ptarmigan, with their white wings, on the top of *Sron a Chro*, also plovers, grouse, and pheasants. We were safely home by a quarter to eight.

Tuesday, October 1.

At a quarter-past eight o'clock we started, and were very very sorry to leave *Blair* and the dear *Highlands!* Every little trifle and every spot I had become attached to; our life of quiet and liberty, everything was so pleasant, and all the Highlanders and people who went with us I had got to like so much. Oh! the dear hills, it made me very sad to leave them behind!

Lord Glenlyon rode with us, and we went back exactly the same road we came; through *Killiecrankie*, *Pitlochrie*, saw *Logierait*, &c. The battle of *Killiecrankie* was fought in a field to your left, as you come from *Blair* and before you come to the pass; and Lord Dundee was shot in a garden immediately above the field at *Urrard* (formerly called *Kinrory*) which belongs to Mr. Stewart of *Urrard*; the Stewarts of *Urrard* used formerly to live on *Craig Urrard*. We reached *Dunkeld* at half-past eleven. Mr. Oswald and Mr. Patrick Small Keir, with a detachment of Highlanders, were there. We drove up to the door of the cottage at

Dunkeld and got out there. It is beautifully situated and the cottage is very pretty, with a good view of the river from the windows. *Craig-y-Barns* is a fine rocky hill to the left as you drive from *Blair*.

We walked to look at the beginning of the new house which the late Duke of Athole commenced, but which has been left unfinished, and also at a beautiful larch-tree, the first that was brought to *Scotland*. I rode back on "Arghait Bhean"[†] for the last time, and took a sad leave of him and of faithful Sandy McAra. We walked into the ruins of the old cathedral and into that part which the late Duke fitted up for service, and where there is a fine monument of him. I should never have recognized the grounds of *Dunkeld*, so different did they look without the encampment.[‡] Beautiful as *Dunkeld* is, it does not approach the beauty and wildness of *Blair*.

After twelve o'clock we set off again, and to our astonishment Lord Glenlyon insisted upon riding on with us to *Dundee*, which is 50 miles from *Blair!* Captain J. Murray also rode with us from *Dunkeld*. It made me feel sad to see the country becoming flatter and flatter. There was a great crowd at *Cupar Angus*, and at *Dundee* a still larger one, and on the pier the crush was very great.

We took leave of Lord Glenlyon with real regret, and he seemed quite unhappy at our going. No one could be more zealous or kinder than he was.

There was a fearful swell when we went in the barge to the yacht.*

Thursday, October 3.

The English coast appeared terribly flat. Lord Aberdeen was quite touched when I told him I was so attached to the dear, dear *Highlands* and missed the fine hills so much. There is a great peculiarity about the *Highlands* and Highlanders; and they are such a chivalrous, fine, active people. Our stay among them was so delightful. Independently of the beautiful scenery, there was a quiet, a retirement, a wildness, a liberty, and a solitude that had such a charm for us.

The day had cleared up and was bright, but the air very heavy and thick, quite different from the mountain air, which was so pure, light, and brisk. At two o'clock we reached *Woolwich*, and shortly after disembarked. We proceeded straight to the railroad, and arrived at *Windsor Castle* at a few minutes past four.*

[†] This pony was given to me by the Duke of Athole in 1847, and is now alive at Osborne.
[‡] *Vide* page 25.

Tour round the West Coast of Scotland,
and Visit to Ardverikie.

Wednesday, August 11, 1847.

We proceeded from the *Osborne Pier* on board the yacht.* Our two eldest children, my brother Charles, the Duke and Duchess of Norfolk, Lord Grey (Secretary of State), Lady Jocelyn, General Wemyss, Sir James Clark, and Miss Hildyard, accompanied us.

We have with us the following steamers:—The "Black Eagle," "Garland," "Undine," "Fairy," and "Scourge" (war-steamers). The two equerries are on board the "Black Eagle."

We were soon under weigh,* and as *Osborne* vanished from our sight, I thought of our poor children left behind.

On Board the Victoria and Albert,
in Dartmouth Harbour,
Thursday, August 12.

I have not much to relate. Our voyage has not been what we intended, *mais l'homme propose et Dieu dispo*se; for instead of being at *Falmouth* we are only at *Dartmouth!* We started at five o'clock, and soon after felt the vessel stop, and on inquiring, heard that the fog was so thick it was impossible to proceed. At last Captain Smithett was sent out in the "Garland" to report on the state of the weather; and he soon returned, saying that all was clear enough to proceed outside *The Needles** (we were in *Alum Bay*). So we started again, and, after breakfast, we came on deck, where I remained working and talking; feeling quite well; but towards one the ground swell had increased, and we decided to run into the harbour we now are in.

On Board the Victoria and Albert,
Milford Haven, South Wales,
Saturday, August 14.*

Arrived here this afternoon at five. I will give an account of what has passed since leaving *Dartmouth*. Thursday evening, after dining with Charles, we went on deck, and found the whole town illuminated, and the effect of its curious high houses running down quite into the still sea, which reflected the illumination, was lovely,—the night being so fine and calm.

Friday, August 13.

We started at four and reached the *Scilly Islands* at three in the afternoon; it had been very rough. The numerous little rocky islands, in the midst of which we are lying, are very curious.

St. Mary's, the principal island, has a little town, a church, and a small harbour. Exactly opposite, on the isle of *Tresco*, is Mr. Smith's house; he has the lease of all the islands from the Duchy of Cornwall. Farther to the left is *St. Agnes*, with a lighthouse and innumerable rocks.

Albert (who, as well as Charles, has not been unwell, while I suffered very much) went with Charles and Bertie to see one of the islands. The children recover from their sea-sickness directly. When Albert and the others returned, soon after five, we went with our ladies and gentlemen in the barge across the harbour,—where, blue as the sea was, it was still rather rough,—and landed at a little pier at *St. Mary's*. The harbour, surmounted by the old fort of the *Star Castle*, reminded me of the harbour of *St. Heliers*. We got into a pony carriage belonging to Mr. Smith, with Charles and Lady Jocelyn, and drove through the place, which looks like a small fishing town, and then round the fortifications of the castle, where there is a very pretty walk overhanging the sea; the rock being covered with fern, and heath, and furze. The extensive view of the islands and rocks around is very beautiful. The town is built upon a very narrow strip of land, with a small bay on either side. We got out at the old castle, which bears the date of one of the Edwards.* The view from the battlements is very fine. We returned the same way we went, a little before seven.

Saturday, August 14.

We started at five o'clock, and the yacht then began to roll and pitch dreadfully, and I felt again very unwell; but I came on deck at three in the afternoon, the sea then was like glass, and we were close to the Welsh coast.

This harbour, *Milford Haven*, is magnificent; the largest we have; a fleet might lie here. We are anchored just off *Milford. Pembroke* in front, in the distance. The cliffs, which are reddish brown, are not very high. Albert and Charles went in the "Fairy" to *Pembroke*, and I sketched. Numbers of boats came out, with Welsh-women in their curious high-crowned men's hats;* and Bertie was much cheered, for the people seemed greatly pleased to see the "Prince of Wales." Albert returned at a quarter to eight.

A very pretty dairymaid, in complete Welsh costume, was brought on board for me to see. We found *Milford* illuminated when we went on deck, and bonfires burning everywhere.

Sunday, August 15.

We started again at four o'clock, but this time had a beautiful day, with the sea smooth the whole way. About eleven we saw the mountainous coast of *Caernarvonshire*; the hills, which are in fact high mountains, are bold and finely shaped, and, Albert said, reminded him much of *Ischia*, with the beautiful deep blue sea and bright sky.

Having arrived at the entrance of the *Menai Straits*, we all left the "Victoria and Albert," and went on board the "Fairy."* The "Victoria and Albert" with the " Black Eagle" (the two equerries having joined us), the "Undine" and "Scourge," proceeded round the *Isle of Anglesea* by *Holyhead*, and, in the "Fairy," accompanied by the "Garland," we went into the *Straits*.* As we entered, the view of the fine mountains with their rich verdure—*Snowdon* rising splendidly in the midst—and of the fields and woods below, was really glorious. To the left the country is extremely flat. Then *Caernarvon** came in sight, with its grand old Castle so finely situated. We stopped for a few moments off here, but did not land. The mountains disappeared for a while, and then re-appeared more beautiful than ever. We passed close to *Plas Newydd*,* where we had spent six weeks fifteen years ago. I felt as if I remembered it all very well; but admired the scenery even more than I had expected from my previous recollection.

We passed the famous *Swilly Rocks*, and saw the works they are making for the tube for the railroad,* and then went under the *Menai Bridge*,* and stopped immediately on the other side. There were crowds of loyal people in steamers and boats, playing "God save the Queen," and cheering tremendously. Albert and Charles landed and walked over the bridge.

When they returned we went on again, and stopped in a most beautiful spot, with almost Swiss scenery, opposite *Penrhyn Castle*,* Colonel Douglas Pennant's (which I saw in the late possessor's time unfinished), and near *Bangor*, with its wooded banks, through which one can see the high-road to *Beaumaris*. The purple hills, with the verdure below, and the blue sea, were extremely picturesque.

Albert and Charles went to see *Penrhyn*. As soon as they returned we dined below in the "Fairy," and at eight we returned, with the children and all our people, to the "Victoria and Albert." The evening was beautiful and the day very successful.

Monday, August 16.

We woke soon after four o'clock, when getting under weigh, and were surprised to feel the yacht stop not an hour after. Something had gone wrong with the paddle-wheel—just as happened last year—and it took full two hours to set it right. Then at seven we started afresh. A beautiful morning with a very smooth sea. By half-past ten we were in sight of the *Isle of Man*, which is a fine island with bold hills and cliffs. A little before twelve we reached the point of the bay, on which is the town of *Douglas*, very prettily situated, with a picturesque castle near the lighthouse, on the extreme point of the bay. We stopped off here for ten minutes or a quarter of an hour,—the rocks were covered with people. From *Douglas* to *Ramsay Bay* the hills and cliffs are high and bold; though *Ramsay* itself is low.

For about two hours we were out of sight of land, and I was below writing. When I came on deck at three o'clock the Scotch coast was quite close; the *Mull of Galloway*, and then *Wigtownshire*. Albert declared he saw the Irish coast, but I could not descry it. At five we came in sight of *Loch Ryan*, and saw, to the left, *Ailsa Craig** rising more than 1,000 feet perpendicularly from the sea. *Loch Ryan* is very fine, and the hills and glens are lovely, particularly little *Glen Finnie*. The loch is very large, and the hills here are very high and wooded. The little town is called *Stranraer*.

Tuesday, August 17.

At six o'clock we began to move. A beautiful morning. At about eight we were close to the *Ailsa Rock* or *Craig*, the formation of which is very curious. There were thousands and thousands of birds,—gannets,—on the rock, and we fired a gun off three times in order to bring them in reach of a shot—Albert and Charles tried, but in vain. We next came in sight of the beautiful *Isle of Arran*. The finest point is when you are before the *Holy Island*,* and in sight of the *Goatfell* range of mountains. The highest is about 2,800 feet; they are peculiarly fine from their bold pointed outlines. Before them is *Lamlash*. After passing *Holy Island* we came to *Brodick Bay*, which is beautiful, with high hills and a glen; in front of which, and surrounded by wood, is the castle which Lord Douglas is building. Not long after this we came in sight of the *Isle of Bute*, and entered the *Clyde*, the view of which from Mr. Stuart's and Lord Bute's property is beautiful: high wooded banks, the river opening out and widening, surrounded by the distant mountains. A small place to the right called *Largs* is very prettily situated.

At half-past twelve we reached *Greenock*, the port of *Glasgow*. The shore and the ships were crowded with people, there being no less (as I since learnt) than thirty-nine steamers, over-filled with people, which almost all followed us! Such a thing never was seen. Add to these steamers boats and ships of all descriptions, moving in all directions; but not getting out of the way! We, however, got safe on board the "Fairy," and steamed up the *Clyde*; it was hazy, and we could not see the distance well. We passed the small town of *Port Glasgow*, and about one o'clock were at *Dumbarton Castle*.* Its situation is very fine, the rock rising straight out of the river, the mountains all round, and the town of *Dumbarton* behind it, making it very picturesque. We landed just below the Castle, and went with Charles and the children in a carriage to the fort. There was a great crowd, but excellent order kept. We went to the battery, but had to mount many steps to get to it. Wallace was confined here; and it was one of the last castles which held out for Mary Queen of Scots. From the battery there is a very extensive view of the *Clyde* and *Dumbarton*, and we ought to have been able to see *Ben Lomond*; but it was in mist.

We got back to the "Fairy" by half-past two, and returned to *Greenock*, escorted by nineteen steamers. Steamed past *Greenock*, and went on towards *Loch Long*, passing *Roseneath* to the right, where the present Duke and Duchess of Argyll live. *Loch Long* is indeed splendid, 15 miles in length, surrounded by grand hills, with such beautiful outlines, and very green—all so different from the eastern part of *Scotland*—the loch winding along most beautifully, so as to seem closed at times. Charles said it reminded him of *Switzerland* and the *Tyrol*. The finest point of *Loch Long* is looking towards *Loch Goil*. We had a very good sight of the mountain called *The Cobbler*; the top of which resembles a man sitting and mending his shoe!* At the end of the loch we got a glimpse of *Ben Lomond*, and were, in fact, very near *Loch Lomond*.

We returned as we came. There was no sun, and once or twice a little mist; but still it was beautiful. We went on to *Rothsay*, which we reached at eight o'clock, and immediately went on board the "Victoria and Albert," greatly tired but much amused and interested.

The children enjoy everything extremely, and bear the novelty and excitement wonderfully. The people cheered the "Duke of Rothsay"+ very much, and also called for a cheer for the "Princess of Great Britain." Everywhere the good Highlanders are very enthusiastic. *Rothsay* is a pretty little town, built round a fine bay, with hills in the distance, and a fine harbour. When we went on deck after dinner, we found the whole town brilliantly illuminated, with every window lit up, which had a very pretty effect.

Wednesday, August 18.

A bright fresh morning, the hills slightly tipped with clouds. At eight o'clock we all went on board the "Fairy," and went up the *Kyles of Bute*, which, as you advance, become very fine, the hills lying so curiously one behind the other, sometimes apparently closing up all outlet.

We saw *Arran* to the left, looking very grand in the distance. We have been turning about a good deal since yesterday, for we went by *Arran* and *Holy Island*, and then left *Little* and *Great Cumbray* to our left, and went up to *Dumbarton* and back, and on to *Loch Long*, and then to *Rothsay*, leaving *Arran* to our left; then, after passing *Arran*, we entered *Loch*

+ A title belonging to the eldest son of the Sovereign of Scotland, and therefore held by the Prince of Wales as eldest son of the Queen, the representative of the ancient Kings of Scotland.

Fyne. I, however, had a headache, and was obliged to lie down below, and only came on deck again when we were within an hour of *Inverary*; where the lake widens, and the hills on either side are very green and undulating, but not very high.

The approach to *Inverary* is splendid; the loch is very wide; straight before you a fine range of mountains splendidly lit up,—green, pink, and lilac; to the left, the little town of *Inverary*; and above it, surrounded by pine woods, stands the Castle of *Inverary*,* square, with turrets at the corners.

Our reception was in the true Highland fashion. The Duke and Duchess of Argyll (dear Lady Elizabeth Leveson Gower), the Duchess of Sutherland, Lord Stafford, Lady Caroline Leveson Gower, and the Blantyres received us at the landing-place, which was all ornamented with heather.* The Celtic Society, including Campbell of Islay, his two sons (one grown up and the other a very pretty little boy), with a number of his men, and several other Campbells, were all drawn up near to the carriage. We got into a carriage with the two Duchesses, Charles and the Duke being on the box (we had left the children on board the "Fairy"), and took a beautiful drive amongst magnificent trees, and along a glen where we saw *Ben Sheerar*, &c. The weather was particularly fine, and we were much struck by the extreme beauty of *Inverary*—presenting as it does such a combination of magnificent timber, with high mountains, and a noble lake.

The pipers walked before the carriage, and the Highlanders on either side, as we approached the house. Outside stood the Marquis of Lorn, just two years old, a dear, white, fat, fair little fellow with reddish hair, but very delicate features, like both his father and mother: he is such a merry, independent little child. He had a black velvet dress and jacket, with a "sporran," scarf, and Highland bonnet. We lunched at two with our hosts; the Highland gentlemen standing with halberds in the room. We sent for our children, who arrived during luncheon time. We left *Inverary* before three, and took the children with us in the carriage. The Argylls, the Duchess of Sutherland, and the others, accompanied us on board the "Fairy," where we took leave of them.

The light on the hills was beautiful as we steamed down *Loch Fyne*. At five we reached *Lochgilp*, and all landed at *Lochgilphead*, a small village where there were numbers of people, and, amongst others, Sir John P. Orde, who lent his carriage and was extremely civil. We and our people drove through the little village to the *Crinan Canal*,* where we entered a most magnificently decorated barge, drawn by three horses, ridden by postilions in scarlet. We glided along very smoothly, and the views of the hills—the range of *Cruachan*—were very fine indeed; but the eleven locks we had to go through—(a very curious process, first passing several by rising, and then others by going down)—were tedious, and instead of the passage lasting one hour and a half, it lasted upwards of two hours and a half, therefore it was nearly eight o'clock before we reached *Loch Crinan*. We instantly went on board the "Victoria and Albert," but it was too late to proceed to *Oban*; we had, therefore, to lengthen our voyage by a day, and spent the night at *Crinan*. It is a very fine spot, hills all round, and, in the distance, those of the island of *Jura*. The yacht had had a good passage round the *Mull of Cantire*. We dined with Charles, and went on deck; and the blaze of the numerous bonfires—the half moon, the stars, and the extreme stillness of the night—had a charming effect.

Thursday, August 19.

A beautiful day. At nine o'clock we left *Crinan*, proceeding to the right, up splendid passes, with myriads of islands, and such enchanting views, that I cannot enumerate them. We passed first up the *Sound of Jura*, where numbers of people met us in small boats, decorated with little flags; then up the *Pass of Kerrera* to *Oban*, one of the finest spots we have seen, with the ruins of the old *Castle of Dunolly* and a range of high mountains in the distance. To the left, after leaving *Oban*, we saw the *Isle of Kerrera* and to the right *Dunstaffnage Castle*,* whence came the famous stone which supports the "Coronation Chair,"* in which the sovereigns are crowned at *Westminster Abbey*. Alexander II. is said to be buried here.* We passed close by the flat rock, called *The Lady's Rock*, on which a McLean left his wife, hoping she would be washed away—she was saved however.*

We then came into the *Sound of Mull* by *Tobermory*, a small place prettily situated, and from thence the views continued beautiful. At one o'clock we were in sight of the *Isles of Rum*, *Eig* and *Muck* (rather large islands, which Lord Salisbury bought a few years ago). Next we passed the long, flat, curious islands of *Coll* and *Tiree*. The inhabitants of these islands have, unhappily, been terrible sufferers during the last winter from famine.* A little further on we saw, to our right, the *Treshinish Isles*, very curiously-shaped rocks: one is called *The Dutchman's Cap*, and has the most strange shape, thus—*

At three we anchored close before *Staffa*, and immediately got into the barge with Charles, the children, and the rest of our people, and rowed towards the cave. As we rounded the point, the wonderful basaltic formation came in sight. The appearance it presents is most extraordinary; and when we turned the corner to go into the renowned *Fingal's Cave*,* the effect was splendid, like a great entrance into a vaulted hall: it looked almost awful as we entered, and the barge heaved up and down on the swell of the sea. It is very high, but not longer than 227 feet, and narrower than I expected, being only 40 feet wide. The sea is immensely deep in the cave. The rocks, under water, were all colours—pink, blue, and green—which had a most beautiful and varied effect. It was the first time the British standard with a Queen of Great Britain, and her husband and children, had ever entered *Fingal's Cave*, and the men gave three cheers, which sounded very impressive there. We backed out, and then went on a little further to look at the other cave, not of basaltic formation, and at the point called *The Herdsman*. The swell was beginning to get up, and perhaps an hour later we could not have gone in.

We returned to the yacht, but Albert and Charles landed again at *Staffa*. They returned in three quarters of an hour, and we then went on to *Iona*; here Albert and Charles landed, and were absent an hour. I and the ladies sketched. We saw from the yacht the ruins of the old cathedral of *St. Oran*.* When Albert and Charles returned, they said the ruins were very curious, there had been two monasteries there, and fine old crosses and tombs of ancient kings were still to be seen. I must see it some other time. On Albert's return we went on again, and reached *Tobermory* at nine. The place was all illuminated.

Friday, August 20.

A wet morning when we rose at half-past seven, and it was pouring with rain when we left *Tobermory* at half-past eight. I went down, and drew and painted. It cleared up about half-past ten, and I came on deck. The scenery in *Loch Linnhe* was magnificent—such beautiful mountains. From *Loch Linnhe* we entered *Loch Eil*, and passed the entrance of *Loch Leven* to the right, at the end of which is *Glencoe*,* so famous for its beautiful scenery and for the horrible massacre of the Macdonalds, in William III.'s time.

A little before one we arrived at *Fort William*,* a very small place. The afternoon was very bright, and the scenery fine. After luncheon Albert and Charles set off in the "Fairy" to see *Glencoe*. They returned at twenty minutes past seven, and Albert thought *Glencoe* was very fine, though not quite as much so as he had expected. They had driven in an extraordinary carriage, with seats for thirty.* The people, who recognized Albert, were so loyal that they took the horses out and insisted on drawing the carriage.

The evening was excessively cold and showery.

I am quite sorry we shall have to leave our yacht tomorrow, in which we have been so comfortably housed, and that this delightful voyage and tour among the Western Lochs and Isles is at an end—they are so beautiful,—and so full of poetry and romance, traditions, and historical associations.

Ardverikie, Loch Laggan,*
Saturday, August 21.

Alas! a very wet morning. We were ready long before nine o'clock, but had to wait, as our carriages were not ready. At last we all landed at *Fort William*, where there was a great gathering of Highlanders, in their different tartans, with Lord Lovat and Mr. Stuart Mackenzie at their head. We got into our carriage with Charles and the two children; there was a great crowd to see us off. We went by a very wild and lonely road, the latter part extremely fine, with mountains and streams that reminded us of *Glen Tilt*. We changed horses only once, and came at length in sight of *Loch Laggan*. It is a beautiful lake (small in comparison to what we have seen) surrounded by very fine mountains: the road by its side is extremely pretty. We saw Lord Abercorn's house of *Ardverikie* long before we came to it. At *Laggan* there is only a small inn, and at the end of the lake, a ferry. Here, in spite of the pouring rain, were assembled a number of Highlanders, with Macpherson of Cluny (always called Cluny Macpherson) and three dear little boys of his, Davidson of Tulloch, and others, with Lord Abercorn, in full Highland dress. We stepped out of our carriage and stood upon the floating bridge, and so crossed over in two or three minutes. We then drove on, in our pony carriages, to *Ardverikie*, and arrived there in about twenty minutes. It is quite close to the lake, and the view from the windows, as I now write, though obscured by rain, is very beautiful, and extremely wild. There is not a village, house, or cottage within four or five miles: one can only get to it by the ferry, or by rowing across the lake. The house is a comfortable shooting-lodge, built of stone, with many nice rooms in it. Stags' horns are placed along the outside and in the passages; and the walls of the drawing-room and ante-room are ornamented with beautiful drawings of stags, by Landseer.

There is little to say of our stay at *Ardverikie*; the country is very fine, but the weather was most dreadful.

On the 28th, about five o'clock, Albert drove me out across the ferry, along the *Kingussie* road, and from here the scenery was splendid: high bold* hills, with a good deal of wood; glens, with the *Pattock*,* and a small waterfall; the meadows here and there, with people making hay, and cottages sprinkled sparingly about, reminded us much of *Thüringen*. We drove to the small farm, where Colonel Macpherson now lives, called *Strathmashie*, and back again, 16 miles in all. We were delighted with the scenery, which is singularly beautiful, wild and romantic,—with so much fine wood about it, which greatly enhances the beauty of a landscape.

Thursday, September 16.

Albert left at six this morning to go to *Inverness* and see the *Caledonian Canal*.*

Friday, September 17.

At two o'clock I left *Ardverikie* with the children, and reached *Fort William* at half-past six, where I had the happiness of finding Albert on board the yacht. All had gone off well; but the weather had been very bad. Albert said *Dochfour** was beautiful; the house new and very elegant, with a fine garden, and Mr. and Lady Georgiana Baillie very pleasant people.

Albert had to go to *Inverness*, and to stay for a ball that was held there; and he was everywhere extremely well received. This morning he saw the *Falls of Foyers*,* which, he tells me, are very grand indeed; and of a great height; and he says that the *Caledonian Canal* is a most remarkable work.

Loch Ryan,
Saturday, September 18.

At five o'clock we left *Fort William*. Rather a fine morning; but very squally, and the sea rough, even where we were. When we came on deck, we were close to the *Isle of Jura*, which has such a fine, bold outline. We went on to *Loch Crinan*, where we got into the barge: here it was very rough and pouring with rain, so unlike the beautiful evening when we were here a month ago. We landed at *Crinan*. Mr. Malcolm, whose castle is just opposite, received us there, and we entered the canal boat at ten. We proceeded more quickly than the last time; the people kept running along as before, and there was a piper at each lock. It rained almost the whole time. We reached *Lochgilphead* at twelve, in pouring rain, and embarked on board the "Black Eagle." The yacht had again to go round the *Mull of Cantire* and meet us at *Campbeltown*. What a contrast to the weather we had when we came!

We got under weigh, and proceeded by *Kilbrannan Sound* and *Arran*. We went on deck for a little while, but were driven below by the rain; later, however, it was possible to keep on deck. We reached *Campbeltown*, a small and not pretty place, at the foot of *Cantire*, at twenty minutes to five. About half an hour after we arrived the yacht came in, with the "Garland," "Fairy," and "Scourge," and we immediately went on board. They had had a very bad passage, and Captain Crispin said he was very glad that we had not been on board the "Victoria and Albert." This rather alarmed us for the next day's voyage, the more so as the evening was squally and the sky very unpromising. There was a long consultation as to what was to be done, and at last it was decided that we should start at four in the morning, and if it were very rough, we should either run into *Loch Ryan*, the *Mull of Galloway*, the *Bay of Ramsay*, or into *Douglas* in the *Isle of Man*.

Loch Ryan,
Sunday, September 19.

We set off at four o'clock, the yacht rolling considerably; but it was quite bearable; however, at seven they came to shut down the port-holes, expecting a heavy sea, and Lord Adolphus saw Albert, who had just got up, and said it would be very rough; upon which it was decided to put back a little way, and to go into *Loch Ryan*; we accordingly did so, and anchored there at half-past eight;—such a dreary rainy day—one could hardly recognize what was so fine when we were last in here.

Both now, and the time before when we were in *Loch Ryan*, Lord Orkney very civilly sent us game and all sorts of things.

At twelve o'clock Lord Adolphus read the short sea service. We then talked over our voyage, and what could be done;—the day was very wretched,—pouring with rain and blowing hard. It was at last decided to start again at three, and get this evening to the *Mull of Galloway*, which would only take us three hours, though it would probably be rough. As soon as we were out of the loch the yacht began to pitch, and the sea was dreadfully rough. I was very ill. Albert, however, stood it perfectly, and the children very tolerably. Presently we came in sight of the *Mull of Galloway*, a great rock with a lighthouse on it;*—and this was our last glimpse of dear *Scotland*.

Monday, September 20.

At six o'clock we got under weigh, and after considerable "rockings," which lasted for nearly two hours, we were near the *Isle of Man*, in smooth water, and at half-past eight anchored in *Ramsay Bay*.*

Albert went on shore, and meantime the Bishop of Sodor and Man, with others, came on board. Albert returned at twelve. At one o'clock we started again. We had to go slowly at first, as our paddle-wheel again got wrong, and because we should otherwise have arrived before we were expected.

We anchored at seven in *Fleetwood Harbour*; the entrance was extremely narrow and difficult. We were lashed close to the pier, to prevent our being turned by the tide; and when I went on deck there was a great commotion, such running and calling, and pulling of ropes, &c. It was a cheerless evening, blowing hard.*

Tuesday, September 21.

At ten o'clock we landed, and proceeded by rail to *London*.

LIFE IN THE HIGHLANDS,
1848 TO 1861.

Land of brown heath and shaggy wood,
Land of the mountain and the flood,
Land of my sires! what mortal hand
Can e'er untie the filial band
That knits me to thy rugged strand!
Still, as I view each well-known scene,
Think what is now, and what hath been,
Seems as, to me, of all bereft,
Sole friends thy woods and streams are left;
And thus I love them better still,
Even in extremity of ill.*

The Lay of the Last Minstrel.

First Impressions of Balmoral.

Balmoral,
Friday, September 8, 1848.

We arrived at *Balmoral* at a quarter to three. It is a pretty little castle in the old Scottish style. There is a picturesque tower and garden in front, with a high wooded hill; at the back there is wood down to the *Dee*; and the hills rise all around.*

There is a nice little hall, with a billiard-room; next to it is the dining-room. Upstairs (ascending by a good broad staircase) immediately to the right, and above the dining-room, is our sitting-room (formerly the drawing-room), a fine large room—next to which is our bed-room, opening into a little dressing-room which is Albert's. Opposite, down a few steps, are the children's and Miss Hildyard's three rooms. The ladies live below, and the gentlemen upstairs.

We lunched almost immediately, and at half-past four we walked out, and went up to the top of the wooded hill opposite our windows, where there is a cairn, and up which there is a pretty winding path. The view from here, looking down upon the house, is charming. To the left you look towards the beautiful hills surrounding *Loch-na-Gar*, and to the right, towards *Ballater*, to the glen (or valley) along which the *Dee* winds, with beautiful wooded hills, which reminded us very much of the *Thüringerwald*. It was so calm, and so solitary, it did one good as one gazed around; and the pure mountain air was most refreshing. All seemed to breathe freedom and peace, and to make one forget the world and its sad turmoils.

The scenery is wild, and yet not desolate; and everything looks much more prosperous and cultivated than at *Laggan*. Then the soil is delightfully dry. We walked beside the *Dee*, a beautiful, rapid stream, which is close behind the house. The view of the hills towards *Invercauld* is exceedingly fine.

When I came in at half-past six, Albert went out to try his luck with some stags which lay quite close in the woods, but he was unsuccessful. They come down of an evening quite near to the house.

First Ascent of Loch-na-Gar.

Saturday, September 16, 1848.

At half-past nine o'clock Albert and I set off in a postchaise, and drove to the bridge in the wood of *Balloch Buie*,* about five miles from *Balmoral*, where our ponies and people were. Here we mounted, and were attended by a keeper of Mr. Farquharson's as guide, Macdonald†—who, with his shooting-jacket, and in his kilt, looked a picture—Grant† on a pony, with our luncheon in two baskets, and Batterbury‡ on another pony. We went through that beautiful wood for about a mile, and then turned and began to ascend gradually, the view getting finer and finer; no road, but not bad ground—moss, heather, and stones. Albert saw some deer when we had been out about three-quarters of an hour, and ran off to stalk them, while I rested; but he arrived just a minute too late. He waited for me on the other side of a stony little burn, which I crossed on my pony, after our faithful Highlanders had moved some stones and made it easier. We then went on a little way, and I got off and walked a bit, and afterwards remounted; Macdonald leading my pony. The view of *Ben-na-Bhourd*, and indeed of all around, was very beautiful; but as we rose higher we saw mist over *Loch-na-Gar*. Albert left me to go after ptarmigan, and went on with Grant, while the others remained with me, taking the greatest care of me. Macdonald is a good honest man, and was indefatigable, and poor Batterbury was very anxious also.

I saw ptarmigan get up, and Albert fire—he then disappeared from my sight, and I rode on. It became cold and misty when we were on

---

† A Jäger of the Prince's, who came from Fort Augustus in the west: he was remarkably tall and handsome. The poor man died of consumption at Windsor, in May, 1860. His eldest son was Attaché to the British Legation in Japan. He died in 1866. The third son, Archie, is Jäger to the Prince of Wales, and was for a year with the beloved Prince.*

† Head-keeper. He had been nearly twenty years with Sir Robert Gordon, nine as keeper; he was born in Braemar, in the year 1810. He is an excellent man, most trustworthy, of singular shrewdness and discretion, and most devotedly attached to the Prince and myself. He has a fine intelligent countenance. The Prince was very fond of him. He has six sons,—the second, Alick, is wardrobe-man to our son Leopold: all are good, well-disposed lads, and getting on well in their different occupations. His mother, a fine, hale, old woman of eighty years, "stops" in a small cottage which the Prince built for her in our village. He, himself, lives in a pretty Lodge called Croft, a mile from Balmoral, which the Prince built for him.*

‡ A groom (now dead some years) who followed me in his ordinary dress, with thin boots and gaiters, and seemed anything but happy. He hardly ever attended me after this.*

Loch-na-Gar. In half an hour, or rather less, Albert rejoined me with two ptarmigan, having come up by a shorter way. Here it was quite soft, easy walking, and we looked down on two small lochs called *Na Nian*,* which were very striking, being so high up in the hills. Albert was tired, and remounted his pony; I had also been walking a little way. The ascent commenced, and with it a very thick fog, and when we had nearly reached the top of *Loch-na-Gar*, the mist drifted in thick clouds so as to hide everything not within one hundred yards of us. Near the peak (the fine point of the mountain which is seen so well from above Grant's house) we got off and walked, and climbed up some steep stones, to a place where we found a seat in a little nook,* and had some luncheon. It was just two o'clock, so we had taken four hours going up.

But, alas! nothing whatever to be seen; and it was cold, and wet, and cheerless. At about twenty minutes after two we set off on our way downwards, the wind blowing a hurricane, and the mist being like rain, and everything quite dark with it. Bowman (Mr. Farquharson's keeper) and Macdonald, who preceded us, looked like ghosts. We walked some way till I was quite breathless, and remounted my pony, well wrapped up in plaids; and we came down by the same path that Albert had come up, which is shorter, but steeper; the pony went delightfully; but the mist made me feel cheerless.

Albert kept ahead a little while for ptarmigan, but he gave it up again. When we had gone on about an hour and a quarter, or an hour and a half, the fog disappeared like magic, and all was sunshine below, about one thousand feet from the top I should say. Most provoking!—and yet one felt happy to see sunshine and daylight again.

The view, as one descends, overlooking *Invercauld* and the wood which is called *Balloch Buie*, is most lovely. We saw some deer in the wood below. We rode on till after we passed the burn, and had nearly got to the wood. We came another way down, by a much rougher path; and then, from the road in the wood, we walked up to the *Falls of the Garbhalt*, which are beautiful. The rocks are very grand, and the view from the little bridge, and also from a seat a little lower down, is extremely pretty. We found our carriages in the road, and drove home by six o'clock.

We met Captain Gordon, and then Lord John Russell and Sir James Clark. They had come to look after us, and when we got home we found the two ladies at the door waiting most anxiously for us.*

A "Drive" in the Balloch Buie.

September 18, 1848.

At a quarter-past ten o'clock we set off in a postchaise with Bertie,* and drove beyond the house of Mr. Farquharson's keeper in the *Balloch Buie*. We then mounted our ponies, Bertie riding Grant's pony on the deer-saddle, and being led by a gillie, Grant walking by his side. Macdonald and several gillies were with us, and we were preceded by Bowman and old Arthur Farquharson, a deer-stalker of Invercauld's.* They took us up a beautiful path winding through the trees and heather in the *Balloch Buie*; but when we had got about a mile or more they discovered deer. A "council of war"* was held in a whisper, and we turned back and went the whole way down again, and rode along to the keeper's lodge, where we turned up the glen immediately below *Craig Daign*, through a beautiful part of the wood, and went on along the track, till we came to the foot of the craig, where we all dismounted.

We scrambled up an almost perpendicular place to where there was a little *box*, made of hurdles and interwoven with branches of fir and heather, about five feet in height. There we seated ourselves with Bertie, Macdonald lying in the heather near us, watching and quite concealed; some had gone round to beat, and others again were at a little distance. We sat quite still, and sketched a little; I doing the landscape and some trees, Albert drawing Macdonald* as he lay there. This lasted for nearly an hour, when Albert fancied he heard a distant sound, and, in a few minutes, Macdonald whispered that he saw stags, and that Albert should wait and take a steady aim. We then heard them coming past. Albert did not look over the box, but through it, and fired through the branches, and then again over the box. The deer retreated; but Albert felt certain he had hit a stag. He ran up to the keepers, and at that moment they called from below that they "had got him," and Albert ran on to see. I waited for a bit; but soon scrambled on with Bertie and Macdonald's help; and Albert joined me directly, and we all went down and saw a magnificent stag, "a royal,"* which had dropped, soon after Albert had hit him, at one of the men's feet. The sport was successful, and every one was delighted,—Macdonald and the keepers in particular;— the former saying, "that it was her Majesty's coming out that had brought the good luck." I was supposed to have "a lucky foot," of which the Highlanders "think a great deal." We walked down to the place we last came up, got into the carriage, and were home by half-past two o'clock.*

The First Stay at Alt-na-Giuthasach.*

August 30, 1849.

After writing our letters, we set off on our ponies, with Miss Dawson,[+] Macdonald, Grant, Batterbury, and Hamis Coutts; Hamis is Gaelic for James, and is pronounced "Hamish." The road has been improved since last year, and though it is still very rough, there are no fords to pass, nor real difficulties any longer. We rode the whole way, and Albert only walked the last two miles. He took a Gaelic lesson during our ride, asking Macdonald, who speaks it with great purity, many words, and making him talk to Jemmie Coutts. Albert has already picked up many words: but it is a very difficult language, for it is pronounced in a totally different way from that in which it is written.

We arrived at our little "bothie" at two o'clock, and were amazed at the transformation. There are two huts, and to the one in which we live a wooden addition has been made. We have a charming little dining-room, sitting-room, bed-room, and dressing-room, all *en suite*; and there is a little room where Caroline Dawson (the Maid of Honour) sleeps, one for her maid, and a little pantry. In the other house, which is only a few yards distant, is the kitchen, where the people generally sit, a small room where the servants dine, and another, which is a sort of store-room, and a loft above in which the men sleep. Margaret French (my maid), Caroline's maid, Löhlein[†] (Albert's valet), a cook, Shackle[‡] (a footman), and Macdonald, are the only people with us in the house, old John Gordon and his wife excepted. Our rooms are delightfully papered, the ceilings as well as walls, and very nicely furnished. We lunched as soon as we arrived, and at three walked down (about twenty minutes' walk) to the loch called "Muich;" which some say means "darkness" or "sorrow."* Here we found a large boat, into which we all got, and Macdonald, Duncan, Grant, and Coutts rowed; old John Gordon and two others going in another boat with the net. They rowed up to the head of the

---

[+] Now Hon. Mrs. Parnell.
[†] This faithful and trusty valet nursed his dear master most devotedly through his sad illness in December, 1861, and is now always with me as my personal groom of the chambers or valet. I gave him a house near Windsor Castle, where he resides when the Court are there. He is a native of Coburg. His father has been for fifty years Förster at Fülbach, close to Coburg.*
[‡] Who was very active and efficient. He is now a Page.

loch, to where the *Muich* runs down out of the *Dhu Loch*, which is on the other side.

The scenery is beautiful here, so wild and grand,—real severe Highland scenery, with trees in the hollow. We had various scrambles in and out of the boat and along the shore, and saw three hawks, and caught seventy trout. I wish an artist could have been there to sketch the scene; it was so picturesque—the boat, the net, and the people in their kilts in the water, and on the shore. In going back, Albert rowed and Macdonald steered; and the lights were beautiful.

We came home at a quarter-past seven. At eight we dined. Löhlein, Macdonald, and Shackle waiting on us. After dinner we played with Caroline Dawson at whist with dummy, and afterwards walked round the little garden. The silence and solitude, only interrupted by the waving of the fir-trees, were very solemn and striking.

A Beat in the Abergeldie Woods.*

September 3, 1849.

At a quarter-past eleven we drove (the three gentlemen going in another carriage) to the road along which we went with Lord Portman the other day, and up to a small path, where I mounted my pony, Albert and the others walking. We came to *Geannachoil*,* and Albert was much pleased with the splendid view. The lights were most beautiful, but the heat was overpowering, and the sun burning.

We turned to the right when out on the moors, where I got off and walked; and we seated ourselves behind a large stone, no one but Macdonald with us, who loaded the guns, and gave notice when anything was to be seen, as he lay upon the ground. The gentlemen were below in the road; the wood was beat, but nothing came, so we walked on and came down a beautiful thickly-wooded glen; and after a good deal of scrambling to get there, and to get up one side of the glen, we sat down again. We then scrambled over to the opposite side, where we again concealed ourselves; in this beat Albert shot a roe, and I think would have shot more had they not been turned back by the sudden appearance of an old woman who, looking like a witch, came along through the wood with two immense crutches, and disturbed the whole thing. Albert killed the roe just as she was coming along, and the shot startled her very much; she was told to come down, which she did, and sat below in the glen, motionless, having covered her head with her handkerchief. When two of the beaters came down and were told to take up the roe, they first saw the old woman, and started, and stared with horror—which was very amusing to see. I rode a little way afterwards, and then we seated ourselves behind a bush, in the rear of the wood, close to the distillery;* but this beat brought nothing. Albert killed a young black cock before we came to the second beat. We were home at a quarter-past three o'clock.

Visit to the Dhu Loch, &c.

September 11, 1849.

The morning was very fine. I heard the children repeat some poetry in German, and then at ten o'clock we set off with Lady Douro[+] in our carriage, and drove on beyond Inch *Bobbard*, changing horses near *Birkhall*, and stopping for a moment at the *Linn of Muich*; here we found the ponies, which we mounted, forded the river, and were almost immediately at the hut.* We stopped there only for an instant, and remounted our ponies directly; Grant, Macdonald (who led my pony the whole time, and was extremely useful and attentive), Jemmie Coutts (leading Lady Douro's pony), Charlie Coutts, and John Brown* going with us: old John Gordon leading the way.* It was half-past twelve when we began ascending the hill immediately behind the house, and proceeded along over the hills, to a great height, whence the view was very fine, quite overhanging the loch, and commanding an extensive view of *Glen Muich* beyond on the opposite side. The road got worse and worse. It was particularly bad when we had to pass the *Burn of the Glassalt*, which falls into the loch, and was very full. There had been so much rain, that the burns and rivers were very full, and the ground quite soft. We rode over the *Strone Hill*, the wind blowing dreadfully hard when we came to the top. Albert walked almost from the first, and shot a hare and a grouse; he put up a good many of them. We walked to a little hollow immediately above the *Dhu Loch*, and at half-past three seated ourselves there, and had some very welcome luncheon. The loch is only a mile in length, and very wild; the hills, which are very rocky and precipitous, rising perpendicularly from it.

In about half an hour we began our journey homewards. We came straight down beside the *Muich*, which falls in the most beautiful way over the rocks and stones in the glen. We rode down, and only had to get off to cross the *Glassalt*, which was an awkward ford to scramble over. The road was rough, but certainly far less soft and disagreeable than the one we came by. I rode "Lochnagar" at first, but changed him for Colonel Gordon's pony, as I thought he took fright at the bogs; but Colonel Gordon's was broken-winded, and struggled very much in the soft ground, which was very disagreeable.

[+] Now Duchess of Wellington.

We were only an hour coming down to the boat. The evening was very fine, but it blew very hard on the lake and the men could not pull, and I got so alarmed that I begged to land, and Lady Douro was of my opinion that it was much better to get out. We accordingly landed, and rode home along a sort of sheep-path on the side of the lake, which took us three-quarters of an hour. It was very rough and very narrow, for the hill rises abruptly from the lake; we had seven hundred feet above us, and I suppose one hundred feet below. However, we arrived at the hut quite safely at twenty minutes to seven, thankful to have got through all our difficulties and adventures, which are always very pleasant to look back upon.

We dined a little before eight with Lady Douro, and played two rubbers of whist with her.

Old John Gordon amused Albert by saying, in speaking of the bad road we had gone, "It's something steep and something rough," and "this is the only best," meaning that it was *very* bad,—which was a characteristic reply.

Ascent of Ben-na-Bhourd.*

September 6, 1850.

At half-past ten o'clock we set off with Lady Douro and Ernest Leiningen,† and drove to *Invercauld*, about three-quarters of a mile beyond the house, where we found our people and ponies, together with Arthur Farquharson, Shewin, and others. We then walked a little way, after which we mounted our ponies and began the ascent towards *Ben-na-Bhourd;* Macdonald leading my pony, good little "Lochnagar," and James Coutts Lady Douro's.* There is an excellent path, almost a narrow road, made up to within the last two miles and a half, which are very steep and rocky. The scenery is beautiful. We first rode up a glen (where a stone of the house in which Finla, the first of the Farquharsons, was born, is still shown,) through which the *Glassalt* runs. Further on comes a very narrow, rocky, and precipitous glen, called the *Sluggan*, said to mean the "swallow," or "swallowing." Some little distance after this the country opens widely before you, with *Ben-na-Bhourd* rising towards the left; and then you enter the *Forest of Mar*, which the Duke of Leeds rents from Lord Fife. There is a very pretty little shooting-box, called *Sluggan Cottage*, which is half way from *Invercauld* to the top of *Ben-na-Bhourd*. Below this is the *Quoich*, which we forded. The last bit of the real road is a long steep ascent on the brow of a hill, the name of which means the "Tooth's craig." (Macdonald translated all the names for us.) The ascent, after the path ceases, is very stony; in fact, nothing but bare granite. Albert had walked a great deal, and we ladies got off after it became more uneven, and when we were no longer very far from the top.* We came upon a number of "cairngorms," which we all began picking up, and found some very pretty ones. At the top, which is perfectly flat, the ground is entirely composed of stones or wet swampy moss, and the granite seems to have stopped just a few feet below. We sat down at a cairn, and had our luncheon. The wind was extremely cold, but whenever we got out of it, the air was very hot. The view from the top was magnificent and most extensive: *Ben-na-Bhourd* is 3,940 feet high. We saw *Ben-y-Ghlo* very clearly, *Cairngorm*, and *Ben Muich Dhui* quite close but in another direction; the *Moray Firth*, and, through the glass, ships

---

† Our nephew.

even could be seen; and on the other side rose *Loch-na-Gar*, still the jewel of all the mountains here.

After luncheon we began our downward progress, and walked the whole of the steep part till we reached the path; we came down very quickly, my pony making great haste, though he had half a mind to kick. Albert found some beautiful little rock crystals in the *Sluggan*, and walked the remainder of the way; we ladies left our horses about a quarter of a mile before we met the carriage. The whole distance from *Invercauld* to the top of *Ben-na-Bhourd* is nine miles, so we must have been at least 18 miles riding and walking. It has been a delightful expedition. It was six o'clock when we reached the carriage, and we were home at a little past seven.

The Gathering.*

September 12, 1850.

We lunched early, and then went at half-past two o'clock, with the children and all our party, except Lady Douro, to the Gathering at the *Castle of Braemar*, as we did last year. The Duffs, Farquharsons, the Leeds's, and those staying with them, and Captain Forbes[+] and forty of his men who had come over from *Strath Don*, were there.[†] Some of our people were there also. There were the usual games of "putting the stone," "throwing the hammer" and "caber," and racing up the hill of *Craig Cheunnich*, which was accomplished in less than six minutes and a half; and we were all much pleased to see our gillie Duncan,[‡] who is an active, good-looking, young man, win. He was far before the others the whole way. It is a fearful exertion. Mr. Farquharson brought him up to me afterwards. Eighteen or nineteen started, and it looked very pretty to see them run off in their different coloured kilts, with their white shirts (the jackets or doublets they take off for all the games), and scramble up through the wood, emerging gradually at the edge of it, and climbing the hill.

After this we went into the castle, and saw some dancing; the prettiest was a reel by Mr. Farquharson's children and some other children, and the "Ghillie Callum" beautifully danced by John Athole Farquharson, the fourth son. The twelve children were all there, including the baby, who is two years old.

Mama, Charles, and Ernest joined us at *Braemar*. Mama enjoys it all very much; it is her first visit to *Scotland*. We left after the dancing.

[+] Now Sir Charles Forbes, of Castle Newe.

[†] A work shortly to be published, entitled *Highlanders of Scotland*, by Kenneth Macleay, Esq., R.S.A., contains excellent portraits of some of the men of these and other of the principal Highland clans, as well as of the Retainers of the Royal Household.*

[‡] One of our keepers since 1851: an excellent, intelligent man, much liked by the Prince. He, like many others, spit blood after running the race up that steep hill in this short space of time, and he has never been so strong since. The running up hill has in consequence been discontinued. He lives in a cottage at the back of Craig Gowan (commanding a beautiful view) called Robrech, which the Prince built for him.

Salmon Leistering.*

September 13, 1850.

We walked with Charles, the boys, and Vicky to the river side above the bridge,* where all our tenants were assembled with poles and spears, or rather "leisters," for catching salmon. They all went into the river, walking up it, and then back again, poking about under all the stones to bring fish up to where the men stood with the net. It had a very pretty effect; about one hundred men wading through the river, some in kilts with poles and spears, all very much excited. Not succeeding the first time, we went higher up, and moved to three or four different places, but did not get any salmon; one or two escaping. Albert stood on a stone, and Colonel Gordon and Lord James Murray waded about the whole time. Duncan, in spite of all his exertions yesterday, and having besides walked to and from the Gathering, was the whole time in the water. Not far from the laundry there was another trial, and here we had a great fright. In one place there was a very deep pool, into which two men very foolishly went, and one could not swim; we suddenly saw them sink, and in one moment they seemed drowning, though surrounded by people. There was a cry for help, and a general rush, including Albert, towards the spot, which frightened me so much, that I grasped Lord Carlisle's arm in great agony. However, Dr. Robertson[+] swam in and pulled the man out, and all was safely over; but it was a horrid moment.

A salmon was speared here by one of the men; after which we walked to the ford, or quarry, where we were very successful, seven salmon being caught, some in the net, and some speared. Though Albert stood in the water some time he caught nothing: but the scene at this beautiful spot was exciting and picturesque in the extreme. I wished for Landseer's pencil. The sun was intensely hot. We did not get back till after three o'clock, and then took luncheon. The Duchess of Gordon came to see us afterwards; and while she was still with us, Captain Forbes (who had asked permission to do so) marched through the grounds with his men, the pipers going in front. They stopped, and cheered three-times-three, throwing up their bonnets. They then marched off; and we listened with pleasure to the distant shouts and the sound of the pibroch.

[+] The gentleman who has had from the beginning the entire management of our property at Balmoral, &c. He is highly esteemed, and is a most amiable man, who has carried out all the Prince's and my wishes admirably.

We heard afterwards that our men had carried all Captain Forbes's men on their backs through the river. They saw the fishing going on, and came to the water's edge on the opposite side; and on being greeted by our people, said they would come over, on which ours went across in one moment and carried them over—Macdonald at their head carrying Captain Forbes on his back. This was very courteous, and worthy of chivalrous times.

Loch Muich.

September 16, 1850.

We reached the hut* at three o'clock. At half-past four we walked down to the loch, and got into the boat with our people: Duncan, J. Brown,⁺ P. Coutts,† and Leys rowing. They rowed mostly towards the opposite side, which is very fine indeed, and deeply furrowed by the torrents, which form glens and corries where birch and alder trees grow close to the water's edge. We landed on a sandy spot below a fine glen, through which flows the *Black Burn*. It was very dry here; but still very picturesque, with alder-trees and mountain-ash in full fruit overhanging it. We afterwards landed at our usual place at the head of the loch, which is magnificent; and rode back. A new road has been made, and an excellent one it is, winding along above the lake.

The moon rose, and was beautifully reflected on the lake, which, with its steep green hills, looked lovely. To add to the beauty, poetry, and wildness of the scene, Coutts played in the boat; the men, who row very quickly and well now, giving an occasional shout when he played a reel. It reminded me of Sir Walter Scott's lines in *The Lady of the Lake:*—

> "Ever, as on they bore, more loud
> And louder rung the pibroch proud.
> At first the sound, by distance tame,
> Mellow'd along the waters came,
> And, lingering long by cape and bay,
> Wail'd every harsher note away."*

We were home at a little past seven; and it was so still and pretty as we entered the wood, and saw the light flickering from our humble little abode.

⁺ The same who, in 1858, became my regular attendant out of doors everywhere in the Highlands; who commenced as gillie in 1849, and was selected by Albert and me to go with my carriage. In 1851 he entered our service permanently, and began in that year leading my pony, and advanced step by step by his good conduct and intelligence. His attention, care, and faithfulness cannot be exceeded; and the state of my health, which of late years has been sorely tried and weakened, renders such qualifications most valuable, and indeed, most needful in a constant attendant upon all occasions. He has since (in December, 1865), most deservedly, been promoted to be an upper servant, and my permanent personal attendant. He has all the independence and elevated feelings peculiar to the Highland race, and is singularly straightforward, simple-minded, kind-hearted, and disinterested; always ready to oblige; and of a discretion rarely to be met with. He is now in his fortieth year. His father was a small farmer, who lived at the Bush on the opposite side to Balmoral. He is the second of nine brothers,—three of whom have died—two are in Australia and New Zealand, two are living in the neighbourhood of Balmoral; and the youngest, Archie (Archiebald) is valet to our son Leopold, and is an excellent, trustworthy young man.*

† Now, since some years, piper to Farquharson of Invercauld.

Torch-Light Ball at Corriemulzie.

September 10, 1852.

We dined at a quarter-past six o'clock in morning gowns, (not ordinary ones, but such as are worn at a "breakfast,") and at seven started for *Corriemulzie*, for a *torch-light ball* in the open air. I wore a white bonnet, a grey watered silk, and (according to Highland fashion) my plaid scarf over my shoulder; and Albert his Highland dress which he wears every evening. We drove in the postchaise; the two ladies, Lord Derby and Colonel Gordon following in the other carriage.

It was a mild though threatening evening, but fortunately it kept fine. We arrived there at half-past eight, by which time, of course, it was quite dark. Mr. and Lady Agnes Duff[†] received us at the door, and then took us at once through the house to the open space where the ball was, which was hid from our view till the curtains were drawn asunder. It was really a beautiful and most unusual sight. All the company were assembled there. A space about one hundred feet in length and sixty feet in width was boarded, and entirely surrounded by Highlanders bearing torches, which were placed in sockets, and constantly replenished. There were seven pipers playing together, Mackay[†] leading—and they received us with the usual salute and three cheers, and "Nis! nis! nis!" (pronounced: "Neesh! neesh! neesh!" the Highland "Hip! hip! hip!") and again cheers; after which came a most animated reel. There were above sixty people, exclusive of the Highlanders, of whom there were also sixty; all the Highland gentlemen, and any who were at all Scotch, were in kilts, the ladies in evening dresses. The company and the Highlanders danced pretty nearly alternately. There were two or three sword dances. We were upon a *haut pas*, over which there was a canopy. The whole thing was admirably done, and very well worth seeing. Albert was delighted with it. I must not omit to mention a reel danced by eight Highlanders holding torches in their hands.

We left at half-past nine o'clock, and were home by a little past eleven. A long way certainly (14 miles I believe).

[†] Now Earl and Countess of Fife.
[†] My Piper from the year 1843, considered almost the first in Scotland, who was recommended by the Marquis of Breadalbane; he unfortunately went out of his mind in the year 1854, and died in 1855. A brother of his was Piper to the Duke of Sussex.

Account of the News of the Duke of Wellington's Death.*

Alt-na-Giuthasach,
Thursday, September 16, 1852.

We were startled this morning, at seven o'clock, by a letter from Colonel Phipps, enclosing a telegraphic despatch with the report, from the sixth edition of the *Sun*, of the Duke of Wellington's death the day before yesterday, which report, however, we did not at all believe. Would to God that we had been right; and that this day had not been cruelly saddened in the afternoon.

We breakfasted with Miss Seymour;[+] and, after writing and reading, we started at a quarter to eleven with her and our Highland party. The day was not cold, and would, in fact, have been very fine, if it had not been for a constant succession of very slight showers, or clouds coming down. We walked along the loch, the road up to which is excellent. It has been widened and would admit of a carriage. We arrived at the *Alt-na-Dearg*, a small burn and fall, which is very fine and rapid. Up this a winding path has been made, upon which we rode; though some parts are rather steep for riding. The burn falls over red granite; and in the ravine grow birch, mountain-ash, and alder. We got off and walked a good long way on the top of the very steep hills overhanging the loch, to the *Stron*, and the *Moss of Mon Elpie*, whence you overlook all the country belonging to Lord Panmure, *Mount Keen*, the *Ogilvie Hills*, &c. We stopped to rest a little while—though the walking is excellent, so hard and dry—on a point overlooking the *Shiel of the Glassalt*, and the head of the loch.* Here I suddenly missed my watch, which the dear old Duke had given me; and, not being certain whether I had put it on or not, I asked Mackenzie[†] to go back and inquire. We walked on until we reached the higher part of the *Glassalt*, which we stepped across. We had passed over the tops of these hills on that expedition to the *Dhu Loch* three years ago, when the ground was so soft, that ponies could scarcely get along, the roads were so very bad.

Then we began the descent of the *Glassalt*, along which another path has been admirably made. From here it is quite beautiful, so wild and grand.

[+] Now Hon. Lady Biddulph.
[†] One of our keepers and a very good man; he lives at Alt-na-Giuthasach.

The falls are equal to those of the *Bruar* at *Blair*, and are 150 feet in height; the whole height to the foot of the loch being 500 feet. It looked very picturesque to see the ponies and Highlanders winding along. We came down to the *Shiel of the Glassalt*, lately built, where there is a charming room for us, commanding a most lovely view. Here we took the cold luncheon, which we had brought with us; and after that we mounted our ponies, and rode to the *Dhu Loch* along a beautiful path which keeps well above the burn, that rushes along over flat great slabs of stone. The scenery is exquisite. We passed a small fall called the *Burn of the Spullan* ("spout"). In half or three quarters of an hour we were at the wild and picturesque *Dhu Loch*.

We got off our ponies, and I had just sat down to sketch, when Mackenzie returned, saying my watch was safe at home, and bringing letters: amongst them there was one from Lord Derby, which I tore open, and alas! it contained the confirmation of the fatal news: that *England's*, or rather *Britain's* pride, her glory, her hero, the greatest man she ever had produced, was no more! Sad day! Great and irreparable national loss!

Lord Derby enclosed a few lines from Lord Charles Wellesley, saying that his dear great father had died on Tuesday at three o'clock, after a few hours' illness and no suffering. God's will be done! The day must have come: the Duke was eighty-three. It is well for him that he has been taken when still in the possession of his great mind, and without a long illness,—but what a *loss!* One cannot think of this country without "the Duke,"—our immortal hero!

In him centered almost every earthly honour a subject could possess. His position was the highest a subject ever had,—above party,—looked up to by all,—revered by the whole nation,—the friend of the Sovereign;— and *how* simply he carried these honours! With what singleness of purpose, what straightforwardness, what courage, were all the motives of his actions guided. The Crown never possessed,—and I fear never *will*—so *devoted*, loyal, and faithful a subject, so staunch a supporter! To *us* (who alas! have lost, now, so many of our valued and experienced friends,) his loss is *irreparable*, for his readiness to aid and advise, if it could be of use to us, and to overcome any and every difficulty, was unequalled. To Albert he showed the greatest kindness and the utmost confidence. His experience and his knowledge of the past were so great too; he was a link which connected us with bygone times, with the last century. Not an eye will be dry in the whole country.

We hastened down on foot to the head of *Loch Muich*; and then rode home, in a heavy shower, to *Alt-na-Guithasach*. Our whole enjoyment was spoilt; a gloom overhung all of us.

We wrote to Lord Derby and Lord Charles Wellesley.

BUILDING THE CAIRN ON CRAIG GOWAN, &C.

Monday, October 11, 1852.

This day has been a very happy, lucky, and memorable one—our last! A fine morning.

Albert had to see Mr. Walpole, and therefore it was nearly eleven o'clock before we could go up to the top of *Craig Gowan*, to see the cairn built, which was to commemorate our taking possession of this dear place;* the old cairn having been pulled down. We set off with all the children, ladies, gentlemen, and a few of the servants, including Macdonald and Grant, who had not already gone up; and at the *Moss House*, which is half way, Mackay met us, and preceded us, playing, Duncan and Donald Stewart+ going before him, to the highest point of *Craig Gowan*; where were assembled all the servants and tenants, with their wives and children and old relations. All our little friends were there: Mary Symons and Lizzie Stewart, the four Grants, and several others.

I then placed the first stone, after which Albert laid one, then the children, according to their ages. All the ladies and gentlemen placed one; and then every one came forward at once, each person carrying a stone and placing it on the cairn. Mr. and Mrs. Anderson were there; Mackay played; and whisky was given to all. It took, I am sure, an hour building; and whilst it was going on, some merry reels were danced on a stone opposite. All the old people (even the gardener's wife from *Corbie Hall*, near *Abergeldie*,) danced; and many of the children, Mary Symons and Lizzie Stewart especially, danced so nicely; the latter with her hair all hanging down. Poor dear old "Monk," Sir Robert Gordon's faithful old dog, was sitting there amongst us all. At last, when the cairn, which is, I think, seven or eight feet high, was nearly completed, Albert climbed up to the top of it, and placed the last stone; after which three cheers were given. It was a gay, pretty, and touching sight; and I felt almost inclined to cry. The view was so beautiful over the dear hills; the day so fine; the whole so *gemüthlich*. May God bless this place, and allow us yet to see it and enjoy it many a long year!

+ One of the keepers, whom we found here in 1848. He is an excellent man, and was much liked by the Prince; he always led the dogs when the Prince went out stalking. He lives in the Western Lodge, close to Grant's house, which was built for him by the Prince.*

After luncheon, Albert decided to walk through the wood for the last time, to have a last chance, and allowed Vicky and me to go with him. At half-past three o'clock we started, got out at Grant's, and walked up part of *Carrop*, intending to go along the upper path, when a stag was heard to roar, and we all turned into the wood. We crept along, and got into the middle path. Albert soon left us to go lower, and we sat down to wait for him; presently we heard a shot—then complete silence—and, after another pause of some little time, three more shots. This was again succeeded by complete silence. We sent some one to look, who shortly after returned, saying the stag had been twice hit and they were after him. Macdonald next went, and in about five minutes we heard "Solomon" give tongue, and knew he had the stag at bay. We listened a little while, and then began moving down hoping to arrive in time; but the barking had ceased, and Albert had already killed the stag; and on the road he lay, a little way beyond *Invergelder*—the beauty that we had admired yesterday evening. He was a magnificent animal, and I sat down and scratched a little sketch of him on a bit of paper that Macdonald had in his pocket, which I put on a stone—while Albert and Vicky, with the others, built a little cairn to mark the spot. We heard, after I had finished my little scrawl, and the carriage had joined us, that another stag had been seen near the road; and we had not gone as far as the "Irons,"[+] before we saw

one below the road, looking so handsome. Albert jumped out and fired—the animal fell, but rose again, and went on a little way, and Albert

[+] These "Irons" are the levers of an old saw-mill which was pulled down, and they were left there to be sold—between thirty and forty years ago—and have remained there ever since, not being considered worth selling, on account of the immense trouble of transporting them.

followed. Very shortly after, however, we heard a cry, and ran down and found Grant and Donald Stewart pulling up a stag with a very pretty head. Albert had gone on, Grant went after him, and I and Vicky remained with Donald Stewart, the stag, and the dogs. I sat down to sketch, and poor Vicky, unfortunately, seated herself on a wasp's nest, and was much stung. Donald Stewart rescued her, for I could not, being myself too much alarmed. Albert joined us in twenty minutes, unaware of having killed the stag. What a delightful day! But sad that it should be the last day! Home by half-past six. We found our beautiful stag had arrived, and admired him much.*

Laying the Foundation Stone of Our New House.*

September 28, 1853.

A fine morning early, but when we walked out at half-past ten o'clock it began raining, and soon poured down without ceasing. Most fortunately it cleared up before two, and the sun shone brightly for the ceremony of laying the foundation stone of the new house. Mama and all her party arrived from *Abergeldie* a little before three. I annex the Programme of the Ceremony, which was strictly adhered to, and was really very interesting:—

Programme.

The stone being prepared and suspended over that upon which it is to rest, (in which will be a cavity for the bottle containing the parchment and the coins):

The workmen will be placed in a semicircle at a little distance from the stone, and the women and home servants in an inner semicircle.

Her Majesty the Queen, and His Royal Highness the Prince, accompanied by the Royal Children, Her Royal Highness the Duchess of Kent, and attended by Her Majesty's guests and suite, will proceed from the house.

Her Majesty, the Prince, and the Royal Family, will stand on the South side of the stone, the suite being behind and on each side of the Royal party.

The Rev. Mr. Anderson will then pray for a blessing on the work. Her Majesty will affix her signature to the parchment, recording the day upon which the foundation stone was laid. Her Majesty's signature will be followed by that of the Prince and the Royal Children, the Duchess of Kent, and any others that Her Majesty may command, and the parchment will be placed in the bottle.

One of each of the current coins of the present reign will also be placed in the bottle, and the bottle having been sealed up, will be placed in the cavity. The trowel will then be delivered to Her Majesty by Mr. Smith of Aberdeen, the architect, and the mortar having been spread, the stone will be lowered.

The level and square will then be applied, and their correctness having been ascertained, the mallet will be delivered to Her Majesty by Mr. Stuart (the clerk of the works), when Her Majesty will strike the stone and declare it to be laid. The cornucopia will be placed upon the stone, and the oil and wine poured out by Her Majesty.

The pipes will play, and Her Majesty, with the Royal Family, will retire.

As soon after as it can be got ready, the workmen will proceed to their dinner. After dinner, the following toasts will be given by Mr. Smith:—

"The Queen."
"The Prince and the Royal Family."
"Prosperity to the house, and happiness to the inmates of Balmoral."

The workmen will then leave the dinner-room, and amuse themselves upon the green with Highland games till seven o'clock, when a dance will take place in the ball-room.

We walked round to the spot, preceded by Mackay. Mr. Anderson[+] made a very appropriate prayer. The wind was very high; but else everything went off as well as could possibly be desired.

The workmen and people all gave a cheer when the whole was concluded. In about three-quarters of an hour's time we went in to see the people at their dinner; and after this walked over to *Craig Gowan* for Albert to get a chance for black game.

We dressed early, and went for twenty minutes before dinner to see the people dancing in the ballroom, which they did with the greatest spirit.

[+] The Minister of Crathie: he died November, 1866.

The Kirk.*

October 29, 1854.

We went to Kirk, as usual, at twelve o'clock. The service was performed by the Rev. Norman McLeod, of *Glasgow*, son of Dr. McLeod, and anything finer I never heard. The sermon, entirely extempore, was quite admirable; so simple, and yet so eloquent, and so beautifully argued and put. The text was from the account of the coming of Nicodemus to Christ by night; St. John, chapter 3. Mr. McLeod showed in the sermon how we *all* tried to please *self*, and live for *that*, and in so doing found no rest. Christ had come not only to die for us, but to show how we were to live. The second prayer was very touching; his allusions to us were so simple, saying, after his mention of us, "bless their children." It gave me a lump in my throat, as also when he prayed for "the dying, the wounded, the widow, and the orphans."* Every one came back delighted; and how satisfactory it is to come back from church with such feelings! The servants and the Highlanders—*all*—were equally delighted.

Arrival at the New Castle at Balmoral.

September 7, 1855.

At a quarter-past seven o'clock we arrived at dear *Balmoral*. Strange, very strange, it seemed to me to drive past, indeed *through*, the old house; the connecting part between it and the offices being broken through. The new house looks beautiful. The tower and the rooms in the connecting part are, however, only half finished, and the offices are still unbuilt: therefore the gentlemen (except the Minister[+]) live in the old house, and so do most of the servants; there is a long wooden passage which connects the new house with the offices. An old shoe was thrown after us into the house, for good luck, when we entered the hall. The house is charming; the rooms delightful; the furniture, papers, everything perfection.

[+] A Cabinet Minister is always in attendance upon the Queen at Balmoral.

Impressions of the New Castle.

September 8, 1855.

The view from the windows of our rooms, and from the library, drawing-room, &c. below them, of the valley of the *Dee*, with the mountains in the background,—which one never could see from the old house, is quite beautiful. We walked about, and alongside the river, and looked at all that has been done, and considered all that has to be done; and afterwards we went over to the poor dear old house, and to our rooms, which it was quite melancholy to see so deserted; and settled about things being brought over.

News of the Fall of Sevastopol.

September 10, 1855.

Mama, and her lady and gentleman, to dinner.

All were in constant expectation of more telegraphic despatches. At half-past ten o'clock two arrived—one for me, and one for Lord Granville. I began reading mine, which was from Lord Clarendon, with details from Marshal Pélissier of the further destruction of the Russian ships; and Lord Granville said, "I have still better news;" on which he read, "From General Simpson—*Sevastopol is in the hands of the Allies.*"* God be praised for it! Our delight was great; but we could hardly believe the good news, and from having so long, so anxiously expected it, one could not realize the actual fact.

Albert said they should go at once and light the bonfire which had been prepared when the false report of the fall of the town arrived last year, and had remained ever since, waiting to be lit. On the 5th of November, the day of the battle of *Inkermann*, the wind upset it, strange to say; and now again, most strangely, it only seemed to *wait* for our return to be lit.

The new house seems to be lucky, indeed; for, from the first moment of our arrival, we have had good news. In a few minutes, Albert and all the gentlemen, in every species of attire, sallied forth, followed by all the servants, and gradually by all the population of the village—keepers, gillies, workmen—up to the top of the cairn. We waited, and saw them light the bonfire; accompanied by general cheering. It blazed forth brilliantly, and we could see the numerous figures surrounding it—some dancing, all shouting;—Ross[†] playing his pipes, and Grant and Macdonald firing off guns continually; while poor old François d'Albertançon[‡] lighted a number of squibs below, the greater part of which would not go off. About three-quarters of an hour after, Albert came down, and said the scene had been wild and exciting beyond everything. The people had been drinking healths in whisky, and were in great ecstasy. The whole house seemed in a wonderful state of excitement. The boys were with

---

[†] My Piper since 1854; he had served seventeen years in the 42nd Highlanders—a very respectable, good man.

[‡] An old servant of Sir R. Gordon's, who had charge of the house, and was a native of Alsace; he died in 1858.

difficulty awakened, and when at last this was the case, they begged leave to go up to the top of the cairn.

We remained till a quarter to twelve; and, just as I was undressing, all the people came down under the windows, the pipes playing, the people singing, firing off guns, and cheering—first for me, then for Albert, the Emperor of the French, and the "downfall of *Sevastopol*."

The Betrothal of the Princess Royal.*

September 29, 1855.

Our dear Victoria was this day engaged to Prince Frederick William of Prussia, who had been on a visit to us since the 14th. He had already spoken to us, on the 20th, of his wishes; but we were uncertain, on account of her extreme youth, whether he should speak to her himself, or wait till he came back again. However, we felt it was better he should do so; and during our ride up *Craig-na-Ban* this afternoon, he picked a piece of white heather, (the emblem of "good luck,") which he gave to her; and this enabled him to make an allusion to his hopes and wishes, as they rode down *Glen Girnoch*, which led to this happy conclusion.

The Kirk.

October 14, 1855.

To Kirk at twelve o'clock. The Rev. J. Caird, one of the most celebrated preachers in *Scotland*, performed the service, and electrified all present by a most admirable and beautiful sermon, which lasted nearly an hour, but which kept one's attention riveted. The text was from the twelfth chapter of Romans, and the eleventh verse: "*Not slothful in business; fervent in spirit; serving the Lord.*" He explained, in the most beautiful and simple manner, what real religion is; how it ought to pervade every action of our lives; not a thing only for Sundays, or for our closet; not a thing to drive us from the world; not "a perpetual moping over 'good' books," but "being and doing good;" "letting everything be done in a Christian spirit." It was as fine as Mr. McLeod's sermon last year, and sent us home much edified.

Finding the Old Castle Gone.

August 30, 1856.

On arriving at *Balmoral* at seven o'clock in the evening, we found the tower finished as well as the offices, and the poor old house gone! The effect of the whole is very fine.

Gardens, &c. round the New Castle.

August 31, 1856.

We walked along the river and outside the house. The new offices and the yard are excellent; and the little garden on the west side, with the eagle fountain which the King of Prussia gave me, and which used to be in the greenhouse at *Windsor*, is extremely pretty; as are also the flower-beds under the walls of the side which faces the *Dee*. There are sculptured arms on the different shields, gilt, which has a very good effect; and a bas-relief under our windows—not gilt—representing St. Hubert, with St. Andrew on one side and St. George* on the other side: all done by Mr. Thomas.†*

---

† He died in March, 1862. The Prince had a high opinion of his taste.

Love for Balmoral.

October 13, 1856.

Every year my heart becomes more fixed in this dear Paradise, and so much more so now, that *all* has become my dearest Albert's *own* creation, own work, own building, own laying out, as at *Osborne*; and his great taste, and the impress of his dear hand, have been stamped everywhere. He was very busy to-day, settling and arranging many things for next year.

[Balmoral Castle from the North-West.]

Opening of the New Bridge over the Linn of Dee.

September 8, 1857.

At half-past one o'clock we started in "Highland state,"—Albert in a royal Stuart plaid, and I and the girls in skirts of the same,*—with the ladies (who had only returned at five in the morning from the ball at *Mar Lodge*) and gentlemen, for the *Linn of Dee*, to open the new bridge there. The valley looked beautiful. A triumphal arch was erected, at which Lord Fife and Mr. Brooke received us, and walked near the carriage, pipers playing—the road lined with Duff men. On the bridge Lady Fife received us, and we all drank in whisky "prosperity to the bridge." The view of the linn is very fine from it.

All the company and a band were outside a tent on the bank overlooking the bridge. Here we took some tea, talked with the company, and then drove back by *Mar Lodge*,—the Fifes preceding us to the end of the grounds. The same people were there as at the Gatherings,—the Campdens, Errolls, Airlies, old Lady Duff, and Mr. and Lady L. Brooke, and others. We were home at half-past five, not without having some rain by the way.

Visits to the Old Women.

Saturday, September 26, 1857.

Albert went out with Alfred for the day, and I walked out with the two girls and Lady Churchill, stopped at the shop and made some purchases for poor people and others; drove a little way, got out and walked up the hill to *Balnacroft*, Mrs. P. Farquharson's, and she walked round with us to some of the cottages to show me where the poor people lived, and to tell them who I was.* Before we went into any we met an old woman, who, Mrs. Farquharson said, was very poor, eighty-eight years old, and mother to the former distiller. I gave her a warm petticoat, and the tears rolled down her old cheeks, and she shook my hands, and prayed God to bless me: it was very touching.

I went into a small cabin of old Kitty Kear's, who is eighty-six years old—quite erect, and who welcomed us with a great air of dignity. She sat down and spun. I gave her, also, a warm petticoat; she said, "May the Lord ever attend ye and yours, here and hereafter; and may the Lord be a guide to ye, and keep ye from all harm." She was quite surprised at Vicky's height; great interest is taken in her. We went on to a cottage (formerly Jean Gordon's), to visit old widow Symons, who is "past four-score," with a nice rosy face, but was bent quite double; she was most friendly, shaking hands with us all, asking which was I, and repeating many kind blessings: "May the Lord attend ye with mirth and with joy; may He ever be with ye in this world, and when ye leave it." To Vicky, when told she was going to be married, she said, "May the Lord be a guide to ye in your future, and may every happiness attend ye." She was very talkative; and when I said I hoped to see her again, she expressed an expectation that "she should be called any day," and so did Kitty Kear.†

We went into three other cottages: to Mrs. Symons's (daughter-in-law to the old widow living next door), who had an "unwell boy;" then across a little burn to another old woman's; and afterwards peeped into Blair the fiddler's. We drove back, and got out again to visit old Mrs. Grant (Grant's mother), who is so tidy and clean, and to whom I gave a dress and handkerchief, and she said, "You're too kind to me, you're over kind to me, ye give me more every year, and I get older every year." After talking some time with her, she said, "I am happy to see ye looking so

---

† She died in Jan. 1865.

nice." She had tears in her eyes, and speaking of Vicky's going, said, "I'm very sorry, and I think she is sorry hersel';" and, having said she feared she would not see her (the Princess) again,* said: "I am very sorry I said that, but I meant no harm; I always say just what I think, not what is fut" (fit).* Dear old lady; she is such a pleasant person.

Really the affection of these good people, who are so hearty and so happy to see you, taking interest in everything, is very touching and gratifying.

Visit to the Prince's Encampment at Feithort.

Tuesday, October 6, 1857.

At twelve o'clock I drove off with the two girls to the "Irons," where we mounted our ponies, and rode up (Brown and Robertson attending on

foot) through the *Corrie Buie*, along the pretty new path through *Feithluie* to the foot of the very steep ascent to *Feithort*,* where we got off and walked up—and suddenly, when nearly at the top of the path, came upon Albert's little encampment, which was just at the edge of the winding path.

Albert was still absent, having gone out at six o'clock, but Löhlein and some of the gillies were there. The little house, with shelves for keeping a few boxes (no seat), and a little stove, was not at all uncomfortable; but the wind was dreadfully high, and blew in. We waited for about a quarter of an hour, and then Albert arrived; he had been out since six o'clock, shot three stags, but only got one bad one. The fine one, yesterday evening, had cost him much trouble. The night had been bitterly cold and windy; but he had slept. We lunched in the little "housie" at the open door. There was a second hut for the people. Luncheon over, we walked down and across the greater part of the *Balloch Buie*, mounting our ponies wherever it was wet. We saw deer as we came lower down, and all of a sudden a stag was seen quite close by the path; Albert shot him, and he fell at once. He had very fine horns, a royal on one side.

Then they beat up to the *Craig Daign*. Poor Albert was much tired, and had to walk all the time, as he had no pony; we rode part of the way. Then the lower part of the road was driven. As we were sitting by a tree close to Albert a stag came out, and Albert killed him at one shot. A fine day, though at times it has been very cold. We got home at half-past six.*

A Fall of Snow.

September 18, 1858.*

Alas! the last day! When we got up the weather seemed very hopeless. Everything was white with snow, which lay, at least, an inch on the ground, and it continued snowing heavily, as it had done since five this morning. I wished we might be snowed up, and unable to move. How happy I should have been could it have been so! It continued snowing till half-past ten or eleven, and then it began to clear up. The hills appeared quite white; the sun came out, and it became splendidly bright. Albert was going to have the woods driven—which are not properly called *Carrop Woods*, but *Garmaddie Woods*—but had first to ride round *Craig Gowan* with Dr Robertson to see *Robrech*, the place where Duncan's new house is to be built, which is above the village, opposite *Craig Luraghain*,* with a most splendid view; and at Grant's house I was to meet him.

At one o'clock I left with Alice and Lenchen[+] for Grant's, where we met Albert, who joined us in the carriage: the day was truly splendid. We got out at the river, and were going down to *Nelly's Bush*, when a stag was heard roaring very near; so we had to stop, and, with our plaids and cloaks to sit upon, really avoided getting very wet. We waited till Albert was near to the stag, saw it move, heard Albert fire twice, and the stag turn, stop, and then disappear. Albert fired again, but the stag had crossed the *Dee*; so we turned up on to the road, and went into the dear old *Corrie Buie*; Albert turning off to see if there were any deer near, while we waited for him. We then came to a place which is always wet, but which was particularly bad after the late rain and snow. There was no pony for me to get on; and as I wished not to get my feet wet by walking through the long grass, Albert proposed I should be carried over in a plaid; and Lenchen was first carried over; but it was held too low, and her feet dangled; so Albert suggested the plaid should be put round the men's shoulders, and that I should sit upon it; Brown and Duncan, the two strongest and handiest, were the two who undertook it, and I sat safely enough with an arm on each man's shoulder, and was carried successfully over. All the Highlanders are so amusing, and really pleasant and instructive to talk to—women as well as men—and the latter so

[+] Princess Helena.

gentlemanlike.+ Albert's shots were heard close by whilst we were at luncheon; and there was a general rush of all the people. Albert joined us soon after; he had had a great deal of trouble in stalking his stag, which he had been after several days, but had killed him at one shot. He was brought for us to see: a very light-coloured one, with fine straight horns, of extraordinary thickness. After this we walked on for a beat quite round *Carrop*; and the view was glorious! A little shower of snow had fallen, but was succeeded by brilliant sunshine. The hills covered with snow, the golden birch-trees on the lower brown hills, and the bright afternoon sky, were indescribably beautiful. The following lines† admirably pourtray what I then saw:—

> "The gorgeous bright October,
> Then when brackens are changed, and heather blooms are faded,
> And amid russet of heather and fern, green trees are bonnie;
> Alders are green, and oaks; the rowan scarlet and yellow;
> One great glory of broad gold pieces appears the aspen,
> And the jewels of gold that were hung in the hair of the birch-tree,
> Pendulous, here and there, her coronet, necklace, and earrings,
> Cover her now, o'er and o'er; she is weary and scatters them from her."*

Oh! how I gazed and gazed on God's glorious works with a sad heart, from its being for the last time, and tried to carry the scene away, well implanted and fixed in my mind, for this effect with the snow we shall not often see again. We saw it like this in 1852; but we have not seen it so since, though we have often had snow-storms and showers with a little snow lying on the highest hills.*

+ A similar view to that given in the text is admirably expressed by the Reverend Frederick W. Robertson in his *Lectures on Literary and Social Topics*, and his description of a Tyrolese is even more applicable to a Highlander.

"My companion was a Tyrolese chamois-hunter, a man who, in point of social position, might rank with an English labourer. I fear there would be a difficulty in England in making such a companionship pleasurable and easy to both parties; there would be a painful obsequiousness, or else an insolent familiarity on the one side, constraint on the other. In this case there was nothing of that sort. We walked together, and ate together. He had all the independence of a man, but he knew the courtesy which was due to a stranger; and when we parted for the night, he took his leave with a politeness and dignity which would have done no discredit to the most finished gentleman. The reason, as it seemed to me, was that his character had been moulded by the sublimities of the forms of the outward nature amidst which he lived. It was impossible to see the clouds wreathing themselves in that strange wild way of theirs round the mountain crests, till the hills seemed to become awful things, instinct with life—it was impossible to walk, as we did sometimes, an hour or two before sunrise, and see the morning's beams gilding with their pure light the grand old peaks on the opposite side of the valley, while we ourselves were still in deepest shade, and look on that man, his very exterior in harmony with all around him, and his calm eye resting on all that wondrous spectacle, without a feeling that these things had had their part in making him what he was, and that you were in a country in which men were bound to be polished, bound to be more refined, almost bound to be better men than elsewhere."*

† *The Bothie of Tober-na-Vuolich*. By Arthur Hugh Clough.

Ascent of Morven.

September 14, 1859.

I felt very low-spirited at my dearest Albert having to leave at one o'clock for *Aberdeen*, to preside at the meeting of the British Association.

I with Alice, the two ladies, Lord Charles Fitzroy, and Brown,* left shortly before for *Morven*. We took post-horses at the foot of *Gairn*, and drove by the right side of the glen, along a new good road, avoiding the ford, and by half-past two we were at the foot of *Morven*, not far from the shooting-lodge there. Here we mounted our ponies, and our caravan started with the gillies—Jemmie Coutts, an old acquaintance, now keeper at the lodge, leading the way. About half-way, at a burn-side, we stopped, seated ourselves on plaids on the fine springy turf, and took luncheon; then walked about, sketched, mounted our ponies, and rode up to the top, which was rather steep and soft,—"foggy," as Brown called it, which is the Highland expression for mossy,—my little pony, being so fat, panted dreadfully. *Morven* is 2,700 feet high, and the view from it more magnificent than can be described, so large and yet so near everything seemed, and such seas of mountains with blue lights, and the colour so wonderfully beautiful. We looked down upon the Duke of Richmond's property, and saw the mountain called the *Buck of Cabrach*, and still further on the *Slate Hills*; to the east, *Aberdeen* and the blue sea, and we could even see the ships with the naked eye: the table-land between *Tarland* and *Ballater*; and stretching out below, due south, *Mount Keen*. To the south-west, *Loch-na-Gar*; to the west, *Ben A'an* and *Ben-na-Bhourd*,—"the land of *Gairn*," as they call it,—and *Muich*; and *Deeside* in the foreground. It was enchanting! We walked down to where we had lunched, and rode to the bottom. Here we found a fire, also tea with cakes, &c., which had been very kindly prepared for us by a lady and gentleman, the daughter and son of Sir J. G. Ratcliff, living in the shooting-lodge. We drank the tea, and left in the carriage at half-past six o'clock, reaching *Balmoral* at half-past seven. So sad not to find my darling Husband at home.

The Prince's Return from Aberdeen.

September 15, 1859.

I heard by telegram last night that Albert's reception was admirable, and that all was going off as well as possible. Thank God. I ascended *Loch-na-Gar* with Alice, Helena, Bertie, Lady Churchill, Colonel Bruce, and our usual attendants, and returned after six o'clock. At ten minutes past seven arrived my beloved Albert. All had gone off most admirably; he had seen many learned people; all were delighted with his speech; the reception most gratifying.* *Banchory House* (Mr. Thomson's) where he lodged (four miles from *Aberdeen*) was, he said, very comfortable.

Fête to the Members of the British Association.*

September 22, 1859.

The morning dawned brightly. Suddenly a very high wind arose which alarmed us, but yet it looked bright, and we hoped the wind would keep off the rain; but after breakfast, while watching the preparations, showers began, and from half-past eleven a fearful down-pour, with that white curtain-like appearance which is so alarming; and this lasted till half-past twelve. I was in despair; but at length it began to clear, just as the neighbours with their families, and some of the farmers opposite (the Herrons, Duncans, Brown's father and brothers) arrived, and then came the huge omnibuses and carriages laden with "philosophers."* At two o'clock we were all ready. Albert and the boys were in their kilts, and I and the girls in royal Stuart skirts and shawls over black velvet bodies.*

It was a beautiful sight in spite of the frequent slight showers which at first tormented us, and the very high cold wind. There were gleams of sunshine, which, with the Highlanders in their brilliant and picturesque dresses, the wild notes of the pipes, the band, and the beautiful background of mountains, rendered the scene wild and striking in the extreme. The Farquharson's men headed by Colonel Farquharson, the Duff's by Lord Fife, and the Forbes's men by Sir Charles Forbes, had all marched on the ground before we came out, and were drawn up just opposite to us,* and the spectators (the people of the country) behind them. We stood on the terrace, the company near us, and the "savants," also, on either side of us, and along the slopes, on the grounds. The games began about three o'clock:

1. "Throwing the Hammer."
2. "Tossing the Caber."
3. "Putting the Stone."

We gave prizes to the three best in each of the games. We walked along the terrace to the large marquee, talking to the people, to where the men were "putting the stone." After this returned to the upper terrace, to see the race, a pretty wild sight; but the men looked very cold, with nothing but their shirts and kilts on; they ran beautifully.* They wrapped plaids round themselves, and then came to receive the prizes from me. Last of all came the dancing—reels and "Ghillie Callum." The latter the judges could not make up their minds about; it was danced over and over again;

and at last they left out the best dancer of all! They said he danced "too well!" The dancing over, we left amid the loud cheers of the people. It was then about half-past five. We watched from the window the Highlanders marching away, the different people walking off, and four weighty omnibuses filling with the scientific men. We saw, and talked to, Professor Owen, Sir David Brewster, Sir John Bowring, Mr. J. Roscoe, and Sir John Ross.[+]

When almost all were gone, we took a short walk to warm ourselves. Much pleased at everything having gone off well. The Duke of Richmond, Sir R. Murchison, General Sabine, Mr. Thomson of *Banchory House*, and Professor Phillipps, Secretary of the Association, all of whom slept here, were additions to the dinner-party. I sat between our cousin Philip (Count of Flanders) and the Duke of Richmond. All the gentlemen spoke in very high terms of my beloved Albert's admirable speech, the good it had done, and the general satisfaction it had caused.

We could see the fire of the Forbes's encampment on the opposite side.

[+] During the Fête, we heard from Sir R. Murchison and others that news had been received this morning of the finding of poor Sir John Franklin's remains—or, rather, of the things belonging to him and his party.

Expedition to Inchrory.

September 30, 1859.

At twenty minutes past eleven we started with Helena and Louise in the sociable, Grant on the box, for *Loch Bulig*, passing the farms of *Blairglass* and of *Dall Dounie*, and the shooting-lodge of *Corndavon*, ten miles distant. Here we found our ponies (mine being "Victoria"), and rode along the edge of the lake, up a beautiful glen, by a path winding through the valley, which appeared frequently closed. We then rode along a small river or burn, of which no one knew the name; none of our party having ever been there before. The hills were sprinkled with birch-trees, and there was grass below in the valley; we saw deer. As we approached *Inchrory* (a shooting-lodge of Lord H. Bentinck's) the scenery became finer and finer, reminding us of *Glen Tilt*, and was most beautiful at *Inchrory*, with the fine broad water of the *Avon* flowing down from the mountains.

We inquired of the people at *Inchrory* whether there was any way of getting round over the hills by *Gairn Shiel*, and they said there was; but that the distance was about 11 miles. Neither Grant nor Brown had been that way. However we accepted it at once, and I was delighted to go on *à l'improviste*,* travelling about in these enchanting hills in this solitude, with only our good Highlanders with us, who never make difficulties, but are cheerful, and happy, and merry, and ready to walk, and run, and do anything. So on we went, turning up above *Inchrory* by a winding road between hillocks and commanding a glorious view towards *Laganaul*. Here, on a little grassy knoll, we lunched in a splendid position.

After our luncheon, and walking a little way, we remounted, and proceeded by the so-called "Brown Cow" (on the other side of which we had driven,) over a moor, meeting a shepherd, out of whom Grant could get little information. Soon we came to corn-fields in the valley; passed *Favanché* and *Inchmore*, and got on to a good road, on which Brown and Grant "travelled" at a *wonderful* pace, upwards of five miles an hour without stopping; and the former with that vigorous, light, elastic tread which is quite astonishing. We passed *Dal-na-Damph Shiel* (a shooting-lodge of Sir Charles Forbes); and went along the old "Military Road,"* leaving *Cockbridge*, a small straggling "toun," which is on the road to *Inverness*, to our left, and the old *Castle of Corgarf* to our right. We looked over into *Donside*. The road was soon left for a mountain one in the hills, above one of the tributary streams of the *Don*, and was wild and desolate; we passed *Dal Choupar* and *Dal Vown*, and, as we ascended we saw *Tornahoish*, at a distance to the left. After going along this hill-track, over some poor and tottering bridges, we joined the road by which we had driven to *Tornahoish*. It was fast getting dark, but was very fine. I and the girls got off and walked sharply some little distance. Albert had walked further on, Grant riding his pony meantime. P. Robertson and Kennedy, besides those I have named, carried the basket alternately.

We remounted our ponies, and Brown led mine on at an amazing pace up the *Glaschoil Hill*, and we finally reached *Gairn Shiel* after seven, quite in the dark. There, at the small public-house, we found the carriage, and drove off as soon as we could; the ponies were to be given half a feed, and then to come on. We had to drive home very slowly, as the road is not good, and very steep in parts.

A mild night. Home by ten minutes past eight, enchanted with our day. How I wish we could travel about in this way, and see *all* the wild spots in the *Highlands!* We had gone 35 miles, having ridden 19 and a half! The little girls were in great glee the whole time.

Ascent of Ben Muich Dhui.*

Friday, October 7, 1859.

Breakfast at half-past eight. At ten minutes to nine we started, in the sociable, with Bertie and Alice and our usual attendants. Drove along the opposite side of the river. The day very mild and promising to be fine, though a little heavy over the hills, which we anxiously watched. At *Castleton* we took four post-horses,* and drove to the *Shiel of the Derry*, that beautiful spot where we were last year—which Albert had never seen—and arrived there just before eleven. Our ponies were there with Kennedy, Robertson, and Jemmie Smith. One pony carried the luncheon-baskets. After all the cloaks, &c. had been placed on the ponies, or carried by the men, we mounted and began our "journey." I was on "Victoria," Alice on "Dobbins." George McHardy, an elderly man who knew the country (and acts as a guide, carrying luggage for people across the hills "on beasts" which he keeps for that purpose), led the way. We rode (my pony being led by Brown most of the time both going up and down) at least four miles up *Glen Derry*, which is very fine, with the remnants of a splendid forest, *Cairn Derry* being to the right, and the *Derry Water* running below. The track was very bad and stony, and broken up by cattle coming down for the "Tryst."* At the end of the glen we crossed a ford, passed some softish ground, and turned up to the left by a very rough, steep, but yet gradual ascent to *Corrie Etchan*, which is in a very wild rugged spot, with magnificent precipices, a high mountain to the right called *Ben Main*, while to the left was *Cairngorm of Derry*. When we reached the top of this very steep ascent (we had been rising, though almost imperceptibly, from the *Derry Shiel*), we came upon a loch of the same name, which reminded us of *Loch-na-Gar* and of *Loch-na-Nian*. You look from here on to other wild hills and corries—on *Ben A'an*, &c. We ascended very gradually, but became so enveloped in mist that we could see nothing—hardly those just before us! Albert had walked a good deal; and it was very cold. The mist got worse; and as we rode along the stony, but almost flat ridge of *Ben Muich Dhui*, we hardly knew whether we were on level ground or the top of the mountain. However, I and Alice rode to the very top, which we reached a few minutes past two; and here, at a cairn of stones, we lunched, in a piercing cold wind.

Just as we sat down, a gust of wind came and dispersed the mist, which had a most wonderful effect, like a dissolving view—and exhibited the grandest, wildest scenery imaginable! We sat on a ridge of the cairn to take our luncheon,—our good people being grouped with the ponies near us. Luncheon over, Albert ran off with Alice to the ridge to look at the splendid view, and sent for me to follow. I did so; but not without Grant's help, for there were quantities of large loose stones heaped up together to walk upon. The wind was fearfully high, but the view was well worth seeing. I cannot describe all, but we saw where the Dee rises between the mountains called the *Well of Dee*—*Ben-y-Ghlo*—and the adjacent mountains, *Ben Vrackie*—then *Ben-na-Bhourd*—*Ben A'an*, &c.—and such magnificent wild rocks, precipices, and corries. It had a sublime and solemn effect; so wild, so solitary—no one but ourselves and our little party there.

Albert went on further with the children, but I returned with Grant to my seat on the cairn, as I could not scramble about well. Soon after, we all began walking and looking for "cairngorms," and found some small ones. The mist had entirely cleared away below, so that we saw all the beautiful views. *Ben Muich Dhui* is 4,297 feet high, one of the highest mountains in *Scotland*. I and Alice rode part of the way, walking wherever it was very steep. Albert and Bertie walked the whole time. I had a little whisky and water, as the people declared pure water would be too chilling. We then rode on without getting off again, Albert talking so gaily with Grant. Upon which Brown observed to me in simple Highland phrase, "It's very pleasant to walk with a person who is always 'content.'" Yesterday, in speaking of dearest Albert's sport, when I observed he never was cross after bad luck, Brown said, "Every one on the estate says there never was so kind a master; I am sure our only wish is to give satisfaction." I said, they certainly did.[†]

By a quarter-past six o'clock we got down to the *Shiel of Derry*, where we found some tea, which we took in the "shiel,"[†] and started again by moonlight at about half-past six. We reached *Castleton* at half-past seven—and after this it became cloudy. At a quarter-past eight precisely we were at *Balmoral*, much delighted and not at all tired; everything had been so well arranged, and so quietly, without any fuss. *Never* shall I forget this day, or the impression this very grand scene made upon me; truly sublime and impressive; such solitude!

[†] We were always in the habit of conversing with the Highlanders—with whom one comes so much in contact in the Highlands. The Prince highly appreciated the good breeding, simplicity, and intelligence, which make it so pleasant, and even instructive to talk to them.*
[†] "Shiel" means a small shooting-lodge.*

First Great Expedition:—To Glen Fishie and Grantown.

Hotel Grantown,
Tuesday, September 4, 1860.

Arrived this evening after a most interesting tour; I will recount the events of the day. Breakfasted at *Balmoral* in our own room at half-past seven o'clock, and started at eight or a little past, with Lady Churchill and General Grey, in the sociable (Grant and Brown on the box as usual) for *Castleton*, where we changed horses. We went on five miles beyond the *Linn of Dee*, to the *Shepherd's Shiel of Geldie*, or, properly speaking, *Giuly*, where we found our ponies and a guide, Charlie Stewart. We mounted at once, and rode up along the *Geldie*, which we had to ford frequently to avoid the bogs, and rode on for two hours up *Glen Geldie*, over a moor which was so soft and boggy in places, that we had to get off several times. The hills were wild, but not very high, bare of trees, and even of heather to a great extent, and not picturesque till we approached the *Fishie*, and turned to the right up to the glen which we could see in the distance. The *Fishie* and *Geldie** rise almost on a level, with very little distance between them. The *Fishie* is a fine rapid stream, full of stones. As you approach the glen, which is very narrow, the scenery becomes very fine—particularly after fording the *Etchart*, a very deep ford. Grant, on his pony, led me through: our men on foot took off their shoes and stockings to get across. From this point the narrow path winds along the base of the hills of *Craig-na-Go'ar*—the rocks of the "Goat Craig;"—*Craig-na-Caillach*; and *Stron-na-Barin*—"the nose of the queen." The rapid river is overhung by rocks, with trees, birch and fir; the hills, as you advance, rise very steeply on both sides, with rich rocks and corries, and occasional streamlets falling from very high—while the path winds along, rising gradually higher and higher. It is quite magnificent!

We stopped when we came to a level spot amongst the trees. The native firs are particularly fine; and the whole is grand in the extreme. We lunched here—a charming spot—at two o'clock; and then pursued our journey. We walked on a little way to where the valley and glen widen out, and where there is what they call here a green "hard." We got on our ponies again and crossed the *Fishie* (a stream we forded many times in the course of the day) to a place where the finest fir-trees are, amidst some of the most beautiful scenery possible.

Then we came upon a most lovely spot—the scene of all Landseer's glory—and where there is a little encampment of wooden and turf huts, built by the late Duchess of Bedford; now no longer belonging to the family, and, alas! all falling into decay*—among splendid fir-trees, the mountains rising abruptly from the sides of the valley. We were quite enchanted with the beauty of the view. This place is about seven miles from the mouth of the *Fishie*. Emerging from the wood we came upon a good road, with low hills, beautifully heather-coloured, to the left; those to the right, high and wooded, with noble corries and waterfalls.

We met Lord and Lady Alexander Russell at a small farm-house, just as we rode out of the wood, and had some talk with them. They feel deeply the ruin of the place where they formerly lived, as it no longer belongs to them. We rode on for a good long distance, 12 miles, till we came to the ferry of the *Spey*. Deer were being driven in the woods, and we heard several shots. We saw fine ranges of hills on the *Spey-side*, or *Strathspey*, and opening to our left, those near *Loch Laggan*. We came to a wood of larch; from that, upon cultivated land, with *Kinrara* towards our right, where the monument to the late Duke of Gordon* is conspicuously seen on a hill, which was perfectly crimson with heather.

Before entering the larch wood. Lord Alexander Russell caught us up again in a little pony carriage, having to go the same way, and he was so good as to explain everything to us. He showed us "The Duke of Argyll's Stone"—a cairn on the top of a hill to our right, celebrated, as seems most probable, from the Marquis of Argyll having halted there with his army.* We came to another larch wood, when I and Lady Churchill got off our ponies, as we were very stiff from riding so long; and at the end of this wood we came upon *Loch Inch*,* which is lovely, and of which

I should have liked exceedingly to have taken a sketch, but we were pressed for time and hurried. The light was lovely; and some cattle were crossing a narrow strip of grass across the end of the loch nearest to us, which really made a charming picture. It is not a wild lake, quite the contrary; no high rocks, but woods and blue hills as a background. About a mile from this was the ferry. There we parted from our ponies, only Grant and Brown coming on with us. Walker, the police inspector, met us, but did not keep with us. He had been sent to order everything in a quiet way, without letting people suspect who we were: in this he entirely succeeded. The ferry was a very rude affair; it was like a boat or coble, but we could only stand on it, and it was moved at one end by two long oars, plied by the ferryman and Brown, and at the other end by a long sort of beam, which Grant took in hand.* A few seconds brought us over to the road, where there were two shabby vehicles, one a kind of barouche, into which Albert and I got, Lady Churchill and General Grey into the other—a break; each with a pair of small and rather miserable horses, driven by a man from the box. Grant was on our carriage, and Brown on the other. We had gone so far 40 miles, at least 20 on horseback. We had decided to call ourselves *Lord and Lady Churchill and party*, Lady Churchill passing as *Miss Spencer*, and General Grey as *Dr. Grey!* Brown once forgot this, and called me "Your Majesty" as I was getting into the carriage; and Grant on the box once called Albert "Your Royal Highness;" which set us off laughing, but no one observed it.

We had a long three hours' drive; it was six o'clock when we got into the carriage. We were soon out of the wood, and came upon the *Badenoch* road—passing close by *Kinrara*, but unfortunately not through it, which we ought to have done. It was very beautiful—fine wooded hills—the high *Cairngorm* range, and *Ben Muich Dhui*, unfortunately much obscured by the mist on the top—and the broad *Spey* flowing in the valley, with cultivated fields and fine trees below. Most striking, however, on our whole long journey was the utter, and to me very refreshing, solitude. Hardly a habitation! and hardly meeting a soul! It gradually grew dark. We stopped at a small half-way house for the horses to take some water; and the few people about stared vacantly at the two simple vehicles.

The mountains gradually disappeared,—the evening was mild, with a few drops of rain. On and on we went, till at length we saw lights, and drove through a long and straggling "toun," and turned down a small court to the door of the inn. Here we got out quickly—Lady Churchill and General Grey not waiting for us. We went up a small staircase, and were shown to our bed-room at the top of it—very small, but clean—with a large four-post bed which nearly filled the whole room. Opposite was the drawing and dining-room in one—very tidy and well-sized. Then came the room where Albert dressed, which was very small. The two maids (Jane Shackle[+] was with me) had driven over by another road in the waggonette, Stewart driving them. Made ourselves "clean and tidy," and then sat down to our dinner. Grant and Brown were to have waited on us, but were "bashful" and did not. A ringletted woman did everything; and, when dinner was over, removed the cloth and placed the bottle of wine (our own which we had brought) on the table with the glasses, which was the old English fashion. The dinner was very fair, and all very clean:—soup, "hodge-podge," mutton-broth with vegetables, which I did not much relish, fowl with white sauce, good roast lamb, very good potatoes, besides one or two other dishes, which I did not taste, ending with a good tart of cranberries.* After dinner, I tried to write part of this account (but the talking round me confused me), while Albert played at "patience." Then went away, to begin undressing, and it was about half-past eleven, when we got to bed.*

Wednesday, September 5.

A misty, rainy morning. Had not slept very soundly. We got up rather early, and sat working and reading in the drawing-room till the breakfast was ready, for which we had to wait some little time. Good tea and bread and butter, and some excellent porridge. Jane Shackle (who was very useful and attentive) said that they had all supped together, namely, the two maids, and Grant, Brown, Stewart, and Walker (who was still there), and were very merry in the "commercial room." The people were very amusing about us. The woman came in while they were at their dinner, and said to Grant, "Dr. Grey wants you," which nearly upset the gravity of all the others: then they told Jane, "Your lady gives no trouble;" and Grant in the morning called up to Jane, "Does his lordship want me?" One could look on the street, which is a very long wide one, with detached houses, from our window. It was perfectly quiet, no one stirring, except here and there a man driving a cart, or a boy going along on his errand. General Grey bought himself a watch in a shop for 2*l.*!

At length, at about ten minutes to ten o'clock, we started in the same carriages and the same way as yesterday, and drove up to *Castle Grant*,

---

[+] One of my wardrobe-maids, and daughter to the Page mentioned earlier.

Lord Seafield's place,—a fine (not Highland-looking) park, with a very plain-looking house, like a factory, about two miles from the town. It was drizzling almost the whole time. We did not get out, but drove back, having to pass through *Grantown* again; where evidently "the murder was out," for all the people were in the street, and the landlady waved her pocket-handkerchief, and the ringletted maid (who had curl-papers in the morning) waved a flag from the window. Our coachman evidently did not observe or guess anything. As we drove out of the town, turning to our right through a wood, we met many people coming into the town, which the coachman said was for a funeral. We passed over the *Spey*, by the *Bridge of Spey*. It continued provokingly rainy, the mist hanging very low on the hills, which, however, did not seem to be very high, but were pink with heather. We stopped to have the cover of leather put over our carriage, which is the fashion of all the flys here. It keeps out the rain, however, very well.

The first striking feature in this country is the *Pass of Dal Dhu*, above which the road winds,—a steep corrie, with green hills. We stopped at a small inn, with only one other house near it; and here the poor wretchedly-jaded horses got a little water, and waited for about ten minutes. Further on we came to a very steep hill, also to a sort of pass, called *Glen Bruin*, with green hills, evidently of slate formation. Here we got out, and walked down the hill, and over the *Bridge of Bruin*, and partly up another hill, the road winding amazingly after this—up and down hill. We then came in sight of the *Avon*, winding below the hills; and again got out at a little wood, before the *Bridge of Avon*; the river is fine and clear here. We re-entered our carriages (Lady Churchill and I for this short time together), and drove about a mile further up a hill to *Tomintoul*; our poor horses being hardly able to drag themselves any longer, the man whipping them and whistling to them to go on, which they could not, and I thought every instant that they would stop in the village. We took four hours to drive these 14 miles; for it was two o'clock when we were outside the town, and got out to mount our ponies. *Tomintoul* is the most tumble-down, poor-looking place I ever saw—a long street with three inns, miserable dirty-looking houses and people,* and a sad look of wretchedness about it. Grant told me that it was the dirtiest, poorest village in the whole of the *Highlands*.

We mounted our ponies a short way out of the town, but only rode for a few minutes as it was past two o'clock. We came upon a beautiful view, looking down upon the *Avon* and up a fine glen. There we rested and took luncheon. While Brown was unpacking and arranging our things, I spoke to him and to Grant, who was helping, about not having waited on us, as they ought to have done, at dinner last night and at breakfast, as we had wished; and Brown answered, he was afraid he should not do it rightly; I replied we did not wish to have a stranger in the room, and they must do so another time.

Luncheon (provisions for which we had taken with us from home yesterday) finished, we started again, walked a little way, till we were overtaken by the men and ponies, and then rode along *Avonside*, the road winding at the bottom of the glen, which is in part tolerably wide; but narrows as it turns, and winds round towards *Inchrory*, where it is called *Glen Avon*. The hills, sloping down to the river side, are beautifully green. It was very muggy—quite oppressive, and the greater part of the road deep and sloppy, till we came upon the granite formation again. In order to get on, as it was late, and we had eight miles to ride, our men,— at least Brown and two of the others,—walked before us at a fearful pace, so that we had to trot to keep up at all. Grant rode frequently on the deer pony; the others seemed, however, a good deal tired with the two long days' journey, and were glad to get on Albert's or the General's pony to give themselves a lift; but their willingness, readiness, cheerfulness, indefatigableness, are very admirable, and make them most delightful servants. As for Grant and Brown they are perfect—discreet, careful, intelligent, attentive, ever ready to do what is wanted; and the latter, particularly, is handy and willing to do everything and anything, and to overcome every difficulty, which makes him one of my best servants anywhere.

We passed by *Inchrory*—seeing, as we approached, two eagles towering splendidly above, and alighting on the top of the hills. From *Inchrory* we rode to *Loch Bulig*, which was beautifully lit up by the setting sun. From *Tomantoul* we escaped all real rain, having only a slight sprinkling every now and then. At *Loch Bulig* we found our carriage and four ponies, and drove back just as we left yesterday morning, reaching *Balmoral* safely at half-past seven.

What a delightful, successful expedition! Dear Lady Churchill was, as usual, thoroughly amiable, cheerful, and ready to do everything. Both she and the General seemed entirely to enjoy it, and enter into it, and so I am sure did our people. To my dear Albert do we owe it, for he always thought it would be delightful, having gone on many similar expeditions in former days himself. He enjoyed it very much. We heard since that the secret came out through a man recognizing Albert in the street yesterday morning; then the crown on the dog-cart made them think that it was some one from *Balmoral*, though they never suspected that it could be ourselves! "The lady must be terrible rich," the woman observed, as I had so many gold rings on my fingers!—I told Lady Churchill she had on many more than* I had. When they heard who it was, they were ready to drop with astonishment and fright. I fear I have but poorly recounted this very amusing and never to be forgotten expedition, which will always be remembered with delight.

I must pay a tribute to our ponies. Dear "Fyvie" is perfection, and Albert's equally excellent.

Second Great Expedition:—To Invermark and Fettercairn.

Friday, September 20, 1861.

Looked anxiously at the weather at seven o'clock—there had been a little rain, there was still mist on the hills, and it looked doubtful. However, Albert said it would be best to keep to the original arrangements, and so we got up early, and by eight the sun shone, and the mist began to lift everywhere. We breakfasted at half-past eight, and at half-past nine we started in two sociables—Alice and Louis[+] with us in the first, and Grant on the box; Lady Churchill and General Grey in the second, and Brown on the box. We drove to the *Bridge of Muich*, where we found our six ponies, and five gillies, (J. Smith, J. Morgan, Kennedy, C. Stewart, and S. Campbell.) We rode up the peat-road over the hill of *Polach* and down it again for about four miles, and then came to a very soft bit; but still with careful management we avoided getting into any of the bogs, and I remained on my pony all the time. Albert and Louis had to get off and walk for about two hundred yards. The hills of *Loch-na-Gar* were very hazy, but *Mount Keen* was in great beauty before us, and as we came down to the *Glen of Corrie Vruach*, and looked down *Glen Tanar*, the scenery was grand and wild. *Mount Keen* is a curious conical-shaped hill, with a deep corrie in it. It is nearly 3,200 feet high, and we had a very steep rough ascent over the shoulder, after crossing the *Tanar Water*. It was six and a half miles from the *Bridge of Muich* to *Corrie Vruach*.

When we were on the level ground again, where it was hard and dry, we all got off and walked on over the shoulder of the hill. We had not gone far when we descried Lord Dalhousie (whom General Grey had in confidence informed of our coming) on a pony. He welcomed us on the border of his "March," got off his pony and walked with us. After walking some little time Alice and I remounted our ponies, (Albert riding some part of the time,) and turned to the left, when we came in sight of a new country, and looked down a very fine glen—*Glen Mark*. We descended by a very steep but winding path, called *The Ladder*, very grand and wild: the water running through it is called *The Ladder Burn*. It is very fine indeed, and very

---

[+] Prince Louis of Hesse.

striking.* There is a small forester's lodge at the very foot of it. The pass is quite a narrow one; you wind along a very steep and rough path, but still it was quite easy to ride on it, as it zigzags along. We crossed the burn at the bottom, where a picturesque group of "shearers" were seated, chiefly women, the older ones smoking. They were returning from the south to the north, whence they came.* We rode up to the little cottage; and in a little room of a regular Highland cabin, with its usual "press bed," we had luncheon. This place is called *Invermark*,* and is four and a half miles from *Corrie Vruach*. After luncheon I sketched the fine view. The steep hill we came down immediately opposite the keeper's lodge is called *Craig Boestock*, and a very fine isolated craggy hill which rises to the left—over-topping a small and wild glen—is called the *Hill of Doun*.

We mounted our ponies a little after three, and rode down *Glen Mark*, stopping to drink some water out of a very pure well, called *The White Well*;* and crossing the *Mark* several times. As we approached the *Manse of Loch Lee*, the glen widened, and the old *Castle of Invermark* came out extremely well; and, surrounded by woods and corn-fields, in which the people were "shearing," looked most picturesque. We turned to the right, and rode up to the old ruined castle, which is half covered with ivy. We then rode up to Lord Dalhousie's shooting-lodge, where we dismounted. It is a new and very pretty house, built of granite, in a very fine position overlooking the glen, with wild hills at the back. Miss Maule (now Lady C. Maule) was there. We passed through the drawing-room, and went on a few yards to the end of a walk whence you see *Loch Lee*, a wild, but not large, lake closed in by mountains—with a farm-house and a few cottages at its edge. The hall and dining-room are very prettily fitted up with trophies of sport, and the walls panelled with light wood. We had a few of the very short showers which hung about the hills. We then got into our carriages. The carriage we were in was a sort of double dog-cart which could carry eight—but was very narrow inside. We drove along the glen—down by the *Northesk* (the *Ey* and *Mark* meeting become the *Northesk*), passing to the right another very pretty glen—*Glen Effach*, much wooded, and the whole landscape beautifully lit up. Before us all was light and bright, and behind the mist and rain seemed to come down heavily over the mountains.

Further on, we passed *Poul Skeinnie Bridge* and *Tarf Bridge*, both regular steep Highland bridges.* To the right of the latter there is a new Free Kirk—further on *Captain Wemyss's Retreat*, a strange-looking place,—to the left *Mill Dane*—and, on a small eminence, the *Castle of Auch Mill*, which now resembles an old farmhouse, but has traces of a terrace garden remaining. The hills round it and near the road to the left were like small mounds. A little further on again we came to a wood, where we got out and walked along *Major McInroy's Burn*. The path winds along through the wood just above this most curious narrow gorge, which is unlike any of the other lynns; the rocks are very peculiar, and the burn very narrow, with deep pools completely overhung by wood. It extends some way. The woods and grounds might be in *Wales*, or even in *Hawthornden*. We walked through the wood and a little way along the road, till the carriages overtook us. We had three miles further to drive to *Fettercairn*, in all 40 miles from *Balmoral*. We came upon a flat country, evidently much cultivated, but it was too dark to see anything.

At a quarter-past seven o'clock we reached the small quiet town, or rather village, of *Fettercairn*, for it was very small—not a creature stirring, and we got out at the quiet little inn, "Ramsay Arms," quite unobserved, and went at once upstairs. There was a very nice drawing-room, and next to it, a dining-room, both very clean and tidy—then to the left our bed-room, which was excessively small, but also very clean and neat, and much better furnished than at *Grantown*. Alice had a nice room, the same size as ours; then came a mere morsel of one, (with a "press bed,") in which Albert dressed; and then came Lady Churchill's bed-room just beyond. Louis and General Grey had rooms in an hotel, called "The Temperance Hotel," opposite. We dined at eight, a very nice, clean, good dinner. Grant and Brown waited. They were rather nervous, but General Grey and Lady Churchill carved, and they had only to change the plates, which Brown soon got into the way of doing. A little girl of the house came in to help—but Grant turned her round to prevent her looking at us! The landlord and landlady knew who we were, but *no one else* except the coachman, and they kept the secret admirably.

The evening being bright and moonlight and very still, we all went out, and walked through the whole village, where not a creature moved;—through the principal little square, in the middle of which was a sort of pillar or Town Cross on steps, and Louis read, by the light of the moon, a proclamation for collections of charities which was stuck on it. We walked on along a lane a short way, hearing nothing whatever—not a leaf moving—but the distant barking of a dog! Suddenly we heard a drum and fifes! We were greatly alarmed, fearing we had been recognized; but Louis and General Grey, who went back, saw nothing whatever. Still, as we walked slowly back, we heard the noise from time to time,—and when we reached the inn door we stopped, and saw six men march up with fifes and a drum (not a creature taking any notice of them), go down the street, and back again. Grant and Brown were out; but had no idea what it could be. Albert asked the little maid, and the answer was, "It's just a band," and that it walked about in this way twice a week. How odd! It went on playing some time after we got home. We sat till half-past ten working, and Albert reading,—and then retired to rest.

Saturday, September 21.

Got to sleep after two or three o'clock. The morning was dull and close, and misty with a little rain; hardly any one stirring; but a few people at their work. A traveller had arrived at night, and wanted to come up into the dining-room, which is the "commercial travellers' room;" and they had difficulty in telling him he could *not* stop there. He joined Grant and Brown at their tea, and on his asking, "What's the matter here?" Grant answered, "It's a wedding party from *Aberdeen*."* At "The Temperance Hotel" they were very anxious to know whom they had got. All, except General Grey, breakfasted a little before nine. Brown acted as my servant, brushing my skirt and boots, and taking any message, and Grant as Albert's valet.

At a quarter to ten we started the same way as before, except that we were in the carriage which Lady Churchill and the General had yesterday. It was unfortunately misty, and we could see no distance. The people had just discovered who we were, and a few cheered us as we went along. We passed close to *Fettercairn*, Sir J. Forbes's house; then further on to the left, *Fasque*, belonging to Sir T. Gladstone, who has evidently done a great deal for the country, having built many good cottages. We then came to a very long hill, at least four miles in length, called the *Cairnie Month*, whence there is a very fine view; but which was entirely obscured by a heavy driving mist. We walked up part of it, and then for a little while Alice and I sat alone in the carriage. We next came to the *Spittal Bridge*, a curious high bridge with the *Dye Water* to the left, and the *Spittal Burn* to the right. Sir T. Gladstone's shooting-place is close to the *Bridge of Dye*—where we changed carriages again, reentering the double dog-cart—Albert and I inside, and Louis sitting behind. We went up a hill again and saw *Mount Battock* to the north-west, close to Sir T. Gladstone's shooting-lodge. You then come to an open country, with an extensive view towards *Aberdeen*, and to a very deep, rough ford, where you pass the *Feugh*, at a place called *White Stones*. It is very pretty and a fine glen with wood. About two miles further to the north-west, on the left, is *Finzean*; and, a little beyond, is "King Durdun's Stone,"* as they call it, by the roadside—a large, heavy, ancient stone,—the history of which, however, we have not yet discovered. Then we passed *Mary's Well*, to the left of which is *Ballogie House*, a fine property belonging to

Mr. Dyce Nicol. The harvest and everything seemed prosperous, and the country was very pretty. We got out at a very small village, (where the horses had some water, for it was a terribly long stage,) and walked a little way along the road. Alice, Lady Churchill, and I, went into the house of a tailor, which was very tidy, and the woman in it most friendly, asking us to rest there; but not dreaming who we were.

We drove on again, watching ominous-looking clouds, which, however, cleared off afterwards. We saw the woods of Lord Huntly's forest, and the hills which one sees from the road to *Aboyne*. Instead of going on to *Aboyne* we turned to the left, leaving the *Bridge of Aboyne* (which we had not seen before) to the right. A little beyond this, out of sight of all habitations, we found the postmaster, with another carriage for us. This was 22 miles from *Fettercairn*. We crossed the *Tanar Water*, and drove to the left up *Glen Tanar*—a really beautiful and richly-wooded glen, between high hills—part of Lord Huntly's forest. We drove on about six miles, and then stopped, as it was past two, to get our luncheon. The day kept quite fair in spite of threatening clouds and gathering mist. The spot where we lunched was very pretty. This over, we walked on a little, and then got into the carriages again, and drove to the end of the glen— out of the trees to *Eatnoch*, on to a keeper's house in the glen—a very lonely place, where our ponies were. It was about four when we arrived. A wretched idiot girl was here by herself, as tall as Lady Churchill; but a good deal bent, and dressed like a child, with a pinafore and short-cut hair. She sat on the ground with her hands round her knees, rocking herself to and fro and laughing; she then got up and walked towards us. General Grey put himself before me, and she went up to him, and began taking hold of his coat, and putting her hand into his pockets, which set us all off laughing, sad as it was. An old man walked up hastily soon after, and on Lady Churchill asking him if he knew that poor girl, he said, "Yes, she belongs to me, she has a weakness in her mind;" and led her off hurriedly.

We walked on a few hundred yards, and then mounted our ponies a little higher up, and then proceeded across the other shoulder of the hill we had come down yesterday—crossed the boggy part, and came over the *Polach* just as in going. The mist on the distant hills, *Mount Keen*, &c., made it feel chilly. Coming down the peat-road[+] to the *Bridge of*

[+] Grant told me in May, 1862, that, when the Prince stopped behind with him, looking at the Choils which he intended as a deer-forest for the Prince of Wales, and giving his directions as to the planting in Glen Muich, he said to Grant,—"You and I may be dead and gone before that." In less than three months, alas! his words were verified as regards himself! He was ever cheerful, but ever ready and prepared.

Muich, the view of the valleys of *Muich*, *Gairn*, and *Ballater* was beautiful. As we went along I talked frequently with good Grant.*

We found my dearest Mother's sociable, a fine large one, which she has left to Albert, waiting to take us back. It made me very sad, and filled my eyes with tears. Oh, in the midst of cheerfulness, I feel so sad! But being out a great deal here—and seeing new and fine scenery, does me good.

We got back to *Balmoral*, much pleased with our expedition, at seven o'clock. We had gone 42 miles to-day, and 40 yesterday, in all 82.

Expedition to Loch Avon.

Saturday, September 28, 1861.

Looked out very anxiously. A doubtful morning; still gleams of sunshine burst through the mist, and it seemed improving all round. We breakfasted at a quarter to eight, with Alice and Louis, in our sitting-room; and started at half-past eight. Louis and Alice with us, Grant and Brown on the box, as usual. The morning greatly improved.

We drove along the north side of the river, the day clearing very much, and becoming really fine. We took post-horses at *Castleton*, and drove up to the *Derry* (the road up *Glen Luie* very bad indeed); and here we mounted our ponies, and proceeded the usual way up *Glen Derry*, as far as where the path turns up to *Loch Etchan*. Instead of going that way, we proceeded straight on—a dreadfully rough, stony road, though not steep, but rougher than anything we ever rode upon before, and terrible for the poor horses' feet. We passed by two little lakes called the *Dhoolochans*, opposite to where the glen runs down to *Inchrory*, and after crossing them, there was a short boggy bit, where I got off and walked some way on the opposite side, along the "brae" of the hill, on the other side of which the loch lies, and then got on again. It was so saturated with water, that the moss and grass and everything were soaked,—not very pleasant riding, particularly as it was along the slope of the hill. We went on and on, nearly two miles from the foot of this hill, expecting to see the loch, but another low hill hid it from us, till at length we came in sight of it; and nothing could be grander and wilder—the rocks are so grand and precipitous, and the snow on *Ben Muich Dhui* had such a fine effect.

We saw the spot at the foot of *Loch Etchan* to which we scrambled last year, and looked down upon *Loch Avon*. It was very cold and windy. At length, at a quarter-past two, we sat down behind a large stone a little above the loch (unfortunately, we could not go to the extreme end, where the water rushes into it). We lunched as quickly as we could, and then began walking back, and crossed the hill higher up than in coming. I walked for some time, but it was not easy, from the great wet and the very uneven ground. Good Louis helped me often; Albert and Alice running along without assistance. Remounted my pony, which, as well as Albert's, went beautifully, carefully led by that most attentive of servants, Brown. I had again to get off before we crossed by the *Dhoolochans*; but after that we rode back the whole way.

We had the same guide, Charlie Stewart, who took us to *Glen Fishie* last year, and who walks wonderfully. We had two slight showers going down, and saw that there had been much more rain below. We found the *Ford of the Derry* very deep, nearly up to the ponies' girths; and the roughness and stoniness of the road is beyond everything, but the ponies picked their way like cats. We were down at the *Derry* by nearly six o'clock; the distance to *Loch Avon* being ten miles. Found our carriages there: it was already getting darkish, but still it was quite light enough to enable the post-boys to see their way.

At the bridge at *Mar Lodge*, Brown lit the lanterns. We gave him and Grant our plaids to put on, as we always do when they have walked a long way with us and drive afterwards. We took our own horses at *Castleton*, and reached *Balmoral* at ten minutes past eight, much pleased with the success of our expedition, and really *not* tired. We dined *en famille*.

Third Great Expedition:—To Glen Fishie, Dalwhinnie, and Blair Athole.

Tuesday, October 8, 1861.

The morning was dull and rather overcast; however, we decided to go. General Grey had gone on before. We three ladies drove in the sociable: Albert and Louis in a carriage from *Castleton*. The clouds looked heavy and dark, though not like mist hanging on the mountains. Down came a heavy shower; but before we reached *Castleton* it cleared; blue sky appeared; and, as there was much wind, Grant thought all would be well, and the day very fine. Changed horses at *Castleton*, and drove beyond the *Linn of Dee* to the *Giuly* or *Geldie Water*—just where last year we mounted our ponies, 18 miles from *Balmoral*. Here we found our ponies—"Inchrory" for me, and a new pony for Alice—a tall grey one, ugly but safe. The others rode their usual ones. The same guide, Charlie Stewart, was there, and a pony for the luncheon panniers, and a spare one for Grant and others to ride in turn.

We started about ten minutes past eleven, and proceeded exactly as last year, fording the *Geldie* at first very frequently. The ground was wet, but not worse than last year. We had gone on very well for about an hour, when the mist thickened all round, and down came heavy, or at least beating, rain with wind. With the help of an umbrella, and waterproofs and a plaid, I kept quite dry. Dearest Albert, who walked from the time the ground became boggy, got very wet, but was none the worse for it, and we got through it much better than before; we ladies never having to get off our ponies. At length at two o'clock, just as we were entering that beautiful *Glen Fishie*, which at its commencement reminds one of *McInroy's Burn*, it cleared, and became quite fine and very mild. Brown waded through the *Etchart* leading my pony; and then two of the others, who were riding together on another pony, dropped the whole bundle of cloaks into the water!

The falls of the *Stron-na-Barin*, with that narrow steep glen, which you ride up, crossing at the bottom, were in great beauty. We stopped before we entered the wood, and lunched on the bank overhanging the river, where General Grey joined us, and gave us an account of his arrangements. We lunched rather hurriedly, remounted our ponies and rode a short way—till we came near to a very steep place, not very pleasant to ride. So fine! numberless little burns running down in cascades. We walked a short way, and then remounted our ponies; but as we were to keep on the other side of the river, not by the *Invereshie* huts,* we had to get off for a few hundred yards, the path being so narrow as to make it utterly unsafe to ride. Alice's pony already began to slip. The huts, surrounded by magnificent fir-trees, and by quantities of juniper-bushes, looked lovelier than ever; and we gazed with sorrow at their utter ruin. I felt what a delightful little encampment it must have been, and how enchanting to live in such a spot as this beautiful solitary wood in a glen surrounded by the high hills. We got off, and went into one of the huts to look at a fresco of stags of Landseer's, over a chimney-piece. Grant, on a pony, led me through the Fishie (all the fords are deep) at the foot of the farm-houses, where we met Lord and Lady Alexander Russell last year—and where we this time found two carriages. We dismounted and entered them, and were off at five o'clock—we were to have started at four.

We four drove together by the same way as we rode last year (and nothing could be rougher for driving), quite to the second wood, which led us past *Loch Inch*; but we turned short of the loch to the left along the high road. Unfortunately by this time it was nearly dark, and we therefore lost a great deal of the fine scenery. We had ridden 15 miles. We drove along the road over several bridges—the *Bridge of Carr*, close below the ruined *Castle of Ruthven*,* which we could just descry in the dusk—and on a long wooden bridge over the *Spey* to an inn at *Kingussie*, a very straggling place with very few cottages. Already, before we arrived there, we were struck by people standing at their cottage doors, and evidently looking out, which made us believe we were expected. At *Kingussie* there was a small, curious, chattering crowd of people—who, however, did not really make us out, but evidently suspected who we were. Grant and Brown kept them off the carriages, and gave them evasive answers, directing them to the wrong carriage, which was most amusing. One old gentleman, with a high wide-awake, was especially inquisitive.

We started again, and went on and on, passing through the village of *Newtonmoore*, where the footman McDonald[+] comes from. Here the *Spey* is crossed at its junction with the *Truim*, and then the road ascends for ten miles more to *Dalwhinnie*. It became cold and windy with occasional rain. At length, and not till a quarter to nine, we reached the inn of *Dalwhinnie*,—29 miles from where we had left our ponies,—which

---

[+] He died at Abergeldie last year of consumption; and his widow, an excellent person, daughter of Mitchell the blacksmith at Balmoral, is now my wardrobe-maid.

stands by itself, away from any village. Here, again, there were a few people assembled, and I thought they knew us; but it seems they did not, and it was only when we arrived that one of the maids recognized me. She had seen me at *Aberdeen* and *Edinburgh*. We went upstairs: the inn was much larger than at *Fettercairn*, but not nearly so nice and cheerful; there was a drawing-room and a dining-room; and we had a very good-sized bedroom. Albert had a dressing-room of equal size. Mary Andrews[+] (who was very useful and efficient) and Lady Churchill's maid had a room together, every one being in the house; but unfortunately there was hardly anything to eat, and there was only tea, and two miserable starved Highland chickens, without any potatoes! No pudding, and no *fun*; no little maid (the two there not wishing to come in), nor our two people—who were wet and drying our and their things—to wait on us! It was not a nice supper; and the evening was wet. As it was late we soon retired to rest. Mary and Maxted (Lady Churchill's maid) had been dining below with Grant, Brown, and Stewart (who came, the same as last time, with the maids) in the "commercial room" at the foot of the stairs. They had only the remnants of our two starved chickens!*

Wednesday, October 9.

A bright morning, which was very charming. Albert found, on getting up, that Cluny Macpherson, with his piper and two ladies, had arrived quite early in the morning; and, while we were dressing, we heard a drum and fife—and discovered that the newly-formed volunteers had arrived—all indicating that we were discovered. However, there was scarcely any population, and it did not signify. The fat old landlady had put on a black satin dress, with white ribbons and orange flowers! We had breakfast at a quarter to nine o'clock; at half-past nine we started. Cluny was at the door with his wife and daughters with nosegays, and the volunteers were drawn up in front of the inn. They had all assembled since Saturday afternoon!

We drove as we did yesterday. Fine and very wild scenery, high wild hills, and no habitations. We went by the *Pass of Drumouchter*, with fine hills on both sides and in front of us; passed between two, the one on our left called *The Boar of Badenoch*, and that on the right, *The Athole Sow*.* The *Pass of Drumouchter* separates *Perthshire* from *Inverness-shire*.

[+] One of my wardrobe-maids—now dresser to Princess Helena (Princess Christian). Her father was thirty-eight years with my dear uncle the King of the Belgians.

Again, a little farther on, we came to *Loch Garry*, which is very beautiful—but the mist covered the furthest hills, and the extreme distance was clouded. There is a small shooting-lodge, or farm, charmingly situated, looking up the glen on both sides, and with the loch in front; we did not hear to whom it belonged. We passed many drovers, without their herds and flocks, returning, Grant told us, from *Falkirk*. We had one very heavy shower after *Loch Garry* and before we came to *Dalnacardoch Inn*, 13 miles from *Dalwhinnie*. The road goes beside the *Garry*. The country for a time became flatter; but was a good deal cultivated. At *Dalnacardoch Inn* there was a suspicion and expectation of our arrival. Four horses with smart postilions were in waiting; but, on General Grey's saying that this was *not* the party, but the one for whom only two horses had been ordered, a shabby pair of horses were put in; a shabby driver driving from the box (as throughout this journey), and off we started.*

The *Garry* is very fine, rolling along over large stones—like the *Quoich* and the *Fishie*, and forming perpetual falls, with birch and mountain-ash growing down to the water's edge. We had some more heavy showers. A few miles from *Dalnacardoch* the Duke of Athole (in his kilt and shooting-jacket, as usual) met us on a pretty little chestnut pony, and rode the whole time near the carriage. He said, there were vague suspicions and rumours of our coming, but he had told no one anything. There was again a shower, but it cleared when we came in sight of *Ben-y-Ghlo*, and the splendid *Pass of Killiecrankie*, which, with the birch all golden,—not, as on *Deeside*, bereft of leaves,—looked very beautiful.

We passed by the *Bruar*, and the road to the *Falls of the Bruar*, but could not stop. The Duke took us through a new approach, which is extremely pretty; but near which, I cannot help regretting, the railroad will come,* as well as along the road by which we drove through the *Pass of Drumouchter*. The Duke has made great improvements, and the path looked beautiful, surrounded as it is by hills; and the foliage still full, though in all its autumn tints—the whole being lit up with bright sunshine. We drove through an avenue, and in a few minutes more were at the door of the old castle.* A thousand recollections of seventeen years ago crowded upon me—all seemed so familiar again! No one there except the dear Duchess, who stood at the door, and whom I warmly embraced; and Miss MacGregor. How well I recognized the hall with all the sporting trophies; and the staircase, which we went up at once. The Duchess took us to a room which I recognized immediately as the one where Lady Canning lived. There we took off our things—then went to look at the old and really very handsome rooms in which we had lived—the one in which

Vicky had slept in two chairs, then not four years old! In the dining-room we took some coffee, which was most welcome; and then we looked at all the stags' horns put up in one of the corridors below; saw the Duke's pet dog, a smooth-haired black terrier, very fat; and then got into the carriage, a very peculiar one, viz., a *boat*—a mere boat (which is very light), put on four wheels, drawn by a pair of horses with a postilion. Into this we four got, with the Duke and Duchess and the dog;—Lady Churchill, General Grey, and Miss MacAra going in another carriage; with our two servants on the box, to whom all this was quite new and a great treat. The morning was beautiful. It was half-past twelve—we drove up by the avenue and about a favourite walk of ours in '44, passed through the gate, and came on to *Glen Tilt*—which is most striking, the road winding along, first on one side of the Tilt, and then on the other; the fine high hills rising very abruptly from each side of the rapid, rocky, stony river Tilt—the trees, chiefly birch and alder, overhanging the water.

We passed the *Marble Lodge*, in which one of the keepers lives, and came to *Forest Lodge*, where the road for carriages ends, and the glen widens. There were our ponies, which had passed the night at the *Bainoch* or *Beynoch* (a shooting "shiel" of Lord Fife's). They came over this morning; but, poor beasts, without having had any corn! *Forest Lodge* is eight miles from *Blair*. There we took leave of the dear Duchess; and saw old Peter Frazer, the former head-keeper there, now walking with the aid of two sticks! The Duke's keepers were there, his pipers, and a gentleman staying on a visit with him.

It was barely two o'clock when we started. We on our ponies, the Duke and his men (twelve altogether) on foot—Sandy McAra, now head-keeper, grown old and grey, and two pipers, preceded us; the two latter playing alternately the whole time, which had a most cheerful effect. The wild strains sounded so softly amid those noble hills; and our caravan winding along—our people and the Duke's all in kilts, and the ponies, made altogether a most picturesque scene.

One of the Duke's keepers, Donald Macbeath, is a guardsman, and was in the Crimea. He is a celebrated marksman, and a fine-looking man, as all the Duke's men are. For some little time it was easy riding, but soon we came to a rougher path, more on the "brae" of the hill, where the pony required to be led, which I always have done, either when it is at all rough or bad, or when the pony has to be got on faster.

The Duke walked near me the greater part of the time; amusingly saying, in reference to former times, that he did not offer to lead me, as he knew I had no confidence in him. I replied, laughingly, "Oh, no, only I like best being led by the person I am accustomed to."

At length, at about three, we stopped, and lunched at a place called *Dalcronachie*, looking up a glen towards *Loch Loch*—on a high bank overhanging the *Tilt*. Looking back the view was very fine; so, while the things were being unpacked for lunch, we sketched. We brought our own luncheon, and the remainder was as usual given to the men, but this time there were a great many to feed.* After luncheon, we set off again. I walked a few paces; but as it was very wet, and the road very rough, by Albert's desire I got on again. A very few minutes brought us to the celebrated ford of the *Tarff*,* (*Poll Tarff* it is called,) which is very deep—and after heavy rain almost impassable. The Duke offered to lead the pony on one side, and talked of Sandy for the other side, but I asked for Brown (whom I have far the most confidence in) to lead the pony, the Duke taking hold of it (as he did frequently) on the other side. Sandy McAra, the guide, and the two pipers went first, playing all the time. To all appearance the ford of the *Tarff* was not deeper than the other fords, but once in it the men were above their knees—and suddenly in the middle, where the current, from the fine, high, full falls, is very strong, it was nearly up to the men's waists. Here Sandy returned, and I said to the Duke (which he afterwards joked with Sandy about) that I thought he (Sandy) had better take the Duke's place; he did so, and we came very well through, all the others following, the men chiefly wading—Albert (close behind me) and the others riding through—and some of our people coming over double on the ponies. General Grey had little Peter Robertson up behind him.

The road after this became almost precipitous, and indeed made riding very unpleasant; but being wet, and difficult to walk, we ladies rode, Albert walking the greater part of the time. Only once, for a very few steps, I had to get off, as the pony could hardly keep its footing. As it was, Brown constantly could not walk next to the pony, but had to scramble below, or pull it after him. The Duke was indefatigable.

The *Tilt* becomes narrower and narrower, till its first source is almost invisible. The *Tarff* flows into the *Tilt*, about two miles or more beyond the falls. We emerged from the pass upon an open valley—with less high hills and with the hills of *Braemar* before us. We crossed the *Bainoch* or *Bynack*, quite a small stream, and when we came to the "County March"—where *Perth* and *Aberdeen* join—we halted. The Duke gave Albert and me some whisky to drink, out of an old silver flask of his own, and then made a short speech proposing my health, expressing the pleasure with which he and all had received me at *Blair*, and hoping that I would return as often as I liked, and that I should have a safe return home; ending by the true Highland "Nis! nis! nis! Sit air a-nis! A-ris! a-ris! a-ris!" (pronounced: "Neesh! neesh! neesh! Sheet eir, a-neesh! A-rees! a-rees! a-rees!") which means: "Now! now! now! That to him, now! Again! again! again!" which was responded to by cheering from all. Grant then proposed "three cheers for the Duke of Athole," which was also very warmly responded to;—my pony (good "Inchrory"), which went admirably, rather resenting the vehemence of Brown's cheering.

We then went on again for about three miles to the *Bainoch*, which we reached at ten minutes to six, when it was already nearly dark. As we approached the "shiel," the pipers struck up, and played. The ponies went so well with the pipes, and altogether it was very pleasant to ride and walk with them. They played "the Athole Highlanders" when we started, and again in coming in.*

Lady Fife had very kindly come down to the *Bainoch* herself, where she gave us tea, which was very welcome. We then got into our carriages, wishing the good Duke of Athole goodby. He was going back the whole way—which was certainly rather a hazardous proceeding, at least an adventurous one, considering the night, and that there was no moon—and what the road was! We got home safely at a quarter-past eight. The night was quite warm, though slightly showery—but became very clear and starlight later.

We had travelled 69 miles to-day, and 60 yesterday. This was the pleasantest and most enjoyable expedition I *ever* made; and the recollection of it will always be most agreeable to me, and increase my wish to make more! Was so glad dear Louis (who is a charming companion) was with us. Have enjoyed nothing as much, or indeed felt so much cheered by anything, since my great sorrow.[+] Did not feel tired. We ladies did not dress, and dined *en famille*; looking at maps of the *Highlands* after dinner.

[+] The death of the Duchess of Kent.

Last Expedition.

Wednesday, October 16, 1861

To our great satisfaction it was a most beautiful morning. Not a cloud was on the bright blue sky, and it was perfectly calm. There had been a sharp frost which lay on parts of the grass, and the mountains were beautifully lit up, with those very blue shades upon them, like the bloom on a plum. Up early, and breakfasted with Alice, Louis, and Lenchen, in our room. At twenty minutes to nine o'clock we started, with Alice, Lenchen, and Louis. The morning was beyond everything splendid, and the country in such beauty, though the poor trees are nearly leafless.

Near *Castleton*, and indeed all along the road, in the shade, the frost still lay, and the air was very sharp. We took post-horses at *Castleton*, and proceeded up *Glen Clunie* to *Glen Callater*, which looked lovely, and which Albert admired much. In a little more than two hours we were at *Loch Callater**—the road was very bad indeed as we approached the loch, where our ponies were waiting for us. After walking a few paces we remounted them, I on my good "Fyvie," and Alice on "Inchrory."

The day was glorious—and the whole expedition delightful, and very easily performed. We ascended *Little Cairn Turc*, on the north side of *Loch Callater*, up a sort of footpath very easy and even, upon ground that was almost flat, rising very gradually, but imperceptibly; and the view became wonderfully extensive. The top of *Cairn Turc* is quite flat—with moss and grass—so that you could drive upon it. It is very high, for you see the high table-land behind the highest point of *Loch-na-Gar*. On that side you have no view; but from the other it is wonderfully extensive. It was so clear and bright, and so still there, reminding us of the day on *Ben Muich Dhui* last year.

There rose immediately behind us *Ben Muich Dhui*, which you hardly ever see, and the shape of which is not fine, with its surrounding mountains of *Cairngorm*, *Brae Riach*, *Ben Avon* or *A'an*, *Ben-na-Bhourd*, &c. We saw *Ben-y-Ghlo* quite clearly, and all that range of hills; then, further west, *Shichallion*,* near *Loch Tay*; the mountains which are near the *Black Mount*; and, quite on the horizon, we could discern *Ben Nevis*, which is above *Fort William*.

Going up *Cairn Turc* we looked down upon *Loch Canter*, a small loch above *Loch Callater*, very wild and dark. We proceeded to *Cairn Glaishie*, at the extreme point of which a cairn has been erected. We got off to take a look at the wonderful panorama which lay stretched out before us. We looked on *Fifeshire*, and the country between *Perth* and *Stirling*, the *Lomond Hills*, &c. It was beautifully clear, and really it was most interesting to look over such an immense extent of the *Highlands*. I give a very poor description of it; but here follows a rough account of the places we saw:—

To the North—*Ben Muich Dhui, Brae Riach, Cairngorm, Ben Avon, Ben-na-Bhourd*.

To the East—*Loch-na-Gar*, &c.

To the South-West—*Ben-y-Ghlo* or *Ben-y-Gloe*, and the surrounding hills beyond *Shichallion*, and the mountains between *Dunkeld* and the *Black Mount*.

Quite in the extreme West—*Ben Nevis*.

To the South—the *Lomond Hills; Perth* in the middle distance.

We walked on a little way, and then I got upon my pony. Another half hour's riding again over such singular flat table-land, brought us on to the edge of the valley of *Cairn Lochan*,* which is indeed "a bonnie place." It reminded me and Louis of *Clova*; only there one did not see the immense extent of mountains behind. *Cairn Lochan* is a narrow valley, the river *Isla* winding through it like a silver ribbon, with trees at the bottom. The hills are green and steep, but towards the head of the valley there are fine precipices. We had then to take a somewhat circuitous route in order to avoid some bogs, and to come to a spot where we looked right up the valley for an immense distance; to the left, or rather more to the south, was *Glen Isla*, another glen, but wider, and not with the same high mountains as *Cairn Lochan*. Beyond *Glen Isla* were seen the *Lomond Hills* behind *Kinross*, at the foot of which is *Loch Leven*.

We sat on a very precipitous place, which made one dread any one's moving backwards; and here, at a little before two o'clock, we lunched. The lights were charmingly soft, and, as I said before, like the bloom on a plum. The luncheon was very acceptable, for the air was extremely keen, and we found ice thicker than a shilling on the top of *Cairn Turc*, which did not melt when Brown took it and kept it in his hand.

Helena was so delighted, for this was *the only really great* expedition in which she had accompanied us.

Duncan and the keeper at *Loch Callater* (R. Stewart) went with us as guides.

I made some hasty sketches; and then Albert wrote on a bit of paper that we had lunched here, put it into the Selters-water bottle, and buried it there, or rather stuck it into the ground. Grant had done the same when we visited *Ben Muich Dhui* the first time. This over, we walked part of the way back which we had ridden to avoid the bogs,—we ladies walking only a short way, and then riding. We altered our course, and left *Cairn Glaishie* to our right, and went in the direction of the *Cairn Wall*. Looking back on the distant hills above *Glen Isla* and *Cairn Lochan* (Lord Airlie's "Country"), it was even more beautiful; for, as the day advanced, the mountains became clearer and clearer, of a lovely blue, while the valleys were in shadow. *Shichallion*, and those further ranges, were also most perfectly to be seen, and gave me such a longing for further Highland expeditions! We went over *Garbchory*, looking down on the road to the *Spittal*; and on the lower mountains, which are most curiously connected one with another, and which, from the height we were, we could look down upon.

Here follows the account of our route, with all the names as written down by Duncan. I cannot "mind" the names, as they say here.

From *Balmoral* to—
  Loch Callater, four miles,
  Left *Loch Callater* at 11 o'clock, A.M.,
  Little Cairn Turc,
  Big Cairn Turc,
  Loch Canter,
  Cairn Glaishie,
  Cairn Lochan,
  Ca-Ness, six miles.

Returning route:—
  Cairn Lochan,
  Cairn Glashie,
  Garb Chory,
  Month Eigie Road,
  Glass Meall,
  Fian Chory,
  Aron Ghey,
  Shean Spittal Bridge, 4.30 P.M.,
  Shean Spittal Bridge to *Balmoral*, 16 miles.

This gave one a very good idea of the geography of the country, which delighted dear Albert, as this expedition was quite in a different direction from any that we had ever made before. But my head is so very ungeographical, that I cannot describe it. We came down by the *Month Eigie*, a steep hill covered with grass—down part of which I rode, walking where it was steepest; but it was so wet and slippery that I had two falls. We got down to the road to the *Spittal Bridge*, about 15 miles from *Castleton*, at nearly half-past four, and then down along the new road, at least that part of it which is finished, and which is to extend to the *Cairn Wall*. We went back on our side of the river; and if we had been a little earlier, Albert might have got a stag—but it was too late. The moon rose and shone most beautifully, and we returned at twenty minutes to seven o'clock, much pleased and interested with this delightful expedition. Alas! I fear our *last* great one!

(IT WAS OUR LAST ONE!—1867.)

TOURS

IN

ENGLAND AND IRELAND,

AND

YACHTING EXCURSIONS.*

First Visit to Ireland.

On Board the Victoria and Albert,
in the Cove of Cork,
Thursday, August 2, 1849.

ARRIVED here after a quick but not very pleasant passage. The day was fine and bright, and the sea to all appearance very smooth; but there was a dreadful swell, which made one incapable of reading or doing anything. We passed the *Land's End* at nine o'clock in the morning. When we went on deck after eight in the evening, we were close to the *Cove of Cork*, and could see many bonfires on the hill, and the rockets and lights that were sent off from the different steamers. The harbour is immense, though the land is not very high, and entering by twilight it had a very fine effect. Lady Jocelyn, Miss Dawson, Lord Fortescue (Lord Steward), Sir George Grey (Secretary of State for the Home Department), Miss Hildyard, Sir James Clark, and Mr. Birch are on board with us. The equerries, Colonel Phipps and Colonel Gordon, are on board the "Black Eagle."

Friday, August 3.

The day was grey and excessively "muggy," which is the character of the Irish climate. The ships saluted at eight o'clock, and the "Ganges" (the flag-ship and a three-decker) and the "Hogue"* (a three-decker cut down, with very heavy guns, and with a screw put into her), which are both very near us, made a great noise. The harbor is very extensive, and there are several islands in it, one of which is very large. *Spike Island* is immediately opposite us, and has a convict prison; near it another island with the depot, &c. In a line with that is the town of *Cove*, picturesquely built up a hill. The two war-steamers have only just come in. The Admiral (Dixon) and the Captains of the vessels came on board. Later, Lord Bandon (Lord-Lieutenant of the county), Lord Thomond, General Turner, Commander of the Forces at Cork, presented their respects, and Albert went on shore, and I occupied myself in writing and sketching. Albert returned before our luncheon, and had been walking about and visiting some of the cabins.

We left the yacht at two with the ladies and gentlemen, and went on board the "Fairy," which was surrounded with rowing and sailing boats.

We first went round the harbour, all the ships saluting, as well as numbers of steamers and yachts. We then went in to *Cove* and lay alongside the landing-place, which was very prettily decorated; and covered with people; and yachts, ships and boats crowding all round. The two Members, Messrs. Roche and Power,* as well as other gentlemen, including the Roman Catholic and Protestant clergymen,* and then the members of the Yacht Club, presented addresses. After which, to give the people the satisfaction of calling the place *Queenstown*,* in honour of its being the first spot on which I set foot upon Irish ground, I stepped on shore amidst the roar of cannon (for the artillery were placed so close as quite to shake the temporary room which we entered); and the enthusiastic shouts of the people. We immediately re-embarked and proceeded up the river *Lee* towards *Cork*. It is extremely pretty and richly wooded, and reminded me of the *Tamar*. The first feature of interest we passed was a little bathing-place, called *Monkstown*, and later *Blackrock Castle*; at which point we stopped to receive a salmon, and a very pretty address from the poor fishermen of *Blackrock*.

As we approached the city we saw people streaming in, on foot, on horseback, and many in jaunting-cars. When we reached *Cork* the "Fairy" again lay alongside, and we received all the addresses: first, from the Mayor and Corporation (I knighted the Mayor immediately afterwards), then from the Protestant Bishop and clergy; from the Roman Catholic Bishop and clergy; from the Lord-Lieutenant of the county,* the Sheriffs, and others. The two Judges, who were holding their courts, also came on board in their robes. After all this was over we landed, and walked some few paces on to where Lord Bandon's carriage was ready to receive us. The ladies went with us, and Lord Bandon and the General rode on each side of the carriage. The Mayor preceded us, and many (Lord Listowel among the number,) followed on horseback or in carriages. The 12th Lancers escorted us, and the Pensioners and Infantry lined the streets.

I cannot describe our route, but it will suffice to say that it took two hours; that we drove through the principal streets; twice through some of them; that they were densely crowded, decorated with flowers and triumphal arches; that the heat and dust were great; that we passed by the new College which is building—one of the four which are ordered by Act of Parliament;* that our reception was most enthusiastic; and that everything went off to perfection, and was very well arranged. *Cork* is not at all like an English town, and looks rather foreign. The crowd is a noisy, excitable, but very good-humoured one, running and pushing about, and laughing, talking, and shrieking. The beauty of the women is very remarkable, and struck us much; such beautiful dark eyes and hair, and such fine teeth; almost every third woman was pretty, and some remarkably so. They wear no bonnets, and generally long blue cloaks; the men are very poorly, often raggedly dressed; and many wear blue coats and short breeches with blue stockings.

We re-embarked at the same place and returned just as we came.

Kingstown Harbour, Dublin Bay,
Sunday, August 5.

Safely arrived here: I now continue my account. For the first two hours and a half the sea, though rough, was not disagreeable. We entered *Waterford Harbour* yesterday at twenty minutes to four o'clock. The harbour is rocky on the right as one enters, and very flat to the left; as one proceeds the land rises on either side. We passed a little fort called *Duncannon Fort*,* whence James II. embarked after the battle of the *Boyne*,* and from which they had not saluted for fifty years.* Further up, between two little villages, one on either side, each with its little chapel, picturesquely situated on the top of the rock or hill, we anchored. The little fishing place to our left is called *Passage*, and is famous for salmon; we had an excellent specimen for our dinner. Albert decided on going to *Waterford*, ten miles up the river, in the "Fairy," with the boys, but as I felt giddy and tired, I preferred remaining quietly on board sketching. Albert returned after seven o'clock; he had not landed.

Viceregal Lodge, Phœnix Park,*
Monday, August 6.

Here we are in this very pretty spot, with a lovely view of the *Wicklow Hills* from the window. But now to return to yesterday's proceedings. We got under weigh at half-past eight o'clock; for three hours it was dreadfully rough, and I and the poor children were very sea-sick. When we had passed the *Tuscar Rock* in *Wexford* the sea became smoother, and shortly after, quite smooth, and the evening beautiful. After we passed *Arklow Head*, the *Wicklow Hills* came in sight—they are beautiful. The *Sugarloaf* and *Carrick Mountain* have finely pointed outlines, with low hills in front and much wood. At half-past six we came in sight of *Dublin Bay*, and were met by the "Sphynx" and "Stromboli" (which had been sent on to wait and to come in with us), the "Trident," and, quite close to the harbour, by the "Dragon," another war-steamer. With this large squadron we steamed slowly and majestically into the harbour of

Kingstown, which was covered with thousands and thousands of spectators, cheering most enthusiastically. It is a splendid harbour, and was full of ships of every kind. The wharf, where the landing-place was prepared, was densely crowded, and altogether it was a noble and stirring scene. It was just seven when we entered, and the setting sun lit up the country, the fine buildings, and the whole scene with a glowing light, which was truly beautiful. We were soon surrounded by boats, and the enthusiasm and excitement of the people were extreme.

While we were at breakfast the yacht was brought close up to the wharf, which was lined with troops. Lord and Lady Clarendon and George[+] came on board; also Lords Lansdowne and Clanricarde, the Primate, the Archbishop of Dublin, and many others. The address was presented by the Sheriff and gentlemen of the county. As the clock struck ten we disembarked, stepping on shore from the yacht, Albert leading me and the children, and all the others following us. An immense multitude had assembled, who cheered most enthusiastically, the ships saluting and the bands playing, and it was really very striking. The space we had to walk along to the railroad was covered in; and lined with ladies and gentlemen strewing flowers. We entered the railway-carriages with the children, the Clarendons, and the three ladies; and in a quarter of an hour reached the Dublin station. Here we found our carriages with the postilions in their Ascot liveries. The two eldest children went with us, and the two younger ones with the three ladies. Sir Edward Blakeney, Commander-in-Chief in Ireland, rode on one side of the carriage and George on the other, followed by a brilliant staff, and escorted by the 17th Lancers and the Carabiniers.

It was a wonderful and striking scene, such masses of human beings, so enthusiastic, so excited, yet such perfect order maintained; then the numbers of troops, the different bands stationed at certain distances, the waving of hats and handkerchiefs, the bursts of welcome which rent the air,—all made it a never-to-be-forgotten scene; when one reflected how lately the country had been in open revolt and under martial law.*

Dublin is a very fine city; and *Sackville Street* and *Merrion Square* are remarkably large and handsome; and the *Bank*, *Trinity College*, &c. are noble buildings. There are no gates to the town, but temporary ones were erected under an arch; and here we stopped, and the Mayor presented me the keys with some appropriate words.* At the last triumphal arch a poor little dove was let down into my lap, with an olive branch round its

---

[+] The Duke of Cambridge.

neck, alive and very tame. The heat and dust were tremendous. We reached *Phœnix Park*, which is very extensive, at twelve. Lord and Lady Clarendon and all the household received us at the door. It is a nice comfortable house, reminding us of *Claremont*, with a pretty terrace garden in front (laid out by Lady Normanby), and has a very extensive view of the *Park* and the fine range of the *Wicklow Mountains*. We are most comfortably lodged, and have very nice rooms.*

Tuesday, August 7.

We drove into *Dublin*—with our two ladies—in Lord Clarendon's carriage, the gentlemen following; and without any escort. The people were very enthusiastic, and cheered a great deal. We went, first, to the *Bank*, where the Directors received us, and then to the printing-room, and from thence viewed the old Houses of Lords and Commons, for what is now the *Bank* was the old Parliament House.* From here we drove to the *Model-School*, where we were received by the Archbishop of Dublin, the Roman Catholic Archbishop Murray (a fine venerable-looking old man of eighty), and the other gentlemen connected with the school. We saw the *Infant*, the *Girls'*, and the *Boys' Schools*; in the latter, one class of boys was examined in mental arithmetic and in many very difficult things, and they all answered wonderfully. Children of all creeds are admitted, and their different doctrines are taught separately, if the parents wish it; but the *only* teaching enforced is that of the Gospel truths, and love and charity. This is truly Christian and ought to be the case everywhere.* About 1,000 children are educated here annually, of which 300 are trained as school-masters and mistresses. From here we visited *Trinity College*, the Irish University, which is not conducted upon so liberal a system, but into which Roman Catholics are admitted. Dr. Todd, the secretary, and a very learned man, well versed in the Irish language,* showed us some most interesting ancient manuscripts and relics, including St. Columba's Book* (in which we wrote our names), and the original harp of King O'Brian,* supposed to be the one from which the Irish arms are taken. The library is a very large handsome room, like that in *Trinity College, Cambridge*. We then proceeded towards home, the crowd in the streets immense, and so loyal. It rained a little at intervals. Home by a little past one. Albert went into *Dublin* again after luncheon, and I wrote and read, and heard our children say some lessons.

At five we proceeded to *Kilmainham Hospital*, very near here; Lord Clarendon going in the carriage with the ladies and myself—Albert and the other gentlemen riding. Sir Edward Blakeney and his staff, and George, received us. We saw the old pensioners, the chapel, and the hall, a fine large room (where all the pensioners dine, as at *Chelsea**), and then Sir Edward's private apartments. We afterwards took a drive through all the principal parts of *Dublin*,—*College Green*, where the celebrated statue of William the III.* is to be seen; *Stephens' Green*, by *The Four Courts*, a very handsome building; and, though we were not expected, the crowds were in many places very great. We returned a little before seven. A large dinner. After dinner above two or three hundred people arrived, including most of the Irish nobility and many of the gentry; and afterwards there was a ball.

Wednesday, August 8.

At twenty minutes to one o'clock we left for *Dublin*, I and all the ladies in evening dresses, all the gentlemen in uniform. We drove straight to the Castle.* Everything here as at *St. James's* Levée. The staircase and throne-room quite like a palace. I received (on the throne) the addresses of the Lord Mayor and Corporation, the University, the Archbishop and Bishops, both Roman Catholic and Anglican, the Presbyterians, the non-subscribing Presbyterians, and the Quakers.* They also presented Albert with addresses.+ Then followed a very long Levée, which lasted without intermission till twenty minutes to six o'clock! Two thousand people were presented!

Thursday, August 9.

There was a great and brilliant review in the *Phœnix Park*— six thousand one hundred and sixty men, including the Constabulary. In the evening we two dined alone, and at half-past eight o'clock drove into *Dublin* for the Drawing-room. It is always held here of an evening. I should think between two and three thousand people passed before us, and one thousand six hundred ladies were presented. After it was over we walked through *St. Patrick's Hall* and the other rooms, and the crowd was very great.* We came back to the *Phœnix Park* at half-past twelve—the streets still densely crowded. The city was illuminated.

+ Lord Breadalbane (Lord Chamberlain) was in attendance, having joined us on our arrival in Dublin.

Friday, August 10.

At a quarter to twelve o'clock we set out, with all our suite, for *Carton*, the Duke of Leinster's; Lord and Lady Clarendon in the carriage with us. We went through *Woodlands*, a place belonging to Mr. White, in which there are beautiful lime-trees; and we passed by the "Preparatory College" for *Maynooth*; and not far from *Carton* we saw a number of the Maynooth students. The park of *Carton* is very fine. We arrived there at a little past one, and were received by the Duke and Duchess of Leinster, the Kildares, Mr. and Lady C. Repton, and their two sons. We walked out into the garden, where all the company were assembled, and the two bands playing; it is very pretty: a sort of formal French garden with rows of Irish yews. We walked round the garden twice, the Duke leading me, and Albert the Duchess. The Duke is one of the kindest, and best of men.

After luncheon we walked out and saw some of the country people dance jigs, which was very amusing. It is quite different from the Scotch reel; not so animated, and the steps different, but very droll. The people were very poorly dressed in thick coats, and the women in shawls. There was one man who was a regular specimen of an Irishman, with his hat on one ear. Others in blue coats, with short breeches and blue stockings. There were three old and tattered pipers playing. The Irish pipe is very different from the Scotch; it is very weak, and they don't blow into it, but merely have small bellows which they move with the arm. We walked round the pleasure-grounds, and after this got into a carriage with the Duke and Duchess—our ladies and gentlemen following in a large jaunting-car, and the people riding, running, and driving with us, but extremely well-behaved; and the Duke is so kind to them, that a word from him will make them do anything. It was very hot, and yet the people kept running the whole way, and in the thick woollen coats, which it seems they always wear here. We drove along the park to a spot which commands an extensive view of the *Wicklow Hills*. We then went down an entirely new road, cut out of the solid rock, through a beautiful valley, full of the finest trees, growing among rocks close to a piece of water. We got out and walked across a little wooden bridge to a very pretty little cottage, entirely ornamented with shells, &c. by the Duchess. We drove back in the jaunting-car, which is a double one, with four wheels, and held a number of us—I sitting on one side between Albert and the Duke; the Duchess, Lady Jocelyn, Lord Clarendon, and Lady Waterford, on the opposite side; George at the back, and the equerries on either side of the coachman.

As soon as we returned to the house we took leave of our hosts, and went back to the *Phœnix Park* a different way from the one we came, along the banks of the *Liffey*, through Mr. Colson's park, in which there were the most splendid beeches I have ever seen—feathering down quite to the ground; and farther along the road and river were some lovely sycamore-trees. We drove through the village of *Lucan*, where there were fine decorations and arches of bays and laurel. We passed below *The Strawberry-beds*, which are really curious to see—quite high banks of them—and numbers of people come from *Dublin* to eat these strawberries; and there are rooms at the bottom of these banks on purpose. We were home a little after five.*

On Board the Victoria and Albert,
in Loch Ryan,
Sunday, August 12.*

We arrived after a dreadfully rough though very short passage, and have taken refuge here. To return to Friday. We left the *Phœnix Park*, where we spent so pleasant a time, at six o'clock, Lord Clarendon and the two elder children going in the carriage with us, and drove with an escort to the Dublin Railway Station. The town was immensely crowded, and the people most enthusiastic. George met us there, and we took him, the Clarendons, and Lord Lansdowne and our ladies in the carriage with us. We arrived speedily at *Kingstown*, where there were just as many people and as much enthusiasm as on the occasion of our disembarkation. We stood on the paddle-box as we slowly steamed out of *Kingstown*, amidst the cheers of thousands and thousands, and salutes from all the ships; and I waved my handkerchief as a parting acknowledgment of their loyalty. We soon passed *Howth* and *Ireland's Eye*. The ship was very steady, though the sea was not smooth, and the night thick and rainy, and we feared a storm was coming on.

Saturday, August 11.

We reached *Belfast Harbour* at four o'clock. The wind had got up amazingly, and the morning was a very bad and stormy one.

We had not had a very quiet night for sleeping, though very smooth. The weather got worse and worse, and blew a real gale; and it was quite doubtful whether we could start as we had intended, on our return from *Belfast*, for *Scotland*.

We saw the Mayor and General (Bainbrigg), who had come on board after breakfast.

At a quarter-past one we started with the ladies and gentlemen for the "Fairy." Though we had only two minutes' row in the barge, there was such a swell that the getting in and out, and the rolling and tossing in the boat, were very disagreeable. We had to keep in the little pavilion, as the squalls were so violent as to cover the "Fairy" with spray. We passed between *Holywood* and *Carrickfergus*, celebrated for the first landing of William III.* We reached *Belfast* in half an hour, and fortunately the sun came out.

We lay close alongside the wharf, where a very fine landing-place was arranged, and where thousands were assembled. Lord Londonderry* came on board, and numerous deputations with addresses, including the Mayor (whom I knighted), the Protestant Bishop of Down and clergy, the Catholic Bishop Denvir (an excellent and modest man), the Sheriff and Members for the county, with Lord Donegal (to whom the greater part of *Belfast* belongs), Dr. Henry, from the new College, and the Presbyterians (of whom there are a great many here). Lady Londonderry and her daughter also came on board. There was some delay in getting the gang-board down, as they had made much too large a one. Some planks on board were arranged, and we landed easily in this way. The landing-place was covered in, and very tastefully decorated. We got into Lord Londonderry's carriage with the two ladies, and Lord Londonderry himself got on the rumble behind with the two sergeant-footmen, Renwick and Birbage, both very tall, large men; and the three must have been far from comfortable.

The town was beautifully decorated with flowers, hangings, and very fine triumphal arches, the galleries full of people; and the reception very hearty. The people are a mixture of nations,* and the female beauty had almost disappeared.

I have all along forgotten to say that the favourite motto written up on most of the arches, &c., and in every place, was: "Cead mile failte,"* which means "A hundred thousand welcomes" in Irish, which is very like Gaelic; it is in fact *the* language, and has existed in books from the earliest period, whereas Gaelic has only been *written* since half a century, though it was always *spoken*. They often called out, "Cead mile failte!" and it appears in every sort of shape.

Lord Donegal rode on one side of the carriage and the General on the other. We stopped at the *Linen Hall* to see the exhibition of the flax and linen manufacture.* Lord Downshire and several other gentlemen received us there, and conducted us through the different rooms, where we saw the whole process in its different stages. First the plant, then the flax after being steeped; then the spun flax; lastly, the linen, cambric, and cloth of every sort and kind. It is really very interesting to see, and it is wonderful to what a state of perfection it has been brought.

We got into our carriages again. This time Lord Londonderry did not attempt to resume his uncomfortable position.

We went along through the *Botanic Garden*, and stopped and got out to look at the new College which is to be opened in October. It is a handsome building. We passed through several of the streets and returned to the place of embarkation. *Belfast* is a fine town, with some good buildings—for instance, the *Bank* and *Exchange*,—and is considered the *Liverpool* and *Manchester* of *Ireland*.*

I have forgotten to mention the Constabulary, who are a remarkably fine body of men, 13,000 in number (altogether in *Ireland*), all Irish, and chiefly Roman Catholics; and not one of whom, during the trying times last year, fraternised with the rebels.

We left amid immense cheering, and reached the "Victoria and Albert" at half-past six. It was blowing as hard as ever, and the getting in and out was as disagreeable as before. We decided on spending the night where we were, unless the wind should drop by three or four o'clock in the morning. Many bonfires were lighted on the surrounding hills and coasts.

Sunday, August 12.

The weather no better, and as there seemed no hope of its improvement, we decided on starting at two o'clock, and proceeding either to *Loch Ryan* or *Lamlash*. Lord Adolphus read the service at half-past ten, at which the two eldest children were also present.

I intend to create Bertie "Earl of Dublin," as a compliment to the town and country; he has no Irish title, though he is *born* with several Scotch ones (belonging to the heirs to the Scotch throne, and which we have inherited from James VI. of Scotland and I. of England); and this was one of my father's titles.*

The preparations on deck for the voyage were not encouraging; the boats hoisted up, the accommodation ladders drawn quite close up, every piece of carpet removed, and everything covered; and, indeed, my worst fears were realized. We started at two, and I went below and lay down shortly after, and directly we got out of the harbour the yacht began rolling for the first three-quarters of an hour, in a way which was dreadful, and there were two rolls, when the waves broke over the ship, which I never shall forget. It got gradually better, and at five we entered *Loch Ryan*, truly thankful to be at the end of our voyage. Albert came down to me and then I went up on deck, and he told me how awful it had been. The first great wave which came over the ship threw everybody down in every direction. Poor little Affie[+] was thrown down and sent rolling over the deck, and was drenched, for the deck was swimming with water. Albert told me it was quite frightful to see the enormous waves rising like a wall above the sides of the ship. We did not anchor so high up in *Loch Ryan* as we had done two years ago;* but it was a very safe quiet anchorage, and we were very glad to be there. Albert went on shore.

Monday, August 13.

We started at four o'clock in the morning, and the yacht rolled a little, but the motion was an easy one. We were in the *Clyde* by breakfast-time, but the day was very bad, constant squalls hiding the scenery. We left *Greenock* to our left, and proceeded a little way up *Loch Goil*, which opens into *Loch Long*, and is very fine; it seems extraordinary to have such deep water in a narrow loch and so immediately below the mountains, which are very rocky. We turned back and went up *Loch Long*, which I remembered so well, and which is so beautiful. We let go the anchor at *Arrochar*, the head of the lake, intending to land and proceed to *Loch Lomond*, where a steamer was waiting for us; but it poured with rain most hopelessly. We waited an hour in vain, and decided on stopping till after luncheon and making the attempt at three o'clock. We lunched and stepped into the boat, as it had cleared a little; but just then it began pouring again more violently than before, and we put back much disappointed, but Albert persevered, and he went off with Mr. Anson, Sir James Clark, and Captain Robinson almost directly afterwards. Just then it cleared and I felt so vexed that we had not gone; but there have been some terrible showers since. We left *Arrochar* a little before four, *Loch Long* looking beautiful as we returned.

Perth,
Tuesday, August 14.

We anchored yesterday in *Roseneath Bay*, close to *Roseneath*—a very pretty spot—and looking towards the mountains which you see in *Loch Goil*. One of them is called "The Duke of Argyll's Bowling-green."* Albert only returned soon after eight o'clock, having been able to see a

---

[+] Prince Alfred.

good deal of *Loch Lomond*, and even *Rob Roy's Cave*,* in spite of heavy showers. Captain Beechey (who was with us during the whole voyage in '47, and again the whole of this one to pilot us), Captain Crispin, and Captain Robinson (who met us this morning and piloted Albert in *Loch Lomond*, and did the same for us in '47), dined with us also, and we had much interesting conversation about the formation of glaciers, &c., in all of which Captain Beechey (who is a very intelligent man, and has been all over the world) took part. He was with Sir Edward Parry at the *North Pole*,* and told us that they had not seen daylight for four months. They heaped up snow over the ship and covered it in with boards to keep the cold off.

Balmoral,
Wednesday, August 15.

It seems like a dream to be here in our dear Highland home again; it certainly does not seem as if it were a year since we were here!* Now I must describe the doings of yesterday. We embarked on board the "Fairy" at a quarter to nine o'clock, and proceeded up the *Clyde* in pouring rain and high wind, and it was very stormy till after we had passed *Greenock*. We steamed past *Port Glasgow*, then came *Dumbarton* and *Erskine*. The river narrows and winds extraordinarily here, and you do not see *Glasgow* until you are quite close upon it. As we approached, the banks were lined with people, either on estrades or on the sea-shore, and it was amusing to see all those on the shore take flight, often too late, as the water bounded up from the swell caused by the steamer.

The weather, which had been dreadful, cleared up, just as we reached *Glasgow*, about eleven, and continued fine for the remainder of the day. Several addresses were presented on board, first by the Lord Provost, who was knighted, (Colonel Gordon's sword being used,) then one from the county, the clergy (Established Church and Free Kirk),* and from the Houses of Commerce. We landed immediately after this; the landing-place was very handsomely decorated. We then entered our carriage with the two eldest children, the two others following. Mr. Alison (the celebrated historian, who is the Sheriff) rode on one side of the carriage, and General Riddell (the Commander of the Forces in Scotland) on the other. The crowds assembled were quite enormous, but excellent order was kept and they were very enthusiastic. Mr. Alison said that there were 500,000 people out.* The town is a handsome one with fine streets built in stone, and many fine buildings and churches. We passed over a bridge commanding an extensive view down two quays, which Albert said was very like *Paris*. There are many large shops and warehouses, and the shipping is immense.

We went up to the old cathedral, where Principal MacFarlane, a very old man, received us, and directed our attention, as we walked through the church gates, to an immensely high chimney,* the highest I believe in existence, which belongs to one of the manufactories. The cathedral is a very fine one, the choir of which is fitted up as a Presbyterian church. We were shown the crypt and former burial-place of the bishops, which is in a very high state of preservation. The architecture is beautiful. It is in this crypt that the famous scene in *Rob Roy** is laid, where Rob Roy gives Frank Osbaldistone warning that he is in danger. There is an old monument of St. Kentigern, commonly called St. Mungo, the founder of the cathedral. We re-entered our carriages and went to the *University*, an ancient building, and which has produced many great and learned men. Here we got out and received an address. We only stopped a few minutes, and then went on again towards the *Exchange*, in front of which is Marochetti's equestrian statue of the Duke of Wellington,* very like and beautifully executed. We got out at the railway station and started almost immediately.

We passed *Stirling* in the distance, and a little before four we reached *Perth*, where the people were very friendly. We took the four children in our carriage and drove straight to the "George Inn," where we had the same rooms that we had last time.

Albert went out immediately to see the prison,* and at six we drove together along the *London Road* (as they rather strangely call it), towards *Moncrieffe*. The view was perfectly beautiful, and is the finest of *Perth* and the grand bridge over the *Tay*.

Wednesday, August 15.

At a quarter to eight o'clock we started. The two boys and Vicky were in the carriage with us, Alice followed with the ladies. It was a long journey, but through very beautiful scenery. We saw the *Grampians* as we left *Perth*. We first changed horses at *Blairgowrie*, 15 miles. Then came a very long stage of 20 miles, to the *Spittal of Glenshee*. We first passed the house of a Lieut.-Colonel Clark Rattray, called *Craig Hall*, overhanging a valley or glen above which we drove, and after this we came into completely wild Highland scenery, with barren rocky hills, through which the road winds to the *Spittal of Glenshee*,* which can scarcely be called a village, for it consists of only an inn and two or three cottages. We got out at the inn, where we found Mr. Farquharson and his son, and some of his men. Here we had some luncheon, and then set off again. The next stage of 15 miles to *Castleton* is over a very bad, and at night, positively dangerous road, through wild, grand scenery, with very abrupt turns and steep ascents. One sharp turn is called *The Devil's Elbow*. The Farquharson men joined us again here, some having gone on before, and others having followed from the inn, skipping over stones and rocks with the rapidity and lightness peculiar to Highlanders. They remained with us till we were able to trot on again.

We drove through a very fine pass called *Cairn Wall* and were overtaken by a heavy shower. When we reached *Castleton* the day had cleared, and we were able to open the carriage again. Here we were met by Sir Alexander Duff and the Duke of Leeds at the head of their men. Lady Duff, Mr. and Lady Agnes Duff, Miss Farquharson, and several of the children, and the Duchess of Leeds, came up to the carriage. The drive from *Castleton* to *Balmoral*, particularly the beautiful part from the *Balloch Buie*, was well known to us; and it was a great pleasure to see it all again in its beauty. Grant had met us at the *Spittal of Glenshee*, and ridden the whole way with us. At the door at *Balmoral* were Mackay, who was playing, and Macdonald in full dress. It was about four when we arrived.

Yachting Excursion.*

*On Board the Victoria and Albert,
Dartmouth,
Thursday, August* 20, 1846.

We steamed past the various places on the beautiful coast of *Devonshire* which we had passed three years ago—*Seaton, Sidmouth,* off which we stopped for ten minutes, *Axmouth, Teignmouth,* &c.;—till we came to *Babbicombe,* a small bay,* where we remained an hour. It is a beautiful spot, which before we had only passed at a distance. Red cliffs and rocks with wooded hills like *Italy,* and reminding one of a ballet or play where nymphs are to appear—such rocks and grottos, with the deepest sea, on which there was not a ripple. We intended to disembark and walk up the hill; but it came on to rain very much, and we could not do so. We tried to sketch the part looking towards *Torbay.* I never saw our good children looking better, or in higher spirits. I contrived to give Vicky a little lesson, by making her read in her English history.*

We proceeded on our course again at half past one o'clock, and saw *Torquay* very plainly, which is very fine. The sea looked so stormy and the weather became so thick that it was thought best to give up *Plymouth* (for the third time), and to put into that beautiful *Dartmouth,* and we accordingly did so, in pouring rain, the deck swimming with water, and all of us with umbrellas; the children being most anxious to see everything. Notwithstanding the rain, this place is lovely, with its wooded rocks and church and castle at the entrance. It puts me much in mind of the beautiful *Rhine,* and its fine ruined castles, and the *Lurlei.**

I am now below writing, and crowds of boats are surrounding us on all sides.

Plymouth Harbour,
Friday, August* 21.

We got under weigh by half-past six o'clock, and on looking out we saw the sea so calm and blue and the sun so bright that we determined to get up. It was a very fine day, but there was a great deal of swell. At length at half-past nine we entered the splendid harbour of *Plymouth,* and anchored again below *Mount Edgcumbe;** which, with its beautiful trees, including pines, growing down into the sea, looks more lovely than ever. I changed my dress and read innumerable letters and despatches, and then went on deck and saw the authorities—the Admirals and Generals. I did Vicky's lessons and wrote; and at half-past one we went on board the "Fairy," (leaving the children on board the "Victoria and Albert,") with all our ladies and gentlemen, as well as Sir James Clark, who has joined us here. We steamed up the *Tamar*,* going first a little way up the *St. Germans* river, which has very prettily wooded banks. *Trematon Castle** to the right, which belongs to Bertie as Duke of Cornwall, and *Jats* to the left, are extremely pretty. We stopped here and afterwards turned back and went up the *Tamar*, which at first seemed flat; but as we proceeded the scenery became quite beautiful—richly wooded hills, the trees growing down into the water, and the river winding so much as to have the effect of a lake. In this it reminded me so much of going up the *Rhine*,—though I don't think the river resembles the *Rhine*. Albert thought it like the *Danube*. The finest parts begin about *Saltash*, which is a small but prettily built town. To the right as you go up all is un-English looking; a little farther on is the mouth of the *Tavy*; here the river becomes very beautiful. We passed numbers of mines at work.* Further on, to the left, we came to *Pentillie Castle** situated on a height most beautifully wooded down to the water's edge, and the river winding rapidly above and below it. Albert said it reminded him of the situation of *Greinburg* on the *Danube*. Not much further on we came to the picturesque little village and landing-place of *Cothele*, at the foot of a thickly wooded bank, with a valley on one side. Here the river is very narrow. We landed, and drove up a steep hill under fine trees to the very curious old *House of Cothele*,* where we got out of the carriage. It is most curious in every way—as it stands in the same state as it was in the time of Henry VII. and is in great preservation—the old rooms hung with arras, &c.

We drove down another way under beautiful trees and above the fine valley; embarked and proceeded down the river. The evening was beautiful, the sun bright, and the sky and sea so blue. We arrived just too late for the launch of the frigate "Thetis." It reminded me so much of when we were here three years ago,* as we approached our yacht, surrounded by myriads of boats, and had to row through them in our barge. We returned at half-past five. The evening was delightful—clear, calm, and cloudless, but a good deal of noise in the boats around us. Lord and Lady Mount Edgcumbe and Sir James Clark dined with us.

Plymouth,
Saturday, August 22.

Albert was up at six o'clock, as he was to go to *Dartmoor Forest*.* At ten I went in the barge with the two children, the ladies, Baron Stockmar, and Lord Alfred Paget, and landed at *Mount Edgcumbe*, where we were received by Lady Mount Edgcumbe, her two boys, her sister and nieces, and beyond the landing-place by Lord Mount Edgcumbe. There were crowds where we landed, and I feel so shy and put out without Albert. I got into a carriage with the children and Lady Mount Edgcumbe—Lord Mount Edgcumbe going before us and the others following—and took a lovely drive along the road which overhangs the bay, commanding such beautiful views on all sides, and going under and by such fine trees. We had been there three years ago; but it is always a pleasure to see it again. The day very hot and a little hazy. We came to the house at eleven. The children went with their governess and the other children into the shade and had luncheon in the house, and I remained in the gallery—a very pretty room, with some fine pictures, and with a door opening on the garden, and commanding a lovely little bit of sea view, which I tried to sketch. A little after twelve we returned to the yacht, which had been beset with boats ever since six in the morning. Albert returned safely to me at one o'clock, much pleased with his trip; and said that *Dartmoor Forest* was like *Scotland*.

At two we went with our ladies and gentlemen, and without the children, again to the landing-place at *Mount Edgcumbe*, where we were received as before, and drove up to the house. There are some of the finest and tallest chestnut-trees in existence here, and the beech-trees grow very peculiarly—quite tall and straight—the branches growing upwards. We walked about the gallery and looked into Lady Mount Edgcumbe's little room at one end of it, which is charming, and full of pretty little things which she has collected, and then we took luncheon in a room where there are some fine portraits by Sir Joshua Reynolds.* They are all of the Mount Edgcumbe family, one of whom was his great patron. Sir Joshua was born a few miles from *Plymouth*. There are in the same room pictures by him when he first began to paint, which have kept their colour; then when he made experiments—and these are quite faded; and again of his works when he discovered his mistakes, and the colour of his pictures is then beautiful. We walked about the garden near the house, and then drove to the "Kiosk,"* by beautiful stone pines and pinasters, which interested Albert very much, and put me so much in mind of Mr. Lear's drawings.* The view from this "Kiosk," which is very high over the sea and town, is most beautiful, and the sea was like glass, not a ripple to be seen. We walked down a very pretty road or path through the woods and trees till we met the carriage, and we drove along that beautiful road, which is said to be a little like the *Cornice*,* overhanging the sea, down to the place of embarkation, where we took leave of them all, and returned to our yacht by half-past four. Poor Lord Mount Edgcumbe is in such a sad, helpless state; but so patient and cheerful. We went on board just to fetch the children, and then on to the "Fairy," and steamed in her round the harbour, or rather bay, in which there are such pretty spots; into the *Cat Water*, from whence we rowed in one of the barges a little way up the river to look at *Saltram*, Lord Morley's; after that back to the "Fairy," went in her into *Mill Bay*, *Sutton Pool*, and *Stonehouse*, and returned to the yacht by half-past six.

In Guernsey Bay, off St. Pierre, Guernsey,
Sunday, August 23.

On waking, the morning was so lovely that we could not help regretting that we could not delay our trip a little, by one day at least, as the Council* which was to have been on the 25th is now on the 29th. We thought, however, we could do nothing but sail for *Torbay*, at half-past nine, and for *Osborne* on Monday. While dressing, I kept thinking whether we could not manage to see *Falmouth*, or something or other. Albert thought we might perhaps manage to see one of the *Channel Islands*, and accordingly he sent for Lord Adolphus Fitzclarence, and it was settled that we should go to *Guernsey*,* which delighted me, as I had so long wished to see it. The day splendid. The General and Admiral came on board to take leave. Sir J. West is the Admiral, and General Murray, the General; and at about half-past nine we set off, and the sea the whole way was as calm as it was in '43. *Plymouth* is beautiful, and we shall always be delighted to return there.

For two hours we were in expectation of seeing land; but it was very hazy, and they did not know where we were—till about six, when land was seen by the "Fairy," who came to report it, and then all the other vessels went on before us. As we approached we were struck by the beauty of the *Guernsey* coast, in which there are several rocky bays, and the town of *St. Pierre* is very picturesquely built, down to the water's edge. You see *Sark* (or *Sercq*) as you enter the harbour to the right, and further on, close opposite *St. Pierre*, two islands close together—*Herm* and *Jethou*.* The bay with these fine islands is really most curious. We anchored at seven, immediately opposite *St. Pierre*, and with the two islands on the other side of us. We dined at eight, and found on going on deck the whole town illuminated, which had a very pretty effect, and must have been done very quickly, for they had no idea of our coming. It is built like a foreign town. The people speak mostly French amongst themselves.*

August 24.

St. Pierre is very picturesque-looking—with very high, bright-coloured houses built down almost into the sea. The College and Church are very conspicuous buildings. This island with its bold point, and the little one of *Cornet* with a sort of castle on it (close to which we were anchored), and the three islands of *Herm, Jethou,* and *Sark,* with innumerable rocks, are really very fine and peculiar,—especially as they then were in bright sunlight. We both sketched, and at a quarter to nine got into our barge with our ladies. The pier and shore were lined with crowds of people, and with ladies dressed in white, singing "God save the Queen," and strewing the ground with flowers. We walked to our carriage, preceded by General Napier, brother to Sir Charles (in *Scinde*), a very singular-looking old man, tall and thin, with an aquiline nose, piercing eyes, and white moustaches and hair. The people were extremely well-behaved and friendly, and received us very warmly as we drove through the narrow streets, which were decorated with flowers and flags, and lined with the *Guernsey* militia, 2,000 strong, with their several bands. Some of the militia were mounted.

The vegetation beyond the town is exceedingly fine; and the evergreens and flowers most abundant. The streets and hills steep, and the view from the fort, which is very high, (and where General Napier presented me with the keys,) is extremely beautiful. You look over the bay of *Guernsey,* and see opposite to you the islands of *Herm, Jethou,* and *Sark*; with *Alderney,** and the coast of *France, Cape de la Hague,* to the left in the distance, and to the right in the distance, *Jersey.* The island appears very flourishing. In the town they speak English, but in the country French, and this is the same in all the islands. They belonged to the Duchy of Normandy, and have been in our possession ever since William the Conqueror's time. King John was the last of their sovereigns who visited them. We drove along the pier, and then embarked amidst great cheering. It was all admirably managed; the people are extremely loyal.

We got under weigh a little before one and in about an hour-and-a-half we came close to *Alderney,* seeing all the time the French coast, *Cape de la Hague,* very plainly to our right, and leaving the *Casquets Lights** to our left. *Alderney* is quite different from all the other islands, excessively rocky and barren, and the rocks in and under the sea are most frightful.

SECOND YACHTING EXCURSION.

On Board the Victoria and Albert,
Off St. Heliers, Jersey,
Wednesday, September 2, 1846.

At a quarter-past seven o'clock we set off with Vicky, Bertie, Lady Jocelyn, Miss Kerr, Mdlle. Gruner, Lord Spencer, Lord Palmerston, and Sir James Clark (Mr. Anson and Colonel Grey being on board the "Black Eagle"), and embarked at *Osborne Pier.* There was a good deal of swell. It was fine, but very cold at first. At twelve we saw *Alderney,* and between two and three got into the *Alderney Race,* where there was a great deal of rolling, but not for long. We passed between *Alderney* and the French coast—*Cape de la Hague*—and saw the other side of *Alderney*; and then, later, *Sark, Guernsey,* and the other islands. After passing the *Alderney Race* it became quite smooth; and then Bertie put on his sailor's dress,* which was beautifully made by the man on board who makes for our sailors. When he appeared, the officers and sailors, who were all assembled on deck to see him, cheered, and seemed delighted with him.

The coast of *Jersey* is very beautiful, and we had to go nearly all round, in order to get to *St. Heliers.** We first passed the point called *Rondnez,* then *Grosnez* with a tower, *St. Ouen's Bay, La Rocca,* a curious old tower on a rock, and then *Brelade's Bay.* The red cliffs and rocks, with the setting sun gilding and lighting them all up, were beautiful. At last, at a quarter to seven, we arrived in this fine large bay of *St. Aubin,* in which lies *St. Heliers*; and after dinner we went on deck to see the illumination and the bonfires.

Off St. Heliers,
Thursday, September 3.

A splendid day. I never saw a more beautiful deep blue sea, quite like *Naples*; and Albert said that this fine bay of *St. Aubin,* in which we lie, really is like *Naples. Noirmont Point* terminates in a low tower to our left, with *St. Aubin* and a tower on a rock in front of it; farther in, and to our right, *Elizabeth Castle,* a picturesque fort on a rock, with the town of *St. Heliers* behind it.

The colouring and the effect of light were indescribably beautiful. We got into our barge with our ladies and gentlemen, and then went on board the "Fairy," until we were close to the harbour, and then we got into the barge again. We landed at the stairs of the *Victoria Harbour*, amid the cheers of the numberless crowds, guns firing, and bands playing; were received, as at *Guernsey*, by all the ladies of the town, very gaily dressed, who, strewing flowers on our way, conducted us to a canopy, where I received the address of the States and of the militia.

We then got into our carriage and drove along the pier: Colonel Le Couteur, my militia aide-de-camp, riding by my side, with other officers, and by Albert's side Colonel Le Breton, commanding the militia, who, 5,000 strong, lined the streets, and were stationed along the pier. The States walking in front. The crowds were immense, but everything in excellent order, and the people most enthusiastic, though not more so than the good *Guernsey* people; the town is much larger, and they had much longer time for preparations; the decorations and arches of flowers were really beautifully done, and there were numberless kind inscriptions. All the country people here speak French, and so did the police who walked near us. It was a very gratifying reception. There was a seat in one of the streets filled by Frenchwomen from *Granville*, curiously dressed with white handkerchiefs on their heads. After passing through several streets we drove up to the *Government House*, but did not get out. General Gibbs, the Governor, is very infirm.

We then proceeded at a quicker pace—the walking procession having ceased—through the interior of the island, which is extremely pretty and very green,—orchards without end, as at *Mayence*. We passed the curious old tower of *La Hougue Bic*, of very ancient date, and went to the *Castle of Mont Orgueil*,* in *Grouville Bay*, very beautifully situated, completely overhanging the sea, and where Robert, Duke of Normandy, son of William the Conqueror, is said to have lived. We walked part of the way up, and from one of the batteries, where no guns are now mounted, you command the bay, and the French coast is distinctly seen, only 13 miles distant. The people are very proud that *Mont Orgueil* had never been taken; but I have since learnt it was taken by surprise and held for a few days; *Guernsey*, however, *never* was taken.

We then returned to our carriage, and proceeded to the pier by a shorter road, and through a different part of the town. There is a peculiar elm-tree in the island, which is very pretty, and unlike any other,—the leaf and the way it grows almost resembling the acacia. The crowd was very great and the heat very intense in going back.

We re-embarked in the barge, but had only to go a few yards to the "Fairy." The situation of the harbour is very fine,—and crowned with the fort, and covered by numbers of people, was like an amphitheatre. The heat of the sun, and the glare, had made me so ill and giddy that

I remained below the greater part of the afternoon, and Albert went out for an hour on the "Fairy."

Falmouth Harbour,
Friday, Sept. 4.

A beautiful day again, with the same brilliantly blue sea. At a quarter to eight o'clock we got under weigh. There was a great deal of motion at first, and for the greater part of the day the ship pitched, but getting up the sails steadied her. From five o'clock it became quite smooth; at half-past five we saw land, and at seven we entered *Falmouth Harbour*, where we were immediately surrounded by boats. The evening was beautiful and the sea as smooth as glass, and without even a ripple. The calmest night possible, with a beautiful moon, when we went on deck; every now and then the splashing of oars and the hum of voices were heard; but they were the only sounds, unlike the constant dashing of the sea against the vessel, which we heard all the time we were at *Jersey*.

Mount's Bay, Cornwall,
Saturday, September 5.

At eight o'clock we left *Falmouth* and proceeded along the coast of *Cornwall*, which becomes bold and rugged beyond the *Lizard Point* and as one approaches *Land's End*. At about twelve we passed *Land's End*, which is very fine and rocky, the view from thence opening beautifully. We passed quite close by the *Longships*,* some rocks on which stands a lighthouse. The sea was unusually smooth for the *Land's End*. We went beyond a point with some rocks near it, called *The Brisons*,* and then steamed back; the famous Botallack mine* lies here. A little before two we landed in this beautiful *Mount's Bay*, close below *St. Michael's Mount*,* which is very fine. When the bay first opened to our view the sun was lighting up this beautiful castle, so peculiarly built on a lofty rock, and which forms an island at high water.

In entering the bay we passed the small village of *Mousehole* and the town of *Penzance*, which is prettily situated, about one mile and a half from *St. Michael's Mount*. The day brightened just as we arrived, and the sea again became so blue. Soon after our arrival we anchored; the crowd of boats was beyond everything; numbers of Cornish pilcher fishermen,* in their curious large boats, kept going round and round, and then anchored, besides many other boats full of people. They are a very noisy, talkative race, and speak a kind of English hardly to be understood.*

During our voyage I was able to give Vicky her lessons. At three o'clock we all got into the barge, including the children and Mdlle. Gruner, their governess, and rowed through an avenue of boats of all descriptions to the "Fairy," where we went on board. The getting in and out of the barge was no easy task. There was a good deal of swell, and the "Fairy" herself rolled amazingly. We steamed round the bay to look at *St. Michael's Mount* from the other side, which is even more beautiful, and then went on to *Penzance*. Albert landed near *Penzance* with all the gentlemen, except Lord Spencer (who is most agreeable, efficient, and useful at sea, being a Captain of the Navy) and Colonel Grey, and went to see the smelting of copper and tin, and the works in serpentine stone at *Penzance*. We remained here a little while without going on, in order to sketch, and returned to the "Victoria and Albert" by half-past four, the boats crowding round us in all directions; and when Bertie showed himself the people shouted:—"Three cheers for the Duke of Cornwall!" Albert returned a little before seven, much gratified by what he had seen, and bringing home specimens of the serpentine stone.*

Mount's Bay.
Sunday, September 6.

A hazy, dull-looking morning, but as calm as it possibly could be. At half-past eight o'clock we got into our barge, with Miss Kerr and Lord Spencer, and proceeded without any standard to the little harbour below *St. Michael's Mount*. Behind *St. Michael's Mount* is the little town of *Marazion*, or "Market Jew,"* which is supposed to have taken its name from the Jews having in former times trafficked there. We disembarked and walked up the *Mount* by a circuitous rugged path over rocks and turf, and entered the old castle, which is beautifully kept, and must be a nice house to live in; as there are so many good rooms in it. The dining-room, made out of the refectory, is very pretty; it is surrounded by a frieze, representing ancient hunting. The chapel is excessively curious. The organ is much famed; Albert played a little on it, and it sounded very fine. Below the chapel is a dungeon, where some years ago was discovered the skeleton of a large man without a coffin; the entrance is in the floor of one of the pews. Albert went down with Lord Spencer, and afterwards went up with him and Sir James Clark (who, with Lord Palmerston and Colonel Grey, had joined us,) to the tower, on the top of which is "St. Michael's chair," which, it is said, betrothed couples run up to, and whoever gets first into the chair will have at home the government of the house; and the old house-keeper—a nice tidy old woman—said many a couple "does go there!" though Albert and Lord Spencer said it was the awkwardest place possible to get at. *St. Michael's Mount* belongs to Sir J. St. Aubyn. There were several drawings there of *Mont St. Michel* in *Normandy*, which is very like this one; and was, I believe, inhabited by the same order of monks as this was, *i.e.* Benedictines. We walked down again, had to step over another boat in order to get into our barge, as the tide was so very low, and returned on board the yacht before ten.

The view from the top of *St. Michael's* is very beautiful and very extensive, but unfortunately it was too thick and hazy to see it well. A low ridge of sand separates *St. Michael's Mount* from *Marazion* at low water, and the sea at high water. From the sand to the summit of the castle is about 250 feet. The chapel was originally erected, they say, for the use of pilgrims who came here; and it owes its name to a tradition of St. Michael the Archangel having rested on the rock.

At half-past eleven Lord Spencer read on deck the short morning service generally read at sea, which only lasted twenty or twenty-five minutes. The awning was put up, and flags on the sides; and all the officers and sailors were there, as well as ourselves. A flag was hoisted, as is usual when the service is performed on board ship, and Lord Spencer read extremely well.

Albert made a most beautiful little sketch of *St. Michael's Mount*. Soon after two we left *Mount's Bay*. About four we came opposite to some very curious serpentine rocks, between *Mount's Bay* and *Lizard Point*, and we stopped, that Albert might land. The gentlemen went with him. Lord Spencer soon returned, saying that Albert was very anxious I should see the beautiful little cave in these serpentine rocks; and accordingly I got into the barge, with the children, and ladies, and Lord Spencer, and we rowed to these rocks, with their caves and little creeks. There were many cormorants and seagulls on the rocks. We returned again, and were soon joined by Albert, who brought many fine specimens which he had picked up. The stone is really beautifully marked with red and green veins.

We proceeded on our course, and reached *Falmouth* before seven. The fine afternoon was changed to a foggy, dull, cold evening. We have had on board with us, since we left *Falmouth*, Mr. Taylor, mineral agent to the Duchy of Cornwall,* a very intelligent young man, married to a niece of Sir Charles Lemon's.

Falmouth, Monday, September 7.

Immediately after breakfast, Albert left me to land and visit some mines. The corporation of *Penryn* were on board, and very anxious to see "The Duke of Cornwall," so I stepped out of the pavilion on deck with Bertie, and Lord Palmerston told them that that was "The Duke of Cornwall;" and the old mayor of *Penryn* said that "he hoped he would grow up a blessing to his parents and to his country."

A little before four o'clock, we all got into the barge, with the two children, and rowed to the "Fairy." We rowed through a literal *lane* of boats, full of people, who had surrounded the yacht ever since early in the morning, and proceeded up the river by *St. Just's Pool*, to the left of which lies Sir C. Lemon's place, and *Trefusis** belonging to Lord Clinton. We went up the *Truro*, which is beautiful,—something like the *Tamar*, but almost finer, though not so bold as *Pentillie Castle* and *Cothele*,—winding between banks entirely wooded with stunted oak, and full of numberless creeks. The prettiest are *King Harry's Ferry* and a spot near *Tregothnan* (Lord Falmouth's), where there is a beautiful little boat-house, quite in the woods, and on the river, at the point where the *Tregony* separates from the *Truro*. Albert said the position of this boat-house put him in mind of Tell's Chapel in *Switzerland*. We went a little way up the *Tregony*, which is most beautiful, with high sloping banks, thickly wooded down to the water's edge. Then we turned back and went up the *Truro* to *Malpas*, another bend of the river, from whence one can see *Truro*, the capital of *Cornwall*. We stopped here awhile, as so many boats came out from a little place called *Sunny Corner*, just below *Truro*, in order to see us; indeed the whole population poured out on foot and in carts, &c. along the banks; and cheered, and were enchanted when Bertie was held up for them to see. It was a very pretty, gratifying sight.

We went straight on to *Swan Pool** outside *Pendennis Castle,** where we got into the barge, and rowed near to the shore to see a net drawn. Mr. Fox, a Quaker, who lives at *Falmouth*, and has sent us flowers, fruit, and many other things, proposed to put in his net and draw, that we might see all sorts of fish caught, but when it was drawn there was not one fish! So we went back to the "Fairy." The water near the shore in *Swan Pool* is so wonderfully clear that one could count the pebbles.

Tuesday, September 8.

A wet morning when we rose and breakfasted with the children. At about ten o'clock we entered *Fowey*, which is situated in a creek much like *Dartmouth*, only not so beautiful, but still very pretty. We got into the barge (leaving the children on board, and also Lord Spencer, who was not quite well), and landed at *Fowey* with our ladies and gentlemen, and Mr. Taylor, whom we had brought with us from *Falmouth*. We got into our carriage with the ladies, the gentlemen following in others, and drove through some of the narrowest streets I ever saw in *England*, and up perpendicular hills in the streets—it really quite alarmed one; but we got up and through them quite safely. We then drove on for a long way, on bad and narrow roads, higher and higher up, commanding a fine and very extensive view of the very hilly country of *Cornwall*, its hills covered with fields, and intersected by hedges. At last we came to one field where there was no road whatever, but we went down the hill quite safely, and got out of the carriage at the top of another, where, surrounded by woods, stands a circular ruin, covered with ivy, of the old castle of *Restormel*,* belonging to the Duchy of Cornwall, and in which the last Earl of Cornwall lived in the thirteenth century. It was very picturesque from this point.

We visited here the Restormel mine,* belonging also to the Duchy of Cornwall. It is an iron mine, and you go in on a level. Albert and I got into one of the trucks and were dragged in by miners, Mr. Taylor walking behind us. The miners wear a curious woollen dress, with a cap like this:  and the dress thus:

and they generally have a candle stuck in front of the cap. This time candlesticks were stuck along the sides of the mine, and those who did not drag or push the truck carried lights. Albert and the gentlemen wore miners' hats. There was no room for any one to pass between the trucks and the rock, and only just room enough to hold up one's head, and not always that. It had a most curious effect, and there was something unearthly about this lit-up cavern-like place. We got out and scrambled a little way to see the veins of ore, and Albert knocked off some pieces; but in general it is blown by gunpowder, being so hard. The miners seemed so pleased at seeing us, and are intelligent, good people. It was quite dazzling when we came into daylight again.

We then got into our carriage and passed through the small town of *Lostwithiel*, where an address was presented to us, and then we passed through Mr. Agar Robarts' Park, which reminded one of *Cothele*. We returned by the same road till near *Fowey*, when we went through some of the narrowest lanes I almost ever drove through, and so fearfully stony. We drove along high above the river to *Place*, belonging to Mr. Treffry,* which has been restored according to drawings in his possession, representing the house as it was in former times. A lady of that name defended the house against the French during the absence of her husband, in the fourteenth or fifteenth century. The old gentleman showed us all over the house, and into an unfinished hall, lined with marble and porphyry, all of which came from *Cornwall*. We then walked down to the place of embarkation and proceeded at once to the yacht. Mr. Taylor deserved the greatest credit for all the arrangements. He and his father are what are called "Adventurers" of the mine.

Osborne,
Wednesday, September 9.

We got up about seven o'clock and found we had just passed *The Needles*.

Visit to the Lakes of Killarney.

Tuesday, August 27, 1861.

At eleven o'clock we all started in our own sociable, and another of our carriages, and on ponies, for *Ross Castle*,* the old ruin which was a celebrated stronghold, and from which the Kenmare family take their name. Here there was an immense crowd and a great many boats. We got into a very handsome barge of eight oars—beautifully rowed. Lord Castlerosse steering. The four children,* and Lady Churchill, Lady Castlerosse, and Lord Granville were with us.

We rowed first round *Innisfallen Island** and some way up the *Lower Lake*. The view was magnificent. We had a slight shower, which alarmed us all, from the mist which overhung the mountains; but it suddenly cleared away and became very fine and very hot. At a quarter to one we landed at the foot of the beautiful hill of *Glena*, where on a small sloping lawn there is a very pretty little cottage. We walked about, though it was overpoweringly hot, to see some of the splendid views. The trees are beautiful,—oak, birch, arbutus, holly, yew,—all growing down to the water's edge, intermixed with heather. The hills, rising abruptly from the lake, are completely wooded, which gives them a different character from those in *Scotland*, though they often reminded me of the dear *Highlands*. We returned to the little cottage, where the quantity of midges and the smell of peat made us think of *Alt-na-Guithasach*. Upstairs, from Lady Castlerosse's little room, the view was towards a part of the *Lower Lake*, the outline of which is rather low. We lunched, and afterwards re-embarked, and then took that most beautiful row up the rapid, under the *Old Weir Bridge*, through the channel which connects the two lakes, and which is very intricate and narrow. Close to our right as we were going, we stopped under the splendid hill of the *Eagle's Nest** to hear the *echo* of a bugle; the sound of which, though blown near by, was not heard. We had to get out near the *Weir Bridge* to let the empty boats be pulled up by the men. The sun had come out and lit up the really magnificent scenery splendidly; but it was most oppressively hot. We wound along till we entered the *Upper Lake*, which opened upon us with all its high hills—the highest, *The Reeks*, 3,400 feet high—and its islands and points covered with splendid trees;—such arbutus (quite large trees) with yews, making a beautiful foreground. We turned into a small bay or creek, where we got out and walked a short way in the shade, and up to where a tent was placed, just opposite a waterfall called *Derricaunihy*, a lovely spot, but terribly infested by midges. In this tent was tea, fruit, ice, cakes, and everything most tastefully arranged. We just took some tea, which was very refreshing in the great heat of this relaxing climate. The vegetation is quite that of a jungle—ferns of all kinds and shrubs and trees,—all springing up luxuriantly. We entered our boats and went back the same way we came, admiring greatly the beauty of the scenery; and this time went down the rapids in the boat. No boats, except our own, had followed us beyond the rapids. But below them there were a great many, and the scene was very animated and the people very noisy and enthusiastic. The Irish always give that peculiar shrill shriek—unlike anything one ever hears anywhere else.

Wednesday, August 28.

At a quarter-past eleven we started on a most beautiful drive, of which I annex the route.* We drove with Mrs. Herbert and Bertie in our sociable, driven from the box by Wagland;[†] and, though the highest mountains were unfortunately occasionally enveloped in mist, and we had slight showers, we were enchanted with the extreme beauty of the scenery. The peeps of the lake; the splendid woods full of the most magnificent arbutus, which in one place form, for a few yards, an avenue under which you drive, with the rocks,—which are very peculiar—all made it one of the finest drives we had ever taken. Turning up by the village and going round, the *Torc* mountain reminded us of *Scotland*—of the woods above *Abergeldie*, of *Craig Daign* and *Craig Clunie*. It was *so* fine. We got out at the top of the *Torc Waterfall* and walked down to the foot of it. We came home at half-past one. At four we started for the boats, quite close by. The *Muckross Lake* is extremely beautiful; at the beginning of our expedition it looked dark and severe in the mist and showers which kept coming on, just as it does in the *Highlands*. Mr. Herbert steered. Our girls, Mrs. Herbert, Lady Churchill, and Lord Granville were in the boat with us. The two boys went in a boat rowed by gentlemen, and the rest in two other boats. At Mr. and Mrs. Herbert's request I christened one of the points which runs into the lake with a bottle of wine, Albert

---

[†] My coachman since 1857; and a good, zealous servant. He entered the Royal service in 1831, and rode as postilion for seventeen years. His father has been thirty-two years porter in the Royal Mews at Windsor, and is now seventy-five years old; and has been sixty years in the service. His grandfather was also in the Royal service, having entered it in 1788; and his daughter is nursery-maid to the Prince of Wales's children. Four generations, therefore, have served the Royal Family.

holding my arm when we came close by, so that it was most successfully smashed.

When we emerged from under *Brickeen Bridge* we had a fine view of the *Lower Lake* and of the scenery of yesterday, which rather puzzled me, seeing it from another *point de vue*. At *Benson's Point* we stopped for some time, merely rowing about backwards and forwards, or remaining stationary, watching for the deer (all this is a deer forest as well as at *Glena*), which we expected the dogs would find and bring down into the water. But in vain: we waited till past six and no deer came. The evening had completely cleared and became quite beautiful; and the effect of the numbers of boats full of people, many with little flags, rowing about in every direction and cheering and shouting, lit up by the evening light, was charming. At *Darby's Garden** the shore was densely crowded, and many of the women in their blue cloaks waded into the water, holding their clothes up to their knees.

We were home by seven o'clock, having again a slight sprinkling of rain.

MORE LEAVES
FROM THE JOURNAL
OF
A LIFE IN THE HIGHLANDS,
FROM 1862 TO 1882

1866.

MORE LEAVES
FROM THE JOURNAL
OF
A LIFE IN THE HIGHLANDS,
FROM 1862 TO 1882.

FOURTH EDITION

LONDON:
SMITH, ELDER, & CO., 15 WATERLOO PLACE.
1884.

All rights reserved.

PREFACE.

The little volume "Our Life in the Highlands," published fifteen years ago, with its simple records of the never-to-be-forgotten days spent with him "who made the writer's life bright and happy," was received with a warmth of sympathy and interest which was very gratifying to her heart. The kind editor of that volume is no longer here to advise and help her, though friendly assistance has not been wanting on the present occasion. But remembering the feeling with which that little book was received, the writer thinks that the present volume may equally evoke sympathy, as, while describing a very altered life, it shows how her sad and suffering heart was soothed and cheered by the excursions and incidents it recounts, as well as by the simple mountaineers, from whom she learnt many a lesson of resignation and faith, in the pure air and quiet of the beautiful Highlands.

The writer wishes at the same time to express her gratitude to those who are mentioned throughout this volume for the devotion and kindness which contributed so much to her enjoyment of the varied scenes and objects of interest of which these pages contain the unpretending record.

Osborne:
December 22, 1883.

TO

MY LOYAL HIGHLANDERS

AND ESPECIALLY

TO THE MEMORY OF

MY DEVOTED PERSONAL ATTENDANT

AND FAITHFUL FRIEND

JOHN BROWN

THESE RECORDS OF MY WIDOWED LIFE

IN SCOTLAND

ARE

GRATEFULLY DEDICATED

VICTORIA R. I.

CONTENTS.

	DATE	PAGE
Building of the Prince's Cairn	21 Aug. 1862	183
Visit to the Old Cairn on the Prince's Birthday	26 Aug. 1862	185
First Visit to the Prince's Cairn after its Completion	19 May 1863	186
Visit to Blair	15 Sept. 1863	187
Carriage Accident	7 Oct. 1863	189
Unveiling of the Prince's Statue at Aberdeen	13 Oct. 1863	192
Expedition to Invermark	19 Sept. 1865	197
First Visit to Dunkeld	9 Oct. 1865	201
Second Visit to Dunkeld	1 Oct. 1866	209
Opening of the Aberdeen Waterworks	16 Oct. 1866	219
Halloween	31 Oct. 1866–7	221
Visit to Floors and the Scotch Border Country	20 Aug. 1867	222
Visit to Glenfiddich	24 Sept. 1867	231
Unveiling of the Prince's Statue at Balmoral	15 Oct. 1867	238
A House-warming at the Glassalt Shiel	1 Oct. 1868	240
"Juicing the Sheep"	21 Oct. 1868	242
A Highland "Kirstnin" (Christening)	24 Oct. 1868	243
A Second Christening	1 Nov. 1868	244
Widow Grant	22 Aug. 1869	245
Visit to Invertrossachs	1 Sept. 1869	246
Sheep Clipping	13 June 1870	260
Betrothal of Princess Louise to the Marquis of Lorne	3 Oct. 1870	261

Communion Sunday at Crathie	13 Nov. 1871	262
The "Spate"	11 June 1872	264
Visit to Holyrood and Edinburgh	13 Aug, 1872	267
Visit to Dunrobin	6 Sept. 1872	274
Dr. Norman Macleod	March 1873	288
Visit To Inverlochy	9 Sept. 1873	301
Home-coming of their Royal Highnesses the Duke and Duchess of Edinburgh	29 Aug. 1874	321
Departure of the Prince of Wales from Abergeldie before leaving for India	17 Sept. 1875	322
Visit to Inveraray	21 Sept. 1875	324
Highland Funeral	21 Oct. 1875	338
Unveiling of the Statue of the Prince Consort at Edinburgh	17 Aug. 1876	340
Presentation of Colours to "The Royal Scots"	26 Sept. 1876	343
Expedition to Loch Maree	12 Sept. 1877	345
Visit to Broxmouth	23 Aug. 1878	356
Death of Sir Thomas Biddulph at Abergeldie Mains	28 Sept. 1878	363
Memorial Cross to the Princess Alice, Grand Duchess of Hesse	22 May 1879	365
Death of the Prince Imperial	19 June 1879	367
Home-Coming of their Royal Highnesses the Duke and Duchess of Connaught	5 Sept. 1879	371
His Royal Highness the Duke of Connaught's Cairn	8 Sept. 1879	372
Visit to the Glen Gelder Shiel	6 Oct. 1879	374
Victory of Tel-el-Kebir and Home-Coming of their Royal Highnesses the Duke and Duchess of Albany	11 Sept. 1882	375
Conclusion		378

LIST OF ILLUSTRATIONS.

Portrait of Her Majesty the Queen	*To face Title*
" Mr. John Grant	*page* 184
" H.R.H. the Princess Helena	198
" Mr. John Brown	202
" H.R.H. the Princess Louise	210
" General Grey	220
" Lady Churchill	230
Sharp, the Queen's Collie	236
View of the Glassalt Shiel	239
Portrait of H.R.H. the Princess Beatrice	268
Noble, the Queen's Collie	302
Memorial Cross to H.R.H. the Princess Alice	366
View of Glen Gelder Shiel	373

CALEDONIA! thou land of the mountain and rock,
   Of the ocean, the mist, and the wind—
Thou land of the torrent, the pine, and the oak,
   Of the roebuck, the hart, and the hind!
   .   .   .   .   .   .
Thou land of the valley, the moor, and the hill,
   Of the storm and the proud-rolling wave—
Yes, thou art the land of fair liberty still,
   And the land of my forefathers' grave!
THE ETTRICK SHEPHERD.*

A nation famed for song and beauty's charms,—
Zealous yet modest, innocent though free;
Patient of toil, serene amidst alarms,
Inflexible in faith, invincible in arms.
BEATTIE'S *Minstrel*.*

Building of the Prince's Cairn.

Balmoral,
Thursday, August 21, 1862.

At eleven o'clock started off in the little pony-chair (drawn by the *Corriemulzie* pony, and led by Brown), Bertie, who had come over from *Birkhall*,* on foot, the two girls on ponies, and the two little boys, who joined us later, for *Craig Lowrigan*; and I actually drove in the little carriage to the very top, turning off from the path and following the track where the carts had gone. Grant and Duncan pushed the carriage behind. Sweet Baby (Beatrice) we found at the top. The view was so fine, the day so bright, and the heather so beautifully pink—but no pleasure, no joy! all dead!

And here at the top is the foundation of the cairn*—forty feet wide—to be erected to my precious Albert, which will be seen all down the valley. I and my poor six orphans all placed stones on it; and our initials, as well as those of the three absent ones, are to be carved on stones all round it. I felt very shaky and nervous.

It is to be thirty-five feet high, and the following inscription to be placed on it:—

TO THE BELOVED MEMORY

OF

ALBERT, THE GREAT AND GOOD

PRINCE CONSORT,

RAISED BY HIS BROKEN-HEARTED WIDOW,

VICTORIA R.

AUGUST 21, 1862.

"He being made perfect in a short time fulfilled a long time;
For his soul pleased the Lord,
Therefore hastened He to take him
Away from among the wicked."
Wisdom of Solomon, iv. 13, 14.

Walked down to where the rough road is, and this first short attempt at walking in the heather shook me and tired me much.

Visit to the Old Cairn on the Prince's Birthday.

Balmoral,
August 26, 1862.

I went out at twelve with the two girls on ponies (I in the little carriage), Bertie on foot. We went to see the obelisk building to His dear memory: Bertie left us there, and we went on round by the village, up *Craig-Gowan*, in the little carriage, over the heather till we reached near to the old cairn of 1852. Grant said: "I thought you would like to be here to-day, on His birthday!"—so entirely was he of opinion that this beloved day, and even the 14th of December, must not be looked upon as a day of mourning. "That's not the light to look at it." There is so much true and strong faith in these good, simple people.

Walked down by the *Fog[+] House*,* all pink with heather; the day beautifully fine and bright.

[+] Scotch for "Moss."

First Visit to the Prince's Cairn After its Completion.

Balmoral,
Tuesday, May 19, 1863.*

I went out in the little carriage (Donald Stewart leading the pony, as John Brown was unwell) with Lenchen and Dr. Robertson (Grant following), and drove up to the cairn on the top of *Craig Lowrigan*, which is a fine sharp pyramid admirably constructed out of granite without any mortar. The inscription is very well engraved and placed. There is a good path made up to the top of the hill.

Visit to Blair, 1863.

Balmoral,
Tuesday, September 15, 1863.

At twenty minutes to eight we reached *Perth*, where we breakfasted and dressed, and at twenty minutes past nine I left with Lenchen, Augusta Bruce, and General Grey, for *Blair*, going past *Dunkeld*, where we had not been since 1844,* and which is so beautifully situated, and *Pitlochry*, through the splendid *Pass of Killiecrankie* (which we so often drove through in 1844), past Mr. Butter's place *Faskally*, on to *Blair*, having a distant peep at the entrance to *Glen Tilt*, and *Schiehallion*, which it made and makes me sick to think of.* At the small station were a few people—the poor Duke's Highlanders (keepers), the dear Duchess, Lord Tullibardine, and Captain Drummond of *Megginch*.

The Duchess was much affected, still more so when she got into the carriage with me. Lenchen and the others went in the boat carriage, the one we had gone in not two years ago!

We drove at once to the house which we had visited in such joyful and high spirits October 9, two years ago.* The Duchess took me to the same room which I had been in on that day, and, after talking a little to me of this dreadful affliction,+ she went to see if the Duke was ready. She soon returned, and I followed her downstairs along the passage, full of stags' horns, which we walked along, together with the poor Duke, in 1861. When I went in, I found him standing up very much altered; it was very sad. He kissed my hand, gave me the white rose which, according to tradition, is presented by the Lords of Athole on the occasion of the Sovereign's visit, and we sat a little while with him. It is a small room, full of his rifles and other implements and attributes of sport—now for ever useless to him! A sad, sad contrast. He seemed very much pleased and gratified.

We went upstairs again and took some breakfast, in the very same room where we breakfasted on that very happy, never-to-be-forgotten day, full of joy and expectation. While we were breakfasting the door opened, and in walked the Duke in a thick MacDougal. Mrs. Drummond and Miss Moncreiffe (the Duchess's pretty, amiable future daughter-in-law) were there, and also Miss MacGregor, but we did not see her. The poor

---

+ The Duke was suffering from an incurable illness.

Duke insisted on going with me to the station, and he went in the carriage with the Duchess and me. At the station he got out, walked about, and gave directions. I embraced the dear Duchess and gave the Duke my hand, saying, "Dear Duke, God bless you!" He had asked permission that his men, the same who had gone with us through the glen on that happy day two years ago, might give me a cheer, and he led them on himself. Oh! it was so dreadfully sad! To think of the contrast to the time two years ago, when my darling was so well and I so happy with him, and just beginning to recover from my great sorrow for dearest Mama's death—looking forward to many more such delightful expeditions; and the poor Duke then full of health and strength, walking the whole way, and at the "March"[+] stopping to drink to our health and asking us to come again whenever we liked, and giving a regular Highland cheer in Highland fashion, returned by our men, the pipers playing, and all, all so gay, so bright! And I so eager for next year's expeditions, which I ought not to have been! Oh! how little we know what is before us! How uncertain is life! I felt very sad, but was so much occupied with the poor Duke,[†] for whom I truly grieve, that I did not feel the trial of returning to *Blair* in such terribly altered circumstances, as I should otherwise have done.

At *Stanley Junction* we joined the others, and proceeded as usual to *Aboyne*, whence we drove in open carriages—Lenchen, Alfred, and Baby with me—and reached *Balmoral* at twenty minutes past six. It was very cold. Bertie and Alix were at the door, and stayed a little while afterwards. How strange they should be at *Abergeldie*! A few years ago dear Mama used to receive us.

[+] The boundary of the Duke's property. "March" is the word commonly used in Scotland to express the outer limit or boundary of land.

[†] He died in the following year, January 16, 1864.

Carriage Accident.

Wednesday, October 7, 1863.

 A hazy morning. I decided by Alice's advice, with a heavy heart, to make the attempt to go to *Clova*. At half-past twelve drove with Alice and Lenchen to *Altnagiuthasach*, where we lunched, having warmed some broth and boiled some potatoes, and then rode up and over the *Capel Month* in frequent slight snow-showers. All the high hills white with snow; and the view of the green *Clova* hills covered with snow at the tops, with gleams of sunshine between the showers, was very fine, but it took us a long time, and I was very tired towards the end, and felt very sad and lonely. *Loch Muich* looked beautiful in the setting sun as we came down, and reminded me of many former happy days I spent there. We stopped to take tea at *Altnagiuthasach*. Grant was not with us, having gone with Vicky.[†] We started at about twenty minutes to seven from *Altnagiuthasach*, Brown on the box next Smith,[†] who was driving, little Willem (Alice's black serving boy) behind. It was quite dark when we left, but all the lamps were lit as usual; from the first, however, Smith seemed to be quite confused (and indeed has been much altered of late), and got off the road several times, once in a very dangerous place, when Alice called out and Brown got off the box to show him the way. After that, however, though going very slowly, we seemed to be all right, but Alice was not at all reassured, and thought Brown's holding up the lantern all the time on the box indicated that Smith could not see where he was going, though the road was as broad and plain as possible. Suddenly, about two miles from *Altnagiuthasach*, and about twenty minutes after we had started, the carriage began to turn up on one side; we called out: "What's the matter?" There was an awful pause, during which Alice said: "We are upsetting." In another moment—during which I had time to reflect whether we should be killed or not, and thought there were still things I had not settled and wanted to do—the carriage turned over on its side, and we were all precipitated to the ground! I came down very hard, with my face upon the ground, near the carriage, the horses both on the ground, and Brown calling out in despair, "The Lord Almighty have mercy on us!

[†] She and Fritz Wilhelm had come three days before to stay at Abergeldie with their children.
[†] Smith was pensioned in 1864 and died in 1866, having been thirty-one years in the Royal service.

Who did ever see the like of this before! I thought you were all killed." Alice was soon helped up by means of tearing all her clothes to disentangle her; but Lenchen, who had also got caught in her dress, called out very piteously, which frightened me a good deal; but she was also got out with Brown's assistance, and neither she nor Alice was at all hurt. I reassured them that I was not hurt, and urged that we should make the best of it, as it was an inevitable misfortune. Smith, utterly confused and bewildered, at length came up to ask if I was hurt. Meantime the horses were lying on the ground as if dead, and it was absolutely necessary to get them up again. Alice, whose calmness and coolness were admirable, held one of the lamps while Brown cut the traces, to the horror of Smith, and the horses were speedily released and got up unhurt. There was now no means of getting home except by sending back Smith with the two horses to get another carriage. All this took some time, about half an hour, before we got off. By this time I felt that my face was a good deal bruised and swollen, and, above all, my right thumb was excessively painful and much swollen; indeed I thought at first it was broken, till we began to move it. Alice advised then that we should sit down in the carriage—that is, with the bottom of the carriage as a back—which we did, covered with plaids, little Willem sitting in front, with the hood of his "bournous" over his head, holding a lantern, Brown holding another, and being indefatigable in his attention and care. He had hurt his knee a good deal in jumping off the carriage. A little claret was all we could get either to drink or wash my face and hand. Almost directly after the accident happened, I said to Alice it was terrible not to be able to tell it to my dearest Albert, to which she answered: "But he knows it all, and I am sure he watched over us." I am thankful that it was by no imprudence of mine, or the slightest deviation from what my beloved one and I had always been in the habit of doing, and what he sanctioned and approved.

The thought of having to sit here in the road ever so long was, of course, not very agreeable, but it was not cold, and I remembered from the first what my beloved one had always said to me, namely, to make the best of what could not be altered. We had a faint hope, at one moment, that our ponies might overtake us; but then Brown recollected that they had started before us. We did nothing but talk of the accident, and how it could have happened, and how merciful the escape was, and we all agreed that Smith was quite unfit to drive me again in the dark. We had been sitting here about half an hour when we heard the sound of voices and of horses' hoofs, which came nearer and nearer.* To our relief we found it was our ponies. Kennedy (whom dear Albert liked, and who always went out with him, and now generally goes with us) had become fearful of an accident, as we were so long coming; he heard Smith going back with the ponies, and then, seeing lights moving about, he felt convinced something must have happened, and therefore rode back to look for us, which was very thoughtful of him, for else we might have sat there till ten o'clock. We mounted our ponies at once and proceeded home, Brown leading Alice's and my pony, which he would not let go for fear of another accident. Lenchen and Willem followed, led by Alick Grant. Kennedy carried the lantern in front. It was quite light enough to see the road without a lantern. At the hill where the gate of the deer-fence is, above the distillery, we met the other carriage, again driven by Smith, and a number of stable-people come to raise the first carriage, and a pair of horses to bring it home. We preferred, however, riding home, which we reached at about twenty minutes to ten o'clock. No one knew what had happened till we told them. Fritz and Louis were at the door. People were foolishly alarmed when we got upstairs, and made a great fuss. Took only a little soup and fish in my room, and had my head bandaged.

I saw the others only for a moment, and got to bed rather late.

Unveiling of the Prince's Statue at Aberdeen.

Thursday, October 13, 1863.

I was terribly nervous. Longed not to have to go through this fearful ordeal. Prayed for help, and got up earlier.

A bad morning. The three younger children (except Baby), William of Hesse,[†] and the ladies and gentlemen all gone on. I started sad and lonely, and so strange without my darling, with dear Alice, Lenchen, and Louis. We could not have the carriage open. At *Aboyne* we met Vicky and Fritz, and both the couples went with me in the railway;* the Princes in Highland dress. I felt bewildered. It poured with rain, unfortunately. To describe the day's proceedings would be too painful and difficult; but I annex the account. Vicky and Alice were with me, and the long, sad, and terrible procession through the crowded streets of *Aberdeen*, where all were kindly, but all were silent, was mournful, and as unlike former blessed times as could be conceived. Unfortunately it continued pouring. The spot where the Statue is placed is rather small, and on one side close to the bridge, but Marochetti chose it himself.*

I got out trembling; and when I had arrived, there was no one to direct me and to say, as formerly, what was to be done. Oh! it was and is too painful, too dreadful!

I received (only handed) the Provost's address, and knighted him (the first since all ended) with General Grey's sword. Then we all stepped onto the uncovered and wet platform directly opposite the Statue, which certainly is low, and rather small for out of doors, but fine and like. Principal Campbell's prayer was very long—which was trying in the rain—but part of it (since I have read it) is really very good.

I felt very nervous when the Statue was uncovered, but much regretted that when they presented arms there was no salute with the drums, bugles, or the pipes, for the bands below were forbidden to play. I retired almost immediately.

Just below and in front of where we stood were Löhlein, Mayet, Grant, Brown, Cowley, P. Farquharson, D. Stewart, Nestor,[†] Ross, and Paterson,

---

[†] Youngest brother of Prince Louis of Hesse.

[†] Löhlein, the Prince Consort's valet. Mayet, the Prince Consort's second valet, then with Prince Leopold. Cowley, the Prince Consort's Jäger from 1848, pensioned in 1848, formerly in the Blues. Nestor Tirard, the Queen's hairdresser since 1846.

whom we had brought with us—and why was my darling not near me? It was dreadfully sad.

Took a little luncheon in a room upstairs with our girls, our footmen serving us. After this we left as we came. Affie met us there, and then took leave at the station, William of Hesse joining him. It was quite fair, provokingly so, when we got to *Aboyne*. Here we parted, took leave of Vicky and Fritz, and drove back in an open carriage, reaching *Balmoral* at half-past six. Very tired; thankful it was over, but the recollection of the whole scene, of the whole journey, without my dear Albert, was dreadful! Formerly how we should have dwelt on all!

[The following account of the ceremonial is taken from the "Scotsman" newspaper of October 14, 1863.

The preparations made at the North-Eastern Station at Aberdeen for the reception of Her Majesty and the Princes and Princesses, were very simple and undemonstrative. Two huge flags were suspended across the inside entrance, and the floor of the passage leading into the portico at Guild Street was laid with crimson cloth. The following gentlemen were in waiting at the station, and received the royal party on the platform: The Duke of Richmond; the Lord Provost and Magistrates; the Earl of Aberdeen; Lord Saltoun; Sir J. D. H. Elphinstone; Sir Alexander Bannerman, Bart.; Lord Barcaple; Mr. Thomson of Banchory; Colonel Fraser of Castle Fraser; Colonel Fraser, younger, of Castle Fraser; Mr. Leslie of Warthill, M.P.; Mr. Irvine of Drum, convener of the county; Colonel Farquharson of Invercauld; Sheriff Davidson; John Webster, Esq., and several of the railway directors and officials.

On leaving the station, the procession was formed into the following order, and proceeded by way of Guild Street, Regent Quay, Marischal Street, Castle Street, and Union Street, to the site of the Memorial:—

Body of Police.
Detachment of Cavalry.
The Convener and Master of Hospital of the
Incorporated Trades.
The Principal and Professors of the University of Aberdeen.
The City Architect.
His Grace the Duke of Richmond, the Convener and Sheriff
of the County, and the Committee of Subscribers to the
Memorial.
The Lord Provost,
and Magistrates, and Town Council.
The Suite in Attendance on Her Majesty and Royal Family.
Lady Augusta Bruce (in attendance on the Queen).
Countess Hohenthal (in attendance on Crown-Princess).
Baroness Schenck (in attendance on Princess Louis of Hesse).

Sir George Grey.
The Princes Alfred, Arthur, and Leopold.
Lady Churchill (Lady-in-Waiting).
The Princess Helena.
The Princess Louise.
The Crown-Prince of Prussia.
The Prince Louis of Hesse.
The Princess Louis of Hesse.
The Crown-Princess of Prussia.
THE QUEEN.
Cavalry Escort.

The procession wound its way along the densely packed streets amid the deepest silence of the assemblage, everybody seeming to be animated by a desire to abstain from any popular demonstrations that might be distasteful to Her Majesty. On reaching the Northern Club buildings, Her Majesty, accompanied by the Prince and Princesses, Sir Charles Phipps,[†] Lord Charles Fitz-roy, Major-General Hood, Dr. Jenner, General Grey, and the ladies and gentlemen of the suite, passed from their carriages into the lobby, and thence into the billiard room—a handsome lofty room, which forms a half oval at the end towards Union Terrace. The Lord Provost then presented the following address to Her Majesty:—

TO THE QUEEN'S MOST EXCELLENT MAJESTY.

The humble Address of Her Majesty's loyal and dutiful subjects, the contributors to the erection in Aberdeen of a Memorial Statue of His Royal Highness the Prince-Consort.

May it please your Majesty,

We, your Majesty's most loyal and dutiful subjects, the contributors to the erection in Aberdeen of a Memorial Statue of His Royal Highness the Prince-Consort, humbly beg leave to approach your Majesty with the expression of our devoted attachment to your Majesty's person and government.

We are enabled this day to bring to completion the work which we undertook in sorrowing and grateful remembrance of that illustrious Prince, whose removal by the inscrutable will of Providence we, in common with all your Majesty's subjects, can never cease to deplore.

No memorial is necessary to preserve the name of one who adorned the highest station of the land by the brightest display of intellectual and moral greatness, as well as the purest and most enlightened zeal for the public good; whose memory is revered throughout the world, as that of few Princes has ever

---

[†] Keeper of the Privy Purse, who died February 24, 1866, to my great regret, for he was truly devoted and attached to the dear Prince and me, with whom he had been for twenty years.

been; and whose example will ever be cherished as a most precious inheritance by this great nation. Yet, in this part of the United Kingdom, which was honoured by the annual presence of the illustrious Prince, and in this city, which a few years ago was signally favoured by the exertion of his great talents as President of the British Association for the Advancement of Science,* an earnest desire pervaded all ranks to give permanent expression to the profound reverence and affection he had inspired.

How inadequate for such a purpose the memorial we have erected must be, we ourselves most deeply feel. But that your Majesty should have on this occasion graciously come forth again to receive the public homage of your loyal and devoted people, we regard as a ground of heartfelt thankfulness; and viewing it as a proof that your Majesty approves the humble but sincere tribute of our sorrow, we shall ever be grateful for the exertion which your Majesty has made to afford us this proof.

That Almighty God, the source of all strength, may comfort your Majesty's heart, prospering all your Majesty's designs and efforts for your people's good; that He may bestow His choicest favours on your royal offspring, and continue to your devoted subjects for many years the blessings of your Majesty's reign, is our earnest and constant prayer.

In name of the Contributors,
ALEX. ANDERSON,
Lord Provost of Aberdeen,
Chairman of the Committee of Contributors.

Aberdeen, October 13, 1863.

On receiving the address, Her Majesty handed the following reply to the Lord Provost:—

Your loyal and affectionate address has deeply touched me, and I thank you for it from my heart.

It was with feelings which I fail in seeking words to express that I determined to attend here to-day to witness the inaugurating of the statue which will record to future times the love and respect of the people of this county and city for my great and beloved husband. But I could not reconcile it to myself to remain at Balmoral while such a tribute was being paid to his memory without making an exertion to assure you personally of the deep and heartfelt sense I entertain of your kindness and affection; and at the same time proclaim in public the unbounded reverence and admiration and the devoted love that fill my heart for him whose loss must throw a lasting gloom over all my future life.

Never can I forget the circumstances to which you so feelingly alluded—that it was in this city he delivered his remarkable address to the British Association a very few years ago; and that in this county we had for so many years been in the habit of spending some of the happiest days of our lives.

After the Queen's reply had been handed to the Lord Provost, Sir George Grey commanded his Lordship to kneel, when Her Majesty, taking a sword from Sir George, touched the Provost on each shoulder and said—"Rise, Sir Alexander Anderson."* This ceremony concluded, the Queen and the whole of the royal party then proceeded to the platform, Her Majesty's appearance on which was the signal for the multitude gathered outside to uncover their heads. Her Majesty, who appeared to be deeply melancholy and much depressed, though calm and collected, advanced to the front of the platform, while the Princes, who were all dressed in Royal Stewart tartan, and the Princesses, who wore blue silk dresses, white bonnets, and dark grey cloaks, took up a position immediately behind her. The proceedings were opened with a prayer by Principal Campbell, who spoke for about ten minutes, the assemblage standing uncovered in the rain, which was falling heavily at the time. During the time the learned Principal was engaged in prayer, Her Majesty more than once betrayed manifest and well-justified signs of impatience at the length of the oration. At the conclusion of the prayer, a signal was given, the bunting which had concealed the statue was hoisted to the top of a flagstaff, and the ceremony was complete.

Her Majesty, having scanned the statue narrowly, bowed to the assemblage and retired from the platform, followed by the royal party. After the illustrious company had lunched in the club, the procession was reformed and proceeded the same way as it came to the Scottish North-Eastern Station in Guild Street. Her Majesty left Aberdeen about three o'clock.]

Expedition to Invermark.

Tuesday, September 19, 1865.

On waking I felt very low and nervous at the thought of the expedition. All so sadly changed.* Started at eleven o'clock with Lenchen and Jane Churchill, Grant and Brown on the box—like in former happy times. General Grey had preceded us, and we found him at the *Bridge of Muich*, where our ponies were waiting. We had four gillies, three of whom were with us in 1861 (Smith, Morgan, and Kennedy). The heat was intense going up the *Polach*. I got well enough through the bog, but Jane Churchill's pony floundered considerably. We lunched when we had crossed the *Tanar* and gone a little way up *Mount Keen*, and General Grey then went on to meet Lord Dalhousie. Two of his foresters had come to show us the way. We remounted after sitting and resting a little while, and ascended the shoulder of *Mount Keen*, and then rode on. The distance was very hazy. We got off and walked, after which I rode down that fine wild pass called the *Ladder Burn*; but it seemed to strike me much less than when I first saw it, as all is flat now. At the foot of the pass Lord Dalhousie met us with General Grey, and welcomed us kindly; and at the Shiel, a little further on, where we had lunched in 1861, Lady Christian Maule, Lord Dalhousie's sister, met us. She was riding. We then went on a few yards further till we came to the *Well*,* where we got off. It is really beautiful, built of white stones in the shape of the ancient crown of *Scotland*; and in one of the pillars a plate is inserted with this inscription: "Queen Victoria with the Prince Consort visited this well and drank of its refreshing waters on the 20th September, 1861, the year of Her Majesty's great sorrow;" and round the spring, which bubbles up beautifully, and quite on a level with the ground, is inscribed in old English characters the following legend:—

> Rest, traveller, on this lonely green,
> And drink and pray for Scotland's Queen.

We drank with sorrowing hearts from this very well, where just four years ago I had drunk with my beloved Albert; and Grant handed me his flask (one I had given him) out of which we had drunk on that day! Lord Dalhousie has kindly built this well in remembrance of that occasion. It was quite a pilgrimage.

We afterwards had some tea, close by; and this fine wide glen was seen at its best, lit up as it was by the evening sun, warm as on a summer's day, without a breath of air, the sky becoming pinker and pinker, the hills themselves, as you looked down the glen, assuming that beautifully glowing tinge which they do of an evening. The Highlanders and ponies grouped around the well had a most picturesque effect. And yet to me all seemed strange, unnatural, and sad.*

We mounted again, and went on pursuing the same way as we had done four years ago, going past the old *Castle of Invermark*. As there was time, however, we rode on to *Loch Lee*, just beyond it, which we had only seen from a distance on the last occasion. It is quite small, but extremely pretty, and was beautifully lit up, reminding me of the farthest end of *Loch Muich*. After this we rode up to the house, the little drawing-room of which I well remembered; it brought all back to me. Lady Christian took us upstairs. I had two nice small rooms. The two maids, Lenchen and Lady Churchill, and Brown were all in our passage, away from the rest of the house. I felt tired, sad, and bewildered. For the first time in my life I was alone in a strange house, without either mother or husband, and the thought overwhelmed and distressed me deeply. I had a dear child with me, but those loving ones above me were both gone,—their support taken away!* It seemed so dreadful! How many visits we paid together, my darling and I, and how we ever enjoyed them! Even when they were trying and formal, the happiness of being together, and a world in ourselves, was so great.*

Dinner was below, in a pretty room which I also remembered. Only Lord Dalhousie, Lady Christian, the General, Lady Churchill, Lenchen, and I. I stayed but a short while below after dinner, and then went up with Lenchen and Jane Churchill, and afterwards walked out a little with Jane. It was very warm.

Wednesday, September 20.

A beautiful morning. Breakfasted alone with Lenchen in my own little sitting-room—waited on by Brown, who is always ready to try to do anything required. At eleven we went out, and I planted two trees, and Lenchen one (instead of her blessed Father, alas!) We then mounted our ponies as yesterday, and proceeded (accompanied by Lord Dalhousie, Lady Christian, and several of his foresters) by a shorter road past the well, where we did not get off, up the *Ladder Burn*, on our homeward journey. We went the same way, stopping at the "March," where, in a high wind, we got off and lunched under some stones. Good Lord

Dalhousie[+] was most hospitable and kind. The luncheon over, they took leave and went back, and General Grey went on in advance. As it was only one o'clock when we sat down to luncheon, we remained sitting some little time before we commenced our downward course. It was to-day—strange to say—the anniversary of our first visit to *Invermark*. Then we proceeded down the same way we had come up, across the *Tanar*, and when we had gone up some little way we stopped again, as we were anxious not to hurry home, and moreover the carriage would not have been ready to meet us. We had some tea, sketched a little, and rode on again; the sky had become dark and cloudy, and suddenly down came a most violent shower of rain which beat fiercely with the wind. We were just then going over the boggy part, which, however, we got across very well. As we came over the *Polac*h the rain ceased. The view of the *Valley of the Gairn* and *Muich* as you descend is beautiful, and reminded me forcibly of our last happy expedition in 1861, when Albert stopped to talk to Grant about the two forests, and said he and Grant might possibly be dead before they were completed!* There lay the landscape stretched out—the same as before; and all else was changed!

We got home at ten minutes past seven o'clock, when it was still raining a little.

[+] He died in 1874.

First Visit to Dunkeld.*

Monday, October 9, 1865.

A thick, misty, very threatening morning! There was no help for it, but it was sadly provoking. It was the same once or twice in former happy days, and my dear Albert always said we could not alter it, but must leave it as it was, and make the best of it. Our three little ones breakfasted with me. I was grieved to leave my precious Baby and poor Leopold behind. At ten started with Lenchen and Janie Ely (the same attendants on the box), General Grey had gone on an hour and a half before. We took posthorses at *Castleton*. It rained more or less the whole time. Then came the long well-known stage to the *Spital of Glenshee*, which seemed to me longer than ever. The mist hung very thick over the hills. We changed horses there, and about a quarter of an hour after we had left it, we stopped to lunch in the carriage. After some delay we went on and turned into *Strathardle*, and then, leaving the *Blairgowrie* road, down to the farm of *Pitcarmich*, shortly before coming to which Mr. Small Keir[+] of *Kindrogan* met us and rode before us to this farm. Here we found General Grey and our ponies, and here the dear Duchess of Athole and Miss MacGregor met us, and we got out and went for a short while into the farmhouse, where we took some wine and biscuit. Then we mounted our ponies (I on dear Fyvie, Lenchen on Brechin), and started on our course across the hill. There was much mist. This obscured all the view, which otherwise would have been very fine. At first there was a rough road, but soon there was nothing but a sheep-track, and hardly that, through heather and stones up a pretty steep hill. Mr. Keir could not keep up with the immense pace of Brown and Fyvie, which distanced every one; so he had to drop behind, and his keeper acted as guide. There was by this time heavy driving rain, with a thick mist. About a little more than an hour took us to the "March," where two of the *Dunkeld* men met us, John McGregor, the Duke's head wood-forester, and Gregor McGregor, the Duchess's gamekeeper; and the former acted as a guide. The Duchess and Miss MacGregor were riding with us. We went from here through larch woods, the rain pouring at times violently. We passed (after crossing the *Dunkeld March*) *Little Loch Oishne*, and *Loch Oishne*, before coming

---

[+] His father was presented to me at Dunkeld in 1842.

to *Loch Ordie*.* Here dripping wet we arrived at about a quarter-past six, having left *Pitcarmich* at twenty minutes to four. It was dark already from the very bad weather. We went into a lodge here, and had tea and whisky, and Lenchen had to get herself dried, as she was so wet. About seven we drove off from *Loch Ordie*. There was no outrider, so we sent on first the other carriage with Lenchen, Lady Ely, and Miss MacGregor, and General Grey on the box, and I went with the Duchess in a phaeton which had a hood—Brown and Grant going behind. It was pitch-dark, and we had to go through a wood, and I must own I was somewhat nervous.

We had not gone very far when we perceived that we were on a very rough road, and I became much alarmed, though I would say nothing. A branch took off Grant's cap, and we had to stop for Brown to go back and look for it with one of the carriage-lamps. This stoppage was most fortunate, for he then discovered we were on a completely wrong road. Grant and Brown had both been saying, "This is no carriage-road; it is full of holes and stones." Miss MacGregor came to us in great distress, saying she did not know what to do, for that the coachman, blinded by the driving rain, had mistaken the road, and that we were in a track for carting wood. What was to be done, no one at this moment seemed to know—whether to try and turn the carriage (which proved impossible) or to take a horse out and send the postilion back to *Loch Ordie* to get assistance. At length we heard from General Grey that we could go on, though where we should get out, no one could exactly tell. Grant took a lamp out of the carriage and walked before the horses, while Brown led them; and this reassured me. But the road was very rough, and we had to go through some deep holes full of water. At length, in about twenty minutes, we saw a light and passed a lodge, where we stopped and inquired where we were, for we had already come upon a good road. Our relief was great when we were told we were all right. Grant and Brown got up behind, and we trotted along the high road fast enough. Just before we came to the lodge, General Grey called out to ask which way the Duchess thought we should go, and Brown answered in her name, "The Duchess don't know at all where we are," as it was so dark she could not recognise familiar places. At length at a quarter to nine we arrived quite safely at *Dunkeld*, at the Duchess's nice, snug little cottage, which is just outside the town, surrounded by fine large grounds. Two servants in kilts, and the steward, received us at the door. You come at once on the middle landing of the staircase, the cottage being built on sloping ground. The Duchess took me to my room, a nice little room, next to which was one for my wardrobe maid, Mary Andrews.[+] Lenchen was upstairs near Miss MacGregor on one side of the drawing-room, which was given up to me as my sitting-room, and the Duchess's room on the other. Brown, the only other servant in the house, below, Grant in the adjoining buildings to the house. The General and Lady Ely were at the hotel. We dined at half-past nine in a small dining-room below, only Lenchen, the Duchess, Miss MacGregor, and I. Everything so nice and quiet. The Duchess and Miss MacGregor carving, her three servants waiting. They were so kind, and we talked over the day's adventures. Lenchen and every one, except the Duchess and myself, had been drenched. The Duchess and her cousin stayed a short while, and then left us, and I wrote a little. Strange to say, it was four years to-day that we paid our visit to *Blair* and rode up *Glen Tilt*. How different!

Tuesday, October 10.

A hopelessly wet morning. I had slept well, but felt sad on awaking. Breakfasted alone with Lenchen downstairs, each day waited on by Brown. A dreadful morning, pouring rain. Sat upstairs in the drawing-room, and wrote a good deal, being perfectly quiet and undisturbed.

Lenchen and I lunched with the Duchess and Miss MacGregor, and at four we drove up to the Duchess's very fine model farm of *St. Colme's*, about four miles from *Dunkeld*; the Duchess and I in the phaeton, Lenchen, Janie Ely, and Miss MacGregor going in the other carriage. We went all over the farm in detail, which is very like ours at *Osborne* and *Windsor*, much having been adopted from our farms there;* and my dearest Husband had given the Duchess so much advice about it, that we both felt so sad *he* should not see it.

We took tea in the farmhouse, where the Duchess has kept one side quite for herself, and where she intends to live sometimes with Miss MacGregor, and almost by themselves. From here we drove back and stopped at the "*Byres*," close by the stables, which were lit up with gas, and where we saw all the cows being milked. Very fine Ayrshire cows, and nice dairymaids. It is all kept up just as the late Duke wished it. We came home at past seven. It never ceased raining. The Cathedral bell began quite unexpectedly to ring, or almost toll, at eight o'clock, which the Duchess told us was a very old custom—in fact, the curfew-bell. It sounds very melancholy.

Dinner just as yesterday.

[+] She left my service in 1866.

Wednesday, October 11.

Another wretchedly wet morning. Was much distressed at breakfast to find that poor Brown's legs had been dreadfully cut by the edge of his wet kilt on Monday, just at the back of the knee, and he said nothing about it; but to-day one became so inflamed, and swelled so much, that he could hardly move.* The doctor said he must keep it up as much as possible, and walk very little, but did not forbid his going out with the carriage, which he wished to do. I did not go out in the morning, and decided to remain till Friday, to give the weather a chance. It cleared just before luncheon, and we agreed to take a drive, which we were able to do almost without any rain. At half-past three we drove out just as yesterday. There was no mist, so that, though there was no sunshine, we could see and admire the country, the scenery of which is beautiful. We drove a mile along the *Blair Road* to *Polney Loch*, where we entered the woods, and, skirting the loch, drove at the foot of *Craig y Barns* on grass drives—which were very deep and rough, owing to the wet weather, but extremely pretty—on to the *Loch Ordie* road. After ascending this for a little way we left it, driving all round *Cally Loch* (there are innumerable lochs) through *Cally Gardens* along another fine but equally rough wood drive, which comes out on the *Blairgowrie* high road. After this we drove round the three *Lochs* of the *Lowes*—viz. *Craig Lush*, *Butterstone*, and the *Loch of the Lowes* itself (which is the largest). They are surrounded by trees and woods, of which there is no end, and are very pretty. We came back by the *Blairgowrie* road and drove through *Dunkeld* (the people had been so discreet and quiet, I said I would do this), crossing over the bridge (where twenty-two years ago we were met by twenty of the Athole Highlanders,* who conducted us to the entrance of the grounds), and proceeded by the upper road to the *Rumbling Bridge*, which is Sir William Stewart of *Grandtully's* property. We got out here and walked to the bridge, under which the *Braan* flowed over the rocks most splendidly; and, swollen by the rain, it came down in an immense volume of water with a deafening noise. Returning thence we drove through the village of *Inver* to the *Hermitage* on the banks of the *Braan*, which is *Dunkeld* property. This is a little house full of looking-glasses, with painted walls, looking on another fall of the *Braan*, where we took tea almost in the dark. It was built by James, the second Duke of Athole, in the last century. We drove back through *Dunkeld* again, the people cheering. Quite fair. We came home at half-past six o'clock. Lady Ely and General Grey dined with us. After dinner only the Duchess came to the drawing-room, and read to us again. Then I wrote, and Grant waited instead of Brown, who was to keep quiet on account of his leg.

Thursday, October 12.

A fair day, with no rain, but, alas! no sunshine. Brown's leg was much better, and the doctor thought he could walk over the hill to-morrow.

Excellent breakfasts, such splendid cream and butter! The Duchess has a very good cook, a Scotchwoman, and I thought how dear Albert would have liked it all. He always said things tasted better in smaller houses. There were several Scotch dishes, two soups, and the celebrated "haggis," which I tried last night, and really liked very much. The Duchess was delighted at my taking it.

At a quarter past twelve Lenchen and I walked with the Duchess in the grounds and saw the Cathedral, part of which is converted into a parish church, and the other part is a most picturesque ruin. We saw the tomb of the Wolf of Badenoch,* son of King Robert the Second. There are also other monuments, but in a very dilapidated state. The burying-ground is inside and south of the Cathedral. We walked along the side of the river *Tay*, into which the river *Braan* flows, under very fine trees, as far as the American garden,* and then round by the terrace overlooking the park, on which the tents were pitched at the time of the great déjeuner that the Duke, then Lord Glenlyon, gave us in 1842, which was our first acquaintance with the *Highlands* and Highland customs; and it was such a fine sight! Oh! and here we were together—both widows!

We came back through the kitchen-garden by half-past one o'clock. After the usual luncheon, drove with Lenchen, the Duchess, and Miss MacGregor, at twenty minutes to four, in her sociable to *Loch Ordie*, by the lakes of *Rotmell* and *Dowally* through the wood, being the road by which we ought to have come the first night when we lost our way. It was cold, but the sky was quite bright, and it was a fine evening; and the lake, wooded to the water's edge and skirted by distant hills, looked extremely pretty. We took a short row on it in a "coble" rowed by the head keeper, Gregor M'Gregor. We took tea under the trees. The evening was very cold, and it was getting rapidly dark. We came back safely by the road the Duchess had wished to come the other night, but which her coachman did not think safe on account of the precipices! We got home at nine. Only the Duchess and Miss MacGregor dined with us. The Duke's former excellent valet, Christie (a Highlander, and now the Duchess's house-steward), and George McPherson, piper, and Charles McLaren, footman, two nice, good-looking Highlanders in the Athole tartan, waited on us. The Duchess read again a little to us after dinner.

Friday, October 13.

Quite a fine morning, with bright gleams of sunshine lighting up everything. The piper played each morning in the garden during breakfast. Just before we left at ten, I planted a tree, and spoke to an old acquaintance, Willie Duff, the Duchess's fisherman, who had formerly a very long black beard and hair, which are now quite grey. Mr. Carrington, who has been Secretary in the Athole family for four generations, was presented. General Grey, Lady Ely, and Miss MacGregor had gone on a little while before us. Lenchen and I, with the Duchess, went in the sociable with four horses (Brown and Grant on the box). The weather was splendid, and the view, as we drove along the *Inverness Road*—which is the road to *Blair*—with all the mountains rising in the distance, was beautiful.

We passed through the village of *Ballinluig*, where there is a railway station, and a quarter of a mile below which the *Tay* and the *Tummel* unite, at a place called *Logierait*. All these names were familiar to me from our stay in 1844. We saw the place where the monument to the Duke* is to be raised, on an eminence above *Logierait*. About eleven miles from *Dunkeld*, just below *Croftinloan* (Captain Jack Murray's), we took post-horses. You could see *Pitlochry* in the distance to the left. We then left the *Inverness Road*, and turned to the right, up a very steep hill past *Dunavourd* (Mr. Napier's, son of the historian), past *Edradour* (the Duke's property), over a wild moor, reminding one very much of *Aberarder* (near *Balmoral*), whence, looking back, you have a beautiful view of the hills *Schiehallion*, *Ben Lomond*, and *Ben Lawers*. This glen is called *Glen Brearichan*, the little river of that name uniting with the *Fernate*, and receiving afterwards the name of the *Ardle*. On the left hand a shoulder of *Ben-y-Gloe* is seen.

We lunched in the carriage at ten minutes past twelve, only a quarter of a mile from the West Lodge of *Kindrogan* (Mr. Keir's). Here were our ponies, and General Grey, Lady Ely, and Miss MacGregor. We halted a short while to let General Grey get ahead, and then started on our ponies, Mr. Keir walking with us. We passed Mr. Keir's house of *Kindrogan*, out at the East Lodge, by the little village of *Enoch Dhu*, up the rather steep ascent and approach of *Dirnanean*, Mr. Small's place; passing his house as we went. Mr. Small was absent, but two of his people, fine, tall-looking men, led the way; two of Mr. Keir's were also with us. We turned over the hill from here, through a wild, heathery glen, and then up a grassy hill called the *Larich*, just above the *Spital*.* Looking back the view was splendid, one range of hills behind the other, of different shades of blue. After we had passed the summit, we stopped for our tea, about twenty minutes to four, and seated ourselves on the grass, but had to wait for some time till a kettle arrived which had been forgotten, and had to be sent for from the *Spital*. This caused some delay. At length, when tea was over, we walked down a little way, and then rode. It was really most distressing to me to see what pain poor Brown suffered, especially in going up and down the hill. He could not go fast, and walked lame, but would not give in. His endurance on this occasion showed a brave heart indeed, for he resisted all attempts at being relieved, and would not relinquish his charge.

We took leave of the dear kind Duchess and Miss MacGregor, who were going back to *Kindrogan*, and got into the carriage. We were able to ascend the *Devil's Elbow* before it was really dark, and got to *Castleton* at half-past seven, where we found our own horses, and reached *Balmoral* at half-past eight.

Second Visit to Dunkeld.

Monday, October 1, 1866.

A very fine morning. Got up earlier, and breakfasted earlier, and left at a quarter to ten with Louise and Janie Ely (attended by Brown and Grant as formerly); Arthur having gone on with General Grey. We met many droves of cattle on the road, as it was the day for the tryst at *Castleton*. It was very hot, the sun very bright, and the *Cairn Wall* looked wild and grand. But as we went on the sky became dull and overcast, and we almost feared there might be rain. We walked down the *Devil's Elbow*, and when within a mile and a half of the *Spital* we stopped and lunched in the carriage, and even sketched a little. A little way on the north side of the *Spital* were the ponies, Gordon for me, Brechin for Louise, and Cromar for Janie Ely. There was a pony for Arthur, which he did not ride, and for Grant or any one who was tired. The dear Duchess of Athole and Miss MacGregor came to meet us here, and when we had reached the spot where the road turns up the hill, we found Mr. Keir and his son, and Mr. Small of *Dirnanean*—a strong, good-looking, and pleasing person about thirty-two—and his men, the same two fine tall men, preceding us as last year. It was a steep climb up the hill which we had then come down, and excessively hot. The views both ways beautiful, though not clear. The air was very heavy and oppressive. We went the same way as before, but the ground was very wet from the great amount of rain. We stopped a moment in passing, at *Dirnanean*, to speak to Miss Small, Mr. Small's sister, a tall, stout young lady,[+] and then went on to *Kindrogan*, Mr. Keir's. All about here the people speak Gaelic, and there are a few who do not speak a word of English. Soon after entering Mr. Keir's grounds we got off our ponies, and went along a few yards by the side of the river *Ardle* to where Mr. Keir had got a fire kindled and a kettle boiling, plaids spread and tea prepared. Mrs. Keir and her two daughters were there. She is a nice quiet person, and was a Miss Menzies, daughter of Sir Niel Menzies, whom I saw at *Taymouth* in 1842. Only we ladies remained. The tea over, we walked up to the house, which is a nice comfortable one. We waited here a little while, and I saw at the door Major Balfour of *Fernie*, the intended bridegroom of Mr. Keir's youngest daughter. At a little over a quarter-past five started in my sociable, with

---

[+] Their father, a man of immense size, was presented to me at Dunkeld in 1842.

Louise

Louise and the Duchess. We came very fast and well with the Duchess's horses by exactly the same road we drove from *Dunkeld* last year. The horses were watered at the small halfway house of *Ballinluig*, and we reached *Dunkeld* in perfect safety at ten minutes past seven. I am where I was before, Louise in Lenchen's room, and Arthur in a room next to where Brown was before, and is now. All the rest the same, and snug, peaceful, and comfortable.

Dunkeld, Tuesday, October 2.

Mild and muggy, the mist hanging on the hills. Breakfasted with the children. Andrew Thomson attends to Arthur. Emilie[+] and Annie Macdonald[†] are with me here; they help Louise, who, however, is very handy and can do almost everything for herself.

At half-past eleven I drove out alone with the Duchess through the woods to *Polney*, and then along the road, and turned in at *Willie Duff's Lodge*, and down the whole way along the river under splendid trees which remind me of *Windsor Park*. How dearest Albert would have admired them! We ended by a little walk, and looked into the old ruin. At twenty minutes to four we drove, the Duchess, Louise, and I—Janie Ely and Miss MacGregor following—to *Crieff*-gate on the road of the *Loch of the Lowes*, where we got on ponies and rode for about an hour and a half through beautiful woods (saw a capercailzie, of which there are many here), but in a very thick mist (with very fine rain) which entirely destroyed all idea of view and prevented one's seeing anything but what was near. We came down to *St. Colme's*,* where we got off, but where again, like last year, we saw nothing of the beautiful view. Here we took tea out of the tea-set I had given the Duchess. She has furnished all her rooms here so prettily. How Albert would have liked all this!

Dinner as yesterday. Brown waited at dinner.

Wednesday, October 3.

Just returned from a beautiful and successful journey of seventy miles (in ten hours and a half). I will try and begin an account of it. At nine the Duchess sent up to say she thought the mist would clear off (it was much the same as yesterday), and to suggest whether we had not better try and

---

[+] Emilie Dittweiler, my first dresser, a native of Carlsruhe, in the Grand Duchy of Baden, who has been twenty-four years in my service.

[†] My first wardrobe woman, who has been twenty seven years in my service, daughter of Mitchel, the late blacksmith at Clachanturn, near Abergeldie, and widow of my footman, John Macdonald, who died in 1865 (*vide* "Our Life in the Highlands").

go as far as her horses would take us, and return if it was bad. I agreed readily to this. Arthur left before our breakfast to go to the *Pass of Killiecrankie* with Lady Ely and General Grey. At a quarter past ten, well provided, we started, Louise, the Duchess, Miss MacGregor, and I (in our riding habits, as they take less room). The mist was very thick at first, and even accompanied by a little drizzling rain, so that we could see none of the distant hills and scenery. We crossed the *Tay Bridge*, drove through *Little Dunkeld* and along the *Braan* through *Inver* (where Niel Gow, the fiddler, lived), afterwards along the *Tay* opposite to *St. Colme's*. Four miles from *Dunkeld*, at *Inchmagranachan Farm*, the *Highlands* are supposed to begin,* and this is one of the boundaries of *Athole*. We drove through some beautiful woods—oak and beech with brushwood, reminding one of *Windsor Park*—overtopped by rocks. A mile further *Dalguise* begins (the property of Mr. Stewart, now at the *Cape of Good Hope*), which is remarkable for two large orchards at either end, the trees laden with fruit in a way that reminded me of *Germany*. *Kinnaird** is next, the jointure house of the late Lady Glenlyon (mother to the late Duke). Just beyond this the *Tummel* and the *Tay* join at the point of *Logierait*.

We now entered *Strath Tay*, still the Duke of Athole's property, on the side along which we drove. The *Tay* is a fine large river; there are many small properties on the opposite side in the woods. The mist was now less thick and there was no rain, so that all the near country could be well seen. Post-horses from Fisher of *Castleton*'s brother, the innkeeper at *Dunkeld*, were waiting for us at *Skituan*, a little beyond *Balnaguard* (where we changed horses in 1842, and this was the very same road we took then). Now an unsightly and noisy railroad* runs along this beautiful glen, from *Dunkeld* as far as *Aberfeldy*. We passed, close to the road, *Grandtully Castle*, belonging to Sir William Stewart, and rented by the Maharajah Duleep Singh.* It is a curious old castle, much in the style of *Abergeldie*, with an avenue of trees leading up to it.

At *Aberfeldy*, a pretty village opposite to *Castle Menzies*, one or two people seemed to know us. We now came in among fine high-wooded hills, and here it was much clearer. We were in the *Breadalbane* property and approaching *Taymouth*. We passed, to the left, *Bolfrax*, where Lord Breadalbane's factor still lives, and to the right the principal lodge of *Taymouth*, which I so well remember going in by; but as we could not have driven through the grounds without asking permission and becoming known, which for various reasons we did not wish, we decided on not attempting it, and contented ourselves with getting out at a gate, close to a small fort, into which we were admitted by a woman from the gardener's house, close to which we stopped, and who had no idea who we were. *We got out and looked down from this height upon the house below, the mist having cleared away sufficiently to show us everything; and here unknown, quite in private, I gazed, not without deep inward emotion, on the scene of our reception, twenty-four years ago, by dear Lord Breadalbane in a princely style, not to be equalled for grandeur and poetic effect! Albert and I were only twenty-three, young and happy. How many are gone who were with us then! I was very thankful to have seen it again. It seemed unaltered.*+ Everything was dripping from the mist. *Taymouth* is twenty-two miles from *Dunkeld*.

We got into the carriage again; the Duchess this time sitting near to me to prevent our appearance creating suspicion as to my being there. We drove on a short way through splendid woods with little waterfalls, and then turned into the little village of *Kenmore*, where a tryst was being held, through the midst of which we had to drive; but the people only recognised the Duchess. There was music going on, things being sold at booths, and on the small sloping green near the church cattle and ponies were collected—a most picturesque scene. Immediately after this we came upon the bridge, and *Loch Tay*, with its wooded banks, clear and yet misty, burst into view. This again reminded me of the past—of the row up the loch, which is sixteen miles long, in 1842, in several boats, with pibrochs playing, and the boatmen singing wild Gaelic songs.* The McDougall steered us then, and showed us the real Brooch of Lorne taken from Robert Bruce.

To the right we could see the grounds and fine park, looking rather like an English one. We stopped at *Murray's Lodge*, but, instead of changing horses here, drove five miles up the loch, which was quite clear, and the stillness so great that the reflection on the lake's bosom was as strong as though it were a real landscape. Here we stopped, and got out and sat down on the shore of the loch, which is covered with fine quartz, of which we picked up some; took our luncheon about half-past one, and then sketched. By this time the mist had given way to the sun, and the lake, with its richly wooded banks and changing foliage, looked beautiful.

At half-past two we re-entered our carriage, the horses having been changed, and drove back up a steep hill, crossing the river *Lyon* and going into *Glenlyon*, a beautiful wild glen with high green hills and rocks and trees, which I remember quite well driving through in 1842—then also on a misty day: the mist hung over, and even in some places below

---

+ The passage between the asterisks was quoted in a note in "Our Life in the Highlands," page 26.

the tops of the hills. We passed several small places—*Glenlyon House*, the property of F. G. Campbell of *Troup*. To the left also *Fortingal* village—Sir Robert Menzies'—and a new place called *Dunæven House*. Small, picturesque, and very fair cottages were dotted about, and there were others in small clusters; beautiful sycamores and other trees were to be seen near the riverside. We then passed the village of *Coshieville*, and turned by the hill-road—up a very steep hill with a burn flowing at the bottom, much wooded, reminding me of *M'Inroy's Burn*—passed the ruins of the old castle of the Stewarts of *Garth*, and then came on a dreary wild moor—passing below *Schiehallion*, one of the high hills—and at the summit of the road came to a small loch, called *Ceannairdiche*.

Soon after this we turned down the hill again into woods, and came to *Tummel Bridge*, where we changed horses. Here were a few, but very few people, who I think, from what Brown and Grant—who, as usual, were in attendance—said, recognised us, but behaved extremely well, and did not come near. This was at twenty minutes to four. We then turned as it were homewards, but had to make a good long circuit, and drove along the side of *Loch Tummel*, high above the loch, through birch wood, which grows along the hills much the same as about *Birkhall*. It is only three miles long. Here it was again very clear and bright. At the end of the loch, on a highish point called after me *"The Queen's View"*—though I had not been there in 1844—we got out and took tea. But this was a long and unsuccessful business; the fire would not burn, and the kettle would not boil. At length Brown ran off to a cottage and returned after some little while with a can full of hot water, but it was no longer boiling when it arrived, and the tea was not good. Then all had to be packed, and it made us very late.

It was fast growing dark. We passed *Alleine*, Sir Robert Colquhoun's place, almost immediately after this, and then, at about half-past six, changed horses at the *Bridge of Garry*, near, or rather in the midst of, the *Pass of Killecrankie*; but from the lateness of the hour and the dulness of the evening—for it was raining—we could see hardly anything.

We went through *Pitlochry*, where we were recognised, but got quite quietly through, and reached *Ballinluig*, where the Duchess's horses were put on, at a little before half-past seven. Here the lamps were lit, and the good people had put two lighted candles in each window! They offered to bring "Athole brose," which we, however, declined. The people pressed round the carriage, and one man brought out a bull's-eye lantern which he turned upon me. But Brown, who kept quite close, put himself between me and the glare. We ought to have been home in less than an hour from this time, but we had divers impediments—twice the plaid fell out and had to be picked up; and then the lamp which I had given to the Duchess, like the one our outrider carries, was lit, and the coachman who rode outrider, and who was not accustomed to use it, did not hold it rightly, so that it went out twice, and had to be relit each time. So we only got home at a quarter to nine, and dined at twenty minutes past nine. But it was a very interesting day. We must have gone seventy-four miles.

Thursday, October 4.

Again heavy mist on the hills—most provoking—but without rain. The Duchess came to ask if I had any objection to the servants and gillies having a dance for two hours in the evening, to which I said, certainly not, and that I would go to it myself. At a quarter to twelve I rode in the grounds with the Duchess, going round *Bishop's Hill* and up to the *King's Seat*, a good height, among the most splendid trees—beeches, oaks, Scotch firs, spruce—really quite like *Windsor*, and reminding me of those fine trees at the *Belvidere*, and a good deal of *Reinhardtsbrunn* (in the forest of *Thuringia*). But though less heavy than the two preceding mornings and quite dry, it was too hazy to see any distant hills, and *Craig y Barns*, that splendid rocky, richly wooded hill overtopping the whole, only peeped through the mist occasionally. From the *King's Seat* we came down by the fort and upon the old "*Otter Hound Kennels*," where we saw Mrs. Fisher, the mother of Agnes Brierly, who was formerly schoolmistress to the *Lochnagar* girls' school* near *Balmoral*. We came in at a little after one, expecting it would clear and become much finer, instead of which it got darker and thicker.

At twenty minutes to four drove with the Duchess, Miss MacGregor and Janie Ely following, to *Loch Clunie* by the *Loch of the Lowes*, and passed *Laighwood Farm*. We drove round the loch; saw and stopped to sketch the old castle of *Clunie*, on a little island in the loch, the property of Lord Airlie. The scenery is tame, but very pretty with much wood, which is now in great beauty from the change of the leaf. The distance was enveloped in mist, and, as we drove back towards *Dunkeld* by the *Cupar Angus Road*, it was quite like a thick *Windsor* fog, but perfectly dry.

We stopped to take tea at *Newtyle*, a farm of the Duchess, about two miles from *Dunkeld*, where she has a small room, and which supplies turnips, etc. for the fine dairy cows. We got home by five minutes to seven. We passed through the town, where the people appeared at their doors cheering, and the children made a great noise. Dinner as before.

At half-past ten we went down (through the lower passages) to the servants' hall, in which the little dance took place. All the Duchess's servants, the wives of the men-servants, the keepers, the wood-forester (J. M'Gregor, who has an extensive charge over all the woods on the *Athole* property), the gardener, and some five or six others who belong to my guard (eight people, belonging to the Duchess or to the town, who take their turn of watching two by two at night), besides all our servants, were there; only Grant and two of the gillies did not appear, which vexed us; but the gillies had not any proper shoes, they said, and therefore did not come.* Janie Ely came; also Mr. Keir, and both were very active; General Grey only looked in for a moment, as he was suffering severely from cold. The fiddlers played in very good time, and the dancing was very animated, and went on without ceasing. Louise and Arthur both danced a good deal. Nothing but reels were danced. Even the Duchess's old French maid, Clarice, danced! She no longer acts as the Duchess's maid, but still lives near, in the adjacent so-called "brick buildings."*

Friday, October 5.

A brighter morning, though still hazy. The sun came out and the mist seemed dispersing. At twenty minutes to one started with the Duchess and Louise, the two ladies following, for *Loch Ordie*. Several times during the drive the mist regained its mastery, but then again the sun struggled through, blue sky appeared, and the mist seemed to roll away and the hills and woods to break through. We drove by *Craig Lush* and *Butterstone Lochs*, and then turned by the *Riechip Burn*—up a very steep hill, finely wooded, passing by *Riechip* and *Raemore*, two of the Duke of Athole's shooting lodges, both let. After the last the road opens upon a wild moor (or "muir") for a short while, before entering the plantations and woods of *Loch Ordie*. Here, quite close to the lodge, on the grass, we took luncheon. The Duchess had had a hot venison pie brought, which was very acceptable. The sun had come out, and it was delightfully warm, with a blue sky and bright lights, and we sat sketching for some time. The good people have made a cairn amongst the trees where we had tea last year.

At four we drove away, and went by the road which leads towards *Tullymet*, and out of the woods by *Hardy's Lodge*, near a bridge. We stopped at a very picturesque place, surrounded by woods and hills and little shiels, reminding me of the *Laucha Grund* at *Reinhardtsbrunn*.* Opposite to this, on a place called *Ruidh Reinnich*, or the "ferny shieling," a fire was kindled, and we took our tea. We then drove back by the upper *St. Colme's Road*, after which we drove through the town, up *Bridge Street*, and to the *Market Cross*, where a fountain is being erected in memory of the Duke. We went to see the dairy, and then came home on foot at a quarter to seven. Rested on the sofa, as my head was bad; it got better, however, after dinner.

Saturday, October 6.

A beautiful, bright, clear morning, most provokingly so. After breakfast at half-past nine, we left, with real regret, the kind Duchess's hospitable house, where all breathes peace and harmony, and where it was so quiet and snug. It was a real holiday for me in my present sad life. Louise and the Duchess went with me; the others had gone on. Some of the principal people connected with the Duchess stood along the approach as we drove out. We went the usual way to *Loch Ordie*, and past the lodge, on to the east end of the loch, the latter part of the road being very rough and deep. Here we all mounted our ponies at half-past eleven, and proceeded on our journey. A cloudless sky, not a breath of wind, and the heat intense and sickening. We went along a sort of cart-road or track. The burn of *Riechip* runs out of this glen, through which we rode, and which really is very beautiful, under the shoulder of *Benachallie*. The shooting tenant of *Raemore*, a Mr. Gordon, was out on the opposite side of the glen on a distant hill. We rode on through the woods; the day was very hazy. After a few miles the eastern shore of *Loch Oishne* was reached, and we also skirted *Little Loch Oishne* for a few hundred yards. We followed from here the same road which we had come on that pouring afternoon in going to *Dunkeld* last year, till at a quarter to one we reached the *Kindrogan March*. Here Mr. Keir, his son, and his keeper met us. Thence we rode by *Glen Derby*, a wild open glen with moors. Descending into it, the road was soft but quite safe, having been purposely cut and put in order by Mr. Keir. We then ascended a steepish hill, after passing a shepherd's hut. Here Arthur and General Grey rode off to *Kindrogan*, young Mr. Keir with them, whence they were to drive on in advance. As we descended, we came upon a splendid view of all the hills, and also of *Glen Fernate*, which is the way to *Fealar*.

At half-past two we five ladies lunched on a heathery knoll, just above Mr. Keir's wood, and were indeed glad to do so, as we were tired by the great heat. As soon as luncheon was over, we walked down through the wood a few hundred yards to where the carriage was. Here we took leave, with much regret, of the dear kind Duchess and amiable Miss MacGregor, and got into the carriage at half-past three, stopping for a moment near

Kindrogan to wish Mrs. Keir and her family good-bye. We drove on by *Kirkmichael*, and then some little way until we got into the road from *Blairgowrie*.* The evening was quite splendid, the sky yellow and pink, and the distant hills coming out soft and blue, both behind and in front of us. We changed horses at the *Spital*, and about two miles beyond it—at a place called *Loch-na-Braig*—we stopped, and while Grant ran back to get from a small house some hot water in the kettle, we three, with Brown's help, scrambled over a low stone wall by the roadside, and lit a fire and prepared our tea. The kettle soon returned, and the hot tea was very welcome and refreshing.

We then drove off again. The scenery was splendid till daylight gradually faded away, and then the hills looked grim and severe in the dusk. We cleared the *Devil's Elbow* well, however, before it was really dark, and then many stars came out, and we reached *Balmoral* in safety at half-past eight o'clock.

Opening of the Aberdeen Waterworks.

Tuesday, October 16, 1866.

At a quarter-past ten left for *Ballater* with Lenchen and Louise; Christian, Arthur, the Duchess of Roxburghe, and Emily Cathcart in the second; the gentlemen (General Grey,[+] etc.) having gone on in front. We went by the railway, which was useful on this occasion. We went about three-quarters of an hour by railway, and then stopped close to *Inchmarlo*, Mr. Davidson's place, not far from *Kincardine O'Neil*. Here we got into carriages—Lenchen and Louise with me,—Christian, Arthur, and the two equerries, etc., in the next. About twenty minutes' drive took us to *Invercannie*, where the ceremony took place. I got out and stood outside the tent while the Lord Provost (whom I knighted at *Aberdeen* in 1863) read the address. Then I had to read my answer, which made me very nervous; but I got through it well, though it was the first time I had read anything since my darling Husband was taken from me. Then came the turning of the cock, and it was very pretty to see the water rushing up.

These waterworks are on a most extensive scale, and are estimated to convey to the city 6,000,000 gallons of water daily. The water is from the river *Dee*, from which it is diverted at *Cairnton*, about four miles above *Banchory*. The principal features of the works are a tunnel 760 yards in length, which is cut through the hill of *Cairnton*, composed of solid rock of a very hard nature. At the end of the tunnel is the *Invercannie* Reservoir, where the ceremony took place. This reservoir is estimated to contain 15,000,000 gallons of water. It is just two years and a half since the first turf of the undertaking was cut, and the cost of the works is 130,000*l*. The ceremony was over in less than a quarter of an hour, and we returned as we came, stopping a moment at the door of Mr. Davidson's house, where his daughter presented me with a nosegay. The day was fine and mild. The people were very kind, and cheered a good deal.

We got back at twenty minutes past two.*

[+] He died on March 31, 1870. He had been with me as equerry from the tine I came to the Throne. In 1846 he became Private Secretary to the Prince, and from December 1861 held the same position with me till his death. He was highly esteemed and valued by us both, and his loss grieved me deeply.

Halloween,
October 31, 1866–1867.*

While we were at Mrs. Grant's we saw the commencement of the keeping of Halloween. All the children came out with burning torches, shouting and jumping. The Protestants generally keep Halloween on the old day, November 12, and the Catholics on this day; but hearing I had wished to see it two years ago, they all decided to keep it to-day. When we drove home we saw all the gillies coming along with burning torches, and torches and bonfires appeared also on the opposite side of the water. We went upstairs to look at it from the windows, from whence it had a very pretty effect.

On the same day in the following year, viz., Thursday, October 31, 1867, we had an opportunity of again seeing the celebration of Halloween, and even of taking part in it. We had been out driving, but we hurried back to be in time for the celebration. Close to Donald Stewart's house we were met by two gillies bearing torches. Louise got out and took one, walking by the side of the carriage, and looking like one of the witches in "Macbeth." As we approached *Balmoral*, the keepers and their wives and children, the gillies and other people met us, all with torches; Brown also carrying one. We got out at the house, where Leopold joined us, and a torch was given to him. We walked round the whole house, preceded by Ross playing the pipes, going down the steps of the terrace. Louise and Leopold went first, then came Janie Ely and I, followed by every one carrying torches, which had a very pretty effect. After this a bonfire was made of all the torches, close to the house, and they danced reels whilst Ross played the pipes.

Visit to
Floors* and the Scotch Border Country,
August 20, 1867.

Tuesday, August 20, 1867.

At ten o'clock I left *Windsor* (those night departures are always sad) with Louise, Leopold, and Baby (Beatrice); Lenchen, Christian, and their little baby boy meeting us at the station.* Jane Churchill, Harriet Phipps, the two governesses, Sir Thomas Biddulph, Lord Charles Fitz-Roy, Colonel G. Gordon, Mr. Duckworth, and Dr. Jenner were in attendance. I had been much annoyed to hear just before dinner that our saloon carriage could not go under some tunnel or arch beyond *Carlisle*, and that I must get out and change carriages there.

Wednesday, August 21.

The railway carriage swung a good deal, and it was very hot, so that I did not get much sleep. At half-past seven I was woke up to dress and hurry out at *Carlisle*, which we did at a quarter to eight. Here in the station we had some breakfast, and waited an hour till our carriage was taken off and another put on (which they have since found out was quite unnecessary!) The morning, which had been gloomy, cleared and became very fine, and we went on along such a pretty line through a very pretty country, through *Eskdale* and past *Netherby*, as far as *Riddings*, and then leaving the E*sk* entered *Liddesdale*, the railway running along the *Liddel Water* to *Riccarton* station, where we stopped for a moment. We next came along the *Slitrig Water* to *Hawick*, where we went slowly, which the people had begged us to do, and where were great crowds. Here we entered *Teviotdale* and descended it, entering the valley of the *Tweed* at *St. Boswell's*. Between *St. Boswell's* and *Kelso* at *Roxburgh* station, we crossed the *Teviot* again. We passed close under the *Eildon Hills*, three high points rising from the background. The country is extremely picturesque, valleys with fine trees and streams, intermingled with great cultivation. Only after half-past eleven did we reach *Kelso* station, which was very prettily decorated, and where were standing the Duke and Duchess of Roxburghe, Lord Bowmont, the Duke of Buccleuch, and Lord C. Ker, as well as General Hamilton, commanding the forces in *Scotland*. We got out at once. I embraced the dear Duchess, and shook hands with the two Dukes, and then at once entered the carriage (mine) with Lenchen, Louise, and the Duchess; Beatrice, Leopold, and Christian going in the second, and the others following in other carriages.

The morning beautiful and very mild. We drove through the small suburb of *Maxwell Heugh*, down into the town of *Kelso*, and over the bridge which commands a beautiful view of the broad stream of the *Tweed* and of the *Park of Floors*, with the fine house itself. Everywhere decorations, and great and most enthusiastic crowds. The little town of *Kelso* is very picturesque, and there were triumphal arches, and no end of pretty mottoes, and every house was decorated with flowers and flags. Fifty ladies dressed in white strewed flowers as we passed. Volunteers were out and bands playing. At the Market Place the carriage stopped; an address was presented, not read; and a little girl was held up to give me an enormous bouquet. Immense and most enthusiastic cheering. We then drove on, amidst continued crowds and hearty cheers, up to the very park gates, where the old Sheriff, eighty-five years old, was presented. The park is remarkably fine, with the approach under splendid beech, sycamore, and oak trees. The house very handsome, built originally by Sir John Vanbrugh in 1718, but much improved by the present Duke. You drive under a large porch, and then go up a flight of steps to the hall. The Duke's band was stationed outside. Mr. and Lady Charlotte Russell, Mr. Suttie, and Lady Charles Ker were in the hall. The Duchess took us into the library, where the Duke of Buccleuch joined us, and, after waiting a little while, we had breakfast (ourselves alone) in the really splendid dining-room adjoining, at ten minutes past twelve. This over, the Duchess showed us to our rooms upstairs. I had three that were very comfortable, opening one into the other: a sitting-room, dressing-room, and the largest of the three, the bedroom, simple, with pretty chintz, but very elegant, nice and comfortable. The children were close at hand. But the feeling of loneliness when I saw no room for my darling, and felt I was indeed alone and a widow, overcame me very sadly! It was the first time I had gone in this way on a visit (like as in former times), and I thought so much of all dearest Albert would have done and said, and how he would have wandered about everywhere, admired everything, looked at everything—and now! Oh! must it ever, ever be so?

At half-past two lunched (as at home) in the fine dining-room. A lovely day. The view from the windows beautiful. The distant *Cheviot* range with a great deal of wood, *Kelso* embosomed in, rich woods, with the bridge, and the *Tweed* flowing beneath natural grass terraces which go down to it. Very fine. It reminded me a little of the view from the *Phœnix Park* near *Dublin*.

At half-past five walked out with Lenchen and the kind Duchess to a spot where I planted a tree,[+] and then we walked on to the flower-garden, where there are a number of very fine hot-houses, and took tea in a pretty little room adjoining them, which is entirely tiled. After this we took a pleasant drive in the fine park which is full of splendid timber, along the *Tweed*, and below the ruins of the celebrated old *Castle of Roxburgh*,* of which there is very little remaining. It is on a high eminence; the *Tweed* and *Teviot* are on either side of it, so that the position is remarkably strong. It stood many a siege, and was frequently taken by the English and retaken by the Scotch. Scotch and even English kings, amongst them Edward III., held their Court there.

We came home at eight. The Duke and Duchess dined with us, and after dinner we watched the illuminations and many bonfires from the library, and afterwards went for a moment into the drawing-room to see the ladies and gentlemen, after which I went up to my room, where I sat and rested, feeling tired and only able to read the newspapers.

Thursday, August 22.

A fine morning, though rather hazy. The night and moonlight had been beautiful. Breakfasted with our family in the breakfast-room. At twenty minutes to eleven went and sat out under some trees on the lawn near the house writing, where I was quite quiet and undisturbed, and remained till half-past twelve, resting, reading, etc. Immediately after luncheon started in two carriages, the Duchess and our two daughters with me; Christian, the Duke, Lady Charlotte Russell, and Lord Charles Fitz-Roy in the second carriage (with post-horses). We had the Duke's horses as far as *Ravenswood*. We drove through *Kelso*, which was full of people, crossed the *Tweed* and *Teviot* (where the waters join), and passed below the old *Castle of Roxburgh*. The country is very pretty, hilly, wooded, and cultivated. Not long after we started, the second carriage disappeared, and we waited for it. It seems that, at the first hill they came to, the wheelers would not hold up. So we stopped (and this delayed us some time), the leaders replaced the wheelers, and they came on with a pair. Then we drove up to *St. Boswell's Green*, with the three fine *Eildon* hills before us—which are said to have been divided by Michael Scott, the wizard*—seeing *Mertoun*, my excellent Lord Polwarth's place, on the other side of the road. Alas! he died only last Friday from a second stroke, the first of which seized him in February; and now, when he had intended

---

[+] The gardener, Hector Rose, became head gardener at Windsor in the spring of 1868, and died, alas! June 5, 1872, after having filled his situation admirably.

to be at the head of the volunteers who received me at *Kelso*, he is lying dead at his house which we passed so near! It lies low, and quite in among the trees. I lament him deeply and sincerely, having liked him very much, as did my dearest Albert also, ever since we knew him in 1858.

We changed horses at *Ravenswood*, or old *Melrose* (where I had my own), having caught a glimpse of where *Dryburgh Abbey** is, though the railway almost hides it. The Duke of Buccleuch met us there, and rode the whole way. Everywhere, wherever there were dwellings, there was the kindest welcome, and triumphal arches were erected. We went by the side of the *Eildon Hills*, past an immense railway viaduct, and nothing could be prettier than the road. The position of *Melrose* is most picturesque, surrounded by woods and hills. The little village, or rather town, of *Newstead*, which we passed through just before coming to *Melrose*, is very narrow and steep. We drove straight up to the *Abbey** through the grounds of the Duke of Buccleuch's agent, and got out and walked about the ruins, which are indeed very fine, and some of the architecture and carving in beautiful preservation. David I., who is described as a "sair Saint," originally built it, but the Abbey, the ruins of which are now standing, was built in the fifteenth century. We saw where, under the high altar, Robert Bruce's heart is supposed to be buried; also the tomb of Alexander II., and of the celebrated wizard, Michael Scott. Reference is made to the former in some lines of Sir Walter Scott's in the "Lay of the Last Minstrel," which describes this Border country:—

> They sat them down on a marble stone;
> A Scottish monarch slept below.*

And then when Deloraine takes the book from the dead wizard's hand, it says—

> He thought, as he took it, the dead man frowned.*

Most truly does Walter Scott say—

> If thou wouldst view fair Melrose aright,
> Go visit it by the pale moonlight.*

It looks very ghostlike, and reminds me a little of *Holyrood Chapel*. We walked in the churchyard to look at the exterior of the Abbey, and then re-entered our carriages and drove through the densely crowded streets. Great enthusiasm and hearty affectionate loyalty. Many decorations. A number of people from *Galashiels*, and even from the North of *England*, had come into the town and swelled the crowd; many also had spread themselves along the outskirts. We took the other side of the valley returning, and saw *Galashiels*, very prettily situated, a flourishing town famous for its tweeds and shawls; the men are called the "braw lads of *Gala Water*."

Another twenty minutes or half-hour brought us to *Abbotsford*,* the well-known residence of Sir Walter Scott. It lies low and looks rather gloomy. Mr. Hope Scott and Lady Victoria† (my goddaughter and sister to the present Duke of Norfolk) with their children, the young Duke of Norfolk, and some other relations, received us. Mr. Hope Scott married first Miss Lockhart, the last surviving grandchild of Sir Walter Scott, and she died leaving only one daughter, a pretty girl of eleven, to whom this place will go, and who is the only surviving descendant of Sir Walter. They showed us the part of the house in which Sir Walter lived, and all his rooms—his drawing-room with the same furniture and carpet, the library where we saw his MS. of "Ivanhoe," and several others of his novels and poems in a beautiful handwriting with hardly any erasures, and other relics which Sir Walter had himself collected. Then his study, a small dark room, with a little turret in which is a bust in bronze, done from a cast taken after death, of Sir Walter. In the study we saw his journal, in which Mr. Hope Scott asked me to write my name (which I felt it to be a presumption in me to do), as also the others.

We went through some passages into two or three rooms where were collected fine specimens of old armour, etc., and where in a glass case are Sir Walter's last clothes. We ended by going into the dining-room, in which Sir Walter Scott died where we took tea....

We left at twenty minutes to seven—very late. It rained a little, but soon ceased. We recrossed the *Tweed*, and went by *Gattonside* to *Leaderfoot Bridge*. Here we were met by the *Berwickshire* Volunteers, commanded by Lord Binning (Lord Haddington's son), who as Deputy Lieutenant rode a long way with us. Here was a steep hill, and the road surrounded by trees. We passed soon after through *Gladswood*, the property of Mr. Meiklam, at whose house-door we stopped, and he and Mrs. Meiklam were presented, and their daughter gave me a nosegay. Just after this we entered *Berwickshire*. Changing horses and leaving this place, going over *Gateheugh*, we came upon a splendid view, overlooking a great extent of country, with a glen deep below the road, richly wooded, the river at the bottom, and hills in the distance; but unfortunately the "gloaming"† was already commencing—at least, the sun was gone down, and the evening was grey and dull, though very mild. We passed *Bemersyde*, which is eventually to belong to Alfred's Equerry, Mr. Haig,‡ and through the

---

† She died in 1870.   † The Scotch word for "twilight."
‡ He succeeded to the property in 1878.

village of *Mertoun*, behind the park; and it was striking to see the good feeling shown by the people, who neither displayed any decorations nor cheered, though they were out and bowed, as their excellent master, Lord Polwarth, was lying dead in his house.

It was nearly dark by this time, but we got well and safely home by ten minutes to nine. The Duke of Buccleuch rode with us some way beyond *Gladswood*. We did not come through *Kelso* on our way back. In passing *Mertoun* we left the old tower of *Smailholm* to the left, the scene of the "Eve of St. John."* We only sat down to dinner at half-past nine, and I own I was very tired. The Duke of Buccleuch was only able to come when dinner was half over. Besides him the Duke and Duchess of Roxburghe, Lord Bowmont, Lady Charles Ker, and Mr. Suttie made the party at dinner. Lady Susan was prevented by indisposition from being there. Nobody could be kinder, or more discreet, or more anxious that I should be undisturbed when at home, than the Duke and Duchess. I only stopped a few minutes downstairs after dinner, and then went up to my room, but it was then nearly eleven. The others went into the drawing-room to meet some of the neighbours.

Friday, August 23.

A dull morning, very close, with a little inclination to rain, though only for a short time. Breakfast as yesterday. At twenty minutes to eleven we started: I with our daughters and the Duchess; Christian with dear Beatrice, the Duke of Marlborough (the Minister in attendance), and Lady Susan Melville, in the second carriage; and the Duke of Roxburghe, Lord Charles Fitz-Roy, Sir Thomas Biddulph, in the third, with Colonel Gordon and Dr. Jenner on the box.[+] We proceeded through *Kelso*, which was very full, and the people most loyal; by the village of *Heiton*, prettily decorated with an arch (two young girls dressed in white threw nosegays), and up the rivers *Teviot* and *Jed*, which flow through charming valleys. The town of *Jedburgh* is very prettily situated, and is about the same size as *Kelso*, only without its large shops. It is, however, the capital of the county. It was very crowded, and very prettily decorated. The town is full of historical recollections. King Malcolm IV. died there; William the Lion and Alexander II. resided there; Alexander III.* married his second wife, Joletta, daughter of the Comte de Dreux, there; and Queen Mary* was the last sovereign who came to administer severe justice. The Duchess pointed out to me a house up a side street in the town

---

[+] Brown and the sergeant footman, Collins, were (as usual) on the seat behind my carriage.

where Queen Mary had lived and been ill with fever. In the square an address was presented, just as at *Kelso*, and then we went on down a steep hill, having a very good view of the old Abbey,* as curious in its way as *Melrose*, and also founded by David I. There is a very fine ruined abbey in *Kelso* also.

There were four pretty triumphal arches; one with two very well chosen inscriptions, viz., on one side "Freedom makes all men to have lyking," and on the other side "The love of all thy people comfort thee."

We went on through a beautiful wooded valley up the *Jed*, in the bank of which, in the red stone, are caves in which the Covenanters were hid.* We passed Lord Cranstoun's place, *Crailing*, and then turned, and close before the town we turned into *Jed Forest*—up an interminable hill, which was very trying to the horses and the postilions—and returned through the grounds of *Hartrigge*, the late Lord Campbell's, now occupied by a Mr. Gordon.

We then returned by the same road we came, passing *Kirkbank*, belonging to the Duke of Buccleuch, where his late brother, Lord John Scott, used to live. Here the horses were watered. We stopped for a few minutes, and the Duke of Buccleuch, who had ridden with us the greater part of the way, into *Jedburgh* and back to this place, took leave.

We only got home near three o'clock. We lunched at once, and then I rested. Only at half-past six did I go out with Lenchen and the good Duchess, and walked with them to the flower-garden, where, as it began to rain, we took tea in the small room there. Lenchen walked back with the Duchess, who returned to me, and I sat out a little while with her, and then walked back to the house. It was a very oppressive evening.

At half-past eight we dined. The Duke and Duchess, Mr. and Lady Charlotte Russell, and Lord Charles Ker dined. Went upstairs and wrote. At ten minutes to eleven we left *Floors*, where I had been most kindly received, and had been very comfortable and enjoyed all I saw, and felt much all the kindness of high and low. The carriages were open, and the night very warm and starlight. There were lamps all along the drive in the Park; the bridge was illuminated, and so was the whole town, through which we went at a foot's pace. It was densely crowded, the square especially, and the people very enthusiastic. The dear Duchess went with us to the station, whither the Duke and his sons had preceded us with the others. It was a very pretty sight. The *Free Kirk*, a pretty building, was lit up with red light, which almost gave it the appearance of being on fire.* We took leave of the dear Duchess and the Duke, got into our railway carriage, and started at once.

Saturday, August 24.

We passed through *Edinburgh*. At eight a.m. we were at *Ballater*. Some coffee and tea were handed in to us before we left the train and got into our carriages.

A fine and very mild morning, the heather hardly out, but all very green; and at ten minutes to nine we were at our dear *Balmoral*.*

Jane Churchill
1875

Visit to Glenfiddich.

Tuesday, September 24, 1867.

A bright morning, but a fearful gale blowing. The maids, Emilie and Annie and Lady Churchill's maid, with Ross and the luggage, started at a little past seven.

Breakfasted at a quarter past nine; and at ten, taking leave of Lenchen, darling Beatrice, and the boys, and Christian, started with Louise and Jane Churchill—Brown, as usual, on the box. Sir Thomas Biddulph had gone on at eight. We drove up by *Alt Craichie* on to *Gairnshiel*, and anything like the wind I cannot describe. It blew through everything. Just beyond *Gairnshiel* we took another change of my own horses, which took us up that very steep hill called *Glaschoil*. Here we met the luggage with Blake,[†] which had stuck completely, but was going on with the help of four cart or farm horses, and then we went on by *Tornahoish* and *Cock Brigg*, where we crossed the *Don*. At the small inn at the foot of the hill, called *Bridge End*, we found the maids' carriage halting. They were waiting for the luggage, but we sent them on. Our postilions next took a wrong road, and we had to get out to enable them to turn. Then came a very steep hill, the beginning of very wild and really grand scenery. Louise and Jane Churchill walked up to the top of this hill, and then we went down another very steep one, seeing a fearfully long ascent before us. We changed horses, and took a pair of post-horses here. Steep green hills with a deep ravine on our left as we went up, and then down again, this fearful hill—surely three miles in length—called *Lecht*. At the bottom we entered a glen, or rather pass, very wild, and the road extremely bad, with rapid turnings. Near this there are iron mines belonging to the Duke of Richmond. Here we met a drove of very fine Highland cattle grazing.* Turning out of this glen we came into much more cultivated land with farms and trees, skirted by hills in the distance—all very clear, as the views had been all along, By half-past one we came close by *Tomintoul*, which lies very prettily amongst the trees, hills, and fields; then leaving it to our left, we went on about a mile and a half beyond the town; and here by the roadside, on some grass below a heathery bank, at about a quarter-past two, we took our luncheon, and walked a little. The Duke of Richmond's keeper, Lindsay by name, joined us here and rode

---

[†] A footmen, now one of the Pages of the Presence.*

before us. We changed horses (again a pair) and drove on, entering *Glen Livet* through the small village of *Knockandhu*—*Blairfindy Castle* on the left, just behind the celebrated *Glenlivet Distillery*.* We drove on six miles; pretty country all along, distant high hills and richly cultivated land, with houses and cottages dotted about. At *Tomnavoulin*, a farm, not far from a bridge, we met Sir Thomas Biddulph (who had driven on in a dogcart) and our ponies. Though the wind had gone down a good deal, there was quite enough to make it disagreeable and fatiguing, and so we decided to drive, and Sir Thomas said he would ride across with the ponies and meet the Duke, while his head keeper was to come on the box with Brown and show us the way (Grant did not go with us this time). We drove on for an hour and more, having entered *Glen Rinnes* shortly after *Tomnavoulin*, with the hills of *Ben Rinnes* on the left. There were fine large fields of turnips, pretty hills and dales, with wood, and distant high hills, but nothing grand. The day became duller, and the mist hung over the hills; and just as we sat down by the roadside on a heathery bank, where there is a very pretty view of *Glenlivet*, to take our tea, it began to rain, and continued doing so for the remainder of the evening. Lindsay, the head keeper, fetched a kettle with boiling water from a neighbouring farmhouse. About two miles beyond this we came through *Dufftown*—a small place with a long steep street, very like *Grantown*—and then turned abruptly to the right past *Auchindoun*, leaving a pretty glen to the left. Three miles more brought us to a lodge and gate, which was the entrance of *Glenfiddich*. Here you go quite into the hills. The glen is very narrow, with the *Fiddich* flowing below, green hills rising on either side with birch trees growing on them, much like at *Inchrory*, only narrower. We saw deer on the tops of the hills close by. The carriage-road—a very good one—winds along for nearly three miles, when you come suddenly upon the lodge, the position of which reminds me very much of *Corn Davon*,† only that the glen is narrower and the hills just round it steeper. It is a long shooting lodge, covering a good deal of ground, but only one story high. We reached it at half-past six, and it was nearly dark. Sir Thomas received us, but he had missed the Duke! A message had, however, at once been sent after him. On entering the house there is one long, low passage, at the end of which, with three windows, taking in the whole of each side and looking three different ways, is the drawing-room, where tea was prepared. We went along the passage to our rooms, which were all in a row. Another long

---

† Near Balmoral, not far from Loch Bulig.

passage, a little beyond the hall door, went the other way at right angles with the first, and along that were offices and servants' bedrooms. Next to the drawing-room came the dining-room, then Sir Thomas Biddulph's room, then the Duke's, then Brown's and Ross's (in one), then Louise's, then mine, then Emilie's and Annie's (in one), then, a little further back, Jane Churchill's and her maid's—all very comfortably and conveniently together. But though our maids had arrived, not a bit of luggage. We waited and waited till dinner-time, but nothing came. So we ladies (for Sir Thomas had wisely brought some things with him) had to go to dinner in our riding-skirts, and just as we were. I, having no cap, had to put on a black lace veil of Emilie's, which she arranged as a coiffure. I had been writing and resting before dinner. The Duke (who remained at *Glenfiddich*) and Sir Thomas dined with us ladies.

None of the maids or servants had any change of clothing. Dinner over, I went with Louise and Jane to the drawing-room, which was given me as my sitting-room, and Jane read. While at dinner at half-past nine, Ross told us that Blake, the footman, had arrived with some of the smaller things, but none of the most necessary—no clothes, etc. The break with the luggage had finally broken down at *Tomintoul*; from thence Blake had gone with a cart to *Duffiown*, where he had got a small break, and brought the light things on, but the heavier luggage was coming in a cart, and they hoped would be here by twelve o'clock. At first it seemed as if no horses were to be had, and it was only with the greatest difficulty that some were at last obtained. Louise and Jane Churchill left me at near eleven o'clock.

I sat up writing and waiting for this luggage. A man was sent out on a pony with a lantern in search of it, and I remained writing till a quarter-past twelve, when, feeling very tired, I lay down on the sofa, and Brown (who was indefatigable) went out himself to look for it. At one, he came back, saying nothing was to be seen or heard of this luckless luggage, and urged my going to bed. My maids had unfortunately not thought of bringing anything with them, and I disliked the idea of going to bed without any of the necessary toilette. However, some arrangements were made which were very uncomfortable; and after two I got into bed, but had very little sleep at first; finally fatigue got the better of discomfort, and after three I fell asleep.*

Wednesday, September 25.

Slept soundly till half-past seven, and heard that the luggage had only arrived at half-past four in the morning. Breakfasted with Louise, who made my coffee beautifully with Brown, who waited at breakfast, Ross coming in and out with what had to be carried. It rained soon after I got up, and continued raining till near eleven. I read and wrote, etc. At half-past eleven, it having cleared, I rode up the small narrow glen, down which flows a "burnie" (called the *Garden Burn*), the banks covered with fern and juniper, heather and birch, etc., past the kitchen-garden. Louise walked with me. Went up nearly to the top and walked down it again, then on to the stables, which are at a small distance from the house, where I saw an old underkeeper, P. Stewart by name, seventy-four years old, with a Peninsular and Waterloo medal,* who had been in the 92nd Highlanders, and was a great favourite of the late Duke's. Home by twenty minutes to one. The day became very fine and warm. Lunched in my own room with Louise at the same small table at which we had breakfasted, Ross and the Duke's piper playing outside the window.

After luncheon rode (on Sultan, as this morning) with Louise and Jane Churchill, the Duke walking (and Jane also part of the way), down to the end of *Glenfiddich*; turning then to the left for *Bridgehaugh* (a ford), and going on round the hill of *Ben Main*. We first went along the road and then on the heather "squinting" the hill—hard and good ground, but disagreeable from the heather being so deep that you did not see where you were going—the Duke's forester leading the way, and so fast that Brown led me on at his full speed, and we distanced the others entirely. At five we got to the edge of a small ravine, from whence we had a fine view of the old ruined castle of *Achendown*, which formerly belonged to the old Lords Huntly. Here we took our tea, and then rode home by another and a shorter way—not a bad road, but on the steeper side of the hill, and quite on the slant, which is not agreeable. We came down at the ford, and rode back as we went out, getting home at seven. A very fine evening. It was very nearly dark when we reached home. I was very tired; I am no longer equal to much fatigue.

Thursday, September 26.

Slept very well and was much rested. At half-past twelve I started with Louise on ponies (I on Sultan), and Jane Churchill, the Duke of Richmond, and Sir Thomas walking, rode past the stables on a good road, and then turned to the right and went up *Glenfiddich* for about four miles. The scenery is not grand, but pretty; an open valley with green and not very high hills, some birches, and a great deal of fern and juniper. After about three miles the glen narrows and is extremely pretty; a narrow steep path overhanging a burn leads to a cave, which the Duke said went a long way under the hill. It is called the *Elf House.** There is a small space of level ground, and a sort of seat arranged with stones, on which Louise and I sat; and here we all lunched, and then tried to sketch. But I could make nothing of the cave, and therefore scrambled up part of the hill with great trouble, and tried again but equally unsuccessfully, and had to be helped down, as I had been helped up, by Brown. We were here nearly an hour, and then, after walking down the steep path, we got on our ponies and rode up to the left, another very steep and narrow path, for a short while on the brink of a steep high bank with the *Fiddich* below. We emerged from this ravine and came upon moors in the hills (the whole of this is "the forest"), and rode on a mile and a half till near the head of the *Livet* on the right of the *Sowie*, a high, bare, heathery, mossy hill; *Cairn-ta-Bruar* to the left. Here we had a fine view of *Ben Aven* and *Ben-na-Bourd*, and this was the very way we should have ridden from *Tomnavoulin*. We had a slight sprinkling of rain, but very little at this time. We saw eight stags together at a distance. Oh! had dearest Albert been here with his rifle! We rode on and back till we came to a sheltered place near the burnside, about one mile and three-quarters from *Glenfiddich Lodge*, where one of the Duke's keepers had prepared a fire and got a kettle boiling, and here we took our tea. Afterwards I sketched, but we were surrounded by a perfect cloud of midges which bit me dreadfully. The gentlemen left us, after tea, and walked home. I walked a little while, and then rode back by a quarter to seven. A beautiful mild evening, the sky a lovely colour. Dear good Sharp[+] was with us and out each day, and so affectionate.

A. Thomson, S. Forbes, Kennedy, and J. Stewart, the latter with the ponies, as well as the Duke's forester Lindsay, were out with us. Dinner as yesterday. Jane Churchill finished reading "Pride and Prejudice"* to us after dinner. A very clear starlight night.

Friday, September 27.

A fair but dull morning. These quiet breakfasts with dear Louise, who was most amiable, attentive, and cheerful, were very comfortable, just as they had been in 1865 with good Lenchen, and in 1866 with Louise at *Dunkeld*. Sketched hastily the stables from one window, and the approach from the other. The house in itself is really a good one, the rooms so well-sized and so conveniently placed, all close to each other. The cuisine, though very simple, was excellent, and the meat etc. the very best—only a female cook.* The Duke was very kind.

At a quarter-past ten we left, taking leave of the Duke at the door. Sir Thomas sat with Brown on the box. The day was raw. We drove

---

[+] A favourite collie of mine.

SHARP

precisely the same way as we came. In *Duftown* the people had turned out, the bell was rung and the band played, but they seemed hardly sure till we had passed who it was. We drove through at a great rate. The day being fair, we could see the country better. At one we got to the same place where we had lunched on Tuesday, and here changed horses, and Sir Thomas left us and got into his dogcart and drove after us. The sun had come out, and the day was fine and warm. As we passed *Tomnavoulin*, and in various other places, people were out. We drove on for about two or three miles, and then stopped at twenty minutes to two, just before we turned into the glen of the *Lecht Hills*; and here just below the road, under a bank on the grass, we sat down and took our luncheon, and sketched. Sir Thomas drove on, and we saw him again near the top of the hills, while we began the first very steep ascent, which seemed almost beyond the horses' power; but though only a pair, they got us up admirably. Brown walked by the carriage all the time, being very anxious about the road. Then down ever so long, having a splendid view of the hills—the road being dreadfully rough and bad besides—then up again, and when it came to that very steep winding hill going down to *Bridge End*, we got out and walked to the bottom and across the ford at *Tornahoish* over a foot-bridge. The view here was splendid, all the hills rising around, with the old *Castle of Corgarff,* and the river *Don* with the valley of the *Don-side* in the foreground.

Here we found our horses and drove on. It was raining at this time (about four), and it rained several times during the evening. We drove on, and after we passed *Tornahoish* two or three miles, and had got up the long hill, we found a sort of hole in the bank (such as are often met with where gravel and stones have been taken out), where we took our tea. The kettle took some time boiling, as we had only cold water from the burn. When we go out only for the afternoon we take two bottles filled with hot water, which saves much time. Poor Louise had been suffering from toothache all the time. We got safely home at ten minutes past seven o'clock.

Unveiling of the Prince's Statue at Balmoral.

Tuesday, October 15, 1867.

Our blessed Engagement Day! A dear and sacred day—already twenty-eight years ago. How I ever bless it! A wet morning—most annoying and provoking!*

At a quarter-past eleven in this distressing rain, which twice had given hopes of ceasing, I, with all the family and Janie Ely, drove to the spot, just above *Middleton's Lodge*, where were assembled all the servants and tenants, and the detachment of the 93rd Highlanders* drawn up opposite, just behind the Statue.* I and the children stood just in front of the Statue, which was covered. A verse of the 100th Psalm was sung, and Mr. Taylor then stepped forward and offered up a beautiful prayer (in pelting rain at that moment), after which the order was given to uncover the Statue; but (as happened at *Aberdeen*) the covering caught, and it was a little while before it could be loosened from the shoulder.

The soldiers presented arms, and the pipes played, as we gazed on the dear noble figure of my beloved one, who used to be with us here in the prime of beauty, goodness, and strength.

Then Dr. Robertson stepped forward, and made a very pretty little speech in the name of the servants and tenants, thanking me for the gift of the statue. He spoke remarkably well. This was followed by the soldiers firing a *feu de joie*; then all cheered, and the whole concluded by "God save the Queen" being sung extremely well.

GLASSALT SHIEL.

First Visit to the Glassalt Shiel.*
A House-warming.

Thursday, October 1, 1868.

At nearly four o'clock left with Louise and Jane Churchill for the *Glassalt Shiel*. It was a beautiful evening, clear and frosty. We drove by *Birkhall* and the *Linn of Muich*, where we stopped to take tea; we had just finished when Arthur arrived from *Ballater* with Grant, who had gone to meet him there. He had travelled straight from *Geneva*, and looked rather tired, having besides had a bad passage. After walking a little we drove on, Arthur getting into the carriage with us, and Grant going with Brown on the box. We arrived at half-past six at the *Glassalt Shiel*, which looked so cheerful and comfortable, all lit up, and the rooms so cozy and nice. There is a wonderful deal of room in the compact little house. A good staircase (the only one)* leads to the upper floor, where are the rooms for Louise, Jane Churchill, her maid, and Arthur, in one passage; out of this there is another, where are three rooms for Brown, the cook, and another servant; in one of these Grant and Ross slept, and C. Thomson in the other. Below are my sitting-room, bedroom, and my maids' room; and on the other side of our little hall the dining-room; then a nice kitchen, small steward's room, store-closet, and another small room where two menservants slept. The small passage near my bedroom shuts off the rest, and makes it quite private and quiet. Good stables, and the keeper's cottage, where our gillies sleep, just outside at the back.

We dined at about half-past eight in the small dining-room. This over, after waiting for a little while in my sitting-room, Brown came to say all the servants were ready for the house-warming, and at twenty minutes to ten we went into the little dining-room, which had been cleared, and where all the servants were assembled, viz., my second dresser,+ C. Wilmore, Brown, Grant, Ross (who played), Hollis (the cook), Lady Churchill's maid, Maxted, C. and A. Thomson, Blake (the footman), the two housemaids, Kennedy, J. Stewart (the stableman), and the policeman (who only comes to do duty outside at night). We made nineteen altogether. Five animated reels were danced, in which all (but myself) joined. After the first reel "whisky-toddy" was brought round for every one, and Brown begged I would drink to the "fire-kindling." Then

---

+ She was in my service for thirteen years, and left in 1881.

Grant made a little speech, with an allusion to the wild place we were in, and concluding with a wish "that our Royal Mistress, our good Queen," should "live long." This was followed by cheers given out by Ross in regular Highland style, and all drank my health. The merry pretty little ball ended at a quarter-past eleven. The men, however, went on singing in the steward's room for some time, and all were very happy, but I heard nothing, as the little passage near my bedroom shuts everything off.

Sad thoughts filled my heart both before dinner and when I was alone and retired to rest. I thought of the happy past and my darling husband whom I fancied I must see, and who always wished to build here, in this favourite wild spot, quite in amidst the hills. At *Altnagiuthasach* I could not have lived again now—alone. It is far better to have built a totally new house; but then the sad thought struck me that it was the first *Widow's house*, not built by him or hallowed by his memory. But I am sure his blessing does rest on it, and on those who live in it.*

"Juicing the Sheep," 1868.

Thursday, October 21.

At a quarter to twelve I drove off with Louise and Leopold in the waggonette up to near the "*Bush*" (the residence of William Brown,[+] the farmer) to see them "juice the sheep." This is a practice pursued all over the *Highlands* before the sheep are sent down to the low country for the winter. It is done to preserve the wool.* Not far from the burnside, where there are a few hillocks, was a pen in which the sheep were placed, and then, just outside it, a large sort of trough filled with liquid tobacco and soap, and into this the sheep were dipped one after the other; one man (James Brown,[†] my shepherd, the elder brother, who came up on purpose to help) took the sheep one by one out of the pen and turned them on their backs; and then William and he, holding them by their legs, dipped them well in, after which they were let into another pen into which this trough opened, and here they had to remain to dry. To the left, a little lower down, was a cauldron boiling over a fire and containing the tobacco with water and soap; this was then emptied into a tub, from which it was transferred into the trough. A very rosy-faced lassie, with a plaid over her head, was superintending this part of the work, and helped to fetch the water from the burn, while children and many collie dogs were grouped about, and several men and shepherds were helping. It was a very curious and picturesque sight.

[+] Brown's fourth brother.   [†] Brown's eldest brother.

A Highland "Kirstnin" (Christening), 1868.*

Sunday, October 24.

At a quarter to four I drove, with Louise, Beatrice, and Lady Ely, to John Thomson the wood forester's house for the christening of their child, three weeks old. Here, in their little sitting-room, in front of the window stood a table covered with a white cloth, on which was placed a basin with water, a bible, and a paper with the certificate of the child's birth.

We stood on one side, and John Thomson in his Highland dress next the minister, who was opposite me at the head of the table. Barbara, his wife, stood next to him, with the baby in her arms, and then the old Thomsons and their unmarried daughter, the Donald Stewarts, Grants, and Victoria, Morgan and sister, and Brown.

Dr. Taylor (who wore his gown) then began with an address and prayer, giving thanks "for a living mother and a living child," after which followed another prayer; he then read a few passages from Scripture, after which came the usual questions which he addressed to the father, and to which he bowed assent. Then the minister told him—"Present your child for baptism." After this the father took the child and held it while the minister baptised it, sprinkling it with water, but not making the sign of the cross, saying first to those present: "The child's name is Victoria;" and then to the child:

Victoria, I baptise thee in the name of the Father, and of the Son, and of the Holy Ghost, One God blessed for ever.—Amen.

The Lord bless thee and keep thee! The Lord make His face to shine upon thee and be gracious unto thee! The Lord lift up His countenance upon thee and give thee peace!

The service was concluded with another short prayer and the usual blessing. I thought it most appropriate, touching, and impressive. I gave my present (a silver mug) to the father, kissed the little baby, and then we all drank to its health and that of its mother in whisky, which was handed round with cakes. It was all so nicely done, so simply, and yet with such dignity.

A Second Christening, 1868.

On Monday, November 1, I drove down at a quarter to four with Louise, Beatrice, Leopold (who was on the box with Brown), and Lady Ely, to the *Bush* (William Brown's) to witness the christening of his first child, just a week old, which was to be called Albert. The service was nearly the same, only two instead of three prayers, and the young mother with the child, who was only a week old, was seated by the fire, looking very nice, with the baby on her lap. The old mother, Mrs. Brown, in her white mutch, the three brothers, and a few neighbours stood round the room. I gave my present. It was a touching and impressive sight to see the young father holding his child with an expression of so much devotion and earnestness. On this occasion a dinner was given by the father after we left, in which Dr. Taylor took part.

Widow Grant, 1869.

On Sunday, August 22, 1869, I went to see old Mrs. Grant, whom I was grieved to see sitting in her chair supported by pillows, and her poor feet raised upon cushions, very much altered in her face, and, I fear, dying of dropsy.

On August 26 I again saw her, and gave her a shawl and pair of socks, and found the poor old soul in bed, looking very weak and very ill, but bowing her head and thanking me in her usual way. I took her hand and held it.

On the 27th she died.

On the 28th I stopped at her cottage and went in with Louise and Leopold. We found all so clean and tidy, but all so silent. Mrs. Gordon, her daughter, was there, having arrived just in time to spend the last evening and night with her; and then she lifted the sheet, and there the poor old woman, whom we had known and seen from the first here these twenty-one years, lay on a bier in her shroud, but with her usual cap on, peaceful and little altered, her dark skin taking away from the usual terrible pallor of death. She had on the socks I gave her the day before yesterday. She was in her eighty-ninth year.

Visit to Invertrossachs, 1869.*

Wednesday, September 1, 1869.

We got up at half-past seven, breakfasted at eight, and at half-past eight left *Balmoral* with Louise, Beatrice, and Jane Churchill (Brown as always, unless I mention to the contrary, on the box), for *Ballater*. A high and rather cold wind, but very bright sun, dreadfully dusty. Colonel Ponsonby met us at the railway station. Emilie Dittweiler and Annie Macdonald, Ocklee (for the two girls), Jane Churchill's maid, Charlie Thomson, and the footman Cannon, went with us; Blake, Spong with the luggage, A. Thomson, with Sharp (my faithful collie dog), and Annie Gordon (housemaid), Kennedy, Arthur Grant, and Hiley (the groom) with the ponies, all went yesterday, and three cooks came from *London*. We had a saloon carriage, but not my own. It grew hot in the railway train. We stopped at *Aberdeen* and the *Bridge of Dun*, where Jane Churchill got into our carriage, and had luncheon with us; but we could have no one to help to pack and unpack it, which is now so comfortably arranged in my own railway carriage where there is a communication with the attendants.

Stopping a moment at *Cupar-Angus*, we passed through *Perth*, and had another short halt at *Dunblane*, where the people crowded very much. Here we got a view of the old Cathedral, and turned off to *Callander*,* which we reached at a quarter-past three. There was a very well-behaved crowd at the quiet station. Mr. and Lady Emily Macnaghten,[†] to whose house (which they had most kindly lent us) we were going, and Sir Malcolm and Lady Helen MacGregor (he is Miss MacGregor's nephew, she Lady Emily Macnaghten's niece), received us there. Their little girl gave me a nosegay. We at once got into our celebrated sociable, which has been to the top of the *Furca* in *Switzerland*, etc., and had been sent on before, Colonel Ponsonby and Brown going on the box. We drove off at once with post-horses through the small town of *Callander*, which consists of one long street with very few shops, and few good houses, but many poor ones. Poor Kanné[†] (who was to have managed everything, but had fallen ill) was still laid up there. We drove on, and, after about

---

[†] She died in 1874.

[†] My Director of Continental journeys, who had been sent to look at the house and to make arrangements for my reception.

three-quarters of a mile's drive, came to *Loch Vennachar*, a fine lake about four miles long, with *Ben Venue* and other high and beautiful mountains rising behind and around it. The road is thickly wooded with oak, birch, beech, mountain-ash, etc. The house stands extremely well on a high eminence, overlooking the loch and surrounded by trees, and you drive up through evergreens and trees of all kinds. Half an hour brought us to the door of the house, *Invertrossachs*,* which is small and comfortable. At the entrance is a nice little hall in which there is a small billiard table; to the left, beyond that, a very nice well-sized dining-room with one large window. To the right of the hall is the drawing-room, very much like the one at *Invermark* (Lord Dalhousie's); altogether the house is in that style, but larger. The staircase is almost opposite the hall-door, and there is a narrow passage which goes on to the left and right, along which are Louise's, Baby's (Beatrice's), my sitting-room (a snug little room), and my bedroom (very good size); and out of that, two little rooms which I use as dressing- and bath-rooms, and Emilie Dittweiler's. Further on, round a corner as it were, beyond Louise's, are Lady Churchill's, her maid's, and Colonel Ponsonby's rooms, all very fair-sized and comfortable. Close to my dressing-rooms is a staircase which goes upstairs to where Brown and our other people live. The rooms are very comfortably and simply furnished, and they have put down new carpets everywhere. In the absence of poor Kanné, whom we are so sorry for, Jungbluth, the cook, acts as steward, and showed us over the rooms.

We took tea and rested a little, and at twenty minutes to six drove out with the two girls (sweet Beatrice very happy and very good, the first time she had been without a governess) and Lady Churchill. We drove along the loch, which has always to be done, as there is no road on the *Invertrossachs* side further than *Invertrossachs* itself, and crossed over the bridge at *Coilantogleford* celebrated in the "Lady of the Lake,"* then to the right down a steep hill and over the bridge by *Kilmahog*, where there are a few cottages and a turnpike, on through the *Pass of Leny*, which is now (like every other burn and river) nearly dry, overhung by beautiful trees with very grand hills, reminding me much of *Switzerland* from their greenness, the rugged rocks, and the great amount of wood which grows at their base and a good way up. It reminded Louise and me very much of *Pilatus** with its meadows and fine trees on the way to *Hergessvyl*. We went as far as the beginning of *Loch Lubnaig*, a very fine wild, grand-looking loch; turning there and going back the same way. The view of *Loch Vennachar*,* with the beautiful deep blue of *Ben Venue* and the other hills, was lovely. We came in at half-past seven.

Darling Beatrice took her supper on coming in, but she came and sat with us while we were at dinner for a short while. Only four at dinner. We went out for a moment afterwards. Very mild and starlight. Louise went to bed. Jane read a little to me in the drawing-room, but I went upstairs soon, as I was tired.

Thursday, September 2.

A very fine, bright, warm morning. We decided to go on an expedition, but not to *Loch Lomond*, as we should have to start so early. Breakfasted in the drawing-room with Louise and Beatrice. Then writing, etc. At twenty minutes to twelve I started in the sociable with Louise, Beatrice, Jane Churchill, and Colonel Ponsonby and Brown on the box, and drove (excellent post-horses, always only a pair) to *Callander*, but turned to the right short of it, and went on some little way.* On coming to the top of a hill we saw *Ben Ledi*, a splendid hill; to the north *Ben Voirlich*, and to the east the heights of *Uam Var*, a pink heathery ridge of no great elevation; and in the distance, rising up from the horizon, *Dun Myat*, and the *Wallace Monument* on the *Abbey Craig*,* near *Stirling*. We went across a moor, and then soon passed *Loch Ruskie*, quite a small lake. The country about here is rather lowland, but as we proceeded it was extremely pretty, with very fine trees and cornfields, and harvesting going on; and soon after, descending a hill, we came upon the Loch of "*Menteith*" (the only loch in Scotland which is ever called lake). It reminds one very much of *Loch Kinnord* near *Ballater*, and very low blue and pink hills rise in the distance. There are two or three islands in it; in the large one, *Inchmahome*,* you perceive amongst the thick woods the ruins of the ancient priory. Queen Mary lived there once, and there are monuments of the Menteiths to be seen on it. To the right we passed the ruin of *Rednock Castle*, and to the left the gates of the Park of *Rednock*, with very fine large trees, where Mr. Graham, the proprietor, was standing. We went on and passed the *Clachan of Aberfoyle* (renowned in Sir Walter Scott's "Rob Roy"),* and here the splendid scenery begins— high, rugged, and green hills (reminding me again of *Pilatus*), very fine large trees and beautiful pink heather, interspersed with bracken, rocks, and underwood, in the most lovely profusion, and *Ben Lomond* towering up before us with its noble range. We went on perhaps a quarter of a mile, and, it being then two o'clock, we got out and lunched on the grass under an oak at the foot of *Craig More*. It was very hot, the sun stinging, but there were many light white clouds in the blue sky, which gave the most beautiful effects of light and shade on this marvellous colouring. After luncheon and walking about a little, not finding any good view to sketch, we got into the carriage (our horses had been changed), but had not gone above a few yards when we came upon *Loch Ard*, and a lovelier picture could not be seen. *Ben Lomond*, blue and yellow, rose above the lower hills, which were pink and purple with heather, and an isthmus of green trees in front dividing it from the rest of the loch. We got out and sketched. Only here and there, far between, were some poor little cottages with picturesque barefooted lasses and children to be seen. All speak Gaelic here. Louise and I sat sketching for half an hour, Beatrice running about merrily with Jane Churchill while we drew. We then drove on, and certainly one of the most lovely drives I can remember, along *Loch Ard*, a fine long loch, with trees of all kinds overhanging the road, heather making all pink; bracken, rocks, high hills of such a fine shape, and trees growing up them as in *Switzerland*; the road rough and bad, with very steep bits of hill (but the post-horses went remarkably well) overhanging the loch, which reminded me very much of the drive along the *Lake Zug* in *Switzerland*. Altogether, the whole drive along *Loch Ard*, then by the very small *Loch Dow* and the fine *Loch Chon*, which is very long, was lovely. The heather in full bloom, and of the richest kind, some almost of a crimson colour, and growing in rich tufts along the road. One can see, by the mounds or heaps of stone, all along *Loch Chon*, where the *Glasgow* waterworks* are carried, but they have not disfigured the landscape.

Emerging from this road we came upon the *Loch Lomond Road*, having a fine view of *Loch Arklet*, on the banks of which Helen MacGregor* is said to have been born. The scene of our drive today is all described in "Rob Roy." *Loch Arklet* lies like *Loch Callater*, only that the hills are higher and more pointed. Leaving this little loch to our left, in a few minutes we came upon *Loch Katrine*,* which was seen in its greatest beauty in the fine evening light. Most lovely! We stopped at *Stronachlachar*, a small inn where people stay for a night sometimes, and where they embark coming from *Loch Lomond* and *vice versâ*. As the small steamer had not yet arrived, we had to wait for about a quarter of an hour. But there was no crowd, no trouble or annoyance, and during the whole of our drive nothing could be quieter or more agreeable. Hardly a creature did we meet, and we passed merely a very few pretty gentlemen's places, or very poor cottages with simple women and barefooted long-haired lassies and children, quiet and unassuming old men and labourers. This solitude, the romance and wild loveliness of everything here, the absence of hotels and beggars, the independent simple people, who all speak Gaelic here, all make beloved *Scotland* the proudest, finest country in the world. Then there is that beautiful heather, which you do not see elsewhere. I prefer it greatly to *Switzerland*, magnificent and glorious as the scenery of that country is.

It was about ten minutes past five when we went on board the very clean little steamer "Rob Roy"—the very same we had been on under such different circumstances in 1859 on the 14th of October, in dreadful weather, thick mist and heavy rain, when my beloved Husband and I opened the *Glasgow Waterworks*.* We saw the spot and the cottage where we lunched.

We took a turn and steamed a little way up the bay called *Glen Gyle*, where there is a splendid glen beautifully wooded, which is the country of the MacGregors, and where there is a house which belonged to MacGregor of *Glen Gyle*, which, with the property, has been bought by a rich Glasgow innkeeper of the same clan. We turned and went on, and nothing could be more beautiful than the loch, wooded all along the banks. The rugged *Ben Venue*, so famed in the "Lady of the Lake" (which we had with us as well as several guide-books, of which we find Black's far the best),* rises majestically on the southern side of the lake, and looking back you see the *Alps of Arrochar*, which well deserve the name, for they are quite pointed and most beautiful; their names are *Ben Vean, Ben Voirlich, Ben Eim,* and *Ben Crosh*. Next came the well-known "*Silver Strand*," "*Helen's Isle*,"* which is most lovely, and the narrow creek so beautifully wooded below the splendid high hills, and the little wooden landing-place which I remembered so well; and very melancholy and yet sweet were my feelings when I landed and found on the path some of the same white pebbles which my dearest Albert picked up and had made into a bracelet for me. I picked up and carried off a handful myself.

We had taken our tea on board on deck. We now entered two hired carriages, the girls and I in the first, with Brown on the box, and Jane Churchill and Colonel Ponsonby in the second. The evening was lovely, and the lights and pink and golden sky as we drove through the beautiful *Trossachs* were glorious indeed—

> So wondrous wild, the whole might seem
> The scenery of a fairy dream—*

and along *Loch Achray*—the setting sun behind *Ben Venue*, which rose above most gloriously, so beautifully described by Sir W. Scott:

> The western waves of ebbing day
> Rolled o'er the glen the level way.
> Each purple peak, each flinty spire
> Was bathed in floods of living fire.*

We passed the fine *Trossachs Inn* where Louise had stopped with Alice and Louis in 1865, and a lovely little church in a most picturesque position, and lastly the *Brig of Turk*. It is a long way round *Loch Vennachar* to *Invertrossachs*: you see the house for three-quarters of an hour before you can get to it. Home at eight. The drive back was lovely, for long after the sun had set the sky remained beautifully pink behind the dark blue hills. A most successful day. Dinner as yesterday. I felt very tired.

Friday, September 3.

A very dull, dark thick morning, and the hills beyond *Callander* hardly visible. Still, no rain. Went up to my room and wrote a little, and at twelve took a walk in a very pretty wood quite close below the house, from several points of which there are beautiful views, but the atmosphere was too thick to see them to-day.... We lunched all together.... At half-past three we started again (just as yesterday), and drove up the noble *Pass of Leny*, past *Kilmahog*, where a little boy tried to give me a nosegay which was fixed to a pole, and in trying to catch it Colonel Ponsonby let it fall. The little boy screamed "Stop, stop!" and ran in such an agony of disappointment that I stopped the carriage, and took it from him to his mother's great delight. On our way we saw on a hill among woods *Leny House* (belonging to Mr. Buchanan Hamilton), where Sir W. Scott lived when he wrote "Rob Roy."

We went along that truly beautiful *Loch Lubnaig*,* driving along its windings like the *Axenstrasse* on the *Lake of Lucerne*, the high, jagged, and green hills rising precipitously from it. It is four miles long, and very romantic. There is a railway unfinished, only a single line, on the western side, and as it ran along the loch it again reminded me of the *Axenstrasse* at the points where it goes low near the water. The road leads under beautiful sycamore trees. We passed on the right a farmhouse called *Ardhullary*, where formerly the Abyssinian traveller Bruce* used to live, and next entered *Strathyre*, a fine broad open strath, wooded and with cornfields, the heather on the hills quite pink. The village of *Strathyre* is composed of a row of a few peasants' houses, with very poor people, and a nice well-built little inn. A little way on again you come to a picturesque little inn called the *King's House*, covered with pretty creepers and convolvulus, and here you turn short to the left and go up *Balquhidder*, another most lovely glen, with a beautiful view of *Loch Voil* with its beautiful sweeping green hills, the *Braes of Balquhidder*, the strath itself very rich with its fine trees and cornfields, the small river *Balvaig* running through it. We drove about two miles, passing some pretty cottages covered with creepers like the inn I mentioned, and stopped outside a neat-looking little village, the *Kirkton of Balquhidder* (twelve miles from *Callander*), composed of only a few cottages. We got out and walked up a steep knoll overhanging the road, on which, under a splendid plane tree (we passed some most beautiful limes just before), is the old kirkyard with the ruins of the old church. We went at once to look at the tomb of Rob Roy*—a flat stone on which is carved a figure in a kilt, and next to it a stone where his wife is buried, and on which a sword is rudely carved.† His son's tomb is next to his, but looks far more modern. We went on to look at a very curious old font, and then at two or three other tombstones. On one of these were some verses, which Mr. Cameron, the school-master, an intelligent young man, recited, and afterwards wrote out for me.†

We afterwards went into the very pretty new church, which is close to the old ruin. Nothing can surpass the beauty of the position of this spot, for it overlooks *Loch Voil* and a glen, or rather mere ravine or corry, with a hill rising behind it. We walked down again and re-entered our carriage, driving back the same way, and passing about half a mile from the *Kirkton*, on our road back, the present burial-place of the MacGregors (whose country this is, or, alas! rather was),* which is a chapel standing in a wood, the whole enclosed by a wall and iron gateway. We drove past the *King's House* a very short way, and then got out, scrambled up the hillside, sat down on a bank overhanging a burn, kindled a fire, and had our tea. This was on Lord Breadalbane's property. We got home from this very interesting and beautiful drive by a quarter-past eight. The day

---

† These stones are supposed to be very ancient, and carved centuries before they were adapted to their present use.

† The words of the inscription are:—

ISABEL CAMBELL,
SPOUSE TO MR. ROBERT KIRK, MINISTER,
DIED 25 DECEMBER, 1680.
SHE HAD TWO SONS, COLIN AND WILLIAM.
HER AGE 25.

Stones weep tho' eyes were dry;
Choicest flowers soonest die:
Their sun oft sets at noon,
Whose fruit is ripe in June.
Then tears of joy be thine,
Since earth must soon resign
To God what is divine.

Nasci est aegrotare, vivere est saepe mori, et mori est vivere.*

LOVE AND LIVE.

had not been bright—dark and dull, but quite clear enough to see everything in this truly beautiful country.

Dinner as before. We always sit in the drawing-room, and Jane read out the newspaper to us.

Saturday, September 4.

Up by half-past seven, and breakfasting at a quarter to eight. Got on my pony Sultan[+] at nine, the others walking, and went through the wood to the loch's edge, where we three got into a small boat and were rowed across to the other side by the keeper and underkeeper, Brown sitting in the bow, Colonel Ponsonby and Jane Churchill going across in another very small boat rowed by one man. Here we got into our carriage as before. Dear Beatrice enjoys it all very much, and is so good and cheerful.

We drove on through the beautiful *Trossachs* to *Loch Katrine*.* It was a very dark thick morning; no distance to be seen at all, and *Ben Venue* very imperfectly. We embarked by ten o'clock on board the steamer "Rob Roy," and steamed off for *Stronachlachar*. No distant view was visible, and the colour of the sky was really that of a thick November fog. However, by the time we reached *Stronachlachar*, it was much lighter to the left, towards where we were going.

Here we got into two hired carriages again, Jane and Colonel Ponsonby preceding us this time. We drove along *Loch Arklet*, a lovely drive with pink heathered hills to the right, and gradually the mist cleared off, and allowed us to see rugged peaks above and in front of us. We met (as we had done from the first) several large coaches, but with only outside seats, full of tourists. This reminded me, as did the whole tour this day and on Thursday, of *Switzerland* and our expeditions there, especially now when we suddenly came upon *Loch Lomond*, and drove down a very steep hill to *Inversnaid*, where there is only one house (a small inn), and saw high mountains, looking shadowy in the mist (dry mist), rising abruptly from the loch. We went at once on board the fine steamer "Prince Consort" (a pleasant idea that that dear name should have carried his poor little wife, alas! a widow, and children, on their first sail on this beautiful lake which he went to see in 1847). She is a fine large vessel, a good deal larger than the "Winkelried" (in which we used to go on the *Lake of Lucerne*), with a fine large dining-cabin below, a very high upper deck, and a gallery underneath on which people can stand and smoke without incommoding the others above. The following people were on

---

[+] I rode him up to the top of the Righi (near Lucerne) 5,000 feet high, in 1868.

board: Mr. A. Smollett, late M.P., Mr. Wylie, factor to Sir T. Colquhoun, and Mr. Denny, the auditor, and Mr. Young, the secretary.

We steamed southward, and for the first half nothing could be finer or more truly Alpine, reminding me much of the *Lake of Lucerne*; only it is longer—*Loch Lomond* being twenty-two miles long. We kept close to the east shore, passing under *Ben Lomond* with its variously called shoulders—*Cruachan, Craig a Bochan,* and *Ptarmigan*—to *Rowardennan* pier, where there is a pretty little house rented from the Duke of Montrose (to whom half *Loch Lomond* belongs) by a Mr. Mair, a lovely spot from whence you can ascend *Ben Lomond*, which is 3,192 feet high, and well wooded part of the way, with cornfields below. After you pass this, where there are fine mountains on either side, though on the west shore not so high, the lake widens out, but the shores become much flatter and tamer (indeed to the east and south completely so); but here are all the beautifully wooded islands, to the number of twenty-four. Some of them are large; on *Inchlonaig Island* the yews are said to have been planted by Robert Bruce to encourage the people in the use of archery. Another, *Inch Cailliach*, is the ancient burial-place of the MacGregors.

On the mainland we passed *Cornick Hill*, and could just see *Buchanan House*, the Duke of Montrose's, and to the right the island of *Inch Murrin*, on which the Duke has his deer preserve. The sun had come out soon after we went on board, and it was blowing quite fresh as we went against the wind. At two o'clock we stopped off *Portnellan* for luncheon, which we had brought with us and took below in the handsome large cabin, where fifty or sixty people, if not more, could easily dine. Colonel Ponsonby also lunched with us.... This over, we went to the end of the lake to *Balloch*, and here turned. It became very warm. To the left we passed some very pretty villas (castles they resembled) and places, amongst others *Cameron* (Mr. Smollett's), *Arden* (Sir J. Lumsden's, Lord Provost of Glasgow), *Ross-Dhu* (Sir J. Colquhoun's), the road to *Glen Fruin*, the islands of *Inch Connachan, Inch Tavanach*, the point of *Stob Gobhlach, Luss*, a very prettily situated village, the mountain of *Ben Dubh*, and the ferry of *Inveruglas*, opposite *Rowardennan*. Then *Tarbet*, a small town, where dearest Albert landed in 1847, and here began the highest and finest mountains, with splendid passes, richly wooded, and the highest mountains rising behind. A glen leads across from *Tarbet* to *Arrochar* on *Loch Long*, and here you see that most singularly shaped hill called the *Cobbler*, and a little further on the splendid *Alps of Arrochar*. All this and the way in which the hills run into the lake reminded me so much of the *Nasen* on the *Lake of Lucerne*.*

The head of the lake with the very fine glen (*Glen Falloch*), along which you can drive to *Oban*, is magnificent. We (Louise and I) sketched as best we could, but it is most difficult to do so when the steamer keeps moving on; and we were afterwards much vexed we had not asked them to go more slowly, as we had to wait again for the "Rob Roy" steamer at *Stronachlachar*. From the head of *Loch Lomond* (where is the *Hotel of Inverarnan*) we turned; we were shown a hole in the rock, on the east side, which they called *Rob Roy's Cave*,* and landed at *Inversnaid*. The people (quite a small crowd) threw bunches of heather as we passed. Heather is everywhere the decoration, and there is indeed no lovelier, prettier ornament. It was in such full bloom. The mountains here are peculiarly fine from the sharp serrated outline and wonderful clothing of grass and trees. It was a very bright warm evening, and the drive back, which we had to take slowly, not to arrive too soon, was extremely pretty. At *Stronachlachar*, both on embarking and disembarking, there were a few people collected. On board we had again our tea, and Mr. Blair, the very obliging gentlemanlike host of the *Trossachs Inn* (and possessor of the *Loch Katrine* steamer), who was in attendance each time, gave us some clotted cream.

It was a splendid sail over this most lovely loch, and delightful drive back by the *Trossachs*. We got into the boat again where we left it this morning, and rowed across; but this time it was most unpleasant, for it blew and was very rough, and the little boat rolled and danced. The second smaller one with the two others shipped water. Rode back and got up to the house by half-past seven. This was the only *contretemps* to our most successful, enjoyable day. How dearest Albert would have enjoyed it!

Dinner just as before, Jane reading the newspapers. This day year we went to the *Brünig Pass*.

Sunday, September 5.

A dull muggy morning. Decided not to go to kirk, as it would have been very public. So at eleven rode (on Sultan) with dear Beatrice (on her little Beatrice) for an hour, first up at the back of the farm, and then a little way on the beautiful pink heathery and bracken hills just behind the house, and saw *Loch Drunkie* almost dry from the drought, and looked over to the *Brig of Turk*, then back by the stables to the house. Read the collect, epistle, and gospel, and the second lesson for the day, with the two girls, Beatrice reading the last-named.

While we were at luncheon it rained, but it soon ceased, and the afternoon became quite fine and was very warm. At half-past five walked out with Louise, Beatrice, and Jane Churchill, stopping at the lodge where McIsaacs, the keeper, and his wife live. Walked some way on, and then drove with Beatrice round a short way on the *Trossachs Road*, coming home at half-past seven.

Monday, September 6.

Misty early, then beautiful and clear and very hot. Got up with a bad headache. At five minutes to eleven rode off with Beatrice, good Sharp going with us and having occasional "collie-shangies"+ with collies when we came near cottages (A. Thomson and Kennedy following). We rode out the same way we came back yesterday, and then up the same hill overlooking *Loch Drunkie*—which really is nearly dry—and on down the other side of the hill, as fast as we could go along a rough but very pretty road, which brought us, over perfumed pink heather interspersed with bracken, to a spot where you get a lovely glimpse of *Loch Achray* and *Ben Venue*. We then continued along a wood past a few miserable cottages, but as private as if I were riding at *Balmoral*, out into the high road just at the *Brig of Turk*, and stopped at what is called "*Fergusson's Inn*," but is in fact the very poorest sort of Highland cottage. Here lives Mrs. Fergusson, an immensely fat woman and a well-known character, who is quite rich and well dressed, but will not leave the place where she has lived all her life selling whisky. She was brought out and seemed delighted to see me, shaking hands with me and patting me. She walks with a crutch, and had to sit down. We only stopped a very few minutes, and then went home as fast as we came, and got back by one. But Brown and the other two men were as hot as the day we went up the *Righi*, and it was indeed very hot. Our ride must have been eight miles altogether. My head still aching.

At three, after luncheon, we started just as yesterday, and drove the same way as last Friday up the *Pass of Leny* by *Loch Lubnaig*, *Strathyre* and the *King's House*: here, instead of turning to the left to *Balquhidder*, we went straight on for four miles, till we came to *Loch Earn Head*. It was a beautiful and very hot afternoon. We stopped at the inn, which is quite a small place commanding a beautiful view of *Loch Earn*, which was splendidly lit up, the loch deep blue and the hills all lilac and violet. Sir Malcolm† and Lady Helen MacGregor with their two little children

---

+ A Scotch word for quarrels or "rows," but taken from fights between "collies."
† He died in 1879.

received us at the door and took us upstairs. They have got a very pretty little drawing-room (looking on to the loch), which they have arranged nicely and comfortably. The two little girls are dear little things, Malvina four and Margaret two years old. Sir Malcolm wore the kilt. He is a captain in the Navy, and showed us some curiosities brought home from *New Zealand*, also a bottle which is said to have belonged to Rob Roy, and was given to Lady Helen by an old man in the parish, and a silver quaich out of which Prince Charles Edward had drunk, and which had belonged to Sir Malcolm's great-great-grandfather. Lady Helen is the late Lord Antrim's only child. Both were most kind and gave us some tea, and at half-past five we left on our return. There was a small friendly crowd collected at the door, who cheered both when we arrived and when we left. We changed horses here, or at least very near, in 1842 on our way back from *Taymouth*. They said I mentioned the circumstance in my book.[+] We drove through the grounds of *Edenchip*, which belongs to Sir Malcolm MacGregor (but was then let), on the way home, and came back the same road, reaching home by half-past seven.

My headache, which had been very bad all day, got much better just before we got home.

Tuesday, September 7.

Received a letter from Colonel Elphinstone, dated 22nd from *Halifax*, with excellent accounts of dear Arthur.* The passage had been a very good one; he had mixed with every one on board, and been a general favourite—three hundred emigrants on board. Walked, and rode a little, while the others walked. Tired and feeling ill. It turned wet and continued so all the evening. We, however, determined to go to *Loch Katrine*, having ordered the steamer, and boats to row to the *Silver Strand*. So off I went with the girls and Lady Churchill just as on the other days, but when we got there it was too wet to do anything; so we only went on board the steamer, took our tea in the cabin below, and then drove back again by half-past seven.

Wednesday, September 8.

A very bad night from a violent attack of neuralgia in my leg. I only got up after nine, and could hardly walk or stand, but was otherwise not ill. I took a little, but very little, breakfast, alone. I remained at home reading, writing, and resting on the sofa or in an arm-chair. I came down

[+] *Our Life in the Highlands*, p. 30.

to luncheon, Brown helping me down and up, but took it alone with the children in the drawing-room. Rested afterwards, and at twenty minutes to four took a quiet but enjoyable drive with Jane Churchill. It was not very bright, nor the distance very clear, but there were occasional gleams of bright sunshine which lit up the fine scenery. We drove to *Loch Menteith*, just the same way as on Thursday, and were surprised to find how short the distance was. After passing the gate of *Rednock Castle* we turned to the left and drove a short way close along the lochside past the kirk and small village (composed of only two or three houses) of *Port Menteith*, getting a good view of *Inchmahome* on the way. We stopped to take our tea (which had been made before we went out, but was quite hot still) outside *Rednock* grounds, and then drove back again, but took another turn through *Callander*, and then along a road (above which a number of pretty villas are built, and where you have a very pretty view) which comes out at *Kilmahog Turnpike*. Then home by a quarter past seven. Found Sir William Jenner, whom we had sent for, arrived. I dined below (hobbling along a little better and downstairs without help) in the drawing-room with Louise and Jane Churchill.

Thursday, September 9.

I had a really very fair night, and on getting up found I could walk much better, for which I was most thankful. I went down to breakfast as usual. Received again letters from dear Arthur and Colonel Elphinstone with excellent and favourable accounts of the good his presence had already done. At half-past eleven drove with Louise and Beatrice up the *Pass of Leny* as far as the commencement of *Loch Lubnaig*, intending to sketch, but it was too late. We met first two large coaches covered with people on the narrowest part of the bridge going to *Kilmahog*, and then endless droves of wild-looking, and for the most part extremely small, shaggy Highland cattle with their drovers and dogs—most wild and picturesque—going to *Falkirk* Tryst. They stop for nights on the road—we saw some droves grazing on the lower parts of the hills on our way to *Loch Earn Head*—and the drovers get shelter with friends in the cottages and villages about. Home at half-past one. Planted two (very small) trees in front of the house, as did Louise and Beatrice also. Luncheon as yesterday, only with the children. My leg very stiff, so that, with great regret, I had to give up going to *Loch Katrine* for the last time, which I had so much wished. However, I did drive with Beatrice as far as the *Trossachs Inn* and back, and got a glimpse of the beautiful *Trossachs* and *Loch Achray*, with *Ben Venue* rising gloriously above it. I even made a slight outline of it, and returned, quite pleased at this, by half-past seven, stopping to make and take our tea not far from home, I remaining in the carriage. Felt better altogether, and was able to come to the usual dinner, to which also Sir W. Jenner came. Dear Beatrice sat with us during part of the dinner, as she had done almost every night. Brown (the only upper servant in attendance, as I brought no page), who waited at all my meals, and did all the outdoors attendance on me besides, with the greatest handiness, cheerfulness, and alacrity, and the three very good footmen, Blake, Cannon, and Charlie Thomson (one of seven brothers, two of whom are also in my service, and one a gillie at *Balmoral*), did all the waiting at dinner and luncheon. Good Sharp was always in the dining-room, but remained quietly lying down.

Friday, *September* 10.

Raining early, which made me feel I had done right in giving up going by the *Spital*, as I had intended up to yesterday afternoon. Felt, however, better, and could walk with much greater ease. At half-past eleven we left *Invertrossachs*, the recollection of the ten days at which—quiet and cozy—and of the beautiful country and scenery I saw in the neighbourhood, though the last two days were spoilt by stupid indisposition, will ever be a very pleasant one. The two girls and I drove in a *Callander* carriage, with Brown on the box, perched up alarmingly high, Jane Churchill and the two gentlemen having preceded us to the station at *Callander*. All our luggage, ponies and all, went with our train. We stopped outside *Perth* for luncheon for a few minutes—and Jane Churchill came in again at *Aberdeen* for our tea—to enable Brown to come and help us. When we reached *Ballater*, where we got into two carriages, it began to rain.

Reached *Balmoral* at half-past six.

Sheep Clipping, 1870.

Balmoral,
Monday, June 13, 1870.

Drove off at half-past eleven on past J. Thomson's house. Here, in the nearest adjoining field, close to the wall, all the sheep (mine) were in a pen, and James Brown, the shepherd, and Morrison, my grieve at *Invergelder*, assisted by others (one, a brother of the Morgans), took them out one by one, tied their legs together, and then placed them on the laps of the women who were seated on the ground, and who clipped them one after the other, wonderfully well, with huge scissors or clippers. Four were seated in a sort of half-circle, of whom three were Mrs. Durran, Mrs. Leys (both these did their work admirably), and Mrs. Morrison, who seemed rather new at it, and had some difficulty with these great heavy sheep, which kick a good deal. The clippers must take them between their knees, and it is very hard work. Four other women were sitting close under the wall, also clipping. Then the sheep were all marked; and some, before being clipped, had to have their horns sawn to prevent them growing into their heads. It was a very picturesque sight, and quite curious to see the splendid thick wool peel off like a regular coat.

BETROTHAL OF PRINCESS LOUISE TO THE MARQUIS OF LORNE, OCTOBER 3, 1870.

Balmoral,
October 3, 1870.

This was an eventful day! Our dear Louise was engaged to Lord Lorne.

The event took place during a walk from the *Glassalt Shiel* to the *Dhu Loch*. She had gone there with Janie Ely, the Lord Chancellor (Lord Hatherley), and Lorne. I had driven with Beatrice and the Hon. Mrs. Ponsonby to *Pannanich Wells*, two miles from *Ballater*, on the south side of the *Dee*, where I had been many years ago. Unfortunately almost all the trees which covered the hills have been cut down.*

We got out and tasted the water, which is strongly impregnated with iron, and looked at the bath and at the humble but very clean accommodation in the curious little old inn, which used to be very much frequented. Brown formerly stayed there for a year as servant, and then quantities of horses and goats were there.

The same perfectly cloudless sky as on the two preceding days. We got home by seven. Louise, who returned some time after we did, told me that Lorne had spoken of his devotion to her, and proposed to her, and that she had accepted him, knowing that I would approve.* Though I was not unprepared for this result, I felt painfully the thought of losing her. But I naturally gave my consent, and could only pray that she might be happy.

Communion Sunday at Crathie, 1871.*

Balmoral,
Sunday, November 13, 1871.

A very bright morning with deep snow. At twelve o'clock I went to the kirk with my two ladies (the Duchess of Roxburghe and Lady Ely), Lord Bridport being also in attendance. At the end of the sermon began the service of the Communion, which is most touching and beautiful, and impressed and moved me more than I can express. I shall never forget it.

The appearance of the kirk was very striking, with the tables in the cross seats, on either side facing the pulpit, covered with a white cloth. Neither Brown, though he came with us, nor any of our Scotch servants sat behind us, as usual, but all below, as every one does who intends taking the sacrament at the "first table." A table, also covered with a white cloth, was placed in front of the middle pew, directly facing the pulpit.

The service was the same as that on ordinary Sundays until after the sermon, excepting that every psalm and prayer had reference to the Lord's Supper, and the sermon was on the *perfect obedience of the Son* (Hebrews ii. 10).

The prayer after the sermon was very short, after which Dr. Taylor delivered an address from the pulpit, in which he very beautifully invited all true penitents to receive the communion, the hardened sinner alone to abstain. It was done in a very kind and encouraging tone. Dr. Taylor adopted part of one of the English prayers, only shortened and simplified.... After this address—"the Fencing of the Tables," as it is called—the minister came down to the small table in front of the pulpit, where he stood with the assistant minister, and the elder son either side, and while the 35th Paraphrase was being sung the elders brought in the Elements, and placed them on the table, viz. the bread cut into small pieces, and two large plates lined with napkins, and the wine in four large silver cups. The minister then read the words of the institution of the Lord's Supper, from I Corinthians xi. 23, and this was followed by a short but very impressive prayer of consecration.

This done, he handed the bread first, and then the wine, right and left to the elders, Francis Leys (Brown's uncle), Symon "the merchant," Hunter, and Dr. Robertson, to dispense; himself giving both to one or two people nearest to him, who were in the middle pew, where the Thomsons all sit generally, and in which, on this occasion, were old

Donald Stewart and his wife (eighty-six and eighty-one, looking so nice and venerable), the young Donald Stewarts, the Thomsons, old Mr. and Mrs. Brown (he eighty-one and very much bent, and she seventy-one). Old John Brown and old Donald Stewart wore large plaids; old Smith of *Kintore* was likewise in this pew. The bread was then reverently eaten, and the wine drunk, sitting, each person passing it on one to the other; the cup being replaced by each on the table before them after they had partaken of the wine, and then the elder carried it on to the next pews, in which there were tables, until all those in that portion of the church prepared for the Lord's Supper, had communicated. After which the elders replaced the Elements on the table before the minister, who delivered a short address of thankfulness and exhortation. He then gave out the 103rd Psalm, which was sung while the communicants were leaving the tables, to be occupied in turn by others.

We left after this. It would indeed be impossible to say how deeply we were impressed by the grand simplicity of the service. It was all so truly earnest, and no description can do justice to the perfect devotion of the whole assemblage. It was most touching, and I longed much to join in it.[+] To see all these simple good people in their nice plain dresses (including an old woman in her mutch), so many of whom I knew, and some of whom had walked far, old as they were, in the deep snow, was very striking. Almost all our own people were there. We came home at twenty minutes before two o'clock.

[+] Since 1873 I have regularly partaken of the Communion at Crathie every autumn, it being always given at that time.

The "Spate," 1872.

Tuesday, June 11, 1872.

Brown came in soon after four o'clock, saying he had been down at the waterside, for a child had fallen into the water, and the whole district was out to try and recover it—but it must be drowned long before this time. I was dreadfully shocked. It was the child of a man named Rattray, who lives at *Cairn-na-Craig*, just above where the new wood-merchant has built a house, and quite close to the keeper Abercrombie's house, not far from *Monaltrie Farmhouse* in the street. At a little before five, set off in the waggonette with Beatrice and Janie Ely, and drove along the north side of the river. We stopped a little way beyond *Tynebaich*, and saw the people wandering along the riverside. Two women told us that two children had fallen in (how terrible!), and that one "had been gotten—the little een" (as the people pronounce "one"), but not the eldest. They were searching everywhere. While we were there, the old grandmother, Catenach by name, who lives at *Scutter Hole*, came running along in a great state of distress. She is Rattray's mother. We drove on a little way, and then turned round.

We heard from the people that the two boys, one of ten or eleven and the other only three, were at *Monaltrie Burn* which comes down close to the farmhouse and below Mrs. Patterson's shop, passing under a little bridge and running into the *Dee*. This burn is generally very low and small, but had risen to a great height—the *Dee* itself being tremendously high—not a stone to be seen. The little child fell in while the eldest was fishing; the other jumped in after him, trying to save his little brother; and before any one could come out to save them (though the screams of Abercrombie's children, who were with them, were heard) they were carried away and swept by the violence of the current into the *Dee*, and carried along. Too dreadful! It seems, from what I heard coming back, that the poor mother was away from home, having gone to see her own mother who was dying, and that she purposely kept this eldest boy back from school to watch the little one.

We drove back and up to Mrs. Grant's, where we took tea, and then walked up along the riverside, and heard that nothing had been found and that the boat had gone back; but as we approached nearer to the castle we saw people on the banks and rocks with sticks searching: amongst them was the poor father—a sad and piteous sight—crying and looking so anxiously for his poor child's body.

Wednesday, June 12.

Drove up to the *Bush* to warn Mrs. William Brown never to let dear little Albert* run about alone, or near to the burn, of the danger of which she was quite aware. She said her husband, William, had started off early at three this morning. Some people went down to *Abergeldie* and as far as the *Girnoch* to search, and others were up and below the castle.

No word of the poor child being found. All were to start early to search.

Thursday, June 13.

At half-past ten drove out in the waggonette with Beatrice and Janie Ely, and drove beyond Mrs. Patterson's "shoppie" a little way, and turned up to the right off the road behind the wood-merchant's new cottage, and got out just below Abercrombie the keeper's house, and walked a few paces on to the small cottage called *Cairn-na-Craig*, at the foot of *Craig Noerdie*, in a lovely position, sheltered under the hill, yet high, with a beautiful view of *Lochnagar*. Brown went in first, and was received by the old grandmother; and then we went in, and on a table in the kitchen covered with a sheet, which they lifted up, lay the poor sweet innocent "bairnie," only three years old, a fine plump child, and looking just as though it slept, with quite a pink colour, and very little scratched, in its last clothes—with its little hands joined—a most touching sight. I let Beatrice see it, and was glad she should see death for the first time in so touching and pleasing a form.

Then the poor mother came in, calm and quiet, though she cried a little at first when I took her hand and said how much I felt for her, and how dreadful it was. She checked herself, and said, with that great resignation and trust which it is so edifying to witness, and which you see so strongly here, "We must try to bear it; we must trust to the Almighty."

The poor little thing was called Sandy. She herself is a thin, pale, dark, very good, and respectable-looking woman. She had no wish to go away that day, as the old grandmother told us, but her husband wished her to see her mother. She has one boy and two girls left, and the eldest and youngest are taken.

They were playing at the burnside, but some way above the road, where there is a small bridge. As we were leaving I gave her something, and she was quite overcome, and blessed me for it.

We walked down again, and then drove back, and walked at once past the stables to the riverside, where, on both sides, every one was assembled, four in the boat (Donald Stewart and Jemmie Brown amongst them), and all with sticks, and up and down they went, searching under every stone. They had been up to the boat pool and back, but nothing appeared. I remained watching till one o'clock, feeling unable to tear myself away from this terrible sight. The poor father was on our side, William Brown amongst the others on the other side. I sat on the bank with Janie Ely for some time (Beatrice having gone in earlier than I), Grant as well as Brown standing near me. When they came to that very deep pool, where twenty-two years ago a man was nearly drowned when they were leistering for salmon, they held a piece of red cloth on a pole over the water, which enabled them to see down to the bottom. But all in vain. The river, though lower, was still very high.

At four took a short drive in the single pony carriage with Janie Ely, and back before five. Saw and talked to the schoolmaster, Mr. Lubban, a very nice little man, and he said that this poor child, Jemmie, the eldest, was such a good, clever boy. Every one shows so much feeling and kindness. It is quite beautiful to see the way in which every one turned out to help to find this poor child, from the first thing in the morning till the last at night—which, during these long days, was very hard work—and all seemed to feel the calamity deeply. We heard by telegraph during dinner that the poor boy's body had been found on an island opposite *Pannanich*, below *Ballater*, and that steps would be taken at once to recover it.*

Saturday, June 15.

After luncheon, at a quarter to three, drove with the two children up as far as the *West Lodge*, and then just descried the sad funeral procession slowly and sadly wending its way along the road; so we drove back again, catching glimpses of it as we went along, and drove on a little way beyond the bridge, when, seeing the first people not far off, we turned and drove back, stopping close to the bridge, and here we waited to see them pass. There were about thirty people, I should say, including the poor father, Jemmie and Willie Brown, Francie's brother, Alick Leys, Farmer Patterson, etc. The poor father walked in front of one of the coffins; both covered with white, and so small. It was a very sad sight. Dr. Taylor walked last with another gentleman. He had of course been up to the house and performed the service there, as is always done throughout *Scotland* by all the Protestant denominations except the Episcopalian, and no service whatever near the grave.⁺ We watched the sad procession as long as we could, and drove home again.

⁺ A change has taken place since this was written, and now (1883) a prayer is sometimes said as well at the grave.

Visit to Holyrood and Edinburgh, August 13, 1872.

Tuesday, August 13.

At six I left sweet *Osborne* with Leopold and Beatrice, Marie Leiningen, and the Duchess of Roxburghe, Flora Macdonald,[+] Colonels Ponsonby and De Ros, Mr. Collins, and Fräulein Bauer. It was very warm. The yachts, which were out, had a very pretty effect. At *Gosport*, where we had to wait about ten minutes before landing, as we arrived too soon, I took leave of dear Marie Leiningen, who was to return to *Germany* next day. We had our own usual large travelling railway carriages, which are indeed charming.

It was a splendid night. Sir W. Jenner joined us at *Basingstoke*, and at *Banbury* at half-past ten we stopped for refreshments, and lay down before twelve.

Wednesday, August 14.

I had a good deal of rest, and was up and dressed by eight, or a little past. But we had already passed *Melrose*, and there was so much fog, and the air so thick, that we could see very little. The last station (not in a village or town) was *Fountainhall*, where old Mr. Lawson, the former Lord Provost of *Edinburgh* and famous seedsman, came up to the carriage, and some little girls presented Baby (as Beatrice is always called by us still) with a nosegay. We passed *Portobello*, and a few minutes more brought us to the very station—the private one, outside *Edinburgh*—which for eleven years my beloved Albert and I had always arrived at, and where we left it together eleven years ago.* There it was, all unaltered, and yet all so altered!

The General, Sir J. Douglas,[+] the Lord Provost, and other official people received us there, and we got into our carriage. The two children and the Duchess of Roxburghe went in the carriage with me.

It was a dull, gloomy, heavy morning, but a great many people were out, and all most enthusiastic, reminding me forcibly and sadly of former days. We had an escort of the Scots Greys.* We drove up to the door of the old, gloomy, but historical Palace of *Holyrood*,* where a guard of

---

[+] The Hon. Flora Macdonald, Maid of Honour, now Bedchamber Woman.
[+] Commanding the forces in Scotland.

honour with a band of the 93rd Highlanders were stationed in the quadrangle of the court. We got out, walked up the usual stairs, and passed through two of the large gloomy rooms we used to occupy, and then went past some passages up another and very steep staircase to the so-called "*Argyll rooms*," which have been arranged for me, with very pretty light paper, chintz, and carpets (chosen by Louise). There is a suite, beginning with a dining-room (the least cheerful) at the farthest end, and then my sitting-room, a large and most cheerful room, the nicest of all, with very light paper; next to this the bedroom, almost too large a room, and out of this the dressing-room. All open one out of the other, and have, except the dining-room, the same pretty carpets and chintzes (red geraniums on a white ground). The page's room and a wardrobe and dresser's room are just opposite, across a small passage.

We three took breakfast directly in the dining-room. Our rooms are above the old rooms, and have the same look-out.

It cleared up, and though still thick and hazy, the sun shone out brightly, and at a quarter to twelve I went out into the garden, going through our old rooms, which looked sadly deserted: all open and some few things removed from them; the gloomy bedroom with its faded tapestry and green silk bed, and the wretched little dark box-room in which I undressed at night, all full of many recollections. I went through the long picture gallery, down the small steps into the garden, where I met Beatrice, who walked with me. We walked about the garden, which is improved, but terribly overlooked, and quite exposed to public view on the side looking towards the street. We walked about the fine old chapel with its beautiful window and its tombstones, and then went in—Beatrice and I with Brown (who was much interested by all)—conducted by the keeper, an intelligent sensible man called Anderson, and visited the rooms of Queen Mary, beginning with the Hamilton apartments (which were Lord Darnley's rooms) and going up the old staircase to Queen Mary's chamber. In Lord Darnley's rooms there are some fine old tapestry and interesting portraits of the Royal family, and of the Dukes and Duchesses of Hamilton. There are some other curious old pictures in this room.

We saw the small secret staircase which led up in the turret to Queen Mary's bedroom, and we went up another dark old winding staircase at the top of which poor Rizzio was so horribly murdered*—whose blood is still supposed to stain the floor. We entered the Presence Chamber, the ceiling of which, in panels, is from the time of Queen Mary, and contains her mother's and her own initials and arms as Dauphine of France and Queen of Scotland, with Darnley's initials. Here is the bed provided for

Charles I. when he came to *Holyrood* to be crowned King of Scotland. Thence we were shown into poor Queen Mary's bedroom, where are the faded old bed she used, the baby-basket sent her by Queen Elizabeth when King James I. was born, and her work-box. All hung with old tapestry, and the two little turret rooms; the one where she was supping when poor Rizzio was murdered, the other her dressing-room. Bits of the old tapestry which covered the walls at the time are hung up in frames in the rooms. Beatrice is immensely interested by all she sees, and delighted with everything.

At half-past five drove off in the open landau and four with Beatrice, Leopold, and the Duchess of Roxburghe, the two equerries riding. We drove up through the *Canongate*, that curious old street with its very high-storied houses, past *Knox's House* and quaint old buildings, with the lowest, poorest people about, down *Bank Street*, and eastward along *Princes Street*, that splendid street with its beautiful shops, hotels, etc., on one side, and its fine monuments on the other, the gardens and institutions and other parts of the town rising above it and crowned by the picturesque *Castle*; then by *Saint Andrew Street*, across *Saint Andrew Square* (where Lord Melville's statue is), along *George Street*, a fine wide street, at the end of which is *Charlotte Square*, where my dear one's Monument* is to be placed, and where I was to have stopped to look at the site. But the crowd, which was very great everywhere and would run with us (facilitated by the great steepness and slipperiness of the streets), as well as the great number of cabs and vehicles of all kinds which would drive along after us everywhere, made this impossible. We turned to the left with some difficulty—one or two carriages coming in contact with ours—and went on by *Hope Street*, *Queen's Ferry Street*, where we took a wrong turn, and went by *Clarendon Crescent* and *Forres Street* till we got to the *Water of Leith*, where we found we could not go on.

We had to turn, with considerable difficulty, owing to the narrowness of the road, and go back again by *Moray Place*, *Heriot Row*, and thence down by *Pitt Street* on to *Inverleith Row* (outside the town), past the *Botanic Garden*, then along the *Queen's Ferry Road*, *Pilrig Street*, and *Leith Walk* (which I remembered from our having taken the same drive in 1861), then along a broad street, under the *Calton Hill*, and *Regent Terrace*, past *Holyrood*, into the beautiful *Queen's Drive*, right round *Arthur's Seat* with its fine grass, its rocks and small lochs. Unfortunately, however, no clear distant view could be obtained on account of the fog. Home to *Holyrood* at half-past seven. It was a fatiguing drive.

The crowds were very great, but the people behaved remarkably well; only they kept cheering and shouting and running with us, for the postilions drove very slowly whenever there was the slightest descent, and there were many in the town, and one long one coming down home from the *Queen's Drive*. A good many flags were out, but there were hardly any decorations. The equerries kept extremely well close up to the carriage, which was no easy task.

Thursday, August 15.

Again a very foggy morning. Breakfasted at half-past nine. Beatrice and Leopold started to go and see *Roslin Chapel*. Walked a little in the garden at half-past ten, and then sat for half an hour under the only tree which afforded shade and was not overlooked by the street, a thorn, with very overhanging long branches, on a small grassy mound or "hillock." Here I read out of a volume of Poems by the "Ettrick Shepherd,"* full of beautiful things (which Brown had given me some years ago), and wrote till half-past twelve.

At half-past five I started as yesterday with Beatrice, Leopold, and the Duchess of Roxburghe, the two equerries riding, and took a very long—rather too long—drive. It would have been quite beautiful and most enjoyable from the very fine scenery with rich vegetation, fine trees, and hills, and dales, with the *Pentlands* in the distance, had it not been for a dark, heavy, leaden fog and sky like November, but warmer, which obscured all the distance in the most provoking way, and at one time even came down in a rather heavy shower. We went out by the *Queen's Drive*, going to the right as we left *Holyrood*. Numbers of people surrounded the entrance, and, as there is a long ascent part of the way, some of them, especially boys, ran along with us. We proceeded by the *Liberton Road*, on past the villages of *Straiton*, *Lasswade* (very picturesque, and which I well remember from 1842), and *Bonnyrigg*, to *Dalhousie Castle*, where we had visited the late Marquis and Marchioness from *Dalkeith* in 1842 (the Duchess of Buccleuch drove me over), an old Scotch castle in red stone, where, however, we did not get out. It had been raining, but we did not shut the carriage, and just as we had thought of doing so the rain ceased. From here we drove under a very fine viaduct along the *South Esk*, past *Newbattle* (not into the grounds)—where there is an arch which was built for George IV. to drive through,* but he never went there—on through the small town of *Dalkeith*, where many people, as indeed in almost every other place, had collected, into the *Park of Dalkeith*. Here, as well as everywhere in the neighbourhood, there are beautiful trees, especially some very fine sycamores. We drove up to the house, and got out, as I wished the children to see the rooms where we had lived. The staircase and the gallery where I held the Drawing-room I remembered well, as also the dining-room. Our former rooms were shown us; but though the bed and even the washing-basin still exist, the rooms which had been arranged for us are altered.

We visited it last in September 1859. The population of *Dalkeith* and of all the villages about here are colliers and miners, and are very poor.* We came home straight, coming into the same road as we started by, and going down the hill of the *Queen's Drive*. We collected again a goodly and most good-humoured crowd, and saw the little boys and girls rolling down the steep hill, and people pouring in from the town to get a sight of us.

Friday, August 16.

A thoroughly wet day. At half-past eleven I walked out with Flora Macdonald* (whose name attracted great attention in *Edinburgh*), right across the court to the stables, which are very good, and saw all belonging to them—harness-room, coach-house, etc. Then I looked into the guard-room next door, where the guard, who were called out and drawn up thinking I was coming by, did not know us. I went in behind them, and I found a sergeant (I think) of the 93rd in full dress, with four medals, and I asked him his years' service, which were twenty, and where he came from—"*Perthshire*." Two other men, who were cooking and had their coats off, were in the room where they also slept. The newspapers have reported an absurd conversation of mine with them, but none took place. We then walked back through the house into the garden, and finally came home through the chapel at half-past twelve.

It was raining hard, but nevertheless we started at half-past four in the open landau, Beatrice and the two ladies with me, the two equerries riding. We drove by way of *Princes Street*, which overlooks the *Mound* with its gardens and fine buildings, and is always so animated and full of people on foot and in carriages; crossed the *Dean Bridge*, which commands a most beautiful view, though then it was obscured by the pelting rain; passed *Stewart's Asylum*, a fine new building, getting from the road a good view of another fine institution, *Fettes College*, built only within the last few years; and so on to the edge of *Barnton Park*, where we turned back to *Granton*. By this time it had begun to blow most violently, in addition to the rain, and the umbrellas dripped and the carriage became soaked. Our road lay close to the sea, past *Granton Pier* where we had landed in 1842; *Trinity* came next, a place with some good houses, and then *Newhaven*—where we saw many fishwives who were very enthusiastic, but not in their smartest dress—and then *Leith*, where here were numbers of people looking out for us in spite of the dreadful rain; but indeed everywhere the poor people came out and were most loyal. We took a wrong turn here, and had to come back again to go to the *Albert Docks*—new and very splendid large docks, with the ships all decked out. We stopped a moment to speak to the Provost of *Leith*, who said the people were very grateful for my coming; and I have since had repeated expressions of thanks, saying the good people felt my coming out in the rain more than anything. We drove on along the shore, with a distant view of the *Island of Inchkeith*, by *Leith Links*, the *London Road*, the *Cavalry Barracks*, *St. Margaret's Station* and *Queen's Park*, home. We got home by ten minutes past seven. We were all more or less wet, and had to change our things. The waterproofs seemed not to have done their work. After dinner, at twenty minutes past eleven, we left *Holyrood*; a gardener presented me with a bouquet, and said it was "the proudest day in his life." It did not rain, so we had the carriage open. The two children and the Duchess of Roxburghe were in our carriage, and we had an escort. Numbers of people were out. The whole way was splendidly lit up by red, blue, and yellow lights from *Salisbury Crags* and *Arthur's Seat*, and the effect was most dazzling and beautiful. There were besides some torches near the station, which was the same we arrived at. The Provost hoped I "was leaving well," and I thanked him for the very kind reception which I had met with, and for the beautiful illuminations.

Saturday, August 17.

Did not sleep much or well—it was so very hot, and I was too much excited, and then we had to be roused up and to dress hurriedly before seven, by which time we were at *Ballater*. There were many people out, and so there were at *Balmoral*, where we arrived at a quarter to eight. The heather beautiful, but not completely out yet. The air sweet and soft.

Beloved Mama's birthday! That dear, dear mother! so loving and tender, so full of kindness! How often I long for that love! She frequently spent this day at *Abergeldie*, but we were not here then.

Visit to Dunrobin, 1872.

Friday, September 6, 1872.

A dull but fair morning. Breakfasted with the children before nine o'clock, and at half-past nine I left dear *Balmoral* in the open landau and four with Beatrice and Leopold, Jane Churchill, Fräulein Bauer, and Lord Granville, and drove to *Ballater*, where Colonel Ponsonby, Sir W. Jenner, and Mr. Collins met us. Besides Brown, who superintends everything for me, Emilie Dittweiler, Annie Macdonald, Jemmie Morgan, my second piper Willie Leys, Beatrice's, Leopold's, and Lady Churchill's attendants, three footmen and Goddard went with us. We passed into the station at *Aberdeen*, which was immensely crowded. An address and the keys were presented by Provost Leslie; then Lord Kintore (who gave me a nosegay and some fruit) and young Lord Aberdeen were presented. The day was becoming fine, and it was excessively hot. From *Aberdcen* we went by a line totally new to me—past *Inverurie*, close past the hill of *Benachie*, and got a good sight of the *Buck of Cabrach* and the surrounding hills, past *Huntly* and the ruined *Castle of Huntly* to *Keith*, where the *Banff* Volunteers were drawn up and there were many people close to the station, but no one on the platform. Here we were delayed by one of the doors, from the bedroom into the little dressing-room, refusing to open. Annie had gone through shortly before we got to *Keith*, and when she wanted to go back, the door would not open, and nothing could make it open. Brown tried with all his might, and with knives, but in vain, and we had to take in the two railway men with us, hammering and knocking away as we went on, till at last they forced it open. We were at *Keith* at 1.20, and at *Elgin* at 1.58. The station here was beautifully decorated; there were several arches adorned with flowers and heather, and a platform with raised seats for many ladies. The Provost and the Duke of Richmond and Lord March were there. The Provost presented an address, and then I spoke to the Duke of Richmond, who told me that dear Uncle Leopold had received the freedom of the city when he was staying in the neighbourhood in 1819. The ruins of the Cathedral are said to be the finest in *Scotland*, and the town is full of ancient recollections. No British sovereign has ever been so far north. The Provost's daughter presented me with a nosegay.

We stopped here about ten minutes. It was broiling hot. The corn and oats looked ripe, and were cut in many places. After this we took our luncheon (cold), and as we were sitting at the small table we suddenly found ourselves passing slowly, without stopping, the station of *Forres*, near which is the wild "muir" which Shakespeare chose as the scene of Macbeth's meeting with the witches. *Nairn* lies very prettily on the shore of the *Moray Frith*. We passed *Culloden*,* and the moor where that bloody battle, the recollection of which I cannot bear, was fought. The heather beautiful everywhere, and now the scenery became very fine. At half-past three we were at *Inverness*, the capital of the *Highlands*,* the position of which is lovely. We stopped here for ten minutes, but outside the station. There was an immense crowd, but all very well managed, and no squeeze or crush. There were numbers of seats in galleries filled with ladies, among whom I recognised Mrs. Cluny Macpherson. Cluny Macpherson himself was in command of the Volunteers. On the platform to the left (the Volunteers and the galleries with seats were to the right) was the Provost, Dr. Mackenzie, a fine-looking old man in a kilt, with very white hair and a long white beard, who presented an address. Lord Seafield, the Master of Lovat, Mr. Baillie of *Dochfour*, and his son Mr. Evan Baillie, were all there, and I said a word to each. The Provost's grand-daughter presented a bouquet. There was an immense crowd at the back of the platform.

As our train proceeded, the scenery was lovely. Near the ruins of the old *Priory of Beauly* the river of the same name flows into the *Beauly Frith*,+ and the frith looks like an enormous lake with hills rising above it which were reflected on the perfectly still water. The light and colouring were rather grey, but had a charming effect. At twenty minutes to four we reached Dingwall, where there were Volunteers, as indeed there were everywhere, and where another address was presented and also flowers. Sir J. Matheson, Lord Lieutenant of the county, was named to me, also the Vice-Lieutenant; and some young ladies gave Beatrice nosegays. The position of *Dingwall*, in a glen with hills rising above it, is extremely pretty, and reminds me of a village in *Switzerland*. The head of the *Cromartie Frith* appears here. After this and passing slowly *Tain* and *St. Duthus* (called after the Cathedral there), we thought, as we did not stop, and were not to do so, that we would take our tea and coffee—which kept quite hot in the Norwegian kitchen—when suddenly, before we had finished, we stopped at *Bonar Bridge*, and the Duke of Sutherland came up to the door. He had been driving the engine (!) all the way from *Inverness*, but only appeared now on account of this being the boundary of his territory, and the commencement of the *Sutherland* railroad. He expressed

---

+ Beauly, so called from the French "Beau lieu."

the honour it was to him that I was coming to *Dunrobin*. Lord Ronald L. Gower also came up to the carriage-door. There was a most excited station-master who would not leave the crowd of poor country-people in quiet, but told them to cheer and "cheer again," another "cheer," etc., without ceasing.

Here the *Dornoch Frith*, which first appears at *Tain*, was left behind, and we entered the glen of the *Shin*. The railway is at a very high level here, and you see the *Shin* winding below with heathery hills on either side and many fine rocks, wild, solitary, and picturesque. The Duchess of Sutherland's own property begins at the end of this glen. At six we were at *Golspie* station, where the Duchess of Sutherland received us, and where a detachment of the *Sutherland* Volunteers, who look very handsome in red jackets and Sutherland tartan kilts, was drawn up. I got into the Duchess's carriage, a barouche with four horses, the Duke riding, as also Lady Florence and their second son Lord Tarbat, and drove through the small town—one long street like *Dufftown*—which is inhabited chiefly by a fishing population, and was extremely prettily decorated with heather and flowers, and where there were many triumphal arches with Gaelic inscriptions (which I annex) and some very pretty English ones.

"Ar Buidheachas do 'n Bhuadhaich."

"Our gratitude to Victoria."

"Na h-uile lath chi's nach fhaic, slainte duibh 'is solas"

"Health and happiness, far or near."
(Literally—"Every day see we you, or see we not,
health to you and happiness.")

"Ceud mile failte do Chattaobh."
"A hundred thousand welcomes to Sutherland."

"Failte do 'n laith Buidhe."
"Hail to the lucky day,"

"Better lo'ed you canna' be;
Will you no come back again?"*

Everywhere the loyalty and enthusiasm were very great. In about ten minutes we were at *Dunrobin Castle*.* Coming suddenly upon it as one does, or rather driving down to it, it has a very fine imposing appearance with its very high roof and turrets, a mixture of an old Scotch castle and French chateau. Constance Westminster (the Marchioness of Westminster, the Duke's youngest sister) was at the door, and Annie Sutherland's little girl in the hall, which is, as also the staircase, all of stone, with a sort of gallery going round opening into a corridor. But I will describe this and the rooms to-morrow.

The Duchess took me to my rooms, which had been purposely arranged and handsomely furnished by the dear late Duke and Duchess* for us both, and consist of a sitting-room next to the drawing-room, with a little turret communicating by a small passage with the dressing-room, which opens into the bedroom and another room which is my maid's room, and was intended for dearest Albert's dressing-room. I went to see Beatrice's room, which is close by, down three steps in the same passage. Fraulein Bauer, and Morgan, her dresser, are near her. Brown lives just opposite in the room intended for Albert's valet. It was formerly the prison.

Rested a little while, for I felt very tired. Dined at half-past eight alone in my sitting-room with Beatrice and Leopold, Brown waiting. Shortly afterwards Annie Sutherland came to see us for a little while, and later Jane Churchill. The children went early to bed.

Dunrobin,
Saturday, September 7.

I will now describe my rooms. They are very high; the bedroom is the largest and very handsome, with a beautiful bed with white and gold flowers and doves at each corner (just like one at *Clieveden*), with light blue furniture, and gold and white round the cornice of the ceiling; pale blue and white panels; blue satin spangled with yellow leaves (which look just like gold) on the walls; and furniture and carpet to match. The dressing-room the same, but pale blue and pink silk fluted, on the walls. The sitting-room pale sea-green satin, with the cyphers of the late Duke and Duchess and their daughters on the ceiling. The furniture of light wood, and the sofas, chairs, tables, etc., remind me greatly of *Clieveden* and *Stafford House.** The little boudoir has a small domed ceiling, spangled with golden stars, and the same furniture. There are some pretty pictures in the sitting-room and prints in the other rooms. At half-past nine we breakfasted in the sitting-room, and soon after saw the Duchess. At twenty minutes to eleven, I walked out with the Duchess and Beatrice to the steps, of which there are several flights, leading down to the garden, which is very pretty, and where there are fountains, and from here straight on to the sea, which is closer to the house, by half a mile I should say, than at *Osborne*. We walked along here, and then up and into the pretty byre for Ayrshire cows, and a little farther on to the dairy, a very nice, cool round one. The Duchess told Brown to open the sitting-room, and we found it occupied by a policeman in bed, which we were not at all prepared for, and which caused much amusement. Florence, Jane Churchill, and Fräulein Bauer had joined us here, and shortly after the Duke did so too. We walked back through the kitchen garden, which is very well kept, and the Duke also showed us where he has a quantity of young salmon which are artificially hatched, and also a new apparatus for watering grass. We came home by the steps again. There is plenty of shade, but rather too many trees. The old part of the Castle is as old as the twelfth century. The late Duke enlarged it and added on the towers, and finished the new part in 1849–50.

In at a quarter to twelve. A dull muggy day. We lunched as we breakfasted. Afterwards reading, etc., and at twenty minutes past four drove out in the waggonette (Bourner[+] driving, as I had sent my own carriage and ponies) with the Duchess, Constance Westminster, and Jane Churchill. We drove past the monument of the late Duke,* which faces the Castle and is outside the gates, close to which is the Duke's private little station, used only by the family; rather near, for it cannot be above five hundred yards from the house, but it is very well managed, so as to be but little seen. We drove by the four crossroads, turning to the left through *Dunrobin Wood*, which is really very pretty, with fine Scotch firs and other trees of all kinds, beech, oak, ash, and birch, above and below the drives, with quantities of lovely pink heather and ferns—some parts of the drive are rather steep—on to *Bacchies*, then by the *Dutch Cottage*, on to *Benabhraghie Drive*, and stopped at the four cross-roads to take our made tea and coffee, the warmth of which surprised Constance and Annie very much. We saw some deer. Drove on by the same drive (*Benabhraghie*, the name of the hill on which the old Duke's very colossal statue* stands). We stopped a little farther on to look at a fine view of the Castle and village, and to the right the hills which are seen farther inland, and the blue distant hills above the coast of *Ross-shire*; then came out at *Culmallie Lodge* and passed through the village of *Golspie* with all its pretty decorations, and stopped at two cottages outside, when Annie called out a nice-looking girl who makes beautiful Shetland shawls in the one, and an oldish woman, a character, who worked me a book-marker and lives in the other (a double cottage under one roof). We drove through the *Golspie Burn* and dairy park, along the grass drive on the seashore below the woods, as far as *Strathstephen*, and looking back had one of the finest views of the Castle, with the hills of *Cambusmore* rising behind, and, turning up into the *Caithness* high road, came back to the Castle.

[+] My coachman and postilion, who has been thirty-eight years in my service.—1883.

Home at half-past six. A dull evening. Tried to sketch a bit of sea-view. At a quarter past eight we had dinner in the dining-room with the Duke and Annie (between whom I sat), Leopold, Constance Westminster, the Granvilles, Jane Churchill, and Ronald. I felt strange—such a dinner in a strange place for the first time without my dear one! Brown waited on me, and did so at all meals, attending on me indoors and out of doors, most efficiently and indefatigably. Then went for a short time into the drawing-room, which is next my sitting-room. Here we were joined by Mrs. Sumner (Miss Kingscote by birth, half-sister to Colonel Kingscote and niece to Lord Bloomfield), a great friend of the Duchess's and who is staying in the house with her husband, who is a great friend of the Duke's; Constance Pitt, a younger sister of Mary Pitt, and travelling with her uncle and Lady Granville; Dr. Fayrer (a distinguished physician, who was for two years in *India*),[†] Mr. Sumner, and Mr. Edwin Lascelles, brother to Mary. I remained for a few minutes, and then went to my room.

Sunday, September 8.

A fine bright morning. Breakfast as yesterday. Directly after it, at a quarter-past ten, walked with Beatrice along the *Lady's Walk*, as it is called, which commences near the Castle and goes for a mile and a half entirely amongst trees, very shady, and overlooking the sea, and with paths leading down to the sea, and seats commanding lovely views of the sea and distant coast. It was very warm, and the thickness of the adjoining woods made the air feel close. We walked back the same way, and got home at a quarter-past eleven. At twelve there was quite a short service performed by Dr. Cumming in the gallery which runs round the staircase, Dr. Cumming being opposite to us. It was over by a quarter to one. Annie then took me up to her room, which is a very pretty one; long, but not high, and very light, with a very fine view above all the trees; very simply furnished. Her dressing-room and bedroom equally nice and airy, like those they have at *Stafford House*. The Duke's dressing-room is very simply and plainly furnished; he is wonderfully plain and simple in his tastes. The Duchess took me along the passage to where Florence lives, and to the nursery where we saw little Alix in her bed, and then by a staircase, which belongs to the very old part of the Castle, to the rooms which were the dear late Duke's and Duchess's,

---

[†] He travelled with Alfred, and has written a remarkable book on snakes.

though the last time she came here she lived in my rooms. Everywhere prints of ourselves and of people I know. After this came down again. Luncheon as yesterday.

At twenty minutes past four walked to the nearest seat in the *Lady's Walk*, and sketched the view, and about half-past five drove out in the waggonette with Beatrice and Lady Granville. We drove through the *Uppat Woods*, along the big burn drive, past the *Pictish Tower* up to Mr. Loch's Memorial,* which has the following inscription on it by the late Duchess:—

TO THE HONOURED MEMORY OF

JAMES LOCH,

WHO LOVED IN THE SERENE EVENING OF HIS LIFE
TO LOOK AROUND HIM HERE.

May his children's children gather here, and think of him whose life was spent in virtuous labour for the land he loved and for the friends he served, who have raised these stones, A.D. 1858.

OBIIT JUNII 28° 1855.

The heather is very rich all round here. We got out and went into it, and there is a very fine view looking up *Dunrobin Glen* and over the sea, and *Birk Head*, which is the extreme point of the land which runs into the sea. You also get a very pretty glimpse of the Castle at the end of a path cut through the wood. We drove down again, and before we were out of the lower wood, which is close down upon the sea-shore, we stopped to take our tea and coffee, but were half devoured by midges. We then came out upon the high road, and got into the sea-shore road, about half a mile beyond where we went yesterday, and drove along it and in by the Dairy—home at seven. Resting, writing. Dined in our sitting-room with our two children and Annie. Afterwards we went into the drawing-room where the ladies and gentlemen were, but I only stayed a short time.

Monday, September 9.

Raining a little early in the day. After breakfast drove in the waggonette with Beatrice and Jane Churchill to the Kennel, a remarkably nice and clean one to the left, and rather farther on than the stables, which are close to the railway station. Mr. Macdonald, the head keeper (who is brother to our poor Macdonald, Albert's late Jäger), whom I saw at *Windsor* two years ago, showed us over them. There are fine deerhounds and pointers and setters. We visited the Macdonalds in their nice house, and saw their daughters, three of whom are very good-looking and remind me of their cousins. He is not the least like his brother. From here we went to the stables, which are small, where my ponies were, and where we also saw some of Annie's ponies and horses. Then walked home, meeting the Duke and Ronald on the way. Two splendid Highland beasts,* which are being fattened for the Christmas show, were brought up to the road for me to see. We passed the herd they belong to yesterday, when driving. These beasts really are beautiful, and most picturesque, with their rough coats, shaggy heads, and immense spreading horns; the greatest number are dun- and mouse-coloured. At twenty-five minutes past twelve I started with the two children and Annie for the laying of the first stone of the Memorial to be raised by the clansmen and servants to the memory of my dear Duchess of Sutherland,* who was adored in *Sutherland*. We drove in the barouche and four. The rain had quite ceased. Everyone else had gone on before; the Duke waited to help us in, and then ran on followed by MacAlister, his piper, valet, and confidential servant—a short stout man of sixty, I should say—an excellent man, and first-rate piper. We got out, and I went up on a platform, which was covered over and close to the stone, with the children, Annie, the Duke, Constance, and Jane Churchill. All the others, and many spectators, stood around. Mr. Joass, the minister there, offered up a short prayer, and after it presented (but did not read) the Address. I then answered what I had thought over, but spoke without reading:

"It gives me great pleasure to testify on this occasion my love and esteem for the dear Duchess, my valued friend, with whose children I am happy to be now staying, and I wish also to express my warm thanks for the loyal and hearty welcome I have met with in *Sutherland*."

This made me very nervous, but it was said without hesitating. Then the usual ceremony of spreading the mortar and of striking the stone with a mallet was gone through. The Duke gave me a drawing of the intended Memorial, which is to be an Eleanor cross, with a bust of the dear Duchess, and a medal of her which Ronald L. Gower had struck. After this we got into the carriage again, amid the cheers of the people, and drove back. Only Leopold walked, and Constance took his place in the carriage. We were in, before one. Almost directly afterwards Beatrice and I went into the ante-room (where all the company who afterwards had luncheon were assembled) with Annie and the Duke, who presented some people to me; amongst others a very old lady, Mrs. Houston by name, who is between eighty and ninety, and was a great friend of the dear Duchess and of the Duchess of Norfolk. She was quite overcome, and said, "Is that my dear Queen," and, taking the Duke's hand, "and my darling Duke?"

Luncheon as usual. After it saw Lord Granville. At a quarter past four drove out in the waggonette, drawn by four of the Duke's horses, with Beatrice, Annie, and Constance. It was fine though not very bright weather, and windy. We drove to the top of *Benabhraghie*, or the *Monument Hill*, on which is the very colossal statue of the Duke's grandfather, the first Duke, who married the Countess of Sutherland, from whom this enormous property came. She died in 1839, and I remember her quite well as a very agreeable, clever old lady. We drove through part of the wood by the way we went the previous days, up the big burn drive and through *Bacchies*, looking up *Dunrobin Glen*, which is very wild; and the pink heathery hills, though not very high, and the moor, with distant hills, were very pretty. It is a long pull upwards on a grass drive, which makes it very hard work for the horses. Halfway up we stopped to take tea and coffee; and before that, Brown (who has an extraordinary eye for it, when driving quite fast, which I have not) espied a piece of white heather,* and jumped off to pick it. No Highlander would pass by it without picking it, for it is considered to bring good luck. We got a very extensive view, though not quite clear, of endless hills between this and the west coast—all the Duke's property—where the Westminsters have two if not three forests of the Duke's.

In fine weather seven counties are to be seen in the other direction, looking towards *Ross-shire* and the *Moray Frith*, but it was not clear enough for this. We saw distinctly *Ben Rinnes*, a highish hill that rises in the distance above a long stretch of low land extending into the sea which belongs to the Duke of Richmond. We drove down the hill the same way, but afterwards took a different turn into the high-road, and home by *Golspie* and the Lodge by seven. The dear pretty little girl came to see me. Beatrice brought in Lilah Grosvenor, who had just arrived. Dined at a quarter-past eight in the dining-room, as on Saturday. The same people exactly, with the addition of Colonel Ponsonby. We had some sheep's head, which I tasted for the first time on Sunday, and think really very good. Remained a little while in the drawing-room, and the Duke presented Mr. Stanley, the discoverer of Livingstone.* He talked of his meeting with Livingstone, who he thinks will require eighteen months to finish the work on which he is bent. Sir Henry Rawlinson was also there.

Then went to my room and Jane read.

Tuesday, September 10.

Very fine. Our usual breakfast. At half-past ten got on my pony Maggie, Annie and Jane Churchill walking, and went to see the *Golspie Burn Falls*. We made two mistakes before we got right. We went out by the usual approach down to the mill, and past the mill under the great arch for the railway, over some very rough stones in the river, and then along a path in the wood full of hazel bushes and trees of all kinds, till the glen narrows very much, and we came to a wooden bridge, where I got off and walked to the head of the falls—over several foot-bridges, along a small path overhung by high rocks and full of rich vegetation. It is extremely pretty, reminding me of *Corriemulzie*, only on a much smaller scale. I mounted my pony again, and rode home the same way about twelve. Very warm. We had a few drops of rain, but it remained very fine all day.

At ten minutes to four started with the two children and Annie Sutherland in my waggonette for *Loch Brora*, which is nine miles off. We drove past the stables out on the main *Caithness* road, through the small fishing village of *Brora*, where all the people were out, and where they had raised a triumphal arch and decorated the village with heather. We turned sharp to the left, and came into a wild moor country, stopping for a moment at a place where one of the new coal mines* which the Duke has found is being worked. One of these, near the sea, we had passed on Sunday. Then on, till we came very soon to the commencement of *Loch Brora*, which is seven miles in length, very narrow at first, and out of which the *Brora* flows into the sea. The hills heighten as the loch widens, and to the left as we drove along the *Carrol Hill* rises very finely with bold rocks up above the loch. An hour's drive took us to the Fishing Cottage, a small wooden house, built like a chalet, which is just off the road, on the grass.* Here we got out. The Duke drove his break, four horses in hand. They had never been together before, and it was not easy to drive them, for the road is full of turnings and rather narrow. Lord Granville sat on the box with him; and Constance Westminster, Jane Churchill, the Duchess de San Arpino (who had just arrived, and is a great friend of the Duchess) and Lady Granville were inside, and two grooms sitting behind. The three young ladies, and Mr. Collins, and Colonel Ponsonby followed in the waggonette. They had started before us, but we caught them up at *Brora*. MacAlister had broiled some fish and got tea ready for us in a very small room upstairs in this little cottage, where there was a fire. I had my coffee. We ladies and Leopold all squeezed into this room. It was a very merry tea. The tea over, we all went down to see a haul of fish. It was very successful; quantities of brilliantly red char, trout, and two salmon, both of which had to be put back again. After this haul I went up and sat sketching on the balcony while there were several more hauls, which Macdonald the keeper superintended, and some walked, and others rowed. The view, looking towards the *Carrol Hill*, was lovely, and the colouring beautiful.

The ladies and gentlemen rowed across, having sent the carriages round, but I preferred *terra firma*, and drove round the loch to where the *Black-Water* runs into *Loch Brora*, and is literally black; we drove over it. The Duchess told us that there was a fine drive into a wild country up that glen.* We drove along the loch side, really a beautiful drive, under the *Carrol Rock* or *Hill*, through the *Carrol Wood*; the trees seem to grow remarkably well there. We saw some deer on the very top of the hills. As we drove along the loch, some high hills were seen rising up behind the low ones on the opposite side, one of which, called *Ben Arlmin*, is in the Duke's nearest deer-forest.

We turned to the right, passing by moors which the Duke has cultivated wonderfully with the steam plough, and came back through *Uppat* stopping near Mr. Loch's place, *Uppat*, where, in early days, the late Duke and Duchess used to live when they were Lord and Lady Gower. Mr. Loch's father was the commissioner for the late Duke, and the present Mr. Loch (whom I remember in a similar capacity at *Worsley*, Lord Ellesmere's, in 1851) is commissioner to the present Duke. Mrs. Loch, and her daughter, and little granddaughter, who gave me a nosegay, were there. And the *Dol* schoolchildren were drawn up outside the school. We got home through the woods at twenty minutes past seven. Dinner was at half-past eight in the dining-room, the same as before, only with the addition of the Duchess of San Arpino and Sir Henry Rawlinson, and the omission of Lord Ronald L. Gower and Colonel Ponsonby.

I must now describe the dining-room. It is not a very large room, but a pretty one; with wood panelling and a portrait of the first Duchess's father, the Earl of Sutherland, at one end, and a beautiful chalk drawing, by Landseer, of two deer in the snow, one having been killed by the other. Stags' heads are round the room, and behind one (a very fine one) gaspipes have been introduced, which light up each point. In each panel along the sides of the room are paintings after Thorwaldsen's statues.* By daylight the room is dark. We had some haggis at dinner to-day, and some sheep's head yesterday. MacAlister had walked round the table each of the previous days playing, but to-day it was my piper,[+] Willie Leys; and afterwards they played together in the next room. Went again for a little while into the drawing-room, which is handsome, and about the size of the dining-room, and cheerfully arranged with tables and ornaments. The paper on the walls is dark red. There is a little turret at one end of it, and windows on two sides, and it opens into the ante-room,

---

[+] He left my service in 1876.

which again opens into the library. There is a full-length picture of me in the ante-room. The dining-room is a detached room on the other side; and the billiard-room is close opposite to my sitting-room. Jane Churchill again read to me in my room.

Wednesday, September 11.

A dull morning. The military manoeuvres in the South seem to be going on very satisfactorily, and every one praises dear Arthur, his indefatigable zeal and pains.* It is very gratifying. At a quarter to eleven walked with Jane Churchill and the Duke down to the small museum in the garden, which is very nicely arranged, and where there is a very interesting collection of Celtic ornaments, some of which are quite perfect, and have been very well imitated, and of all sorts of odd and curious Celtic remains, weapons, utensils, etc., and a very fine large collection of all the birds found at or near *Dunrobin*.* Mr. Joass, the minister, was there to explain everything to us.

We took a short turn, and came home at half-past eleven, as it rained. We met little Alix on her wee pony. We also saw the Duchess's Norwegian cariole and pony. (Busy choosing presents to give away; and after our usual luncheon there was some more arranging about these presents.) Painting the view of the sea from my window. At ten minutes to four started in the waggonette, with the two children and Annie. The Duke, the other ladies, Ronald L. Gower, Colonel Ponsonby, and Sir Henry Rawlinson had gone on in the drag. We drove out by the *West Lodge*, through *Golspie*, on the road (on part of which we had come before) under the *Silver Hill*, a very pretty wooded road, and turned to the right across the Mound, an embankment constructed by the first Duke to make a communication across an arm of the sea, called *Loch Fleet*, which comes in there. This Mound "spans *Strathfleet*." Near it is a railway station.

We then drove through a very pretty glen, with fine hills, to *Dornoch*, along the shore of *Dornoch Frith*, past *Cambusmore* (though not near the house, which lies up in the wood at the foot of the fine hill of that name), on through woods for some way, till we suddenly emerged on lower ground and saw the steeple of *Dornoch Church*, formerly a cathedral.

We turned sharp to the left, and went into *Dornoch*; quite a small place, but the capital of *Sutherland*, now much out of the world, as the railway does not go near it. It is a small fishing town, smaller than *Golspie*. There was an arch with a Gaelic inscription, and the houses were decorated with flowers, heather, and green boughs, and many people out. We drove to the door of the so-called cathedral; though

I had not intended doing it, I got out there, and walked up the large kirk. The late Duke's father and mother are buried there, as were sixteen Earls of Sutherland; and there is a statue of the old Duke in marble. The cathedral was built by Gilbert de Moravia, Bishop from 1223 to 1260, at his own expense. St. Gilbert was related to the Sutherlands, who had then recently acquired that vast territory, "the Southern land of *Caithness*," which now gives the title to their descendant, the present and third Duke. In a very ancient stone sarcophagus are the bones of Richard Murray, brother to the Bishop. We only remained a few minutes in the church, and then went out by another door, where we got into the carriage. There is a curious old tower opposite the church, which was part of the Bishop's Palace. The people were very enthusiastic, and an old fish-wife, with her creel on her back, bare legs and feet, and very short petticoat (we met many such about *Dunrobin*), began waving a handkerchief, and almost dancing, near the end of the place as we drove away. Brown motioned to her to come on, and threw her something, which the poor old thing ran to pick up.* We stopped when we had regained the wood to take our tea and coffee, and were joined by the Duke's drag just as we had finished.

We changed our road, going by *Embo* and *Skelbo*, the model farm of the late Duke, and drove up to *Cambusmore*, the pretty little cottage of Mr. and Mrs. Bateson. There is a small garden in front. The two children got out, and so did all the others, but I begged to remain in the carriage, as I was tired. However, I afterwards got out; and certainly the little cottage is most charmingly fitted up with deer's heads, pretty prints, and pretty things of all kinds. They asked me to write my name in a book, which I did, sitting in the carriage.

From here we drove back again the same way; and the evening was very fine, and the sky beautiful, red and every possible bright colour. As we drove along, before reaching *Cambusmore* we saw the high land of *Caithness*, a good way beyond *Brora*. Back by seven. Dined with the two children in my own room, and then went for a short while into the drawing-room; then wrote, and at half-past eleven left *Dunrobin*, with the two children and Annie, in the Duke's carriage, the Duke (in the kilt) helping us in, and then walking, with MacAlister after him, up the approach, straight to the private station, which is about five hundred yards from the house.

There were many people out, and the whole was brilliantly illuminated by Egyptian and red and blue lights. At the station all the ladies and gentlemen were assembled, and I wished them all good-bye, and then got into the train, having kissed Annie, and Constance, and the two girls, and shaken hands with the Duke, who, as well as the Duchess, had been most kind.

It was half-past twelve before I lay down. Beatrice did so sooner.

Thursday, September 12.

I had not slept much, but the journey was very quiet. At eight we were at *Ballater*. A splendid morning. We drove off at once, Beatrice, Leopold, and I in one carriage, and reached dear *Balmoral* safely at a quarter to nine A.M.

Felt as though all had been a dream, and that it was hardly possible we should have been only last night at *Dunrobin*, and dined there.

Dr. Norman Macleod.*

[March, 1873.—I am anxious to put on record all my recollections of my dear and valued friend Dr. Norman Macleod, who has been taken from us, and whose loss is more deeply felt every day.

I have therefore made the following extracts from my journal since the year 1861, when my heavy misfortune brought me into very close contact with him.]

Balmoral,
Sunday, May 11, 1862.

Hurried to be ready for the service which Dr. Macleod was kindly going to perform.* And a little before ten I went down with Lenchen and Affie (Alice being still in bed unwell) to the dining-room, in which I had not yet been. The ladies and gentlemen were seated behind me, the servants, including Grant and some of the other Highlanders, opposite. And never was service more beautifully, touchingly, simply, and tenderly performed. There was the opening prayer, then the reading from Scripture, which was most beautifully selected as follows: the twenty-third chapter of Job, the forty-second Psalm, the fourteenth chapter of St. John, some of the first verses, and then from the twenty-third verse to the end, and the seventh chapter of Revelations to the end.* All so applicable. After this came another prayer, and then the sermon, entirely extempore, taken from the twelfth chapter of the Epistle to the Hebrews to the thirteenth verse, also alluding to the tenth chapter, and occasionally turning to the Corinthians. The sermon was admirable, all upon affliction, God's love, our Saviour's sufferings, which God would not spare Him, the blessedness of suffering in bringing us nearer to our eternal home, where we should all be together, and where our dear ones were gone on before us. He concluded with another prayer, in which he prayed most touchingly for me. The children and I were much affected on coming upstairs.

Monday, May 12.

On coming home in the afternoon, Dr. Macleod came to see me, and was so clever, agreeable, kind and good. We talked of dear Albert's illness, his readiness to go hence at all times, with which Dr. Macleod was much struck, and said what a beautiful state of mind he must always have been in—how unselfish—how ready to do whatever was necessary; and

I exemplified this by describing his cheerfulness in giving up all he liked and enjoyed, and being just as cheerful when he changed to other circumstances, looking at the bright and interesting side of them; like, for instance, going from here to *Windsor* and from *Windsor* to *London*, leaving his own dear home, etc., and yet being always cheerful, which was the reverse with me. He spoke of the blessing of living on with those who were gone on before. An old woman, he said, whom he knew, had lost her husband and several of her children, and had had many sorrows, and he asked her how she had been able to bear them, and she answered: "Ah! when *he* went awa' it made a great hole, and all the others went through it."[+] And so it is, most touchingly and truly expressed, and so it will ever be with me.

Balmoral,
Sunday, August 24, 1862.

At ten service was performed by Dr. Macleod downstairs, again very beautifully. His selections were very good: the hundred and third Psalm, part of the eleventh chapter of Isaiah, and then before his sermon, the fourth chapter of Philippians, sixth verse, which was the text: "Be careful for nothing; but in every thing by prayer and supplication with thanksgiving let your requests be made known unto God," and part of the eleventh chapter of St. Luke, fifth verse: "Which of you shall have a friend, and shall go unto him at midnight, and shall say unto him, Friend, lend me three loaves?" As usual, it made a deep impression.

After dinner, in the evening, I went over to Mrs. Bruce's room, and there Dr. Macleod joined us, and was so kind, so comforting, and so cheering. He expressed great admiration of my dearest Albert's statue (the cast of which was standing in the vestibule below). His eyes were full of tears, and he said his loss was felt more and more. I showed him a drawing of the mausoleum, and he said, "Oh! *he* is not there," which is so true; and again, when admiring the photograph of the reclining statue by Marochetti, he added, "But I think *he* is more like the statue below," which is a beautiful and a true idea. He looks so truly at the reality of the next life.

[+] I since hear that this poor woman was not personally known to Dr. Macleod, but that her remark was related to him by Dr. Black, his predecessor in the Barony Parish, Glasgow. Her words were: "When *he* was ta'en, it made sic' a hole in my heart that a' other sorrows gang lichtly through."

Sunday, May 24, 1863.

My poor birthday!
At a quarter past ten service was performed by Dr. Macleod. All the children but Baby there. He read the ninetieth and hundred and third Psalms; part of the twenty-fourth chapter of St. Matthew, ninth verse: "All hail." His sermon very fine, but he read it, not having had time to prepare one by thinking the subject over, or even by the help of mere notes. I saw him in the evening, and he was most kind and sympathising.

Sunday, October 9, 1864.

At four, went to kirk with Lenchen and Augusta Stanley. Dr. Macleod performed the service admirably, and gave us a very striking sermon, all extempore, and appealing very strongly to the people's feelings. Saw good Dr. Macleod afterwards, and was much upset in talking to him of my sorrows, anxieties, and overwhelming cares; and he was so kind and sympathising, so encouraging and full of that *faith* and *hope* which alone can comfort and sustain the broken heart.* In his sermon he spoke of there being *peace without happiness,* and *happiness without peace,* which is so true.

Balmoral,
Sunday, June 11, 1865.

At twelve, went (a great effort) to the kirk with the girls and the Duchess of Athole. I had only been once at the end of our stay last year in October, in the afternoon, and it made me very nervous. Still, as no one expected me to go, it was better so. Dr. Macleod performed the service most impressively. His sermon was from 1 Thessalonians iv. 10. No one reads the Bible better than he does, and his prayers were most beautiful. In the one for me, which he always words so expressively and touchingly, he prayed for Alix and her dear babe very beautifully. The singing and the whole service brought tears to my eyes. I felt so alone! All reminded me of former blessedness.

Balmoral,
Saturday, October 14, 1865.

After dinner Dr. Macleod gave us a long account of that dreadful Dr. Pritchard,[†] and his interviews with him. Never in his life had he seen

---

[†] He had poisoned his wife and his wife's mother, and Dr. Macleod attended him in prison.

anything so dreadful as this man's character and his wonderful untruthfulness.

Dr. Macleod afterwards came upstairs, and read to Lenchen and me out of Burns most beautifully.

Sunday, October 15, 1865.

At twelve we went to the kirk, where dear Dr. Macleod performed the service more beautifully than I ever heard it. The sermon was touching, and most striking and useful. It touched and struck all. The text was from Genesis iii. 13: "And the Lord God said unto the woman, What is this that thou hast done?"

And then he showed how we all had a secret life which no one knew but God, and showed the frightful danger of living a life of deception till you deceived yourself, and no longer knew wrong from right. I wish I could repeat *all* he said, but it was admirable. Then in his beautiful prayers he brought in a most touching allusion to Lord Palmerston,[†] and prayed for him.

Balmoral,
Sunday, June 17, 1866.

We went at twelve to the kirk, and Dr. Macleod gave us a beautiful sermon from St. Mark ix. 38, etc. It was very fine, so large-minded and charitable, much against party spirit and want of charity, and showed how thoroughly charity, in its highest form, existed in our Saviour.

... The Duchess of Athole and Dr. Macleod dined with me. He was so amiable, and full of sympathy; he also suffers much from constant work and worry, and must go abroad for relaxation. Told him how much I required it, and that I came here for it, and had had a hard fight for it. He said he quite felt this, and entreated me—"as you work for us"—always to insist upon coming here. I said my dearest Albert had injured himself by never giving himself enough rest; and we spoke of the absolute necessity of complete relaxation occasionally, and of the comfort of it.

Balmoral,
Sunday, September 16, 1866.

The church was very full and the atmosphere very close. Dr. Macleod preached admirably, especially the latter part of the sermon, when he preached

---

[†] He was dying, and expired on October 18.

extempore, and spoke of our responsibilities which made us work out our salvation. God wished us all to be saved, but we must work that out ourselves. And we might by our own fault not be saved. The first part was read, he having told me the night before that he felt nervous, and must read it.

Balmoral,
Thursday, September 20, 1867.

Good Dr. Macleod (who arrived yesterday, for two nights) came to talk to me for some little time while I was sitting out. He spoke most kindly, and said enough to show how shocked he was at my many worries, but said also that he was convinced of the great loyalty of the nation, and that I should take courage.

On the next day, the 21st, he came to take leave of me, as he was going to *India*, sent by the General Assembly to look after the missions.* He is only going for six months; still, his life is so valuable that it is a great risk. He was much affected in taking leave of me, and said, "If I should not return, I pray God to carry your Majesty through all your trials."

Balmoral,
Saturday, October 10, 1868.

Mr. Van de Weyer and good Dr. Macleod, who is looking ill, and rather broken, and with a long beard, dined with us.†

Sunday, October 11.

All to kirk at twelve. Christian and Franz† sat in the *Abergeldie* pew. Dr. Macleod performed the service, and I never heard a finer sermon, or more touching prayer for me. The text, St. Luke ix. 33: "Peter said unto Jesus, Master, it is good for us to be here...not knowing what he said."

Saw Dr. Macleod, who talked, as also last night, of *India*, and of the disturbance in the Church.*

Balmoral,
Sunday, June 6, 1869.

To kirk with Louise, Leopold, Baby (Beatrice), and Christian. Dr. Macleod (who arrived last night) performed the service, and admirably, speaking so

---

† He had only lately returned from India.
† The Prince and Princess Christian of Schleswig-Holstein and the Prince and Princess of Teck were on a visit.

much to the heart. The prayers were beautiful, and so was the sermon. It was so full of truth and simple good advice, telling us to act according to the spirit of what is told us, and according to what we felt was right. The text from I Peter iv. 21. Afterwards saw dear Dr. Macleod, whom I find a good deal altered and aged. He is Moderator of the General Assembly for this year, and spoke with much pleasure of the unanimity prevailing, and of the good feeling shown towards him; and regretted much this Irish Church Bill.*

Balmoral,
Sunday, October 3, 1869.

At twelve, went with our children to the kirk. Dr. Macleod preached a fine sermon, and gave us two beautiful prayers as usual. The text was from Matthew xxvi. 30.

I saw Dr. Macleod before dinner. He is greatly alarmed for the Established Church of Scotland, as he fears that an attempt will be made to pull that down also; though, thank God, there is no difference of form or doctrine there, and were this to happen, the Free Church and United Presbyterians, with the present Established Church, would become one very strong Protestant body.* I also asked him about Lord Lorne,* and he said he had a very high opinion of him; that he had long known him, and had prepared him for confirmation, that he thought very highly of him, and had a great respect for him, and that he had fine, noble, elevated feelings.

Sunday, October 2, 1870.

A very fine morning after a frost. The sun intensely hot. Dear Leopold breakfasted with us out of doors. Sat out for a short while. To the kirk at twelve. It was not so stifling. Dr. Macleod gave us such a splendid sermon on the war, and without mentioning *France*, he said enough to make every one understand what was meant (when he pointed out how God would punish wickedness, and vanity, and sensuality; and the chapters he read from Isaiah xxviii., and from Ezekiel, Amos, and one of the Psalms, were really quite wonderful for the way in which they seemed to describe *France*)*. It was all admirable and heart-stirring. Then the prayers were beautiful in which he spoke of the sick, the dying, the wounded, the battlefield, and my sons-in-law and daughters. We all came back deeply impressed.

Monday, October 3.

Dr. Macleod came to wish me good-bye. He yesterday again told me what a very high opinion he had of Lord Lorne, how good, excellent, and superior he thought him in every way, and the whole family so good.

Balmoral,
June—,1871.

Dear Dr. Macleod was unable to come during my present stay here, having been unwell in the winter. He has gone abroad to *Ems.**

Balmoral,
Sunday, November 5, 1871.

At a little before twelve, went to kirk with Baby and Janie Ely, for the first time after a very severe illness—a great pleasure to me who am so fond of going to the dear little church here. Brown helped me up and down the steep staircase, but I found no great difficulty. Dr. Macleod (who arrived yesterday evening at the Castle) performed the service, which he made purposely rather short for me. He gave us a beautiful sermon, the text from St. Matthew vi. 9: "Our Father, who art in heaven;" and he preached upon the great importance, as well as comfort, of our looking on God as a Father, and not as a judge or "magistrate," to use a homely phrase. He also gave an admirable explanation of the Sacrament, which he announced was to be given next Sunday, explaining that it was not a miracle, which people often consider it to be. Back by a quarter-past one, much edified.

He came to see me before dinner.

Monday, November 6, 1871.

Had a long and satisfactory talk with Dr. Macleod after luncheon to-day again.

Balmoral,
Sunday, May 26, 1872.

To kirk at twelve, with Baby and the ladies, etc. Dr. Macleod preached a very fine sermon, full of love and warm feeling, upon future life and hope. The text was from St. Matthew v. 9, "Thy kingdom come." But I was grieved to see him looking ill.

After luncheon saw good Dr. Macleod, who was very depressed and looking very ill, and willingly sat down at my request. He said he was quite broken down from hard work, and would have to give up his house in *Glasgow* (where he has not a moment's rest), and his Indian mission work, etc. He feels all this much, but it is unavoidable. He did too much. He has never recovered from the effects of his visit to *India*. He is, however, going to *America* for some months, and has refused everything in the way of preaching and lectures. He talked much of a future life, and his certainty of there being a continuation there of God's educational purposes, which had commenced in this world, and would work on towards the final triumph of good over evil, and the extinction of sin.

Balmoral,
Monday, May 27, 1872.

Saw and wished good Dr. Macleod good-bye, with real regret and anxiety. Towards the end of dinner, yesterday, he cheered up, having hardly talked at all during the course of it.

Balmoral,
Sunday, June 16, 1872.

We had come home at five minutes past eight; I had wished Brown good-night, and was just going to my dressing-room, when he asked to come in again and say a few words to me. He came in, and said, very kindly, that he had seen Colonel Ponsonby, and that there was rather bad news of Dr. Macleod, who was very ill, in fact that they were afraid he was *dead!* Oh! What a blow! How dreadful to lose that dear, kind, loving, large-hearted friend! My tears flowed fast, but I checked them as much as I could, and thanked good Brown for the very kind way he broke this painful and most unexpected news to me. I sent for and told Leopold, who was quite stunned by it, and all my maids. Every one was most deeply grieved—the Duchess of Athole, Janie Ely, Miss MacGregor, Colonel Ponsonby, and Dr. Taylor, who was so overcome as hardly for some time to be able to speak. The loss, he and we all felt, was quite irreparable. Dr. Taylor knew (which I did not) that he had been very ill for a week, and that he might die at any moment, and that the long and most admirable speech which he made in the Assembly had been far too much for him. That was on the 30th. Still we all hoped that rest would have restored him. How thankful I felt that I had seen him so lately! When the Duchess came upstairs, we could speak of little else. After she left, and I was alone, I cried very bitterly, for this is a terrible loss to me.

Monday, June 17.

When I awoke the sad truth flashed upon me, which is doubly painful, as one is unaware of the reality on first waking.

After breakfast, when I thought of my dear friend Dr. Macleod, and all he had been to me—how in 1862–63–64 he had cheered, and comforted, and encouraged me—how he had ever sympathised with me, and how much I always looked forward to the few occasions I had of seeing him when we went to *Balmoral*, and that this too, like so many other comforts and helps, was for ever gone—I burst out crying.

Yesterday evening we heard by telegraph from Mr. Donald Macleod (for the first news came from the *Glasgow* telegraph clerk to Warren[+]) that his dear brother had died at twelve that morning.

I telegraphed to all my children, and could think of nothing else. I try to dwell on all he said, for there was no one to whom in doubts and anxieties on religion I looked up with more trust and confidence, and no one ever reassured and comforted me more about my children. I remember that he expressed deep satisfaction at hearing such good accounts of them.... And then he seemed so full of trust and gratitude to God. He wrote a beautiful letter to Janie Ely on his birthday (June 3), in answer to my inquiries after him, of which I annex the copy. His words seemed almost prophetic!

June 3, 1872.

Dear Lady Ely,—Whether it is that my head is empty or my heart full, or that both conditions are realised in my experience, the fact, however, is that I cannot express myself as I feel in replying to your Ladyship's kind—far too kind—note, which I received when in the whirlwind or miasma of Assembly business.

Thanks deep and true to you, and to my Sovereign Lady, for thinking of me. I spoke for nearly two hours in the Assembly, which did me no good, nor, I fear, to any other.

I was also to preach yesterday. As I have nice summer quarters, I much hope to recruit, so as to cast off this dull, hopeless sort of feeling.

I ought to be a happy, thankful man to-day. I am today sixty, and round my table will meet my mother, my wife, and all my nine children, six brothers, sisters, and two aunts—one eighty-nine, the other seventy-six; and all these are a source of joy and thanksgiving! Why such mercies to me, and such sufferings as I often see sent to the rest on earth?

God alone knows! I don't see *how* He always acts as a wise, loving, and impartial Father to all His children. What we know not now, we shall know hereafter. Let us trust when we cannot trace.

God bless the Queen for all her unwearied goodness! I admire her as a woman, love her as a friend, and reverence her as a Queen; and you know that what I say I feel. Her courage, patience, and endurance are marvellous to me.

(Signed) N. MACLEOD.

[+] My own telegraph clerk.

March 1873.

Dear Dr. Macleod likewise came to *Balmoral*, and preached there, on the following occasions: October 11, 1863, May 24, 1864 (my birthday, after his visit to the *Holy Land*), on May 27, 1867, and on May 29, 1869.

When I last saw him I was greatly distressed at his depression and sadness, and instead of my looking to him to cheer and encourage *me*, I tried to cheer *him*. He said he had been ordered to give up all work, and to give up his house at *Glasgow*, merely continuing to preach at the *Barony Church*; and that then they gave him hopes of a recovery, but it was not at all certain. He must give up the Indian Mission, which was a great sorrow to him; and he meant to take the opportunity of resigning it in person, to say what he felt so strongly, though others might not be pleased. He meant to go to *America* in August, merely to recruit his health and strength; and he had refused every invitation: for dinners, or to lecture or preach. He had not much confidence, he said, in his recovery, but he might be wrong. All was in God's hands. "It is the nature of Highlanders to despond when they are ill," he added. He hoped God would allow him to live a few years longer, for his children, and to be able to go on with "Good Words." He dwelt then, as always, on the love and goodness of God, and on his conviction that God would give us, in another life, the means to perfect ourselves and to improve gradually. No one ever felt so convinced, and so anxious as he to convince others, that God was a loving Father, who wished all to come to Him, and to preach of a living personal Saviour, One who loved us as a brother and a friend, to whom all could and should come with trust and confidence. No one ever raised and strengthened one's faith more than Dr. Macleod. His own faith was so strong, his heart so large, that all—high and low, weak and strong, the erring and the good—could alike find sympathy, help, and consolation from him.

How I loved to talk to him, to ask his advice, to speak to him of my sorrows, my anxieties!

But, alas! how impossible I feel it to be to give any adequate idea of the character of this good and distinguished man! So much depended on his personal charm of manner, so warm, genial, and hearty, overflowing with kindness and the love of human nature; and so much depended on himself, on knowing and living with him, that no one who did not do so can truly portray him. And, indeed, how can any one, alas, who has not known or seen a person, ever imagine from description what he is really like?

He had the greatest admiration for the beauties of nature, and was most enthusiastic about the beautiful wild scenery of his dear country, which he loved intensely and passionately. When I said to him, on his last visit, that I was going to take some mineral waters when I went south, he pointed to the lovely view from the windows, looking up the glen of the *Dee*, and said: "The fine air in these hills, and the quiet here, will do your Majesty much more good than all the waters." His wife, he said, had urged him to come, though he felt so ill. "It always does you good to go to *Balmoral*," she told him. He admired and loved the national music of his country, and wrote the following description of it, most kindly, as a preface to a book of Pipe Music published by my head piper, William Ross:—

THE BAGPIPE AND ITS MUSIC.
By the Rev. Dr. Norman Macleod.

The music of the *Highlands* is the pibroch of the great war-pipe, with its fluttering pennons, fingered by a genuine Celt, in full Highland dress, as he slowly paces a baronial hall, or amidst the wild scenery of his native mountains. The bagpipe is the instrument best adapted for summoning the clans from the far-off glens to rally round the standard of their chiefs, or for leading a Highland regiment to the attack amidst the roar of battle. The pibroch is also constructed to express a welcome to the chief on his return to his clan, and to wail out a lament for him as he is borne by his people to the old burial-place in the glen or in the sainted *Isle of Graves*. To those who understand its carefully composed music there is a pathos and depth of feeling suggested by it which a Highlander alone can fully sympathise with; associated by him as it always is with the most touching memories of his home and country; recalling the faces and forms of the departed; spreading forth before his inward eye panoramas of mountain, loch, and glen, and reviving impressions of his early and happiest years. And thus, if it excites the stranger to laughter, it excites the Highlander to tears, as no other music can do, in spite of the most refined culture of his after life. It is thus, too, that what appears to be only a tedious and unmeaning monotony in the music of the genuine pibroch, is not so to one under the magic influence of Highland associations. There is, indeed, in every pibroch a certain monotony of sorrow. It pervades even the "welcome," as if the young chief who arrives recalls the memory of the old chief who has departed. In the "lament" we naturally expect this sadness; but even in the "summons to battle," with all its fire and energy, it cannot conceal what it seems already to anticipate, sorrow for the slain. In the very reduplication of its hurried notes, and in the repetition of its one idea, there are expressions of vehement passion and of grief—"the joy of grief," as Ossian terms it,* which loves to brood upon its own loss, and ever repeats the one desolate thought which fills the heart, and which in the end again breaks forth into the long and loud agonising cry with which it began. All this will no doubt seem both meaningless and extravagant to many, but it is nevertheless a deliberately expressed conviction.

The characteristic poetry of the *Highlands* is Ossian, its music the pibroch; and these two voices embody the spirit and sing the praises of "Tir na'm Beann, na'n Gleann's na Gaisgeach" ("the land of the mountains, the glens, and the heroes").

I said I was sure he would rejoice to think that it was a Highlander who had seized O'Connor,[+] and he replied, "I was deeply thankful to hear it."

He possessed a keen sense of wit and great appreciation of humour, and had a wonderful power of narrating anecdotes. He had likewise a marvellous power of winning people of all kinds, and of sympathising with the highest and with the humblest, and of soothing and comforting the sick, the dying, the afflicted, the erring and the doubting. A friend of mine told me that if she were in great trouble, or sorrow, or anxiety, Dr. Norman Macleod was the person she would wish to go to! And so it was! One felt one's troubles, weaknesses, and sorrows would all be lovingly listened to, sympathised with, and entered into.

I detected a sign of illness in dear Dr. Macleod's accepting, contrary to his ordinary usage, my invitation to him to sit down, saying he could not stand well; and I afterwards heard he had complained greatly of fatigue in walking back from the kirk. I said I feared *India* had done him harm. He admitted it, but said, "I don't regret it." I expressed an earnest hope that he would be very careful of himself, and that on his return at the end of October he would take *Balmoral* on his way.

When I wished him good-bye and shook hands with him, he said, "God bless your Majesty," and the tears were in his eyes. Only then did the thought suddenly flash upon me, as I closed the door of my room, that I might never see this dear friend again, and it nearly overcame me. But this thought passed, and never did I think, that not quite three weeks after, his noble, pure spirit would be with the God and Saviour he loved and served so well! I have since heard that he mentioned to several at *Balmoral* that he thought he should never come there again.

I will here quote from my Journal some part of an account of my conversations at *Balmoral* on August 24 and 25, 1872, with Dr. Macleod's excellent and amiable brother, the Rev. Donald Macleod, about his dear brother Norman:—

"He (Norman) was a complete type in its noblest sense of a Highlander and a Celt, which, as Mr. Donald Macleod and I both observed, was peculiarly sympathetic, attaching, and attractive. I said that since my great sorrow in 1861, I had found no natures so sympathetic and so soothing as those of the Highlanders.... He (Donald Macleod) said, 'I went to him for everything; he

---

[+] The young man who rushed up to my carriage with a petition and a pistol in Buckingham Palace Garden on February 29, 1872, and was seized by Brown.

was like a father to me (he is twenty years his junior)! His indefatigable kindness to every one was unequalled, and his patience was so great and he was so good.' His acts of kindness to people whom he did not know were frequent and unknown even to his family. His sense of humour and fun was unbounded, and enabled him to win the confidence of persons of the greatest diversity of character. Mr. Donald Macleod thinks, however, that it was a mercy his dear brother was taken when he was, for that a life of inactivity, and probable infirmity, would have been unbearable to him.... His health had been unsatisfactory already before he went to *India*, but, no doubt, that journey had done him great harm; still he never would have spared himself, if he thought there was a work given to him to do.... His wife and children bore up wonderfully because he had taught them to look on the future state so much as a reality, and as one of such great happiness, that they felt it would be doing wrong not to rejoice in his joy. His faith was so strong that it held others in a marvellous manner, and he realised the future state and its activity, as he believed, in a most remarkable way.

Visit to Inverlochy, 1873.

Tuesday, September 9, 1873.

Got up at ten minutes to seven, and breakfasted with Beatrice at twenty minutes past seven. The morning was splendid. At five minutes past eight I left *Balmoral* with Beatrice and Jane Churchill in the landau and four (Brown on the rumble) for *Ballater*, whither General Ponsonby and Dr. Fox had preceded us. We had our own comfortable train; Jane Churchill came with us. Emilie Dittweiler, Annie Macdonald, Morgan, and Maxtead (Jane's maid) went in the dresser's compartment, and Francie with dear Noble,[+] with Brown next to me. After crossing the *Bridge of Dun*, where we were at half-past eleven, we had some cold luncheon, and by a quarter to one we were at *Stanley Junction*, where we left the main line from *Aberdeen* to the south, and turned into the Highland Railway. Here, alas! the distance became indistinct, the sky grey, and we began fearing for the afternoon. At one we passed the really beautiful valley of *Dunkeld*, catching a glimpse of the cathedral and the lovely scenery around, which interested Beatrice very much, and made me think of my pleasant visits and excursions thence; then passed opposite *St. Colme's*, the Duchess's farm, by *Dalguise*, and saw the large Celtic cross at *Logierait*, put up to the late Duke of Athole; then *Pitlochry*; after which we passed through the magnificent *Pass of Killiekrankie*, which we just skirted in our long drive by *Loch Tay* and *Loch Tummel*, in 1866. The dull leaden sky which overhung *Dunkeld* continued, and soon a white veil began to cover the hills, and slight rain came down.

We passed close by *Blair*, which reminded me much of my sad visit there in 1863, when I came by this same line to visit the late Duke;* and I could now see the great improvements made at the Castle. From here the railway (running almost parallel with the road by which *we* went so happily from *Dalwhinnie* the reverse way in 1861) passes *Dalnaspidal Station*—a very lonely spot—then up *Drumouchter*, with *Loch Garry* and *Loch Ericht*, fine and wild, but terribly desolate and devoid of woods and habitations, and so veiled by mist and now beating rain as to be seen to but very little advantage. Next comes *Dalwhinnie Station*, near the inn where we slept in 1861, having ridden over from *Balmoral* to *Glen Fishie*, and thence down by *Newton More*;* consequently, the distance across

---

[+] Another favourite and splendid collie.

NOBLE

the hill is comparatively nothing, though, to avoid posting in uncertain weather, we had to come all this way round. At thirty-five minutes past two we reached *Kingussie*. The station was decorated with flowers, heather, and flags, and the Master of Lovat (now Lord Lieutenant of *Inverness-shire*) and Cluny Macpherson (both of course in kilts) were there. We waited till all our things were put into our carriage, and then got out, in heavy rain at that moment. We three went in the sociable, General Ponsonby and Brown on the box, Dr. Fox and my maids in the waggonette, the other maids and Francie with the dog and the remainder following in two other carriages. We passed through the village of *Kingussie*, where there were two triumphal arches and decorations, and some of Cluny's men drawn up, and then turned sharp to the left up amongst the hills, through the very poor long village of *Newton More* (which Annie Macdonald, whose late husband came from there, had never seen, but which *we* had driven through in 1861), and on amongst desolate, wild, heathery moors. The road skirts the *Spey*, which meanders through a rich green valley, hills rising grandly in the distance and on either side. We passed the rock of *Craig Dhu*, and a castle amongst trees, where there was an arch, and the owner and his family standing near it, and where a nosegay was presented to me. Next we came to *Cluny Castle*, at the gate of which stood Mrs. Macpherson with her family. We stopped after we had gone past, and she came and presented me with a nosegay.

From here the road was known to me, if I can call going once to see it in 1847* knowing it. Very few inhabitants, and not one village after *Newton More*, only miserable little cottages and farmhouses, with a few people, all very friendly, scattered about here and there. We changed horses first at *Laggan Bridge*, having crossed the *Spey* over a large stone bridge, which I well remember; it is near *Strathmashie*. Here we stopped a few minutes; and a little girl presented me with a nosegay, and the innkeeper gave Brown a bottle with some wine and a glass. We were preceded the whole way by the postmaster of *Banavie*, who supplied the horses; he was called McGregor, and wore a kilt. We had only a pair of horses all along and after the first stage—excellent ones. The roads admirable— hardly any hills, though we drove through such a hilly, wild country. The rain had ceased, and only occasional showers came on, which did not prevent our seeing the very grand scenery, with the high finely pointed and serrated mountains, as we drove along. Shortly after changing horses we left the river and came to the beautiful *Loch Laggan*, seven miles in length, along which the drive goes under birch, mountain-ash laden with bright berries, oak, alders, in profusion, and is really beautiful. I was quite pleased to see the loch again after twenty-five years—recognised it and admired its beauty, with the wooded promontories, its little bays, and its two little islands, its ferry (the only communication to the other side), and the noble hills, the two *Ben Alders*.

We stopped, soon after passing the ferry, in a very secluded spot at five, and had our (made) tea in the carriage, which was very refreshing. We at length came opposite *Ardverikie*, which I so well remember, recalling and relating, as we now drove along, many of the incidents of our month's stay there, which was as wet as this day. Sir John Ramsden, who has bought the property, was standing with some other people by the roadside. At the head of the loch is *Moy Lodge*, a pretty little place in the style of *Ardverikie*, at which Mr. Ansdell, the artist, is staying. A little beyond this we changed horses at *Moy* (only a single house), and drove along through *Glen Spean*, which is very fine and grand in some parts, the road looking down upon the rapid, rushing, gushing river, as it whirls along imbedded in rocks and overhung with wood, while high ranges of hills, fine and pointed in shape, are seen in the distance rising peak upon peak. Along this road I had driven, but I had forgotten it. Before coming to the *Bridge of Roy* Inn, we saw some of the celebrated *Parallel Roads** quite distinctly, which are more clearly seen farther on, and which are very interesting to all geologists as being supposed to mark the beaches of an inland lake, which was pent back by a great glacier in *Glen Spean*, and subsided to different levels, as the glacier sank or broke away at three successive periods.

The rain ceased, and we walked a little before coming to the *Bridge of Roy*, where we changed horses for the last time, and directly afterwards passed a triumphal arch with heather and inscriptions, pipers playing, etc., and Highlanders as well as many other people drawn up, but we unfortunately drove past them too quickly. There was an inscription in Gaelic on one side, and on the other "Loyal Highlanders welcome their Queen." The papers say that it was put up by Mrs. McDonell of *Keppoch*.

About three miles farther on we reached *Spean Bridge*, and it was already getting dark. Here there is only an inn, and Lord and Lady Abinger and their tenantry met us. Lord Abinger said he had been requested to express the people's thanks for my honouring their country with a visit, and his little girl presented me with a large nosegay in the name of the tenantry. We then drove on through rather desolate moors, and the rain began to fall again very heavily. It became quite dark, and we could just descry mountains under which we drove. At ten minutes past eight we arrived at *Inverlochy*,* entering by a lodge, which was lit up and looked cheery enough. The house is entered through a small, neat-looking hall, and I have three nice rooms upstairs, with the maids close by, and Beatrice and Morgan also, just at the other side of the passage. My sitting-room is very nice. It was nine before we got to dinner, which I took with Beatrice and Jane, Brown waiting on us as well as Cannon[+] (the footman). The drawing-room is a large, rather handsome and well-furnished room. We soon went up to our rooms, and all were glad to go to bed.

Inverlochy Castle,
Wednesday, September 10.

Mist on all the hills, and continuous rain! Most disheartening, but the views from the house beautiful, especially from my sitting-room, which has a bow-window, with two small ones on either side, looking towards *Ben Nevis* (which is close in front of it), and commands a lovely view of *Fort William* (farther to the right), and of *Loch Linnhe*, etc., a portion of *Loch Eil* (pronounced *Loch Eel*) which runs up a long way, nearly twelve miles, with the fine *Moidart* range, close to *Glen Finnan*, as a background; and this, with *Banavie* and the hotel, close to the *Caledonian Canal*, is distinctly seen from the other window. This very pretty little room does not open into any other; next to it is Emilie Dittweiler's, next to that my dressing-room, and Annie's room, all narrow and long, and next again is a really large and also long room, my bedroom, in which I had my own bed,* which has been to *Switzerland, Invertrossachs, Sandringham,* and *Baden.* Downstairs is the dining-room, a good-sized room (in which the gentlemen dine), also the drawing-room, and a small library, in which *we* take our meals. No room in the house opens into another. Though some of the bedrooms are larger than those at *Invertrossachs,* the servants are not so well off. After breakfast (which, as well as luncheon, Beatrice and I always took alone) at half-past nine, went upstairs again and looked at Brown's room, which is a few steps lower than mine, in fact, only a very small bathroom. Beatrice is just opposite where I am, or rather round the corner. Jane Churchill and the two gentlemen, upstairs, have also good rooms. As the rain did not cease, Beatrice, Jane Churchill, and I walked out in the grounds to the stables, which we looked at, then out at the lodge and as far as the farm, where, however, no beasts were at the time, and on coming home we went through the house and kitchen, servants' hall, etc., and were in at a quarter to one. There were short gleams of sunshine which lit up the splendid scenery, and I sketched from my window looking up to *Banavie.*

[+] He left my service in 1879.

Played with Beatrice on the piano. The day seemed better, but again and again the sunshine was succeeded by heavy showers; still we determined to go out. So at twenty minutes to five we three started in the sociable, Brown on the box, with a pair of horses and a postilion who drove extremely well. We drove past the distillery (between this and *Fort William*), then turned to the right over the suspension bridge to *Banavie*, about a mile farther, where there is a good hotel, quite close to the *Caledonian Canal*, which we crossed by a bridge, and drove through *Corpach*, a very small village, where the horses made a halt and turned another way, and Brown said nearly put us into a ditch! but we soon got all right again, having to go on a little way to turn. We went along the upper part of *Loch Eil*, the sea loch, on which *Fort William* stands. It is very narrow at first, and then widens out into a large broad loch as you approach the head of it, beyond which is the very fine range of the *Moidart Hills*, high and very serrated and bold. These are close to *Glen Finnan*. The road is excellent and not hilly, though it skirts the hills the whole time and is very winding, with much wood, so that you drive a good deal under trees, ash, oak, alder, and the mountain ash which is now laden with red berries. The bright heather, growing in tufts of the richest colour mixed with a great deal of high tall bracken which is beginning to turn, has a lovely effect. Here and there were some very poor little huts, most miserable, of stone, wretchedly thatched with moss and grass, and weeds growing on the roofs, very dirty and neglected-looking, the little fields full of weeds choking the corn, and neglected bits of garden, bushes and brambles growing into the very window; and yet generally the people who looked most poor had a cow!

We passed *Fassifern*, which belonged to the father of the Colonel Cameron killed at *Quatre Bras*,* now merely a farmhouse, and surrounded by fine trees. I think the drive to near the head of the loch must have been nearly ten miles! It was a beautiful drive, in spite of the frequent very heavy showers of rain.

We came home at twenty minutes to eight. Good accounts of Leopold,* but the weather has been bad. Dined as yesterday. Played on the piano with Beatrice in the drawing-room, and then we went upstairs.

Thursday, September 11.

A pouring wet morning after a pouring wet night. Could not go out all the morning. It, however, cleared up in the afternoon, and became very bright and fine. Just as we decided to go out at a quarter past four, it began raining again; however, as I left with Beatrice and Jane in the sociable, it cleared, and was very fine for some time. We drove out the way we came on Tuesday as far as *Spean Bridge*, and then turned sharp to the left along the *Spean*, under fine trees which abound in the valleys, and in view of scattered birches which creep up the hills. We changed horses after passing *High Bridge* and an old neglected-looking churchyard, from which a funeral party was evidently returning, as we met "a good few" (i.e. a good many) farmers in black, and saw the gate open and a spade near it. The road ascends to *High Bridge*, commanding a very fine view over the *Ben Nevis* range and the hills above *Loch Lochy*, of which, as we approached the *Caledonian Canal* and came to a lock, we caught a glimpse. We changed horses at *Gairlochy* before crossing the canal, by the side of which flows the *Lochy*. The road ascends and goes along the western side high above the canal and river, commanding a splendid view of *Ben Nevis* and the surrounding range of hills, "*the Grampians.*" The road is, as all the roads here are, very good and most picturesque, winding through trees, with small and wretched but picturesque cottages with little bits of fields dotted here and there and with Highland cattle grazing about. It was again rainy and showery after we came to *Gairlochy*. We came down again to *Banavie*, the hotel at which seems excellent, and were at home by a quarter-past six. Beatrice and Jane took some tea in the dining-room, and then took a short walk in the grounds, coming in at seven. Wrote. It was still raining, but not blowing. Played after dinner on the piano with Beatrice, and then went upstairs, and Jane Churchill read.

Friday, September 12.

A most beautiful bright sunshiny day. After breakfast Mr. Newton, the artist, brought some lovely sketches. Sketched and painted, for the views are quite lovely, from my room. At eleven drove in the waggonette with Beatrice and Jane Churchill, General Ponsonby being on the box with Brown, to and through *Fort William*, which is three miles and a half from *Inverlochy*, passing the celebrated *Ben Nevis Distillery*,* which is two miles from here, and through a triumphal arch, just beyond the bridge over the *Nevis Burn*, by an old, very neglected graveyard, to the right, in which is an obelisk to McLachlan, a poet, and past the *Belford Hospital*, a neat building, built by a Mr. and Mrs. Belford; then a little farther on, entered the town, where there was a triumphal arch, the fort, now private property, belonging to Campbell of *Monzie*. Here Glencoe came to take the oath to King William III.*

The town of *Fort William* is small, and, excepting where the good shops are, very dirty, with a very poor population, but all very friendly and enthusiastic. There are four churches (Established, Free Church, Episcopalian, and Roman Catholic). We drove on along *Loch Eil* (called *Loch Linnhe* below *Corran* ferry) a mile, and turned at *Achintee*, and down to old *Inverlochy Castle*,* which is nearer to *Fort William* than the new castle. We got out to look at the ruin, but it is uninteresting, as there is so little of it and literally nothing to see. About a quarter of a mile from the house we got out and walked; home by half-past twelve.

Friday, September 12.

At a quarter-past three, the day being most splendid, started with Beatrice and Jane Churchill, the two gentlemen following in the waggonette (with Charlie Thomson on the box), and drove by *Banavie*, the same road we came home yesterday, as far as where we crossed the canal at *Gairlochy*—only, instead of going down to it, we kept above, and went to the left: it is a beautiful road, coming in sight of *Loch Lochy*, which, with its wooded banks and blue hills, looked lovely. Leaving the main road, we turned into a beautiful drive along the river *Arkaig*, in Lochiel's property, reminding one very much of the *Trossachs*.

As you approach *Achnacarry*, which lies rather low, but is surrounded by very fine trees, the luxuriance of the tangled woods, surmounted by rugged hills, becomes finer and finer till you come to *Loch Arkaig*, a little over half a mile from the house. This is a very lovely loch, reminding one of *Loch Katrine*, especially where there is a little pier, from which we embarked on board a very small but nice screw steamer which belongs to Cameron of *Lochiel*.

He received us (wearing his kilt and plaid) just above the pier, and we all went on board the little steamer. The afternoon was beautiful, and lit up the fine scenery to the greatest advantage. We went about halfway up the *Loch* (which is fourteen miles long), as we had not time to go farther, to the disappointment of Lochiel, who said it grew wilder and wilder higher up. To the left (as we went up) is the deer forest; to the right he has sheep.

Both sides are beautifully wooded all along the lower part of the fine hills which rise on either side, and the trees are all oaks, which Cameron of *Lochiel* said were the "weed of the country," and all natural—none were planted. A good many grow up all the hollows and fissures of the hills and rocks. Right ahead, where we turned, was seen a fine conical-shaped hill called Scour-na-nat, and to the left *Glenmally*, to the north *Muir Logan*, and *Giusach* and *Gerarnan* on either side. Before we came to the turning we three had our tea, which was very refreshing.

I tried to sketch a little, but the sun shone so strongly that I could not do much.

Mr. Cameron, who was with Lord Elgin in *China*, came and explained everything, and talked very pleasantly. His father had to let this beautiful place, and Lord Malmesbury had it for fifteen years. The Cannings used to go there, and I often heard Lady Canning speak of its beauties, and saw many pretty sketches which she made there. Thirteen years ago his father died, and he has lived there ever since. Alfred was there in 1863.

It was, as General Ponsonby observed afterwards, a striking scene. "There was Lochiel," as he said, "whose great-grand-uncle had been the real moving cause of the rising of 1745—for without him Prince Charles would not have made the attempt—showing your Majesty (whose great-great-grandfather he had striven to dethrone) the scenes made historical by Prince Charlie's wanderings. It was a scene one could not look on unmoved."

Yes; and *I* feel a sort of reverence in going over these scenes in this most beautiful country, which I am proud to call my own, where there was such devoted loyalty to the family of my ancestors—for Stuart blood is in my veins, and I am *now* their representative, and the people are as devoted and loyal to me as they were to that unhappy race.*

We landed at the little pier, but walked over the small bridges (the carriages following)—on which a piper was playing—a few hundred yards to a gate (on the side opposite to that by which we came), where we got into the carriages again. We drove through a beautiful road called the *Dark Mile*—dark from the number of very fine trees which overhang it, while on the left it is overshadowed by beetling rocks with a rich tangled undergrowth of bracken and heather, etc. The heather grows very richly and fully in these parts, and in thick tufts. We saw here the cave in which Prince Charles Edward was hid for a week. We came out of this road at the end of *Loch Lochy*, which looked lovely in the setting sun, and drove along the water's edge till nearly where we joined the road by which we had come. It is all Lochiel's for a long way—a splendid possession.

And now came the finest scene of all—*Ben Nevis* and its surrounding high hills, and the others in the direction of *Loch Laggan*, all pink and glowing in that lovely after-glow (*Alpenglühen*), which you see in the *Alps*. It was glorious. It grew fainter and fainter till the hills became blue and then grey, and at last it became almost quite dark before we reached *Banavie*, and we only got home at a quarter-past eight. As we drove out I sketched *Ben Nevis* from the carriage.

Quantities of letters. The post comes in after eight and goes out at ten, which is very inconvenient.

Our usual little dinner only, about nine.

Saturday, September 13.

Another splendid morning, of which we were very glad, as we meant to go to *Glencoe*, which was the principal object of our coming here. Our nice little breakfast as usual. Sketching.

At eleven we started, just as yesterday, Francie Clark[+] and Cannon going on the box of the second carriage. We drove through *Fort William*, on as we did yesterday morning by *Achintee*, and down the eastern side of *Loch Eil*, which was beautifully lit, the distant hills intensely blue. The cottages along the roadside here and there hardly deserve the name, and are indeed mere hovels—so low, so small, so dark with thatch, and overgrown with moss and heather, that if you did not see smoke issuing from them, and some very ragged dirty old people, and very scantily clothed, dishevelled children, you could not believe they were meant for human habitations. They are very picturesque and embedded in trees, with the heathery and grassy hills rising above them, and reminded me of *Switzerland*. There were poor little fields, fuller of weeds than of corn, much laid by the wet, and frequently a "calvie" or "coo" of the true shaggy Highland character* was actually feeding in them.

The road, which runs close above the loch, commands an excellent view of the fine noble hills on the opposite side of the loch. At *Corran Ferry*[†] (eleven miles) are seen across the loch *Conaglen*, and *Ardgour*, Lord Morton's, at the entrance of a very fine glen. He has bought a large property in these parts, which formerly belonged to the Macleans. South of *Corran Ferry* the loch is called *Loch Linnhe*, and the road turns inland westwards, soon after passing up along the shore of *Loch Leven*, which is, in fact, also an arm of the sea. After three miles we passed a few cottages called *Onich*, the high hills of *Glencoe* beginning already to show. All was so bright and green, with so much wood, and the loch so calm, that one was in perpetual admiration of the scenery as one went along. Four miles more from *Corran Ferry* brought us to *Ballachulish* at a little before one o'clock. The situation of the hotel—the large one—on the opposite side, at the foot of the hills close to the ferry, is extremely pretty. There was a smaller and less handsome inn on the north side, by which we had come. Here we got out, after all our things—cloaks, bags, luncheon baskets, etc.—had been removed from the carriage, which we had to leave, and walked down to the boat. The small number of people collected there were very quiet and well behaved. Beatrice and Jane

---

[+] My Highland servant since 1870, and cousin to Brown.
[†] Here Alfred got his very favourite Skye terrier Corran.

Churchill and I, with General Ponsonby and Brown, got into the boat, and two Highlanders in kilts rowed us across to the sound of pipes. On the opposite side there were more people, but all kept at a very respectful distance and were very loyal. A lady (a widow), Lady Beresford, who owns the slate quarries,* and her daughter, in deep mourning, were at the landing-place, and one of them presented me with a bouquet. We got at once into two carriages (hired, but very fair ones), Beatrice, Jane, and I in a sort of low barouche, Brown on the box. We had a pair of horses, which went very well. The two gentlemen occupied the second carriage. The drive from *Ballachulish*, looking both ways, is beautiful, and very Alpine. I remember Louise, and also Alice, making some sketches from here when they went on a tour in 1865.

We went on, winding under the high green hills, and entered the village of *Ballachulish*, where the slate quarries are, and which is inhabited by miners. It was very clean and tidy—a long, continuous, straggling, winding street, where the poor people, who all looked very clean, had decorated every house with flowers and bunches or wreaths of heather and red cloth. Emerging from the village we entered the *Pass of Glencoe*, which at the opening is beautifully green, with trees and cottages dotted about along the verdant valley. There is a farm belonging to a Mrs. MacDonald, a descendant of one of the unfortunate massacred MacDonalds. The *Cona* flows along the bottom of the valley, with green "haughs," where a few cattle are to be seen, and sheep, which graze up some of the wildest parts of this glorious glen. A sharp turn in the rough, very winding, and in some parts precipitous road, brings you to the finest, wildest, and grandest part of the pass. Stern, rugged, precipitous mountains with beautiful peaks and rocks piled high one above the other, two and three thousand feet high, tower and rise up to the heavens on either side, without any signs of habitation, except where, halfway up the pass, there are some trees, and near them heaps of stones on either side of the road, remains of what once were homes, which tell the bloody, fearful tale of woe. The place itself is one which adds to the horror of the thought that such a thing could have been conceived and committed on innocent sleeping people. How and whither could they fly? Let me hope that William III. knew nothing of it.*

To the right, not far on, is seen what is called *Ossian's Cave*; but it must be more than a thousand feet above the glen, and one cannot imagine how any one could live there, as they pretend that Ossian did.* The violence of the torrents of snow and rain, which come pouring down, has brought quantities of stone with them, which in many parts cover the road and make it very rough. It reminds me very much of the

Devil's Bridge, *St. Gothard*, and the *Göschenen Pass*, only that is higher but not so wild. When we came to the top, which is about ten miles from *Ballachulish*, we stopped and got out, and we three sat down under a low wall, just below the road, where we had a splendid view of those peculiarly fine wild-looking peaks, which I sketched.

Their Gaelic names are *Na tri Peathraichean* (*the Three Sisters*), but in English they are often called "*Faith*, *Hope*, and *Charity*."

We sat down on the grass (we three) on our plaids, and had our luncheon, served by Brown and Francie, and then I sketched. The day was most beautiful and calm. Here, however—here, in this complete solitude, we were spied upon by impudently inquisitive reporters, who followed us everywhere; but one in particular (who writes for some of the Scotch papers)* lay down and watched with a telescope and dodged me and Beatrice and Jane Churchill, who were walking about, and was most impertinent when Brown went to tell him to move, which Jane herself had thought of doing. However, he did go away at last, and Brown came back saying he thought there would have been a fight; for when Brown said quite civilly that the Queen wished him to move away, he said he had quite as good a right to remain there as the Queen. To this Brown answered very strongly, upon which the impertinent individual asked, "Did he know who he was?" and Brown answered he did, and that "the highest gentlemen in England would not dare do what he did, much less a reporter"—and he must move on, or he would give him something more. And the man said, "Would he dare say that before those other men (all reporters) who were coming up?" And Brown answered "Yes," he would before "anybody who did not behave as he ought." More strong words were used; but the others came up and advised the man to come away quietly, which he finally did. Such conduct ought to be known. We were there nearly an hour, and then began walking down a portion of the steep part.

The parish clergyman, Mr. Stewart, who had followed us up, and who had met us when we arrived at *Ballachulish*, explained the names of the hills, and showed the exact place of the dreadful massacre. He also said that there were many Episcopalians there from the old Jacobite feeling, and also Roman Catholics.*

There was seldom frost in the glen, he said, but there was a good deal of snow.

A short distance from where Ossian's cave is shown there is a very small lake called *Loch Treachtan*, through which the *Cona* flows; and at the end of this was a cottage with some cattle and small pieces of cultivated land. We drove down on our return at a great pace. As we came through *Ballachulish* the post-boy suddenly stopped, and a very respectable, stout-looking old Highlander stepped up to the carriage with a small silver quaich, out of which he said Prince Charles had drunk, and also my dearest Albert in 1847, and begged that I would do the same. A table, covered with a cloth and with a bottle on it, was on the other side of the road. I felt I could hardly refuse, and therefore tasted some whisky out of it, which delighted the people who were standing around. His name, we have since heard, is W. A. Cameron.

We drove to the same small pier where we had disembarked, and were rowed over again by two Highlanders in kilts. The evening was so beautiful and calm that the whole landscape was reflected in the lake. There is a high, conical-shaped hill, the commencement of the *Pass of Glencoe*, which is seen best from here; and the range of hills above *Ardgour* and *Corran Ferry* opposite was of the most lovely blue. The whole scene was most beautiful. Three pipers played while we rowed across, and the good people, who were most loyal and friendly, cheered loudly. We re-entered our carriages, and drove off at a quick pace. When we were on the shores of *Loch Eil* again, we stopped (but did not get out) to take tea, having boiled the kettle. The setting sun cast a most glorious light, as yesterday, on *Ben Nevis* and the surrounding hills, which were quite pink, and gave a perfectly crimson hue to the heather on the moor below. The sky was pink and lilac and pale green, and became richer and richer, while the hills in the other direction, over *Fort William*, were of a deep blue. It was wonderfully beautiful, and I was still able to make, or at least begin, a sketch of the effect of it, after we came home at a quarter to seven, from Beatrice's window.

Resting and writing. Leopold has had far less fine weather for his excursion than we have had.

Sunday, September 14.

It was dull, and there had been some rain, but it cleared, and the day was fine, though not bright.

At twenty minutes past eleven walked out with Beatrice. We walked first to look at the kitchen garden, which is large, and has some very nice hot-houses with good grapes. From here we went out by the lodge, meeting not a soul, and past the farm, going down a road on the left to a small burn, over which there is a foot-bridge. Finding, however, that it only led to a keeper's house, Brown advised us to return, which we accordingly did, coming by the back and the stables, and in at ten minutes to one o'clock. Rested, wrote, and then read prayers with Beatrice, and part of Mr. Campbell's[+] sermon, which Beatrice was so pleased with that she copied it entirely. Luncheon as usual. Painted and finished the view looking towards *Fort William*.

At five drove out with Beatrice and Jane Churchill in the waggonette. We drove past the distillery; and then just beyond the bridge, which must be very little over two miles from *Inverlochy*, we turned off the main road. We drove up for four miles along the *Nevis*, a fine rapid burn rolling over large stones and almost forming cascades in one or two places, under fine trees with very steep green hills rising on either side, and close under and along the base of *Ben Nevis*, which rose like a giant above us. It was splendid! Straight before us the glen seemed to close; halfway up we came to a large farm, the drive to which is under an avenue of ash trees. But there is no other habitation beyond this of any kind; and soon after the trees become fewer and fewer, though still a good many grow at the burnside and up the gullies of the hills. Sheep were grazing at a great height. The road became so rough and bad that we got out and walked almost a mile, but could go no farther. We were delighted with the solemn solitude and grandeur of *Glen Nevis*; it is almost finer than *Glencoe*. There was no one when we first entered the glen, but as we walked back we met several people coming out to look. After getting into the carriage again, I stopped a little to take a rough sketch.

The farm belongs to Mrs. Campbell of *Monzie*, only daughter of the late Sir Duncan Cameron of *Fassifern*, who owns a good deal of *Ben Nevis*. Every hill has a name, but I cannot remember them, though I have them written down by the keeper at *Inverlochy*. As it was still a little too early to go home, we drove as far as the Fort and turned back, coming in at a quarter past seven. Writing. The post comes in at a most inconvenient hour, a little past eight.

Dinner as usual. My favourite collie Noble is always downstairs when we take our meals, and was so good, Brown making him lie on a chair or couch, and he never attempted to come down without permission, and even held a piece of cake in his mouth without eating it, till told he might. He is the most "biddable" dog I ever saw, and so affectionate and kind; if he thinks you are not pleased with him, he puts out his paws, and begs in such an affectionate way.

Jane Churchill read.

[+] The newly appointed minister at Crathie.

Monday, September 15.

The mist hung about the hills, but the sun struggled through. It was very mild and became beautiful. We decided to go up *Glenfinnan* and to lunch out. Painted and finished two other sketches looking up *Loch Eil* and towards *Banavie*, and then wrote, after which at a quarter to twelve took a short turn in the grounds with Beatrice.

At twenty minutes to one started with Beatrice and Jane Churchill in the sociable (Brown going each day of course with us on the box), the two gentlemen following (with Francie Clark and Charlie Thomson), and drove past *Banavie* through *Corpach* and up *Loch Eil*. When we had come to the head of the loch, the road turned towards the right, winding along through verdant valleys, with that noble range of *Moidart* before you, rather to the left. In one valley, which became very narrow after passing a large meadow in which they were making hay, we turned into a narrow sort of defile, with the stream of the *Finnan* flowing on as slowly as an English river, with trees and fir trees on the rocks, and unlike anything I had seen in *Scotland*, and then you come at once on *Loch Shiel* (a freshwater loch), with fine very high rugged hills on either side. It runs down twenty miles.

At the head of the loch stands a very ugly monument to Prince Charles Edward,* looking like a sort of lighthouse surmounted by his statue, and surrounded by a wall. Here it was that he landed when he was brought by Macdonald of *Borradale*—whose descendant, now Macdonald of *Glenaladale*, has a house here (the only habitation to be seen)—to wait for the gathering of the clans. When Prince Charlie arrived at the spot where the monument stands, which is close to the loch and opposite to *Glenfinnan* (the road we came going past it and on up a hill to *Arisaig*, twenty-five miles farther on), he found only a dozen peasants, and thought he had been betrayed, and he sat down with his head in his hands. Suddenly the sound of the pipes aroused him, and he saw the clans coming down *Glenfinnan*. Soon after the Macdonalds appeared, and in the midst of a cheering host the Marquis of Tullibardine (Duke of Athole but for his attainder) unfurled the banner of King James. This was in August 1745. In 1746 poor Prince Charles was a fugitive hiding in the mountains on the sides of *Loch Arkaig* and *Loch Shiel*. As we suddenly came upon *Loch Shiel* from the narrow glen, lit up by bright sunshine, with the fine long loch and the rugged mountains, which are about three thousand feet high, rising all around, no habitation or building to be seen except the house of *Glenaladale*, which used to be an inn, and a large picturesque Catholic church, reminding one, from its elevated position to the right and above the house, of churches and convents abroad, I thought I never saw a lovelier or more romantic spot, or one which told its history so well. What a scene it must have been in 1745! And here was *I*, the descendant of the Stuarts and of the very king whom Prince Charles sought to overthrow, sitting and walking about quite privately and peaceably.

We got out and scrambled up a high hillock off the road, where I lunched with Beatrice and Jane Churchill and then sketched, but did not attempt to colour. We walked about a little, and then came down to the road to speak to Mr. Macdonald of *Glenaladale*, whom General Ponsonby had been to speak to, and who had never seen me. He is a stout, robust-looking Highlander of about thirty and a widower. He is a Catholic, as are all the people in this district. The priest is his uncle, and lives with him. He showed me some curious relics of Charles Edward. An old-fashioned, strange silver snuff "mull" which had been given by him to Macdonald's ancestor, with the dates 1745 and 1746 engraved on it, for at *Borradale* Prince Charlie slept for the last time in *Scotland*; a watch which had belonged to him, and a ring into which some of his fair hair had been put, were also shown.

This is the district called *Moidart*, and from the highest hills the *Isle of Skye* is seen distinctly. Lord Morton's property comes up close to *Loch Shiel*, and to the right are *Lochiel*, etc., and Macdonald of *Glenaladale*'s in front, at the head of the loch. The family used to live at *Borradale* near *Arisaig*, but acquired *Glenaladale* from the former Macdonalds of *Glenaladale* who emigrated to *Prince Edward's Island* after the Forty-five.*

Beatrice, Jane Churchill, and Brown went up with Mr. Macdonald to the top of the monument, but said the ascent was very awkward and difficult. General Ponsonby had been into the church, and said it was very expensively and handsomely decorated, but we have since heard there are only about fifty people in the neighbourhood. We left this beautiful spot about half-past four, having spent two hours there. The evening was not so bright as on Friday and Saturday, and there was no after-glow on the hills, *Ben Nevis* having its top covered with mist, as it often has. The horses were tired, and went rather slowly. I observed a flower here, which I have not seen with us at *Balmoral*, viz., instead of the large white daisies[+]—"Marguerites," as the French call them, and of

---

[+] *Chrysanthemum Leucanthemum*, White ox-eye daisy.

which such numbers are seen in the fields in England—there is a large yellow one,[+] just the same in form, only the petals are bright yellow.

The heather, as I before observed, is of a very full and rich kind, and, as we drove along, we saw it on the old walls, growing in the loveliest tufts. We met those dreadful reporters, including the man who behaved so ill on Saturday, as we were coming back. We got home at twenty minutes past six. Had some tea. Wrote and put everything in order. All had been settled about money to be given,* etc. Our last nice little dinner, which I regretted. Came up directly after and wrote.

Tuesday, September 16.

Had to get up by seven, and Beatrice and I breakfasted at a quarter to eight. The morning was fine.

The real name of the place used to be *Torlundy*, which is the name of the "lochie," or "tarn," below the house, in the middle of which there is a little island on which there are ducks. The property, which is very large, sixty-four miles in extent, was purchased from the late Duke of Gordon by the late Lord Abinger, who began a house, but it was burnt down; the present Lord built this one, in fact, only ten years ago, and added to it since. He has called it *Inverlochy Castle*, after the old fortress, which is supposed to have belonged to the Pictish kings, but the present ruin is thought to date from the time of Edward I. The Marquis of Montrose defeated the Marquis of Argyle there in 1645, an incident described in Sir Walter Scott's "Legend of Montrose."*

At a quarter-past eight we left *Inverlochy Castle*, where we had spent very pleasant days. The gentlemen had gone on before.

We drove to *Banavie*, where a good many people were assembled, and stepped on board the steamer which was on the *Caledonian Canal*. Here were Lord and Lady Abinger, whom I thanked very much for their kindness. I left an illustrated copy of my book* and prints of Albert's and my portraits at *Inverlochy* for Lord Abinger. She is an American lady from the *Southern States*, a Miss Macgruder, and they have five children, of whom one only is a boy. They left the steamer, and we began moving. The steamer is called the "Gondolier." It is built on the same principle as the one we had on *Loch Lomond*, with a fine large cabin with many windows, almost a deck cabin (though it is down one flight of steps), which extends through the ship with seats below, open at the sides far forward. In this large cabin sixty-two people can dine. We remained

---

[+] *Chrysanthemum segetum*, Yellow ox-eye or corn marigold.

chiefly on deck. We steamed gently along under the road by which we had driven from *Gairlochy* and *Achnacarry*, Lochiel's to the left or west, and Lord Abinger's to the right. *Ben Nevis*, unfortunately, was hid in the mist, and the top invisible, which we hear is very generally the case.

We came to one lock, and then shortly afterwards to *Gairlochy*, after which you enter *Loch Lochy*. The *Caledonian Canal* is a very wonderful piece of engineering, but travelling by it is very tedious. At each lock people crowded up close to the side of the steamer. As the river rises from *Banavie* to *Loch Oich* (which succeeds *Loch Lochy*), the canal has to raise the vessels up to that point, and again to lower them from *Loch Oich* to *Inverness*. The vessel, on entering the lock from the higher level, is enclosed by the shutting of the gates. The sluices of the lower gates are raised by small windlasses (it was amusing to see the people, including the crew of the steamer, who went on shore to expedite the operation, which is not generally done, run round and round to move these windlasses), and holes are thus opened at the bottom of the lower gates, through which the water flows till the water in the lock sinks to the lowest level. The lower gates are then opened, as the water is on the lowest level, while the upper gates keep back the water above. The same process raises the ships in the lock which ascend. About five or six feet can be raised or depressed in this manner at each lock. (I have copied this from an account General Ponsonby wrote for me.)

As we entered *Loch Lochy*, which looked beautiful, we saw where *Loch Arkaig* lay, though it was hid from us by high ground. The hills which rise from *Loch Lochy* are excellent pasture for sheep, but the lower parts are much wooded. After eight miles' sail on *Loch Lochy* we came to *Loch Oich*, which is entered by another lock at *Laggan*. Here Mr. and Mrs. Ellice (who is a first cousin of the Greys) were waiting, and came on board. They had wished me to get out and drive round their fine place, *Invergarry*, to rejoin the steamer at the next lock, but I declined, preferring to remain quietly on board, though the process of going through the locks is slow and necessarily tedious. It is nervous work to steer, for there is hardly a foot to spare on either side. Mrs. Ellice went on shore again, having given us some fine grapes, but Mr. Ellice remained on board till the next lock, *Cullochy*. A road much shaded runs along the side of the loch, and here we passed the small monument by its side, put over the well into which a number of heads of some of the MacDonalds, who had murdered two of their kinsmen of *Keppoch*, were thrown after they had been killed in revenge for this act, by order of MacDonald of the Isles.* It was erected in 1812. We next came to the old ruined castle of *Invergarry*, embosomed in trees, close to which, but not in sight, is

Mr. Ellice's new house. He has an immense deal of property here on both sides. The hills rise high, and one conically shaped one called *Ben Tigh* towers above the rest. At *Cullochy* Mr. Ellice left the steamer. Mr. Brewster, formerly Lord Chancellor of *Ireland* and nearly eighty years old, was standing on the shore here. Francie and one of the policemen got out with good Noble, and walked to meet us again at *Fort Augustus*. While we were stopping to go through one of the locks, a poor woman came and brought us a jug of milk and oat-cake, which with their usual hospitality the country people constantly offer.

After this, and at about ten minutes past twelve, Beatrice, Jane Churchill, and I went below and had some hot luncheon. The people from the locks looked down upon us, but it was unavoidable. We had now reached *Fort Augustus*, where there was again some delay and a great many people, and where there was a triumphal arch. Here on this very day thirty-six years ago* my beloved Albert passed, and he saw poor Macdonald the Jäger here, and took a liking to him from his appearance, and, being in want of a Jäger, inquired after him and engaged him. He was keeper to Lord Digby and Colonel Porter then, and brought some game for dearest Albert from them, and Albert was greatly struck by his good looks. He was very handsome, especially in the kilt, which he habitually wore.

There had been a heavy shower, but it was over when we came up on deck again. We entered *Loch Ness* here. It is twenty-four miles long, and broad, the banks wooded, with many pretty places on them. We passed *Invermorriston* in *Glen Morriston*, the seat of Sir G. Brooke Middleton, formerly Grant property. (So many of the finest, largest estates in the *Highands* have passed into English hands, chiefly by purchase, but also often by inheritance.)* *Foyers*, the celebrated falls, which are much visited, could just be seen, but not the falls themselves. Everywhere, where there were a few houses or any place of note, people were assembled and cheered.

Next, to the left comes the very fine old ruin of *Castle Urquhart*, close upon the *Lochan Rocks*, where there were again a great many people. The Castle has stood several sieges, and one in particular in the fourteenth century in the reign of Edward I. It belongs to Lord Seafield (head of the Grants), who has a very large property here, and whose own shooting-place, *Balmacaan*, is up in the glen just beyond. The fine mountain of *Mealfourvonie* rises above it. It is two thousand seven hundred feet high, but the peak alone is seen from here. I tried to sketch a little, but in vain, the wind in my face was so troublesome.

At about twenty minutes to four (or half-past three) we passed *Dochfour House*, Mr. Baillie's, which I think stands rather low, and in which Albert passed this night twenty-six years ago. A few minutes more brought us to

Dochgarroch, quite a quiet place, but where a good many people had assembled. We waited to see every one and all our luggage landed and packed in and off before we stepped on shore. It was an amusing sight. There must have been two or three carriages besides ours. The last to drive off was the one in which Morgan, Maxted, and Lizzie Stewart[+] got, with Francie Clark and Noble on the box. Mr. Baillie and Lady Georgiana, whom I had not seen for long, were at the end of the landing platform, as well as Mr. Evan Baillie and Mrs. Colville, their son and daughter. Two little girls put down bunches of flax for me to walk upon, which it seems is an old Highland custom. There is a small village where we landed. Lady Georgiana Baillie is quite an old lady, aunt of the Duke of Manchester, and grand-daughter of the celebrated Duchess of Gordon.

Beatrice, Jane, and I got into a hired (not very beautiful) open landau (on the rumble of which Brown sat, as in crowds it is much safer to have a person close behind you) with a pair of post-horses and a postilion. In the second carriage went General Ponsonby, Emilie Dittweiler (sitting next to him), Dr. Fox, and Annie, every available place being necessary. We were escorted by the 7th Dragoon Guards, which was thought better on account of the great crowds in *Inverness*, where no Sovereign had been seen since my poor ancestress Queen Mary.

The mixture of half state and humble travelling (we being in our common travelling dresses) was rather amusing.

The evening was beautiful, and *Inverness* looked extremely well on the blue *Moray Frith*. We passed a magnificent building, which is the county Lunatic Asylum. We had to drive six miles to the town, through a small portion of which only we passed, and had to drive quickly, as it was late. The streets were full of decorations and arches, and lined with volunteers. Great order prevailed, and the people were most enthusiastic. The fine-looking old Provost was there, and the Master of Lovat, who walked up along the station with us. A great squeeze, which Brown, having a great heap of cloaks etc. to carry, had some difficulty in getting through. But every one, including the dog, got safe in, and we travelled by train as before. We went the same way as last year, but never stopped till we got to *Keith*, where last time our door got wrong. After this, about six, we had some warm tea and cold meat, which was very refreshing. A fine evening.

We reached *Ballater* at five minutes to nine, and started at once in the open landau and four, preceded by the outrider with the lamp. There were a few drops of rain, but very slight. At twenty minutes to ten we reached *Balmoral* safely, very thankful that all had gone off so well.

[+] My second wardrobe maid since 1879, a native of *Balmoral*.

Home-coming of their Royal Highnesses the Duke and Duchess of Edinburgh, August 1874.

Saturday, August 29, 1874.

At a quarter to two started in the landau and four with Beatrice and Lady Abercromby, Brown in full dress on the rumble. It was raining, so we kept the carriage shut, but there were decided symptoms of clearing, and by the time we reached *Ballater* the sun began to shine, and the rain ceased as I got out.

The train with Alfred and Marie had already arrived, and Marie got out as I advanced. Alfred was already out of the carriage. I kissed them, and then, with Marie, Alfred, and Beatrice, got in again, the carriage being open, and it was very fine. Marie wore a brown travelling dress with a hat. When we reached the bridge we went slowly. The *Ballater* company of volunteers, to the number of thirty (kilted in Farquharson tartan), were next it, and from here to the arch, and beyond it, stood all our people in full dress with their families, and all the tenants of the three estates with theirs, also the ladies and gentlemen. The pipers walked in front playing, and our keepers and others, who wore full dress,* on either side (Brown remaining in his place on the carriage), followed by all the other people.

In this way we proceeded through the arch up to *Balmoral*, just as when Helena arrived, only then there were fewer people. Leopold was in his carriage. We got out at the door of the Castle, and then Dr. Robertson proposed the health of Alfred and Marie, which was drunk by all with cheers. Then two reels were danced, after which we took Marie and Alfred to their rooms downstairs, and sat with them while they had tea.

Departure of the Prince of Wales from Abergeldie before leaving for India.*

Balmoral,
Friday, September 17, 1875.

Coming home from our drive at twenty minutes past seven, we had passed Bertie's carriage in the *Balloch Buie,* but we heard no sound of a carriage when we went downstairs for dinner a little before nine, and Alix [Princess of Wales] had also not arrived. Their people having come, we consulted with Charlotte Knollys[†] what to do, and sent to beg Alix to come and order Bertie's things to be brought to the Castle. At length, at half-past nine, Bertie arrived, very hot, having lost his way and been separated from the others. He had got four stags (and had been lucky altogether), and he asked us to go to dinner. We accordingly sat down—Lenchen, Beatrice, Jane Churchill, and Lord Carnarvon. Christian had gone on to look after Bertie, but he soon returned. Only at ten did Alix arrive, and at ten minutes past ten, Bertie; and we did not get up from dinner till half-past ten. All the ladies and gentlemen came into the drawing-room after dinner, and *all* felt that this terrible parting was hanging over us. At eleven I took Bertie and Alix upstairs, and talked over various details of this anxious journey to *India.* Then it came to the saying good-night, and Bertie sent for Löhlein and Brown to come and take leave of him. I saw how that began to try him, and it grieved them. He shook hands with both, and I felt nearly upset myself when Brown shook him by the hand, and said: "God bless your Royal Highness, and bring you safe back!" He also wished my maids good-bye, who were standing there. Poor dear Alix seemed to feel it much, and so did I, as I embraced them both several times, and said I would go to see them off next morning.

Saturday, September 18.

A dull and rather raw morning. Breakfasted alone (as Beatrice was not quite well, with a sort of chill) at nine in the cottage.

At half-past nine I drove off with Lenchen to *Abergeldie.* There we found all in considerable confusion. Bertie was out in the garden, where

---

[†] Lady to the Princess of Wales, eldest daughter of General Sir William Knollys, K.C.B., for many years at the head of the Prince of Wales's household.

we waited a little while, and then I went up, and found poor Alix putting up her things in her bedroom—the little girls there—the maids not yet off. At length, at a quarter-past ten, they left. Dear Bertie wished all good-bye. Our ladies and gentlemen and all the people were assembled outside. Poor dear Beatrice was the only one absent. Christian had gone on before. Bertie shook hands with all; I wished him every possible success, and that God would bless and protect him during this long and anxious journey to the East. It was very sad to see him drive off with Alix and the boys (the little girls followed in another carriage), not knowing what might not happen, or if he would ever return. May God bless him!

Visit to Inveraray, September 1875.

Tuesday, September 21, 1875.

We had a family dinner at twenty minutes to nine. At a quarter past ten left *Balmoral* with Beatrice and Jane Churchill, Brown on the rumble. We reached *Ballater* by eleven, when we took the railroad. General Ponsonby and Sir W. Jenner met us there. Emilie, Annie, Morgan (for Beatrice), Francie Clark, and the footmen, Cannon, Charlie Thomson, and Heir, went in attendance, as well as Baldry and three men of the police. The horses (six) with Bourner, Hutchinson, and Goddard with the luggage, had gone on in advance. We started immediately, and very soon after lay down. We went steadily and slowly, but I did not sleep very well.

Inveraray,
Wednesday, September 22.

At eight we reached *Tyndrum*, a wild, picturesque, and desolate place in a sort of wild glen with green hills rising around. Here we breakfasted in the train, Brown having had the coffee heated which we had brought made with us, and some things coming from the nice-looking hotel. The morning was beautiful, just a little mist on the highest hills, which cleared off. There are a few straggling houses and a nice hotel at this station, where we got out and where Lord and Lady Breadalbane met us, as this is his property. The day was beautiful.

We got into the sociable (that is, Beatrice, Jane Churchill, and I) with a pair of posthorses, Brown and Francie Clark on the box, the two gentlemen and four maids in a waggonette following, and further behind the unavoidable luggage with the footmen, etc. The road lay up a broad glen, with green hills on either side, on one of which are lead mines belonging to Lord Breadalbane.* It was very winding, very rough, and continually up and down, and we went very slowly. Looking back, behind *Tyndrum* was a fine range of hills which are in the forest of the *Black Mount*. Passed the entrance of a broad glen with many trees called *Glenorchy* (the second title of Breadalbane), and saw all along where the railway is being made. A small stream flows at the bottom. To the left we saw *Ben Luie*; then as we descended, the country became more and more beautiful, with trees and copsewood sprinkled about, till we came to *Dalmally*, lying embosomed in trees, with *Ben Cruachan* and its adjacent range rising close before us, with the bluest shadows and tints on all the heights, and the sky pure and bright with a hot sun, though a good deal of air. Looking back we still saw the other green hills from which we had come.

As it approaches *Dalmally* the road goes under trees till you reach the inn, which stands quite alone. The church is beautifully situated at the bottom of the glen, and is surrounded by trees. There was no large crowd here, and the people behaved very well. *Dalmally* is thirteen miles from *Tyndrum*. Four horses were put on here to drag us up the first hill, which was long and high, and brought us in view of *Loch Awe*, which looked beautiful. Here the leaders were taken off. *Loch Awe* extends back a good way, and we could just see *Kilchurn Castle*,* of historic celebrity, and the beautiful head of the loch with high hills on the right, and the islands of *Innishail* and *Ardchone*, besides many smaller ones. On the first-named of these is said to be buried an ancestor of the Argylls. The loch is thirty miles in length, and as it stretches out and widens the hills become much flatter. We drove quite round the head of *Loch Awe*, then passed *Cladich*, and here the ground became very broken, and high hills were seen in the background, towering above the nearer ones. Bracken with birch and oak, etc., grow profusely among the green hills and rocks, much as they do near *Inverlochy*, *Loch Eil*, etc. Here and there were small knots of people, but not many. About five or six miles before *Inveraray*, at a place called *Crais-na-Schleacaich*, at the foot of *Glen Aray*, where the Duke's property begins, four of our own horses were waiting, and here dear Louise and Lorne met us, looking pleased and well. Lorne rode, and dear Louise got into her pony-carriage and drove after us. We soon after came to an arch with a Gaelic inscription—"Ceud mille Failte do'n Bhan Rhighinn do Inerara" (A hundred thousand welcomes to the Queen to *Inveraray*). A very stout tenant's wife, Mrs. McArthur, presented me with a nosegay, which a child she held in her arms gave me.

On we went along *Glen Aray*, the road as we approached *Inveraray Castle** being bordered on either side by trees. When we reached the gate there were two halberdiers, whilst others were posted at intervals along the approach, dressed in Campbell tartan kilts with brown coats turned back with red, and bonnets with a black cock's tail and bog-myrtle (the Campbell badge). With them were also the pipers of the volunteers. In front of the house the volunteers in kilts and red jackets, and the artillery volunteers in blue and silver, of whom Lorne is the colonel, were drawn up, and a good many spectators were assembled. The Duke and Duchess of Argyll and their six girls were at the door: the outside steps are now under glass and made into a sort of conservatory.

The Duke and Duchess took us upstairs at once to our rooms, part of which are Louise's; very comfortable, not large but cheerful, and having a beautiful view of *Loch Fyne*. It was one when we arrived, and we lunched at two, only Louise, Beatrice, and Lorne, in a nice room (in fact the Duchess's drawing-room) with tapestry, at the foot of the stairs. Brown (who has attended me at all the meals since we came here) waited, helped by two or three of the Duke's people. After lunch we went into the large drawing-room, next door to where we had lunched in 1847, when Lorne was only two years old.* And now I return, alas! without my beloved Husband, to find Lorne my son-in-law!

In the drawing-room I found Lord and Lady Dufferin (who are staying here) as well as Sir John and Lady Emma McNeill. She is the Duke's only sister, and he a very fine old man (now eighty), who was formerly my minister in *Persia*. Went upstairs to rest and sketch the splendid *Ardkinglass Hills*, from the window of the little turret which forms my dressing-room. Then had tea, and at half-past five drove out with Louise and Beatrice by the lodge called *Creitabhille*, through part of the wood or forest where the beeches are splendid, as also the spruces, on past *Ballachanooran*, by the upper road, green hills, trees, oaks, ferns, and broken ground all along, like at *Loch Eil*, past *Achnagoul*, a little village lying close under the hill, to the *Douglas Water*, a small rapid stream. Here we turned back and went along this pretty little mountain stream, past some cottages and a small farm, and then came upon the shore of *Loch Fyne*, the drive along which is lovely. As we drove, the setting sun bathed the hills in crimson,—they had been golden just before,—the effect was exquisite. Looking up and down the shores, the view was lovely, and the reflections on the calm surface of the lake most beautiful.

We drove back through the small town of *Inveraray*, which is close to the gates of the Castle, and looks pretty from my window with its small pier, where we landed in 1847, and near to which there is a curious old Celtic cross. There are two inns, three churches, and a jail, for it is a county town. On coming home we walked a little in the garden close to the house, and came in at ten minutes past seven. Resting. Writing. Dinner at half-past eight in the room in which we lunched. The Duke and Duchess, Louise, Beatrice, and Lady Churchill dined with me. Then went for a short while into the drawing-room, where, besides the family, which included Lord Colin, were Dr. MacGregor, Mr. Donald Macleod, and Mr. Story (all clergymen staying in the house), and the following gentlemen: Lord Ardmillan (who was there for the assizes), Mr. Campbell, of *Stonefield* (Convener of the county of *Argyll*), Mr. and Mrs. Hector Macneal, of *Ugadale*, etc. Mr. Macneal showed me a brooch which had some resemblance to the *Brooch of Lorne*, and had been given by King Robert Bruce to one of his ancestors.

Thursday, September 23.

This sad anniversary, when my beloved sister was taken from me, whom I miss so continually, returns for the third time.

A fine morning. Breakfasted in my sitting-room at a quarter to ten with Louise and Beatrice. My sitting-room is generally Louise's bedroom, which had been specially arranged by her for me, and in the recess the Duchess had placed a picture of *Balmoral*, copied from A. Becker's picture. This opens into a small apartment, generally used as Lorne's dressing-room, in which my maid Annie sleeps and the two maids sit, next to which comes the bedroom, at the end of which is the nice cozy little turret-room with two windows, one of which looks on the loch with the very fine *Ardkinglass Range* in front, and the other on the front door, the bridge, and splendid trees. My dresser, Emilie Dittweiler, is next door to my bedroom, and Beatrice next to her in Louise's sitting-room.

At a little after eleven I walked out with Louise and Beatrice along the approach, and then turned up through the wood and up the lower walk of *Dunaquoich*, the hill opposite the house, which is wooded nearly to the top, on which is a tower, and walked along under magnificent trees, chiefly beeches and some very fine spruces, that reminded me of *Windsor Park* and *Reinhardtsbrunn*. We walked on some way, passed a well and a small cottage, where the poultry is kept, where there is a funny good-natured woman called Mrs. McNicholl, who kissed Louise's hand and knelt down when I came up, and said to Louise, when she heard I was coming, "How shall I speak to her?" We went into the little cottage, where another old woman of eighty lives. She looked so nice and tidy with a clean white mutch. We then walked down and came back along the river, which flows quite close to the house into the sea, and is full of fish. We were in at twenty minutes to one. Luncheon at two, just like yesterday. The day was dull, but quite fair and clear. Drawing and painting.

At a quarter-past four drove out with Louise, Beatrice, and the Duchess, in my waggonette, driven by Bourner. After going for some distance the same way as yesterday afternoon, we turned into a wooded drive, leading to the *Glen of Essachosan*, where there are the most beautiful spruces, and some silver firs which reminded me in height and size of those on the road to *Eberstein*, near *Baden*, and on by what they call the *Queen's drive*,* made for me in 1871, past *Lechkenvohr*, whence there is a fine view of the loch and surrounding hills, *Ben Een, Ben Buie,* etc. The road is very steep going down to the *Curling Pond* and *Black Bull Cottage*; then over *Carlonnan Bridge* down to some falls, and back along the approach to the *Dhu Loch*, under the avenue of fine old beeches, which, joining as they do, almost form an aisle. Eleven, alas! were blown down two years ago: they were planted by the Marquis of Argyll two hundred years ago. You come rapidly upon the *Dhu Loch*, a small but very pretty loch—a complete contrast to our *Dhu Loch*, for this is surrounded by green and very wooded hills, with the extremely pretty and picturesque *Glen Shira* in the background, which is richly wooded. We drove along the right bank of the *Shira River*, up as far as the small farm of *Drum Lee*, most prettily situated on the hillside some way up, passing one or two other farms—one especially, a very strange old building. We took our (made) tea, and Elizabeth (the Duchess) greatly admired the convenient arrangement (viz. the bag into which cups etc. are fitted), and then drove back the same way and along the shore road. Home at ten minutes to seven. A charming drive, but there was a very high and cold wind.

Louise, Beatrice, the Duchess of Argyll, Lord and Lady Dufferin, and Sir John and Lady Emma McNeill dined with me, as yesterday. Went again for a short while into the drawing-room, where the Duke presented some other people—the sheriff, Mr. F. A. Irvine of *Drum* (in *Aberdeenshire*), Mr. J. Malcolm of *Poltalloch* (a fine-looking man, whose son, a tall large man, dined here yesterday, and whose daughter has just married Mr. Gathorne Hardy's son), and Sir G. and Lady Home, who live just outside the town: he is sheriff-depute, and she a niece of Sir F. Grant. Went upstairs with Beatrice and Jane Churchill, Louise always remaining below.

Friday, September 24.

Raining and blowing. Breakfasted with my two dear daughters. The rain ceased, and at a little past twelve I walked with Louise and Beatrice up by the lodge at the stables, which are in the "*Cherry Park*," and looked at our horses and Louise's, and saw a little dog, the daughter of Louise's poor old Frisky; and then walked along at the back of the stables, where the trees are very fine—most splendid silver firs—and then back by the kitchen-garden and the straightest path, past a magnificent Scotch fir of great height and circumference. In at twenty minutes past one. It was dull and dark.

At a quarter-past five, after tea, started with Louise, Beatrice, and Jane Churchill in the rain, which turned to a heavy downpour. We drove up the way we had previously walked, by the private road, under trees the whole way, to *Lynn a Gluthen*, the highest fall of the *Aray*, which is very pretty. There we had to get out to walk over a wooden bridge, which Louise said they did not like to drive over, and came back by the high road. By this time the weather had quite cleared, and so we drove on past the inn of *Inveraray*, through a gate which is always left open, and up what is called the "*Town Avenue*," consisting entirely of very old beeches joining overhead and nearly a mile long, at the back of the town. We came back by the lime avenue in the deer park, and in by a gate close to the pleasure-ground at half-past six. The halberdiers, all tenants of the Duke, kept guard the whole day.

We dined at a quarter-past eight on account of the ball—only Louise, Beatrice, Jane Churchill, and I. Went into the drawing-room for a moment, where the Duke presented Sir Donald Campbell of *Dunstaffnage* and his wife, and J. A. Campbell of *New Inverawe* (*Loch Awe*). Sir Donald Campbell is deputy-keeper of *Dunstaffnage Castle*, and wears a key in consequence. He is between forty and fifty, and wore a kilt, as did also Malcolm of *Poltalloch* and the other gentlemen. At a quarter-past ten we drove across to the temporary pavilion, where the ball to the tenants was to take place.* Louise, Beatrice, and Jane Churchill went with me in the Duke's coach. The Duke, Lorne, and Colin received us, and the Duchess and all the girls and the other ladies were inside at the upper end on a raised platform, where we all sat. It is a very long and handsome room, I believe a hundred and thirty feet long, and was built at the time of Louise's marriage. It was handsomely decorated with flags, and there were present between seven and eight hundred people—tenants with their wives and families, and many people from the town; but it was not like the Highland balls I have been accustomed to, as there were many other dances besides reels. The band could not play reels (which were played by the piper), and yet came from *Glasgow*! The ball began, however, with a reel; then came a country dance, then another reel. Louise danced a reel with Brown, and Beatrice with one of the Duke's foresters; but the band could only play a country dance tune for it. Another reel with pipes, in which Jane Churchill danced with Brown, and Francie Clark with Annie (Mrs. Macdonald, my wardrobe maid), Louise and Beatrice dancing in another reel with one of the other people and Mr. John Campbell. Then came a "*schottische*," which seemed to be much liked there, and more reels, and lastly a "*tempête*," in which Louise and Beatrice danced. In the early part a Gaelic song was sung by some of the people, including Mr. John Campbell. I remember some which were sung by the boatmen on *Loch Tay* in 1842. After the "*tempête*" we came away at nearly half-past twelve.

Saturday, September 25.

A pouring morning. Breakfast as usual with my two dear children—dear Louise so kind and attentive, so anxious I and all my people should be comfortable, thinking of everything. It cleared, and at half-past eleven I walked out with Louise (Beatrice walked with Jane Churchill and the girls) to the kennel, along the *River Aray*, which had risen a great deal since Thursday, when it was as low as possible. We went to the kennel and saw the dogs and the eagle; from here we went to the kitchen-garden, which is large. There are very fine peaches and a wonderful old laurel and thuja, which have spread to an immense size. Home at twenty minutes to one. Luncheon as before.

Louise introduced me to a good old lady, a Miss McGibbon, who was too ill to come out and see me; she patted Louise on the shoulder and said, "We are all so fond of the Princess; she is a great pet." Louise said, "Lorne was her great pet;" and she answered, "Yes; he is, and so you are a double pet."[†]

At ten minutes past four drove out with Louise, Beatrice, and the Duke in the waggonette, and took a charming drive, the afternoon being very fine and bright. We went out the same way we had been on Wednesday, and once or twice besides, along the avenue called *Ballachanooran*, by the deer park (a great many gates having to be opened, as they must be kept locked to prevent the deer getting out), and struck into the *Lochgilphead Road* beyond *Cromalt*. We then passed, as on the first day, *Dalchenna* and *Killean*, *Achnagoul* and *Achindrain*. The last two places are old Highland villages, where a common old practice, now fallen into disuse, continues, of which the Duke gave me the following account:—*

In the *Highlands* of *Scotland* up to a comparatively recent date the old system of *village communities* prevailed as the common system of land tenure. Under this system the cultivators were collected into groups or villages, the cottages being all built close together on some one spot of the farm. The farm itself was divided into *pasture land* and *arable land*. The pasture land was held in *common* by all the families, and the arable land was divided *by lot* every year, so that each family might get its turn or its chance of the better and the worse qualities of soil. This very rude system is quite incompatible with any improved culture, but is an extremely ancient one. Sir Henry Maine has lately published a very interesting little book on the subject, showing that it once prevailed all over *Europe*, and does still actually prevail over the greater part of *India*. It has

---

[†] She died soon after.

now almost entirely disappeared in the *Highlands*, where such *crofters* or very small cultivators as remain are generally separate from each other—each living on his own *croft*—although there are still remaining many cases of pasture or hill land held in common among several crofters.

Achnagoul, near *Inveraray*, is one of the old *primitive villages*, where all the houses are built close together, and where, as late as the year 1847, the old rude practice still held—that of an *annual casting of lots* for the patches of arable land into which the farm was divided. At that time there were sixteen families, and each of them cultivated perhaps twenty different patches of arable land separated from each other. About that year the families were persuaded with much difficulty to give up this old semi-barbarous system and to divide the arable land into fixed divisions, one being assigned to each tenant, so that he could cultivate on an improved system. But the village remains as it was, and is one of the comparatively few of that class which now remain in the *Highlands*.

They are said to be the only two villages of the kind in existence in the *Highlands*. The inhabitants are very exclusive, and hardly ever marry out of their own villages.

We went on between curious, rather low, grass hills on either side, some higher than others, and several of which have small lochs at the tops with excellent trout, as the Duke told us. He showed us some farms and other glens, and had something to say about each place. We next turned to the left, where we got into oak woods, passing some powder mills* belonging to Sir G. Campbell, and a small village called *Cumlodden*, or rather a row of huts in which the people employed at the mills live, and from here turned to the village of *Furnace*, inhabited by the men who work the Duke's great quarries close to the sea, and which is so called from a number of furnaces which were used in the last century for smelting down lead brought from *England*. The Duke showed us one remaining, though in ruins, and we passed a quarry. The drive went by the shore of *Loch Fyne*, much reminding me of the drive along *Loch Eil* beyond *Banavie*, between trees on either side, oak, ash, beech, etc., with much underwood, hazel, bramble, etc., and we stopped at a point called *Pennymore*, where there is a small battery where Lorne's volunteers practise; and here the view, looking down the loch towards the sea and the *Kyles of Bute* with finely-shaped hills, was very beautiful. The more distant hills were those above *Ardrishaig*. I tried to sketch here after we had taken our tea. We went along by *Kenmore*, *Kilbryde*, and *Dalchenna* (again), and it was a lovely evening, with such soft tints on the distant hills, and the town in front backed by trees. I took another sketch (only very slight, in pencil) of this view from the Duchess's new school-house, called *Creggan's School*.

We got home by half-past six. Besides our two daughters and the Duke and Duchess, Lady Dufferin and Colin Campbell dined with me. Went as usual into the drawing-room for a little while, and then upstairs to my room. Beatrice remained with Jane and me.

Sunday, September 26.

The morning was very wet, so decided after our usual nice breakfast not to go out, but wrote, etc. At a quarter to twelve we attended divine service in the house, in the large dining-room, which is a long room. Dr. MacGregor performed the service. Went afterwards into the drawing-room and the two libraries, the newer of which had been arranged by Louise and Lorne. There are some fine pictures in the drawing-room—one of the Marquis of Argyll who was beheaded, of Field-Marshal Conway by Gainsborough, of Duke Archibald, who built the house, etc., also of the present Duke's handsome grandmother, who married first a Duke of Hamilton, secondly a Duke of Argyll.

Luncheon as usual. Then upstairs, and at twenty minutes to four walked out with Louise, Beatrice, and Jane Churchill, and went along by the river, which had been over the road in the night, on to the "*Miller's Lynn*," the first falls, which are very pretty and were very full, but are not near as high as the *Garbhalt*. We met some of the party coming back, and then some way farther up the river got into the carriage and drove to the "middle fall" or *Essachlay*, where we got out and walked to look at the fall; then drove to *Lynn a Gluthen* and saw the third fall, after which we drove some distance up *Glen Aray*, beyond *Stronmagachan* to *Tullich Hill*, then back again past the stables, and on through the *Town Avenue* back, and in by ten minutes past six.

Took tea with Beatrice and Louise, who came in rather late, afterwards read and wrote. Besides Louise and Beatrice, Lorne, Elizabeth Campbell, Jane Churchill, and General Ponsonby dined with me. We went into the drawing-room for a short while as usual.

Monday, September 27.

It was a dreadfully rough night, pouring and blowing fearfully, and we heard it had thundered and lightened. After our nice little breakfast and writing, I went out at eleven with Louise, and met the Duke and the rest in the pleasure-grounds, where I planted a small cedar of Lebanon, the seed of which Lady Emma McNeill had brought back from the East.* Then went on a little farther to where the road turns near the river, and planted a small silver fir, opposite to a magnificent one which my beloved

Albert had admired in 1847. Beatrice walked up meanwhile with Jane Churchill, Evelyn, and Frances Campbell, to the top of the fine hill of *Dunaquoich*, opposite the Castle, after seeing the trees planted, and was to plant one herself when she came down. I drove off with Louise past the *Creitabhille* Lodge, the granite quarry (not, of course, the large ones which we saw on Saturday in the deer forest), and then got out and walked up a long steep path in the wood to obtain a view, of which, however, we did not see much. I am sure we walked a mile and a half up to the top, and it was a long pull, but I walked well. However, in going down, the wet grass and moss made me slip very much, having no nails to my boots, and twice I came down completely.

We drove back by *Essachosan* as quickly as we could at a quarter to one. The trees are wonderfully thick, and the tangled undergrowth of fern etc. is almost like a jungle. We had hardly any rain. Luncheon as usual. Drawing. The views from my room were so fine. While I was dressing to go out, Louise brought in Archibald Campbell's two lovely little children, little Neil, a dear pretty fair boy of three, very like Archie as a child, and the baby, Elspeth, who is beautiful: brown curly hair, enormous dark blue eyes fringed with very long dark eyelashes, and a small mouth and nose.

At ten minutes to four drove off in the waggonette with Louise, Beatrice, and Lorne, out by the approach along the foot of *Dunaquoich*, past the yew and chestnut avenue, over the *Garonne Bridge*, along the lochside, an excellent road, much wooded, and commanding a beautiful view of the opposite shore and hills of *Ardkinglass*, past the *Strone Point*, *Achnatra*, and the ruins of the old castle or tower of *Dunderave*, which formerly belonged to the McNaghtons, who subsequently settled in *Ireland*, on to the head of *Loch Fyne*. There we turned up to the left and drove up *Glen Fyne*, a very wild narrow glen with hardly any trees, and the water of the *Fyne* running through it. The high green hills with rugged grey rocks reminded me of the *Spital of Glenshee* and of *Altanour* (Lord Fife's). We drove up to a very small shooting-lodge, the property of Mr. Callander, brother-in-law to Lord Archibald, where a keeper with a nice wife lives. As it was beginning to rain, we went into the house and took our (made) tea, and I sketched. Janie Campbell (Lady Archibald) and her two sisters lived here for some time. The Duke was their guardian. We drove back the same way, and encountered a tremendous shower, which only ceased as we were quite near home. We were home at twenty minutes to seven. Besides Louise and Beatrice, the Duke and Duchess and Sir John and Lady Emma McNeill dined with me. Mr. D. Macleod gone; the others remain.

Tuesday, September 28.

Bright and then showery. At a little past eleven drove with Louise and Beatrice along the sea-shore as far as *Douglass Water Point*, where we stopped to sketch between the frequent showers, the view being lovely and the lights so effective.

Home through the town by a quarter to one.

Painting. Luncheon as each day, after which again painting. At a quarter to four started off in a shower in the waggonette, with Louise, Beatrice, and Jane Churchili, for *Glen Shira*. We drove by the approach through the fine old avenue of beeches which suffered so much two years ago. This time along the right side of the *Dhu Loch*, which is three-quarters of a mile long, up to the head of *Glen Shira*, which is seven miles distant from the upper end of the loch, and is lovely. We had driven up a good way last Thursday, as far as *Drumlee*. It is a lovely glen, wilder and much shut in as you advance, with fine rocks appearing through the grassy hills, and thickly wooded at the bottom. We passed two farms, and then went up to where the glen closes, and on the brae there is a keeper's cottage, just above which are the remains of a house where Rob Roy lived for some time concealed, but on sufferance. His army or followers were hidden in *Glen Shira*.

We got out here to look at some fine falls of the river *Shira*, a linn falling from a height to which footpaths had been made. Then drove on a little farther, and stopped to take our tea. We stopped twice afterwards to make a slight sketch of this lovely green glen, so picturesque and peaceful-looking, and then to take another view from the lower end of the *Dhu Loch*, in which Louise helped me. She also sketched the glen, and had done a sketch this morning. She has such talent, dear good child, and I felt so sad to leave her. The evening was quite fine, it having cleared up and all the heavy clouds vanished when we arrived at the head of the glen. In at twenty minutes past six. Busy arranging papers, painting, etc. Besides Louise and Beatrice, the Duke and Duchess, Lady Dufferin and Mr. J. Campbell dined with me. Went again into the drawing-room and took leave of the Dufferins, who were to go next day. He starts on the 8th for *Canada*. Dear Louise came up with me to my room, and stayed a little while talking with me.

Wednesday, September 29.

Vicky's and Fritz's engagement day—already twenty years ago! God bless them!

Got up before eight, and at half-past eight breakfasted for the last time with dear Louise and Beatrice. Then dressed before half-past nine and went downstairs. The early morning was fair, though misty, but unfortunately by half-past eight the mist had come down and it rained. It was decided that the horses should go back overland (having had such a terrible journey from the diffcult embarkation and landing) by *Dalmally*, stopping all night at *Tyndrum* and coming on next day. The van was to go by sea. Some of the things belonging to our toilettes (which were in far too cumbrous boxes) we kept with us. I took leave of the whole family,[+] including the McNeills, and, with a heavy heart, of my darling Louise. It rained very much as we drove off, and for some time afterwards, to make it more melancholy.

We left *Inveraray* at half-past nine, and drove out by the same gateway as on our arrival, but afterwards went along the sea-shore to the head of the loch. We then turned to the right, still along the lochside, and changed horses at twenty minutes to eleven at a small inn called *Cairndow*, where the dear little Campbell children are staying, and who were at the window—such lovely children! There were a few people collected, and the harness as well as the horses had to be changed, and a pair of leaders put on to pull us up the long steep ascent in *Glenkinglass*. This caused a delay of ten minutes or a quarter of an hour. It rained rather heavily, the mist hanging over the hiils most provokingly. We passed *Ardkinglass* (Mr. Callander's), and then turned up to the left through the very wild and desolate *Glenkinglass*. The high green hills with hardly any habitations reminded me of the *Spital of Glenshee*. The mist lifted just enough to let one see the tops of the hills below which we were passing. The road was steep, and, just as we were getting near the top, the leaders, which had repeatedly stopped, refused to pull any farther, reared and kicked and jibbed, so that we really thought we should never get on, and should perhaps have to sleep at some wayside inn. But we stopped, and Brown had the leaders taken off near a small tarn, called *Loch Restel*, and he and Francie walked. We then got on much better. A little farther on we passed a few scattered huts, and at last we reached the top of this long ascent. The rain, which had been very heavy just when our plight was at its worst, stopped, and the day cleared.

At the summit of the pass is the spot called *Rest and be thankful*, from an inscription cut upon a stone by the regiment that made the road, which was one of the military roads to open up the *Highlands* constructed

---

[+] Elizabeth, Duchess of Argyll, died May 25, 1878.

by Government under the superintendence of Marshal Wade.* The stone still remains, but the words are much defaced. Here we came upon the splendid steep wild pass of *Glen Croe*, something like *Glencoe*, but not so fine and the road much steeper. It reminds me of the *Devil's Elbow*, and even of the *Devil's Bridge* in the *Göschenen Pass* on the *St. Gothard*. We got out and walked down the road, which goes in a zigzag. A few people who had walked up from the coach were standing there. As at *Glencoe* the stream flows in the hollow of the pass, and there were some cattle and a house or two. The sun even came out all at once and lit up the wild grand scene. We got into the carriage near the bottom, and drank Fritz and Vicky's healths.

There was no more heavy rain, though there were frequent showers succeeded by most brilliant sunshine. We drove on under and by trees, and saw high hill-tops, including the peak of *Ben Lomond*, and then came upon *Loch Long*, a sea loch, which we sailed up in 1847, and drove part of the way along the shore, on the opposite side of which lie *Arrochar* and several pretty villas. We went round the head of the loch, where stood Lady Welby (formerly Victoria Wortley) and her children, and drove along under an arch near the bridge, passing through the village of *Arrochar*, which is in *Dumbartonshire*, and here had a very good view of the celebrated *Cobbler*, or *Ben Arthur*. We next changed horses at *Tarbet*, quite a small village, where there was a sort of arch, composed of laurels and flowers stretched across the road. There were a good many people here, who pressed in upon us a good deal. Here General Ponsonby presented Mr. H. E. Crum Ewing, Lord Lieutenant of *Dumbartonshire*. He preceded us a little way in his carriage, and then followed us.

The drive along *Loch Lomond*, which we came upon almost immediately after *Tarbet*, was perfectly beautiful. We wound along under trees on both sides, with the most lovely glimpses of the head of the loch, and ever and anon of *Loch Lomond* itself below the road; the hills which rose upon our right reminding me of *Aberfoyle*, near *Loch Ard*, and of the lower part of the *Pilatus*. Such fine trees, numbers of hollies growing down almost into the water, and such beautiful capes and little bays and promontories! The loch was extremely rough, and so fierce was the wind, that the foam was blown like smoke along the deep blue of the water. The gale had broken some trees. The sun lit up the whole scene beautifully, but we had a few slight showers. It reminded me of *Switzerland*. I thought we saw everything so much better than we had formerly done from the steamer. As we proceeded, the hills became lower, the loch widened, and the many wooded islands appeared. We next changed horses at *Luss*, quite a small village—indeed the little inn stands almost alone, and they drove us close up to it, but there was a great crowding and squeezing, and some children screamed with fright; two presented nosegays to Beatrice and me, and a poor woman offered me a bag of "*sweeties.*"

From here we drove along past the openings of *Glen Luss* and *Glen Finlas*, which run up amongst the fine hills to the right, the loch being on our left, and the road much wooded. There are slate quarries close to *Luss*.* About two miles from *Luss* we drove through Sir J. Colquhoun's place, *Rossdhu*, which commands a beautiful view of *Ben Lomond* and the loch, and drove up to the house, where Highland volunteers were drawn up, and where we stopped without getting out of the carriage, and I received a nosegay from a little girl, and a basket of fruit. Sir J. Colquhoun's father was drowned two years ago in the loch, crossing over from an island where he had been shooting, and the body was not found for a fortnight; the keepers with him were also drowned. We drove on, passing several other places, and everywhere were arches of flowers, flags, etc., and the poorest people had hung out handkerchiefs for flags. We were followed by endless "machines" full of people, and many on foot running, and our horses were bad and went very slowly. However, as we approached *Balloch*, through which we did not pass, but only went up to the station, though the crowds were very great, perfect order was kept. The militia was out, and we got quite easily into the train at a quarter-past three.

Here again a nosegay was presented, and Mr. A. Orr Ewing, member for the county, and Mr. Smollett, the Convener, whom we had seen on board the steamer six years ago, were presented. *Balloch* is a manufacturing place for dyeing, and is connected with the trade in *Glasgow*. We had some cold luncheon as soon as we got into the train.

Our next stoppage was at *Stirling*, where there was an immense concourse of people, and the station prettily decorated. The evening was very fine, the pretty scenery appearing to great advantage, and the sky lovely. After this it got rapidly dark. We stopped at *Perth* and at the *Bridge of Dun*, where Jane Churchill got into our carriage and we had some tea; and then at *Aberdeen*, where it poured. At twenty minutes to ten we arrived at *Ballater*, and at once got into our carriage, and reached *Balmoral* at twenty-five minutes to eleven.

HIGHLAND FUNERAL.*
OCTOBER 1875.

Thursday, October 21, 1875.

Much grieved at its being a worse day than ever for the funeral of Brown's father,† which sad ceremony was to take place to-day. The rain is hopeless—the ninth day! Quite unheard of! I saw good Brown a moment before breakfast; he was low and sad, and then going off to *Micras*. At twenty minutes to twelve drove with Beatrice and Janie Ely to *Micras*. As we drove up (unfortunately raining much) we met Dr. Robertson, and all along near the house were numbers of people— Brown told me afterwards he thought above a hundred. All my keepers, Mitchell the blacksmith (from *Clachanturn*), Symon, Grant, Brown's five uncles, Leys, Thomson (postmaster), and the forester, people below *Micras* and in *Aberarder*, and my people; Heale, Löhlein (returned this day from a week's leave), Cowley Jarrett, Ross and Collins (sergeant footman), Brown and his four brothers,† including Donald (who only arrived last night, and went to the *Bush*, his brother William's farm), took us to the kitchen, where was poor dear old Mrs. Brown sitting near the fire and much upset, but still calm and dignified; Mrs. William Brown was most kind and helpful, and the old sister-in-law and her daughter; also the Hon. M. West, Mr. Sahl, Drs. Marshall and Profeit, Mr. Begg, and Dr. Robertson, who came in later. The sons, and a few whom Brown sent out of the kitchen, were in the other small room, where was the coffin. A small passage always divides the kitchen and the sitting-room in this old sort of farmhouse, in front of which is the door—the only door. Mr. Campbell, the minister of *Crathie*, stood in the passage at the door, every one else standing close outside. As soon as he began his prayer, poor dear old Mrs. Brown got up and came and stood near me—able to hear, though, alas! not to see—and leant on a chair during the very impressive prayers, which Mr. Campbell gave admirably. When it was over, Brown came and begged her to go and sit down while they took the coffin away, the brothers bearing it. Every one went out and followed, and we also hurried out and just saw them place the coffin in the hearse,

---

† He had died on the 18th, aged 86, at Micras, opposite Abergeldie, on the other side of the river.
† The fifth, Hugh (who, since May 1883, has been my Highland attendant), was then in New Zealand.

and then we moved on to a hillock, whence we saw the sad procession wending its way sadly down. The sons were there, whom I distinguished easily from their being near good Brown, who wore his kilt walking near the hearse. All walked, except our gentlemen, who drove. It fortunately ceased raining just then. I went back to the house, and tried to soothe and comfort dear old Mrs. Brown,* and gave her a mourning brooch with a little bit of her husband's hair which had been cut off yesterday, and I shall give a locket to each of the sons.

When the coffin was being taken away, she sobbed bitterly.

We took some whisky and water and cheese, according to the universal Highland custom, and then left, begging the dear old lady to bear up. I told her the parting was but for a time. We drove quickly on, and saw them go into the kirkyard, and through my glasses I could see them carry the coffin in. I was grieved I could not be in the kirkyard.

Saw my good Brown at a little before two. He said all had gone off well, but he seemed very sad; he had to go back to *Micras* to meet all the family at tea. All this was terribly trying for the poor dear old widow, but could not be avoided. Already, yesterday morning, she had several of the wives and neighbours to tea. Every one was very kind and full of sympathy, and Brown was greatly gratified by the respect shown to him and his family to-day.

Unveiling of the Statue of the Prince Consort at Edinburgh, 1876.

Holyrood,
August 17, 1876.

Beloved Mama's birthday.

How often she came to *Edinburgh* for a few days on her way to and from *Abergeldie*, and how much she always liked it!

We arrived yesterday morning at *Edinburgh* at eight o'clock. Had had a good night. Unfortunately the weather was misty, and even a little rain fell. No distance could well be seen. Dear Arthur came to breakfast (always in uniform).[+] At eleven o'clock went and sat out till half-past twelve, under an umbrella and with screens, on the side of the Abbey facing *Arthur's Seat*. Wrote and signed, Brown always helping to dry the signatures.

Read also in the papers a very nice account given in the "Courant"* of what passed yesterday. Many interruptions. The day improving. Crowds flocking into the town, troops marching, bands playing—just as when any great event takes place in *London*.

The last time that my dearest Albert ever appeared in public was in *Edinburgh* on October 23 [1861], only six weeks before the end of all, when he laid the first stone of the new Post Office, and I looked out of the window to see him drive off in state, or rather in dress, London carriages, and the children went to see the ceremony. It was in *Edinburgh*, too, that dearest Mama appeared for the last time in public—being with me at the Volunteer Review in 1860, which was the first time she had driven with me in public for twenty years!

Dear Arthur could not come to luncheon, as he was on duty. At half-past three we started in three carriages: Beatrice, Leopold, and I in the third; Brown (in full dress) and Collins behind; Leopold in the Highland dress; dear Arthur, commanding the full Sovereign's escort of the 7th Hussars, riding next to me.

We drove out to the right—by *Abbey Hill*, the *Regent Road*, *Princes Street*, then turning into *St. Andrew Square*, along *George Street* to *Charlotte*

[+] He was then Major in the 7th Hussars, and living at the Piers Hill Barracks, near Edinburgh, where his regiment was quartered.

Square. Enormous crowds everywhere clustering upon the *Calton Hill* and round and upon all the high monuments. The decorations were beautiful along the streets and on the houses, Venetian masts with festoons of flags on either side of *Princes Street* and *St. Andrew Street*. *St. Andrew Square* also was beautifully decorated, and the few inscriptions were very touching and appropriate. The day was quite fair, though dull (which, however, under the circumstances, was better than a very scorching sun like yesterday) and heavy, and not clear as to distance. The crowd, which was all along most hearty and enthusiastic, was densest at *Charlotte Square*. The Duke of Buccleuch received us, and the Royal Archers kept the ground.

We walked up to a dais handsomely arranged, where I stood between Beatrice and Leopold (who were a little behind me). Dear Arthur's sense of duty was so great, that he would not dismount and stand near me, but remained with the escort which he commanded, and which waited near our carriage. The ladies and gentlemen, Mr. Cross (Home Secretary), etc., standing behind them; the Committee, with the Duke of Buccleuch at their head, below. A large enclosure railed off was full of spectators, including all the highest and principal people, the Duchesses of Athole and Roxburghe, the Dowager Lady Ruthven, Sir Thomas Biddulph, etc.; and our maids also were there, but I saw none of them.

The ceremony began by a short prayer (which was somewhat disturbed by a great noise made by the crowd) offered up by Dr. Milligan, one of the Deans of the Chapel Royal. Then my dearest Albert's Chorale,* with words like a National Anthem, was beautifully sung by a choir, accompanied by the band of the 79th,* led by Professor H. Oakeley, Mus. Doc. and Professor of Music in the University of *Edinburgh*. The Duke of Buccleuch then presented the Executive Committee, of which he himself is Chairman, and which consisted of Sir J. McNeill, G.C.B., Sir William Gibson Craig, Sir Daniel McNee, Dr. Lyon Playfair, and Mr. William Walker. After this, the Duke of Buccleuch read a very pretty address, in which, besides my beloved Husband, dear Mama was alluded to, and I read a reply.

Mr. Cross then declared that I wished the Statue* (an equestrian one) to be unveiled, which was done most successfully, without a hitch. The effect of the monument as a whole, with the groups at the angles of the pedestal, is very good. The Coburg March* was played, and its well-known strains+ ever bring back dear and sweet memories.

Mr. Steell, the sculptor, was presented, and this was followed by the singing of another beautiful chorale, with touching words and music, the

---

+ This March was always played for dear Albert, and was originally composed for our grand-uncle, Field-Marshal Prince Francis Josias of Saxe-Coburg-Saalfeld.

latter composed by Professor Oakeley, who is a wonderful musician, and plays beautifully on the organ. We then, followed by our own suite, the Committee, and Mr. Steell, walked round the Statue and examined the groups of bas-reliefs. The three sculptors who had executed the groups were also presented. Brown followed us round, having stood behind us the whole time. He was delighted with the reception.

We drove back by *South Charlotte Street* and *Princes Street*. The horses of the Yeomanry and even some of the Hussars were very restive, and kept plunging and whirling round upon our horses. One of the Hussars, in particular, got in between our horses, and nearly caused an accident. We got back by ten minutes to five o'clock.

We looked out of the window to see Arthur[+] ride off, and then I knighted Mr. Steell, who looked very happy. He has now long white hair—such a kind, good man! I also knighted Professor Oakeley, who is still very lame, having met with a dreadful accident in *Switzerland* some years ago. His mother was a Murray (daughter of Lord Charles Murray Aynsley) and sister to the mother of Mrs. Drummond of *Megginch*, and his sister married an uncle of Fanny Drummond. Dear Augusta Stanley took much interest in him.

I had a large dinner in the old dining-room below, where I had not dined since my darling Albert's time in 1861. I sat in the middle, opposite to where I used to sit. The party consisted of Arthur, who led me in and sat near me, and Leopold and Beatrice, all our people, the Duke of Buccleuch (who sat near me) and Lady Mary Scott, Lord Lothian (the Duke's son-in-law), Lord Dalkeith, young Lord Elgin, Lord Rosebery, the Dowager Lady Dunmore and Lady Adine Murray, Lord and Lady Elphinstone, Sir John and Lady Emma McNeill, Mr. Cross, the Honourable B. Primrose, Major-General J. N. Stuart, and Colonel Hale of the 7th Hussars (Colonel of dear Arthur's regiment). The band of the 7th Hussars played during dinner, and Ross played during dessert. Brown[†] waited on me.

Every one seemed pleased, and talked of the great success of the day. Mr. Cross was delighted. I remained talking some little time in the drawing-room, and then went upstairs and looked with Beatrice out of the window at the rockets. Such a noise in the streets and from the trains!

[+] Arthur was attended by Lieutenant-Colonel Pickard, R.H.A., who had been with him since 1867. He entered the Queen's service 1st January, 1878, as Groom-in-Waiting, and became Assistant Privy Purse and Assistant Private Secretary in October 1878. He was a charming, amiable person, much devoted to Arthur and to me. He died at the age of forty of consumption, at Cannes, March 1, 1880, deeply regretted by us and by all who knew him.

[†] It was hard for him to have to appear on such a festive occasion, having lost his much-loved mother only a fortnight before; but his sense of duty ever went before every feeling of self.

Presentation of Colours to "The Royal Scots," September, 1876.*

*Balmoral,
September 26, 1876.*

An earlier lunch. It had appeared to clear, and the rain was far less heavy. We started at three. The ladies and gentlemen had all gone on before in carriages, and many of our people went to *Ballater*, as it was a great novelty for the people here—William Brown and his wife, who had said yesterday she had never seen so many soldiers together and would therefore like to go; Hugh Brown and his wife. Mrs. Profeit[+] with her children was there also. Alice, Beatrice, and Arthur were with me. The weather held up while we were going to *Ballater*, which we did in a closed landau (Brown and Collins on the rumble). Just outside the village we opened the carriage. We drove to the left of the railway through a wood, avoiding the town, preceded by Captain Charles Phipps, as Assistant Adjutant Quartermaster-General, on to the open space—a beautiful position, with the noble rocky high hill of *Craig an Darrach*, at the foot of which lie the *Pass of Ballater* and the park of *Monaltrie House* with the hills opposite. Nothing could be finer. A great many people were there, it is said between two and three thousand; but none of the spectators were in uniform. Alix was in a carriage, Bertie and the boys (in Highland dress) and Prince John of Glücksburg[†] on foot. They stood near me, so did Arthur (also in his kilt), who had got out of the carriage. Then followed, after the Royal salute, the trooping of the colours,* with all its peculiar and interesting customs, marching and counter-marching, the band playing the fine old marches of the "Garb of old Gaul" and "Dumbarton Drums," also the march from the "Fille du Régiment," which was evidently played as a compliment to me, whom they considered as "born in the regiment," my father having commanded it at the time I was born. Then came the piling of the drums* and the prayer by Mr. Middleton, minister of *Ballater*, after which the new colours were given to me. I handed them to the two sub-lieutenants who were kneeling, and then I said the following words:—

[+] Wife of my Commissioner at Balmoral.
[†] Uncle of the Princess of Wales.

"In entrusting these colours to your charge, it gives me much pleasure to remind you that I have been associated with your regiment from my earliest infancy, as my dear father was your Colonel. He was proud of his profession, and I was always told to consider myself a soldier's child. I rejoice in having a son who has devoted his life to the army, and who, I am confident, will ever prove worthy of the name of a British soldier. I now present these colours to you, convinced that you will always uphold the glory and reputation of my first Regiment of Foot—the Royal Scots."

Colonel M'Guire then spoke a few words in reply, and brought the old colours to me, and begged me to accept them. In doing so, I said I should take them to *Windsor*, and place them there in recollection of the regiment and their Colonel. Then they marched past well (they were fine men), and after the Royal salute gave three cheers for me. The 79th kept the ground and took charge of the old colours. We left at once.

The rain continued persistently, having got worse just as the prayer began; but we kept the carriage open, and were back by half-past five.

I was terribly nervous while speaking.

Expedition to Loch Maree,
September 12–18, 1877.

Wednesday, September 12, 1877.

A dull morning, very mild. Had not a good night. Up at a quarter-past eight, breakfasting at a quarter to nine (I had packed my large boxes with papers etc., with Brown, before breakfast on Monday, as all the heavier luggage had to be sent on in advance), and at a quarter-past nine left *Balmoral* with Beatrice and the Duchess of Roxburghe, leaving Leopold, who was himself to start at ten A.M. for *Dunkeld*. Brown on the rumble of the landau, his leg now really fairly well, but he looks pulled.[+] It began to rain very soon, and went on till we almost reached *Ballater*, when we got into the railway. Here General Ponsonby and Sir William Jenner met us. Wilmore, Morgan, Cannon, Francie Clark (with darling Noble), and Heir went with us. Annie Macdonald, Hollis the cook, Lockwood, Seymour (who replaced poor Goddard), and Lizzie Stewart (the housemaid) went on before us on Monday.

The day cleared and gradually became very fine. Passed through *Aberdeen*, which looked very handsome, and where we much admired a new tower added to a college. Stopped at *Dyce Junction* at nineteen minutes to twelve. Near *Aberdeen* we saw the corn already cut, which is unusually early. Passed close under *Benachie*, the heather beautiful everywhere. At one o'clock we had our luncheon, and dear Noble came in and was so good and quiet. At twenty-five minutes past one stopped at *Keith*, where we had stopped in 1872, and where we had then been obliged to take two people into the carriage to open a door through which the maids passed, and which had got fixed.[†] The volunteers and a number of people were waiting for us here. About *Keith* the corn was sadly destroyed, but around *Elgin* it was better. Soon after this appeared the lovely hills of the *Moray Frith*—really beautiful: the land-locked sea so blue, with heavy fields of yellow corn (harvesting going on) in the undulating ground, with trees and woods here and there, formed a lovely picture. An old ruined church (*Kinloss Abbey*) we passed to the right, and

---

[+] When we went on board the "Thunderer," August 12, at Osborne, Brown had fallen through an open place inside the turret, and got a severe hurt on the shin. He afterwards damaged it again, when it was nearly healed, by jumping off the box of the carriage, so that when he came to Balmoral about a fortnight afterwards, it was very bad, and he was obliged to take care of it for some days previous to the fresh journey.

[†] *Vide* Expedition to Dunrobin, p. 274.

Forres at eighteen minutes past two. Then *Nairn*, lying low on the *Frith*, but very picturesque with the hills rising around. Near here poor Jane Churchill's sister, Cecilia Brinckman, died on August 16, which is the cause that dear Jane is not with us now. The heather was so brilliant, and the sea, though very rough, was blue, which had a lovely effect; but the bracken, and even the trees, have begun to turn here, as well as with us. Good crops about here. We passed near *Fort George*, which lies very prettily on the shore of the *Frith*, but where we did not stop, and *Culloden*. At three minutes past three passed through *Inverness*, where many people were out, and went quickly past *Beauly*. As far as *Dingwall* we had travelled precisely the same way in going to *Dunrobin* in 1872. At twenty minutes to four reached *Dingwall*, charmingly situated in a glen, where we stopped, and where there were a good many people waiting for us.

Here Sir Kenneth and Lady Mackenzie of *Gairloch* met us with their three children, two boys and a girl. He is a pleasing courteous person, and wore the kilt. He has an immense property about here, and all round is the *Mackenzie country*. Lady Mackenzie is the elder sister of Lady Granville, and excessively like her. Soon after this we took tea, which was pleasant and refreshing. From *Dingwall* we turned to the left, and, instead of going on by the main line to *Tain*, went through the celebrated *Strathpeffer*, which is extremely pretty—a wooded glen with houses and cottages dotted about; then on through a wild glen, with hills, partly rocky, but with grass, heather, and bracken, and some trees running up amidst them. The railway goes along above and at some distance from the village, proceeding by way of *Strath Bran* and *Loch Luichart*. There were occasional showers, with gleams of sunshine always between.

We left the railway at *Achnasheen*, where we arrived at a quarter to five, and where there are only a small station and two or three little cottages. We three ladies got into the sociable (Brown and Cannon on the box), the two gentlemen and three maids following in the waggonette, and the other servants in "traps." Sir Kenneth Mackenzie came as far as this small station, where there were a Gaelic inscription and some plaids arranged in festoons. The twenty miles drive from here, through a desolate, wild, and perfectly uninhabited country, was beautiful, though unfortunately we had heavy showers. The first part winds along *Loch Rusque* (Gaelic *Chroisg*), a long narrow loch, with hills very like those at the *Spital* and at *Glen Muich* rising on either side. Looking back you see the three high peaks of *Scour-na-Vuillin*. The road continues along another small loch; and then from the top of the hill you go down a very grand pass called *Glen Dochart*. Here *Loch Maree* came in view most beautifully. Very shortly after this you come upon the loch, which is grand and romantic. We changed horses at *Kinlochewe*, a small inn, near to which is a shooting-lodge, which was for some time rented by Lady Waterpark's son-in-law, Mr. Clowes, and he and his wife used to live there a good deal. They are now living near *Gairloch*, at *Flowerdale*, another shooting-lodge of Sir Kenneth Mackenzie.

The drive along the lochside, for ten miles to the hotel of *Loch Maree*, is beautiful in the extreme. The hills to the right, as you go from *Kinlochewe*, are splendid—very high and serrated, with wood at the base of some of them. One magnificent hill towers above the rest, and is not unlike the *Pilatus* in shape, seen as it is from our hotel, just as the *Pilatus* is seen from the *Pension Wallis*. The windings of, the road are beautiful, and afford charming glimpses of the lake, which is quite locked in by the overlapping mountains. There are trees, above and below it, of all kinds, but chiefly birch, pine, larch, and alder, with quantities of high and most beautiful heather and bracken growing luxuriantly, high rocks surmounting the whole. Here and there a fine Scotch fir, twisted, and with a stem and head like a stone-pine, stands out on a rocky projection into the loch, relieved against the blue hills as in some Italian view. Part of the way the road emerges altogether from the trees, and passes by a mass of huge piled-up and tumbled-about stones, which everywhere here are curiously marked, almost as though they were portions of a building, and have the appearance of having been thrown about by some upheaving of the earth. We had several heavy showers, which produced a most brilliant rainbow, with the reflection of a second, quite perfect. Then it quite cleared up, and the sky was radiant with the setting sun, which gave a crimson hue to all the hills, and lit up *Ben Sleach* just as I remember having seen it light up *Ben Nevis* and the surrounding hills at *Inverlochy*.

It was a little after seven when *Loch Maree Hotel*,* which stands close to the loch and to the road and is surrounded by trees, was reached. At the entrance there is no gate, merely a low wall open at either side to admit carriages etc. It is a very nice little house, neatly furnished. To the left, as you enter, are two good rooms—a large one called the coffee-room, in which we take our meals, and the other, smaller, next to it, in which the gentlemen dine. Up the small but easy short winding staircase to the right come small, though comfortable, rooms. To the left Beatrice's, and Brown's just opposite to the right. Then up three steps is a small passage; at the end, to the left, is my dear little sitting-room, looking on to the loch, and to *Ben Sleach* and the road; it is very full with my things. At the other end is my bedroom, with two small rooms between for Wilmore and Annie.

On arriving heard that the Russians had bombarded *Plevna** on the 9th, and had repulsed a sortie of the Turks with heavy loss. The bombardment continued again the following day, and General Skobeleff occupied the heights. We two and the Duchess dined together. The Duchess read to me a sketch of Thiers' life. Good Brown waited, and brought in my usual glass of water. Felt rather tired.

Dear Louis of Hesse's birthday—God bless him!

Thursday, September 13.

It had rained a great deal through the night, and the morning was dull. Had slept well. Beatrice and I breakfasted together downstairs, where we also lunched. Began to sketch, though there was no light and shade; but the splendid mountain was clear. At eleven walked out with Beatrice on the road to *Kinlochewe*, about a mile, and back, greatly admiring the magnificent hills. There is a bridge over a stream called *Talladale*, and near it was a cottage, a miserable hovel, in which an old man lived; he wore a coat and a high hat, and was much pleased to see me, but said he "had very little English," which is the case with most people here. We gave him something, and when Brown took it to him he asked the old man the names of some of the hills.

The atmosphere was very close. In at half-past twelve, and then I drew and painted. So hot! It turned to rain. Painted, read, wrote, etc., and then we took tea, and at half-past five started with Beatrice and the Duchess of Roxburghe (Brown and Francie on the box), and drove on down the loch (the contrary way to that by which we had come), under trees, through a larch wood, winding above the loch for two miles, till we reached a bridge, which goes over the stream of *Garvaig*, where there is a descent to above *Slatterdale*, and thence drove up a mountain pass to the left. There the hills are much lower and curiously tumbled about, grass, fern, and heather growing up their sides, with rocks at the tops—curious serrated, knobbed hills.

Passed a small loch called *Padnascally*, out of which runs the *Kerrie Water* into another little loch. Here the road winds along almost like the roads in *Switzerland*, and is very precipitous on one side, passing above the fine falls of the *Kerrie*, of which there are two or three successions, with fine rocks and wooded banks, through which the river seems to force its way. As Brown truly observed, it was like *Glenfeshie*; only *Glenfeshie* has no road, but a very narrow path, where one has to ford. Looking back before you come to the falls there is a fine view of *Ben Evy*. We drove quite down this pass to *Kerriesdale*, at the bridge of which is a very pretty spot with wooded hills leading on to *Gairloch*. We turned, as it was late, and drove back the same way, getting home by half-past seven. It was dull, and grey, and dark, but did not rain till we came back. The Duchess finished reading Thiers' life.

Friday, September 14.

An awful storm of rain, with wind, all night and a good part of the morning. Breakfasted as yesterday. At length we two went out, and walked for more than a mile on the road by which we drove yesterday. The rocky hills, rising above the road, with the fine trees and undergrowth beneath them, remind me of the *Lion's Face*, and of the *Trossachs* and *Loch Eil*. It cleared, the rain ceased, and the day became fine, but very hot and oppressive. In at twenty minutes to one. The view from my little sitting-room is quite beautiful, *Ben Sleach* on one side, and the splendid loch, with the other fine rocky mountains and green island, on the other. One would like to sketch all day. More telegrams.*

At half-past three we started in two carriages, we three ladies in one, and the two gentlemen in the waggonette (Brown with us, and Francie with the next). We went just the same way as yesterday, but changed horses at *Kerrie's Bridge*, and turning to the left went a short way down a bad road, through a small wood of oaks, to *Shieldaig*, where there is a small cottage on the sea with a pretty garden, where Lord Bristol and Mr. Bateson live. But there is no road beyond, and we had to turn and go back again. We then drove over the bridge by a lovely wood of larch and other trees, through which flows a small river, and ascended a hill, passing by *Flowerdale* to *Gairloch*, which is on the sea. It consists of only a very few houses dotted about—the kirk, manse, bank, and on the highest point the hotel. The hills immediately to the right and left of the fine bay are not very high. But high wooded hills are at the back of the *Gairloch*, which is open to the *Atlantic*. Here we turned round and drove straight back again the same way, the few inhabitants having come out to greet us. After passing *Kerrie's Bridge*, we stopped to take our (made) tea. The afternoon and evening were beautiful. We got home at a quarter to seven. The post comes in at a quarter to four and at half-past nine. The climate is very warm and muggy. Dinner as usual. After dinner played with Beatrice on the piano.

Saturday, September 15.

A fair morning. Up early after a very good night. There is a perfect plague of wasps, and we are obliged to have gauze nailed down to keep these insects out when the windows are open, which, as the climate is so hot, they have to be constantly. I had to put on quite thin things again. Decided, after some little doubt, to make an expedition for the day to *Torridon*, described as fine and wild. There was a heavy shower before we started. Had been sketching and painting.

At half-past twelve we started in the waggonette, with Beatrice, the Duchess (who is delighted with everything), and General Ponsonby and Brown on the box. The day was very fine; we had only two or three showers, which lasted a few minutes. We drove on to *Kinlochewe*, where we took fresh horses, and a capital pair of bay ones we had. The sun was brilliant, and lit up the magnificent scenery beautifully. Halfway we crossed the bridge of *Grudie* (from which *Ben Sleach* is seen to advantage), a very pretty rapid burn, with fine fir trees, and a glen running up to the right—*i.e.* to the south. At *Kinlochewe* we turned up to the right by the stream of *Garry*, mountains towering up, as we advanced, like mighty giants, and coming one by one and unexpectedly into view. To the left we passed a pretty, small loch, called *Loch Clare*, which runs back into a wooded glen at the foot of high hills. Sir Ivor Guest has a shooting-lodge near, and you can just see a small house amongst the trees.

Soon after this the grand, wild, savage-looking, but most beautiful and picturesque *Glen of Torridon* opened upon us, with the dark mural precipices of that most extraordinary mountain *Ben Liughach*, which the people pronounce *Liarach*. We were quite amazed as we drove below it. The mountains here rise so abruptly from their base that they seem much higher than our *Aberdeenshire* mountains, although, excepting *Ben Sleach* (3,216 feet) and a few others, the hills are not of any remarkable height, and the level of the country or land itself is barely a hundred feet above the sea, whereas *Balmoral* is eight hundred feet to begin with. All the hills about *Loch Maree* and this glen, and elsewhere in this neighbourhood, are very serrated and rocky. *Ben Liarach* is most peculiar from its being so dark, and the rocks like terraces one above the other, or like fortifications and pillars—most curious; the glen itself is very flat, and the mountains rise very abruptly on either side. There were two cottages (in one of which lived a keeper), a few cattle, and a great many cut peats.

We came to the *Upper Loch Torridon*, which is almost landlocked and very pretty. In the distance the hills of *Skye* were seen. Village there really is none,* and the inn is merely a small, one-storied, "harled" house, with small windows. We drove beyond the habitations to a turn where we could not be overlooked, and scrambled up a bank, where we seated ourselves, and at twenty minutes to three took our luncheon with good appetite. The air off the mountains and the sea was delicious, and not muggy. We two remained sketching, for the view was beautiful. To the right were the hills of *Skye*, rising above the lower purple ones which closed in the loch. To the south, nearly opposite to where I sat, was *Applecross* (formerly Mackenzie property), which now belongs to Lord Middleton, and the high mountains of *Ben Hecklish* and *Ben Damph*, with, in the distance northwards, the white peaks of *Ben Liarach*. We were nearly an hour sitting there, and we got down unwillingly, as it was so fine and such a wild uncivilised spot, like the end of the world. There was a school, standing detached by itself, which had been lately built. The property here belongs to a Mr. Darroch, whose two little boys rode past us twice with a groom. An old man, very tottery, passed where I was sketching, and I asked the Duchess of Roxburghe to speak to him; he seemed strange, said he had come from *America*, and was going to *England*, and thought *Torridon* very ugly!

We walked along, the people came out to see us, and we went into a little merchant's shop, where we all bought some trifles—just such a "shoppie" as old Edmonston's,* and the poor man was so nervous he threw almost everything down. I got some very good comforters, two little woven woollen shawls, and a very nice cloak. We had spoken to a woman before, but she could not understand us, only knowing Gaelic, and had to ask another younger woman to help.

A little farther off the road, and more on the slope of the hill, was a row of five or six wretched hovels, before which stood barelegged and very ill-clad children, and poor women literally squatting on the ground. The people cheered us and seemed very much pleased. Hardly any one ever comes here. We had now to get into the carriage, and one of the horses was a little restive; but we soon started off all right, much interested by our adventures. We admired the splendid mountain again on our way back, and enjoyed our expedition very much. One very short shower we had, before coming to *Kinlochewe*, where we again changed horses, and were home at our nice little house by nearly seven, when Beatrice and I had some welcome tea. Later our usual dinner; then Beatrice played, and we afterwards played together.*

Sunday, September 16.

A most beautiful bright morning, with a slight cloud overhanging *Ben Sleach*, which is very often not clear at the top. There was a heavy shower, which came on quite unexpectedly. We walked out at half-past eleven, and after some three hundred yards turned up a path to the right, off the road to *Kinlochewe*, under oak and rowan trees, through very wet grass and fern, to where stood two very poor-looking low cottages. We looked into one, out of which came a tidy-looking woman, but who could hardly understand or speak a word of English. We then looked into the second, where Baldry lodged; it was wet and muddy, almost to the door, and the inside very low and close, but tidy. The "gudewife" came up and spoke to us, also like a foreigner, with difficulty. She was a nice, tidy-looking woman, and gave her name as Mrs. McRae, and the place is called "*Sliorach*." She knew us—at least Brown told her it was the "Bhan Righ" with her daughter, and gave her some money.

We returned as we had come, and went on some way in the other direction, coming in at twenty minutes to one. Read prayers, etc. There is no kirk nearer than *Kinlochewe* and *Gairloch*, and people had been seen passing on foot as early as half-past seven to *Gairloch*. At half-past four Beatrice, the Duchess of Roxburghe, and I started in a four-oared gig, steered by Hormsby the landlord, a very nice, quiet, youngish man, and rowed to the *Isle of Maree* ("*Eilan Maree*"), which is not visible from the house, being concealed by some of the larger islands. Contrary to what is stated in the *Guide*, it is the smallest of them.* It was delightful rowing through these wooded and rocky islands, with the blue, calm loch—not another sound but the oars—the lovely blue and purple distant hills on the one side, and the splendid peaks of *Ben Sleach* and its surrounding mountains on the other.

The boat was pushed on shore, and we scrambled out and walked through the tangled underwood and thicket of oak, holly, birch, ash, beech, etc., which covers the islet, to the well, now nearly dry, which is said to be celebrated for the cure of insanity. An old tree stands close to it, and into the bark of this it is the custom, from time immemorial, for every one who goes there to insert with a hammer a copper coin,* as a sort of offering to the saint who lived there in the eighth century, called Saint Maolruabh or Mulroy. The saint died near *Applecross* in 722, and is said to have rested under a rock, which is still shown, close to *Torridon*. Some say that the name of *Maree* was derived from "*Mulroy*," others from "*Mary*." We hammered some pennies into the tree, to the branches of which there are also rags and ribbons tied. We then went on to where there are some old grave-stones: two belonged to the tomb of a Norwegian or Danish princess, about whose untimely death there is a romantic story. There are also modern graves, and only eight years ago one of the family of the McLeans was buried there, the island being their burying-place. The remains of the old wall of the monastery are still to be seen. The island is barely a quarter of a mile across at the widest part, and not above half a mile in circumference. Some of the larger islands have red deer on them. We walked along the beach and picked up stones, then rowed back as we had come. It took about twenty minutes. Four very respectable-looking men (one a very good-looking young farmer) rowed the boat. After landing, we got into the waggonette and drove to a bridge just beyond where the trees cease on the *Gairloch Road*, about two miles from the hotel. Here we first took our tea, and then got out and scrambled up a steep bank to look at a waterfall, a pretty one, but very inferior to those in our neighbourhood at *Balmoral*; walked down again and drove home by a quarter-past seven.

Reading; writing. Beatrice's room is a very pretty one, but very hot, being over the kitchen. Brown's, just opposite, also very nice and not hot, but smaller. After dinner the Duchess of Roxburghe read a little out of the newspapers. Saw Sir William Jenner.

Monday, September 17.

A splendid bright morning, like July! Have had such good nights since we came, and my own comfortable bed. Sketched and painted after breakfast. At ten minutes past eleven walked out with Beatrice the same way as yesterday, and turned up to the right and looked at the farm, where the horses for the coach are kept. This coach is like a great break, and is generally full of people; we met it each morning when out walking. We then went on past *Talladale*, where lives the old man to whom we spoke on Thursday, and whom we saw get off the coach this morning, having been to *Gairloch* for church, of which he is an elder. Here three or four very poorly dressed bairns were standing and sitting about, and we gave them biscuits and sandwiches out of the luncheon-box. The midges are dreadful, and you cannot stand for a moment without being stung. In at twenty minutes to one. I remained sketching the lovely views from the windows in the dining-room, and then sketched the beautiful mountain also.

After luncheon some doubt as to what should be done, but decided not to go to *Pool Ewe*, beyond *Gairloch*, but on to *Kerrie's Bridge* to meet the good people who had asked permission to come over from *Stornoway*,* in the *Isle of Lewis*, to see "their beloved Queen." Drew again. At ten minutes past four we two and the Duchess of Roxburghe started in the waggonette, General Ponsonby and Brown on the box. We went by the same pretty winding road; but the *Kerrie Falls* were not nearly so full as on Friday after the heavy rain.

As we approached *Kerrie's Bridge*, we saw a number of people standing on the road, and we drew up to where they were and stopped the carriage. General Ponsonby presented the minister, Mr. Greenfield, who had come over with them. They sang "God save the Queen" with most loyal warmth; and their friendly faces and ringing cheers, when we arrived and when we left, were very gratifying. It took them three hours to come over, and they were going straight back. There were two hundred and fifty of them of all classes, from the very well dressed down to the poorest, and many fishermen amongst them. We met many of these on Saturday coming back from having sold their fish, and also on the coaches. As we returned, we met the coach where there was only just room to pass.

We stopped after we had got up to the top of the hill, overlooking the falls, and took our tea (already made, and brought with us), but were much molested by midges. We drove to above *Slatterdale*, where there is such a splendid view of the loch and of *Ben Sleach*; and the hills looked so beautifully pink. We walked on down to the small waterfall which we visited yesterday, and then drove home (General Ponsonby having walked back) by half-past seven. Reading and writing. Continued telegrams. General Ponsonby and Sir William Jenner dined also with us.

Got a few trifles from *Gairloch*, though very few were to be had, to give as souvenirs to my good people. Brown's leg, though he had to stand so much, did not hurt him, which I was thankful for, and he has waited at all our meals, made my coffee in the morning, etc. I was sorry it was our last night here, and would have liked to stay two or three days longer; but dear Arthur has been, since Saturday, at *Balmoral*, and he must leave again on the 29th. Have enjoyed this beautiful spot and glorious scenery very much. The little house was cozy and very quiet, and there were no constant interruptions as at home. Only dear Beatrice suffered much from rheumatism, which was very vexatious. Nearly opposite is a Mr. Banks's place, called *Letter Ewe*, which he lets.

Tuesday, September 18.

A wet, misty morning, no hills whatever to be seen. Got up early and breakfasted at half-past eight, and at a quarter to nine we left with regret our nice cozy little hotel at *Loch Maree*, which I hope I may some day see again. Changed horses at *Kinlochewe*. The beautiful scenery was much obscured, but it got better as we went on, though it was not a really fine day. At a little before half-past eleven we reached *Achnasheen*, where Mr. (now Sir Alexander) Matheson, M.P. (who is chairman of the railway company, and has property farther north), met us. Here we got into the train, and went on without stopping to *Dingwall*; *Strathpeffer*, and

Castle Leod, which belongs to the Duchess of Sutherland, partly hidden among trees, looked very pretty. The lochs of *Luichart* and *Garve* are most picturesque. We stopped at *Dingwall*, and *Keith*, and *Dyce Junction* as before. We had our luncheon at one o'clock, before coming to *Keith*, and tea after the *Dyce Junction*. Dear Noble was so good on the railway, and also at *Loch Maree*, where he came to our meals; but he was lost without his companions.

We reached *Ballater* at six. A very threatening evening. Such dark, heavy clouds, and the air much lighter than at *Loch Maree*. We reached *Balmoral* at a quarter to seven. Dear Arthur received us downstairs, and came up with us and stayed a little while with me. He had been out deer-stalking these two days, but got nothing.

VISIT TO BROXMOUTH.

Friday, August 23, 1878.

Had to dine at half-past five. At six o'clock, with much regret, left dear *Osborne*, with Beatrice and Leopold, and embarked on board the "Alberta" at *Trinity Pier*. We had a delightful passage, but the weather looked very threatening behind us. Passing close to the "Osborne," we saw Bertie, Alix, the boys, and the King of Denmark standing on the paddle-box. As we steamed across we saw the poor "Eurydice"* lying close off what is called "*No Man's Land*" as we had seen her the day of the Review, in fearful contrast to the beautiful fleet! We at once entered the railway train; poor Sir J. Garvock (who has resigned) was too ill to appear. We stopped at *Banbury* for refreshments, and I lay down after eleven o'clock. At *Carlisle* (at five or six in the morning) Lord Bridport, Harriet Phipps, and Mary Lascelles (who had joined at *Banbury*), Fräulein Bauer, and two of my maids left us to go to *Balmoral*, while Janie Ely, General Ponsonby, Sir W. Jenner, Mr. Yorke, Brown, Emilie, Annie, and three footmen went on with us to *Broxmouth*.

Saturday, August 23.*

Had not a very good night, and was suffering from a rather stiff shoulder. It was a very wet morning. At *Dunbar*, which we reached at a quarter to nine (where the station was very prettily decorated), were the Duke and Duchess of Roxburghe, the Grant-Sutties, the Provost, and Lord Haddington, Lord-Lieutenant of the county. We got into one of my closed landaus—Beatrice, Leopold, the Duchess of Roxburghe, and I—the others following, and drove through a small portion of *Dunbar*, Lord Haddington riding to *Broxmouth*, about a mile and a quarter from *Dunbar*. People all along the road, arches and decorations on the few cottages, and very loyal greetings.

The park is fine, with noble trees and avenues. It is only a quarter of a mile from the sea, which we could see dimly as we drove from *Dunbar*. The house* is an unpretending one, the exterior something like *Claremont*, only not so handsome, and without any steps leading up to the entrance. It has been added to at different times, and was much improved and furnished by the Duke's mother, who lived there. It is built on a slope; consequently on one side there is a story more than on the other. The house is entered by a small hall, beyond which is a narrow corridor with windows on one side and doors on the other. Turning to the left and going straight on, we came to my sitting-room (the Duchess's own sitting-room), with bow-windows down to the ground, and very comfortably arranged. Next to it, but not opening into it was Beatrice's sitting-room, a very handsomely furnished room—in fact, the drawing-room. On the other side of the hall is the dining-room—very nice and well furnished, but not large. Just opposite Beatrice's room is the staircase, also not large, and below it you turn to where Leopold had a room. The staircase lands on a corridor like the lower one. My bedroom is just over the sitting-room, with a nice little dressing-room to the right next to it (the Duchess's room). Next to the bedroom on the other side my two maids' rooms, then Janie Ely's, and beyond Beatrice's, and the maids' at the end; just outside the corridor, Brown's. All most comfortable. We came down almost directly again, and had (we three) an excellent breakfast in the dining-room. Brown waited on us with a footman, Cannon, who had gone on before. Charlie Thomson, Lockwood, and Shorter (a new footman) came with us.

As it was raining I did not go out, but soon afterwards went upstairs. After dressing, came down and rested, and read and wrote. Saw Lady Susan Suttie and her two very pretty daughters, Harriet (Haddie), like Susan Dalrymple, only much darker. Rested on the sofa, and while there received the very startling and distressing account of dear Madame Van de Weyer's death, which affected me much. It came direct and was given me straight, there being no telegraph in the house. At home this would not have happened. Sent to tell Brown, who was very much shocked.*

She was not, of course, the friend her beloved and honoured husband was; but we saw so much of her with him ever since 1840, and so much of them both when they were at *Abergeldie* in 1867, 1868, and 1870. They were always most kind to us and to our children, who grew up with theirs; and when my great sorrow came, who was kinder and more ready to help than dear M. Van de Weyer? Then, after his and his poor son Albert's death, she talked so openly to me, and I tried to comfort her. Dear pretty *New Lodge*,† kept just as he left it, was ever a pleasure for us to go to, as there was still a sort of reflected light from former times, when he charmed every one. To feel that for us it is gone for ever is dreadful, and upset me very much. Another link with the past gone!—with my beloved one, with dearest Uncle Leopold, and with *Belgium*! I feel ever more and more alone! Poor Louise Van de Weyer,

---

† It is close to Windsor.

who has been everything to her mother since Albert's death, and Nellie, how I feel for them! It was only on the 16th that their sister Alice was married to the youngest brother of poor Victoria's husband, Mr. Brand.

I had tea with Beatrice, and at a quarter-past five, the weather having cleared, drove out with her, the Duke of Roxburghe, and Leopold; Lady Ely, the Duke, General Ponsonby, and Mr. Yorke in the second carriage, and Lord Haddington on horseback in his uniform. We drove to and through *Dunbar*, escorted by the *East Lothian* Yeomanry.* The town was beautifully decorated and admirably kept. There were triumphal arches, and many very kind inscriptions. We turned into the park in front of the house, formerly occupied by the Lord Lauderdale of that day, facing the old *Castle of Dunbar* (of which very little remains) to which Queen Mary was carried as a prisoner by Bothwell after the murder of Darnley,* and where lies the harbour—a very small one. Thence past the old watch-tower hill, called *Knockenhair*, where some gipsies—in fact, the "gipsy queen"—from *Norwood* had encamped;* and where we saw several women, very dark and rather handsome and well dressed, standing close to the wall.

On through the small villages of *Belhaven* and *West Barns* by the paper mills,* a large and rather handsome building, turning from the high road to the west lodge of *Biel*, Lady Mary Nisbet Hamilton's (dear Lady Augusta Stanley's elder sister) and past the house (a dull-looking stone one, but the park is fine), and by *Belton*, Mr. Baird Hay's, to *Broxburn*. Home by seven. There was a thick fog (or "haar," as they call it in *Scotland*) from the sea, which obscured all the distance, with occasionally some rain, but nothing to signify.

Only ourselves, the Duke and Duchess, and Janie Ely to dinner, in the same dining-room. One of the Duke's people attended, besides Brown and one of our footmen. Went to my room soon after. Wrote a letter, but went early to bed—by twelve o'clock.

Sunday, August 25.

A fine hot morning. After breakfast, walked with Beatrice down under the trees to the left, along a broad walk next to the *Broxburn*, on to the end of the walk which led to the garden wall, on which roses were growing, and which is quite on the sea, which was of a deep blue. The rocks are very bad for boats. There is a walk along the top of the rocks that overhang the sea—the *Links*. This road goes on to *Dunbar*, which, with its fine church that stands so high as to be a landmark, is well seen from here. We walked back again, and I sat out near the house on the grass, under one of the small canopies which we had brought with us, and signed papers and wrote. At twelve there was service in the dining-room, performed by Mr. Buchanan of *Dunbar*, who had been for some little time tutor to Lord Charles Ker. Beatrice, Janie Ely, the Duke and Duchess, General Ponsonby, Mr. Yorke, and the Duke's upper servants were present. It was very well performed. Afterwards wrote and rested. Selected presents for the servants in the house, and things from *Dunbar* for my people.

At a quarter-past five, after tea, drove out with Beatrice, the Duchess, and Janie Ely, in the landau and four. The afternoon very bright and fine. We drove on towards *England*, in the opposite direction from yesterday's drive and parallel to the sea, though well inland. The sea of a deep blue, but a haze so dense that the distance could hardly be seen. We drove past *Baring Hill* (Sir William Miller's) to *Dunglass* (Sir Basil Hall's), a most beautiful place with splendid trees, firs like those near the *Belvidere* in *Windsor Park*, sycamores, beech, oak, etc. The road passes above a deep ravine, at the bottom of which flows a stream, and past the ruins of an old abbey or castle. The house itself (at the door of which we stopped for a few minutes to speak to Sir Basil and Lady Hall) is a large, rather dreary-looking stone house with columns. It must formerly have belonged to the Home family. The distance was so hazy that, as we drove there, we could with great diffculty faintly discern *St. Abb's Head*,[+] and the point on the *Wolf's Craig* mentioned in the "Bride of Lammermoor."* Coming back we took a long round inland, down steepish hills, through the very picturesque villages of *Brankeston* and *Innerwick*.

Home at half-past seven. Dinner as yesterday with the Duke and Duchess of Roxburghe, with the addition of Lord Haddington and General Ponsonby. Lord Haddington's father (who was for a short time one of my lords in waiting,* but never took a waiting) was brother to the late beautiful Marchioness of Breadalbane (wife of my dear old Lord Breadalbane), to the present Dowager Lady Aberdeen, to the late Lady Polwarth, and the present Dowager Lady Ashburnham.

After dinner the other gentlemen were presented, including Mr. Buchanan, who seems a very nice person. Then went to my room, and Janie Ely stayed with me a short while.

Monday, August 26.

Again this dear and blessed anniversary returns, and again without my beloved blessed One! But he is ever with me in spirit.

[+] Belonging to Mr. Home Drummond Moray of Blair Drummond and Abercairny.

When I came down to breakfast, I gave Beatrice a mounted enamelled photograph of our dear Mausoleum, and a silver belt of Montenegrin workmanship. After breakfast I gave my faithful Brown an oxidised silver biscuit-box, and some onyx studs. He was greatly pleased with the former, and the tears came to his eyes, and he said "It is too much." God knows, it is not, for one so devoted and faithful. I gave my maids also trifles from *Dunbar*; and to Janie Ely, the gentlemen, and the servants a trifle each, in remembrance of the dear day and of the place.

Walked out at half-past ten with Beatrice and the Duchess to the very fine kitchen-garden, and into the splendid hothouse where they have magnificent grapes. The peaches are also beautiful. From here we walked again along the burnside to the sea, the Duchess's pretty and very amiable collie (smaller than Noble, but with a very handsome head), Rex, going with us. We looked at the "Lord Warden" (Captain Freemantle) which arrived yesterday from *Spithead*, where we saw her in the Fleet. She had been guardship last year.

There is a pretty view from this walk to the sea over a small lake, with trees, beyond which *Dunbar* is seen in the distance. Then I sat out in the garden and wrote. After that, when Beatrice returned from a walk near the sea with the Duchess, I went to look at the gravestone of Sir William Douglas, which is quite concealed amongst the bushes near the lawn. The battle of *Dunbar* took place (September 3, 1650) close to *Broxmouth*, and Sir Walter Scott says Cromwell's camp was in the park; but this is doubtful, as it is described as on the north of the *Broxburn*. Leslie's camp was on *Doune Hill*,* conspicuous for miles round. When the Scottish army left their strong position on the hill, they came to the low ground near the park wall, Cromwell is said to have stood on the hillock where the tower in the grounds has been built, and the battle must have been fought close to the present park gate. I afterwards planted a deodara on the lawn, in the presence of the Duke and Duchess.

Indoors near one o'clock. Directly after our usual luncheon we saw Lady Susan Suttie with her two youngest children—Victoria, eleven years, and a boy of nine—and afterwards Lord and Lady Bowmont and their two fine children—the eldest, Margaret, three, and the youngest, Victoria, nine months. The boy did not come.

At half-past three started with Beatrice, Leopold, and the Duchess in the landau and four, the Duke, Lady Ely, General Ponsonby, and Mr. Yorke going in the second carriage, and Lord Haddington riding the whole way. We drove through the west part of *Dunbar*, which was very full, and where we were literally pelted with small nosegays, till the carriage was full of them, by a number of young ladies and girls; then on for some distance past the village of *Belhaven, Knochindale Hill,* where were stationed, in their best attire, the queen of the gipsies, an oldish woman with a yellow handkerchief on her head, and a youngish, very dark, and truly gipsy-like woman in velvet and a red shawl, and another woman. The queen is a thorough gipsy, with a scarlet cloak and yellow handkerchief round her head. Men in red hunting-coats, all very dark, and all standing on a platform here, bowed and waved their handkerchiefs. It was the English queen of the gipsies from *Norwood,* and not the Scottish border one.

We next passed the paper mills, where there were many people, as indeed there were at every little village and in every direction. We turned to the right, leaving the *Traprain Law,* a prominent hill, to the left, crossed the *Tyne,* and entered the really beautiful park of *Tyningham*—Lord Haddington's. More splendid trees and avenues of beech and sycamore, and one very high holly hedge. The drive under the avenues is very fine, and at the end of them you see the sea (we could, however, see it but faintly because of the haze). We passed close to the house, a handsome one, half Elizabethan, with small Scotch towers, and a very pretty terrace garden, but did not get out. Driving on through the park, which reminded me of *Windsor* and *Windsor Forest,* we again came upon the high road and passed by *Whitekirk,* a very fine old church, where numbers of people were assembled, and very soon after we saw through the haze the high hill of *North Berwick Law,* looking as though it rose up out of the sea, and another turn or two brought us to *Tantallon,** which is close to and overhangs the sea. We drove along the grass to the old ruins, which are very extensive. Sir Hew Dalrymple, to whom it belongs, received us, and took us over the old remains of the moat, including the old gateway, on which the royal standard had been hoisted. Lady Dalrymple (a Miss Arkwright) received us. No one else was there but Sir David Baird, who had joined us on the way on horseback. Sir Hew Dalrymple showed me about the ruins of this very ancient castle, the stronghold of the Douglases. It belonged once to the Earl of Angus, second husband to Queen Margaret (wife of James IV.), and was finally taken by the Covenanters.

It was unfortunately so hazy that we could not distinguish the *Bass Rock,* though usually it is quite distinctly seen, being so near; and all the fine surrounding coast was quite invisible. There was a telescope, but we could see nothing through it; it was, besides, placed too low. Seated on sofas near the ledge of the rock, we had some tea, and the scene was extremely wild. After this we left, being a good deal hurried to get back (as it was already past six), and returned partly the same way, by *Binning*

Wood, also belonging to Lord Haddington (which reminds one of *Windsor Forest*), but which we could not drive through, through *Tyningham* village to *Bellowford*, where the cross-road turned off. This brought us sooner back, and we reached *Broxmouth* by twenty-five minutes to eight, Lord Haddington riding the whole way.

We dined at half-past eight, only the Duke and Duchess of Roxburghe with ourselves. At ten or eleven o'clock we left *Broxmouth* with regret, as we had spent a most pleasant time there. We went in the same carriage (a landau), the Duchess of Roxburghe with us, and were driven by the same horses which had been out each day, including this day's long drive, the postilion Thomson riding admirably. *Dunbar* was very prettily illuminated, and the paper mills also. We took leave of the kind Duke[+] and Duchess with real regret, having enjoyed our visit greatly. All had gone off so well.

[+] He died April 23, 1879.

Death of Sir Thomas Biddulph, at Abergeldie Mains, September 28, 1878.

Wednesday, September 25, 1878.

At twenty minutes to five drove in the waggonette with the Duchess of Roxburghe and Harriet Phipps to the *Glen Gelder Shiel*,* and had tea there; and then drove to *Abergeldie Mains*, where Sir Thomas Biddulph had been very ill for a week. We got out, and I went upstairs and saw Mary (Lady) Biddulph. Sir William Jenner came into the drawing-room, and said Sir Thomas would like to see me. I went to his room with Sir William, and found Sir Thomas in bed, much the same as when I saw him on Saturday, looking very ill, but able to speak quite loud. He said "I am very bad!" I stood looking at him, and took his hand, and he said, "You are very kind to me," and I answered, pressing his hand, "You have always been very kind to *me*." I said I would come again, and left the room.

Saturday, September 28, 1878.

At eleven o'clock started off with Beatrice for *Abergeldie Mains* to inquire after Sir Thomas. I went upstairs, and Blake, the former nurse, came in much distressed, saying how ill he was. Then she asked if I would like to look at him, which I did from the door. We (Beatrice and I) were both much upset. We left, intending to return in the afternoon, and got back to *Balmoral* by a quarter to twelve. Sat writing in the garden-cottage. While I was writing, at a quarter to one Brown came round with a note in his hand, crying, and said "It's all over!" It was from Sir William, saying that dear "Sir Thomas passed away at twenty minutes past twelve. Lady Biddulph as well as the children were with him to the last." We were so distressed that we had not remained at the house, and Brown so vexed and so kind and feeling.* Dreadful! Such a loss! Dear Sir Thomas was such an excellent, honest, upright, wonderfully unselfish and disinterested man—so devoted to me and mine. Under a somewhat undemonstrative exterior, he was the kindest and most tender-hearted of men. How terrible is this loss for his poor, poor wife and the children who adored him!

Thursday, October 3, 1878.

A most lovely, almost summer day, and very warm. At a quarter-past ten drove with Beatrice, the Duchess of Roxburghe, and Lady Ely

(Harriet Phipps, Fraulein Bauer, and the gentlemen having gone on before), to *Abergeldie Mains*. We got out and went into the dining-room, where the coffin was placed. Poor Mary Biddulph and her two children received us there. Her brother, Captain Conway Seymour, and the female servants, ourselves, and the ladies were present. No men came into the room; they remained in the hall, the door being left open. Mr. Campbell came in a few minutes afterwards, and performed a short but very impressive service, just reading a few verses from Scripture, and offering up a beautiful prayer. The coffin left the house directly after, followed by Captain Conway Seymour. Bertie and his three gentlemen, Lord Bridport, General Ponsonby, Sir William Jenner, and Dr. Profeit[†] followed in carriages to *Ballater*, as also did Lord Macduff and Colonel Farquharson.

We sat a little while with poor Mary, and then left. Lady Biddulph and her children went in the same train with the honoured remains of her dear husband to *Windsor*.

[†] My Commissioner since November 1875; an excellent man, universally beloved.

Memorial Cross to the Princess Alice, Grand Duchess of Hesse.

Balmoral,
May 22, 1879.

We arrived at *Balmoral* at a quarter-past three. At a quarter to six walked with Beatrice to look at the Cross which I have now put up to my darling Alice. It is in *Aberdeenshire* granite, twelve feet three inches high. It is beautiful. The inscription is:—

TO THE DEAR MEMORY
OF

ALICE, GRAND DUCHESS OF HESSE,

Princess of Great Britain and Ireland,

BORN APRIL 25, 1843, DIED DEC. 14, 1878,

THIS IS ERECTED

BY HER SORROWING MOTHER

QUEEN VICTORIA.

"Her name shall live, though now she is no more."*

We then walked on to Donald Stewart's, where we went in; thence down to Grant's. In both places they were quite overcome to see us after darling Alice's loss, and poor Grant began sobbing and could not come into the room where we were.† The arrival at *Balmoral* to-day was most sad. Everything came before me—the dreadful anxiety about little Ernie,† the sorrow about dear little May,‡ and the anxiety about the others. And, to crown all, the thought of darling Alice gone, and, after her, dear little Waldie.§

---

† Grant died November 17, 1878 [*sic*], in his 70th year, at Robrec, close to Balmoral, where he had lived since 1875, when he was pensioned, and where we went very often to see him. I visited him almost daily during the last days of his life, and was present at the funeral service at his house (November 21). He is buried in the churchyard at Braemar.

† Alice's son, who, with four of his sisters and his father, was lying ill of diphtheria in November.

‡ Dear Alice's youngest child, who died of diphtheria November 16, 1878. We received the news while we were at Balmoral.

§ Prince Waldemar, the Crown Princess of Germany's third and youngest son, who died of diphtheria on March 27 of this year.

Death of the Prince Imperial.
June 1879.

Balmoral Castle,
Thursday, June 19, 1879.

At twenty minutes to eleven Brown knocked and came in, and said there was bad news; and when I, in alarm, asked what, he replied, "The young French Prince is killed;" and when I could not take it in, and asked several times what it meant, Beatrice, who then came in with the telegram in her hand, said, "Oh! the Prince Imperial is killed!"* I feel a sort of thrill of horror now while I write the words.

I put my hands to my head and cried out, "No, no! it cannot, cannot be true! It can't be!" And then dear Beatrice, who was crying very much, as I did too, gave me the annexed telegram from Lady Frere:—

Government House, Cape Town, June 19, 1879.

To General Sir Henry Ponsonby, Balmoral Castle.—For the Information of Her Majesty the Queen.

The melancholy tidings have been telegraphed from Natal, that the Prince Imperial, when out on a reconnaissance from Colonel Wood's camp on the 1st of June, was killed by a number of Zulus* concealed in a field in which the Prince Imperial and his party had dismounted to rest and feed their horses. No official particulars yet received by me. The Prince Imperial's body found and buried with full military honours at Camp Itelezi, and after being embalmed will be conveyed to England. This precedes the press telegrams by one hour. I have sent to Lord Sydney to beg him, if possible, to break the sad intelligence to the Empress before the press telegrams arrive.

To die in such an awful, horrible way! Poor, poor dear Empress! her only, only child—her all gone! And such a real misfortune! I was quite beside myself; and both of us have hardly had another thought since.

We sent for Janie Ely, who was in the house when he was born, and was so devoted to him; and he was so good! Oh! it is too, too awful! The more one thinks of it, the worse it is! I was in the greatest distress, Brown so distressed; every one quite stunned.* Got to bed very late; it was dawning! and little sleep did I get.

Friday, June 20.

Had a bad, restless night, haunted by this awful event, seeing those horrid Zulus constantly before me, and thinking of the poor Empress, who did not yet know it. Was up in good time.

My accession day, forty-two years ago; but no thought of it in presence of this frightful event.

Had written many telegrams last night. One came from Lord Sydney, saying he was going down early this morning to break this dreadful news to the poor afflicted mother. How dreadful! Received distressed and horrified telegrams from some of my children. Heard by telegram also from Sir Stafford Northcote that the news arrived in the House of Commons; that much sympathy had been shown. It came to Colonel Stanley. Telegraphed to many.

Packed my boxes with Brown. Was so horrified. Always, at *Balmoral* in May or June, dreadful news, or news of deaths of Royal persons, come, obliging the State parties to be put off.

At twenty minutes past eleven drove to Donald Stewart's and got out to say "Good-bye," as well as to the Profeits, and stopped at the door of the shop to wish Mrs. Symon good-bye, and also at Brown's house, to take leave of the Hugh Browns. Home at twenty minutes past twelve. Writing.

Received a telegram from Lord Sydney, saying that he had informed the poor dear Empress of these dreadful news. She could not believe it for some time, and was afterwards quite overwhelmed.

How dreadful! Took luncheon with Beatrice in my darling Albert's room. Beatrice was much upset, as indeed we all were. Even those who did not know them felt the deepest sympathy, and were in a state of consternation. He was so good and so much beloved. So strange that, as last time, our departure should be saddened, as, indeed, it has been every year, at least for three or four years, by the occurrence of deaths of great people or of relations.

We left *Balmoral* at half-past one, Janie Ely and Leila Erroll (full of feeling) going with Beatrice and me. It was a pity to leave when everything was in its greatest beauty. The lilacs just preparing to burst. Near *Ballater* there was a bush of white lilac already out. The dust dreadful. Very little whin, and far less of that beautiful broom, out, which was always such a pretty sight from the railway at this time of the year. We reached *Aberdeen* at twenty-eight minutes to four, and soon after had our tea.

At the *Bridge of Dun* we got newspapers with some of the sad details. Thence we turned off and passed again close to the sea by *Arbroath, East*

Haven, Carnoustie (where poor Symon went and got so ill he had to be taken back), all lying low, with golf links near each, and the line passing over long grass strips with mounds and small indentations of the sea, such as are seen near sands, where there are no rocks and the coast is flat; but the ground rises as you approach *Dundee*.

We reached the *Tay Bridge* station at six. Immense crowds everywhere, flags waving in every direction, and the whole population out; but one's heart was too sad for anything. The Provost, splendidly attired, presented an address. Ladies presented beautiful bouquets to Beatrice and me. The last time I was at *Dundee* was in September 1844,* just after Affie's birth, when we landed there on our way to *Blair*, and Vicky, then not four years old, the only child with us, was carried through the crowd by old Renwick.† We embarked there also on our way back.

We stopped here about five minutes, and then began going over the marvellous *Tay Bridge*, which is rather more than a mile and a half long.† It was begun in 1871. There were great diffculties in laying the foundation, and some lives were lost. It was finished in 1878.

Mr. Bouch, who was presented at *Dundee*, was the engineer. It took us, I should say, about eight minutes going over. The view was very fine.

The boys of the training-ship, with their band, looked very well. The line through the beautifully wooded county of *Fife* was extremely pretty, especially after *Ladybank Junction*, where we stopped for a few minutes, and where Mr. Balfour of *Balbirnie* brought a basket of flowers. We met him and his wife, Lady Georgiana, in *Scotland* in 1842. We passed near *Loch Leven*, with the ruined castle in which poor Queen Mary was confined (which we passed in 1842), stopping there a moment and in view of the "*Lomonds*," past *Dollar* and *Tillicoultry*, the situation of which, in a wooded green valley at the foot of the hills, is quite beautiful, and reminded me of *Italy* and *Switzerland*, through *Sauchie*, *Alloa*, all manufacturing towns, and then close under *Wallace's Monument*. We reached the *Stirling Station*, which was dreadfully crowded, at eighteen minutes past eight (the people everywhere very enthusiastic), and after leaving it we had some good cold dinner, which reminded me much of our refreshments in the train during our charming Italian journey.

We got Scotch papers as we went along, giving harrowing details (all by telegraph) from the front, or rather from *Natal* to *Cape Town*, then by ship to *Madiera*, and thence again by telegraph here. Of nothing else

---

† Sergeant footman at the time, who died in 1871.
† The Tay Bridge was destroyed in the same year (1879) in the gale of the night of December 29, when a whole train with upwards of eighty passengers was precipitated into the Tay.

could we think. Janie Ely got in at *Beattock Summit*, and went with us as far as *Carlisle*. She showed us a *Dundee* paper, called the "Evening Telegraph," which contained the fullest and most dreadful accounts. Monstrous! To think of that dear young man, the apple of his mother's eye, born and nurtured in the purple, dying thus, is too fearful, too awtul; and inexplicable and dreadful that the others should not have turned round and fought for him.* It is too horrible!

HOME-COMING OF THEIR ROYAL HIGHNESSES
THE DUKE AND DUCHESS OF CONNAUGHT.
SEPTEMBER 1879.

Balmoral Castle,
Friday, September 5, 1879.

At two I started off with Beatrice and Janie Ely (Sir Henry Ponsonby and General Gardiner having gone on to *Ballater*) in the landau and four, the postilions in blue, outriders in red, Brown in full dress, and Power behind our carriage. We arrived at four minutes to three, and waited in the carriage till we heard the train (special) was approaching, when we got out. In two or three minutes more they were there, and dear Arthur and Louise Margaret stepped out, and were warmly embraced by us. I gave her a nosegay of heather. She had also received others. The guard (Royal Scots) were out.

When we reached the *Balmoral* bridge, we went at a slow pace, passing under the arch composed of moss and heather, on which was wrought, in flowers, "Welcome to Balmoral" on one side, and "Ceud mille Failte" on the other, "A. W." and "L. M." on the outside of each; and there all the people stood—all our kilted people. The ladies and gentlemen, including Lord Chelmsford and Mr. Cross, Christian Victor, and Albert (Helena's boys), and also the Misses Pitt, were there.

Arthur spoke a few words from the carriage, and then Dr. Profeit said a few words; after which, preceded by the pipers playing, and all our kilted men and the rest fellowing, we went at a very slow foot's pace to the Castle.

At the gate three pretty little girls of Colonel Clarke's (Bertie's equerry staying at *Birkhall*) threw nosegays into the carriage, one being of *marguerites*. Every one who was there followed on foot.

Only Captain Fitzgerald came with Arthur and Louise Margaret.

When we got out, everybody having come up, Dr. Profeit proposed Arthur's and Louischen's health, which every one drank with cheers. Arthur thanked. Then we went in, and Arthur, Louischen, and the two boys took tea with us in the library.*

His Royal Highness the Duke of Connaught's Cairn.

Monday, September 8, 1879.

A fine morning. Breakfasted with Beatrice, Arthur, and Louischen in the garden cottage, and at eleven we started for Arthur's Cairn, I on my pony "Jessie," Beatrice walking to the top. We were met by Arthur and Louischen, and went on to near the cairn, to the right of Campbell's path. I got off when we were near it; and here were assembled all the ladies and gentlemen, also Dr. Profeit, the keepers and servants belonging to the place with their families, and almost all our servants from the house. When we had got to the top and had our glasses filled, and were standing close to the cairn, Dr. Profeit, with a few appropriate words complimentary to Arthur, and with many good wishes for both, proposed their health, which was drunk with three times three. Then Arthur, with great readiness, returned thanks in a little speech. My health followed, also with loud cheering; and then Brown said they ought to drink the health of Princess Beatrice, which Cowley took up and proposed; and it was received with many cheers. Fern (who with the other dogs was there) resented the cheering, and barked very much. We all placed a stone on the cairn, on which was inscribed—

Arthur Duke of Connaught and Strathearne,

Married to Princess Louise Margaret of Prussia,
March 13, 1879.

After a few minutes we left, I walking down the whole way. We stopped at Dr. Profeit's on our way down, and here I got on my pony again.*

Visit to the Glen Gelder Shiel.

Balmoral,
October 6, 1879.

At ten minutes past four drove with the Empress Eugénie[+] (who had driven up from *Abergeldie*) in the victoria to the *Glen Gelder Shiel*, or *Ruidh na Bhan Righ* (the Queen's Shiel). The evening was perfectly beautiful, warm, and clear, and bright. The Empress was pleased with the little Shiel, which contains only two small rooms and a little kitchen. It stands in a very wild solitary spot looking up to *Lochnagar*, which towers up immediately above the house, though to reach *Lochnagar* itself would take a very long time. We walked on along the footpath above the *Gelder* for a mile and a half, the dogs, which had come up, following us, and the Empress talked a great deal, and most pleasantly, about former times.

When we came back to the little Shiel, after walking for an hour, we had tea. Brown had caught some excellent trout and cooked them with oatmeal, which the dear Empress liked extremely, and said would be her dinner. It was a glorious evening—the hills pink, and the sky so clear.

We got back at twenty minutes past six, and the Empress drove back to *Abergeldie* with her lady.*

[+] The Empress was staying at Abergeldie, to which I had urged her to come for a little quiet and change of air after her terrible misfortune.

Victory of Tel-el-Kebir and Home-Coming of their Royal Highnesses the Duke and Duchess of Albany. September 1882.

Monday, September 11, 1882.

Received a telegram in cipher from Sir John McNeill, marked *very secret*, saying that it was "determined to attack the enemy with a very large force on Wednesday." How anxious this made us, God only knows; and yet this long delay had also made us very anxious. No one to know, though all expected something at the time.*

Tuesday, September 12.

Drove at ten minutes to five, with Beatrice, Louischen, and Harriet, to the *Glen Gelder Shiel*, where we had tea, and I sketched. The sky was so beautiful. We walked on the road back, and came home at twenty minutes past seven. How anxious we felt, I need not say; but we tried not to give way. Only the ladies dined with us.

I prayed earnestly for my darling child, and longed for the morrow to arrive. Read Körner's beautiful "Gebet vor der Schlacht," "Vater, ich rufe Dich" (Prayer before the Battle, "Father, I call on Thee"). My beloved husband used to sing it often. My thoughts were entirely fixed on *Egypt* and the coming battle. My nerves were strained to such a pitch by the intensity of my anxiety and suspense that they seemed to feel as though they were all alive.

Wednesday, September 13.

Woke very often. Raw and dull. Took my short walk, and breakfasted in the cottage. Had a telegram that the army marched out last night. What an anxious moment! We walked afterwards as far as the arch for Leopold's reception, which was a very pretty one, and placed as nearly where it had been on previous occasions, only rather nearer Middleton's lodge, and thence back to the cottage, where I sat and wrote and signed, etc.

Another telegram, also from Reuter, saying that fighting was going on, and that the enemy had been routed with heavy loss at *Tel-el-Kebir*. Much agitated.

On coming in got a telegram from Sir John McNeill, saying, "A great victory; Duke safe and well." Sent all to Louischen. The excitement very great. Felt unbounded joy and gratitude for God's great goodness and mercy.

The same news came from Lord Granville and Mr. Childers, though not yet from Sir Garnet Wolseley. A little later, just before two, came the following most welcome and gratifying telegram from Sir Garnet Wolseley:—

Ismalia, September 13, 1882.
Tel-el-Kebir.—From Wolseley to the Queen, Balmoral.

Attacked Arabi's position at five this morning. His strongly entrenched position was most bravely and gallantly stormed by the Guards and line, while cavalry and horse artillery worked round their left flank. At seven o'clock I was in complete possession of his whole camp. Many railway trucks, with quantities of supplies, fallen into our hands. Enemy completely routed, and his loss has been very heavy; also regret to say we have suffered severely. Duke of Connaught is well, and behaved admirably, leading his brigade to the attack.

Brown brought the telegram, and followed me to Beatrice's room, where Louischen was, and I showed it to her.* I was myself quite upset, and embraced her warmly, saying what joy and pride and cause of thankfulness it was to know our darling safe, and so much praised! I feel quite beside myself for joy and gratitude, though grieved to think of our losses, which, however, have not proved to be so serious as first reported. We were both much overcome.

We went to luncheon after this, having sent many telegrams, and receiving many. At ten minutes past three drove with Beatrice and Lady Southampton to *Ballater*. We got out of the carriage, and the train arrived almost immediately, and Leopold and Helen stepped out; she was dressed in grey with bonnet to match.

The guard of honour, Seaforth Highlanders (Duke of Albany's), out, and many people. Leopold and Helen got at once into the landau with us two, and we drove straight to *Balmoral*. At the bridge Louischen and Horatia[+] were waiting in a carriage, and followed us. Beyond the bridge, and when we had just passed under the arch, the carriage stopped, and Dr. Profeit said a few words of welcome, for which Leopold thanked. Here everybody was assembled—all our gentlemen and ladies, and those from *Birkhall* and the *Mains*, and all the tenants from the three estates, all our servants, etc.

[+] The Hon. Horatia Stopford.

The pipes preceded, playing the "Highland Laddie," Brown and all our other kilted men walking alongside, and before and behind the carriage everybody else close following—and goodly number they were. We got out at the door, and went just beyond the arch, all our people standing in a line headed by our Highlanders. A table with whisky and glasses was placed up against the house, next to which stood all the ladies and gentlemen. Dr. Profeit gave Leopold's and Helen's healths, and after these had been drunk, Brown stepped forward and said, nearly as follows: "Ladies and gentlemen, let us join in a good Highland cheer for the Duke and Duchess of Albany; may they live long and die happy!" which pleased every one, and there were hearty cheers.

Then I asked Leopold to propose "The Victorious Army in *Egypt*," with darling Arthur's health, which was heartily responded to, and poor Louischen was quite upset. After this Dr. Profeit proposed "The Duchess of Connaught," and at Brown's suggestion he also proposed "The little Princess." The sweet little one had witnessed the procession in Chapman's (her nurse's) arms with her other attendants, and was only a little way off when her health was drunk.

This over, we went in and had tea upstairs in my room—Louischen, Beatrice, and I. Louischen had received a very long and most interesting letter from Arthur about that dreadful march on the 25th (dated 26th, but finished later). A telegram from Sir Garnet Wolseley to Mr. Childers, with fuller accounts, arrived. The loss, thank God! is not so heavy as we feared at first. A bonfire was to be lit by my desire on the top of *Craig Gowan* at nine, just where there had been one in 1856 after the fall of *Sevastopol*, when dearest Albert went up to it at night with Bertie and Affie. That was on September 10, very nearly the same time twenty-six years ago!*

Went to Louischen, who read me portions of Arthur's long letter. The description of his and the officers' sufferings and privations, as well as those of the poor men, made me miserable.

Only ourselves to dinner; and at nine Beatrice, Louischen, Lady Southampton, and the gentlemen, and many of our people, walked up (with the pipes playing) to the top of *Craig Gowan*—rather venturesome in the dark; and we three (Leopold, Helen, and I) went up to Beatrice's room, and from there we saw the bonfire lit and blazing, and could distinguish figures, and hear the cheering and pipes. They were soon back, and I went and sat with Beatrice, Louischen, and Lady Southampton, who were having a little supper in Louischen's room.

Endless telegrams! What a day of gratitude and joy, but mingled with sorrow and anxiety for the many mourners and the wounded and dying!

Conclusion.*

A few words I must add in conclusion to this volume.

The faithful attendant who is so often mentioned throughout these Leaves, is no longer with her whom he served so truly, devotedly, untiringly.

In the fulness of health and strength he was snatched away from his career of usefulness, after an illness of only three days, on the 27th of March of this year, respected and beloved by all who recognised his rare worth and kindness of heart, and truly regretted by all who knew him.

His loss to me (ill and helpless as I was at the time from an accident) is irreparable, for he deservedly possessed my entire confidence; and to say that he is daily, nay, hourly, missed by me, whose lifelong gratitude he won by his constant care, attention, and devotion, is but a feeble expression of the truth.

> A truer, nobler, trustier heart,
> More loyal, and more loving, never beat
> Within a human breast.*

BALMORAL: *November* 1883.

EXPLANATORY NOTES

No explanatory note is included for terms defined in the Glossary (449–55).

LEAVES FROM THE JOURNAL OF
OUR LIFE IN THE HIGHLANDS

7 *anything written by herself*: for Arthur Helps's role as editor, see Introduction and Note on the Texts (ix–xi and lii–liv). Lifelong, the Queen kept a diary with daily or near daily entries. Correspondence between Helps and the Queen reveals that she guided his processes of selecting entries about life at Balmoral and of editing them to be read independently from the rest of the diary. The Editor's Preface was heavily revised: twelve distinct proof stages are preserved.

8 *the additions were accordingly made*: see Introduction (xlv–xlviii) and note to *Leaves*, 139, for the addition of these further journeys or royal progresses in the version of *Leaves* to be offered to the public, following the initial printing of entries solely about life at Balmoral for the private edition.

It will easily be seen . . . public cares: this paragraph of the Preface was rewritten several times. In one proof it read: 'All reference to great political events, all those parts of the Journal which [would] hereafter be most valuable to the statesman and the historian, have been studiously omitted, and the book is nothing more than might have been written by any lady possessing considerable powers of observation, a great love of natural scenery, and also an unusual aptitude for rapidly depicting it, for the accounts of these journeys and illustrations of them were previously written down in the most rapid manner, as memoranda to recall the scenes hereafter in the Author's mind, rather than as finished pictures of them.' Most of this passage (starting at 'nothing more') was then crossed out, and a slip of paper tucked into the proof bears a revision in the Queen's handwriting which is closer to the published version, but which describes the Queen's writing as 'artless', her enjoyment as 'relish' (revised to 'delight'), and her practice as a writer as 'jotting rapidly'. This version was further revised before publication.

the notes to the Volume: the footnotes about people who worked for the Queen, with added information about their families, did not appear in the original journal. A few brief footnotes appear in the earliest proof of the private edition (which later served as the first proof of *Leaves*). To compose the footnotes on her servants, the Queen sought the help of her Commissioner at Balmoral, Dr Andrew Robertson, in researching her servants' histories and ancestries. See *Leaves*, 64, 67, and 77 (and notes), for examples of footnotes amplified and edited over the course of several proof volumes, as the Queen learned more about these individuals.

Patriarchal feeling: the claim that the Queen demonstrates 'Patriarchal feeling' by writing the footnotes was added to the Preface after it had already been set in type. Pasted into the last page of one of several proofs of the Preface is a slip of paper, headed with the words '(To be inserted)', on which is handwritten: 'No observant [word missing] can fail to remark the genial—the almost patriarchal manner in which the Royal personages treat their immediate dependents—a point of domestic conduct, which, the Editor has always thought, would, if more generally adopted, tend to make home life more gracious, more beautiful, & much more happy both for Masters and servants.' 'Patriarchal' alludes to the quasi-familial relation between clan chief and vassal that obtained (or was thought to have obtained) in the ancient Highlands, in contrast to the modern relation between a constitutional monarch and the citizens of her nation; see Introduction (xxxiii–xxxiv).

17 *Royal George Yacht*: HMY *Royal George*, named for King George III, was a royal yacht of the Royal Navy, a three-masted sailing ship built in 1817; it was last used by the Queen in 1842 and was broken up in 1905.

for the railroad: the first railway station at Windsor was not built until 1849, so the royal party travelled in horse-drawn carriages to the station at Slough, then by train to London's Paddington Station, and then in horse-drawn carriages to Woolwich.

Woolwich: between the sixteenth and nineteenth centuries, there was a naval dockyard at Woolwich, east of London on the south side of the River Thames. From Woolwich, HMY *Royal George* could sail out to sea, accompanied by a squadron of naval vessels.

Albert and I immediately stepped into our barge: according to Princess Beatrice's transcription of the original diary, written for private perusal, the Queen originally wrote 'we two'.

the Trinity-House steamer goes with us: the Corporation of Trinity House of Deptford Strond is the official authority for lighthouses in England, Wales, the Channel Islands, and Gibraltar. Trinity House also provides and maintains other navigational aids, such as light-vessels, buoys, and maritime communication systems, and it provides pilots for ships trading in northern European waters. The historic right of Trinity House to escort the sovereign when travelling by ship in territorial waters is still exercised on ceremonial occasions, and during this duty the White Ensign is flown.

18 *Flamborough Head*: a chalk headland with sheer white cliffs on the Yorkshire coast just south of Scarborough. The cliff top has two lighthouses, the older one dating from 1669 and Flamborough Head Lighthouse from 1806.

St. Abb's Head: a rocky promontory near the village of St Abbs in Berwickshire, Scotland. St Abb's Head Lighthouse began service in 1862. On a nearby hill are the remains of the monastery settlement of Saint Æbbe, who *c.* AD 643 established a monastery where both monks and nuns lived in beehive huts made from mud and branches.

Bamborough Castle: an ancient castle, dramatically located on a rocky outcrop near the village of Bamburgh on the north-east coast of England. The site was originally the location of a Celtic Brittonic fort known as Din Guarie, and may have been the capital of the kingdom of Bernicia, from *c.*420 to 547. In the nineteenth century, the ruinous site was purchased by the industrialist William Armstrong, who completed its restoration.

Ferne Island . . . Holy Island: Grace Horsley Darling (1815–1844) was the daughter of an English lighthouse keeper, who kept the light on Farne Island (as it is now spelled), one of a group of rocky islands in the North Sea offshore from Bamburgh Castle. In 1838, rowing in a gale and heavy seas, she and her father rescued nine survivors from the shipwrecked steamship *Forfarshire*. Her bravery brought her national fame. Holy Island or Lindisfarne is a tidal island close to the coast, north-west of the Farne Islands; in 635 the first Christian monastery in England was founded there by St Aidan and his fellow monks from Iona, an island off the coast of Scotland.

a little sailor-boy: the original entry, according to Princess Beatrice's transcription, included details about the sailors which were omitted for publication. After 'sailor-boy' the entry continued: 'Kew, one of the good "Emeralders" danced the Hornpipe; he & Swat are on board & so happy to be with me on this voyage.'

many bonfires: according to Thomas Dick Lauder's contemporary *Memorial of the Royal Progress in Scotland* (1843), enormous welcoming bonfires were set ablaze all along the Firth of Forth, on Arthur's Seat in Edinburgh, on the top of Ben Nevis, and as far away as Fort William.

so well conducted: here Princess Beatrice's edited transcription of the original diary continues: 'Always after their supper, they all stand on the deck, while the Officers go past them to see that they are quite sober. The Officer on board, who had the signalling under him, is a very pleasant, intelligent, & good-looking young man, of the name of Inglefield, who was at Acre. He gave us 2 drawings he had made, whilst he was there.' Acre is a coastal city in present-day Israel.

19 *Macduff held out against Macbeth*: in Shakespeare's *Macbeth*, Macduff, Thane of Fife, is Macbeth's main antagonist. Macduff, whose family Macbeth has had murdered, slays Macbeth. The reference to Shakespeare's only play set in Scotland serves here to bring the country into the fold of English literature.

waited for us yesterday: Lauder's *Memorial* estimates that 100,000 people, in addition to local inhabitants, crowded into the streets of Granton Pier and Edinburgh, waited throughout the day of the Queen's expected arrival, and then returned to their vantage points the next day to wait until the delayed royal party finally arrived.

the Provost: 'Lord Provost' is the title of the chief administrative officer of a Scottish municipality, corporation or burgh; the role is equivalent to that of mayor in England.

Burns' Monument: the Burns Monument in Edinburgh, designed by the architect Thomas Hamilton and constructed 1831–9, is an excellent example of Greek Revival architecture. It is situated in a prominent position on the slopes of Regent Road, and overlooks the city to the south. Modelled on the ancient Greek Choragic Monument of Lysicrates in Athens, it originally contained a statue of the poet by the Scottish artist John Flaxman. The Queen mentions the monument not for itself but among a list of other 'magnificent buildings' that add to her impression of a great and unique city.

19 *Arthur's Seat*: (Scottish Gaelic, Suidhe Artair) the main peak in a group of volcanic hills that form most of Edinburgh's Holyrood Park, just west of the city centre. It is traditionally thought to be named for King Arthur; the 'seat' itself is an alcove in a rocky crag near the top of the hill.

Archers Guard: the Royal Company of Archers (or the Royal Archers Body Guard) was and is a ceremonial troop, which was founded as a private archery club in Scotland in 1676 and received a royal charter from Queen Anne in 1704. Although it supported the Jacobite cause in 1745–6, by the time of George IV's visit to Edinburgh in 1822, it served as the British monarch's honorary bodyguard. The Queen is mistaken when she states that it originated as an armed Scots force, bound, since the fifteenth century, to be in attendance on the monarch. James IV of Scotland was killed in a war with England at the Battle of Flodden Field in Northumberland in 1513.

Frederick Enoch, editorial assistant for the publisher Smith, Elder, & Co. had been asked to verify or correct the Queen's historical information. On the proof, Enoch wrote below this footnote, in ink: 'Fullerton says "The Royal Company of Archers was instituted in 1703 by a Charter of Queen Anne, [as] the Queen's body-guard in Scotland."' Enoch's note was then cancelled with a pencil scribble and the Queen's inaccurate but romantic version remained when the book was published. 'Fullerton' is probably a reference to a work produced in 1845 by Fullarton & Co., publishers in Edinburgh, London, and Dublin—the two-volume *Topographical, Statistical and Historical Gazetteer of Scotland*; copies of both volumes are in the Royal Library. Fullarton published various other historical and reference works about Scotland.

20 *Craigmillar Castle*: a ruined medieval castle south-east of Edinburgh's city centre. The Preston family of Craigmillar, the local feudal barons, began building the castle in the late fourteenth century, and construction continued through the sixteenth. The castle is best known for its association with Mary Queen of Scots, who stayed there in 1563 and again in 1566 following an illness after the birth of her son, the future James VI of Scotland and I of England. Before Mary left on 7 December 1566, a pact known as the 'Craigmillar Bond' was made, with or without her knowledge, to dispose of her husband Henry Stewart, Lord Darnley. By 1775 the castle was abandoned and ruined, becoming a popular tourist attraction. A proposal to renovate the building for the use of Queen Victoria was put forward in 1842 but came to nothing.

Dalkeith: Dalkeith Palace, a country house south-east of Edinburgh, was the seat of the Dukes of Buccleuch (1642–1914); the Duchess of Buccleuch was Victoria's Mistress of the Robes. The twelfth-century Dalkeith Castle belonged first to Clan Graham and then to Clan Douglas; the present palace was built in 1701–11. Prince Charles Edward Stuart, Bonnie Prince Charlie, stayed two nights at Dalkeith in 1745, and King George IV slept there on his visit to Edinburgh in 1822, in preference to the Palace of Holyroodhouse, which was in poor condition.

21 *Holyrood Palace*: the Palace of Holyroodhouse has been the official residence of the British monarch in Scotland since the sixteenth century and is used for state occasions. It is located at the bottom of the Royal Mile in Edinburgh. The ruined Augustinian Holyrood Abbey in the palace grounds was founded

in 1128. The name derives either from a vision of the cross witnessed by King David I, or from a relic of the True Cross, known as the Holy Rood or Black Rood, that belonged to St Margaret, David's mother. The abbey became an important administrative centre: Robert I (Robert Bruce), King of Scots, held a parliament at the abbey in 1326, and by the later fifteenth century it had dedicated royal apartments. James IV constructed a new Gothic palace adjacent to the abbey in anticipation of his marriage to Margaret Tudor in 1503.

The Palace of Holyroodhouse as it stands today was built between 1671 and 1678, with the exception of a tower preserved from the sixteenth-century building. The chapel occupied the north range of the quadrangle, with the Queen's apartments located in the south range. On the first visit of Queen Victoria to Scotland in 1842, she was prevented from visiting Holyroodhouse by an outbreak of scarlet fever. In preparation for her 1850 visit, renovations and redecorations were carried out. Victoria was able to take up a second-floor apartment in 1871, freeing up the former royal apartments as dining and drawing rooms and a throne room. From 1854 the historic apartments in the north-west tower were opened to the public.

Knox's House: the traditional name for a historic house in Edinburgh built from 1490 onwards, featuring a fine wooden gallery and hand-painted ceiling. Although it has been called 'John Knox's House' from the mid-nineteenth century onwards, Knox lived elsewhere in the city.

Regent Murray's House: also known as Moray House, this residence in Edinburgh is an amalgamation of three buildings of different ages, originally grouped around a small courtyard. Although much altered by its occupants down the centuries, it remains one of the few original aristocratic houses in the Canongate district of the city's Old Town, and some of its seventeenth- and eighteenth-century decorated ceilings survive. Moray House became a teacher training college in 1848 and is now part of the University of Edinburgh.

Fortunes of Nigel: *The Fortunes of Nigel* (1822), one of Sir Walter Scott's Waverley novels, focuses on the Scottish community in London during the reign of James VI of Scotland and I of England. The Scottish heroine Margaret Ramsay, who rescues the hero from dangerous entanglement in London court intrigue, is the goddaughter of George Heriot, founder of the hospital that the Queen admires here. The novel's phenomenal sales did not match its critical estimation; the Queen's familiarity with it testifies to the popularity of the Waverley novels, Scott's series about the social history of Scotland's contested relationship with England from the Middle Ages through the Jacobite rebellions and their aftermath. Although the Queen does not mention Sir Walter Scott's arrangements for King George IV's visit to Edinburgh in 1822, her visit too reflects Scott's knowledge of the city.

Dalmeny, Lord Roseberry's: Dalmeny House, the home of the Earl and Countess of Rosebery, is a country house built in Tudor Gothic style in the early nineteenth century on the Firth of Forth, west of Edinburgh. The Queen misspells Rosebery's title here, but renders it correctly in *More Leaves*.

the Bass Rock: the Bass Rock, or simply the Bass, is a volcanic island off the south shore of the Firth of Forth, where it meets the North Sea. The rock is uninhabited but was once settled by an early Christian hermit; the remains of an ancient chapel survive. Later it was the site of a castle, which after the Commonwealth period was used as a prison. It is home to a large colony of gannets.

22 *bright-coloured petticoats*: in Princess Beatrice's transcription of the Queen's diary, which in this case appears to represent the original from which the published entries were drawn, this passage reads: 'They look very clean & somewhat Dutch like, in their snowy white caps & bright coloured skirts. I have tried to make the annexed little sketch.' The sketch was not retained with the diary transcription.

accounts of our little children: in Princess Beatrice's transcription, the diary originally read: 'Received from Ldy Lyttelton, good accounts of dear "Pussy," & the Baby': 'Pussy' and the 'Baby' are, respectively, Vicky, almost two years old, and the Prince of Wales, not yet one.

Newbattle, Lord Lothian's place: Newbattle Abbey is a country house near the village of Newbattle in Midlothian, the home of the Earls, later Marquesses, of Lothian. In 1140 a Cistercian monastery was founded on this site. Part of the abbey survives at the core of the current building, rebuilt most recently in 1858.

Dalhousie, Lord Dalhousie's: Dalhousie Castle is near the town of Bonnyrigg, south of Edinburgh. The castle was the seat of the Earls of Dalhousie, the chiefs of Clan Ramsay. The patriarch of the clan was Simundus de Ramesie (Simon of Ramsey), an English knight of Norman descent, who followed David, Earl of Huntingdon, to Scotland in about 1140, when David inherited the Scottish Crown and became David I. The first castle at Dalhousie was of red stone and was situated in a strategic spot overlooking the River Esk (there is another River Esk just south of Balmoral Castle). Most of the current castle was built in the seventeenth century, but a tower remains from the mid-fifteenth century. In 1400 Sir Alexander Ramsay withstood a six-month siege by English forces led by King Henry IV. Oliver Cromwell used the castle as a base for his invasion of Scotland in 1650.

23 *I held a Drawing-room*: a 'Drawing Room' in this sense was a formal court function at which ladies were presented to the monarch (as opposed to a Levee, when gentlemen were presented). During the reign of Queen Victoria, Drawing Rooms took place in the afternoon and Levees in the morning. The name of this ceremony derives from that of the room within the royal residence in which it took place.

In Princess Beatrice's transcription, and therefore probably in the original, the Queen described the day in more detail: 'Albert rode off at 8 to Edinburgh, & I, breakfasted alone.—Continued good news of the Children.—Read & wrote.—Albert returned at ½ 11, having visited the University & various other Institutions. Began reading to him out of Scott's "Tales of my Grandfather." A Drawingroom & Levee followed,—the whole being over by ½ p. 4. There were such curious dresses, but the Ladies not very awkward, "en revouche", the Gentlemen most ludicrously so. Nearly 2000 people went by.—Rested, & read Despatches to Albert.'

the Regalia: the Honours of Scotland, or the Scottish Crown Jewels, were worn by Scottish kings and queens at their coronations from Mary Queen of

Scots, in 1543 until Charles II in 1661. From the Union of the Crowns in 1603 until the Union of 1707, the Honours were taken to sittings of the Parliament of Scotland to signify the monarch's presence. Following the Union of 1707, the Honours were locked away in a chest in Edinburgh Castle. They were rediscovered in 1818 and have been on public display at the castle ever since.

The Honours consist of the Crown of Scotland, the Sceptre, and the Sword of State. It is not known when the original crown was made, but it can be seen in its pre-1540 form in a portrait of James IV in the Book of Hours created for his marriage to Margaret Tudor in 1503. Arches were added to the crown by James V in 1532. In 1540 the base was melted down, recast, and decorated with fleurs-de-lis, crosses, and twenty-two gemstones. Two gold arches, preserved from the original, are surmounted by a gold monde enamelled blue, with stars representing the night sky. On top of the monde is a cross decorated with black enamel, pearls, and a large amethyst.

The Sceptre of Scotland was made in Italy as a gift from Pope Alexander VI to James IV; it is made of silver gilt and topped by a finial of polished rock, and was remodelled and lengthened for James V in 1536. The Sword of State was also a papal gift: Pope Julius II presented it to James IV in 1507. The etched blade, over three feet (a metre) long, includes figures of St Peter and St Paul, as well as the name of Julius II.

Blackness Castle: the Queen and her party are travelling west from Edinburgh. Blackness Castle is a fifteenth-century fortress on a promontory on the south shore of the Firth of Forth. Shaped like a ship with three mast-like towers, guarding what was once the principal port on the Forth, it served over the years as a prison and as an artillery fortification. After the Union in 1707, it became one of the four fortresses where the British Army garrisoned troops.

Hopetoun is the furthest outside Edinburgh that King George IV's visit to Scotland in 1822 took him.

24 *the castle on the lake*: Loch Leven Castle is a ruined castle on an island in Loch Leven. Possibly built c.1300, the castle was the site of military action during the Wars of Scottish Independence (1296–1357). Starting in the late fourteenth century, the castle was in the hands of Clan Douglas for about 300 years. Mary Queen of Scots was imprisoned there in 1567–8 and forced to abdicate, before escaping with the help of her gaoler's family. In 1675 Sir William Bruce, an architect, bought the castle and used it as a focal point for his garden; it was never again used as a residence.

the 42nd Highlanders: originally recruited from Scots who opposed the 1715 Jacobite uprising, the 42nd (Royal Highland) Regiment of Foot was a Scottish infantry regiment in the British Army also known as the Black Watch. The 42nd Regiment fought against the 1745 Jacobite uprising in Scotland, and was one of the first Highland Regiments to fight in North America, beginning with the French and Indian Wars in 1758.

triumphal arches: a triumphal arch is a free-standing monumental structure in the shape of an archway, with one or more arched passageways, often designed to span a road; it is decorated with imagery to signify the person or event it commemorates. The triumphal arch is one of the most influential and distinctive types of architecture associated with ancient Rome. During Victoria's tours of the British Isles, temporary triumphal arches made of lath and plaster were often erected for royal entries, and sometimes a row of arches was constructed through which processions progressed.

25 *the mound . . . always crowned*: a grassy mound, known as Moot Hill or Boot Hill in Scone (north-east of Perth), the historic capital of the Kingdom of Scotland. In the Middle Ages the monastery, later abbey, constructed nearby was used as a royal residence and as the coronation site of the kingdom's monarchs. In 1580 the abbey estates were granted to Lord Ruthven, later the Earl of Gowrie, who rebuilt the Abbot's Lodging as a grand residence. By 1604 the Palace of Scone was the family seat of the Murrays of Scone and the 1st Lord Scone. The medieval town of Scone, which had grown up around the monastery and the palace, was abandoned in the early nineteenth century, when the residents were removed and a new palace was built on the site by the Earl of Mansfield.

a sycamore-tree planted by James VI: King James VI of Scotland and I of England is reputed to have planted sycamore trees in the grounds of the Palace of Scone in the early seventeenth century, one of which survives today.

battle of Luncarty: Luncarty is a village just north of Perth. Hector Boece (1465–1536), in his *History of the Scottish People*, records that, in 990, Kenneth III of Scotland defeated the Danes near Luncarty.

the Druids used to sacrifice to Bel: in the Scottish Highlands, a mock sacrificial tradition associated with the ancient Celtic festival of Beltane is recorded since the eighteenth century. A Highlander would pass around a hat containing slices of bannock, or griddled oatcake. One piece would be marked with charcoal and its recipient was declared the 'cailleach Beal-tine', a scapegoat who must be sacrificed, though as the one chosen is pushed towards a bonfire, others rush in to the rescue. Celebrated from the eve of April 30 to 1 May, Beltane marks the beginning of summer.

Birnam Wood, so renowned in Macbeth: referring to the demise of Macbeth, the line reminds readers of imperial justice. In Act V of Shakespeare's play, soldiers camouflaged as Birnam Wood by holding branches before them attack Macbeth's castle.

Thüringen: Thuringia is a region in central Germany, incorporating the territories of Saxe-Coburg and Gotha, Saxe-Meiningen, and Saxe-Altenburg. Before marrying Victoria, Prince Albert was Prince of Saxe-Coburg and Gotha, and he retained a lifelong love of the area's beautiful countryside. The Thuringian Forest (German, Thüringer Wald) is a mountain range in the southern part of Thuringia, running north-west to south-east.

Dunkeld: (Scottish Gaelic, Dun Chailleann: 'fort of the Caledonians') the site of a ninth-century monastery and later of a cathedral. It lies close to the geological Highland Boundary Fault, and is frequently described as the 'Gateway to the Highlands' owing to its position on main roads and railway lines to the north. Dunkeld House, where this reception took place, is west of the town, built in 1676–84 for the earls, later dukes of Atholl. The first house was replaced in 1828 and the grounds were remodelled for John Murray, 4th Duke of Atholl.

Lord Glenlyon's Highlanders, with halberds: Lord Glenlyon (later 6th Duke of Atholl) had attended the neo-medieval Eglington Tournament in 1839, where he jousted, as the 'Knight of the Gael', attended by a retinue of local men in military costume. He maintained this Highland Guard and marched with them from Blair to Dunkeld to receive Victoria and Albert on this occasion in 1842. A fighting regiment of Atholl Highlanders had been disbanded in 1783 at the end of the American Revolution.

26 *the "sword dance"*: the Ghillie Callum (see Glossary).

Taymouth: Taymouth Castle, about a mile downstream from Loch Tay on the south bank of the River Tay, was the seat of the Campbells of Breadalbane; the original castle of 1552 was demolished in 1806 to be replaced by a lavish neo-Gothic castle, completed in 1842 in time for the three-day visit by the Queen and Prince Albert.

twenty-four years ago: see *More Leaves*, 212–13.

92nd Highlanders: later known as the Gordon Highlanders, a British Army infantry regiment recruited from Aberdeenshire and Invernessshire, from 1794. They fought in the Napoleonic wars, in the Crimean War, and in India following the 'Mutiny' of 1857.

27 *Swiss cottage*: the large ornamental dairy at Taymouth Castle is a single-storey structure with a tower, set on a mound in the park. Constructed in the 1830s, it is built in an Italianate rustic style, with applied timber ornament. A dairy is one of a number of building types popular for folly pavilions constructed to add interest to the estate of a wealthy landowner.

29 *very amusing and pretty to see*: originally, according to Princess Beatrice's transcription, the Queen had written more: 'But the great [s]ight of the evening, was to see Ly Elizabeth Pringle (Ld Breadalbane's sister) dance, which she does in a most peculiar manner, holding her skirts up very high & making most elaborate steps, flying about in such a wild & strange way. I really think she is a little crazy, & she is always dressed in a most extraordinary way. She [never] missed a dance. We also danced a Country Dance, & staid up till 12.' The Queen had also originally included (on a foldout page) a list of those who attended the ball.

a fir and an oak: trees were frequently planted to mark special occasions in the life of a person, a particular locality, or a nation. Queen Victoria regularly planted a tree within the grounds of homes she visited, as well as at her royal houses, typically in memory of a family member who had died. The trees were customarily identified with memorial plaques.

See the proud pipers . . . Highland strain: the quotation is from Sir Walter Scott's *Lady of the Lake* (1810), Canto 2, stanza 16, lines 19–24. This narrative poem in six cantos, widely popular, marked a high point in Scott's poetic career. Written in octosyllabic tetrameter couplets, it draws on Gaelic history set in the Highlands to retell the legend of Ellen Douglas. Victoria is reminded of their voyage on Loch Tay because Scott set the poem along the shores and islands of another Highland lake—Loch Katrine. In these lines, the hero, Roderick Dhu, is arriving at Ellen's Isle (also called Helen's Isle) on Loch Katrine. For the Queen's further references to this poem, see *Leaves*, 77, and *More Leaves*, 247 and 250.

Gaelic boat-songs: rowing-songs (Scottish Gaelic, *iorram*) formed part of the local work-song repertory.

29 *"brooch of Lorn,"* . . . *Robert Bruce in a battle*: the Brooch of Lorn (Scottish Gaelic, Bràiste Lathurna) is a medieval 'turreted' disc brooch, supposedly taken from Robert Bruce (Robert I, King of Scots) at the Battle of Dalrigh in 1306. It contains a large quartz charmstone with a compartment beneath, probably to hold a religious relic. The stone is surrounded by eight detached turrets, each about 1¼ inches (3.2 cm) high and topped by a Scottish freshwater pearl. Sir Walter Scott wrote about the brooch in *The Lord of the Isles* (1815; Canto 2, sections 11–13). The brooch is now owned by the MacDougall of Dunollie Preservation Trust.

30 *Kyber Pass*: the Khyber Pass traverses the Spin Ghar mountains in what is now Pakistan, on the border with Afghanistan. It is the only route through the Hindu Kush between Central Asia and South Asia. It has long had substantial cultural, economic, and geopolitical significance as an integral part of the ancient Silk Road trade route and as a vital strategic military choke point for various states that sought to control it, including Britain in the nineteenth century.

Drummond Castle: situated on a rocky outcrop south of Crieff, the castle consists of a tower house built *c.*1490 and a seventeenth-century mansion. It is known for steeply terraced formal gardens that date from the 1630s and were redesigned in the 1830s (the engraving in the illustrated edition of *Leaves* highlights the terraces). The Drummond family, loyal to King James VII of Scotland and II of England, lost the property in 1688 when James was deposed in favour of William III and Mary II; it was later sold back to Captain James Drummond (1744–1800), who became 1st Baron Perth.

31 *Lay of the Last Minstrel*: Sir Walter Scott's narrative poem in six cantos (1805), set in the Scottish Borders in the mid-sixteenth century. Scott wrote that his intent was 'to illustrate the customs and manners which anciently prevailed on the Borders of England and Scotland'. The ancient minstrel, having been received by Anne, Duchess of Buccleuch, at Newark Castle, recites the story about a deadly feud between two clans and the forbidden romance that eventually resolves it.

Ridinger: German artist Johann Elias Ridinger (1698–1767) was a painter, draughtsman, etcher, and publisher of prints, specializing in animal and hunting subjects.

battle of Bannockburn: 23–4 June 1314, a victory of the army of Robert Bruce (Robert I, King of Scots) over the army of King Edward II of England in the First War of Scottish Independence. Although it did not bring an end to the war—the Scots would not secure victory until fourteen years later—Bannockburn is still a major landmark in Scottish history. The defeat of the English opened up the north of England to Scottish raids, allowed the Scottish invasion of Ireland, and led to the Treaty of Edinburgh–Northampton in 1328, by which the English Crown recognized the full independence of the Kingdom of Scotland and acknowledged Robert Bruce, and his heirs and successors, as the rightful rulers. Bannockburn is an area immediately south of the centre of the city of Stirling, named for a burn that runs through the town before flowing into the River Forth.

Athole men: the spelling 'Athole' was used from 1838; the traditional spelling 'Atholl' was resumed after 1893.

My half-brother . . . died in 1856: the Queen added this footnote in pencil on an early proof, initially writing 'The Queen's brother' but later altering the third person (in this and other cases) to match the 'I' narration of the main text of *Leaves*. Similarly, in another footnote in *Leaves*, 123, 'the Queen' in proof was revised to 'me'.

32 *Ardoch, called the "Lindrum"*: Ardoch Roman Fort is an archaeological site just outside the village of Braco, about seven miles (eleven km) south of Crieff. It comprises a Roman fort and several marching camps, which included a signal tower. It is one of the best-preserved series of Roman military earthworks in the former Roman Empire.

the Castle: Stirling Castle is one of the largest and most important castles in Scotland, both historically and architecturally. It is strategically located, surrounded on three sides by steep cliffs and guarding what was, until the 1890s, the farthest downstream crossing of the River Forth. The first record of the castle dates from around 1110, when King Alexander I dedicated a chapel there. Almost all the present buildings were constructed between 1490 and 1600, when Stirling was a principal royal centre. The architecture shows an eclectic mix of English, French, and German influences, reflecting the international ambitions of the Stuart dynasty. From 1800 the castle was owned by the War Office and run as a barracks.

window out of which he was thrown: a long-standing rivalry between the Stuarts and the Douglas clan for control of Scotland led to a quarrel during a meeting of King James II's council at Stirling Castle on 22 February 1452. William Douglas, 8th Earl of Douglas, was stabbed by James and then killed by members of the council, supposedly by being thrown from a window. The Douglases continued to challenge James's authority in a series of military encounters that ended with their defeat in 1455.

and the "Knoll" . . . yet remain: in an earlier proof this read, 'the Queen's Knoll, where the tournaments took place, and where all the embankments remain'. In Princess Beatrice's transcription (and therefore probably the original), this reads: 'the Queen's Knot, where the Tournaments used to take place. The ramparts are all still remaining.' Successive revisions improved the style but introduced an error: 'Knott' is the correct term for this circular mound.

33 *well worth seeing*: in Princess Beatrice's transcription of the original diary, after 'worth seeing' the Queen wrote: 'The crowd was again dreadful, & the people drunk & disorderly, which made me nervous.' Just below, where the published version has, 'but we were unable to stop', an earlier proof has, 'we trotted through' (suggesting that this was the Queen's original wording, although Princess Beatrice's transcription reads 'we trolled through').

called Loanhead: in Princess Beatrice's transcription of the original diary, the Queen described Loanhead as 'an unpleasant little mining village'.

the chapel: Rosslyn Chapel was built in the fifteenth century in the village of Roslin, south of Edinburgh. It served as the family burial place for the Sinclair family. Although only the chancel and Lady Chapel were completed of a more ambitious plan, the richly decorated chapel is one of the most important architectural treasures of Scotland.

33 *Sir Alexander Ramsay . . . so long a time*: in Princess Beatrice's transcription, the Queen originally wrote, 'went down into some very curious caves, in the solid rock, where Robert Bruce & his brave followers concealed themselves & held out for a long time'. The hero's name was corrected by the time of publication in *Leaves*: in 1342, in the wake of Bruce's military successes over the English, Alexander Ramsay (son of Robert Bruce's ally William Ramsay) recaptured Roxburgh Castle, the last Scottish castle to have been under English control.

34 *General Steam Navigation Company*: founded in 1821, it was London's foremost short sea shipping line for almost 150 years, and the oldest shipping company in the world to begin business with steamships. Their first steamer, the *James Watt*, inaugurated a service between London and Leith, Scotland, in 1824. In 1841 they launched HMS *Trident*, a three-masted schooner, for the Leith to London service. She was considered to be one of the fastest ships then sailing, and this gave the owners a chance for a publicity coup. The company made an offer to convey Queen Victoria to Scotland in the late summer of 1842, but this was declined. The Queen travelled north in the Royal Yacht *Royal George*, but when this was overtaken by *Trident* on her normal service, the Queen made arrangements to charter the vessel for her return south. By 1844 the Queen had built a new royal yacht, HMY *Victoria and Albert*, a steamship.

Tantallon Castle: a ruined fourteenth-century fortress built by William Douglas, 1st Earl of Douglas. It occupies a rocky promontory on the south shore of the outer part of the Firth of Forth, where the firth meets the North Sea. It was famous for being the stronghold of the Douglases. See *More Leaves*, 361, for the Queen's account of its role in the English Civil War.

Marmion: Sir Walter Scott's *Marmion: A Tale of Flodden Field* (1808) is a historical poem in six cantos, each with an introductory epistle and antiquarian notes. The chivalric poem ends with the definitive defeat in September 1513 of King James IV of Scotland by England under Thomas Howard, Earl of Surrey, in a major battle at Flodden Field in Northumberland. Victoria reads not about Lord Marmion or the triumph of the English but about a voyage of nuns to a convent, now in ruins. The long account of the voyage occurs in Canto 2, 'The Convent', stanzas 1–11.

Grace Darling had died: Princess Beatrice's transcription of the Queen's original diary does not include this mention of Grace Darling's death; either Beatrice omitted it or, perhaps more likely, the Queen added it for publication to round off the description of this journey.

35 *tent made of flags, at half-past five*: in Princess Beatrice's transcription of the diary, the details of this day appear in a slightly different order. At about this point the Queen originally continued: 'We read to each other out of Mme d'Arblay's Diary.' *The Diary and Letters of Madame d'Arblay* was originally published in seven volumes in 1842–6. Frances Burney (1752–1840), known as Fanny Burney and later Madame d'Arblay, was an English novelist, diarist, and playwright. In 1786–90 she served as Keeper of the Robes to Charlotte of Mecklenburg-Strelitz, George III's queen. In 1793 she married a French exile, General Alexandre d'Arblay; she spent the years 1802–12 with him in Paris, while England was at war with France.

Explanatory Notes to Leaves   391

half-past twelve o'clock: according to Princess Beatrice's transcription, this entry and thus the entire 'first visit to Scotland' originally included more detail about the Queen's return to Windsor. On arriving home at midday, at first she was told the children were asleep, but 'soon afterwards we heard that dear "Pussy" was awake & we at once went up stairs. We found her so grown, so much more sensible & independent, & looking so well.' 'The Baby' too looked grown but 'a little pulled down'. In the afternoon, they drove around the grounds; 'Windsor is beautiful even after all we have [seen], & it is, in its way unique.'

36 *Visit to Blair Athole.*: this section was first titled 'Second Visit to Scotland in 1844.' Sending the proof to the Queen for her review, an editor wrote beneath this title: 'Would your majesty prefer "Visit to Blair Athol in 1844."' Beneath these words appears a large 'Yes', pencilled in the Queen's handwriting and underscored with a diagonal line.

Blair Castle, near the village of Blair Atholl, is the ancestral home of Clan Murray, and was historically the seat of their chief, the Duke of Atholl. The oldest part of the castle is the six-storey Cummings or Comyn's Tower; some thirteenth-century construction may remain, though it was largely built in the fifteenth century. Additions to the castle were made in the sixteenth century, in the mid-eighteenth century, and following a fire in 1814, and the castle was remodelled again in the 1870s in Scottish Baronial style.

his little girl being very ill: according to Princess Beatrice's transcription, the diary entry originally continued here: 'We lunched & I established myself on deck, but about 4 there began to be a good deal of motion, & I felt very uncomfortable & unwell. This continued most of the evening. The maids were all "hors de combat", & I think there were very few who did not feel ill.' This edit forms part of a consistent pattern of omitting information about the Queen's health and her body.

Vicky: the Queen used the Princess Royal's pet name 'Pussette' in the original entry, according to Princess Beatrice's transcription.

37 *I said . . . when I was . . . pleasant feeling*: these two sentences are not in Princess Beatrice's transcription of the diary. It is not certain whether they were added for the publication of *Leaves* or whether Princess Beatrice cut the lines while transcribing the original. In the early proof where these sentences first appear in print, the words 'I was' are inserted by hand.

38 *Regality Court of the Dukes of Athole*: adjacent to the inn in the village of Logierait in Atholl was the site of the Regality Court house. Demolished in the nineteenth century, this was the largest hall in Atholl, where, as part of their feudal duties, the Duke of Atholl's lairds would gather to act as juries at trials. The associated prison at one time held Rob Roy and, later, one hundred and twenty prisoners captured after the Battle of Prestonpans by the Jacobites in 1745.

Pass of Killiecrankie: a wooded gorge through which the River Garry flows, near the town of Pitlochry. On 27 July 1689 Jacobite Scots won a battle against the English army at Killiecrankie Pass, in the campaign by King James VII and II to regain the throne after being deposed in 1688 in favour of William III and Mary II. Killiecrankie Pass remains an important site in the history of Scotland.

38 *and then left us*: Lord and Lady Glenlyon gave the castle to Victoria and Albert for their use during this three-week stay. Left behind to guard them were two artillery guns and 150 armed members of the Atholl Highland Guard living in tents set up in the castle grounds. For this service, the Queen 'gave them their colours' the following year—that is, permitted them to bear arms: they remain the only private army in Britain to the present day.

39 *Oh! what can equal . . . his dear father*: this short paragraph is not in Princess Beatrice's transcription of the diary. It cannot be determined whether she cut it from the original or the Queen added it for publication.

path on the opposite side: according to Princess Beatrice's transcription, the Queen originally wrote of this 'charming' walk: 'I managed quite well, without using the chair. After the constant trying publicity we are accustomed to, it is so pleasant & refreshing, to be able, amidst such beautiful surrounding, to enjoying such complete privacy & such a simple life.' The phrase 'using the chair' could refer to needing to be carried owing to her having given birth to Prince Alfred only weeks earlier (August 1844).

"Humble Petition of Bruar Water to the Noble Duke of Athole": Bruar Water is a series of waterfalls near Blair Castle, which the poet Robert Burns visited. His poem 'The Humble Petition of Bruar Water' (1787), addressed to the 'noble Duke of Athole', asks him to shade with trees and bushes the treeless hillsides around Bruar Water to protect its environment. The Duke did so, also adding paths, bridges, and 'viewing huts' to frame the picturesque views for visitors.

at six o'clock: in the original diary, according to Princess Beatrice's transcription, the Queen continued here: 'Albert was full of indignation in reading the accounts of the change of Govt in Greece. King Otto has secretly upset his own Govt, & acts in such a manner, as to make one, Albert says, feel sick. Such bad faith, such stupidity, are unconceivable.—Mr Bloomfield has written a most satisfactory account of Pce F. of Hesse's conduct, during the poor Gd Duchess's illness & afterward, & he seems to be much disliked at St. Petersburg. How very distressing & shocking!'

41 *a grey cloth jacket . . . Highland bonnet*: this parenthesis detailing 'Highland costume' does not appear in Princess Beatrice's transcription and was probably added later for the benefit of a readership unfamiliar with Scottish dress.

the Marble Lodge and Forest Lodge: these two lodges are on the road that follows the Tilt River north-east from Blair Atholl; this day's excursion takes the Queen up a series of rugged peaks north of the Tilt.

42 *Landseer with us to sketch our party*: for the Queen's special appreciation of Landseer, see Introduction, xli–xlii.

quite to the top: according to Ian Mitchell, *On the Trail of Queen Victoria in the Highlands* (Edinburgh: Luath, 2000), this is the first recorded ascent of Cairn Chlamain, one of eight Scottish peaks over 3,000 feet (900 metres) that the Queen scaled between 1844 and 1861.

43 *At length . . . to disappoint him*: these two sentences do not appear in Princess Beatrice's transcription of the diary. It is likely that they were cut during the transcription, rather than having been added to *Leaves* later. In one proof, and therefore probably in the original diary, where the text now reads 'as he knew

Explanatory Notes to Leaves 393

how anxious I should be. He had been very unlucky, and had lost his sport', the Queen had written: 'and been in a great state, for he lost his sport and he knew how anxious I should be. He had been very unlucky, for . . .' Princess Beatrice's version reads: 'we met him shortly after. He had had bad luck, I am sorry to say.'

44 *in the barge to the yacht*: in Princess Beatrice's transcription of the diary, this entry continues, describing Albert teaching Vicky to write, what they ate, and their appreciation for a collection of Landseer's artworks.

a few minutes past four: the entry for 3 October was shortened and rewritten for *Leaves*. In Princess Beatrice's transcription, the Queen gave more detail about the journey south, describing their meals and Vicky's presence; after the end of this entry, referring to their arrival at Windsor Castle, she continued: 'It appeared to me like a dream, having still [been] in the Highland, the day before yesterday. Everything looks fresh & green, but so flat.' Then she described greeting the children who had remained at home (Bertie, Alice, and Alfred), walking the castle grounds to see various 'improvements', and reading the letters waiting for them, including one from Calcutta (Kolkata).

45 *Osborne Pier on board the yacht*: for this tour, the Queen and her family depart from Osborne House, their home on the Isle of Wight, travelling on the new royal yacht, the twin-paddle steamship HMY *Victoria and Albert*, built and launched in 1842. The ship, the first of three royal yachts to be named *Victoria and Albert*, was 200 feet (61 metres) long (lengthened to 260 feet, 79 metres, in 1853) and carried two cannons. After the launch of the second HMY *Victoria and Albert* in 1855, the first one was renamed *Osborne* and continued in service, conveying the royal family to Osborne House.

under weigh: now usually 'under way', the phrase refers to weighing or lifting a ship's anchor for departure.

The Needles: a row of chalk stacks (tall rocks) off the western end of the Isle of Wight.

Saturday, August 14.: although this is the first of two entries dated August 14, in apparent error, the Queen starts with this date to introduce the two-day sea voyage from Dartmouth (on the English Channel) via the Scilly Isles to Milford Haven on the south coast of Wales, then goes back in time to detail each day's events. This sequencing is not present in Princess Beatrice's transcription of the diary, and so was probably added for the publication of *Leaves*.

46 *one of the Edwards*: Star Castle is a sixteenth-century castle overlooking the harbour on St Mary's; before Queen Victoria's son Bertie became King Edward VII in 1901, the last king of that name was Edward VI, who reigned 1547–53; earlier kings named Edward reigned in the thirteenth, fourteenth, and fifteenth centuries.

47 *high-crowned men's hats*: neither the description of Welsh dress nor the sketch included here appears in Princess Beatrice's transcription of the diary. They may have been added for the publication of *Leaves* from the visual record the Queen kept of her travels; they might also have been in the original diary and edited out during transcription.

the "Fairy": this royal steam yacht, built in 1844, was smaller than HMY *Victoria and Albert* and could sail in shallower waters.

47 *the Straits*: the Menai Strait (Welsh, Afon Menai) is a narrow stretch of shallow tidal water separating the Isle of Anglesey from the mainland of Wales.

Caernarvon: Caernarvon Castle (Welsh, Castell Caernarfon) is a medieval fortress at the southern end of the Menai Strait, built (starting in 1283) by King Edward I of England to aid his conquest of Wales.

Plas Newydd: a fifteenth-century country house set in parklands and woodlands on the north bank of the Menai Strait, on the Isle of Anglesey. Princess Victoria's visit in 1832 was part of a royal progress through the Midlands and north Wales, arranged by her mother, the Duchess of Kent, with her Comptroller, Sir John Conroy, when the future Queen was greeted at every stop by parades, triumphal arches, and cheering crowds. She described this visit in her childhood diary, published in 1912 as *The Girlhood of Queen Victoria*. The house belonged to the Marquess of Anglesey, who offered its use to the royal travellers. (This house is not to be confused with the home of the famous Ladies of Llangollen, also named Plas Newydd, nearby in north Wales.)

works . . . for the railroad: Britannia Bridge crosses the Menai Strait between the Isle of Anglesey and the mainland of Wales. It was designed and built, from 1846, by Robert Stephenson, as a tubular bridge of wrought-iron rectangular box sections, for carrying rail traffic between Chester and Holyhead, enabling trains to travel directly between London and the port of Holyhead, and thereby facilitating a sea link to Ireland.

Menai Bridge: the Menai Suspension Bridge (Welsh, Pont y Borth or Pont Grog y Borth), designed by Thomas Telford and completed in 1826, was the world's first major suspension bridge.

48 *Penrhyn Castle*: a country house in Llandygai, north Wales. Originally a medieval fortified manor house, the present building—in the form of a Norman castle—was built between *c.*1822 and 1837. One of the most admired of the numerous mock castles built in Britain in the nineteenth century, it is a picturesque composition that stretches over 600 feet (103 metres), from a tall donjon containing family rooms, through the main block built around the earlier house, to the service wing and the stables. The castle also has some specially designed Norman-style furniture, including a slate bed, weighing a ton, made for Queen Victoria when she visited in 1859. Richard Pennant, 1st Baron Penrhyn (*c.*1737–1808), made his fortune from local slate quarries and from sugar plantations and slavery in Jamaica; the considerable cost of constructing the castle was met by compensation paid to the family following the abolition of slavery.

Ailsa Craig: a small, rocky island in the outer Firth of Clyde, 10 miles (16 km) west of mainland Scotland, where 'blue hone' microgranite has long been quarried to make curling stones. The island was a haven for Catholics during the Scottish Reformation in the sixteenth century, but is today a bird sanctuary, inhabited by gannets and puffins.

49 *the Holy Island*: or Holy Isle, a small island in the Firth of Clyde, in Lamlash Bay on the eastern side of the Isle of Arran. The island has a long history as a sacred site, with a spring or holy well held to have healing properties, the hermit cave of the sixth-century monk St Molaise, and evidence of a thirteenth-century monastery. For the view of Holy Island mentioned here and other sights she describes as they travel up the west coast of Scotland, the Queen may be relying on a guidebook (see Introduction, xxviii).

Explanatory Notes to Leaves 395

Dumbarton Castle: overlooking the town of Dumbarton, the castle (Scottish Gaelic, Dùn Breatainn: 'fort of the Brittons') has the longest recorded history of any stronghold in Scotland; it sits on a plug of volcanic basalt known as Dumbarton Rock. From the fifth century to the ninth, it was the centre of the independent Brittonic Kingdom of Strathclyde. In medieval Scotland, Dumbarton was an important royal castle; 'Wallace was confined here' refers to Sir William Wallace (1270–1305), a leader in the First War of Scottish Independence. Mary Queen of Scots lodged there in 1548, during 'the Rough Wooing' (an eight-year phase of England's sixteenth-century war on Scotland, during which the English tried to engage Mary to marry Prince Edward, the heir to King Henry VIII, both of them children at the time) and again in 1563 (see also note to *More Leaves*, 248). Not much survives from the medieval castle; most of the existing structures were built in the eighteenth century, and they demonstrate the struggle by military engineers to adapt an intractable site to contemporary defensive needs.

mending his shoe!: the Cobbler (Scottish Gaelic, Beinn Artair) is a mountain located near the head of Loch Long. Many maps include the name 'Ben Arthur' (an anglicization of the Gaelic), but the name 'the Cobbler' is more widely used. In the nineteenth century the mountain was referred to as the Cobbler and his Wife. In an early proof of *Leaves*, the plural form 'the Cobblers' is used, and the description reads: 'and there is on the top of one the shape of a man sitting and mending his shoe!' As the text was being prepared for publication, an editor has suggested (in a pencil note) two alternate phrasings for 'there is': 'one may imagine? The people have fancied the top of one is like?' The Queen accepted only the correction from plural to singular.

51 *Castle of Inverary*: (Scottish Gaelic, Caisteal Inbhir Aora) a large, imposing country house on the shore of Loch Fyne, the seat of the Dukes of Argyll, chiefs of Clan Campbell. The present castle, built in the Gothic Revival style from 1746, replaced a fifteenth-century castle. The village of Inveraray was moved in the 1770s to give the castle a more secluded setting. The Queen revisited Inveraray Castle in September 1875; see *More Leaves*, 324–35.

ornamented with heather: heather (*Calluna vulgaris*) is a low-growing, hardy, flowering plant—usually pink, sometimes white—that spreads readily on Scotland's boggy moorlands. Its period of most prolific bloom coincides with the time of year when Victoria and Albert typically visited Scotland—namely, late summer and early autumn. It has become an emblem of Scotland; the Queen loved to see heather growing in the landscape and used as a decoration symbolizing good luck.

Crinan Canal: opened in 1801, it takes its name from the village of Crinan located at its western end. The canal connects the village of Ardrishaig on Loch Gilp with the Sound of Jura, providing a navigable route between the Clyde and the Inner Hebrides that bypasses a long diversion around the exposed Mull of Cantire (now spelled Kintyre).

52 *Dunstaffnage Castle*: the partially ruined castle (Scottish Gaelic, Caisteal Dhùn Stadhainis) sits on a rocky promontory at the entrance to Loch Etive, just north of Oban. It dates back to the thirteenth century, though there had been a fortification on this site in earlier centuries. It has been held since the

fifteenth century by the earls of Argyll of Clan Campbell. A new house was built in 1725, but the castle began to decay and in 1810 a fire led to its abandonment.

52 *Coronation Chair*: the Stone of Scone (Scottish Gaelic, An Lia Fàil; Scots, Stane o Scuin)—also known as the Stone of Destiny and referred to in England as the Coronation Stone—is an oblong block of red sandstone that was used for centuries in the coronation of the monarchs of Scotland. Historically it was kept at the now ruined Scone Abbey in Scone (see note to *Leaves*, 25), having been brought from Iona *c.* AD 841. After its forced removal from Scone during Edward I's invasion of Scotland in 1296, it was fitted into a wooden chair, known as King Edward's Chair, which has been used in the coronation of the monarchs of England and, since the Union of 1707, of the United Kingdom.

Alexander II. is said to be buried here: King Alexander II was buried in Melrose Abbey, where the Queen was shown his grave in 1867 (*More Leaves*, 225).

she was saved however: Lady's Rock, south-west of Lismore (a small island at the entrance to Loch Linnhe), is submerged at high tide and now carries a navigation beacon. In 1527 Lachlan Maclean of Duart decided to murder his wife, Lady Catherine Campbell, a sister of Archibald Campbell, 4th Earl of Argyll. He rowed her out to the rock one night at low tide and left her to die. When he observed no one on the rock the following day, he sent a message of condolence to the Earl at Inveraray Castle, indicating that he intended to bring his wife's body there for burial. Maclean duly arrived at Inveraray with an entourage of men and the coffin. He was immediately taken to the dining hall of the castle to discover Lady Catherine waiting for him at the head of the table. She had been rescued during the night by a boat passing by the rock. Maclean was allowed to make his escape but was murdered later by one of Lady Catherine's brothers.

The inhabitants . . . from famine: during the Highland Potato Famine, 1846–56, the potato crop in the Hebrides and the western Scottish Highlands was repeatedly devastated by potato blight. The impact on the local agricultural communities was severe, if less so than in Ireland during the same period (see note to *Leaves*, 141). A government inquiry could suggest no short-term solution other than reduction of the population by emigration to Canada or Australia. Highland landlords organized and paid for the emigration of more than 16,000 of their tenants and an unknown number paid for their own passage; in 1849 the Duke of Argyll, of Inveraray, who owned Tiree at the time, evicted 600 and sent them to Canada. About a third of the population of the western Scottish Highlands emigrated between 1841 and 1861. Originally (according to Princess Beatrice's transcription), after the words 'Coll and Tiree', the Queen had written: 'on the last of which are 6000 inhabitants, who are often half starving. All these islands have last winter been terrible sufferers from the famine.'

strange shape, thus—: Bac Mòr is one of the Treshinish Isles, off the west coast of the island of Mull, sometimes referred to as 'the Dutchman's Cap' because of its shape. Bac Mòr is of volcanic origin: the peak in the middle is a former cone, and the low-lying plain surrounding it is a glassy lava field. The remains of small stone buildings have been found on the island, suggesting that it was inhabited at one time, even though it has no safe landing place.

53 *Fingal's Cave*: a sea cave on the southern end of the uninhabited island of Staffa, off the west coast of Mull. Formed from hexagonally jointed basalt columns, it has a large arched entrance and is known for its natural acoustics. In calm conditions, one can land and walk to the cave, where a row of fractured columns forms a walkway just above high-water level. The cave became a tourist destination from the late eighteenth century onwards, having been brought to public attention by naturalist Sir Joseph Banks in 1772. It became known as Fingal's Cave after the hero of one of James Macpherson's 'Ossian' poems. Composer Felix Mendelssohn visited in 1829 and wrote an overture 'The Hebrides', op. 26, inspired by the weird echoes in the cave. Other famous nineteenth-century visitors included Jules Verne; William Wordsworth; John Keats; Alfred, Lord Tennyson; and J. M. W. Turner, who painted *Staffa, Fingal's Cave* in 1832.

The Queen's architectural language ('vaulted hall') echoes guidebook descriptions. For example, George and Peter Anderson write, 'the arches and floorings of the caves strongly resemble architectural designs, and have been described by terms taken from works of art' (George Anderson and Peter Anderson, *A Guide to the Highlands and Islands of Scotland*, 3rd edn, Edinburgh: Adam and Charles Black, 1851, 603). The curiously precise figure the Queen gives—227 feet (69 metres) long—is also the figure Anderson gives, taken from a scientific paper by Dr Macculloch (605).

Omitted from *Leaves* is this comment in the original diary: 'Staffa which is disappointing from that side & looks green & like a cheese.'

cathedral of St. Oran: Iona is a small island off the south-west end of Mull, where Christianity is said to have first arrived in Britain when St Columba (Irish Gaelic, Colm Cille) and his followers left Ireland to establish a monastery there in AD 563. It remained a centre of Christian learning, art, and worship and a place of pilgrimage. At the time of the Queen's visit, the Benedictine Abbey (founded in 1203), destroyed during the Reformation, lay in ruins (the cathedral was later restored, starting in 1899). St Oran's Chapel and the adjacent Reilig Odhrain are the traditional burial grounds of Scottish monarchs.

Glencoe: Glen Coe, a mountain glen near the eastern shore of Loch Linnhe, is known for its great beauty as well as for the Massacre of Glencoe on 13 February 1692. About thirty members and associates of Clan MacDonald of Glencoe were killed by Scottish government forces, allegedly for the failure of their representative, Maclain of Glencoe, to pledge timely allegiance to the new monarchs, William III and Mary II. According to a nineteenth-century Scottish guidebook, William issued two orders in January 1692, the first 'to proceed with the extremity of fire and sword, with all who might have neglected the proclamation', the second reiterating the order, adding an exemption for those who might need a little extra time to obey, but 'expressly exempting the Macdonalds of Glencoe, who were directed to be extirpated' (Anderson; see note to *Leaves*, 'Fingal's Cave', above on this page).

The brutality of the massacre became a Jacobite symbol of post-1688 oppression. In 1745 Prince Charles Edward Stuart had a pamphlet by the Irish Jacobite Charles Leslie, denouncing William III for his role in the massacre, reprinted in the *Edinburgh Caledonian Mercury* newspaper. But Whig historian Thomas Macaulay's *History of England from the Accession of James the Second* (1859) sought to exonerate William, claiming that the massacre was part of a Campbell–MacDonald clan feud. The Queen herself eventually visited Glen Coe and the site of the massacre in 1873; see *More Leaves*, 310–11.

53 *Fort William*: a town at the north-east end of Loch Linnhe. The earliest recorded settlement on the site is a wooden fort built in 1654 as a base for British troops. Following the overthrow of James VII and II in 1688, William III ordered a new fort to be built here to control the Highland clans.

54 *seats for thirty*: probably a charabanc, a long and light vehicle with transverse seats facing forward. Its large capacity is probably what surprises the Queen and indicates the popularity of Glen Coe as a tourist destination.

Ardverikie: Ardverikie House is on the shore of Loch Laggan, on lands historically belonging to Clan Macpherson. The 20th chief, Ewen Macpherson, leased the stone shooting-lodge in 1844 to the 2nd Marquess of Abercorn, who served as Groom of the Stool to Prince Albert and who vacated the house for Victoria and Albert's three-week stay in 1847. The house was destroyed by fire in 1873 and was rebuilt in the Scottish Baronial style. The Queen made sketches of frescoes by Edwin Landseer that decorated some of the buildings later destroyed in the fire.

55 *splendid: high bold*: before the word 'hills', the illustrated edition of *Leaves* prints an engraving of the Queen's sketch of Ewan MacPherson in a kilt. This is one of seven images based on sketches by the Queen or Prince Albert that were included in the illustrated edition, in addition to those appearing in the regular edition.

the Pattock: Frederick Enoch added, in pen in the margin of a proof, 'try Pattaig (in Fullerton)'. Enoch had been assigned by the publisher, Smith, Elder, & Co. to check the Queen's sometimes phonetic spellings of place names against 'Ordnance maps and authorities'. For 'Fullerton', see note to *Leaves*, 19. Pattaig—now spelled Pattack—is the name of a loch and of a river flowing into Loch Laggan.

Caledonian Canal: the canal links the long, narrow lakes of Scotland's Great Glen to create a shipping passage from the Atlantic Ocean to the North Sea, from Fort William to Inverness. James Watt first proposed a canal in 1774, and in 1803–4 parliament hired engineers to plan construction, the impetus to build it coming at least in part from the need to remedy (by creating jobs) the depopulation and poverty of the Highlands following the Clearances. The motivation was military as well as economic: the canal was to be wide and deep enough to take a 32-gun frigate, fully equipped. The distance from sea to sea is 60 miles (96 km), two-thirds of that distance being occupied by lakes. The canal was opened in 1822, then renovated and reopened in 1847. The Queen herself visited and travelled on the canal in 1873, on her departure from a visit to Inverlochy (*More Leaves*, 317–20). The Andersons' guide says the canal is 'on a scale worthy of the grandeur and genius of the British people' (133).

Dochfour: an eighteenth-century house on the shore of Loch Dochfour, which became the northernmost section of the Caledonian Canal, just south of

Inverness. The house was built in about 1780 after an earlier house was burned down during the Jacobite uprising of 1745–6. In 1839 the Georgian house was remodelled in Italianate style with new terraced gardens, including walled gardens, a water garden, rose gardens, topiary, kitchen gardens, and orchards extending down to the edge of the loch.

Falls of Foyers: (Scottish Gaelic, Eas na Smùide: 'the smoking falls') a waterfall on the River Foyers, which feeds Loch Ness, north-east of Fort Augustus.

57 *Mull of Galloway . . . with a lighthouse on it*: (Scottish Gaelic, Maol nan Gall) the southernmost point of Scotland, at the southern end of the Rhins of Galloway peninsula. The lighthouse at the point, built in 1830 by Robert Stevenson, is a white-painted round tower.

anchored in Ramsay Bay: early proofs of *Leaves* included here a comment: 'we are therefore far away from dear Scotland', later cancelled with a pencil line and the marginal note, 'said over leaf' (because the previous entry ends with a similar remark). In the original diary as transcribed and edited by Princess Beatrice, the entry lacks the clause beginning 'we are therefore . . .', which appears in the early proof, and continues instead with personal details including a visit with a new dog given to her by Albert, 'very affectionate & seems so good tempered'.

a cheerless evening, blowing hard: in the original diary, the evening is not quite so cheerless: although the Queen went into greater detail about the rough weather and heavy seas, she also wrote that they went on deck after dinner 'to hear the sailors sing. Amongst the songs was "Here's a health to all good l[a]sses", which reminded me of our outward voyage & of our dear Highlands. It used to be our favourite song.'

61 *Land of brown heath . . . extremity of ill*: the epigraph is from Sir Walter Scott's 1805 *The Lay of the Last Minstrel*, Canto 6, stanza 2, lines 3–12 (see note to *Leaves*, 31). The Queen described reading the first five cantos with Albert on their first visit to Scotland in 1842. Used as the epigraph to the section of *Leaves* that is about making a home in Scotland, the lines assert her connection to the land which she joins Scott's minstrel in praising.

63 *the hills rise all around*: two sets of revisions to this opening description served to make the old Balmoral Castle and grounds easier for readers to visualize than if the text had simply followed the original diary. There, the Queen mentioned neither garden nor tower, but included a sketch of the castle based on a print she had purchased. In the earliest proof of the private edition (which eventually became the first proof of *Leaves*), a space was left to insert such a sketch after the words 'Scottish style. Thus:' But instead of a sketch, the verbal description is awkwardly inserted, not quite filling the space. The tower is described as 'nice' and only later became 'picturesque'. Also in the earliest proof, the words 'wood down to the Dee' were followed by: 'which you can in consequence not see.' The Queen then used editorial marks to change this phrasing to the more graceful 'which in consequence you cannot see'; at a later stage, this entire clause was cut.

64 *the wood of Balloch Buie*: the forest of Ballochbuie, on the slopes below Lochnagar and adjoining the Balmoral property, is one of the largest

continuous native Scottish forests. In the depths of the forest are the Garbh Allt Falls and the old Invercauld bridge, built in 1752 as part of the military road system (see notes to *Leaves*, 108, and *More Leaves*, 336). The Queen loved the Ballochbuie forest and bought it from the Farquharson family in 1878 to save it from being felled.

64 *A Jäger . . . beloved Prince.*: John Macdonald was a gillie, but the Queen follows Prince Albert's usage of the equivalent German term 'Jäger'. The first two sentences of this footnote are present in print in the second proof; the two sentences about his eldest son were added in pencil in the margin of that proof, and the sentence on the third son was added still later.

Head-keeper . . . built for him.: the first two sentences of this footnote were introduced by the Queen in pen at the bottom of the page in the first proof and appear in print in the second proof (though the second sentence there ends 'the Prince and the Queen'); the remainder of the note was added later.

A groom . . . after this.: a pencilled note on the first proof indicates the intention to write a footnote, but it was not added until after the second proof. The gradual accumulation of information about servants, demonstrated by this and the preceding two notes, is typical of the development of the footnotes in *Leaves*.

65 *two small lochs called Na Nian*: these lochs are probably Loch Nan Eun and Sandy Loch, to the west of Lochnagar's peak, which at 3,789 feet (1,155 metres) dominates the Deeside landscape.

a seat in a little nook: in the earliest proof of the private edition (which in turn served as the first proof of *Leaves*) this reads: 'in a little nook like this:' and a space is left for the sketch whose intended presence is indicated by the colon. In Princess Beatrice's transcription of the original, this reads 'a place where we sat down in the shelter', with no indication of an accompanying sketch. No record remains of the sketch the Queen apparently intended to insert.

most anxiously for us: up until a late proof, this entry ended: 'I felt a little bewildered, but not tired.' This sentence does not appear in Princess Beatrice's transcription, where the entry instead ends with a list of dinner guests. An editor marked this line 'Qy' (for 'query') on the proof and crossed it out in pencil.

66 *Bertie*: in the earliest proof of the private edition, the Queen added a pencil note: 'Name by which the Pce of Wales is always called in the family.' The need for such a note was obviated by the decision to include, before the entries about Balmoral, which start in 1848, the entries on prior trips to Scotland; but her addition of the note indicates her attentiveness to what a public readership would need.

Farquharson, a deer-stalker of Invercauld's: Invercauld Castle is a country house about five miles (eight km) west of Balmoral belonging to the Farquharson family, who had lived in the area since the fourteenth century, had once owned Balmoral Castle, and were staunch supporters of the Jacobite cause. In the original diary as transcribed and edited by Princess Beatrice, the Queen had written: 'old Arthur Farquharson, a shrewd & very ugly deer stalker.'

Explanatory Notes to Leaves 401

A *"council of war"*: a conference of high-ranking military or naval officers, usually for discussing a major emergency or problem in war, or any conference for discussing or deciding upon a course of action. The term is first recorded in the sixteenth century.

Albert drawing Macdonald: Prince Albert's sketch of John Macdonald appears in the illustrated edition of December 1868 in a space between the words 'coming' and 'past', below. This is one of seven images based on sketches by the Queen or the Prince included in the illustrated edition, in addition to those appearing in the regular edition.

"a royal": a red deer with twelve tines or points to its antlers (six per antler) is called a 'royal stag', while fourteen points make an 'imperial stag' and an animal with sixteen points or more is referred to as a 'monarch'. The heads of many of the stags shot by Prince Albert were stuffed and mounted on the walls in Balmoral Castle.

half-past two o'clock: in Princess Beatrice's transcription of the original diary, the Queen continued at the end of this entry: 'Nothing new from Ireland, but the people are burning & attacking houses, & forcing people to join them, but always contrive to get away, when in reach of the troops.' The reference to her 'lucky foot' does not appear in the transcription, either because Princess Beatrice edited it out or because the Queen added it here.

67 *Alt-na-Giuthasach.*: the Queen's sketch of the house appears above this title in the illustrated edition. Alt-na-Giuthasach (or Allt-na-Giubhsaich, as it is now spelled; Scottish Gaelic: 'burn of the fir wood') is a hunting-lodge south-east of Balmoral and just north of Loch Muick (modern spelling of Loch Muich), which was used for day visits and occasional overnight stays by Victoria and Albert during their weeks at Balmoral. A renovated farmhouse, originally sod-roofed, it has one storey with a dormered second storey; a second building was added to accommodate staff.

This faithful and trusty valet . . . Coburg: the Queen began composing this note on Löhlein in the earliest proof of the private edition (which eventually served as the first proof of *Leaves*), in pencil at the bottom of the printed page, and she continued adding to it in successive proofs. Initially she wrote the word 'confidential', then crossed it out and wrote 'personal page', later amended to 'personal groom of the chambers or valet'. The pencilled draft note lacked the sentence starting 'I gave him a house' and concluded: 'He is a native of Coburg. – Jan. 1865'. The sentence about Löhlein's father was added midway through the editing process, and the sentence about the house near Windsor Castle appears only in the finished publication.

which some say means "darkness" or "sorrow": in early proofs this reads, 'which should be pronounced Mûich.' In a later proof, the pronunciation guidance has been cut and the line reads 'which some say means "pigs," others say it means "darkness" or "sorrow".' An editor's pencilled comment in the margin reads: 'to be verified'. The original diary, as transcribed and edited by Princess Beatrice, reads prosaically, 'Its name is Muick, signifying pigs.'

69 *A Beat in the Abergeldie Woods.*: above the title of this entry, in the proof volume annotated 'corrections in the handwriting of Queen Victoria', appears a note in pencil: 'too many *gots*'. Two were eliminated on the first page of this entry:

'I mounted my pony' was originally 'I got on my pony'; 'I got off' was changed to 'I dismounted', but this revision was not used. The handwriting is not that of the Queen, but it is likely she was dictating corrections to someone else.

69 *Geannachoil*: in 1848 Prince Albert purchased a forty-year lease of the Abergeldie estate, as it adjoined Balmoral on the east. The Genechal, or Sean-choille (Scottish Gaelic: 'the old wood'), is a wood just south of Abergeldie, which formed part of these lands. The Queen had a cottage built here; one half was occupied by John Morgan and his family, who served as housekeepers, while the other half was reserved for use by the royal family.

the distillery: the Lochnagar distillery, located between Balmoral and Abergeldie, originated as an illegal still, one of many hidden in the mountain glens of the Highlands to avoid a heavy excise tax. Once parliament reduced the tax in 1823 and the government began selling licences, the distillery was re-established on a legal basis. John Begg became the owner in 1846, and the Queen granted it a royal warrant in 1848, which led to its renaming as the Royal Lochnagar Distillery. The royal family and their guests were frequent visitors.

70 *the hut*: by this the Queen means her substantial house, Alt-na-Giuthasach (see note to *Leaves*, 67). The Dhu Loch (now spelled Dubh Loch) is west of Loch Muick.

John Brown: in an early proof, John Brown's name reads 'J. Brown' and the Queen has inserted 'Johnnie' in the margin. In a subsequent proof, 'Johnnie' has been adopted; in a still later proof, this has been corrected to 'John'. 'Johnnie' was amended to 'John' because, according to a letter from the Queen (referring to herself in the third person) to Arthur Helps, 'Brown has told Queen Victoria that Johnnie is never used except for boys so he must appear in her book as John Brown.'

old John Gordon leading the way: in addition to the series of edits of John Brown's name in this sentence, further edits appear in pencil, including moving the phrase about John Gordon from an earlier position in the list to the end, making the sentence more graceful and giving the prominence he merits to 'old John Gordon'.

72 *Ben-na-Bhourd*: this mountain north-west of Braemar is spelled Beinn a Bhuird on modern maps. The travellers follow a path up a burn that runs south-east through a narrow glen, Allt an t-Slugain (the Sluggan in the Queen's spelling), into the River Dee.

Lady Douro's: in Princess Beatrice's transcription, Lady Douro appears as 'Bessy Douro'; part of the work of revision was converting familiar names to formal names and titles.

far from the top: in the late proof in which the corrections are said to be in the Queen's handwriting, a line has been drawn through a sentence omitted here: 'I scrambled along extremely well and actively.' This sentence appears in the original diary, according to Princess Beatrice's transcription.

74 *The Gathering.*: the Braemar Gathering of the 1850s (see *Leaves*, 106–7, for Victoria and Albert's sponsorship of a related event in 1859) originated, after a lapse following the Disarming Act of 1746, in the clan Gathering that began in the days of armed Highland resistance to the English Crown (see

Explanatory Notes to Leaves 403

Introduction, xx–xxi). In the 1850s the Gathering was based at Braemar Castle, on the eastern side of Clunie Water, where it meets the Dee in Braemar. Races were run up Craig Cheunnich (spelled Creag Choinnich on modern maps) across the military road from the castle; the Highland Gathering now has its own dedicated arena on the west side of the town.

A work . . . the Royal Household.: the full title of the work referred to is *The Highlanders of Scotland: Portraits Illustrative of the Principal Clans and Followings, and the Retainers of the Royal Household at Balmoral, in the Reign of Her Majesty Queen Victoria*. In the later 1860s, the Queen commissioned Edinburgh portrait painter Kenneth Macleay (1802–1878) to paint thirty-one watercolors portraying fifty-seven individuals, and she collaborated with the Dowager Duchess of Atholl to have the book published, in two volumes, in 1870 by Mitchell of London. Amelia Murray MacGregor wrote the accompanying text about the individual men, the clan objects they are holding in the portraits, and the tartans in which they are portrayed. The original images are in the Royal Library at Windsor Castle.

75 *Salmon Leistering.*: the Queen's sketch of this scene appears at the head of this entry in the illustrated edition.

above the bridge: the bridge crosses the Dee between the village of Crathie and the Balmoral grounds to the east of the castle; 'above the bridge' means upstream, to the west of the bridge. A net was stretched across the width of the river, into which people holding the 'leisters' drove the fish.

77 *the hut*: Alt-na-Giuthasach (see note to *Leaves*, 67).

The same who . . . trustworthy young man.: in the earliest proof of the private edition (which later served as the first proof of *Leaves*), the Queen's footnote about Brown was shorter, lacked the information about his family, and concluded with the Queen's first impression of him, quoted from her diary for 1850: 'J. [or, as later revised, Johnnie] Brown is a nice, active, modest lad; very good-humoured; always ready to do whatever is asked, and always with a smile on his face. He is 23, tall and good-looking, with a profusion of fair, curly hair.' She also described the value of his 'attention, care and faithfulness—now that my sorrow and shattered strength have rendered me so dependent and helpless.' To the line about her shattered strength she initially added, 'and his true sympathy in my great sorrow is very soothing to me', before both expressions were cut and replaced. In proof after proof, the list of his good qualities is changed and changed again (for example, in a later proof he is 'honest, simple, steady, fearless, and unselfish'); the account of Brown at 23 with his curly hair is removed; and the information about the family is added. Many additional small revisions throughout the proof volumes attest to the importance of the wording of this note; Enoch comments, 'this note passed many readings'.

"Ever, as on they bore . . . harsher note away.": these lines from Sir Walter Scott's *The Lady of the Lake* (Canto 2, stanza 17) immediately follow the lines ('See the proud pipers on the bow . . .') that the Queen quotes to describe a similar moment in the visit to Loch Tay on her first journey to Scotland in 1842 (see *Leaves*, 29). Both quotations depict the hero Roderick Dhu's boat crossing Loch Katrine to land on Ellen's (or Helen's) Isle. The Queen refers again to this poem in *More Leaves*, 247 and 250.

79 *Account of the News of the Duke of Wellington's Death.*: this entry, like the entry about the Princess Royal's betrothal, was added—along with the earlier trips to Scotland and the four additional journeys—after the completion of the private edition, as the book was being revised for commercial publication. This account was drafted by the Queen on Balmoral stationery.

Shiel of the Glassalt, and the head of the loch: the party has been walking and riding south from Alt-na-Giuthasach along the northern shore of Loch Muick, turning north and uphill along a small stream (Alt-na-Dearg) that runs into it, then overland to a larger stream, the Glassalt, down which they then return south to Loch Muick. The Shiel of the Glassalt, on the northern shore of Loch Muick, was, in 1852, a single-storey, two-bedroom cottage that had been built in 1851 for Charles Duncan, a gillie on the Balmoral estate, and his wife. It had a room reserved for royal parties. In 1866–8 the Queen had it replaced with a larger building to serve as her 'widow's house' (see *More Leaves*, 240–1).

81 *Craig Gowan . . . this dear place*: Craig Gowan, directly south of Balmoral Castle, became the location of several cairns, most of them commemorating the marriages of her children; the cairn described in this entry is known as 'Purchase Cairn'.

One of the keepers . . . by the Prince.: the Queen drafted this footnote in pencil, written over in pen, in the earliest proof of the private edition (which later served as the first proof of *Leaves*). In this draft she wrote '+ very nice looking' before 'much liked by the Prince'. The draft ends with 'stalking'. The rest of the note was added later.

83 *admired him much*: in the original diary (according to Princess Beatrice's transcription), the Queen ended the entry with a tally of Prince Albert's shooting for 1852: 'Albert has shot in all 32 stags. Last year, he got only 18 stags & the preceding year, still fewer.' In the illustrated edition, a second sketch of a dead stag by the Queen appears after the end of the entry.

In the private edition (which became the first proof of *Leaves*), an entry titled 'A Beat in the Corrie Buie and of Carrop Woods' appears here, after 'Building the Cairn on Craig Gowan, &c' and before 'Laying the Foundation Stone of Our New House'. The entry was later cut for the publication of *Leaves*, but was reinstated for the people's edition of March 1868 and the illustrated edition of December 1868. Corrie Buie, a steep-sided hollow, south-west of Balmoral, is Coire Buidhe on modern maps; Carrop Woods (as the Queen explains in *Leaves*, 102) is another name for Garmaddie Woods, south-west of the castle.

In this entry, the Queen accompanies Albert on a hunting expedition; they see 'the finest sight imaginable—thirty or forty hinds with four or five stags;' Albert shoots one, 'a noble animal' that 'struggled and groaned' before Albert kills it with another shot. Victoria calls this 'a most exciting sight'. Then Albert shoots another stag. Before the entry was cut, the Queen marked a short passage for excision: 'In running back after him, which I did very fast, I got such a tumble, my whole length in the heather, and I think on a stone, for I hurt my knee a good deal. Good Affie, who was with me, was so kind about it, so frightened and distressed.'

84 *Laying the Foundation Stone of Our New House.*: see Introduction, xxxi–xxxii, for the two-year process of replacing the original castle at Balmoral with a new building.

86 *The Kirk.*: the date of this entry has been altered from the original: 8 October 1854. The entry originally included domestic and political comments and has been edited to focus on the church visit. The Queen's attendance at services at the Kirk (or Presbyterian Church of Scotland) is 'as usual', but she did not take communion there until 1873; see *More Leaves*, 262–3.

"the dying . . . and the orphans": this is a reference to British soldiers injured and killed in the Crimean War, which began in 1853 as a conflict between Russia and the Ottoman Empire (modern-day Turkey); Britain joined the war in 1854 (along with France) to prevent Russia from expanding its empire and taking control of the Black Sea and trade routes through Turkey into Asia. The war was fought on the Crimean Peninsula and elsewhere around the Black Sea, with contention especially over Sevastopol, a port city on Crimea's south-west coast, which was home to Russia's Black Sea fleet. Notorious for what the British public considered the excessive scale of the casualties, the Crimean War was among the first modern wars, fought with new technology, such as explosive artillery shells, and with the aid of the railways and the telegraph; it also saw the beginning of professional wartime nursing, as Florence Nightingale and nurses she trained pioneered the treatment of war injuries in Britain's military hospitals. As many British soldiers died of disease as in battle.

89 *Sevastopol is in the hands of the Allies*: the siege of Sevastopol had lasted for a year; the success of the allied armies of Britain, France, and the Ottoman Empire in driving the Russian army out of Sevastopol led to the war's end a few months later.

91 *The Betrothal of the Princess Royal.*: like the entry on the death of the Duke of Wellington, this entry was added after the printing of the private edition. The original diary entry, as transcribed and edited by Princess Beatrice, contains extensive discussion of the betrothal, contractual arrangements for the marriage, and the relationships, personal and dynastic, of the couple and their families.

94 *St. Hubert, with . . . St. George*: St Hubert (*c.*656–727), who encountered a stag with a crucifix between its antlers, was the patron saint of hunters and their dogs. St Andrew (one of Jesus's twelve apostles) is the patron saint of Scotland. St George—often portrayed killing a dragon—is the patron saint of England.

Mr. Thomas: John Thomas (1813–1862) was an architectural sculptor and architect who worked on many celebrated public projects, including the monumental lions for the Britannia Railway Bridge over the Menai Strait; he also worked on the interior decoration at Buckingham Palace and Windsor Castle.

97 *girls in skirts of the same*: on this occasion and another two years later (see *Leaves*, 106) the Queen and her daughters wear dresses that combine two distinct fabrics: tartan skirts (probably silk or wool) and silk velvet bodices. See Introduction, xxxii–xxxiii, for the use of tartan at Balmoral.

98 *up the hill . . . who I was*: Balnacroft is a house and small farm just east of Balmoral, near Abergeldie; Mrs Farquharson was the wife of the Abergeldie gamekeeper, and the houses the Queen visits form a cluster around Balnacroft. Princess Beatrice's transcription of the original diary does not include Mrs Farquharson introducing the Queen to the poor cottagers, but this remark is present from the earliest proof for the private edition (which later served as the first proof of *Leaves*).

99 *having said . . . (the Princess) again*: in a proof, Arthur Helps underlined an earlier phrasing ('that she had said she feared she would not see her again') and commented in pencil in the margin, 'This to Mr Helps is rather a puzzling bit. He supposes that the shes apply to the old woman, and the "her" to the princess. If so, may the words "the Princess" be inserted in brackets after her?' To which the Queen replied, with a double underline in the same margin, 'Yes.'

"*I am very sorry . . . not what is fut*" *(fit)*: Mrs Grant's quoted words do not appear in Princess Beatrice's transcription of the original diary entry. Most likely this rather audacious remark was cut for the transcription, which includes only the report (in the third person) of Mrs Grant's fear that she would not see Vicky again.

100 *Feithluie . . . Feithort*: Feithort is at the upper end of a footpath up Feithluie (Feith an Laoigh on modern maps), a narrow burn that runs north-east into Gelder Burn, south of the castle. In 1863 the Queen had a stone placed at Feithort to commemorate the prince's hunting camp, now marked as 'The Prince's Stone'.

101 *half-past six*: in the illustrated edition the Queen's sketch of 'Highland Lad and Lassie' appears at the end of this entry.

102 *September 18, 1858*: in Princess Beatrice's transcription of the diary, this entry is dated October 18, 1858.

Craig Luraghain: the Queen initially wrote 'Craig Lowrican', as the name appears in early proofs. In a later proof, an editor (probably Enoch) has written at the bottom of the page in pen, 'Craig-lour-achin (in a Gaelic book)'. Another editor, probably Helps, then scribbled over this in pencil: 'on Miss McGregor's authority and Brown's'. That yet a third spelling appears in the final publication attests to the significance, as well as the difficulty, of conveying Gaelic terms into English. It is spelled Creag an Lurachain on modern maps. This hill (spelled Craig Lowrigan in *More Leaves*) became the location of Prince Albert's memorial cairn, built in 1862–3.

103 "*My companion . . . than elsewhere.*": Frederick W. Robertson, *Lectures and Addresses on Literary and Social Topics* (London: Smith, Elder, & Co.; Boston: Ticknor & Fields, 1859), 19–20. The passage is accurately transcribed except for the omission of a phrase indicating that the man has 'a rifle on his shoulder' and a 'curling feather in his high green hat'. Robertson's lecture, given to the Working Men's Institute of Brighton in 1848, took as its subject the potential refinement of working men's minds, and after the passage quoted by the Queen he next turns to Wordsworth's appreciation for ordinary country people.

"*The gorgeous bright October . . . from her.*": Arthur Hugh Clough (1819–1861) was born in Liverpool and attended Rugby School and Oxford University.

The Bothie of Tober-na-Vuolich: A Long-Vacation Pastoral (1849) is a lengthy poem in nine parts, written in hexameters; the slightly misquoted passage is from Part VIII, lines 159–66. The title, roughly translated, means 'the hut of the bearded well' and refers to a Highland location where five Oxford University friends gather with a tutor to learn and to explore the lochs, glens, and cliffs. The poem follows the adventures of Philip; in the quoted lines' vibrant setting, 'Elspie gave her troth to Philip', so the quotation also lightly alludes to the Highland romance between Victoria and Albert. The quotation does not appear in Princess Beatrice's transcription of the original diary.

snow lying on the highest hills: neither the lines from Clough nor the rest of this entry as printed in *Leaves* appears in Princess Beatrice's transcription; instead, the entry ends with details about Albert's shooting (a 'fine stag, his 21rst') and their departure, as this was their last evening in Scotland for the year. The Clough quotation was probably added for the publication of *Leaves*, but the subsequent exclamation ('Oh! how I gazed and gazed . . .') and the record of the snow in 1852 and thereafter might have been present in the original diary and omitted from the transcription. In the proof volume said to include corrections in the Queen's handwriting, the last sentence was edited: pencil lines are drawn through a parenthesis '(excepting the last three years)' between 'had' and 'snow-storms', and through a sentence that had ended the passage in proof: 'Snow was even lying on the grass everywhere in the wood.'

104 *and Brown*: Princess Beatrice's transcription of the original diary omits any mention of Brown on the ascent of Morven, referring only to the presence of gillies.

105 *the reception most gratifying*: in 1859, Prince Albert was president of the British Association for the Advancement of Science, and he gave a speech at their twenty-ninth meeting, held in Aberdeen—their first meeting in the Highlands. Among the BAAS's investigative interests were the racial identities and characteristics of the various peoples of Britain, and in his speech praising the association's advancement of the scientific method of objective observation, he spoke of 'nature in its wild and primitive form' in the Highlands, and listed the Highlanders' racial composition: 'Man also, the highest object of our study, is found in vigorous, healthy development, presenting a happy mixture of the Celt, Goth, Saxon, and Dane, acquiring his strength on the hills and the sea.' *The Principal Speeches and Addresses of His Royal Highness the Prince Consort* (London: John Murray, 1862), 206–7.

106 *Fête to the Members of the British Association.*: Prince Albert invited the members of the BAAS to visit Balmoral the week after his speech in Aberdeen, to observe the local performance of Highland games. The Braemar Gathering (see note to *Leaves*, 74) had already been held on 1 September at Braemar Castle, so the Queen and the Prince invited all the participants to Balmoral three weeks later to restage the competition and the military display for the BAAS. About two hundred members attended, travelling by train to Banchory and then by carriage to Balmoral, leaving Aberdeen at 6 a.m. one morning and arriving home at 1 a.m. the next.

carriages laden with "philosophers": members of the BAAS are called 'philosophers' (and later 'savants') because 'natural philosophy' was a contemporary term for science. In several proofs, an additional sentence appeared here: 'We lunched at one, and saw many amusing figures appear outside: from half past twelve they had begun to appear.' In a late proof, an editor (probably Helps) has crossed this sentence out and written beneath it in pencil: 'Will offend.' The sentence with 'amusing figures' does not appear in Princess Beatrice's transcription of the diary.

106 *over black velvet bodies*: see note to *Leaves*, 97; 'bodies' is a variant of 'bodices' (see Glossary).

Farquharson's men . . . opposite to us: these three Highland militias represent local landowners: the Farquharsons, Lairds of Invercauld, had regained ownership of Braemar Castle from the British military in 1831 (see notes to *Leaves*, 66 and 74); Duff was the clan name of the Earl of Fife, whose seat was Mar Lodge, about four miles (about six and a half km) west of Braemar; and Sir Charles Forbes's ancestral home was in Strathdon, north of Balmoral across the Dee.

they ran beautifully: the spectacle of the Highlanders competing in track and field events (running, the hammer throw, tossing the caber, and the shot-put) was recorded by Egron Lundgren, an artist commissioned by Victoria and Albert, who specialized in watercolours of historical and folkloric subjects. His work from 1859 appears in the illustrated edition: his image of tossing the caber appears with this entry from 1859, that of runners in kilts in the entry of 1850.

108 *à l'improviste*: French: 'unexpected', 'improvised'.

the old "Military Road": following the Jacobite rebellion of 1715, a network of military roads was built to ensure the subjection of Scotland. The first four such roads, built under the command of General George Wade, linked the Central Lowlands with a series of fortified barracks located strategically across the Highlands: Inverness to Fort William; Dunkeld to Inverness via the Pass of Drumochter; Crieff to the existing road at Dalnacardoch by Aberfeldy and the Tummel Bridge; and Dalwhinnie to Fort Augustus. Further military roads, including one reaching Braemar from Blairgowrie in the south and continuing north from Braemar to Cockbridge, Tomintoul, and Grantown— the road they travel on briefly here—were built under Major William Caufeild in the 1740s to 1760s; see also *More Leaves*, 335–6.

110 *Ascent of Ben Muich Dhui.*: this mountain, the highest in the Cairngorms (and the second highest in Scotland after Ben Nevis), is now known as Ben Macdui. The Queen gives its height accurately.

At Castleton we took four post-horses: in Braemar, Castleton is the part of the town that lies on the eastern bank of Clunie Water where it joins the Dee; the Queen uses the term to refer to the inn (the Invercauld Arms) where they hired horses for excursions west and north of Balmoral, and where the Earl of Mar first raised the Stuart standard at the start of the Jacobite rising of 1715.

cattle coming down for the "Tryst.": the party is travelling towards the mountain on the Lairig an Laoigh, a cattle drovers' road. The Queen sometimes describes encountering cattle being driven to market or travelling over drovers' roads; more often she uses such roads without seeing what they are. Cattle were an important part of the Highland economy before the Clearances, and drovers' roads were principal arteries in the Highlands before the building of the military roads. Her use of them for pleasure excursions is a sign of the Highlands' economic and social transformation.

111 *We were always . . . talk to them.*: this footnote, initially hand-drafted as an insertion into the printed proof text, was turned into a footnote and heavily revised in various handwritings, including that of the Queen, who changed 'with whom you come so much in contact' to 'one comes'. The draft also included, in parentheses, 'as everyone who has lived in the Highlands knows' after 'which make it.' That 'The Prince' originally read 'Albert' indicates the Queen's particular attention to drafting the note, even though little of it is in her handwriting.

"Shiel" means a small shooting-lodge.: a shiel is a roughly made, temporary hut for herders or fishermen, but the term is sometimes used to refer to a small house or cottage; it does not primarily mean a shooting-lodge, but the Queen rebuilt such small structures into lodges—for example, at Alt-na-Giuthasach or, later, Glassalt Shiel.

112 *The Fishie and Geldie*: the travellers have followed a path west up the River Dee and then up its tributary, Geldie Burn; a short way overland, near where Geldie Burn originates and descends to the east, the River Feshie (as Fishie is now spelled) begins its descent north-west towards the River Spey. Stron-na-Barin, 'the nose of the queen', a steep peak they pass to their left near the beginning of the Feshie, appears as Sron na Banrigh on modern maps.

113 *all falling into decay*: this encampment of huts near Ruigh-aiteachain in Glen Feshie, with their connection to the painter Edwin Landseer, encountered here and on the 'third great expedition' (*Leaves*, 128), were built by Georgiana, Duchess of Bedford (1781–1853), to serve as casual guest accommodation when she and her husband, the Duke of Bedford, stayed on the Invereshie estate, which they leased for hunting from 1825. The Duke hired Landseer to paint the family, the landscape, and the local animals; it was rumoured he became the lover of the Duchess. Landseer decorated some of the chimney pieces with frescoes of deer. Almost nothing remains of these structures, but a copy of Landseer's *Monarch of the Glen* has been hung in a nearby stone bothy that is available for public use.

monument to the late Duke of Gordon: perched high on a hill, Torr Alvie, in the Kinrara estate, south of Aviemore, is the 80-foot (24-metre) column, topped with a statue of the Duke, erected in 1840 to commemorate the 5th Duke of Gordon, who died in 1836. The Waterloo Cairn, also on Torr Alvie, was erected by the 5th Duke to commemorate those local men who fell at the Battle of Waterloo.

"The Duke of Argyll's Stone" . . . with his army: the Argyll Stone (Clach Mhic Calein) is a naturally formed granite tor near the summit of Creag Dubh, south of the River Spey and the monuments on Torr Alvie. It is thought to have been named for Archibald Campbell, the 7th Earl of Argyll (1575–1638), who paused there while retreating south after his Protestant army was defeated by a Catholic force at the Battle of Glenlivet in 1594.

Loch Inch: (now spelled Loch Insh) a widening of the River Spey between the towns of Kingussie and Aviemore. The royal party is travelling north-east along the Spey towards Grantown-on-Spey.

114 *which Grant took in hand*: printed in the second proof for the private edition, the image of the Spey ferry (113) included two errors that were subsequently

corrected. Initially Grant, in the ferry's bow, was pictured wearing a kilt; on the proof, the Queen marked the image with an X and wrote in the lower margin, 'This man with the oar ought to have trowsers & no kilt.' (In Macleay's *Highlanders of Scotland*, Grant is uniquely depicted wearing trousers; all the other men wear the kilt, see note to *Leaves*, 74.) In the same proof image, the Queen and Lady Churchill are wearing veils; these were later removed.

115 *Grant and Brown . . . tart of cranberries*: the three sentences calling Grant and Brown 'bashful' and detailing the service and food at the dinner are not present in Princess Beatrice's transcription of the original diary.

got to bed: in proof, the words 'went away, to begin undressing' were marked 'Qy' (for 'query') by an editor and crossed out, with the pencilled word 'retired' suggested instead, but the revision was not accepted. Following the last words of this entry, the earliest proof for the private edition (which became the first proof for *Leaves*) continued: '—a very hard bed, but quite clean. We had taken the precaution of having our own sheets, which, however, told tales the next day, from the mark of the crown and V. R. on them.' The sentence about the marked sheets had been cut by the time of the later proof in which 'undressing' was queried. Princess Beatrice's transcription includes neither this sentence about the marked sheets nor the previous one about undressing.

116 *dirty-looking houses and people*: in the earliest proof for the private edition, this description of Tomintoul continued at this point: 'and a look of wretched disreputability about it, which reminded Lady Churchill of an Irish village: Grant said they were chiefly Catholics—a large Catholic church there—and he afterwards told me that it was the dirtiest, poorest village in the whole of the Highlands, and that the epithet for a miserable person in this part of the world was a "Tomintouler".' Princess Beatrice's transcription includes the phrase 'with a disreputable look', but not the comments about Ireland and Catholics.

Tomintoul sits on a ridge at the highest elevation of any town in the Highlands. It was planned and built in the 1770s by Alexander, the 4th Earl of Gordon, with a central square and houses lining the military road built twenty years before. The Earl had the farmland around it cleared of the locals' crops, with the aim of starting a linen industry, which, however, failed—hence the poverty the Queen observed.

118 *she had on many more than*: in the illustrated edition, an engraving of the Queen's sketch of Loch Bulig appears after these words, in a space between blocks of text near the end of the entry.

119–20 *It is very fine indeed, and very striking*: in the earliest proof for the private edition, a small indented space, seven lines high and two-thirds of the width of the page, is left in the type just beneath the description of the Ladder Burn (ending with the words 'and very striking'), and a larger space (a little less than half a page) is left on the facing page above the words 'a picturesque group of "shearers"'. The same-sized space is also left at the top of the next page, just after 'the *Hill of Doun*'. Like other such spaces in the earliest proof, these seem to have been left to insert sketches of the scenes indicated (the arrangement would now be called 'text wrap', except that there is no image for the text to surround); the spaces are gone in the next proof.

120 *south to the north, whence they came*: itinerant agricultural workers, probably returning on foot from harvest work in the south. The Queen's party has been following the Mounth road, an old drovers' road.

Invermark: south of Ballater, near Loch Lee and the point where the Water of Mark joins the River Esk. Invermark Castle is a stone tower house, built in the sixteenth century and abandoned in 1803; after passing the ruined castle, the Queen visits Invermark Lodge, Lord Dalhousie's house.

The White Well: see *More Leaves*, 197, for the Queen's return in 1865 to this spot, where Lord Dalhousie had a memorial built in the shape of a royal crown to commemorate the visit described here. It is now called the Queen's Well.

steep Highland bridges: the travellers are following the River Esk as it flows south-east out of the Highlands; the Water of Tarf (not to be confused with the better-known Tarf Water, which flows into the Tilt near Blair Atholl), a tributary flowing from the north, is crossed by a bridge just before it joins the Esk. Fettercairn is on the coastal plain.

122 *"It's a wedding party from Aberdeen."*: at the back of one of the later proof volumes, an editor (noting the two relevant page numbers) writes: 'leave out the falsehoods / The narration of these without reproof touches the author's reputation.' Grant's remark is one of the 'falsehoods' that troubled this editor, committed to enable the Queen's party to travel incognito; for the other, see *Leaves*, 130. The editor might have counted other 'falsehoods' as well—for example, the Queen describes Grant and Brown giving 'evasive answers' to a crowd that gathers around the incognito travellers in the town of Kingussie (*Leaves*, 128).

"King Durdun's Stone,": the travellers return due north from Fettercairn. King Dardanus' Stone is a 4-foot (1.2-metre) tall menhir, or standing stone, which was uncovered in the eighteenth century on the roadside near the town of Finzean. It is alleged to mark the tomb of a first-century king of Scotland, though it is more probably a much older Bronze Age monument. Frederick Enoch, tasked with researching locations and place names, writes in pen in the lower margin, 'King Dardanus's?' followed by a long parenthetical comment: '(Fullerton says: "there is here a long granite stone which is reported to mark the spot where King Dardanus the 20th from Fergus I was put to death").' For Fullerton, see note to *Leaves*, 19.

124 *with good Grant*: after these words, in early proofs this passage continued: 'As we went along, chatted as usual with good Grant; and yesterday I asked him how he liked "Alice's young gentleman?" And he said, "Oh very well, he has not much English, and that makes him bashful; he's very clever; he'll go anywhere; I hope he's *good*." I answered "that he was very good." "That's the main thing, was Grant's observation."' This passage remains in the second proof volume for the private edition, where the Queen edits for clarity and drafts a footnote: '"Clever" is used by the Highlanders to express activity.' Thereafter the entire passage is removed.

128 *the Invereshie huts*: see note to *Leaves*, 113.

128 *ruined Castle of Ruthven*: not a ruined castle but a barracks built for the Hanoverian army in 1716, extended by General Wade in 1734, and burned by the Jacobites in 1746. The barracks were built on the site of a fourteenth-century castle of Alexander Stewart, the Wolf of Badenoch.

129 *They had . . . our two starved chickens!*: in the earliest proof for the private edition, this sentence reads, 'They had only our four starved chickens;' the Queen has inserted 'only the remnants of' in pen in the margin. In a later proof, the four chickens here were reduced to two, to match the count earlier in the paragraph. In the second proof volume, the words 'and no *fun*' earlier in this paragraph were crossed out in pencil, but they remain in subsequent proofs.

on the right, The Athole Sow: in the earliest proof for the private edition (which became the first proof for *Leaves*), a large space for a drawing was left after this sentence.

130 *Four horses . . . and off we started.*: this is the second of two 'falsehoods' that an editor objected to; see note to *Leaves*, 122.

the railroad will come: Scotland's railway network was expanding rapidly in this period. The first railway in Scotland was the Monkland and Kirkintilloch Railway, opened in 1826 and operated using horse traction. By 1850 Scotland's major cities were linked to each other and to the rest of the British rail network. The second half of the nineteenth century saw a rapid expansion of the network, and by 1900 virtually every town with a population greater than 2,000 on the Scottish mainland had a railway station.

the old castle: Blair Castle.

132 *a great many to feed*: at the proof stage, this sentence was the subject of a pencilled marginal discussion between Helps and another editor. 'This is the only place in which we have left this about giving the remnants. Shall it be stet.' To which Helps replied, 'Yes AH.' Feeding servants with the remnants of a royal meal is also mentioned in the 'Third Great Expedition', *Leaves*, 129.

ford of the Tarff: Tarf Water (as it is now spelled) runs south-east to where it joins another stream to form the River Tilt, up which the party has been travelling north-east from Blair; in the narrow glen, fifteen yards above the meeting of waters, is the surprisingly deep ford, Poll Tarf. The illustrated edition includes a full-page engraving of the celebrated painting by Carl Haag depicting this crossing. A bridge was built in 1885.

133 *and again in coming in*: in the earliest proof for the private edition, the text continued here: 'When we crossed the March the Duke said, jokingly, "now we are in the enemy's country." In former times there had been great feuds between the Atholmen and the men of Braemar—the latter having attacked the former.' Here the Queen made a correction in pen in the lower margin, 'Athole, always with an e at the end', and she indicates that 'Athole men' should be 'two words'. Although the passage remained in the next few proofs, incorporating the Queen's spelling correction, the entire passage was later cut.

134 *Loch Callater*: with Cairn Turc, south-west of Balmoral Castle. Loch Canter (nearby) is spelled Loch Kander on modern maps.

Explanatory Notes to Leaves   413

Shichallion: spelled Schiehallion, then and now; the editors did not always correct the Queen's frequent phonetic spellings.

135 *Cairn Lochan*: directly south of Cairn Turc.

139 *Tours in England and Ireland, and Yachting Excursions.*: The inclusion of this section's travelogues in *Leaves* reveals a desire to demonstrate royal interest in the other nations and regions that constitute the United Kingdom, to complement the concentration on Scotland. The narratives seem to have been selected and edited to emphasize royal engagement with local communities. Although each of the volume's three main sections follows chronological order, the 'First Visit to Ireland', 1849, appears out of sequence. It was the first addition selected for inclusion once the decision was made to supplement the entries on life at Balmoral.

141 *the "Ganges" . . . and the "Hogue"*: the 'two war-steamers'—the flagship *Ganges* and the *Hogue*, a sailing ship converted to steam—provide a heavily armed Royal Navy escort for the Queen's first visit to Ireland, which is taking place at a time of great unrest owing to the Great Famine. See Introduction, xlvii–xlviii, for the historical context.

142 *two Members, Messrs. Roche and Power*: the Irish Parliament having been dissolved by the Acts of Union, there were 100 members of parliament (in London) elected from Ireland between 1801 and 1922, when the Irish Free State seceded from Great Britain.

Roman Catholic and Protestant clergymen: the Queen carefully notes the inter-denominational nature of this welcoming event: most Irish people were Catholic (particularly in the south, where this scene takes place), yet the Protestant (Anglican) Church of Ireland was the established church, leading to the exclusion of Catholics from many aspects of civic life. The suppression of Catholicism in Ireland was a chief cause of Irish resistance to British rule.

Queenstown: given this name in honour of Queen Victoria's visit in 1849, the town on Great Island in the city of Cork's harbour had been called the Cove of Cork when the Royal Navy began using it in the 1750s. In 1920 'Queenstown' was replaced by the name 'Cobh', a gaelicization of 'Cove'. It was the departure point for millions of Irish emigrants leaving for North America after 1848.

Lord-Lieutenant of the county: each county in Ireland had its own Lord Lieutenant, the representative of the monarch in that community. He was usually a member of the aristocracy who owned a home there. Lord Lieutenant or Lieutenant General was also the title of the chief governor of Ireland until independence in 1922, though the title Viceroy of Ireland was more commonly used.

one of the four . . . by Act of Parliament: in the 1840s, parliament debated whether to support the education of Catholic priests financially, or, instead, to allow only Protestants to attend Ireland's colleges. The Queen, advocating religious tolerance, had backed Prime Minister Robert Peel's support for non-sectarian education. The Queen's Colleges Bill was passed in 1848, creating provincial non-sectarian Queen's Colleges in Cork (which the Queen now observes under construction), Belfast, and Galway. Trinity College

Dublin (then the sole constituent college of the University of Dublin) had been founded in the sixteenth century and had been closed to all but Anglicans; Maynooth College was founded in 1795 to educate Catholic priests.

143 *Duncannon Fort*: guards the entrance to Waterford Harbour.

battle of the Boyne: fought along the Boyne River, north-west of Dublin, in 1690 between the armies of the deposed Catholic King James VII and II, in alliance with Irish and French forces, and the much larger forces of the Protestant monarchs William III and Mary II. James VII and II had supported Catholicism in Ireland. The battle ended in his defeat, but Jacobite feeling remained strong in Ireland.

they had not saluted for fifty years: the last salute fifty years ago would have marked the Acts of Union of 1800.

Viceregal Lodge, Phœnix Park: the residence of the British ruler in Ireland, now the residence of Ireland's President. Princess Beatrice's transcription of the Queen's diary indicates that the entries for 5 and 6 August have been rearranged, and domestic and travel details eliminated to make a clear narrative.

144 *in open revolt and under martial law*: for the historical context, see Introduction, xlvii; the Queen notes the presence of the military in Dublin (e.g. *Leaves*, 146) and mentions 'the rebels', *Leaves*, 150.

with some appropriate words: in the original diary, as transcribed and edited by Princess Beatrice, this sentence continued: 'spoken in an amazing brogue'. About the dove in the next sentence, the Queen continued, in parentheses, '(I have it in a cage now, & it is a dear little thing).'

145 *and have very nice rooms*: in the original diary, as transcribed and edited by Princess Beatrice, this entry originally included more detail about their rooms and the afternoon's activities, including a drive to 'the Horticultural garden . . . through s[o]me suburbs of Dublin, where there are wretched cottages, & wretchedly raggy, dirty people & children, the latter, very handsome. Everywhere the same enthusiasm, shouting, shrieking, calling out, jumping & making every kind of gesture. Jaunting cars followed us, full of people, who made such a noise,—very amusing & quite unlike anything anywhere else. The raggedness of the people is beyond belief, men & boy having really hardly any proper covering, for they never mend anything.' As they continue their drive, they observe beautiful views in Phoenix Park as well as two regiments of British soldiers camped there.

the old Parliament House: the Irish Parliament had been dissolved with the Acts of Union of 1800.

ought to be the case everywhere: see notes to *Leaves*, 142 and 146; against a norm of discrimination against Irish Catholics, the Queen's views on religious instruction are notably tolerant.

the Irish language: Irish (Standard Irish, Gaeilge), referred to as Irish Gaelic outside Ireland, is a Goidelic language of the Insular Celtic branch of the Celtic language family, which is a part of the Indo-European language family. It is distinct from Scottish Gaelic though both are Celtic languages. Irish was the indigenous population's first language until the late eighteenth century. Its use was officially banned (at first only in interactions with the British colonizers) almost from the beginning of British rule, in the fourteenth century. Although English has been the first language of most residents of the island since the early nineteenth century, Irish was spoken as a first language in broad areas of the south and west.

St. Columba's Book: the Queen is being shown some of the great national treasures of Ireland. St Columba's Book, better known as the Book of Kells, was probably created around the year 800, possibly at the monastery on Iona founded by St Columba (see note to *Leaves*, 53). The book was kept for centuries at the monastery at Kells, north-west of Dublin, until it was sent to Trinity College in the seventeenth century. An elaborately decorated, illuminated manuscript of the four gospels of the New Testament, the book is one of the great art works of medieval Europe.

the original harp of King O'Brian: King O'Brian's harp, known as the Brian Boru harp, allegedly belonged to an early medieval Irish king, though the harp at Trinity College was probably built later. It remains an iconic symbol of Ireland.

146 *as at Chelsea*: the Royal Hospital Chelsea in London, founded by King Charles II, is home to the Chelsea Pensioners, retired veterans of the British Army.

statue of William the III: for William III in Ireland, see notes to *Leaves*, 143 and 149. This equestrian statue of 1701 by Grinling Gibbons, centrally located in Dublin, was surrounded by an iron fence when it was erected to defend it from Jacobite protesters, and indeed it became and remained an object of controversy.

the Castle: built in the early thirteenth century, Dublin Castle was the seat of the British monarch's Viceroy and of the British government in Ireland until 1922. The medieval castle was rebuilt during the eighteenth century following a fire in 1684.

Presbyterians . . . and the Quakers: King James VI and I promoted Presbyterianism in Ireland in the early seventeenth century, by offering land to Scottish settlers, as part of the project to convert Catholic Ireland to Protestantism. Non-subscribing Presbyterians were members of a Protestant sect that originated with eighteenth-century Presbyterian ministers who elevated individual conscience and interpretations of the Bible over Presbyterian doctrine. Quakers, or the Society of Friends, never a large group in Ireland, recorded their first Meeting for Worship in Ireland in the seventeenth century.

the crowd was very great: in Princess Beatrice's transcription of the original diary, this account of the crowd continues: 'They often call out "God spare you", or "God speed you", & shriek instead of cheering. One sees such beautiful women & children, the latter, ever so ragged, & always barefooted. They have such fine dark eyes & hair. Equally remarkable are the beggars, or very poor people, all, in the most dreadful tatters, also the boys who run along by the carriages.' This entry was edited, with details about the procession removed, to focus on the military review in Phoenix Park and the Queen's evening Drawing-Room in Dublin Castle.

148 *home a little after five*: in Princess Beatrice's transcription of the original diary, this passage continues with details about their departure from Phoenix Park,

their arrival at the railway station (filled with 'enthusiastic' crowds), and then (to some extent duplicating the start of her entry for the next day): 'Arrived very speedily at Kingstown, where there were just as many people, & as enthusiastic, as on the occasion of our disembarkation, but it made one feel quite sad to hear these parting shouts & cheers. We feel so deeply [tou]ched at the affect[ion]ate loyalty of the poor Irish, who called out "come every year",—"when will you come back" & one man gave "3 cheers for next summer".'

148 *Sunday, August 12*: the dates of the entries for Sunday 12 August, Saturday 11 August, and Sunday 12 August are out of sequence by design: the Queen narrates her departure from Dublin on 10 August, her rapid visit to Belfast and the sea journey north to Scotland on 11 August and the events of 12 August all from the vantage point of the end of day on 12 August.

149 *the first landing of William III*: British rule and King William III were more welcome in Ireland's northern counties, populated by Protestants descended from English settlers, than in the south.

Lord Londonderry: the name of the city and county of Londonderry in the north of Ireland was Derry until they were renamed by James VI and I in 1613; by the mid-nineteenth century, only the Protestant part of the population used the new name.

a mixture of nations: the Queen refers to the mixture of Celtic and Anglo-Saxon people in the northern parts of Ireland; see Introduction, xxi–xxii, for further discussion of racialization. The six counties of Northern Ireland did not become a distinct political entity until the Government of Ireland Act of 1920 divided six northern counties of Ireland from southern Ireland, which remained part of the Union until 1922.

"Cead Mile failte,": the Queen observes that Irish Gaelic and Scottish Gaelic are distinct if similar languages; Old Irish is the original language from which both derive. Scottish Gaelic became a distinct spoken language some time in the thirteenth century, though a common literary language was shared by Gaels in Ireland and Scotland until the sixteenth century. See also note to *Leaves*, 145. In Scotland as well as Ireland, the Queen is often welcomed, as here, in the native language, despite her representing the English-speaking conquerors.

Commentary on this phrase in a proof indicates the cultural and political weightiness of spelling Gaelic correctly. Someone has changed 'cead mille failte' to 'ceadh mille failthe'; an editor, citing Matthew Arnold as authority, writes (on a slip of paper pasted in): 'Lord Strongford says the right spelling of the Irish is Cead mile failte; and that it is Anglo Irishism & barbarism to spell it otherwise.' On another slip of paper, the same writer adds: 'Yr. Majesty will understand that your text is quite right and does not at all require alteration; but I thought you would like to see what he said about the spelling. It is odd he differs; but of course I shall go by what you have seen.' These comments also confirm that the Queen was reading and approving the proofs.

flax and linen manufacture: flax has been grown in Ireland since the Middle Ages. Restrictions on the Irish woollen trade led to the development of the

Explanatory Notes to Leaves 417

linen industry, which became particularly strong during the eighteenth and early nineteenth centuries in the north of Ireland, where the production of textiles made of flax was a domestic industry. Flax was harvested, retted, broken, scutched, and hackled, before the women in the household spun it into yarn, which was woven into linen cloth and taken for sale at the local market town. An innovation of the 1820s, 'wet spinning', enabled a smoother, more uniform yarn to be spun, and by the late 1820s several wet spinning mills using water power had been built in Ulster. Mechanization allowed linen to compete with the cotton industry. By 1850 there were sixty-two mills in the region, employing 19,000 workers, and by 1871 seventy-eight mills with a workforce of 43,000. At the industry's height, almost a third of all flax mills were located in Belfast, and linen was the catalyst that allowed that place to grow from a town into the region's pre-eminent city.

150 *Liverpool and Manchester of Ireland*: that is, the industrial centre.

one of my father's titles: George III had created the title Earl of Dublin for his younger brother, the Duke of Cumberland, to cement the royal family's connection with Ireland.

151 *as we had done two years ago*: for the visit of 1847, see *Leaves*, 48.

"The Duke of Argyll's Bowling-green.": Argyll's Bowling Green (Scottish Gaelic, Baile na Grèine: 'sunny hamlet' or 'sunny cattle fold') is the most southerly part of the Arrochar Alps, on the Ardgoil peninsula between Loch Goil and Loch Long. The name is marked on James Dorret's *General Map of Scotland and Islands thereto Belonging* (1750). The name is an anglicization of the Gaelic, which may be consciously humorous, as there is very little flat land.

152 *Rob Roy's Cave*: an alleged hideout of Robert Roy MacGregor, a Scottish outlaw turned folk hero, who fought in the Jacobite risings of 1689, 1715, and 1719. It is near Inversnaid (Scottish Gaelic, Inbhir Snàthaid), a rural community on the east bank of Loch Lomond, near the north end of the loch. There is a second cave known as Rob Roy's Cave on the banks of Loch Ard.

Sir Edward Parry at the North Pole: Sir William Edward Parry FRS (1790–1855) was an Anglo-Welsh explorer of the Arctic, best known for his expedition of 1819–20 through the Parry Channel, part of the quest for the North-West Passage between the Atlantic and Pacific oceans. In 1827 Parry attempted to reach the North Pole from the northern shores of Spitsbergen. He reached 82°45′N, which remained the highest latitude attained for the next forty-nine years. He published an account of this journey under the title *Narrative of the Attempt to reach the North Pole, &c.*

since we were here!: this entry is extensively rewritten from the original diary entry, as it appears in Princess Beatrice's transcription, apparently to round off the account of this journey.

(Established Church and Free Kirk): 'Established Church' refers to the Presbyterian Church of Scotland; Free Kirk refers to an independent Presbyterian sect.

500,000 people out: in 1849 Glasgow was Scotland's largest city. The population of Scotland was a little under 3 million, with population heavily concentrated in the cities.

153 *immensely high chimney*: probably the brick chimney at Charles Tennant's chemical works at St Rollox, known as St Rollox Stalk or Tennant's Stalk, built in 1842 and, at 435 feet (133 meters), the tallest chimney in the world at that time.

the famous scene in Rob Roy: *Rob Roy* is one of Sir Walter Scott's Waverley novels (see also notes to *Leaves*, 21, and to *More Leaves*, 248 and 255). The narrator, an Englishman, explains the characters of Highlanders as both wild and rebellious, and chivalrous to the English. The swashbuckling tale involves Highland politics after the Jacobite rebellion. The historical Robert Roy MacGregor chose an outlaw life as a political consequence of English rule. In the novel, the Highlands have been only partly pacified.

Marochetti's . . . statue of the Duke of Wellington: this statue by Carlo Marochetti is located outside the present-day Gallery of Modern Art in Glasgow. Financed by public subscription, it was erected in 1844. In recent times it has frequently been capped with a traffic cone.

to see the prison: Perth Prison was built between 1810 and 1812 by French Napoleonic prisoners of war. It was used initially as a depot for some 7,000 of these prisoners, who were repatriated after the Battle of Waterloo in 1815. Between 1815 and 1839 the depot was used as a military store for uniforms and weapons. In 1839 it was decided to build a civilian prison on the site of the Perth Depot; this became the General Prison at Perth, the oldest occupied prison in Scotland.

the Spittal of Glenshee: the Spital (or Spittal) of Glenshee is at the head of Glenshee, where the confluence of many small streams forms the Shee Water, and where traditionally there has been an inn, and in modern times is a small village. The travellers follow the route of the old military road north to Braemar (Castleton). The Devil's Elbow, mentioned just below, is an especially steep section of the road.

155 *Yachting Excursion.*: in the illustrated edition, this entry was headed by an engraving based on the Queen's sketch of Torquay.

Babbicombe, a small bay: Babbacombe Bay is a broad, sandy bay on the east-facing shore of south-east Devon; the surrounding cliffs and some of the sand are red sandstone. It is just south of Teignmouth, a fishing port that became a fashionable seaside resort in the nineteenth century.

read in her English history: the Princess Royal was four and a half years old at this time.

the Lurlei: or Lorelei, a steep slate rock on the right bank of the River Rhine at Sankt Goarshausen in Germany. The name comes from the old German word *lureln*, Rhine dialect for 'murmuring', and the Celtic term *ley* meaning 'rock'. The murmuring sound is created by heavy currents in the river and a small waterfall nearby.

Plymouth Harbour.: once in the harbour, the Queen is at the border of Cornwall, which had been politically, and remained culturally, a semi-independent region of Britain, with its own language and customs. In the medieval period, Cornwall was more closely tied to Brittany (a peninsula in north-west France) than to the rest of Britain. For the Cornish language, see note to *Leaves*, 162.

In 1337 the title Duke of Cornwall was created, to be held by the monarch's eldest son and heir. On the duchy, see also note to *Leaves*, 165. The Tudor monarchs (1485–1603) consolidated central governance of Cornwall, yet the Cornish Rebellion of 1497 pushed back against taxation from the central government and was put down only when the rebels marched on London.

Mount Edgcumbe: Mount Edgcumbe House, on the Rame Peninsula in southeast Cornwall, overlooks Plymouth Sound. It was the principal seat of the Edgcumbe family from Tudor times, many of whom served as members of parliament, before Richard Edgcumbe was raised to the baronage in 1742. His second son, George, was made an earl in 1789. Sir Richard Edgcumbe built the first house between 1547 and 1553. It was badly damaged by German bombs in 1941 during the Second World War, but later its interiors were restored in eighteenth-century style.

156 *the Tamar*: a river in south-west England that forms most of the border between Devon (to the east) and Cornwall (to the west).

Trematon Castle: with its twelfth-century keep, Trematon Castle is situated near Saltash in Cornwall and overlooks Plymouth Sound. It was probably built by Robert, Count of Mortain, on the ruins of an earlier Roman fort and has remained the property of the earls and dukes of Cornwall since 1270, when Richard, Earl of Cornwall, bought it for £300.

numbers of mines at work: mining in Cornwall began in the early Bronze Age, *c.*2150 BC. Cornwall was one of the most important mining areas in Europe until the early twentieth century. Tin and copper were the most commonly extracted metals, and over the years many other metals such as lead and zinc have been mined. In the nineteenth century, before foreign competition depressed the price of copper and tin, the areas around Gwennap and St Day and on the coast around Porthtowan were among the richest mining areas in the world. Many mines reached under the sea and some went down to great depths. At its height, the Cornish tin-mining industry had around 600 steam engines working to pump out the mines. By the middle and late nineteenth century, Cornish mining was in decline, and miners emigrated to developing mining districts overseas, including South Africa, Australia, and North America.

Pentillie Castle: a country house and estate on the bank of the River Tamar. The house, built by Sir James Tillie (1645–1713), was remodelled from 1809 in a Gothic Revival style by Humphrey Repton.

House of Cothele: Cotehele is a rambling stone manor house on the banks of the River Tamar, and one of the least altered Tudor houses in the UK. It was built by the Edgcumbe family from 1458, after an earlier manor house was pulled down: Sir Richard Edgcumbe received the property and the funds to rebuild the house after fighting for Henry Tudor (King Henry VII from 1485 to 1509) in the Battle of Bosworth (1485).

In the original diary entry, as transcribed and edited by Princess Beatrice, at the end of the next sentence the Queen described the rooms as 'very cheerless.'

156 *three years ago*: entries for this visit in 1843 are not included in *Leaves*.

Dartmoor Forest: Dartmoor is an upland area of moorland capped with many exposed granite hilltops known as 'tors', located in south Devon. The entire area is rich in antiquities and archaeology.

157 *Sir Joshua Reynolds*: (1723–1792) the leading English portrait painter of the eighteenth century and the first president of the Royal Academy of Art in London. Born near Plymouth, Devon, he occasionally returned home to paint the nobility of Devon and Cornwall.

the "Kiosk,": the Kiosk at Mount Edgcumbe, also called the Red Seat, is a platform or 'resting house' built on three stone arches at the top of a steep hill in the park.

Mr. Lear's drawings: Edward Lear (1812–1888) was an English artist, musician, and writer. He is now remembered for his nonsense verse, but in the mid-nineteenth century he was known for his illustrations of birds and animals and for the travel books that he illustrated with his drawings. Soon after the publication of his *Excursions in Italy*, in the summer of 1846 the Queen invited him to Osborne to draw and paint her newly built Italianate house and to give her drawing lessons.

the Cornice: a corniche is a road on the side of a cliff or mountain, with the ground rising on one side and falling away on the other. The word has been absorbed into English from the French term *route à corniche* or 'road on a ledge' (from Italian *cornice*: 'ledge'). The Queen probably refers to the corniche roads cut into steep slopes along the Côte d'Azur in southern France and Monaco, with which she was familiar.

158 *the Council*: a meeting of the Privy Council, which gave advice to the monarch and was composed of the Prime Minister and other senior members of parliament, leaders of the Church of England, justices of the Supreme Court, the sovereign's Private Secretary, and sometimes members of the royal family. Such meetings ordinarily took place at Windsor or Buckingham Palace, but if the Queen was at Balmoral or Osborne, members of the Privy Council were obliged to travel to meet wherever she was.

Guernsey: the Channel Islands, including Guernsey, were part of the Duchy of Normandy when William the Conqueror invaded England in 1066; when he became King of England, they came under English rule. The Bailiwick of Guernsey is a Crown dependency, with a Lieutenant Governor representing the British sovereign, but with its own parliament. Guernsey is the second largest of the Channel Islands; its capital is St Peter Port, which the Queen calls St. Pierre.

Sark (Sercq) . . . Herm and Jethou: these smaller islands close to Guernsey are part of the Bailiwick of Guernsey.

speak . . . French among themselves: French was the legal language of Guernsey until 1971; French and Guernésiais were spoken at the time of the Queen's visit.

159 *Alderney*: the most northerly of the Channel Islands, and part of the Bailiwick of Guernsey.

Casquets Lights: Les Casquets is a cluster of rocky islets west of Alderney; the Casquets Lights, built in 1724, consisted of three towers built on the central islet, giving a distinctive appearance, which would not be confused with lighthouses in nearby France. The lights were originally lit by coal fires, later converted to oil lamps with metal reflectors. Automated in 1990, a single tower remains in use today. Many wrecks occurred in the area; the tides are unusually large (around 30 feet, or 9 metres) and race rapidly.

160 *Bertie put on his sailor's dress*: the Prince of Wales's sailor suit remains in the Royal Collection. He is portrayed wearing it, age 4, hands in pockets, against a background of the sea, in a portrait of him by Franz Xaver Winterhalter (1805–1873) from 1846.

St. Heliers: the capital of Jersey, the largest and most southerly of the Channel Islands, which is (like Guernsey, but independently of it) a self-governing Crown dependency. Its governing body is called the States of Jersey or the States Assembly; the Lieutenant Governor representing the British sovereign may speak at its meetings but may not vote. Both English and French are spoken.

161 *Castle of Mont Orgeuil*: Mont Orgueil Castle, on Jersey, overlooks the harbour of Gorey on a site that was fortified in the prehistoric period. The castle, built following the division of the Duchy of Normandy in 1204, was the primary defence of Jersey until the development of gunpowder made it hard to defend from attack from the high ground nearby. It remained the island's prison until the end of the seventeenth century, and it played a significant part in a Royalist victory in the English Civil War. It was adapted for use as a garrison in the early eighteenth century.

162 *the Longships*: a group of rocky islets about a mile and a quarter (two km) west of Land's End, the westerly tip of Cornwall. The islets are marked by the Longships Lighthouse. Much of the Longships group is submerged at high water, but the three largest islets—Tal-y-Maen, Carn Bras, and Meinek—remain above high water.

The Brisons: north of Land's End is Cape Cornwall, a headland jutting into the Atlantic. The two rocks just off shore are known as the Brisons.

Botallack mine: Botallack was a submarine mine with tunnels extending under the sea. The mine buildings are dramatically sited on the cliff edge near the village of Botallack, just north of Land's End. Over its recorded lifetime, the mine produced around 14,500 tonnes of tin, 20,000 tonnes of copper, and 1,500 tonnes of arsenic. Early records of mining date from the 1500s; archaeological evidence points to mining here in the Roman era or even the Bronze Age. The first steam engine was put to work in the early nineteenth century. The mine became a tourist attraction (charging a guinea for a tour) after the Prince and Princess of Wales visited in 1865 and descended a newly dug diagonal shaft.

St. Michael's Mount: a tidal island in Mount's Bay, Cornwall, about half a mile (nearly one km) offshore and linked to the town of Marazion by a causeway that is passable between mid- and low tide. The island was the site of a monastery from the eighth to the early eleventh centuries, after King Edward the Confessor gifted the site to the Benedictine order of Mont Saint-Michel, a monastery on a similar (and more celebrated) tidal island off the coast of Normandy. St Michael's Mount remained in Crown ownership until 1599, when Queen Elizabeth sold it to Sir Robert Cecil. His descendants sold it to Sir Francis Bassett in 1640, who garrisoned it for King Charles I during the English Civil War. When Parliamentarian forces captured the Mount, Colonel John St Aubyn was appointed Captain of the Mount, and in 1659 he purchased it outright. He was allowed to keep the property after the Restoration of Charles II in 1660. Upgrades were made during the eighteenth and nineteenth centuries, including romanticizing the castle. There is a small village with a chapel, school, and harbour at the foot of the mount.

162 *Cornish pilcher fishermen*: fishing was a traditional mainstay of the economy of Cornwall. Pilchard fishing and processing was a thriving industry from around 1750 to around 1880, after which it went into decline. Seine nets with a fine cotton mesh, often owned by local landowners, were deployed in a horseshoe shape around a shoal of pilchards, trapping it in shallow water until fishermen could scoop out the fish in baskets. The shoals were so large that they could be seen from the cliff tops. Watchers called 'huers' were employed to keep a lookout for the return of the shoals in the late summer and autumn.

a kind of English hardly to be understood: it is not clear if the Queen is hearing Cornish dialect or English spoken in an unfamiliar accent. Cornish (Kernewek or Kernowek) is a Southwestern Brittonic language, a branch of the Celtic language family. Common Brittonic was spoken throughout Britain south of the Firth of Forth during the British Iron Age and Roman period, but, as a result of westward Anglo-Saxon expansion during the early medieval period, the Britons of the south-west were separated from those in modern-day Wales and Cumbria. The western dialects eventually evolved into modern Welsh and the now extinct Cumbric, while Southwestern Brittonic developed into Cornish and Breton, the latter as a result of emigration to Brittany. Cornish became extinct as a living language in Cornwall at the end of the eighteenth century (though it was revived in the twentieth), but many Cornish words survived in the dialect spoken in the region.

163 *serpentine stone*: serpentine is green, brown, or dark red, veined with white. It is especially abundant on the Lizard Peninsula, which juts southward from Cornwall into the Channel just east of St Michael's Mount. It is part of an ophiolite, a piece of ancient oceanic crust that, in molten form, rose up when two tectonic plates moved apart. Serpentine rocks are a source of magnesium and asbestos, and in the nineteenth century there was a strong market for decorative objects made from it, such as mantelpieces, table-tops, and lamp bases. The name is thought to come from the resemblance of the greenish colour to that of a 'serpent' (an archaic synonym for snake) in traditional depictions.

Marazion, or "Market Jew,": Marazion (Cornish, Marhasyow) is a town on the shore of Mount's Bay at the landward end of the causeway to St Michael's Mount. Its medieval charter granted it the right to hold a market on Thursdays, hence its early name Marghasyewe or Marketjew, Cornish for 'Thursday Market.' A Jewish origin has been erroneously ascribed to the place, from the sound of the name.

165 *Duchy of Cornwall*: one of two royal duchies in England. The eldest son of the reigning British monarch inherits possession of the duchy and title of Duke

of Cornwall at birth (or when his parent succeeds to the throne), but may not sell assets for personal benefit. The duchy was established in 1337 by Edward III for his son, Edward, Prince of Wales, the 'Black Prince', who became the first Duke of Cornwall. The majority of the estate lies outside Cornwall. It includes Dartmoor in Devon, most of the Isles of Scilly, and other large holdings in Herefordshire and Somerset.

Trefusis: the manor of Trefusis, near Flushing in Cornwall, was granted to Richard de Trefusis in the second half of the thirteenth century, though the family's association with the area can be traced back to the 1170s. As referred to here by the Queen, Trefusis is a sixteenth-century country house, rebuilt in 1891. By the early eighteenth century, the family had quays built nearby, enabling Flushing to develop as a port.

Swan Pool: Swanpool is the name of both a sandy cove to the west of Falmouth and the lagoon just behind the beach. All swans in Britain technically belong to the sovereign.

Pendennis Castle: an artillery fort constructed by Henry VIII near Falmouth in 1540–42. It formed part of Britain's defences against invasion from France and the Holy Roman Empire, and protected the Carrick Roads waterway at the mouth of the River Fal. The original circular keep with gun platform was enlarged later in the sixteenth century to cope with the increasing threat of invasion by Spanish forces. Pendennis was held by Royalists during the English Civil War until taken by the Parliamentarians after a long siege in 1646. Charles II renovated the fortress after his Restoration in 1660. Pendennis's defences were modernized and upgraded in the eighteenth and nineteenth centuries.

166 *the old castle of Restormel*: Restormel Castle lies by the River Fowey near Lostwithiel in Cornwall. It is one of the four chief Norman castles of Cornwall and is notable for its perfectly circular design. Although once a luxurious residence of the Earl of Cornwall, the castle was all but ruined by the sixteenth century. It was briefly reoccupied and fought over during the English Civil War, but was subsequently abandoned.

Restormel mine: renamed Restormel Royal Iron Mine after this visit from the Queen and the Prince. Following the royal visit, the Queen commanded fifty gold sovereigns to be distributed among the miners.

167 *Place, belonging to Mr. Treffry,*: located in the port of Fowey, Place has been the home of the Treffry family since the fifteenth century. Originally a fortified house dating from 1457, it was extended and remodelled during the seventeenth and eighteenth centuries, but retains a Gothic aspect.

168 *Ross Castle*: on the shore of the Upper Lake (of the two Lakes of Killarney, in south-west Ireland), Ross Castle is a fortified fifteenth-century tower and keep, the ancestral home of Clan O'Donoghue. It was a Royalist stronghold during the Civil War and remained a military garrison until 1835.

The four children: Vicky, Bertie, Alice, and Alfred.

Innisfallen Island: a monastery was founded in the seventh century on Innisfallen Island in the Lower Lake of the two Lakes of Killarney; legend has it that King Brian Boru studied there. The ruins of twelfth-century ecclesiastical structures remain and would have been visible at the time of the Queen's visit.

168 *hill of the Eagle's Nest*: MacGillycuddy's Reeks (Irish Gaelic, Na Cruacha Dubha: 'the black stacks') is a sandstone and siltstone mountain range 19 miles (30.5 km) long in the Iveragh Peninsula in County Kerry, which includes most of the highest peaks and sharpest ridges in Ireland. Carrauntoohil is the central and highest peak, and high up on its side lies the Eagle's Nest, a deep corrie or amphitheatre-like valley carved by a glacier.

169 *I annex the route*: a foldout page was included in the original diary but was not duplicated for publication. For her account of the 'Last Expedition', 16 October 1861, she likewise resorted to attaching a list of places visited; see *Leaves*, 136.

170 *Darby's Garden*: Derby's Garden is a small island on the south-west side of Lough Leane, at the northern end of the Upper Lake.

MORE LEAVES FROM THE JOURNAL OF A LIFE IN THE HIGHLANDS, FROM 1862 TO 1882

182 *The Ettrick Shepherd.*: the first epigraph consists of the first and last lines from *Caledonia*, a short poem by James Hogg, known as the Ettrick Shepherd.

Beattie's Minstrel.: the second epigraph, by the Scottish poet James Beattie (1735–1803), is from *The Minstrel, or The Progress of Genius*, 2 books (1771–4), Book I, stanza 11, lines 6–9. The poem, written in Spenserian verse, traces the development of the poet's mind. Samuel Johnson admired every line; the poem influenced Sir Walter Scott and inspired a generation of Romantic poets, but it subsequently fell out of favour. The minstrel, a shepherd–swain named Edwin, dwells in the Scottish Highlands and tends his flock, singing peaceful praise of the natural world.

183 *Birkhall*: a house on the Balmoral estate on the banks of the River Muick near Ballater, built in 1849. It was given to Albert Edward, Prince of Wales (Bertie), but taken back from his charge by Queen Victoria in 1884.

the cairn: Victoria and Albert erected eleven roughly cut drystone cairns at Balmoral, most of them conical in shape and ranging from 8 to 22 feet (2½ to 7 metres) tall. The majority were built to celebrate their children's marriages and are on Craig Gowan, just behind the castle, along with 'Purchase Cairn' of 1852. Prince Albert's memorial cairn, by contrast, on the top of the nearby taller peak, Creag an Lurachain (as it is now spelled), is a huge, smoothly dressed pyramid, visible across the valley.

185 *Fog House*: now known as Moss House, and part of the Balmoral estate, the cottage is located on Craig Gowan with views over the River Dee.

186 *Balmoral, Tuesday, May 19, 1863.*: after Albert's death, Victoria spent more time at Balmoral than they had spent there together, visiting annually in May as well as at the end of summer, and lengthening her summer visit from weeks to months.

187 *since 1844*: see *Leaves*, 38–43, for the Queen's visit to Blair Castle in 1844, with mentions of Pitlochry and the Pass of Killiecrankie.

Schiehallion . . . sick to think of: traditionally considered a volcano because of its conical shape, Mount Schiehallion had a mythic reputation for danger.

October 9, two years ago: Victoria and Albert visited Blair Castle briefly on the second day of their 'Third Great Expedition', 8–9 October 1861, *Leaves*, 130–1. In the next paragraph, the Queen recalls the Duke of Atholl stopping at the County March to drink their health, with a Highland cheer; see *Leaves*, 132.

190 *which came nearer and nearer*: in the original diary, as transcribed and edited by Princess Beatrice, the Queen's account of her swollen face and injured thumb, and of their sitting down covered with plaids appeared here instead of in the previous paragraph.

192 *the railway*: the Deeside Railway ran between Aberdeen and Ballater. Opened in 1853 to Banchory, the line reached Aboyne in 1859 and Ballater in 1866. It was used by the royal train for travel to and from Balmoral Castle from 1853, and a special 'Messenger Train' ran daily when the royal family was in residence. Although the line was closed in 1966, the Queen's private car and waiting room can still be viewed at Ballater station, now a teashop.

Marochetti chose it himself: the statue was commissioned from Carlo Marochetti and represents the Prince seated, his hat doffed, wearing the uniform of a field marshal with the robes and insignia of the Order of the Thistle, the highest order of chivalry in Scotland. It was erected in Union Street, Aberdeen, remaining there until 1914 when it was moved to the pavement opposite His Majesty's Theatre, Rosemount Viaduct, to make way for a statue of Edward VII.

195 *President of the British Association for the Advancement of Science*: for the Prince's presidency of the BAAS and his speech in 1859, see *Leaves*, 104, and note to *Leaves*, 105.

196 *"Rise, Sir Alexander Anderson."*: the Lord Provost of Aberdeen was knighted by Queen Victoria in 1863 in recognition of his leadership of the Committee of Contributors which ensured the raising of a memorial statue to Prince Albert.

197 *all so sadly changed*: Victoria and Albert visited Invermark on their 'Second Great Expedition', 20–21 September, 1861; in 1861 the scene was 'fine . . . and . . . striking', *Leaves*, 119–20.

the Well: now known as 'the Queen's Well', the Well is a 20-foot (6-metre) high, open-arched, white stone monument, erected by Fox Maule-Ramsay, 11th Earl of Dalhousie. A black marble plaque is inscribed with the first message the Queen records; the basin of the well bears the second inscription, concluding, 'drink and pray for Scotland's Queen'.

199 *strange, unnatural, and sad*: Princess Beatrice's transcription of Queen Victoria's journal omitted this sentence, but the Queen chose to include it from her original journal manuscript, or possibly added it for publication.

and distressed me . . . their support taken away!: this passage does not appear in Princess Beatrice's transcription.

Even when . . . was so great.: this sentence, too, is missing from Princess Beatrice's edited version of the Queen's diary.

200 *dead before they were completed*: see the Queen's footnote to *Leaves*, 123.

201 *First Visit to Dunkeld.*: in visiting the Murray family, the Dukes of Atholl, the Queen now goes to Dunkeld House rather than Blair Castle, which she visited in 1844 and 1861 with the Prince, and for the day in 1863 (*More Leaves*, 187), when the Duke was ill. Two years later, the Duke is dead, and her visit is to his widow, who now lives in one of the smaller family houses. (The Queen and the duchess are 'both widows', *More Leaves*, 206.) For previous brief visits to Dunkeld (the town and the house), see *Leaves*, 25–6 (7 September 1842), and (on the way to and from the visit to Blair Castle) *Leaves*, 37–8 (11 September 1844) and 43 (1 October 1844).

201–3 *Loch Oishne, before coming to Loch Ordie*: Loch Ordie and Loch Oishne (now spelled Oisinneach) are north of Dunkeld and east of the River Tay.

204 *adopted from our farms there*: Prince Albert established model farms at Osborne House and at Windsor Castle. Their purpose was to try out and display the latest agricultural technology: for example, a steam-driven plough was in operation at Osborne in the 1850s.

205 *he could hardly move*: the Queen's attention to this injury became the occasion for a satire: *John Brown's Legs, or Leaves from a Journal in the Lowlands*, by Kenward Philip (New York: Norman L. Munro, 1884). Princess Beatrice omitted this description when she later transcribed the diary, along with the mention of his improvement the next day (*More Leaves*, 206) and three sentences on his continued suffering two days later (208), in keeping with her regular practice of reducing or eliminating mentions of Brown throughout the transcription.

twenty of the Athole Highlanders: see *Leaves*, 26.

206 *Wolf of Badenoch*: Alexander Stewart (*c.*1343–1405), 1st Earl of Buchan; he held a large territory in the north of Scotland and had a reputation for cruelty. He was a son of King Robert II, great-grandson of King Robert I (Robert Bruce), who defeated the English at the Battle Bannockburn in 1314; his brother was Robert III.

the American garden: located along the banks of the River Tay between Dunkeld House and Dunkeld Cathedral, the gardens, established in the mid-nineteenth century, were planted with rhododendrons, azaleas, kalmias, and other botanical species from North America. The plant stock was supplied from the Atholl estate.

207 *monument to the Duke*: the Atholl Monument, a towering stone monument in the shape of a Celtic cross, commemorating the 6th Duke of Atholl, was erected in 1865 (the year after his death) on the site of an old execution mound known as 'Gallows Knoll' above the village of Logierait.

208 *just above the Spital*: the Spital of Glenshee; see note to *Leaves*, 153.

211 *St. Colme's*: the model farm at Dunkeld that Queen Victoria had visited the previous year.

212 *Four miles from Dunkeld . . . the Highlands . . . begin*: the Highland Line, sometimes drawn on maps of Scotland though it is not a legal boundary (like a county boundary), demarcates the cultural and geological boundary dividing

the Highlands and Islands of the north and west of Scotland from the Lowlands to the south and along the eastern coast. Both Dunkeld and Balmoral sit close to the Highland Line.

Kinnaird: a late eighteenth-century house, built for the Kinnaird family and sold to the Duke of Atholl in 1826.

noisy railroad: for the expansion of Scotland's railways, see note to *Leaves*, 130.

Grandtully Castle . . . Duleep Singh: this castle is a three-storey tower house belonging to the Stewart family, near Aberfeldy, built in 1560–1625; it was said to be the inspiration for Tully-Veolan, the home on the border between the Highlands and Lowlands belonging to the Baron of Bradwardine in Sir Walter Scott's *Waverley* (1814). The Queen gave the Maharajah Duleep Singh a copy of *Leaves*, inscribing it 'from his affectionate friend Victoria R'.

213 *boatmen singing wild Gaelic songs*: See *Leaves*, 29, 10 September 1842. Clan MacDougall is a Highland clan historically based in and around the county of Argyll in the west of Scotland.

215 *Lochnagar girls' school*: the village school in Crathie near Balmoral was opened by Queen Victoria in 1871.

216 *All the Duchess's servants . . . did not come*: Princess Beatrice's edited transcription mentions 'a little dance the Duchess was giving her servants', but omits the detailed list of the Duchess's staff and any mention of the Queen's servants and staff attending.

so-called "brick buildings.": Princess Beatrice's version of the diary includes a final sentence at the end of this entry, omitted in *More Leaves*: 'Such gaieties always leave me very sad now, when I return to my solitary room.'

Laucha Grund at Reinhardtsbrunn: Reinhardsbrunn, near Gotha in the German state of Thuringia, is the site of a medieval Benedictine abbey that was converted into a castle and park by the Dukes of Saxe-Coburg and Gotha from 1827. Duke Ernest I, the father of Prince Albert, built his summer residence there in an English style, surrounded by the first English-style landscape garden park in Thuringia. Queen Victoria visited Reinhardsbrunn in 1845 and 1862. The Laucha Grund is a picturesque river valley in Thuringia.

218 *the road from Blairgowrie*: the party has travelled overland north and east from Dunkeld, till they reach the old military road from Blairgowrie to Braemar. The 'Spital' mentioned below is the Spital of Glenshee.

219 *twenty minutes past two*: at the end of this entry, keeping the focus on the waterworks ceremony, the Queen has omitted details about the return of the royal party to Balmoral that are present in Princess Beatrice's transcription. Again for literary effect, the next entry combines two entries a year apart.

221 *October 31, 1866–1867.*: here, literary effect overrides strict chronology, and the Queen combines two entries a year apart; the same motive inspired the omission at the end of the preceding entry.

222 *Floors*: Floors Castle is the seat of the Dukes of Roxburgh, built in the 1720s but incorporating parts of an older house. In the mid-nineteenth century it was embellished with turrets and battlements in the gothick style. The name

Floors is thought to derive either from 'flowers' (or French *fleurs*) or from the 'floors' or terraces on which the castle is built.

222 *at the station*: this visit to the Scottish counties bordering England is the Queen's first such 'progress' by train; she records for the first time being greeted by crowds at elaborately decorated train stations.

224 *old Castle of Roxburgh*: the ruins of a royal house overlook the junction of the River Tweed and River Teviot, in what became the grounds of Floors Castle. Probably built by King David I *c.*1128, it was fought over by the English and the Scots in a series of border disputes, then used by King Edward III of England and his successors as a base for military campaigns in Scotland, until it was retaken and destroyed by the Scots in 1460.

Michael Scott, the wizard: born in Scotland and educated at Oxford and Paris, Michael Scott (or Scot) (*c.*1175–1235) translated works from Arabic (including making a new translation of Aristotle and its Arabian commentaries) into Latin and studied astrology and alchemy. He worked at the court of the Holy Roman Emperor and was widely known in Europe. His association with Islamic and other Eastern cultures and his studies in the occult led to his reputation as a 'wizard'. Dante places him in the eighth circle of his *Inferno*, with false prophets and sorcerers. Legends about his wizardry include his changing the course of the River Tweed and dividing the Eildon Hills into three peaks; these are cited in Sir Walter Scott's *The Lay of the Last Minstrel* (see note to *Leaves*, 31), which is also the source of the claim that he is buried, together with his magic books, in Melrose Abbey.

225 *Dryburgh Abbey*: founded in 1150 on the banks of the Tweed River, Dryburgh Abbey was fought over and burned in the struggle over Scottish independence starting in the thirteenth century. It has been a ruin since the Protestant Reformation in the mid-sixteenth century, when many Catholic monasteries were destroyed. Sir Walter Scott is buried in its grounds.

the Abbey: Melrose Abbey was founded near the River Tweed in 1136 by Cistercian monks; damaged in a sixteenth-century battle and bombarded during the English Civil War in the seventeenth century, its buildings fell into ruin, but the church remained in use as a parish church into the eighteenth century. As the Queen notes, it is celebrated for the beauty of its carved stone decorations and the legends that Michael Scott and the heart of Robert Bruce are buried there.

They sat them down . . . slept below: Sir Walter Scott, *The Lay of the Last Minstrel* (see note to *Leaves*, 31), Canto 2, stanza 12; in the original, the second line is in parentheses. Sir William Deloraine, sent by the Lady of Branksome Hall (the heroine's mother in the plot of the romance) to retrieve Michael Scott's book of magic from his grave, has entered the abbey with the monk who buried it. The 'Scottish monarch' is King Alexander II. Like the Queen, nineteenth-century guidebooks borrow from *The Lay of the Last Minstrel* to describe the abbey.

He thought . . . the dead man frowned: *The Lay of the Last Minstrel*, Canto 2, stanza 21.

If thou wouldst . . . pale moonlight: *The Lay of the Last Minstrel*, Canto 2, stanza 1, as Deloraine arrives at the abbey. This description, in Scott's widely

Explanatory Notes to More Leaves

read poem, helped to make the abbey a popular nineteenth-century tourist destination.

226 *Abbotsford*: Sir Walter Scott created his baronial, turreted mansion Abbotsford near the town of Galashiels, on the south bank of the River Tweed, from a farm that he purchased in 1811, and which he expanded in the 1810s and 1820s. Its neo-medieval construction embodied his romantic conception of early Scottish history, and it would house his enormous collection of books, armour, antique furniture, and historical relics. Scott took the name Abbotsford from a ford across the Tweed used by the monks at nearby Melrose Abbey, and interior decoration found in the house was influenced by the architecture of the abbey. Scott wrote the Waverley novels at Abbotsford. The house was opened to the public as a museum in 1833, soon after the writer's death, though Scott's descendants continued to live there until 2004. The Queen's visit may have influenced her later plans for opening her own residence Kensington Palace to the public.

227 *tower of Smailhome . . . the "Eve of St. John."*: near Kelso, a typical tower house built in 1450 with five storeys, each of one room. The tower and estate were leased by a kinsman of Sir Walter Scott. As a child, Scott spent time at Smailholm, which is described in his poem 'The Eve of St. John' (1799); subtitled 'A Border Ballad', the poem is an imitation of the authentic ballads Scott collected, and he included it in his *The Minstrelsy of the Scottish Border* (1802–3).

King Malcolm IV. . . . Alexander III.: Malcolm IV (1141–65), grandson and successor of King David I, reigned 1153–65; William the Lion, also known as William I, was Malcolm's brother and succeeded him, reigning until 1214; William I was succeeded by his son, Alexander II (1198–1249), whose son and successor was Alexander III (1241–1286).

Queen Mary: usually called Mary Queen of Scots.

228 *the old Abbey*: Jedburgh Abbey was an Augustinian monastery founded in the twelfth century; its construction was completed in 1370. With the Reformation it fell into disrepair, but it remained in use as a parish church until 1870. More of its stone structure remains than does that of the other ruined abbeys the Queen visits—at Melrose, Dryburgh, and Kelso. Kelso Abbey, mentioned in the next sentence is also a twelfth-century foundation.

caves in which the Covenanters were hid: the seventeenth-century Scottish Covenanters, those who signed the National Covenant of 1638, supported the existence of the Presbyterian Church in Scotland and objected to the Stuart monarchy's interference in religious matters. Scottish Covenanters supported Oliver Cromwell during the English Civil War but later championed the Restoration of the monarchy under Charles II, who was crowned King of Scotland in 1651. On Charles's Restoration to the throne of England in 1660, he reneged on earlier promises to allow Presbyterian religious autonomy in Scotland; Covenanters were persecuted and executed in large numbers, and some sought refuge in caves in Jedburgh.

appearance of being on fire: this striking description of the lit-up Free Kirk is not present in Princess Beatrice's transcription of the original diary. A Free Kirk was one that had, in 'The Disruption' of 1843, left the Church of

Scotland in order to maintain its congregation's control over the selection of ministers, when ministers in the official Church were chosen by patrons or town councils. The Queen's Kirk at Crathie remained part of the Church of Scotland.

229 *our dear Balmoral*: in the diary as transcribed and edited by Princess Beatrice, the entry continues beyond this point, describing the rest of the Queen's day; the entry has been truncated to make a concise conclusion to the journey narrative.

231 *Pages of the Presence*: senior staff in the Royal Household who serve as personal attendants to royal visitors; they are usually promoted from the rank of footman. The Presence Chamber was a room in the Royal Apartments where the monarch received visitors. During Queen Victoria's reign, there were three First-Class and three Second-Class Pages, who attended to the Queen's guests, lit fires, and arranged seating.

Highland cattle grazing: Highland cattle, with long coats and horns, were bred to withstand the rough weather conditions in northern Scotland; by the time of the Queen's visit a curiosity, they were once an important part of the Highland economy, when small farmers raised these cattle for beef for the southern market.

232 *Glenlivet Distillery*: founded by George Smith in 1827, the Glenlivet Distillery makes single malt Scotch whisky.

233 *after three I fell asleep*: in the original diary, as transcribed and edited by Princess Beatrice, the Queen gave more detail: 'Slept soundly till ½ p. 7, but only got to bed after 2, having in vain waited for my clothes. A makeshift was arranged and pinned together as a night dress, but it was very uncomfortable & cold & I was long getting to sleep. Awoke feeling very tired & stiff.'

234 *Peninsular and Waterloo medal*: the Waterloo Medal was awarded in 1816 to every officer and soldier of the British Army who took part in any one of the battles fought in 1815 at Ligny, Quatre Bras, and Waterloo. This medal was the first to be awarded to the next of kin of men killed in action. Waterloo was the culminating battle in the Napoleonic Wars. For the 92nd Highlanders, see note to *Leaves*, 26.

the Elf House: a natural cave lying near the River Fiddich, a tributary to the River Spey. It was noted from the eighteenth century for its picturesqueness.

235 *"Pride and Prejudice"*: the novel (1813) by English author Jane Austen (1775–1817). The heroine, Elizabeth Bennett, a high-spirited, independent woman, might have been particularly enjoyed by Victoria: like the Queen, Elizabeth initially resists marriage before marrying for love.

only a female cook: the Queen implies that a female cook is inferior; male cooks were paid more than women, and employers paid a tax on male servants that was not paid for female servants.

238 *annoying and provoking!*: in Princess Beatrice's transcription of the original diary, immediately after this remark about the rain, the Queen mentions a disturbance that she omitted from the published book: 'Gen; Grey received from Manchester, the repetition, in full, of what the Mayor had let Mr Hardy know, but no one had started. The story leaked out, so I told my daughters. Police &

detectives have arrived & every precaution is being taken.' The previous day, the Queen had been informed of a plot originating in Manchester by 'the Fenians . . . to try and seize me here'; General Grey had asked that an infantry regiment and additional police be sent right away. On receiving the news of the plot, the Queen commented: 'Too foolish!!'

93rd Highlanders: the 93rd Regiment of Foot (Sutherland Highlanders) was an infantry regiment of the British Army, raised in 1799.

the Statue: the cast-bronze statue of Prince Albert by William Theed, located south-east of Balmoral Castle (now on the edge of a golf course), is set high up on a plinth made to resemble a rocky crag. The Prince wears a kilt and takes a step forward, with one hand on the head of a hunting dog and in the other a rifle.

240 *the Glassalt Shiel*: Glas-allt-Shiel is a fifteen-room, three-storey lodge built of grey stone on the shore of Loch Muick next to Glas-allt Burn. Completed in 1868, it replaced a small cottage built for a gillie and his wife in 1851; see *Leaves*, 79. The earlier cottage had a room reserved for royal parties.

A good staircase (the only one): the Queen's remark indicates how unusual it is for her to occupy a house with only one staircase. The main staircase in a substantial residence was often restricted to the use of family and visitors. Servants and other staff would use an alternative staircase of simpler construction, often located at the back of a house (hence the term 'back stairs').

241 *But I am sure . . . live in it.*: the published version of this entry is sequenced differently from the original entry as transcribed and edited by Princess Beatrice, where the dance party follows the Queen's 'sad thought', rather than preceding it. The closing sentence, 'But I am sure his blessing does rest on it, and on those who live in it,' does not appear in Princess Beatrice's edited transcription.

242 *It is done to preserve the wool.*: sheep dipping, using substances that vary by locality, prevents infestations of parasites, such as ticks and lice. Princess Beatrice omitted this description from her transcription of the original diary.

243 *A Highland "Kirstnin" (Christening), 1868.*: Princess Beatrice's transcription of Queen Victoria's journal does not include either of the two accounts of christenings (see also *More Leaves*, 244). She may have omitted them in transcribing the original diary, or it is possible that the Queen composed these entries for the publication of *More Leaves*.

246 *Visit to Invertrossachs, 1869.*: on this visit to the Trossachs, a celebrated mountain region of Scotland just north of Glasgow (now within Loch Lomond and the Trossachs National Park), the Queen follows closely the tourist itineraries of *Black's Guide to the Trossachs*, of which she owned a copy of the 1853 edition and probably a more recent one from the 1860s. *Black's Guides* were published by Adam and Charles Black of Edinburgh (later London) from 1839. Contributors included David T. Ansted, Charles Bertram Black, and A. R. Hope Moncrieff.

Black's Guide to the Trossachs in turn follows closely and quotes Sir Walter Scott's depictions of various locations in *The Lady of the Lake* and *Rob Roy*, treating fictional events as if they had really occurred. As noted below, the Queen sometimes chooses the same passages from Scott quoted by *Black's*, having encountered them in Scott's original texts but perhaps having also rediscovered them in *Black's*. Relying on Scott was a common practice in guidebook composition: George Anderson and Peter Anderson, *A Guide to the Highlands and Islands of Scotland* (3rd edn, Edinburgh: Adam and Charles Black, 1851) uses some of the same quotations, as does *Maclure and Macdonald's Illustrated Guide to the Western Highlands of Scotland* (Glasgow: Maclure and Macdonalds, 1861), a copy of which is in the Royal Library.

246 *Callander*: just as for the Queen's excursions, Callander is the starting point for the Trossachs itineraries in *Black's Guide*.

247 *Invertrossachs*: the house, on the south shore of Loch Vennachar, is described in *Black's Guide to the Trossachs* (1864): 'at the head of the loch is Invertrossachs, a shooting-lodge belonging to Stewart McNaughten, Esq.' The house the Queen visited was replaced in 1912 but a tree she planted allegedly remains in the garden.

Coilantogleford, celebrated in "The Lady of the Lake,": here the Queen begins noting the same locations in Scott's *Lady of the Lake* as *Black's Guide* does. She assumes, as does *Black's Guide*, that readers are familiar with the poem and that they share her eagerness to see the real places where Scott sets his fictional events. Coilantogleford (at the eastern outlet of Loch Vennachar) is where Roderick Dhu challenges Fitz-James to single combat, as *Black's* points out, quoting from the poem.

Pilatus: Mount Pilatus overlooks Lucerne in central Switzerland.

The view of Loch Vennachar: *Black's Guide* also commends this view.

248 *went on some little way*: this day's tour of Lake Mentieth, Aberfoyle, Loch Ard, Loch Chon, and onwards follows one of *Black's* itineraries.

Wallace Monument on the Abbey Craig: a 220-foot (67-metre) Victorian Gothic sandstone tower overlooking the city of Stirling. Completed in 1869, it commemorates Sir William Wallace, legendary fighter for Scottish freedom and leader in the First War of Scottish Independence (1296–1328). Abbey Craig is a volcanic crag above Cambuskenneth Abbey, from which, in 1297, Wallace is said to have watched the gathering of the army of King Edward I, just before he defeated the English at the Battle of Stirling Bridge. Artefacts believed to have belonged to Wallace are on display inside the monument, including the Wallace Sword. There is also a Hall of Heroes—a series of sculpted busts of famous Scots.

Inchmahome: the largest of three islands in Lake Mentieth, the location of Inchmahome Priory, founded in 1238. In 1547 it served as a refuge for Mary Queen of Scots, aged 4, for a few weeks following the defeat of the Scots during the Anglo-Scottish war known as 'the Rough Wooing' (see note to *Leaves*, 49). Although the girl was on the island only for a matter of weeks, fanciful stories abounded that she started to learn languages there, held a mock court with 'the Four Marys', her female attendants all named Mary, planted a box hedge, and did needlework.

Clachan of Aberfoyle (renowned in . . . "Rob Roy"): a clachan is a small cluster of houses; in *Black's Guide* the Clachan of Aberfoyle (on the River Forth) is described as 'the scene of many of the incidents alluded to in the novel of Rob Roy'. *Black's* also quotes the novel's description of 'miserable' houses made of loose stones, clay, and thatch. *Rob Roy* is one of Scott's Waverley novels, published in 1817. Set in 1715, it is told in the first person by a young Englishman, Frank Osbaldistone, who often sympathizes with the Highlanders and the Jacobite rising, but whose English perspective also accommodates that of tourists from the south. The title character is based on the historical figure of Robert Roy MacGregor, a Highland outlaw (often compared to Robin Hood of English legend), who participated in the Jacobite risings.

249 *Glasgow waterworks*: canals, pipes, and tunnels carved through the hills and carrying water from Loch Katrine to Glasgow. *Black's Guide* gives a detailed account of the hydraulics in a footnote to the tour of Loch Katrine. In contrast to the Queen's assurance here, *Black's* says the lake's 'picturesque features' are 'much impaired' by the waterworks.

Helen MacGregor: the wife of Robert Roy MacGregor (the original of the legendary figure Rob Roy); she appears in Scott's *Rob Roy*.

Loch Katrine: here the Queen departs from the itinerary in *Black's Guide*, combining elements of the Mentieth–Aberfoyle excursion and the Trossachs and Loch Katrine route, but doing the latter in reverse (west to east instead of east to west).

250 *opened the Glasgow Waterworks*: Victoria and Albert opened the Glasgow waterworks on 14 October 1859, an event she recorded in her diary, but which she omits from *Leaves*. An elaborate stone royal cottage was built on the southern shore of Loch Katrine for her reception that day.

Black's far the best: on *Black's Guides*, see note to *More Leaves*, 246.

"Silver Strand," "Helen's Isle,": the Queen's description of her visit to Loch Katrine exemplifies her own and *Black's Guide*'s way of treating *The Lady of the Lake* (along with *Rob Roy* and other works by Scott) as if it were a guidebook to actual, not fictional, places. *Black's* uses Scott repeatedly to describe Loch Katrine and its vicinity—for example, inserting the entire rowing song of Roderick Dhu's retainers (Canto 2, stanzas 19–20) in place of a description of the loch itself. Helen's Isle, also called Ellen's Isle, is named for the poem's heroine. For the Queen's earlier references to *The Lady of the Lake*, see *Leaves*, 29 and 77. The steamer pier is still in use for ships named 'Rob Roy', 'Sir Walter Scott', and 'The Lady of the Lake.'

So wondrous wild . . . a fairy dream—: these are the closing lines of *The Lady of the Lake*, Canto 1, stanza 12, which *Black's* also quotes to describe the Trossachs. The Trossachs is the name both of the region and of a narrow gorge between Loch Achray and Loch Katrine. *Black's* describes it as 'a singularly romantic defile, where nature is displayed in all her most picturesque aspects. Nothing is more striking than the rich and varied diffusion of vegetation . . .'. After quoting Scott's 'fairy dream' couplet, the description continues: 'Near the entrance of the gorge Fitz-James lost his "gallant grey." . . . so imbued has the whole scenery become with the incidents related by the poet, that we are almost tempted to look for the bleached bones of the generous steed; nor will the guide fail to show the exact spot where he fell.'

The western waves . . . living fire: *The Lady of the Lake*, Canto 1, stanza 11.

251 *Loch Lubnaig*: Here the Queen follows *Black's* itinerary: 'Callander to Loch Lubnaig, Loch Voil, Balquhidder, and Rob Roy's Country.' Visiting Balquhidder, the Queen looks at the old kirk, then at the new church, then at the view of Loch Voil, exactly as *Black's* suggests.

the Abyssinian traveller Bruce: James Bruce (1730–1794) was a Scottish writer who spent more than a dozen years in north Africa and Ethiopia. He claimed, incorrectly, to be the first European to trace the origins of the Blue Nile. He returned home to Kinnaird in 1774; in 1785 he began writing up his travels, which were published in five volumes: *Travels to Discover the Source of the Nile, In the Years 1768, 1769, 1770, 1771, 1772, and 1773* (Edinburgh and London, 1790).

252 *tomb of Rob Roy*: *Black's* likewise describes these three carved stones outdoors in the churchyard, though slightly differently. Both *Black's* and the Queen note that the stone with the sword (on the left, facing the row of tombs) is not Rob Roy's, which is in the centre, but that of his wife Helen. In Scott's novel, she is a fierce military leader and armed.

Nasci est aegrotare, . . . et mori est vivere.: 'To be born is to be ill, to live is often to die, and to die is to live.'

or, alas! rather was: the Queen's expression of regret could relate generally to the defeat of independent Scotland, or might be a specific reference to the MacGregors' particular losses; *Black's* gives an account of the MacGregors' dispossession in a note: after they massacred the Colquhoun clan, their lands were forfeit to King James VI of Scotland and I of England.

253 *to Loch Katrine*: the Queen is now following *Black's* Loch Katrine itinerary, which she had previously explored in reverse on 2 September.

254 *the Nasen on the Lake of Lucerne*: Lake Lucerne is located in central Switzerland, between steep limestone mountains. Great promontories or 'noses' (German, *Nasen*) project into its waters, giving it an irregular shape.

255 *Rob Roy's Cave*: *Rob Roy* locations continue to crop up along the Queen's tour (as in *Black's* and other guides); this location is associated with the historical Rob Roy, and in the novel an important meeting between Rob Roy and the novel's English narrator, Frank Osbaldistone, takes place in the cave.

257 *excellent accounts of dear Arthur*: Prince Arthur, Victoria and Albert's third son, who served in the British Army from the age of 18, went to Canada in August 1869 to join the Montreal detachment of the Rifle Brigade. He toured Canada, attended the opening of parliament in Ottawa (the first member of the royal family to do so), fought against Fenian Raiders, and was made an honorary chief of the Six Nations (Iroquois). Major General Sir Howard Craufurd Elphinstone served as Governor to Prince Arthur.

261 *have been cut down*: at this point in Princess Beatrice's transcription, but omitted from the entry for publication, is this reference to the Franco-Prussian War, which had begun in July 1870: 'The Prussians have got to St. Cloud & shots are being frequently exchanged with the Garde Municipale. The state of Paris is dreadful.'

knowing that I would approve: when *More Leaves* appeared in print, Princess Louise objected to her mother's representation of her engagement. Louise

Explanatory Notes to More Leaves 435

wanted the Queen to acknowledge that she accepted John Campbell, Marquess of Lorne, later 9th Duke of Argyll, to please her mother. She asked her mother to add, in the next edition, 'that you "very much wished the engagement shd. take place"' and to say 'knowing how much I wished it' in place of 'knowing that I would approve'. In reply, the Queen strongly objected to Louise's version of events, and the requested changes were not made. Louise's letter and the Queen's reply are in the Royal Archives.

262 *Communion Sunday at Crathie, 1871*.: the Queen describes her observation of the Presbyterian communion ritual in detail as it differs from the rituals familiar to her in the Anglican Church of England. Although she had been attending services at the Kirk since the purchase of Balmoral (see, for example, *Leaves*, 86), and later invited Dr Macleod to perform Presbyterian services for the family in the castle (see *More Leaves*, 288–90), it was a weightier decision for her to participate in the holy communion following the Presbyterian rite—as, she reports, was her practice from 1873—rather than in that of the Church of England. This entry does not appear in Princess Beatrice's transcription of the original diary.

265 *dear little Albert*: Albert Brown is the child whose christening was the second of the two that the Queen describes earlier (*More Leaves*, 244).

266 *to recover it*: in the original diary as transcribed and edited by Princess Beatrice, the Queen ended this entry by describing a dance held outdoors in a tent that evening; omitting the dance preserves her sombre and respectful tone regarding 'the calamity'.

267 *eleven years ago*: *Leaves* does not record a visit to Edinburgh in 1861, but the 'First Visit to Scotland' (1842; *Leaves*, 19–23) describes an earlier stay in Edinburgh extensively.

the Scots Greys: the Royal Scots Greys was a cavalry regiment of the British Army. The soldiers rode grey horses and were early referred to as the Grey Dragoons. Despite being formally renamed the Royal North British Dragoons ('North Britain' then being put forward as a name for Scotland) in 1707, they continued to be referred to as the Scots Greys, and in 1857 this nickname was made official.

Palace of Holyrood: for the Queen's account of her visit to Holyrood Palace in 1842, see *Leaves*, 21.

269 *poor Rizzio was so horribly murdered*: David Rizzio (1533–1566) was Queen Mary's Catholic Italian private secretary; he was stabbed to death by Mary's husband, Lord Darnley, and a group of conspirators, nominally because Darnley suspected Rizzio and Mary of being lovers, but also as part of a plot to restore Protestantism to Scotland.

270 *my dear one's Monument*: for information about the monument, unveiled in 1876, see note to *More Leaves*, 341.

271 *Poems by the "Ettrick Shepherd," . . . some years ago*: the volume Brown gave the Queen could be *The Royal Jubilee: A Scottish Mask* (1822), by 'the Ettrick Shepherd' (James Hogg), of which there is a nineteenth-century Edinburgh edition in the Royal Library; it could also be one of the collections of songs that Hogg published in the last ten years of his life, or a posthumous selection, *Works of the Ettrick Shepherd* (1865).

271 *arch... to drive through*: for King George IV's entry into Edinburgh in August 1822, arranged by Sir Walter Scott and a source of comparisons for Victoria's visits, see Introduction, xxviii–xxix.

272 *are very poor*: in the diary as transcribed and edited by Princess Beatrice, this sentence originally read: 'The population of Dalkeith & the surrounding villages, all colliers & miners, very poor, wretched, dirty, ill clothed & unhealthy looking turned out to see me pass.' As in *Leaves*, comments that could be seen as derogatory have been edited out. In the next entry, beginning with the 'wet day', the published version omits a reference to choosing 'stuffs & jewellery from the shops here'.

Flora Macdonald: this companion's name attracts attention because an earlier Flora Macdonald (1722–1790) was famous for helping Prince Charles Edward Stuart (Bonnie Prince Charlie) to evade government troops in the Outer Hebrides, to which he had retreated after the Battle of Culloden in April 1746.

275 *Culloden*: the Battle of Culloden was the final confrontation of the Jacobite rising of 1745. On 16 April 1746, the Jacobite army of Charles Edward Stuart was decisively defeated by a British government force under Prince William Augustus, Duke of Cumberland, on Drummossie Moor near Inverness. Charles Edward Stuart lodged at nearby Culloden House in the days leading up to the battle. It was the last pitched battle fought on British soil.

Inverness, the capital of the Highlands: the largest town in the Highlands, at the eastern end of the Great Glen; it was traditionally known as the Highland capital, though in a cultural rather than a political sense.

276 *Better lo'ed ... come back again?*: these are lines from a Jacobite song inviting Prince Charles Edward Stuart to return.

Dunrobin Castle: on the north-east coast of Scotland just north of Golspie, described in Anderson's guidebook as 'the largest and most ornamented edifice in the Highlands'. The first house dated from the eleventh century but it was rebuilt in the fifteenth and sixteenth centuries in a French style. The detailed guidebook account recommends to the tourist a point of view on the seashore from which 'the numerous pinnacles, and variously elevated roofage, with the gigantic entrance tower looming high at one corner, forms a very striking and picturesque sky outline'; George Anderson and Peter Anderson, *A Guide to the Highlands and Islands of Scotland*, 3rd edn (1851), 536, 538.

277 *the dear late Duke and Duchess*: the 'late Duke' is the 2nd Duke of Sutherland, father of the present 3rd Duke. The late Duchess Harriet, the 2nd Duchess of Sutherland, was a close friend of Victoria's.

Clieveden and Stafford House: Cliveden House overlooking the River Thames in Buckinghamshire and Stafford House near St James's Palace in London were other grand properties then belonging to the Dukes of Sutherland. Queen Victoria is said to have remarked to the 2nd Duchess of Sutherland on arriving at Stafford House, 'I have come from my House to your Palace.'

278 *the monument of the late Duke*: 'the late Duke' refers to the 2nd Duke of Sutherland. The Queen refers to his father, the 1st Duke, as 'the old Duke', and to his son, the 3rd Duke, as 'the Duke'.

Explanatory Notes to More Leaves 437

the old Duke's very colossal statue: George Granville Leveson-Gower, 1st Duke of Sutherland (1758–1833), who was Lord Stafford from 1803, was raised to the dukedom only in the year of his death. The monument erected in his memory was completed in 1837, and is known locally as the 'Mannie'. Financed by public subscription, the statue was sculpted by Sir Francis Chantrey. Over 100 feet (30 metres) tall and located atop Ben Bhraggie, it dominates the skyline above the village of Golspie. The 1st Duke of Sutherland remains a controversial figure for his role in the Highland Clearances; see Introduction, xxxvii.

280 *Mr Loch's memorial*: James Loch was the Commissioner for Lord and Lady Stafford (later the 1st Duke and Duchess of Sutherland) from 1815. At their direction, he cleared Sutherland of many of its small farms to replace them with more profitable sheep grazing. He instituted 'Loch Policy', which transformed both the landscape and the traditional way of life of the people, who were forced either to emigrate or to accept resettlement on small lots on the inhospitable coast. In 1815 he published a defence of his practices: *An Account of the Improvements on the Estate of Sutherland Belonging to the Marquess and Marchioness of Stafford* (enlarged edn. 1820). Although the violence occasioned by some of these removals brought bad publicity to the Sutherlands, and evictions slowed after 1821, Loch remained in their service, and on this visit the Queen meets Loch's son, Commissioner to the present Duke (*More Leaves*, 284). On the Highland Clearances, see Introduction, xxxv–xxxviii.

281 *Highland beasts*: see note to *More Leaves*, 231 ('Highland cattle'). In Sutherland, evicted farmers who were removed to the coast were required to sell their cattle.

my dear Duchess of Sutherland: the memorial is to Harriet, the 2nd Duchess.

282 *white heather*: white mountain heather (*Cassiope mertensiana*), is found less frequently than purple-flowered heather and is gathered for good luck.

Mr. Stanley, the discoverer of Livingstone: Dr David Livingstone was a celebrated Scottish missionary and explorer, who, in 1866, went in search of the source of the Nile River in east Africa. In 1871, when he appeared to be missing, the *New York Herald* sent the journalist Henry Morton Stanley (1841–1904) to look for him; in November 1871, Stanley located Livingstone in a village in what is now Tanzania. Livingstone died in 1873, still searching for the source of the Nile ('the work on which he is bent'); in 1874 Stanley completed Livingstone's search, and went on to serve Belgium's King Leopold II in creating and administering the brutally exploitative Congo Free State. Queen Victoria knighted him in 1897.

283 *new coal mines*: coal mining had been undertaken at Brora on the east coast of Sutherland since the sixteenth century. In 1811 the 1st Duke of Sutherland sank the Ross Mine on the banks of the River Brora, which continued in production until 1976.

the Fishing Cottage . . . on the grass: this wooden structure near Gordonbush farm on Loch Brora, known locally as the Luncheon Cottage, was built for the Queen's visit and survived until the 1980s.

284 *the Black-Water . . . wild country up that glen*. The 'fine drive into a wild country' up the Black Water which the Duchess recommends was the location of particularly violent clearances earlier in the century.

284 *Thorwaldsen's statues*: the Queen is referring to the work of Bertel Thorvaldsen (1770–1844) (also spelled Thorwaldsen), Danish sculptor and medalist.

285 *The military . . . zeal and pains*: this sentence does not appear in Princess Beatrice's transcription of the diary and seems to have been text from the original diary, or was added by the Queen for *More Leaves*. Prince Arthur, aged 22 in 1872, served from 1869 as an officer in the Rifle Brigade (the Prince Consort's Own), an infantry rifle regiment of the British Army, and saw service in South Africa.

birds found at or near Dunrobin: the collection of artefacts in this small museum was largely assembled, starting in 1866, by the Revd Dr J. M. Joass, minister at Golspie, who was an enthusiast for local archaeology. It includes large carved 'Pictish Symbol Stones', stone mortars, and other items taken from nearby burial cairns, souterrains, and ruined brochs. Dr Joass was also responsible for the collection of taxidermied local wildlife that the Queen saw, now dwarfed by an extensive collection of hunting trophies from all over the world.

286 *Brown motioned . . . ran to pick up*: this sentence about Brown is absent from Princess Beatrice's transcription of the original diary.

288 *Dr. Norman Macleod.*: in a departure from her usual procedure in compiling journal entries in chronological sequence, the Queen collected her entries on Dr Macleod in this chapter, and added a eulogy (dated March 1873), which does not appear in Princess Beatrice's transcription of the diary.

service which . . . going to perform: for her attendance at other Presbyterian services, see *Leaves*, 86, and *More Leaves*, 243–4, 262–3, and 289–94.

twenty-third chapter . . . to the end: Princess Beatrice's transcription of the diary does not include this listing of Dr Macleod's selection of biblical readings and of texts for his sermon, nor does it include the Queen's warm expressions of enthusiasm for his sermon and his prayers. The same is true of the entry for 24 August 1862 (*More Leaves*, 289), describing another service conducted by Dr Macleod. Either the princess omitted these from her edited transcription to minimize discussion of her mother's involvement in a Church of Scotland service, or the Queen added these expressions to amplify her original journal text for *More Leaves*.

290 *sustain the broken heart*: Princess Beatrice's transcription of the diary shortens this sentence to omit the Queen's depiction of herself as 'much upset in talking to him of my sorrows, anxieties, and overwhelming cares'.

292 *sent . . . to look after the missions*: the General Assembly of the Church of Scotland is the Church's highest court and governing body. It met yearly in Edinburgh and was chaired by an elected Moderator. The Foreign Mission Committee (later Board of World Mission and Unity) was responsible for the Church's global missionary work. The first Church of Scotland missionary, Alexander Duff, arrived in India in 1830 and founded the General Assembly's Institution, which offered higher education based on Western principles, taught in English and directed towards religious conversion.

disturbance in the Church: throughout this period there were tensions between the established Presbyterian Church of Scotland and several independent Presbyterian sects, including the Free Kirk and the Reformed Church of Scotland; the last major division had occurred with 'The Disruption' in 1843.

293 *Irish Church Bill*: the Anglican Church of Ireland had few adherents in majority Catholic Ireland. The Irish Church Act of 1869 separated the Church of Ireland from the Church of England and disestablished the former. Strongly opposed by conservatives in both houses of parliament, the Irish Church Act meant that the Church of Ireland was no longer entitled to collect tithes from the people of Ireland, and it ceased to send bishops to the House of Lords in Westminster.

one very strong Protestant body: the Queen and Dr Macleod share the conservative view that the state should have an established church, which in Scotland is Presbyterian; they worry that, following the disestablishment of the Irish Church, the Church of Scotland might also be disestablished and lose its state sponsorship. The Free Church (or Free Kirk) and the United Presbyterians were institutionally separate from, but doctrinally similar to, the Church of Scotland, so that in the eventuality of disestablishment, the majority of the population would remain united in religious practice and belief.

Lord Lorne: for Princess Louise's engagement to Lord Lorne, see note to *More Leaves*, 261.

seemed to describe France: On the Franco-Prussian or Franco-German War, see also note to *More Leaves*, 261. 'Sensuality' was a supposed French national characteristic for which Britain habitually disparaged the French. The Queen, who was raised speaking German and married a German prince, tended to sympathize with Germany. The war began as a French effort to prevent independent German states from uniting; Germany's unification and subsequent victory over the French meant that it ended the war as the dominant political force in Europe.

294 *Ems*: Bad Ems is a health resort on the River Lahn in western Germany, with mineral and thermal springs.

298 *as Ossian terms it*: Ossian, 'the Homer of the North', is the persona devised by Scottish poet James Macpherson to embody the poetic voice of ancient Scotland. Macpherson presented the poems as translations of a third-century Scottish epic. By 1872 it was generally understood that Ossian was a literary hoax, yet readers continued to love his authentic-sounding verse, which was derived at least in part from Scottish Gaelic oral traditions and authentic fragments of ancient verse.

301 *to visit the late Duke*: for this visit to Blair Castle on 15 September 1863, see *More Leaves*, 187–8.

down by Newton More: for this journey in September 1861 (the 'First Great Expedition'), see *Leaves*, 112–18.

303 *in 1847*: for this visit to Loch Laggan and Ardverikie in western Scotland in August 1847, see *Leaves*, 54–5.

304 *Parallel Roads*: in describing this unusual geological feature, the Queen echoes contemporary guidebooks. The Andersons' *Guide to the Highlands and Islands of Scotland* (1851) describes the Parallel Roads of Glen Roy as 'perfectly horizontal' bands of sand appearing at three different levels of the steep sides of this glen and others nearby. They were once thought by those who are 'zealous for the greatness and antiquity of their Celtic ancestors' to be man-made, but (as the Queen notes) are now understood by geologists to be

'alluvial banks . . . of a lake, the barrier of which, whether of rock, gravel, or ice, had given way at successive elevations' (Anderson and Anderson, 186–8).

304 *arrived at Inverlochy*: this relatively small, recently built stately home north of Fort William replaced earlier fortified castles closer to Loch Eil. The Queen uses the house (which is now a hotel with a marked 'Victoria Walk' in its grounds) as her base for exploring the locations of the Jacobite cause.

305 *my own bed*: Queen Victoria often travelled with her own special 'travelling' beds, which could be taken apart for easy transportation. There are examples in the Royal Collection.

306 *Quatre Bras*: this battle, fought on 16 June 1815 between the armies of the Duke of Wellington and Napoleon Bonaparte, was a preliminary engagement to the decisive Battle of Waterloo two days later, won by Wellington's forces.

Good accounts of Leopold: Prince Leopold, Victoria and Albert's fourth son, had (at the age of 20) just begun studying at Christ Church in the University of Oxford.

307 *Ben Nevis Distillery*: in Lochy Bridge, Fort William, the Ben Nevis Distillery was founded in 1825 by John 'Long John' McDonald, who passed it down to his son Donald in 1856. A second distillery was sited nearby in 1878 and named Nevis Distillery. The two distilleries became one in the twentieth century.

the oath to King William III: for Glencoe's belated oath of allegiance to William III, and the ensuing Massacre of Glencoe, see note to *Leaves*, 53.

308 *old Inverlochy Castle*: built in the thirteenth century on the banks of the River Lochy, a moated castle with towers at the four corners, old Inverlochy Castle was the site of historic battles, including some during the English Civil War. In 1645 the Campbells were defeated by the royalist Marquess of Montrose, a victory that was followed by the massacre of 1,300 of the Campbell defenders. Shortly afterwards, the castle was abandoned for a new fortification at the mouth of the River Lochy where it joins Loch Linnhe. The town that grew up around the new castle (which the Queen is visiting) became the modern Fort William. See also the Queen's account of this history, *More Leaves*, 317.

309 *that unhappy race*: for the Queen's view that in her person she represents the reconciliation of the Hanoverians and the Stuarts, England and Scotland, see Introduction, xxix–xxx. The German Hanoverians had become Britain's monarchs after Queen Anne (a Stuart, the great-granddaughter of King James VI and I) died without an heir, and the Crown passed to George I, a German descendant of James VI and I; King George I was Victoria's great-great-great-grandfather. Referring to Charles Edward Stuart as 'Prince Charles Edward' or 'Prince Charles' in these entries (rather than 'the Pretender') confirms her sympathy with the romance of the Jacobite–Stuart cause.

310 *a "calvie" or "coo" of the . . . Highland character*: a calf or cow of the Highland breed; see note to *More Leaves*, 231.

311 *the slate quarries*: Ballachulish Slate Quarry, near Glencoe, was established in 1692 and thrived during the eighteenth and nineteenth centuries, producing roof tiles for the surrounding area and for Edinburgh and Glasgow. In 1845 the quarry supplied 26 million slates, though owing to the presence of small

quantities of iron pyrite, which weathered rapidly in the Scottish climate, they deteriorated quickly. Many local villagers were employed in the mine.

Let me hope that William III. knew nothing of it: on King William III's role in the Massacre of Glencoe, see note to *Leaves*, 53.

Ossian's Cave . . . pretend that Ossian did: this cave is located on the northern face of the Three Sisters' peak of Aonach Dubh in Glencoe. For Ossian, see note to *More Leaves*, 298; he was reputedly born at nearby Loch Achtriochtan. It is not clear whether the Queen considers everything about Ossian to be 'pretend', or only this unlikely dwelling-place.

312 *some of the Scotch papers*: that reporters from several Scottish newspapers have trailed the Queen and her party ten miles up this rugged glen indicates the newsworthiness of the Queen's sightseeing visit to Glencoe in the context of increasing celebrity culture.

old Jacobite feeling . . . Roman Catholics: for these political–religious alignments, see Introduction, xx–xxi.

315 *monument to Prince Charles Edward*: the Glenfinnan Monument at the head of Loch Shiel is described in the Andersons' *Guide to the Highlands and Islands of Scotland* (1851) as 'a round narrow tower which no traveller can behold with indifference . . . surmounted by a colossal statue . . . of the unfortunate but chivalrous prince' (177). The monument was commissioned in 1815 to commemorate the spot where Prince Charles Edward Stuart raised his standard in 1745 at the start of the Jacobite rebellion. It is 60 feet (18 metres) high and was designed by Scottish architect James Gillespie Graham.

316 *after the Forty-five*: the Jacobite rising of 1745, also known as the Forty-five Rebellion or simply the '45; see Introduction, xx–xxii and xxx.

317 *money to be given*: tips, at the end of their stay.

Scott's "Legend of Montrose": a novel of 1819, set in the 1640s, one of Sir Walter Scott's historical novels in his series Tales of My Landlord.

illustrated copy of my book: the Queen is giving Lord Abinger a copy of the illustrated edition of *Leaves*, published in December 1868.

318 *the small monument . . . MacDonald of the Isles*: the monument marking the Well of the Heads is on the north shore of Loch Oich, near Invergarry. On 25 September 1663 the young chief of Keppoch, Alexander MacDonald, and his younger brother Ranald were stabbed to death by rivals within the clan. In 1665 the seven criminals were hunted down at Inverlair, killed and decapitated. The heads were taken to Invergarry Castle and washed in the well before being displayed to the local population.

319 *thirty-six years ago*: for these remembered events of 16–17 September 1847 (twenty-six, not thirty-six years before), see *Leaves*, 55.

often by inheritance: on the transformation of ancestral clan lands into English investment properties, see Introduction, xxxiii–xl.

321 *who wore full dress*: this is the first formal appearance of the Queen's Balmoral Highlanders, her own clan 'volunteers' or militia, formed in imitation of the militias she admired at Blair Atholl and the Deeside estates of Farquharson of

Invercauld and the Duke of Fife. Starting in 1887 (for her Golden Jubilee) the Braemar Gathering was sometimes held at Balmoral, where the Balmoral Highlanders marched with these other militias.

322 *Departure of the Prince of Wales . . . India.*: the inclusion of this entry is the result of a dispute between the Queen and two of her children in February 1884, after *More Leaves* had been published. Princess Louise passed on to their mother a complaint from the Prince of Wales about not being mentioned ('very many people remark on there being no mention of Bertie and his taking leave of you at Balmoral before his great journey to India'). The Queen replied that her book wasn't a compendium of family events: 'As for Bertie's departure for India that is not [an] event which took place there. I do not record family events as such but a few of them which occurred in Scotland, and Highland customs, Excursions. But Bertie merely took leave before a journey which so many take and did not go for some little time afterwards. Not one of the newspapers (and I am sure I have seen between 30 and 40) allude to that as an omission. There are many other family events the news of which I received at Balmoral, which might be mentioned if I had wished to publish a record of them. But such was not my intention.' Nonetheless she added this entry in subsequent editions, his farewell having taken place in Scotland. This correspondence is preserved in the Royal Archives among other letters about *More Leaves*. For more on her children's objections to her published writing, see note to *More Leaves*, 261, and Introduction, xv. The Prince of Wales's tour of India, October 1875 to May 1876, took him to twenty-one cities and towns, was thoroughly reported in the British newspapers, and reaffirmed Britain's hold over India.

324 *lead mines . . . Lord Breadalbane*: in 1730 Sir Robert Clifton of Nottinghamshire took a mining lease on part of the Breadalbane estate owned by the Campbell family in the vicinity of Loch Lomond, and in 1741 discovered a rich lead deposit at Tyndrum. From 1838 John Campbell, 2nd Marquess of Breadalbane, took on the management of the failing mine himself, employing German engineers and prolonging the useful life of the venture.

325 *Kilchurn Castle*: the castle was a fifteenth-century fortress with a five-storey tower house, built on a rocky peninsula in Loch Awe as a stronghold of the Campbells; it was abandoned and in ruins by the time of the Queen's visit.

Inveraray Castle: the ancestral home of the Campbell family and the Dukes of Argyll (see note to *Leaves*, 51). It became the home of Princess Louise on her marriage in 1871 to John Campbell, Marquess of Lorne, later 9th Duke of Argyll. The glass 'sort of conservatory' surrounding the front entry steps was created for the Queen's visit, as were the costumes for the halbardiers who lined the approach.

326 *Lorne was only two years old*: in *Leaves* (51), the lunch visit to Inveraray takes place on 18 August 1847.

327 *Queen's drive*: an avenue that was cut through the Inveraray estate to the north of Inveraray House in 1871.

329 *ball to the tenants was to take place*: in describing this enormous party, the Queen shows her appreciation for traditional Highland music and for the mixing of social classes enabled by Highland dancing. These details were,

however, left out of Princess Beatrice's transcription of the original diary. According to the transcription, 'Louise & Beatrice danced, a good deal', but it does not say that Louise danced with Brown and Beatrice with one of the foresters. Princess Beatrice's version simplifies the odd matter of the Glasgow band that cannot play reels, eliminating the Queen's exclamation of surprise; and it leaves out the *schottische*, the *tempête*, and the Gaelic song that the Queen mentions at the end of her account.

330 *the following account*: this two-paragraph account by the Duke of Argyll summarizes Henry Sumner Maine, *Village Communities in the East and West: Six Lectures Delivered at Oxford* (London: John Murray, 1871). Maine describes this 'old, primitive' practice of communal ownership of arable farmlands, known as 'runrig', in which collectively held lands were divided into narrow strips that changed hands periodically, sometimes by lottery, so that no one kept the best or worst pieces for long. Maine emphasizes the similarities both in law and in practice between villages in India (which his readers would accept as 'semi-barbaric') and Scots villages such as Achnagoul. Individual crofting, the privatized farming practice preferred by the Duke, was also under pressure of extinction by the Highland Clearances, though these two villages were not cleared.

Auchindrain (though not Achnagoul) continued to be farmed collectively by descendants of the same families until 1961 (runrig having been given up voluntarily in the 1840s) and has since been preserved as an outdoor museum of traditional farm life. It is the last of what were once about 4,000 self-governing townships that farmed and paid their taxes collectively. As elsewhere in Scotland, the faintest traces of the runrig strips can still be seen.

331 *powder mills*: the Argyll gunpowder industry consisted of four factories known locally as 'powder mills'. The works at Furnace closed in 1883.

332 *brought back from the East*: as the Queen explains earlier in *More Leaves* (326), Sir John McNeill 'was formerly my minister in Persia'.

336 *under . . . Marshal Wade*: Rest and Be Thankful is the top of the pass dividing Glen Kinglas from Glen Croe on the military road between Tarbet and Campbeltown on the Kintyre peninsula; a stone was erected by soldiers with the inscription 'Rest and Be Thankful' to commemorate the completion of the road in 1750. The road, constructed under Marshal Wade's successor, Major William Caufeild, was part of the network of roads, often referred to as Wade's Roads, designed to ensure the subjection of Scotland following the Jacobite rebellion. For the military roads, see also *Leaves*, 108.

337 *slate quarries close to Luss*: Luss is a village on the west bank of Loch Lomond, developed in the eighteenth century by the Colquhouns of nearby Rossdhu Castle to house workers for the Camstraddan slate quarries.

338 *Highland Funeral.*: this account of the elder John Brown's funeral does not appear in Princess Beatrice's transcription of the original diary.

339 *comfort dear old Mrs. Brown*: by custom, only men attended burials; not even the Queen accompanies the procession to the kirkyard.

340 *the "Courant"*: the *Edinburgh Evening Courant* began publication in 1718, printed by John McQueen (or McEwen) on the Royal Mile, and was passed to

his protégé Alexander Kincaid in 1735. It survived until the *Edinburgh Evening News* came into existence in 1873.

341 *Albert's Chorale*: two chorales composed by Albert were published and found their way into hymnals in the nineteenth century under the names 'Coburg' and 'Gotha'. They are included in *The Collected Compositions of His Royal Highness the Prince Consort*, ed. W. G. Cusins (London: Metzler & Co., 1882).

the 79th: the Queen's Own Cameron Highlanders, a line infantry regiment of the British Army, raised in 1793 at Fort William from members of Clan Cameron.

the Statue: the cast-bronze equestrian statue of Prince Albert in Charlotte Square, which Victoria is in Edinburgh to unveil, is by Sir John Steell. It depicts Albert in a field marshal's uniform. Designated Sculptor in Ordinary to Her Majesty for Scotland by Queen Victoria in 1838, Steell earned a reputation as Scotland's finest sculptor. The plinth, designed by the architect David Bryce, incorporates sculptural contributions by David Watson Stevenson (Science and Learning; Labour), George Clarke (Army and Navy), and William Brodie (Nobility). The monument stands 30 feet (9 metres) tall.

The Coburg March: based on a tune composed by Haydn, the Coburg March was adopted by the Royal Hussars as their regimental slow march.

343 *Presentation of Colours . . . September 1876.*: 'colours' in this context are military flags or banners. The presentation of colours is a ceremony that marks an anniversary or event in the history of a regiment, when a new regimental colour is presented to a regiment or equivalent formation in the armed forces, and an earlier colour is retired. This tradition began with the British armed forces and is today used in most Commonwealth countries.

trooping of the colours: part of the military ceremonial known as 'mounting the guard', in which the colour (standard or flag) is received from the commander-in-chief and is paraded.

piling of the drums: a ceremony in which regimental drums are stacked to serve as a temporary table or more usually as an altar for a religious service.

347 *Loch Maree Hotel*: apart from the three nights of the 'great expeditions' described in *Leaves* (112–18, 119–24, and 127–33), when the royal party travelled incognito, and a night spent at the George Inn in Perth on the way to Balmoral from Ireland (see *Leaves*, 153), this is the only occasion in the two volumes when the Queen describes staying in a hotel, as if she were an ordinary tourist, rather than in an aristocratic castle or mansion. This trip did not involve any social interactions with nobility. The hotel, which she calls 'a very nice little house', was built in 1872 on the southern shore of Loch Maree and had sixteen bedrooms. A large grey boulder outside the entrance, inscribed in Gaelic, commemorates the Queen's six-night stay.

348 *Russians . . . bombarded Plevna*: the siege of Plevna (or Pleven), a city in northern Bulgaria, was a major engagement in the Russo-Turkish War of 1877–8, fought by the combined armies of Russia and Romania against the Ottoman Empire. The Russian general Mikhail Dmitriyevich Skobelev (1843–1882) became famous for his conquest of Central Asia and for his heroism during this war. Princess Beatrice's transcription of the diary reveals that the Queen originally commented more often on the ongoing war.

Explanatory Notes to More Leaves 445

349 *More telegrams.*: In Princess Beatrice's transcription, the original continues here: 'More telegrams & the following cypher from Col: Mansfield: "Col: Wellesley telegraphs that on the 11th Russians made 3 desperate attacks on the west of Plevna, but were repulsed with heavy loss. The Roumanians have also suffered severely." '

350 *Village there . . . is none*: this almost non-existent village is Torridon; the remote village on the shore beyond Torridon, described in the rest of the paragraph, is probably Lower Diabaig.

351 *a "shoppie" as old Edmonston's*: probably a shop in Crathie or Ballater.

we . . . played together: Princess Beatrice's edited transcription of the Queen's journal continued: 'Heard that after 5 unsuccessful attempts, the Turks had retaken the forts, taken by Gen: Skobeleff on the 12th, also that Col: Wellesley reported the loss of Grivitza, not of vital importance. The Russians lost 1000 in taking the town & 5000 men & over 125 Officers in unsuccessful attempt on the redoubt. This is extraordinary.'

352 *the Guide . . . smallest of them*: Isle Maree (Scottish Gaelic, Eilean Maolruibhe) is a small island in Loch Maree to the north of a group of larger islands that obscure the view of it from the hotel on the southern shore. It is not clear which Highland guide the Queen is following here, and in any case she places more trust in local informants.

An old tree . . . copper coin: this 'wish tree' on Isle Maree died long ago from copper poisoning, though it remained in place near the ruins of the monastery of St Maol Rubha and its graveyard.

353 *over from Stornoway*: the distance from Stornoway to Kerrie's Bridge (a short walk inland from the pier at Gairloch) is about fifty miles (eighty km), a long sea voyage for these 250 loyal subjects to undertake in an afternoon. Because the Queen had seen the fishermen among them two days earlier, Ian Mitchell speculates that the group was already onshore and stayed, after selling their fish, from Saturday until this encounter on Monday, travel on the Sabbath being discouraged in their strict Presbyterian (Free Kirk) code (*On the Trail of Queen Victoria in the Highlands* (Edinburgh: Luath, 2000), 124–5).

356 *the poor "Eurydice"*: HMS *Eurydice* was a 26-gun navy ship designed to operate in shallow waters. It saw service in the waters off North America, the West Indies, and South Africa, as well as a brief period in the Black Sea during the Crimean War. In 1877 it was refitted as a training ship. On 24 March 1878 *Eurydice* was caught in a heavy snowstorm off the Isle of Wight, capsized, and sank. Only two of the ship's 319 crew and trainees survived; most of those who were not carried down with the ship died of exposure in the freezing waters.

Saturday, August 23.: this entry is for Saturday 24 August.

The house: Broxmouth House, near Dunbar, Lothian, was inherited in 1644 by the Dukes of Roxburgh, who still hold the title Viscount Broxmouth. Oliver Cromwell garrisoned the house and used it as his headquarters in 1650 during the Battle of Dunbar. The present house, built in the late eighteenth century, incorporated elements of the earlier one, and was used by the family as a dower house. See *More Leaves*, 222–8, for the Queen's visit to another Roxburgh estate.

446 *Explanatory Notes to* More Leaves

357 *Brown . . . very much shocked*: Princess Beatrice omits this mention of Brown, as is often her practice, despite the Queen's elaboration of an important feature of their relationship: normally Brown would have brought such news and, presumably, would have softened it.

358 *East Lothian Yeomanry*: the East Lothian Yeomanry Cavalry was raised in 1797, disbanded in 1838, and then re-raised in 1846. They were amalgamated with the Berwickshire Yeomanry to become the 'Lothians and Berwickshire Regiment of Yeomanry Cavalry' in 1888 and the 'Lothians and Berwickshire Imperial Yeomanry' in 1901.

Bothwell after the murder of Darnley: these events occurred in 1567. Bothwell was James Hepburn, 1st Duke of Orkney and 4th Duke of Bothwell (c.1534–1578). Darnley, Queen Mary's second husband, having plotted the murder of the Queen's secretary David Rizzio (see *More Leaves*, 269–70), was in turn murdered, probably on the orders of Bothwell, whose servants were executed for the crime. Mary married Bothwell three months later.

some gipsies . . . had encamped: identifying this community of Roma (*More Leaves*, 361), Queen Victoria knowledgeably specifies that this 'gipsy queen' is English 'and not the Scottish border one'. In 1836, before her accession, Queen Victoria describes in some detail in her diary encountering a Roma encampment at Esher in Surrey, noting names of some of the individuals and discussing their customs. Over the next months she made a series of watercolours of members of the community, and sought out publications addressing the history of the Roma.

West Barns by the paper mills: Alexander Annandale of Lasswade was a successful paper manufacturer in Midlothian, who (responding to increased demand for paper) bought the farm and estate of West Barns to create a new paper-making venture, the Beltonford Paper Mill. Reservoirs were dug and sewage rights secured, and a factory, stores, engine house, and housing were built, as well as a railway link; the mill was complete in 1865 and produced 20 tons of printing paper weekly.

359 *mentioned in the "Bride of Lammermoor."*: a historical novel (1819) set in 1707, the time of the Union between Scotland and England, in Sir Walter Scott's Tales of My Landlord series. The setting is the Lammermuir Hills near Dunbar, and the Wolf's Craig in the novel had been identified with a rocky outcropping called Fast Castle on the coast nearby.

one of my lords in waiting: a lord-in-waiting was a government whip in the House of Lords. George Baillie-Hamilton, 10th Earl of Haddington, served in this capacity in 1867–8.

360 *Leslie's camp was on Doune Hill*: 2 miles (3.2 km) south of Dunbar, Doon Hill was the site of the camp of General Leslie and the Covenanter army during the English Civil War, immediately before their defeat at the Battle of Dunbar by Oliver Cromwell's Parliamentarian army. Sir Walter Scott's version of this history is in his three-volume *Tales of a Grandfather*, a history of Scotland written for young people (1828–30).

361 *Tantallon*: for Tantallon Castle, see note to *Leaves*, 34.

363 *Glen Gelder Shiel*: built in 1865 on open moorland south of Balmoral Castle, on the banks of the Gelder Burn, Glen Gelder Shiel is a single-storey, gabled,

T-plan granite lodge, still in use as a hikers' bothy (for the Queen's description, see *More Leaves*, 374). Visitors to it would have passed the ruins of the 'cleared', abandoned settlements of Rhacaish and Ruighachail.

Brown . . . so kind and feeling: all the references to Brown in this entry are missing from Princess Beatrice's transcription of the diary.

365 *though now she is no more."*: in addition to creating this monument, the Queen also collaborated with her daughter Princess Helena on a memorial volume that combines a short account of Alice's life with extracts from her letters to her mother, selected by Queen Victoria herself: *Alice, Grand Duchess of Hesse, Princess of Great Britain and Ireland: Biographical Sketch and Letters, with Portraits* (London: John Murray, 1884).

367 *the Prince Imperial is killed!*: Louis-Napoleon, Prince Imperial (1856–1879), was the only child of Emperor Napoleon III and Empress Eugenie of France. When his father was deposed in 1870, the family moved to England, where the prince trained as a soldier and volunteered to serve in the British forces in South Africa. Had the Second Empire not been overthrown, he would have ruled France as Napoleon IV after his father's death in 1873. Queen Victoria had a memorial cross erected on the spot where he was killed, at Qweqwe, Eastern Cape, South Africa.

killed by a number of Zulus: the Anglo-Zulu War was fought in 1879 between Britain and the Zulu Kingdom. Following the Constitution Act of 1867 for the federation of Canada, it was thought that similar political effort, coupled with military campaigns, might succeed with African kingdoms, tribal areas, and Boer republics in South Africa. In 1874 Sir Bartle Frere was sent to South Africa as High Commissioner for the British Empire to effect the plan, which would include overcoming the armed independent states of the South African Republic and the Zulu Kingdom. Frere (whose wife has sent this telegram to the Queen) sent a deliberately provocative, untenable ultimatum to the Zulu king Cetshwayo on 11 December 1878, and when this was rejected Lord Chelmsford was dispatched to invade Zululand. The war is notable for several hard-fought battles, including an opening victory for the Zulu at the Battle of Isandlwana, followed by their defeat at Rorke's Drift by a small British force. The British eventually won the war, ending the Zulu nation's dominance of the region.

every one quite stunned: all references to Brown in this episode are missing from Princess Beatrice's transcription of the diary.

369 *in September 1844*: for the Queen's visit to Dundee with Vicky in September 1844, see *Leaves*, 36–7.

370 *and fought for him*: in Princess Beatrice's transcription of the diary, the Queen's description of Louis-Napoleon's death is elaborated: 'dying by the ruthless cruel hands of savages, found stripped & bleeding, with 7 wounds in him, is too awful! Quite inexplicable, & monstrous, that the others should not have turned round & fought for him.'

371 *in the library*: remaining in Princess Beatrice's transcription after this point are further remarks about Britain's conquest of South Africa: 'Ld Chelmsford brought me a map & showed the distances, on which he had written & pointed out the impossibilities of proceeding in directions people thought he could,

owing to the broken ground.—He considers the war virtually at an end, as so many important Chiefs, & the Prime Minister Umseyana, one of the principal, & most influential men, had surrendered.'

372 *on my pony again*: Princess Beatrice's edited transcription of the Queen's journal continues: 'More telegrams. One feels quite bewildered, as the Afghan affairs had seemed to have been finished, the Zulu war had absorbed our thoughts for so long. It is terribly distressing. But I think there are enough troops. As yet, the Ameer appears to be innocent, & helpless.'

374 *with her lady*: *More Leaves* omits the French empress's remarks about her son, which are retained in Princess Beatrice's transcription: 'She talked a great deal of former times,—of Pce Napoleon, & his dreadful, worthless life, & said he was her "plus cruel ennemi". . . . When I said I so much regretted there was no young relation, no child, she could take interest in, she said there was none, but after all "ils ne pourraient pas remplacer mon Enfant", & that she found most comfort in her dear son's friends, & his young officer friends.'

375 *something at the time*: the Battle of Tel El Kebir was the decisive engagement of the British conquest of Egypt (the Anglo-Egyptian War). It was fought on 13 September 1882 at Tel El Kebir in Egypt, north-east of Cairo. An entrenched Egyptian force under the command of Ahmed 'Urabi was defeated by a British army led by Sir Garnet Wolseley, consisting largely of Highland regiments, in a sudden assault preceded by a march under cover of darkness. The British sought to retain control over the Suez Canal, to maintain its shipping route to India. The Queen is especially anxious because Prince Arthur is participating in the battle.

376 *and I showed it to her*: Princess Beatrice's transcription of the diary omits Brown's bringing the telegram and participating in this emotional scene.

377 *twenty-six years ago*: for the bonfire to celebrate the end of the Crimean War, see *Leaves*, 89. The Queen misdates this celebration; it was in 1855, twenty-seven years before.

378 *Conclusion.*: the conclusion was thoughtfully revised, in correspondence between the Queen and her secretary, Sir Henry Ponsonby, which is in the Royal Archives among other letters about *More Leaves*. Ponsonby suggests a revision (to an original now lost): 'he is not sure whether the final words of the 3rd paragraph run quite easily'. The Queen revises, and he writes again with his approval. The exchange captures Ponsonby's delicacy in approaching the Queen's style: 'Your Majesty's sentences, written with the true feeling that inspire them, strike the reader as the real expression of Your Majesty's thoughts and therefore Sir Henry Ponsonby scarcely liked to meddle with the paragraph more than was necessary. But this one now written by Your Majesty is he thinks very good indeed.'

A truer . . . a human breast: from *The Two Foscari: An Historical Tragedy* (1821), a verse drama in five acts, set in fifteenth-century Venice, by Lord Byron. Byron originally planned to dedicate the work to Sir Walter Scott. In the quoted lines, Marina Foscari is defending her husband to his father, the Doge.

GLOSSARY

Athole brose A traditional Scots fortifying drink made by pouring boiling water on oatmeal and adding whisky, honey, and sometimes cream.
awful In the archaic sense, awe-inspiring.
balloch A narrow mountain pass.
barge Generally, a flat-bottomed freight boat, chiefly used for canal and river navigation, but here a shallow sailing or rowing boat used as a ferry or tender.
barouche A four-wheeled carriage with a partial covering that can be raised or lowered, with a seat in front for the driver and two facing pairs of seats inside.
battery (i) A fortified platform on or within which artillery is mounted. (ii) An embankment.
beat (noun) A tract over which a hunter ranges in pursuit of game; 'beating' is the action of striking at bushes or ground cover to rouse or drive out birds or animals to be killed.
ben A mountain peak; hence, 'Ben' in the names of Scottish mountains.
boat carriage Generally, a style of landau, a four-wheeled carriage with a folding two-part hood and a distinctively rounded underbody; in the case of the boat carriage at Blair Castle, an actual boat made into a carriage.
bodies (i) Variant of 'bodice', the tight-fitting upper part of a woman's dress, made either in one piece with the skirt or as a separate garment. (ii) A corset.
bonnet [Highland bonnet] A head-covering for men and boys, soft, and lacking the stiff brim that characterizes a hat. The term 'cap' had replaced 'bonnet' in England by the seventeenth century, but 'bonnet' persisted in Scotland.
bothie A hut or small cottage, typically inhabited by servants on a farm; here sometimes used interchangeably with 'shiel' (q.v.) and 'hut'.
box In the context of transportation, the seat on which the driver of a carriage sits.
brace In hunting, two, a pair; used, especially, of animals and other game (as in 'a brace of grouse').
brae A steep bank bounding a river valley, or any steep hillside; Old English, but retained only in northern England and Scotland.
broom In a botanical context, a yellow-flowering shrub (*Cytisus scoparius*), widespread in Scotland.
burn A spring or a small stream or brook; Old English, but retained only in northern England and Scotland.
burnous A mantle or cloak with a hood.
caber A rough-hewn pine trunk from which the branches have been stripped. In the sport known as 'tossing the caber', the competitor holds the caber at chest level, upright, by the narrow end, and throws it in an arc so that the thick end lands first and the trunk falls beyond it.

cairn A pyramid or pile of rough stones, raised as a memorial to a person or an event; a cairn may also be a boundary mark or a landmark on a mountain-top or a high point of land.

cairngorm A gemstone, a type of rock crystal (chemically, silicon dioxide SiO_2), coloured yellow, brown, or purple by iron oxide; it is found particularly in the Cairngorm mountain range, and is used for ornamenting Highland weapons and items of clothing, and as jewellery.

Caledonia The Roman name for northern Britain, later used as a poetical term for Scotland.

capercailzie The wood grouse (*Tetrao urogallus*), the largest European grouse and a favourite game bird; native to Scotland, it became extinct in the eighteenth century and was reintroduced in the early nineteenth from Scandinavia.

Celt A native of a country or region in which a Celtic language is spoken—Brittany, Cornwall, Wales, Ireland, and Scotland—but in the nineteenth century, a term denoting a racial category; see the Introduction, xxi–xxii and xxxix, and note to *Leaves*, 105.

chanters The pipes with finger holes that form part of a bagpipe, on which the melody is played.

coble In Celtic languages, a short, open, flat-bottomed rowing boat, used in salmon fishing or for crossing lakes or rivers.

collier (i) A coal-miner. (ii) A colliery village or hamlet built (often by the mine owner) near mine workings for the accommodation of the workforce.

commercial room A public room in an inn or hotel for the use of commercial travellers (sales agents for manufacturers) and their customers.

corn The seeds of cereal plants, such as wheat, rye, barley, and oats; in mid-nineteenth-century Britain, the grain or 'corn' fed to horses was typically oats, barley, and beans.

corrie (from Scottish Gaelic *coire*: 'kettle') In the Highlands, a circular hollow on a mountain-side, surrounded by steep slopes and often filled with water, from which a stream usually flows.

countess *See* earl.

coup-d'oeil (French) A quick glance taking in a general view, or a view or scene as it strikes the eye at a glance.

craig (Scots) Variant of 'crag'.

deer-stalking [stalking] The stealthy pursuit of deer on foot, a technique used in hunting deer for their meat (venison), as a pastime or sport, or to control their numbers as part of wildlife management to reduce environmental and crop damage.

dog-cart An open, horse-drawn cart, with a box under the seat for a hunter's dogs; later, an open cart with two transverse seats back to back, the rear seat taking the form of an enclosed box.

dowager A widow who retains a title or property that has come to her from her late husband, after her son has succeeded his father; the word is often added to the woman's title, as in 'Dowager Duchess' or 'Dowager Lady'.

drag A private vehicle resembling a stage coach, pulled by four horses, having seats inside and on the top.

drive (verb) In hunting, to impel animals forward so as to force them into a place, sometimes an enclosure, where they can be killed.

dropsy Swelling caused by fluid retention (now called oedema), usually in the feet, legs, or ankles or other extremities; it was thought to be a disease in itself, but it is a symptom of congestive heart failure or other organ failure.

duke (duchess, duchy) In England, Scotland, and Ireland, a hereditary title of nobility, the highest in the peerage below that of prince (the ranks in descending order are prince, duke, marquess, earl, viscount, baron, knight); the female form of the title is 'duchess'. The land owned by a duke is sometimes referred to as a 'duchy'.

earl In England, Scotland, and Ireland, a hereditary title beneath that of duke (q.v.) and marquess and above the rank of viscount; the equivalent female title is countess.

Episcopalian A member of the Episcopalian Church. The Scottish Episcopal Church was established in 1582, when the Church of Scotland rejected government by bishops (episcopal government) and adopted government by elders (presbyterian government), as well as Reformed theology.

equerry Originally an officer charged with the care of the royal horses (a shortened form of 'officer of the equerry', referring to the royal stables); at the English court, an office holder in the Royal Household whose duty is attendance on the sovereign.

estrade A raised platform or dais.

factor In land management, the manager of an estate; the word used in this sense is archaic except in Scotland.

feu de joie A rifle salute fired by soldiers as part of ceremonial. Each soldier fires in succession along the ranks to make a continuous sound.

Finnan haddies Pieces of haddock cured with the smoke of green wood or peat; a local specialty of north-eastern Scotland, traditionally served poached in milk for breakfast.

fly A lightweight, fast-moving one-horse carriage, typically for hire.

gannet A large seabird, white with black wing tips (*Morus bassanus*), which dives for fish and roosts in large flocks on offshore rocks.

Ghillie [Gillie] **Callum** [sword dance] The most celebrated of Scottish folk dances, danced to the tune of that name, the Ghillie Callum is a traditional dance of war and is said to date back to the eleventh century. The victorious combatant's claymore (two-handed broadsword of Scotland) was crossed over the sword of the defeated chief, and the victor danced over them both in exultation; three, four, or even eight swords were sometimes used. Dancing to slow (strathspey) time, followed by quick (reel) time, the dancer normally travels anti-clockwise round the swords. Completion of the dance without inflicting self-injury necessitates appropriate placing of the feet and rapid body turns, and as a result is an exciting visual display. The Ghillie Callum is usually the last dance at a Highland ball (q.v.).

gillie [ghillie] In the Highlands, a male servant, especially an attendant of a clan chief; by extension, a hunter's or fisherman's attendant.

Gipsy A member of the Roma community in Britain (an archaic term, now regarded as pejorative).

glen A narrow mountain valley traversed by a stream.

Gothic A style of architecture prevalent in Europe from the twelfth to the sixteenth century, characterized by pointed arches; from the eighteenth century onwards, 'gothic' (or 'gothick') may also mean a romantically medieval style.

grouse moor A moorland area where grouse (*Lagopus scoticus*) are prevalent, and where they may be hunted.

haggis A dish consisting of the heart, lungs, and liver of a sheep or calf, minced and mixed with suet, oatmeal, onion, and seasonings, and boiled in a sheep's stomach; now regarded as traditionally Scottish.

halberdier A soldier carrying a halberd, a weapon combining an axe blade with a spear head and mounted on a pole five to seven feet long; in a military context, the halberd was used in the fifteenth and sixteenth centuries, but by the nineteenth it featured only in romantic ceremonial displays.

hart A male deer, especially a red deer, usually over five years old.

haut pas An area of floor that is raised one or more steps above the rest; a dais.

Highland ball A social assembly for the purpose of dancing, especially Scottish reels.

hind A female red deer, especially one over three years old.

hodge-podge A thick broth made from a mixture of various meats and vegetables.

Jäger (German: 'hunter') The German or Swiss term for the attendant of a wealthy or high-ranking hunter; the equivalent Scottish term is 'gillie' (q.v.).

jaunting-car A light, two-wheeled, one-horse carriage, carrying four or more people who are seated either back to back or facing each other, with another seat in front for the driver.

jig A lively, rapid, springy kind of dance, or the music for it, typically Irish or Scottish.

jointure Property settled on a person in consideration of marriage, to be owned by that person after the spouse's death; typically, a jointure house is a house left to a widow for her use during her lifetime.

kilt A component of modern Highland dress, consisting of a skirt reaching from the waist to the knee. It is usually of tartan cloth and is deeply pleated at the back and sides. In the nineteenth century, the tartan kilt, or philibeg, was a relatively recent innovation, which had replaced the traditional belted plaid, a single length of fabric wrapped around the body. The short kilt is said to have evolved in the 1720s, encouraged by an English Quaker factory owner near Inverness, who found the traditional belted plaid too cumbersome for his workers.

kirk Northern English and Scots term for 'church'. 'Kirk' is also used, in contrast to 'Church', to distinguish the Presbyterian Church of Scotland—the official Church of Scotland—from the Church of England or the Episcopal Church of Scotland. 'Free Kirk' or 'Free Church' refers to Presbyterian denominations that had separated from the official Church of Scotland.

kyle A narrow channel between two islands, or between an island and the mainland; in the plural, the word is found in place names, such as the Kyles of Bute.

landau A four-wheeled carriage, with a top made in two parts that may be closed or thrown open.

leister A pronged spear for striking and taking fish; 'leistering' is thus a method of fishing using this tool.

linn A pool below a waterfall; or a cascade, waterfall, or torrent of water running over rocks.

loch A lake, or an arm of the sea, especially when narrow and partly landlocked.

Lord Provost The chief administrative officer of a Scottish municipality, corporation, or burgh; similar to a mayor in England.

manufactory A factory or workshop.

march A boundary, border, or frontier, or a tract of land on the border; the boundary of an estate.

militia A military force made up of citizens, as distinguished from mercenaries or professional soldiers. *See also* volunteers.

mull In Scotland, a headland or promontory.

mutch A cap, usually made of linen, worn by women and young children.

neuralgia An affection of one or more nerves, causing pain.

outrider An attendant mounted on horseback, who rides in advance of, or beside a carriage.

peat Semi-carbonized, decayed vegetable matter that lies under the turf in boggy moorland; cut into roughly brick-shaped pieces and dried, it is burned as fuel. A peat-road is the route across moorland, formed by the sledges carrying the cut peat.

phaeton A lightweight, four-wheeled, open carriage, drawn by a pair of horses, with one or two seats facing forwards; named for the son of Apollo, in Greek mythology, who stole the chariot of the sun and nearly set the world on fire.

philosopher Until the end of the nineteenth century, any lover of wisdom, including one who would now be called a scientist or a naturalist.

pibroch Music for the bagpipe, consisting of a theme and variations, usually martial or elegiac; sometimes the term is (mistakenly) used for the bagpipe itself.

postchaise A fast-moving carriage, designed to carry the post, with a closed body and seating for one to three people, and drawn by two or four horses, the driver being seated on one of the horses.

postillion The rider of a horse that is pulling a carriage; especially, the rider of one of a pair of horses when there is no driver on the box.

progress (noun) In the sense of a journey, an itinerary followed by a monarch or other dignitary, typically to visit the nations, regions, and noble families of the realm, so as to reaffirm ties between the one who travels and the territory and its elite society.

ptarmigan A bird of the grouse family (*Lagopus alpinus* or *Lagopus mutus*) that inhabits high altitudes of Scotland and northern Europe; the feathers change from gray and black in summer to white in winter.

quadrille A square dance, originally French, performed by four couples.

quaich A traditional Scots drinking vessel, a two-handled shallow cup made of wood or silver, or of wood rimmed with silver.

reel A lively traditional Scottish dance, in which the basic movements are a setting step (movement on the spot), followed by a travelling figure; it is danced by groups of three or four, or by a set of four couples.

roebuck The male of the roe deer.

schottische A partnered country dance, which originated in Germany, incorporating elements of the polka; it must have once appeared to have Scottish attributes.

screw The propeller on an engine-driven ship.

shiel A temporary or roughly made shed or shanty, typically made of turf or rough stones, with a dirt floor and thatched roof, used by shepherds in mountainous areas, or by salmon fishermen; the word sometimes forms part of a place name, such as Galashiels. The term was also in use by the nineteenth century to describe a bothie (q.v.), or a small dwelling or cottage, especially one that includes a public house (a hostelry for the sale of alcohol).

shooting lodge [shooting box] A small house, cottage, or hut for use as a residence or shelter, located in or near an area used for game hunting.

sociable (noun) [sociable coach; barouche-sociable] An open, four-wheeled carriage, drawn by a single horse in shafts or by a matching pair in pole gear; it had two facing pairs of seats and a box seat for a driver, and a pair of folding hoods were raised to protect the passengers.

spate A flood; a sudden rise of water in a stream or river.

spittal A charitable institution for the accommodation of the poor or sick; in Scotland, a shelter, hostel, or inn for travellers, especially in mountainous country. The word is found in place names, such as Spittal of Glenshee.

sporran A leather pouch, ornamented with goat hair, fur, or brass, worn suspended from a belt in front of the kilt (q.v.), and used to hold money and other small articles.

squadron A division of a fleet of ships forming one body under the command of a flag officer.

squint (verb) To cross a surface obliquely or on the slant (from the noun meaning a diagonal); by extension, to drift.
steam-plough A steam-powered traction engine used for ploughing.
strath A wide, shallow river valley.
sword dance *See* Ghillie Callum.
tempête (French: (lit.) 'tempest') A popular Scottish reel (q.v.).
three-decker A sailing ship with three decks, traditionally or presumptively a warship carrying guns on three decks.
tryst A meeting place, and by extension a market, or fair, especially for the sale of sheep and cattle.
victoria A light, low, four-wheeled carriage with a collapsible hood, for two passengers, with a box seat for a driver.
volunteers In a military context, an organized force (as in the Berwickshire Volunteers), formed by volunteer enrolment, and distinct from the regular army of the state; similar to a militia (q.v.).
wheelers In a carriage drawn by a team of horses, the pair of horses closest to a carriage, as opposed to the leaders; they provide the main braking effort, slowing the vehicle and controlling it downhill by pulling back on the pole or shafts. The strength of the wheelers is often the limiting factor in determining the maximum safe load for a vehicle. While all the animals can pull uphill, only the wheelers can hold the vehicle when it is travelling downhill; for this reason, the strongest pair in a team may be chosen as the wheelers. Wheelers also steer the vehicle by turning the pole or shafts.
whin A yellow-flowering thorny shrub gorse or furze (*Ulex europaeus*), widespread in Scotland.
whist (whist with dummy) A card game for four players in two couples, similar to bridge; in whist with dummy, played with only three, the dummy is an imaginary player represented by an exposed hand of cards, serving as partner to one of the others.